PALMYRENE SARCOPHAGI

STUDIES IN PALMYRENE ARCHAEOLOGY AND HISTORY
VOLUME 10

FOUNDING EDITOR
Professor **Rubina Raja**, *Centre for Urban Network Evolutions, Aarhus University, Denmark*

ADVISORY BOARD
Professor **Nathanael Andrade**, *Binghamton University, New York, USA*
Dr **Olympia Bobou**, *Aarhus University, Denmark*
Professor **Maura K. Heyn**, *University of North Carolina, Greensboro, USA*
Dr **Emanuele Intagliata**, *Università degli Studi di Milano, Italy*
Professor **Ted Kaizer**, *Durham University, UK*
Professor **Eivind Heldaas Seland**, *University of Bergen, Norway*
Dr **Jean-Baptiste Yon**, *Laboratoire HiSoMA, CNRS, Lyon*

Previously published volumes in this series are listed at the back of the book.

Palmyrene Sarcophagi

Volume 2

OLYMPIA BOBOU and RUBINA RAJA

BREPOLS

British Library Cataloguing in Publication Data
A catalogue record for this book is available from the British Library.

© 2023, Brepols Publishers n.v., Turnhout, Belgium.

All rights reserved. No part of this publication may be reproduced,
stored in a retrieval system, or transmitted, in any form or by any means,
electronic, mechanical, photocopying, recording, or otherwise without
the prior permission of the publisher.

D/2023/0095/19
ISBN: 978-2-503-60466-4 (2 volumes)
eISBN: 978-2-503-60754-2 (2 volumes)
10.1484/M.SPAH-EB.5.134891

Printed in the EU on acid-free paper.

Table of Contents

Colour Plates 573

Catalogue

Objects with Indication of General Context (Cat. 278–288) 596

Sarcophagi with No Known Provenance or from Secondary Contexts (Cat. 289–444) 607

Sarcophagi Reliefs (Cat. 445–450) 750

Fragments from either Sarcophagus Lids or Boxes (Cat. 451–476) 761

Possible Sarcophagus Fragments (Cat. 477–488) 776

Heads from Sarcophagi (Cat. 489–683) 783

Banqueting Reliefs (Cat. 684–729) 900

Appendix 1. Lost Dated Reliefs 963

Appendix 2. Lost Reliefs from Tower Tombs 965

Appendix 3. Lost Reliefs from Temple Tombs 967

Appendix 4. Marble Sarcophagi from Attica 969

Appendix 5. Sarcophagi without Portraits 972

Appendix 6. Objects Known Only through Publications 982

Appendix 7. Reliefs with Frame, without Portraits 991

Credits

Catalogue Image Credits 994

Plate 55. Female head, cat. no. 288.

574 COLOUR PLATES

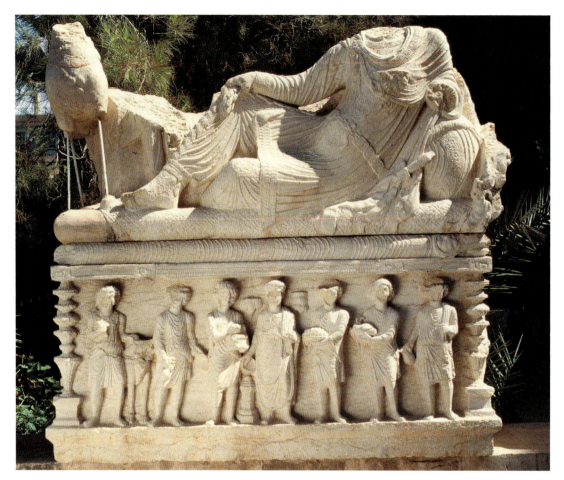

Plate 56. Complete sarcophagus with banqueting scene, horse, and religious scene, cat. no. 290.

Plate 57. Lateral side of sarcophagus, cat. no. 290.

Plate 58. Lateral side of sarcophagus, cat. no. 290.

Plate 59. Sarcophagus lid with banqueting scene, cat. no. 291.

Plate 60. Lateral side of sarcophagus, cat. no. 298.

Plate 61. Figure of child from sarcophagus lid, cat. no. 329.

Plate 62. Fragment of sarcophagus lid with banqueting scene, cat. no. 333.

Plate 63. Figure of child from sarcophagus lid, cat. no. 351.

COLOUR PLATES 581

Plate 64. Female figure, cat. no. 360.

Plate 65. Female figure, cat. no. 365.

Plate 66. Male figure, cat. no. 386.

Plate 67. Female figure, cat. no. 387.

582 COLOUR PLATES

Plate 68. Fragment of sarcophagus lid wth banqueting scene, cat. no. 389.

Plate 69. Fragment of sarcophagus lid wth banqueting scene, cat. no. 390.

COLOUR PLATES 583

Plate 70. Fragment of sarcophagus lid wth banqueting scene, cat. no. 391.

Plate 71. Fragment of sarcophagus lid wth banqueting scene, cat. no. 392.

Plate 72. Fragment of sarcophagus box with portrait busts, cat. no. 403.

Plate 73. Fragment of sarcophagus - fulcrum, cat. no. 417.

COLOUR PLATES 585

Plate 74. Fragment of sarcophagus box with portrait busts, cat. no. 420.

586 COLOUR PLATES

Plate 75. Fragment of a sarcophagus box with standing figure, cat. no. 424.

Plate 76. Fragment of a sarcophagus box with standing figures, cat. no. 430.

Plate 77. Fragment of sarcophagus - fulcrum, cat. no. 443.

COLOUR PLATES 587

Plate 78. Sarcophagus relief with banqueting scene, cat. no. 445.

Plate 79. Sarcophagus relief with portrait busts, cat. no. 445.

588 COLOUR PLATES

Plate 80. Head of priest, cat. no. 494.

Plate 81. Head of priest, cat. no. 507.

Plate 82. Head of priest, cat. no. 520.

Plate 83. Head of priest, cat. no. 524.

COLOUR PLATES 589

Plate 84. Head of youth, cat. no. 555.

Plate 85. Head of youth, cat. no. 565.

Plate 86. Head of youth, cat. no. 574.

590 COLOUR PLATES

Plate 87. Head of youth, cat. no. 575.

Plate 88. Male head, cat. no. 576.

Plate 89. Male head, cat. no. 577.

Plate 90. Male head, cat. no. 583.

COLOUR PLATES 591

Plate 91. Head of youth, cat. no. 584.

Plate 92. Male head, cat. no. 593.

Plate 93. Female head, cat. no. 616.

Plate 94. Female head, cat. no. 622.

Plate 95. Female head, cat. no. 632.

Plate 96. Banqueting relief, cat. no. 689.

COLOUR PLATES 593

Plate 97. Banqueting relief, cat. no. 694.

Plate 98. Banqueting relief, cat. no. 695.

Plate 99. Banqueting relief, cat. no. 700.

Plate 100. Banqueting relief, ct. no. 714.

COLOUR PLATES 595

Plate 101. Banqueting relief, cat. no. 716.

Plate 102. Banqueting relief, cat. no. 719.

Catalogue

Objects with Indication of General Context

SARCOPHAGUS LIDS

A.D. 200–220

278. FRAGMENT OF A BANQUETING RELIEF

DATABASE NUMBER: PM579.
LOCATION: Palmyra, Palmyra Museum, inv. no. A 88.
CONTEXT: South-west necropolis. Excavated by Ingholt.
ACQUISITION HISTORY: —
MEASUREMENTS: —
MATERIAL: Limestone.
PRESERVATION: The head is broken off at the base of the neck. The feet are broken off. The left hand is chipped. The surface is weathered.
TECHNICAL DESCRIPTION: —
DATE: A.D. 200–220.
REFERENCES: Ingholt Archives, PS 974.

OBJECT DESCRIPTION
The sarcophagus lid depicts a reclining male. He rests the left arm against a cushion. Curving grooves indicate the texture of the fabric.

PORTRAIT
The figure is shown frontally. The legs appear short in relation to the body. The right arm is extended along the body. The left arm is bent. The right leg is bent; the left leg is slightly bent and rests along the mattress.

He wears a tunic and a himation. The tunic has a wide, v-shaped neckline and short, wide sleeves. It covers his chest and shoulders. The folds of the tunic are rendered by curving grooves. Over the tunic, he wears a himation. The himation covers most of his body and legs. It is wrapped around the left shoulder and arm. One end of the himation crosses the waist diagonally and falls over his right side. Two s-shaped folds fall from under his left hand and over the cushion. The folds of the himation are rendered by oblique and curving grooves.

Cat. 278

FRAGMENTS FROM LIDS, LID RELIEFS, OR BANQUETING RELIEFS

A.D. 140–160

279. FEMALE FIGURE

DATABASE NUMBER: DamascusUNK012.
LOCATION: Damascus, unknown location.
CONTEXT: South-west necropolis. Excavated by Ingholt in 1924.
ACQUISITION HISTORY: —
MEASUREMENTS: Height: 79 cm. Width: 35 cm.
MATERIAL: Limestone.
PRESERVATION: The lower right corner and the bottom of plinth are chipped. The lower half of the left side of the object is chipped. The surface of the lower right arm and both knees is chipped.

Cat. 279

TECHNICAL DESCRIPTION: —
DATE: A.D. 140–160.
REFERENCES: Ingholt Archives, PS 647; Krag 2018, 43 n. 164; 238 cat. 273.

OBJECT DESCRIPTION

The lid depicts a female sitting in a chair. The chair has a round back, decorated with a beaded band. The back of the chair supports the figure up to the height of the shoulder. The armrests are decorated with an outer beaded band, and a band with a crisscross pattern, possibly indicating a high-backed wicker chair.

PORTRAIT

The figure is shown frontally with the head turned to her left. The arms appear short in relation to the body. The right arm is slightly bent. The left arm is bent and held to the chest. She sits with her legs apart with both feet resting on a protruding plinth.

She wears three headdresses: a headband, turban, and veil. The headband is placed low on the forehead, with rectangular panels separated by vertical grooves (details unclear). The turban is coiled. It is divided into three layers and the upper two layers are looped into each other creating a knot in the middle. Horizontal grooves indicate the coiling of the fabric. The veil is heavy. It falls behind her right shoulder and is folded around her left shoulder and arm. A thick, wavy lock of hair falls down her neck and shoulders on each side. The individual strands of hair are indicated by incised lines. Her face is square. The eyebrows are curving. The eyes are large and almond-shaped, with thick eyelids. The upper eyelids extend beyond the end of the lower ones. The ears are depicted with the helix (details unclear). Small horizontal lines on the helix may indicate the presence of ear hoops. The nose is short and straight with incised alae. The cheeks are fleshy and the mouth is large with a full lower lip. The chin is wide, and the neck is short and wide. Two wide, curving grooves form a protruding mass at the middle of the neck.

She wears a tunic and a himation. The tunic falls to the ankles. It has a wide, round neckline and short, wide sleeves. The folds of the tunic are rendered by curving grooves on the chest, oblique grooves on the sleeves, and vertical grooves over the feet. The himation crosses the chest diagonally from the left shoulder to the right side, and covers the left breast. It is fastened at the shoulder with a trapezoidal brooch with a rosette finial (Colledge classification: b). The himation covers the lower body and legs and ends at the shins, revealing the tunic underneath. The folds of the himation are rendered by oblique grooves on the body and thighs, and curving grooves on the lower legs.

She appears to rest her right hand on the right thigh (details unclear). With the left hand, she holds a conical object incised with fine, wavy lines, with a bowl-shaped tip, and a thick, short staff topped by a polygonal mass with a crisscross pattern and a small cylinder. These are reduced versions of a spindle and a distaff. She wears a ring on the ring finger of the right hand (other details unclear). Her left index and middle finger are extended.

A.D. 170–200

280. FRAGMENT OF A MALE FIGURE

DATABASE NUMBER: PM588.
LOCATION: Palmyra, Palmyra Museum.
CONTEXT: South-west necropolis. Excavated by Ingholt in 1925.
ACQUISITION HISTORY: —
MEASUREMENTS: —
MATERIAL: Limestone.
PRESERVATION: The upper part is broken off horizontally through the right elbow, the chest, and upper left arm. The tip of the left foot is broken off. The surface is weathered.
TECHNICAL DESCRIPTION: —
DATE: A.D. 170–200 (Starcky 1941: A.D. 100–150).
REFERENCES: Ingholt Archives, PS 534; Ingholt 1926, 140 pl. 34; Seyrig 1937, 10. 14 n. 5 fig. 2; Starcky 1941, 40 fig. 35; Tanabe 1986, 44 pl. 448; Yatsenko 2013, 120 fig. 6:2.

OBJECT DESCRIPTION

The object depicts a male standing on a protruding plinth.

Cat. 280

PORTRAIT

The figure is shown frontally. The right arm is extended along the body. The left arm is bent and held to the torso. He stands with legs parted and feet planted on the ground.

He wears a >Parthian-style< tunic, >Parthian-style< trousers, and over-trousers. The tunic has long, tight-fitting sleeves. The cuffs of the sleeves are decorated with beaded bands. The edge of the tunic runs in a curving line from the right to the left side of the waist, covering the uppermost part of the thighs. The lower border is decorated with a beaded band. The folds of the tunic are rendered by curving and oblique grooves. He wears a plain band belt, knotted at the centre with the ends looped under on either side of the waist. The trousers are visible at the upper thighs. In the middle, each trouser leg has a band extending downwards and decorated with a running dog. The folds of the trousers are rendered by curving grooves. The over-trousers are fastened on each side of the waist and fall in a curving line across the upper thighs. The over-trousers end at the ankles. The folds of the garment are rendered by curving grooves. He also wears plain shoes with a round tip.

With the right hand, he holds the handle of a jug. It has a conical foot and body and a straight lip. With the left hand, he holds a ladle. It has a long shaft with a round end at the top indicated by a drill hole. The index finger is extended.

A.D. 220–240

281. FRAGMENT OF A BANQUETING RELIEF

DATABASE NUMBER: InSitu198.
LOCATION: Palmyra, in situ.
CONTEXT: Possibly from the north necropolis. House tomb no. 150, tomb of Marona.
ACQUISITION HISTORY: —
MEASUREMENTS: —
MATERIAL: Limestone.
PRESERVATION: The object is broken off on all sides. The head of the figure is broken off at the base of the neck. The left arm and the legs are broken off. The right arm is heavily chipped and the left shoulder and arm are chipped.
TECHNICAL DESCRIPTION: —
DATE: A.D. 220–240.
REFERENCES: Anderson – Ousterhout 2016, pl. 41.

OBJECT DESCRIPTION

The object depicts a reclining male.
Anderson – Ousterhout 2016 suggest that the object is possibly from the tomb of Marona.

PORTRAIT

The figure is shown frontally. The right arm is extended and held away from the body.

He wears a >Parthian-style< tunic and a chlamys. The tunic has long sleeves and a vertical band running downwards in the middle, decorated with a running scroll with central rosettes. The folds of the tunic are indicated by curving and oblique grooves. He also wears a plain band belt knotted at the centre with the ends looped under on either side. The chlamys falls over the shoulders and covers most of the chest. It is fastened at the right shoulder (details unclear), and a zigzag-shaped fold falls underneath. The edge of the chlamys is scalloped, visible in a curving fold across the chest. Along his right thigh he has an object with a triangular end, a rectangular main body, and two lateral round elements: a sheathed dagger.

The outline of an object, possibly a bowl, is visible at the centre of the torso.

A.D. 240–273

282. MALE FIGURE

DATABASE NUMBER: PM954.
LOCATION: Palmyra, Palmyra Museum, inv. no. A 217.
CONTEXT: West necropolis. Valley of the Tombs. Found near Temple/house tomb no. 85b, tomb of Aʿaîlamî and Zebîdâ (›Tomb Cantineau‹).
ACQUISITION HISTORY: —
MEASUREMENTS: Height: 83 cm.
MATERIAL: Limestone, yellow.
PRESERVATION: The right side, the upper part, the left side, and the lower left corner are broken off. The surface is weathered. The head is broken off at the neck.
TECHNICAL DESCRIPTION: —
DATE: A.D. 240–273.
REFERENCES: Ingholt Archives, PS 1317.

OBJECT DESCRIPTION

The object is rectangular in shape and depicts a standing male. The relief background is visible to the left of the figure. The figure is standing on a mattress. It is decorated with an intersecting lozenges pattern with beaded elements at the intersections. There are four-petal flowers at the centre of the lozenges with the veins of the petals incised.

INSCRIPTION

SCRIPT: Palmyrene Aramaic.
LOCATION ON RELIEF: Unclear.
TRANSCRIPTION: ṢLM ʾPRHT GWYʾ MHYMNʾ ḤBL.
TRANSLATION: Image of Afrahat, the trusted confidant/eunuch (?), alas!

CIS no. 4239; PAT no. 0595.

COMMENT: The meaning of GWYʾ MHYMNʾ is not certain. GWYʾ could be ›Eunuch‹ (as in Syriac) or ›Treasurer‹. Besides, MHYMNʾ in Hatran may mean ›Eunuch‹ as well (Beyer 1998, 174, for H100, 139 and 290).

Cat. 282

PORTRAIT

The figure is shown frontally. The right arm appears short in relation to the body. The right arm is bent and held in front of the torso. The left arm is slightly bent and held in front of the waist. The figure stands on the mattress.

He wears a tunic and a himation. The folds of the tunic are rendered by curving grooves on the chest. The himation falls over both shoulders and is folded around the arms, leaving the right hand free. It is wrapped around the left wrist (›arm-sling‹ type). The himation covers the lower body and legs, and ends just above the ankles. The folds of the tunic are rendered by curving grooves. Horizontal lines at the ankles indicate shoes (details unclear).

His right hand is in front of the torso and holds a fold of the himation. The fingers are slightly bent. The left hand is at the waist and holds a fold of the himation. A large edge of the himation falls from underneath the hand, in a zigzag-shaped fold.

SARCOPHAGUS BOXES

A.D. 100–150

283. SARCOPHAGUS BOX WITH PORTRAIT BUSTS

DATABASE NUMBER: InSitu225.
LOCATION: Palmyra, in situ.
CONTEXT: West necropolis. Valley of the Tombs. Found near tomb no. 51.
ACQUISITION HISTORY: —
MEASUREMENTS: —
MATERIAL: Limestone, white.

PRESERVATION: At the centre, the upper section of the relief ground has broken off. The surface is badly weathered. The surface around the heads of the figures is chipped.
TECHNICAL DESCRIPTION: —
DATE: A.D. 100–150.
REFERENCES: Ingholt Archives, PS 1013, 1320; Makowski 1985a, 97; Wielgosz 1997, 71–73 pl. 4, 2; Krag 2018, 7 n. 77; 32 n. 63; 87 n. 182. 184; 89 n. 208; 98 n. 23; 244 cat. 290. Inscription: Wielgosz 1997, 72; Krag 2018, 244 cat. 290.

OBJECT DESCRIPTION
The sarcophagus box is rectangular in shape and is rendered as a kline. Five figures are depicted between the kline legs: a female, a male, a female, and two males. The kline legs are turned. They are composed of a plinth, above is a torus, a reversed bell-shaped element, a thin torus, a reversed bell-shaped element, a ball, and a torus.

Wielgosz 1997 suggests that the object is from tomb no. 80.

INSCRIPTION
INSCRIPTION 1
SCRIPT: Palmyrene Aramaic.

Cat. 283

OBJECTS WITH INDICATION OF GENERAL CONTEXT 601

LOCATION ON RELIEF: Next to portrait A, at the height of the head.
TRANSCRIPTION: P[Ṣ]ʾ B[RT] | ḤG[GW] | M[Lʾ].
TRANSLATION: Paṣâ, daughter of Ḥagegû Malê.

INSCRIPTION 2
SCRIPT: Palmyrene Aramaic.
LOCATION ON RELIEF: Next to portrait B, at the height of the head.
TRANSCRIPTION: ḤGGW [BR ML]ʾ.
TRANSCRIPTION: Ḥagegû, son of Malê.

INSCRIPTION 3
SCRIPT: Palmyrene Aramaic.
LOCATION ON RELIEF: Next to portrait C, at the height of the head.
TRANSCRIPTION: PṢʾ BR[T] | NŠʾ ḤGGW | ʾMH ḤBL.
TRANSLATION: Paṣâ, daughter of Neŝâ Ḥagegû, his mother, alas!

INSCRIPTION 4
SCRIPT: Palmyrene Aramaic.
LOCATION ON RELIEF: Next to portrait D, at the height of the head.
TRANSCRIPTION: PṢYʾL BR [- - -] | ḤGGW BR MLʾ | WHBLT ḤBL.
TRANSLATION: Paṣîêl, son of - - -Ḥagegû, son of Malê Wahballath, alas!

INSCRIPTION 5
SCRIPT: Palmyrene Aramaic.
LOCATION ON RELIEF: Next to portrait E, at the height of the head.
TRANSCRIPTION: MLKW BR | ḤGGW WHBLT.
TRANSLATION: Malkû, son of Ḥagegû Wahballath.

CIS no. 4232; PAT no. 0588.

PORTRAIT A: FEMALE BUST, PAṢÂ
The figure is shown frontally. Both arms are bent and held to the torso.
She wears a veil, which is wrapped around her shoulders and draped around both arms.
She holds a spindle and distaff in her left hand (details unclear).

PORTRAIT B: MALE BUST, ḤAGEGÛ
The figure is shown frontally. Both arms are bent and held to the torso.
He wears a tunic and a himation. The tunic has a round neckline. The folds are rendered by curving grooves. The himation is draped around both arms (›arm-sling‹ type). The folds are rendered by curving grooves on the chest and oblique grooves on the right arm.

PORTRAIT C: FEMALE BUST, PAṢÂ
The figure is shown frontally. Both arms are bent and held to the torso.

She wears a veil that falls over her head and shoulders and is further wrapped around her arms. The folds of the veil are rendered by oblique grooves.
She wears a tunic and a himation. The tunic has a round neckline. The folds are rendered by curving grooves. The himation falls across her torso and is fastened at the left shoulder (details unclear).
She holds a spindle and a distaff in her hands (details unclear).

PORTRAIT D: MALE BUST, PAṢÎÊL
The figure is shown frontally. Both arms are bent and held to the torso.
He wears a tunic and a himation. The tunic has a wide, round neckline. The folds of the tunic are rendered by curving grooves. Over the tunic, he wears a himation. The himation covers most of the body: it is wrapped around the right shoulder and arm, leaving only the upper part of the torso and the hand free. One fold of the himation crosses the chest diagonally and falls over the left shoulder (›arm-sling‹ type). The folds of the himation are indicated by diagonal grooves.
He holds the diagonal fold of the himation with his right hand. The left hand is clenched (details unclear).

PORTRAIT E: MALE BUST, MALKÛ
The figure is shown frontally. Both arms are bent and held to the torso.
He wears a tunic and a himation. The tunic has a wide, round neckline. The folds of the tunic are rendered by curving grooves. Over the tunic, he wears a himation. The himation covers most of the body: it is wrapped around the right shoulder and arm, leaving only the upper part of the torso and the hand free. One fold of the himation crosses the chest diagonally and falls over the left shoulder (›arm-sling‹ type). The folds of the himation are indicated by diagonal grooves.
He holds the diagonal fold of the himation with his right hand. The left hand is clenched (details unclear).

284. SARCOPHAGUS BOX WITH A PORTRAIT BUST

DATABASE NUMBER: PM583.
LOCATION: Palmyra, Palmyra Museum, inv. no. unknown.
CONTEXT: North necropolis. South of the House tomb no. 150, tomb of Marona.
ACQUISITION HISTORY:
MEASUREMENTS: Height: 60 cm. Width: 80 cm.
MATERIAL: Limestone.
PRESERVATION: The central part of the turban is chipped. The central part of the face, including the nose, mouth, and jaw, is broken off.
TECHNICAL DESCRIPTION: —
DATE: A.D. 100–150.
REFERENCES: Ingholt Archives, PS 1318.

Cat. 284

OBJECT DESCRIPTION
The object is rectangular in shape and depicts a female within a frame.

INSCRIPTION
SCRIPT: Palmyrene Aramaic.
LOCATION ON RELIEF: Along the top of the frame.
TRANSCRIPTION: ḤBL ŠLMT BRT YRḤY ʾTT ŠḤRW BR ḤYRN ḤBL.
TRANSLATION: Alas, Šalmat, daughter of Yarḥaî, wife of Šaḥarû, son of Ḥaîran, alas.

CIS no. 4234; PAT no. 0590.

COMMENT: See PM621 for ŠḤRY.

PORTRAIT
The figure is shown frontally. Both arms are bent and placed in front of the chest.

She wears three headdresses: a headband, a turban, and a veil. The headband is placed low on the forehead and is divided into three undecorated rectangular panels separated by narrow bands. The turban is depicted with two layers (other details unclear). Over the turban she wears a veil. It falls over the back of the head and covers both shoulders, as well as the left arm. Two wavy locks of hair fall on either side of the neck. The individual strands of hair are depicted by curving grooves. Her face is triangular. The eyebrows are curving and the eyes are large. The ears are large and protruding (other details unclear). The neck is short and wide.

She wears a tunic and a himation. The tunic has a wide, round neckline and short, wide sleeves. The folds of the garment are indicated by oblique grooves. Over the tunic she wears a himation. It is fastened at the left shoulder with a polygonal brooch, perhaps hexagonal, enclosing another polygon (details unclear) (Colledge classification d or j). The himation falls diagonally over the chest. The folds of the himation are indicated by oblique grooves.

It is unclear if she holds any attributes. The thumb, the index, and the middle fingers of both hands are extended.

A.D. 200–273

285. SARCOPHAGUS BOX WITH PORTRAIT BUSTS

DATABASE NUMBER: PalmyraUNK004.
LOCATION: Palmyra, in situ.
CONTEXT: West necropolis. Found east of the tower tomb of Elahbel.
ACQUISITION HISTORY: —
MEASUREMENTS: —
MATERIAL: Limestone.
PRESERVATION: All edges of the relief are broken off. The surface is heavily weathered.

Cat. 285

TECHNICAL DESCRIPTION: —
DATE: A.D. 200–273.
REFERENCES: Gawlikowski 1970b, 85 f. figs. 15–17; Colledge 1976, 73.

OBJECT DESCRIPTION

The relief is rectangular in shape and depicts five figures framed by a bull and a shield. There are two standing figures on the right side of the relief. In the middle, there is a kline with turned legs (other details unclear) with a standing figure and a reclining male. To the left of the kline there is a female seated on a chair (no details visible), turned towards the kline.

According to Gawlikowski 1970b, the objects comes either from tower tomb no. 17 or tower tomb no. 18.

PORTRAIT A: STANDING MALE

The figure is shown frontally. The arms appear bent, the right raised in front of the chest, the left to the side of the chest. The legs are slightly parted.
He has short hair.
He wears a knee-length tunic.
He appears to hold an object with both arms in front of the chest.

PORTRAIT B: STANDING MALE

The figure is shown frontally.

PORTRAIT C: STANDING FIGURE

The figure is shown frontally.

The figure is dressed.

PORTRAIT D: RECLINING FIGURE

The figure's torso is shown frontally. The arms and legs are in profile.

PORTRAIT E: SEATED FEMALE

The figure's head and torso are shown frontally. The arms are shown in profile. The legs are shown in three-quarter view, the knees are parted, and the ankles are crossed.
She is dressed.

A.D. 240–273

286. SARCOPHAGUS BOX RELIEF WITH PORTRAIT BUSTS

DATABASE NUMBER: KMW012.
LOCATION: Vienna, Kunsthistorisches Museum, inv. no. ANSA I 1523.
CONTEXT: West necropolis. Müller (1885) writes that it was found »near a tower tomb at the ›feet‹ of the mountain, south-west of the temple of the Sun« (Temple of Bel).
ACQUISITION HISTORY: Acquired by Dr James Samson in 1896; acquired by the museum in 1926.
MEASUREMENTS: Height: 33 cm. Width: 44 cm. Depth: 14.5 cm. Depth (of field): 7.5 cm.

Cat. 286

MATERIAL: Limestone.
PRESERVATION: The relief is broken off on all sides. The edges are chipped. There are small cracks on the surface of the relief. Portrait A: The upper part of the chest is lightly chipped. Portrait B: The nose and the left cheek are chipped. The upper part of the chest is chipped.
TECHNICAL DESCRIPTION: There are traces of red pigment in the inscriptions. There are tool marks on the surface. Portrait A: The lower eyelids are not carved. Portrait B: The lower eyelids are not carved.
DATE: A.D. 240–273.
REFERENCES: Ingholt Archives, PS 70; Müller 1885, 976 f. cat. 4; Ingholt 1928, 96 PS 70; Colledge 1976, 253. 264; Plattner 2010, 173 cat. 12 fig. 26; Krag 2018, 31 n. 54; 58 n. 300; 59 n. 323; 61 n. 332. 336; 72. 75 n. 62; 76 n. 67. 70. 71. 74; 101 n. 63; 103 n. 74; 345 cat. 670; <www.khm.at/de/object/389941c918/> (15.11.2022). Inscription: Krag 2018, 345 cat. 670.

OBJECT DESCRIPTION
The sarcophagus box is rectangular in shape and depicts two portrait busts, a male and a female.

INSCRIPTIONS
INSCRIPTION 1
SCRIPT: Palmyrene Aramaic.
LOCATION ON RELIEF: To the left of the male's head.
TRANSCRIPTION: RBT | BR | BLʿQB | ḤBL.
TRANSLATION: Rubat, son of Belʿaqab, alas!

INSCRIPTION 2
SCRIPT: Palmyrene Aramaic.
LOCATION ON RELIEF: To the right of the female's head.
TRANSCRIPTION: MQY ʾTTH | ḤBL.
TRANSLATION: Maqqaî, his wife, alas!

CIS no. 4353; PAT no. 0711.

COMMENT: Inscription 2: Vertical writing.

PORTRAIT A: ARMLESS MALE BUST

The figure is shown frontally. The head of the figure is turned slightly to his left.

His hair is short, arranged in five rows of diamond-shaped locks. He has a receding hairline. The head is oval. The eyebrows are plastically rendered as a thick curving band with oblique incised lines indicating individual hairs. The eyes are almond-shaped. The upper eyelids are distinguished from the eyeballs by the carving of the planes of the eyes. The eyeballs are blank. The ears are large and protruding with helix, concha, and scapha indicated. The nose is straight and wide. The alae are carved. The mouth is small, with full lips. He has a beard that starts from the temples, covers the cheeks, the upper lip, and the chin. The facial hair of the beard is indicated by diamond-shaped locks. The moustache is rendered by oblique lines centred over the philtrum that curve downwards and to the left and right of the face. The neck is short and wide.

He wears a tunic and a chlamys. The tunic has a small, v-shaped neckline and wide sleeves. The folds of the tunic are indicated by curving grooves over the chest and oblique lines over the arms. The chlamys falls in a wide, curving fold over the chest. It is fastened at the right shoulder with a round brooch with an incised border (Colledge classification: h). A small fold that ends in two triangles falls from under the brooch.

PORTRAIT B: ARMLESS FEMALE BUST

The figure is shown frontally.

She wears three headdresses: a headband, a second headcloth, and a veil. The headband is placed high on her forehead and is divided into rectangular decorated panels separated by vertical, plain bands. The second headcloth is indicated by a thin, undulating strip. The veil is heavy and has a scalloped edge. It falls over her right shoulder and proceeds in a curving fold across the chest and over the left shoulder. Part of the hair is covered by the headdresses. Several strands of hair above the ears are pushed back over the edge of the headband and disappear under the veil. Her face is square. Her eyebrows are curving, rendered as thin ridges. The eyes are almond-shaped. The upper eyelids are distinguished from the eyeballs by the carving of the planes of the eyes. The eyeballs are blank. Only the earlobes are visible under the hair and she is wearing earrings composed of three juxtaposed beads (Colledge classification: K). The nose is straight and wide and the alae are carved. The mouth is small, with full lips. The chin is pointed. The neck is wide with two curving grooves.

She wears a beaded necklace at the base of the neck. She wears a tunic with a wide, round neckline. The folds of the tunic are indicated by curving grooves.

HEADS: MALES

A.D. 200–220

287. MALE HEAD

DATABASE NUMBER: MBE013.
LOCATION: Beirut, Musée de Beyrouth, inv. no. unknown.
CONTEXT: South-west necropolis. Excavated by Ingholt in 1925.
ACQUISITION HISTORY: —
MEASUREMENTS: —
MATERIAL: Limestone.
PRESERVATION: The lower part of the figure is broken off at the neck. The nose is chipped.
TECHNICAL DESCRIPTION: There are traces of dark paint in the eyes.
DATE: A.D. 200–220.
REFERENCES: Ingholt Archives, PS 265; Ingholt 1928, 121 n. 2.

OBJECT DESCRIPTION

The fragment depicts the head of a male figure.

Cat. 287

PORTRAIT

His hair is arranged in three rows of snail-shell curls around the head. The individual locks of hair are indicated by incised lines. His face is square. The eyebrows are curving and plastically rendered with oblique, incised lines indicating individual hairs. The eyes are almond-shaped, with thick upper eyelids. The upper eyelids extend beyond the end of the lower ones. The irises are indicated by coloured black circles. The ears are small and protruding, with the helix, scapha, tragus, and earlobe depicted. The nose is straight. The alae are incised, and the nostrils drilled. He has a beard: it starts at the temples, covers the outer side of the cheek, the chin, and upper lip. The facial hair is rendered as snail-shell curls, and in the moustache, it is rendered by vertical, incised lines. The mouth is small, with thin lips. The chin is square.

Cat. 288, Pl. 55

HEADS: FEMALES

A.D. 150–200

288. FEMALE HEAD

DATABASE NUMBER: RGZM001.
LOCATION: Mainz, Römisch-Germanischen Zentralmuseum, inv. no. O.38870.
CONTEXT: Found at Tell Nebi Mind (15 km south-west of Homs).
ACQUISITION HISTORY: —
MEASUREMENTS: Height: 25 cm. Width: 18 cm. Depth: 22 cm.
MATERIAL: Marble.
PRESERVATION: The background is broken off. The lower part of the figure is broken off at the neck. The upper edge of the veil is broken off. The tip of the nose is broken off.
TECHNICAL DESCRIPTION: —
DATE: A.D. 150–200 (Künzl 2001: A.D. 100–200).
REFERENCES: Künzl 2001, 519–520; Krag 2018, 107 n. 110; 212 cat. 169.

OBJECT DESCRIPTION

The object depicts a female head.

PORTRAIT

The figure is shown frontally.

She wears three headdresses: a headband, a turban, and a veil. The headband is placed low on the forehead and is divided into decorated, rectangular panels separated by vertical, beaded bands. The central panel has a motif of leaves placed in an opposite arrangement on a stem. The two panels next to the central one are decorated with a diagonal cross intersecting with a cross. The two outer panels are undecorated except for a horizontal groove in the middle. The turban is coiled. It is divided into two layers and the ends are looped into each other creating a knot in the middle. Curving grooves indicate the coiling of the fabric. The veil is heavy and has a scalloped edge. It falls over the back of the head and the shoulders. Three locks of hair are brushed back over the temples, and disappear under the veil. The individual strands of hair are rendered by incised lines. Her face is square. The eyebrows are indicated by curving grooves. The eyes are wide-set, almond-shaped, with thick, upper eyelids. The irises are indicated by incised circles and the pupils by punch holes. Only the earlobes are visible under the hair. She wears earrings in the shape of horizontal bars with three round beads hanging from three twisted, rectangular elements (Colledge classification: G). The nose is straight. The alae are incised. The philtrum is carved. The mouth is small, with thin lips. The chin is round with a small cleft. The neck is slender with three curving grooves.

Sarcophagi with No Known Provenance or from Secondary Contexts

Sarcophagi with No Known Provenance or from Secondary Contexts

SARCOPHAGI

A.D. 150–200

289. COMPLETE SARCOPHAGUS RELIEF

DATABASE NUMBER: PM1072.
LOCATION: Palmyra, Palmyra Museum, inv. no. unknown.
CONTEXT: —
ACQUISITION HISTORY: —
MEASUREMENTS: —
MATERIAL: Limestone.
PRESERVATION: Well preserved. The sides of the lid are lightly chipped. The legs of the kline are chipped. The front left side of the box is fragmented. Portrait A: there is a chip on the left side of the headdresses. Portrait B: The right arm is broken off. Portrait C: The top of the head and the lower part of the legs are broken off. Portrait D: The head and the lower part of the legs are broken off. Portrait E: There are small cracks on the surface, especially on the areas of the legs and the torso. The chest appears to have been broken off and then reconstructed. There are small chips on the face. Portrait F: There are two large cracks on the surface; one across the chest and one across the torso. Part of the veil on the right side is broken off. Portrait G: The lower part of the body, including the legs are lightly chipped. Portrait G: The right side of the chest is fragmented and has been reconstructed.
TECHNICAL DESCRIPTION: There are traces of red pigment in the inscription. There are reconstructions on portraits E and G.
DATE: A.D. 150–200.
REFERENCES: <https://www.gettyimages.dk/detail/news-photo/the-tomb-of-the-three-brothers-warehouse-of-the-museum-of-news-photo/111026118> (06.05.2022).

OBJECT DESCRIPTION

The sarcophagus relief is rectangular with an arched top and depicts a banqueting scene on the lid with five figures: a seated female, three standing males, and a reclining male. The reclining male rests on two cushions on the left side. Under these figures is a box in the shape of a kline with a male and a female bust flanking a standing male between the kline legs. The female figure on the lid is seated on a low back chair. Beneath these figures there is a mattress. It has a wide band with a vegetal motif set between beaded bands. Curving grooves indicate the texture of the fabric. The stretcher is depicted with a rectangular panel over the legs. The legs are turned. They are composed of a thin plinth and above is a concave quarter, a reversed, long, concave quarter, a bell-shaped element, a torus followed by another torus.
NOTE: the relief has been erroneously associated with the tomb of the Three Brothers: <https://www.gettyimages.dk/detail/news-photo/the-tomb-of-the-three-brothers-warehouse-of-the-museum-of-news-photo/111026118?adppopup=true> (06.05.2022).

INSCRIPTIONS
INSCRIPTION 1
SCRIPT: Palmyrene Aramaic.
LOCATION ON RELIEF: Above portrait A. The head of the female seated on the left.
TRANSCRIPTION: - - - | ʿLYMH.
TRANSLATION: - - - his slave.

INSCRIPTION 2
SCRIPT: Palmyrene Aramaic.
LOCATION ON RELIEF: On the plinth.
TRANSCRIPTION: - - - - BRT ḤGGW Ḥ. .H.
TRANSLATION: - - - daughter of Ḥagegû - - -.

INSCRIPTION 3
SCRIPT: Palmyrene Aramaic.
LOCATION ON RELIEF: On the box, to the left of portrait F, at the height of the head.
TRANSCRIPTION: ḤBL GDʿ.ʾ | BRT ḤGGW | - - -ʾ - - BL | - - - YWM | - - - | 4.
TRANSLATION: Alas, - - daughter of Ḥagegû - - -, day - - - 4.

INSCRIPTION 4
SCRIPT: Palmyrene Aramaic.
LOCATION ON RELIEF: On the box, to the right of portrait G, at the height of the head.
TRANSCRIPTION: HRMS | ʿLMH.
TRANSLATION: Hermes, his slave.

INSCRIPTION 5
SCRIPT: Palmyrene Aramaic.
LOCATION ON RELIEF: On the box, to the left of portrait H, at the height of the head.
TRANSCRIPTION: - - - | 24 | ḤBL.
TRANSLATION: - - -, 24, alas!

RES no. —; CIS no. —; PAT no. —.

COMMENT: Several inscriptions are visible on the relief, above the reclining male and the seated female, on the plinth of the couch, and below for the two busts and the standing boy. Only parts of the texts are legible. There are obviously dates for two of the busts below. Inscription 3: Uncertain reading except for l. 2. At the end, a date with mention of the day. >4< is the end of the date. Inscription 5: Several illegible lines, numerical signs. >24< must be the end of the date.

PORTRAIT A: SITTING FEMALE

The figure is shown frontally. Her arms are bent; the right arm is raised to the height of the chest. The left arm is held in front of the chest. She sits with her feet apart. The left leg is obscured by the reclining male.

She wears three headdresses: a headband, a turban, and a veil. The headband is placed low on the forehead and is divided into decorated panels separated by vertical, beaded bands. The turban is coiled. It is divided into two layers and the ends are looped into each other creating a knot in the middle. Curving grooves indicate the coiling of the fabric. The veil is heavy. It falls over both shoulders and is wrapped around both arms. Her face is square. The eyebrows are curving. The eyes are almond-shaped. The eyeballs appear blank. The ears are large and protruding with the helix and lobe depicted. The nose is short and straight. The mouth is small, with thin lips. The chin is pointed. The neck is short. She wears a necklace at the base of the neck, likely a string of round beads (details unclear).

She wears a tunic and a himation. The tunic has a round neckline. The tunic ends at the feet. The folds of the tunic are indicated by wide, curving grooves. Over the tunic, she wears a himation. It falls over the left shoulder, crosses the chest diagonally, and runs under the right arm. It is fastened at the shoulder with a trapezoidal brooch. The himation ends at the knees. The folds of the himation are indicated by vertical and wide, oblique grooves. She also wears soft, round-toed boots or shoes.

She turns the palm of her right hand outwards. All the fingers are extended. With the left hand, she holds a conical object with a bowl-shaped tip, and a thick, short staff topped by a polygonal mass and a small cylinder. These are reduced versions of a spindle and a distaff. All the fingers are extended. On the left wrist, she wears a bracelet (details unclear).

PORTRAIT B: STANDING MALE

The figure is shown frontally. His arms are bent, the left arm is held in front of the torso. The left arm appears large in relation to the body. He stands with his legs together. The lower part of the legs and the feet are obscured by the reclining male.

His hair is arranged in a row of comma-shaped curls around the head. The individual strands of hair are indicated by incised lines. His face is round. The eyebrows are curving. The eyes are almond-shaped. The eyeballs appear blank. The ears are large and protruding (details unclear). The nose is short. The mouth small. The chin is square. The neck is short.

He wears a tunic, trousers, and over-trousers. The tunic has a v-shaped neckline and long, tight-fitting sleeves. The tunic ends at the knees. The folds of the tunic are rendered by wide, curving grooves. An overfold at the waist indicates that he wears a belt. Under the tunic, he wears trousers and over-trousers: the trousers are visible above the knee. The folds of the trousers are indicated by curving and oblique grooves. The over-trousers cover the knee, and their folds are indicated by wide, vertical grooves.

With his left hand, he holds an oblong object (details unclear).

PORTRAIT C: STANDING MALE

The figure is shown frontally. His arms are bent; the right arm is held to the side, the left arm is held in front of the torso. The arms appear large in relation to the body. He stands with his legs together. The shins and feet are obscured by the reclining male.

His hair is voluminous, arranged in snail-shell curls around the head. The individual strands of hair are indicated by incised lines. His face is square. The eyebrows are curving. The eyes are almond-shaped. The eyeballs appear blank. Only the earlobes are visible under the hair. The nose is short and straight. The mouth is small. The chin is square. The neck is short.

He wears a tunic, trousers, and over-trousers. The tunic has a v-shaped neckline and long, tight-fitting sleeves. The tunic ends at the knees. The folds of the tunic are rendered by wide, curving grooves. An overfold at the waist indicates that he wears a belt. Under the tunic, he wears trousers and over-trousers: the trousers are visible above the knee. The folds of the trousers are indicated by curving and oblique grooves. The over-trousers cover the knee, and their folds are indicated by wide, vertical grooves.

With his right hand, he holds an oblong object, possibly a dagger (details unclear). With his left hand, he holds a flat object (details unclear).

PORTRAIT D: STANDING MALE

The figure is shown in frontal to three-quarter view. His arms are extended and held outwards from the body. The arms appear large in relation to the body. He stands with his legs together. The shins and feet are obscured by the reclining male.

He wears a tunic, trousers, and over-trousers. The tunic has a v-shaped neckline and long, tight-fitting sleeves. The tunic ends at the knees. The folds of the tunic are rendered by wide, curving grooves. An overfold at the waist indicates that he wears a belt. Under the tunic, he wears trousers and over-trousers: the trousers are visible above the knee. The folds of the trousers are indicated by curving and oblique grooves. The over-trousers cover the knee, and their folds are indicated by wide, vertical grooves.

With his right hand, he touches the wreath worn by the reclining figure. With his left hand, he holds an object composed of two semicircles and a straight horizontal line, a bow.

PORTRAIT E: RECLINING MALE

The figure is shown in frontal to three-quarter view. His arms are bent; the right arm is held outwards from the body. The left arm rests on the cushions of the kline. The legs are bent and the left leg is placed under the right leg. The left foot is obscured by the right leg.

His hair is arranged in two rows of comma-shaped curls around the head. The individual strands of hair are indicated by incised lines. He wears a wreath high on the head (details unclear). His face is square. There are two horizontal grooves across his forehead. The eyebrows are curving. The eyes are almond-shaped. The eyeballs appear blank. The ears are large and protruding with the helix and lobe depicted. The nose is wide with carved nostrils. The mouth is wide with thin lips. The corners of the mouth curve downwards, giving him a frowning expression. The chin is square and pointed. The neck is short.

He wears a tunic, a chlamys, trousers, and over-trousers. The tunic has long, tight-fitting sleeves. It ends above the knees. Over the tunic, he wears a chlamys that falls over both shoulders, and covers most of the chest. The folds of the chlamys are indicated by wide, curving grooves. He wears a plain band belt, knotted at the centre with the ends looped tightly under either side of the waist. Under the tunic, he wears trousers and over-trousers: the trousers are visible above the knee. The over-trousers cover the knee, and their folds are indicated by wide, vertical grooves. He also wears soft, round-toed boots tied with laces.

With his right hand, he touches his knee. All fingers are extended. With his left hand, he holds a drinking bowl with convex sides.

PORTRAIT F: FEMALE BUST

The figure is shown frontally. Her arms are bent and held in front of the torso. The arms appear short in relation to the body.

She wears three headdresses: a headband, a turban, and a veil. The headband is placed low on the forehead and is divided into decorated panels separated by vertical, beaded bands. The turban is coiled. It is rendered in two layers. The veil is heavy. It falls over both shoulders and it is wrapped around both arms. Her face is oval. The eyebrows are curving. The eyes are almond-shaped. The eyeballs appear blank. The ears are protruding with the helix and lobe depicted. She wears earrings (details unclear). The nose is straight. The mouth is small, with thin lips. The chin is round. The neck is short.

She wears a tunic and a himation. The tunic has a wide, round neckline. The folds of the tunic are indicated by wide, curving grooves. Over the tunic, she wears a himation. It falls over the left shoulder, crosses the chest diagonally, and runs under the right arm. It is fastened at the shoulder with a circular brooch (details unclear). The folds of the himation are indicated by vertical and wide, oblique grooves.

The index finger of the right hand is extended. With the left hand, she holds a conical object and a thick, short staff topped by a polygonal mass and a small cylinder. These are reduced versions of a spindle and a distaff. The index finger is extended.

PORTRAIT G: STANDING MALE

The figure is shown frontally. His right arm is held to the side. The left arm is bent and held in front of the torso. The arms appear large in relation to the body. He stands with his legs slightly apart.

His hair is arranged in a single row of comma-shaped locks. The individual strands of hair are indicated by incised lines. His face is square. The eyes are almond-shaped. The eyeballs appear blank. The ears are protruding (details unclear). The chin is round. The neck is short.

The moustache is rendered with narrow, oblique and vertical incised lines: they are centred over the philtrum, and curve downwards and to the left.

He wears a tunic and trousers. The tunic has long-tight fitting sleeves. The folds of the tunic are indicated by wide, curving grooves. Under the tunic, he wears trousers. The folds of the trousers are indicated by curving and oblique grooves.

With his right hand, he possibly holds an object (details unclear). With his left hand, he holds a large vessel with straight sides and round handles.

PORTRAIT H: MALE BUST

The figure is shown frontally. His arms are bent and held in front of the chest torso.

His hair is arranged in comma-shaped locks. The individual strands of hair are indicated by incised lines. His face is square. There are two horizontal grooves across his forehead. The eyebrows are curving. The eyes are almond-shaped. The eyeballs appear blank. The ears are protruding with the helix and lobe depicted. The nose is wide. The mouth is small. The corners of the mouth curve downwards, giving him a frowning expression. The chin is round and pointed. The neck is short.

He wears a tunic and a himation. The tunic has a wide, round neckline. The folds of the tunic are rendered by wide, curving grooves. Over the tunic, he wears a himation. The himation is wrapped around the right shoulder and arm, leaving only part of the upper torso and the right hand free. One fold of the himation crosses the chest diagonally and falls over the left shoulder (>arm-sling< type), covering the left arm. The folds of the himation are indicated by oblique grooves.

With his right hand, he lightly holds the diagonal fold of the himation.

A.D. 240–273

290. COMPLETE SARCOPHAGUS WITH BANQUETING SCENE AND RELIGIOUS SCENE

DATABASE NUMBER: PM494.
LOCATION: Palmyra, Palmyra Museum, inv. no. 2677B/8983.
CONTEXT: Secondary context: Found (10.09.1990) built into temple tomb no. 176.
ACQUISITION HISTORY: —

Cat. 290, Pl. 56

MEASUREMENTS: Length of box: 232 cm. Width of box: 107 cm. Height of box: 110 cm. Height of figures on box: 70 cm. Length of lid: 226 cm. Width of lid: 97–105 cm. Height of lid: 115 cm (highest point on horse).

MATERIAL: Limestone, white/yellow.

PRESERVATION: The head and the front legs of the horse are broken off. The top right corner under the horse is chipped. The heads of the standing figures are chipped and the surface is weathered. Portrait A: The lower part is broken off diagonally at the knees. The surface of the left leg is chipped. Portraits B and C: Only the bases of the figures are preserved. Portrait D: The head is broken off at the base of the neck. The left lower arm and at the front of the right foot are broken off. Portrait E: The surface is weathered. The upper part is broken off at the waist. Portrait F: A crack runs horizontally through the waist. Portrait G: The surface of the face is shipped. A crack runs diagonally from the right side of the waist and through the head of the calf. Portraits H–K: The surfaces of the faces are chipped. Portrait L: The nose, mouth, and the chin are chipped. Portrait M: The surface is weathered and the head is chipped. Portrait N: The surface of the face is chipped. Portrait O: The surface of the face is chipped. Portrait P: The surface of the face is chipped. The surface is weathered.

TECHNICAL DESCRIPTION: There are traces of red pigment in the tondo of the patera.

DATE: A.D. 240–273 (al-Asʿad – Schmidt-Colinet 1995: A.D. 200–273).

REFERENCES: Colledge 1992, 49 fig. 49; al-Asʿad – Schmidt-Colinet 1995, 41 figs. 48–51; Schmidt-Colinet 1997, 164 fig. 4.12; Wielgosz 1997, 70 pl. 2.1; Parlasca 1998, 313 pl. 126, 1; Rumscheid 2000, 223 f. cat. 272 pl. 66, 1; Kaizer 2002, 179 pl. 4; Yon 2002, 132 fig. 35; Schmidt-Colinet 2004, 193 f. figs. 7–10; al-Asʿad – Schmidt-Colinet 2005, 42 figs. 60–66; Sommer 2005, 199 f. pls. 4–5; Schmidt-Colinet – al-Asʿad 2007, 271–276 pls. 84–89; Hekster 2008, 51 pl. 40; Fejfer 2009, 108 fig. 67; Schmidt-Colinet 2009,

223–227 figs. 1–8; Gawlikowski 2010a, 66; Andrade 2013, 184 f. fig. 14; Wielgosz-Rondolino 2016a, 77 f. fig. 16, a–c; Ciliberto 2017, 49. 54 fig. 2; Curtis 2017, 63 f. fig. 15; Raja 2017a, 220 f. 227 cat. 19; Raja 2017f, 64 f. 75 cat. 19; Raja 2017g, 64 f. 75 cat. 19; Sommer 2017, 185–186; Krag 2018, 32 n. 63; 49 n. 229; 53 n. 260; 58 n. 304; 62 n. 349. 351–353; 64 n. 361. 362; 65 n. 367. 372. 373; 66 n. 382; 73 n. 47. 54; 87 n. 183; 103 n. 73; 396 cat. 854; Kaizer 2018, 84 fig. 8; Sommer 2018, 175 fig. 8,3; Cussini 2019b, 58 fig. 5.5.

OBJECT DESCRIPTION

The sarcophagus is rectangular in shape and depicts the torso and neck of a horse, two standing figures, a reclining figure, and a standing figure. Underneath these figures is a box in the shape of a kline with seven male figures and an animal between the kline legs. On top of the kline are two mattresses. The mattress at the top is decorated with an intersecting lozenge pattern with four-petal flowers inside them. The lower mattress is decorated with five bands. The outer bands are decorated with a running scroll with rosettes, set between beaded bands. The bands on either side of the central one are decorated with lobed leaves in an opposite arrangement on the stem, set between beaded bands. The central band is decorated with four-petal flowers separated by beaded bands. The centre of the flower petals is rendered by fine, incised lines. It is set between beaded bands. Curving grooves indicate the texture of the mattress. The largest figure on the lid, the reclining figure, rests the left arm against a cushion. It is decorated with a band with a sequence of narrow, rib-shaped flowers, six-petal rosettes and serrated six-petal flowers in circles. The band is set between beaded bands. A folded cloth with tassels lies on top of the cushion. It is decorated with a floral motif set between beaded bands. A fulcrum is shown on the left side of the kline. It is decorated with a small armless bust of a male (portrait: M) rendered in a clipeus. From the fulcrum, a male figure protrudes. The right arm is held along the body and the left is bent. The left leg is bent under the right with the knee pointing forwards. He wears a himation that covers his left shoulder and arm, leaving the chest free. The himation proceeds in a curving fold across his waist, covers his legs and falls back at his right side. The chest musculature and the navel are rendered by narrow depressions. In his right hand, he holds a large staff that rests against the upper arm. A row of curving grooves is rendered over his head, possibly depicting a garment of another figure. A female figure is positioned over the male figure. She is seated. Her legs are turned towards her right and her torso is turned toward her left. The left arm is bent and raised, and the right arm is lowered at the height of the waist. She wears a chiton.

The central stretcher of the kline is decorated. The central part is divided into two sections by a thin, horizontal line. The upper section is decorated with leaves placed at either end from where a crisscross pattern extends. The lower section is decorated with a tongue pattern. On either side of the stretcher are rectangular indentations flanked by two square inlays or appliqués. The rectangular indentations are decorated with

Cat. 290

a wave pattern and the inlays with animals. The kline legs are turned. They are composed of a plinth, above is a concave quarter, a long reversed concave quarter, a concave quarter, a torus, a reversed bell-shaped element, a ball, a biconical element, a reversed concave quarter, and a bell-shaped element. All elements are decorated with a tongue pattern.

On the right side of the sarcophagus lid, a horse is shown. It is fragmented, only the lower part of the neck, the body, and the upper part of the tail is preserved. The chest musculature of the horse is modelled and rendered by deep grooves. The tail is long and voluminous. The individual hairs of the tail are rendered by incised lines. The horse is equipped with a cushioned saddle, a rein at the buttock, and a wide strap around the neck. The saddle cushion is decorated with four-petal flowers in squares separated by beaded bands. The lower part of the pommels at the front and the back of the saddle is preserved. The rein at the buttock is decorated with a wave pattern and circles with a beaded edge. The neck strap is decorated with a scroll with concentric, incised circles. At the middle, the strap is fastened with a circular medallion with a beaded border and a central, undecorated inlay.

Cat. 290

Cat. 290

Cat. 290, Pl. 57

The left lateral side of the sarcophagus lid is decorated with a relief divided into two registers. A part of the upper edge is preserved, decorated with a band with oblique grooves. The upper register depicts five figures in architectural aediculae, alternating between triangular and circular pediments supported by columns on bases. Larger figures are shown between the aediculae. The lower register depicts five figures in architectural aediculae, alternating between triangular and circular pediments supported by columns on bases. The lower edge of the sarcophagus lid is decorated with a sequence of squares with four-petal flowers. The midribs of the leaves are incised.

The sarcophagus box depicts seven standing male figures. Between portraits F and G the front legs and part of the torso of an animal are shown frontally. The head of the animal is chipped. The hooves of the animal are rendered, and they have an incised line down the middle, suggesting that the animal is a calf. A small rectangular altar is shown between portraits H and I: the base is composed of two juxtaposed hexagonal plinths, the body is rectangular, and has a trapezoidal upper end, with a circular top. Above the altar, between the heads of portraits H and I, a wreath with a folded cloth underneath is shown. The cloth is folded into two circular loops on either side. Between portraits I and J is a high, cylindrical, flat-top headdress (Palmyrene priestly hat) shown at the height of their heads. It is divided into three sections by two vertical grooves. A wreath with the leaves pointing towards a central medallion is depicted at the middle of the headdress. A folded cloth is shown underneath the headdress. It has two circular, looped folds on either side.

The right lateral side of the sarcophagus box depicts a standing female and a reclining female. The figures are resting on a kline with a mattress. The mattress is decorated with two bands. They are decorated with running scrolls with rosettes. Curving grooves indicate the texture of the fabric. The reclining female rests the right arm against a cushion. The cushion is decorated with a wide, central band (details unclear). The central stretcher of the kline is decorated with two rectangular indentations followed by a square inlay on each side. The central section appears to be decorated (details unclear). The kline legs are composed of two trapezoidal turning. The kline legs are decorated with a tongue pattern. Between the figures, a hexagon-shaped chest placed on a pillar is depicted. The narrow upper part of the chest also, in a hexagon-shape, is decorated with rows of oblique grooves. Each section on the lower part of the chest is decorated with inlays (details unclear).

The left lateral side depicts a standing female and a camel. The camel is rendered in profile. The neck is slender and curving,

Cat. 290, Pl. 58

the body is oval and oblong. The legs are slender. The tail of the camel is crescent-shaped and the hairs are rendered by incised lines. The camel is equipped with a tall saddle covered by a woollen skin, possibly sheep. The texture is indicated by fine, incised lines. On the back of the saddle is a coiled fabric. Underneath the saddle is an embroidered cloth decorated with rhombi. Each diamond has a raised dot at the centre and the edge of the cloth has a beaded band. The saddle is attached to the camel by three lanyards, which form a single band on the belly. The lanyards are covered at the top of the saddle by the skin. On the hip of the camel is a round shield decorated with circular incisions, connected to the saddle by a strap.

SARCOPHAGUS LID

PORTRAIT A: STANDING MALE

The figure is standing with the legs slightly apart. The feet of the figure are obscured by the right foot of the reclining figure to his left.

He wears a ›Parthian-style‹ tunic and ›Parthian-style‹ trousers. The tunic ends at the knees and has a decorated lower border with a running scroll with rosettes and a beaded band at the hem. He also wears trousers tucked into his boots. Each trouser leg is decorated in the middle with a vegetal motif extending downwards. The folds of the trousers are indicated by wide, curving grooves. He wears ankle boots.

PORTRAIT B: STANDING FIGURE
(Details unclear).

PORTRAIT C: STANDING FIGURE
(Details unclear).

PORTRAIT D: RECLINING MALE

The figure is shown in frontal to three-quarter view. The right arm appears short in relation to the body. The right arm is extended and rests on his raised right knee. The left arm is bent and held to the chest. His right leg is bent and his foot is resting on the mattress. The left leg is bent under the right leg with the knee pointing outwards.

He wears a ›Parthian-style‹ tunic, a chlamys, and ›Parthian-style‹ trousers. The tunic has a wide, round neckline decorated with squares and rhombi. The tunic has long, tight-fitting sleeves. The cuffs of the sleeves are decorated with a beaded band, followed by acanthus leaves, each with two opposite volutes, followed by another beaded band. At the middle, the tunic has a wide band decorated with nude male figures holding baskets and picking grapes, extending downwards. The figures are rendered within concentric circles that are tied together by a vine scroll. Surrounding the circles are vines and bunches of grapes. The tunic ends above the knees and has a decorated border with lobed leaves in an opposite arrangement on a stem, set between beaded bands. At the right thigh, the border of the tunic is folded upwards revealing the inner side. The folds of the tunic are rendered by curving, wide grooves. Over the tunic, he wears a chlamys that falls over both shoulders and covers most of the chest. One edge of the chlamys has a scalloped border decorated with rosettes followed by a beaded band, visible on the fold across the chest and the four folds falling down the left shoulder and along the cushion. Attached to the fold in the middle is a pendant or a weight. It is rendered in the shape of a flower with four lanceolate leaves with a round inlay within. The edge of the fold to the left ends in a tassel. The chlamys is fastened at the right shoulder with a circular brooch (details unclear). A zigzag-shaped fold falls from under the brooch. The folds of the chlamys are rendered by wide, curving grooves. Alongside his right thigh lies an object with a pointed end, a rectangular main body, and a lateral semicircle: a sheathed dagger. He also wears a belt across the lower torso. It is composed of round and square bezels with incised borders linked by beaded elements. The bezels and the strap of the belt are fastened to a star-shaped element. The straps are knotted at the centre with the ends looped under on either side of the knot. A sword is fastened to the belt. It has a pommel decorated with a rosette while the scabbard is decorated with an upper curving rim and a central fuller. The trousers are visible from above the knees. Each trouser leg is decorated with a broad, central band extending downwards, decorated with five-petal flowers in circles, and set between beaded bands. The folds of the trousers are rendered by curving grooves. His trousers are tucked into his round-toe boot. The boot is decorated with vines that meander across the surface. The upper edge is decorated with a panel with squares and rhombi between thin lines, followed by panels with a wave pattern. The boot has a wide band running above the ankle. It is decorated with concentric circles and fastened to the boot with a button in the shape of a rosette.

With his right hand, he holds a pinecone facing downwards. The scales of the pinecone are outlined. At the centre of the chest, the outline of an object, possibly a bowl is recognizable.

PORTRAIT E: STANDING MALE

The figure is shown frontally. The legs are obscured by the reclining figure to his right.

He wears a garment, possibly a ›Parthian-style‹ tunic, which ends at the knees. The lower edge of the tunic has a decorated band (details unclear). The folds of the garment are rendered by oblique grooves.

SARCOPHAGUS BOX

PORTRAIT F: STANDING MALE

The figure is shown in three-quarter view. The right arm is bent and held to the chest. The left arm is bent and held out from the body towards the animal. He stands with his legs apart and rests his weight on the right leg. The left leg is slightly bent with the knee rendered under the drapery.

His hair is arranged in snail-shell curls around the head.

He wears a tunic with short sleeves. The tunic ends at the knees. An overfold, possibly created by a belt, is rendered in a curving line at the waist. The folds of the tunic are rendered by oblique and curving grooves. He does not wear shoes.

His right hand is clenched around a thin, oblong object, possibly a dagger.

PORTRAIT G: STANDING MALE

The figure is shown frontally. The head appears to be turned slightly to his right. The right arm is held along the side of the body. The left arm is slightly bent and held out from the body. He stands with his legs apart. He rests his weight on the left leg while the right leg is slightly bent with the knee rendered under the drapery.

The neck is short.

He wears an undergarment and a tunic. The undergarment has a tasselled edge and is visible proceeding in a diagonal line from the left knee and over the right. The tunic has a wide, round neckline and long, tight-fitting sleeves. An overfold, possibly created by a belt, is rendered in a curving line at the waist. The folds of the tunic are rendered by oblique and curving grooves. He wears sandals (other details unclear).

With the right hand, he holds the handle of a jug. The jug has an ovoid body and a narrow neck. With the palm turned outwards, he holds the handle of a patera in his left hand.

PORTRAIT H: STANDING MALE

The figure is shown frontally. The head appears to be turned slightly to his right. Both arms are bent and held to the torso. He stands with his legs set apart and rests his weight on the left leg. The right leg is slightly bent with the knee rendered in the drapery.

The outline of his hair is recognizable and it appears to be voluminous and reaching the neck.

He wears an undergarment and a tunic. The undergarment has a tasselled edge and is visible proceeding in a diagonal line from the left knee and over the right. The tunic has a wide, round neckline and short, loose sleeves. An overfold, possibly created by a belt, is rendered in a curving line at the waist. The folds of the tunic are rendered by oblique and curving grooves. He wears sandals (other details unclear).

The outline of a rectangular chest is visible at the left side of his waist. With the right hand, he holds the lid of the chest. He holds the bottom of the chest with the left hand.

PORTRAIT I: STANDING MALE

The figure is shown frontally. The right arm is extended and held out from the body. The left arm is bent and held to the torso. He stands with his legs apart. The left leg is slightly bent with the knee rendered in the drapery.

He wears a wreath with a central element (details unclear). The neck is wide.

He wears a tunic and a toga. The tunic has a wide, round neckline and short sleeves. On the right side of the chest, the tunic has a wide band (clavus) extending downwards. The folds of the tunic are rendered by curving grooves. The toga is folded over his left shoulder and arm, leaving the hand free. A wide fold of the toga is wrapped around his abdomen, coming from the right side and extends downwards with two large, curving folds (the sinus) rendered. The fold (umbo) coming from the left shoulder is folded under the wide fold at the abdomen. The toga ends at the ankles. The folds of the toga are rendered by curving and oblique grooves. He also wears sandals (details unclear).

With the right hand he holds a patera above the altar. With the left hand, he holds an oblong object, possibly a book-roll. The index finger is extended.

PORTRAIT J: STANDING MALE

The figure is shown in three-quarter view. Both arms are bent and held to the torso. He stands with his legs slightly apart. He rests his weight on the right leg and the left leg is slightly bent with the knee rendered in the drapery.

The outline of the hair is recognizable and appears to have been voluminous and covering the ears.

He wears an undergarment and a tunic. The undergarment has a tasselled edge and is visible proceeding in a diagonal line from the left knee and over the right. The tunic has a wide, round neckline and wide sleeves reaching the elbows. An overfold, possibly created by a belt, is rendered in a curving line at the waist. The folds of the tunic are rendered by oblique and curving grooves. He wears sandals (other details unclear).

He holds a large bowl filled with round objects, possibly fruit, in his hands.

PORTRAIT K: STANDING MALE

The figure is shown in three-quarter view. The head is seen frontally. The arms are bent and held to the torso. He stands with his legs slightly apart. He rests his weight on the right leg and the left leg is slightly bent with the knee rendered in the drapery.

His hair is centrally parted and brushed to each side of the forehead. On the sides of the head, the hair becomes curly and covers the ears. The neck is long.

He wears an undergarment and a tunic. The undergarment has a tasselled edge and is visible proceeding in a diagonal line from the left knee and over the right. The tunic has a wide, round neckline and wide sleeves reaching the elbows. An overfold with a tasselled edge, possibly created by a belt, is rendered in a curving line at the waist. The folds of the tunic are rendered by oblique and curving grooves. He does not wear shoes.

He is holding a bird in his hands. The individual feathers are outlined by incised lines and the tail by horizontal grooves.

PORTRAIT L: STANDING MALE

The figure is shown frontally. The right arm is extended and held out from the body. The left arm is bent and held to the torso. He stands with his legs apart. He rests his weight on the right leg and the left leg is slightly bent with the knee rendered in the drapery.

He wears an undergarment, a tunic, and a himation. The undergarment has a tasselled edge and is visible proceeding in a diagonal line from the left knee and over the right. The tunic has a wide, v-shaped neckline and short, wide sleeves. An overfold with a tasselled edge, possibly created by a belt, is rendered in a curving line at the waist. The folds of the tunic are rendered by oblique and curving grooves. Over the tunic, he wears a himation. It is wrapped around his left shoulder and arm, leaving the left side of the body and the hand free. The himation falls in a wide fold along the left side of the body and falls back at the waist. He wears sandals (other details unclear).

With the right hand, he holds the handle of a jug. The jug has an ovoid body and a wide neck. With the left hand, he holds the thick fold of the himation. The thumb and the index finger are extended.

PORTRAIT M: ARMLESS BUST OF A MALE IN FULCRUM

The figure is shown frontally, rendered in a clipeus (details unclear).

THE RIGHT LATERAL SIDE OF SARCOPHAGUS BOX

PORTRAIT N: STANDING FEMALE

The figure is shown in three-quarter view. The right arm is bent and held to the torso and the left arm is bent and held out from her body towards the reclining figure. She stands with the legs slightly parted. Her feet are obscured by the reclining female to her left.

She wears a tunic and a himation. The tunic has a wide, round neckline and short sleeves. The folds of the tunic are rendered by curving grooves. Over the tunic, she wears an ankle-length himation. It is wrapped around her left shoulder and arm, covering the left breast and the body. The folds of the himation are rendered by curving and vertical grooves.

She holds the ends of a necklace in her hands, directing it towards the reclining female to her left. The necklace is composed of a central rectangular pendant and oval pendants on each side. The pendants are linked by beaded elements.

PORTRAIT O: RECLINING FEMALE

The figure is shown in frontal to three-quarter view. The right arm is bent and rests on her right raised knee. The left arm is bent and raised to the neck. The right leg is bent. The left leg is slightly bent and extended along the mattress. The right foot is obscured by the left leg.

She wears a veil. It falls down on each side of the face and back at the shoulders. She wears two necklaces: one composed of round beads in a string worn at the base of the neck. One composed of a loop-in-loop chain with a central, oval pendant. The chain and pendant are linked by oval terminals on each side.

She wears a tunic and a himation. The tunic has a wide, v-shaped neckline and short, wide sleeves. The folds of the tunic are rendered by curving and oblique grooves. Over the tunic, she wears a himation. It is wrapped around her left shoulder and upper arm. It proceeds in a curving fold across the chest and covers the left breast and the body. A wide, zigzag-shaped fold of the himation falls from under her left arm across the cushion and the mattress. The edge of the fold is tied into a small knot. The himation ends at the ankles. The folds are rendered by curving and oblique grooves.

Her right hand is placed on her right raised knee. She wears a wide hoop bracelet around her right wrist. Her left hand is raised to the neck, and she appears to pull a fold of the veil with her hand.

THE LEFT LATERAL SIDE OF SARCOPHAGUS BOX

PORTRAIT P: STANDING FEMALE

The figure is shown frontally. The right arm is bent and held away from the body. The left arm is slightly bent and held to the lower body. She stands with her legs apart.

She wears a tunic and a himation. The tunic has a wide, round neckline and short, tight-fitting sleeves. The folds of the tunic are rendered by curving grooves. Over the tunic, she wears a himation. It is folded around her left shoulder and upper arm. It proceeds in a slightly curving fold along the left side of the chest and body. Another end of the himation is folded from the right side across the waist, covers the legs, and reaches the ground. The folds of the himation are rendered by deep, diagonal and curving grooves.

Her right hand is clenched around a long staff. The left hand is pulling the fold of the himation coming across the waist.

SARCOPHAGUS LIDS

A.D. 130–150

291. FRAGMENT OF A BANQUETING RELIEF

DATABASE NUMBER: NMD046.
LOCATION: Damascus, National Museum of Damascus, inv. no. Damaskus 19.
CONTEXT: —
ACQUISITION HISTORY: —
MEASUREMENTS: Height: 55 cm. Width: 94 cm.
MATERIAL: Limestone, white.
PRESERVATION: Most of the background is broken off. The lower left side of the relief is chipped. Portrait A: The nose is chipped. Portrait B: The nose is chipped. The part of the body along the mattress is lightly chipped.
TECHNICAL DESCRIPTION: There are traces of pigment in the eyes of the figures.
DATE: A.D. 130–150 (Parlasca 1982a: A.D. 100–150).

REFERENCES: Ingholt Archives, PS 62; Ingholt 1928, 94; Ingholt 1935, 68 pl. 28, 1; Abdul-Hak – Abdul-Hak 1951, 30 cat. 4 pl. 10, 2; Drijvers 1976, 22. 37 pl. 76; Parlasca 1982a, 197–199 cat. 177; Taha 1982, 119 fig. 3; Parlasca 1985, 397 f. cat. 189; Krag 2018, 28 n. 9; 33 n. 77. 78; 41 n. 142. 143; 66 n. 382; 104 n. 78; 242 cat. 282; Raja 2019e, 98. 147 cat. 91 fig. 43. Inscription: Ingholt 1928, 94; Krag 2018, 242 cat. 282.

OBJECT DESCRIPTION
The sarcophagus lid is rectangular in shape and depicts a seated female and a reclining male. She sits on a chair with solid sides and a high back. The edges of the chair are delineated with a groove. He rests against a round cushion decorated with a wide band with four-petal rosettes. The texture and fabric of the cushion are indicated by curving grooves.

INSCRIPTIONS
INSCRIPTION 1
SCRIPT: Palmyrene Aramaic.
LOCATION ON RELIEF: On the right side of the chair.
TRANSCRIPTION: —

Cat. 291, Pl. 59

TRANSLATION: —

INSCRIPTION 2
SCRIPT: Palmyrene Aramaic.
LOCATION ON RELIEF: To the left of the male's head.
TRANSCRIPTION: —
TRANSLATION: —

CIS no. —; PAT no. —.

COMMENT: The inscription is fake.

PORTRAIT A: SEATED FEMALE

The figure is shown frontally. Her arms are bent; the right hand is held at the height of the shoulder, the left in front of the torso. Her legs are bent with the knees rendered under the drapery, and her feet are on the relief ground. The left foot is obscured by the reclining figure.

She wears three headdresses: a headband, a turban, and a veil. The headband is placed low on the forehead and is decorated with three rectangular panels each separated by three narrow bands. The turban is coiled rendered in two layers. Over the turban she wears a heavy veil that is folded around both arms and runs along each side. Several locks of hair, indicated by curving grooves, are depicted over the ears and are brushed back over the edge of the turban. Two long, curving locks of hair fall down on either side of the neck. Her face is square. The eyebrows are curving. The eyes are large and round with thick eyelids. The irises and pupils are indicated by concentric, incised lines. She wears earrings shaped as a miniature bunch of grapes (Colledge classification: E). The nose is straight with a wide base. The mouth is wide with a full lower lip. The chin is square. The neck is long and wide.

She wears a tunic and a himation. The tunic has a wide, round neckline. The folds of the tunic are indicated by wide, curving grooves. Over the tunic, she wears a himation. It is fastened at the left shoulder with a trapezoidal brooch with an animal head finial (Colledge classification: a). The details of the animal are unclear. The himation crosses the chest diagonally and covers the lower body. She wears closed shoes (visible on the right foot).

With her right hand, she holds a fold of the veil near the shoulder. Her index and the middle finger are extended. With her left hand, she holds an oblong shape with oblique grooves and a narrow end, and a round object with a crisscross pattern on a narrow end. This is a reduced version of a spindle and distaff respectively.

PORTRAIT B: RECLINING PRIEST

The figure's head, torso, and upper legs are shown frontally, the arms and lower legs in profile. The head appears large in relation to the body. The right arm is extended and rests on the raised right knee, the left is bent in front of the torso. The right leg is bent and the foot rests on the mattress. The left leg is bent under the right, and the foot is obscured by the right leg.

He wears a tall, cylindrical, flat-top headdress divided into three sections by two vertical grooves low on the forehead: a Palmyrene priestly hat. A wreath is depicted at the lower part of the hat. It has three rows of long, narrow leaves pointing towards an armless bust. Two round objects, possibly berries, are located on either side of the central leaves next to the bust. The bust depicts a beardless male with a Palmyrene priestly hat. The nose is wide, and he wears a tunic with a wide, round neckline and a chlamys that is folded and covers most of the chest, fastened at the right shoulder with a circular brooch. His face is triangular. The eyebrows are indicated by curving ridges. The eyes are large, deep-set, and round with thick eyelids. The irises and pupils are indicated by concentric, incised circles. The ears are small and slightly protruding with the helix, scapha, and lobe shown. The nose is straight. The mouth is small, with a full lower lip. The chin is pointed with a small, round depression. The neck is long and slender.

He wears a tunic, a ›Parthian-style‹ tunic, a chlamys, ›Parthian-style‹ trousers, and over-trousers. The first tunic has a wide, round neckline and tight-fitting, long sleeves. The tunic over it has a beaded neckline, and its lower hem is decorated with a wide band with rosettes inside circles or a running scroll (›Parthian-style‹). It also has a small slit on the right side, with a button-like object at the top of the slit. The folds of the tunic are indicated by curving grooves in the area of the torso and legs, and oblique ones at the arms. The tunic is tied at the waist with a narrow band belt tied with a double knot. Over the ›Parthian-style‹ tunic, he wears a chlamys that falls over both shoulders, and covers most of the chest. The edge of the chlamys is decorated with a running scroll motif between two narrow ridges. It is fastened at the right shoulder with a circular brooch with an incised border and a raised, circular centre (Colledge classification: i). A zigzag-shaped fold falls from under the brooch. The folds of the chlamys are indicated by curving grooves in the area of the left shoulder, and oblique ones on the right side. Under the tunic, he wears trousers. They are decorated with a wide band that extends downwards. The band is framed by beaded borders, and has a running scroll with clusters of grapes. He also wears over-trousers that cover the lower legs. The folds of the over-trousers are indicated by wide grooves. He wears a closed boot tied at the ankle with a band with a double knot.

With the left hand, he holds a skyphos with double-looped handles, without decoration.

A.D. 140–160

292. SARCOPHAGUS LID RELIEF WITH BANQUETING SCENE

DATABASE NUMBER: PM546.
LOCATION: Palmyra, Palmyra Museum, inv. no. A 218/218.
CONTEXT: —
ACQUISITION HISTORY: In 1890 it was in front of the schoolhouse of the village of Palmyra. Already in 1908 it was at the ›praetorium‹ or ›serail‹ of Palmyra. In the collection of the French military commander at Palmyra in 1928. Later moved to Palmyra Museum.
MEASUREMENTS: Height: 85 cm. Width: 178 cm. Depth: 18 cm.
MATERIAL: Limestone, white/yellow.
PRESERVATION: The state of preservation is described as when photographed by al-Asʿad and Gawlikowski (1997). When the object was photographed by Ingholt (1928), it was in a better condition. The surface is weathered. The upper right corner of the sarcophagus lid is broken off. Portrait A: The surface of the face, of the hands, and of the right shoulder is chipped. Portrait B: The surface of the face, of the right shoulder, and of both arms is chipped. Portrait C: The upper part of the head is broken off. The surface of the face, of the right arm, and of the left hand is chipped. Portrait D: The surface of the face, of the right lower arm, and of the left hand is chipped. The surface is weathered. Portrait E: The front of his right foot is broken off. The surface of the face is chipped.
TECHNICAL DESCRIPTION: —
DATE: A.D. 140–160.
REFERENCES: Ingholt Archives, PS 61; Post 1891, 36; Uspensky 1902, 128 pl. 14; Kelman 1908, 308 fig. inserted between 206 f.; Chabot 1922, 111 f. pl. 27, 13; Ingholt 1928, 94; Kammerer 1929, 310 n. 2 pl. 120, 1; Seyrig 1934, 174 pl. 24, 2; Ingholt 1935, 68 n. 50; Seyrig 1937, 5 n. 9; Gawlikowski 1966, 75. 85 fig. 4; Ingholt 1974, 40–43 pl. 1, 3; al-Asʿad – Gawlikowski 1997, 68 cat. 104 fig. 104; Savignac 2001, 167; Yon 2002, 81 n. 161; 133 n. 10; 178 n. 91; Heyn 2008, 170–173. 178 fig. 6, 2; Gawlikowski 2010a, 77; Krag – Raja 2017, 199 n. 24; 203. 204 n. 72. 73. 75; 205 n. 76. 81; 208 n. 99; 209 n. 100; 210 n. 107; 212. 214 cat. 9; Heyn 2018, 111. 117 fig. 2; Krag 2018, 28 n. 9; 33 n. 77. 78. 80. 82; 47 n. 208; 65 n. 377; 66 n. 382; 67 n. 4; 86 n. 178; 87 n. 182. 184. 185; 88 n. 190. 192. 195; 89 n. 204. 205. 207. 208. 210; 98 n. 23; 242 f. cat. 284; Raja 2019e, 98. 147 f. cat. 92 fig. 44; <http://www.gerty.ncl.ac.uk/photo_details.php?photo_id=540> (06.05.2022); <http://www.gerty.ncl.ac.uk/photo_details.php?photo_id=312> (06.05.2022); <https://virtual-museum-syria.org/palmyra/banquet-scene-of-a-barateh-son-of-barnabou-with-his-mother-and-three-children/> (06.05.2022). Inscription:

Cat. 292

Chabot 1922, 112; Ingholt 1974, 41–43; al-Asʿad – Gawlikowski 1997, 68 cat. 104 fig. 104; Krag 2018, 242 f. cat. 284.

OBJECT DESCRIPTION
The sarcophagus lid is rectangular in shape and depicts a seated female, three standing males, and a reclining male. The female sits on a cushion in a wicker chair, indicated by a crisscross pattern. She rests her feet on a footstool: it has a rectangular flat stretcher and short, rectangular legs. The reclining male rests his left arm on a cushion. Curving grooves indicate the texture of the fabric.

INSCRIPTIONS
INSCRIPTION 1
SCRIPT: Palmyrene Aramaic.
LOCATION ON RELIEF: To the right of the seated female.
TRANSCRIPTION: ʿTMʾ [BT] | MQYMW | GDYBWL | ʾMHWN.
TRANSLATION: ʿAtemaʿ daughter of Moqîmû Gaddîbôl, their mother.

INSCRIPTION 2
SCRIPT: Palmyrene Aramaic.
LOCATION ON RELIEF: To the right of the standing male to the right.
TRANSCRIPTION: NBWGDY BR | BRNBW ʾḤWHY.
TRANSLATION: Nabûgaddî son of Barnabû, his brother.

INSCRIPTION 3
SCRIPT: Palmyrene Aramaic.
LOCATION ON RELIEF: To the right of the central standing male.
TRANSCRIPTION: BRNBW BR BRNBW | ʾḤWHY.
TRANSLATION: Barnabû son of Barnabû, his brother.

INSCRIPTION 4
SCRIPT: Palmyrene Aramaic.
LOCATION ON RELIEF: To the right of the standing male to the left.
TRANSCRIPTION: BRʿTH BR | BRNBW ʾḤWHY.
TRANSLATION: Barʿateh son of Barnabû, his brother.

INSCRIPTION 5
SCRIPT: Palmyrene Aramaic.
LOCATION ON RELIEF: To the right of the reclining figure.
TRANSCRIPTION: ṢLM BRʿTH | BR BRNBW BR | BRNBW.
TRANSLATION: Image of Barʿateh son of Barnabû son of Barnabû.

CIS no. 4231; PAT no. 0587.

COMMENT: Inscription 1: ʿAtemaʿ is the mother of Nabûgaddî, of Barnabû, and maybe of the younger Barʿateh. Inscription 4: Alternatively, this Barʿateh may be a son of Barnabû, the brother of the first Barʿateh (the reclining male). Likewise, the two other men may be nephews of the first Barʿateh.

PORTRAIT A: SEATED FEMALE, ʿATEMAʿ
The figure is shown in three-quarter view. The arms appear short in relation to the body. Her right arm is bent and raised to the shoulder, the left is bent and held to the torso. The legs are bent with the knees rendered under the drapery.

She wears a veil. It falls over the shoulders and is wrapped around her arms. It proceeds downwards at her right side and falls back at her ankles. Her face is oval. When photographed by Ingholt (1928) several features were still visible: a headband and a turban were depicted. The eyebrows were curving and depicted as thin ridges. The eyes were close-set and almond-shaped, with heavy upper eyelids. Only the earlobes were visible under the hair. She was wearing earrings. Her nose was large and the cheeks fleshy. The chin was oval.

She wears a tunic and a himation. The tunic falls to the ankles and has a wide, v-shaped neckline. The folds of the tunic are rendered by curving grooves on the body and vertical grooves between her legs. The himation crosses the chest diagonally from the left shoulder to the right side, and covers the left breast. It is fastened at the left shoulder with a brooch (details unclear). The himation ends at her thighs, creating an overfold. The folds of the himation are rendered by curving and oblique grooves. She also wears pointed shoes.

Her right hand is raised to the shoulder were she lightly holds a fold of the veil. The left hand is held to the torso. When photographed by Ingholt (1928) she was holding a conical object and a short staff. These were reduced versions of a spindle and a distaff.

PORTRAIT B: STANDING MALE, NABÛGADDÎ
The figure is shown frontally. The arms appear short in relation to the body. Both arms are bent and held to the torso. He is standing with the legs set slightly apart. The right leg is slightly bent with the knee visible in the drapery and he rests his weight on the left leg. The right foot is obscured by the seated female to his right. The lower left leg is obscured by the reclining figure.

His face is oval and the neck is slender. When photographed by Ingholt (1928), the facial details were better preserved: the hair was curly, arranged in crescent-shaped locks around the head. The eyebrows were curving, depicted as thin ridges. The eyes were close-set and almond-shaped, with thick upper eyelids. The ears were large and protruding. The nose was straight and wide at the tip. The mouth was small with thin lips and the chin was pointed with a cleft.

He wears a tunic and a himation. The tunic falls to the ankles and has a wide, v-shaped neckline. The folds of the tunic are rendered by curving, wide grooves. Over the tunic, he wears a himation. The himation covers only part of the chest: it is wrapped around the right shoulder and arm, leaving only part of the upper torso and the hand free. One end of the himation crosses the chest diagonally and falls over the left shoulder (›arm-sling‹ type). A fold of the himation is wrapped around his left lower arm and falls vertically down on each side of the wrist. The folds of the himation are indicated by diagonal grooves.

With his right hand, he holds the diagonal fold of the himation. With his left hand, he holds a small rectangular object, possibly a schedula. The index finger and thumb are extended on the left hand. The right index finger is extended.

PORTRAIT C: STANDING MALE, BARNABÛ

The figure is shown frontally. The arms appear short in relation to the body. The right arm is bent and held to the chest. Both arms are bent and held to the torso. The legs are obscured by the reclining figure.

The neck is wide. When photographed by Ingholt (1928), the facial details were better preserved: the hair was curly, arranged in crescent-shaped locks around the head. The eyebrows were curving, depicted as thin ridges. The eyes were close-set and almond-shaped, with thick upper eyelids. The ears were large and protruding. The nose was thin. The cheeks were fleshy. The mouth was small with thin lips and the chin was pointed with a cleft.

He wears a tunic and a himation. The tunic has a wide, v-shaped neckline. The folds of the tunic are rendered by curving, wide grooves. Over the tunic, he wears a himation. The himation covers only part of the chest: it is wrapped around the right shoulder and arm, leaving only the upper part of the torso and the hand free. One fold of the himation crosses the chest diagonally and falls over the left shoulder (›arm-sling‹ type). A fold of the himation is wrapped around his left lower arm and falls vertically down on each side of the wrist. The folds of the himation are indicated by diagonal grooves.

With his right hand, he holds the diagonal fold of the himation. With his left hand, he holds a small, rectangular object, possibly a schedula. The index finger and thumb are extended on the left hand. The right index finger is extended.

PORTRAIT D: STANDING MALE, BARʿATEH

The figure is shown frontally. The arms appear short in relation to the body. Both arms are bent and held to the torso. The legs are obscured by the reclining figure on the left.

When photographed by Ingholt (1928), the facial details were better preserved: the hair was curly, arranged in crescent-shaped locks around the head. The eyebrows were curving, depicted as thin ridges. The eyes were close-set and almond-shaped, with thick upper eyelids. The ears were large and protruding. The nose was thin. The cheeks were fleshy. The mouth was small with thin lips and the chin was pointed. The neck is slender.

He wears a tunic and a himation. The tunic has a wide, v-shaped neckline. The folds of the tunic are rendered by curving, wide grooves. Over the tunic, he wears a himation. The himation covers only part of the chest: it is wrapped around the right shoulder and arm, leaving only the upper part of the torso and the hand free. One fold of the himation crosses the chest diagonally and falls over the left shoulder (›arm-sling‹ type). The folds of the himation are indicated by diagonal grooves.

With the right hand, he holds the diagonal fold of the himation. With his left hand, he holds a small, rectangular object, possibly a schedula. The index finger and thumb are extended on the left hand. The right index finger is extended.

PORTRAIT E: RECLINING PRIEST, BARʿATEH

The figure is shown in frontal to three-quarter view. His head appears small in relation to his body. His head is turned slightly to his left. The right arm is extended and rests on his raised right leg. The left arm is bent and held to the torso. His right leg is bent with the foot resting on the mattress. The left is bent under the right with the knee pointing forwards. The lower left leg is obscured by the right leg.

He is wearing a cylindrical headdress divided into three sections by two vertical grooves: a Palmyrene priestly hat. A wreath is depicted at the lower part of the hat. It has three rows of leaves pointing towards a medallion with the bust of a male figure. His face is square. The eyebrows are curving, depicted as thin ridges. The cheeks are fleshy and the neck is wide. When photographed by Ingholt (1928), the facial details were better preserved: his eyes were close-set and almond-shaped, with heavy eyelids. The ears were large with the helix, scapha, and concha depicted. The nose was wide. The mouth was large with a full lower lip. The chin was oval.

He wears a ›Parthian-style‹ tunic, a chlamys, ›Parthian-style‹ trousers, and over-trousers. The tunic has a wide, round neckline decorated with a geometric pattern that leaves the upper part of the torso bare. The tunic has long, tight-fitting sleeves. The cuffs of the sleeves are decorated with a beaded band and a floral motif. The tunic ends above the knees and has a decorated lower border with a running scroll with rosettes and a beaded band at the hem. The folds of the tunic are rendered by curving, wide grooves. Over the tunic, he wears a chlamys that falls over both shoulders and covers most of the chest. One edge of the chlamys has a border decorated with squares between vines, visible on the fold across the chest. A wide, zigzag-shaped fold falls from under the left hand. The chlamys is fastened at the right shoulder with a circular brooch with a hollowed centre as indication of inlay (Colledge classification: h). A zigzag-shaped fold falls from under the brooch. The folds of the chlamys are indicated by narrow, deep grooves. He wears a plain band belt, knotted at the centre with the ends looped under on either side of the waist. Along his right thigh is an object with a round end, a rectangular main body, and a lateral round element: a sheathed dagger. The trousers are visible above the knee, and they have a decorated band with a running scroll and rosettes motif extending downwards in the middle. The over-trousers cover the knees, and end at the ankles. Their folds are indicated by wide, vertical grooves. The folds of the garments are indicated by wide, curving grooves. He wears round boots.

He rests his right hand at his raised right knee. He holds a skyphos in his left hand. It has a conical foot, a straight body, a wide rim, and small looped handles. His thumb, index, and the little finger are extended.

A.D. 150–200

293. FRAGMENT OF A BANQUETING RELIEF

DATABASE NUMBER: DGAM008.
LOCATION: Palmyra, Antiquities Department.
CONTEXT: —
ACQUISITION HISTORY: —
MEASUREMENTS: —
MATERIAL: Limestone.
PRESERVATION: Portrait A: The head and neck of the figure, as well as part of the right arm, are broken off. Portrait B: The figure is broken off diagonally across the upper chest; the head, neck, shoulders, and the right arm from above the elbow are broken off. Portrait C: The head and neck of the figure are broken off. Portrait D: The head and neck of the figure are broken off.
TECHNICAL DESCRIPTION: —
DATE: A.D. 150–200.
REFERENCES: Ali 2015, 50 cat. 8; Krag 2018, 58 n. 304; 62 n. 353; 65 n. 369; 66 n. 382; 66 n. 385; 88 n. 193; 385 cat. 826.

OBJECT DESCRIPTION

The relief is rectangular in shape and depicts a seated female, two standing children, and a reclining male. The reclining male rests against a cushion, decorated with a wide band with leaves.

PORTRAIT A: SEATED FEMALE

The figure is shown frontally. The right arm is bent and rests on the thigh. The left arm is obscured by the figure to her left. The legs are bent and spread.

She wears a veil. It falls over the left shoulder and covers the left arm.

She wears a tunic and a himation. The folds of the tunic are rendered by oblique grooves (other details unclear). The himation crosses the chest diagonally from the left shoulder to the right side, covers the chest and the body, and falls to her ankles. The folds of the himation are rendered by oblique grooves.

She lightly holds the fold of the veil that covers the left arm with her right hand.

PORTRAIT B: STANDING CHILD

The figure is shown frontally. The right arm falls to the side. The left arm is bent and held to the lower torso. The lower body is obscured by the legs of the reclining figure.

The child wears a tunic. It has long, tight-fitting sleeves. The folds of the tunic are rendered by curving grooves.

With the right hand, the child holds a cluster of small, globular elements, a bunch of grapes. With the left hand, the child holds an object close to the body (other details unclear).

PORTRAIT C: STANDING CHILD

The figure is shown frontally. The arms are bent and held to the chest. The lower body is obscured by the legs of the reclining figure.

The child wears a tunic. It has a wide, round neckline and long, tight-fitting sleeves. The folds of the tunic are rendered by curving grooves.

With both hands, the child holds an object close to the chest. It appears to be a cluster of small, globular elements, a bunch of grapes.

PORTRAIT D: RECLINING MALE

The torso of the figure is shown frontally, the left arm and leg are shown in three-quarter view, and the right arm and leg are shown in profile. The right arm is bent and rests on his right leg. The left arm is bent and rests against a cushion. The right leg is bent. The left leg is slightly bent and extended.

He wears a tunic and a himation. The tunic has a wide, round neckline and short, wide sleeves. The folds of the tunic are rendered by curving grooves over the torso and oblique grooves over the arms. Over the tunic, he wears a himation. It is wrapped around his left shoulder and arm, falling along his left side and across his waist, covering the legs and ending at the ankles. An s-shaped fold falls from under the left hand. The fold of the himation that crosses the waist has a scalloped edge. The folds of the himation are rendered by curving grooves. He wears footwear (other details unclear).

His right hand is placed on his raised right knee. With the left hand, he holds a bowl. It has a conical foot and body and small, looped handles. The lower body is decorated with a fluting. The thumb, index, and the little finger are extended.

294. SARCOPHAGUS LID RELIEF WITH BANQUETING SCENE

DATABASE NUMBER: BeirutPriv004.
LOCATION: Private Collection, exhibited in a café in Beirut, Lebanon.
CONTEXT: —
ACQUISITION HISTORY: —
MEASUREMENTS: —
MATERIAL: Limestone, white/yellow.
PRESERVATION: The relief is preserved in two rejoined parts; the right part depicts a seated female and a standing male and the left part depicts a standing male and two reclining males. The head of the left standing male has been reattached. The head of the left standing male and the left reclining male are missing. The right foot of the right reclining male is broken off. The surface is chipped. The mattress is heavily chipped.
TECHNICAL DESCRIPTION: —
DATE: A.D. 150–200.
REFERENCES: — (seen by Jean-Baptiste Yon in 2021).

OBJECT DESCRIPTION

The sarcophagus lid is rectangular in shape and depicts a seated female, two standing males, and two reclining males. The right reclining male rests his left arm on a cushion. Curving grooves indicate the texture of the fabric.

PORTRAIT A: SEATED FEMALE

The figure is shown frontally. The arms appear short in relation to the body. Her left is bent and resting on her side and leg. The legs are bent with the knees rendered under the drapery (more details unclear).

She wears three headdresses: a headband, a turban, and a veil. The headband is placed low on the forehead (details unclear). The turban appears to have two layers (other details unclear). Over the turban she wears a veil. It falls over the back of the head and covers the left shoulder, as well as the left upper arm. Her face is triangular. The eyebrows were curving and depicted as thin ridges. The eyes are wide-set and almond-shaped, with heavy eyelids. The nose is short and straight. The mouth is large with full lips.

She most likely wears a tunic and a himation. The tunic falls to the ankles and has short, loose sleeves. The folds of the tunic are rendered by curving grooves. The himation crosses the chest diagonally from the left shoulder to the right side, and covers the left breast. It is most likely fastened at the left shoulder with a brooch (details unclear). The himation ends at her ankles, right above the tunic. The folds of the himation are rendered by curving and oblique grooves. She also wears pointed shoes.

Her left hand rests on her left knee. She wears a bracelet on her right wrist. It is composed of twisted wire.

PORTRAIT B: STANDING MALE

The figure is shown frontally. Both arms are bent and held to the torso. He is standing with the legs set slightly apart. The right leg is slightly bent with the knee visible in the drapery and he rests his weight on the left leg. The feet are obscured by the reclining figure.

His hair is short and arranged in a row of straight strands falling to the forehead. His face is round. The eyebrows are slightly curving, depicted by thin grooves. The eyes are almond-shaped and slanting with thick eyelids. The ends of the upper eyelids extend beyond that of the lower ones (further details unclear). The nose is thin and short. The mouth is small, with full lips. The chin is pointed. The neck is short and slender.

He wears a tunic and a himation. The tunic has a narrow, round neckline and long, tight-fitting sleeves. The folds of the tunic are rendered by curving, wide grooves. Over the tunic, he wears a himation. The himation covers only part of the body: it is wrapped around the left shoulder and arm, falling down his side and crossing his lower body where it disappears behind his right side. The folds of the himation are indicated by diagonal grooves.

With his right hand, he holds a jug by the handle. The jug has a conical foot and a plain, conical body. With his left hand, he holds the diagonal fold of the himation. The index finger and thumb are extended on the left hand. The right thumb finger is extended.

PORTRAIT C: STANDING MALE

The figure is shown frontally. The arms appear short in relation to the body. Both arms are bent and held to the torso. The legs are obscured by the reclining figure.

He wears a tunic. The tunic has a wide, round neckline and short, loose sleeves. The folds of the tunic are rendered by curving, wide grooves on the chest and oblique folds on the arms.

With his right hand, he holds a jug (details unclear). His left hand rests on the reclining male's arm.

PORTRAIT D: RECLINING MALE

The figure is shown in frontal to three-quarter view. The right arm is extended and rests on his raised right leg. The left arm is bent and held to the torso, resting on a cushion. His right leg is bent with the foot resting on the mattress. The left is bent under the right with the knee pointing forwards. The lower left leg is obscured by the right leg.

His hair is short and rendered in two rows of comma-shaped locks around the head. His face is square. The eyebrows are curving, depicted as thin ridges. His eyes are large with heavy eyelids. The ears are large with the helix, scapha, and concha depicted. The nose is short. The mouth is large with full lips. The chin is wide and pointed.

He wears a ›Parthian-style‹ tunic, a himation, and trousers. The tunic has a wide, round neckline decorated with round elements and sleeves that end right below the elbows. It has a plain band running down the centre of the body. The tunic ends right below the knees. The folds of the tunic are rendered by curving, wide grooves. A wide band belt is tied with a ribbon tied in a double knot at the waist. The himation covers the left shoulder and arm. A fold of the himation falls across the left side of the chest, and is wrapped around the lower body. A fold of the himation is wrapped around the wrist and falls on either side of the arm in two zigzag-shaped folds onto the cushion and the mattress. The folds of the himation are indicated by oblique and curving grooves. The trousers are visible at the right shank: the folds are indicated by narrow vertical and oblique grooves. He wears a boot that covers his ankle.

He holds a small jug in his right hand. His thumb and index finger are extended. With the palm turned upwards, he holds a wide bowl with the fingertips of his left hand. The upper part of the bowl is decorated with horizontal lines and the lower part with a tongue pattern.

PORTRAIT E: RECLINING MALE

The figure is shown in frontal to three-quarter view. His left arm is bent and held to the torso.

He wears a tunic and a himation. The folds of the tunic are indicated by curving grooves.

A.D. 170–200

295. SARCOPHAGUS LID WITH BANQUETING SCENE

DATABASE NUMBER: DGAM007.
LOCATION: Damascus, Directorate-General of Antiquities and Museums, inv. no. unknown.
CONTEXT: —
ACQUISITION HISTORY: Confiscated by authorities in Palmyra, March 2014.
MEASUREMENTS: —
MATERIAL: Limestone.
PRESERVATION: The surface is weathered.
TECHNICAL DESCRIPTION: There are traces of red pigment in the inscriptions.
DATE: A.D. 170–200.
REFERENCES: Ali 2011, 51 cat. 8; Ali 2015, 50 cat. 8; Krag – Raja 2017, 199 n. 24; 204 n. 72. 73; 205 n. 75; 208 n. 99. 100; 210 n. 109; 220 cat. 42; Krag 2018, 28 n. 9; 33 n. 82. 84; 66 n. 382; 88 n. 193. 195. 197; 314 cat. 561; Raja 2019e, 98. 138 cat. 68.

OBJECT DESCRIPTION

Sarcophagus lid with five figures: a seated female, three standing males, and a reclining male. The lid is shaped like a mattress, decorated with a pattern of four-petal rosettes inside lozenges. Part of a fulcrum is visible at the lower left corner of the relief. The first figure sits on two cushions, depicted as half-round objects with wide, curving grooves. The last figure rests against a large cushion, depicted as a cylindrical object, decorated with a central band with arrow-shaped patterns and wide, curving grooves.

INSCRIPTIONS

INSCRIPTION 1
SCRIPT: Palmyrene Aramaic.
LOCATION ON RELIEF: To the right of portrait B.
TRANSCRIPTION: —
TRANSLATION: —

INSCRIPTION 2
SCRIPT: Palmyrene Aramaic.
LOCATION ON RELIEF: To the right of portrait C.
TRANSCRIPTION: - - - | - - - | ʿTʿQB | ḤBL.
TRANSLATION: - - - ʿAteʿaqab | alas!

INSCRIPTION 3
SCRIPT: Palmyrene Aramaic.
LOCATION ON RELIEF: To the right of portrait D.
TRANSCRIPTION: - - -S BR | ʿTʿQB BR | YRḤY BRH.
TRANSLATION: - - - son of ʿAteʿaqab son of Yarḥaî his son.

INSCRIPTION 4
SCRIPT: Palmyrene Aramaic.
LOCATION ON RELIEF: To the right of portrait E.
TRANSCRIPTION: ʿTʿQB BR | YRḤY - - WNYʾ | ḤBL.
TRANSLATION: ʿAteʿaqab, son of Yarḥaî - - -, alas!

CIS no. —; PAT no. —.

COMMENT: Inscription 1: Illegible.

PORTRAIT A: SEATED FEMALE

The figure is shown frontally. The arms are bent; the right arm is held in front of the torso and the left arm is raised to the shoulder. The index finger of the left hand appears too large in relation to the body.

She wears three headdresses: a headband, a turban, and a veil. The headband is placed low on the forehead and is decorated. The turban is coiled. Horizontal grooves indicate the coiling of the fabric. The veil has a scalloped edge(?) and falls over the neck and shoulders. It is wrapped around the left arm, covers the right elbow, and falls across the right leg. Part of the hair is covered by the headdresses: several strands of hair on each side of the face and above the ears are brushed back over the edge of the headband and disappear under the veil. The individual strands of hair are rendered by incised lines. Her face is square. The eyebrows are curving, indicated by thin ridges. The eyes are small and almond-shaped. The earlobes are visible under the hair. She wears dumbbell-shaped earrings (Colledge classification: H). The nose is small. The mouth is small, with full lips. The chin is pointed. The neck is short and wide.

She wears a tunic and a himation. The tunic has short sleeves and ends at the ankles. The folds of the tunic are indicated by curving grooves. Over the tunic, she wears a himation. It falls over the left shoulder, crosses the chest diagonally, and covers the left breast and the lower body, leaving only the hemline of tunic and the feet exposed. It is fastened at the left shoulder with a circular brooch (Colledge classification: i). The border of the himation that falls across the torso is decorated with a broad band. The folds of the himation are indicated by oblique grooves.

With her right hand, she holds the edge of the veil over her lap; the end of the veil falls down between the legs in a zigzag-shaped fold. The index finger is extended. With her left hand, she holds the veil at the height of the shoulder.

PORTRAIT B: STANDING MALE

The figure is shown frontally. The arms are bent; the right arm is held to the torso and the left arm is held in front of the chest. The feet are obscured by the reclining figure.

His hair is arranged in a row of s-shaped curls. His face is square and fleshy. The eyebrows are curving rendered by thin ridges. The eyes are small. The ears are small, slightly protruding. The nose is small. The mouth is small, with full lips. The chin is pointed. The neck is short and wide.

He wears a tunic and a himation. The tunic has a small, v-shaped neckline and short sleeves. The folds of the tunic are rendered by curving grooves. Over the tunic, he wears a himation. The himation is wrapped around the left shoulder and arm, falls diagonally across the torso, and covers the lower body. The fold that is wrapped around the left side has a scalloped edge.

With his right hand, he holds an oblong curving object. With his left hand, he holds a fold of the himation, the end of which falls down in a zigzag-shaped fold. The index finger is extended.

PORTRAIT C: STANDING MALE

The figure is shown frontally. The arms are bent and held in front of the torso. The lower part of the figure is obscured by the reclining figure. The arms appear small in relation to the body.

He wears a headdress, perhaps a turban or a headcloth with a central decoration or loop of coiled fabric. His face is square and fleshy. The eyes are small. The ears are large and protruding. The nose is small. The mouth is small, with full lips. The chin is wide. The neck is short and wide.

He wears a tunic and a himation. The tunic has a round neckline. Over the tunic, he wears a himation. The himation is wrapped around the right shoulder and arm, leaving only part of the upper chest and the right hand free. One fold of the himation crosses the chest diagonally and falls over the left shoulder (>arm-sling< type). The folds of the himation are indicated by oblique grooves.

With his right hand, he lightly holds the diagonal fold of the himation. The index finger is extended. With his left hand, he holds a rectangular object (details unclear). The index finger is extended.

PORTRAIT D: STANDING PRIEST

The figure is shown frontally. The right arm is bent in front of the torso and the left arm is held to the side. The lower part of the figure is obscured by the reclining figure. Both arms appear short in relation to the body.

He wears a tall, cylindrical, flat-top headdress divided into three sections by two vertical grooves: a Palmyrene priestly hat. A wreath with the leaves pointing towards a central decoration (bust?) is depicted at the lower part of the hat. His face is square and fleshy. The eyes are small. The ears are large and protruding. The nose is wide. The mouth is small. The chin is pointed. The neck is short and wide.

He wears a tunic and a himation. The tunic has a v-shaped neckline. Over the tunic, he wears a himation. It is wrapped around the right arm, leaving the shoulder, part of the upper chest, and the right hand free. One fold of the himation crosses the chest diagonally and falls over the left shoulder (>arm-sling< type). The folds of the himation are indicated by oblique grooves.

With his right hand, he lightly holds the diagonal fold of the himation. The index and the middle fingers are extended. With his left hand, he touches the upper arm of the reclining figure.

PORTRAIT E: RECLINING PRIEST

The figure is shown in frontal to three-quarter view. His right arm is extended and rests on his knee and the left arm is bent and held in front of the torso. The right leg is bent and the foot rests on the mattress. The left leg is bent under the right leg with the knee pointing outwards. The left foot is obscured by the right leg.

He wears a tall, cylindrical, flat-top headdress divided into three sections by two vertical grooves: a Palmyrene priestly hat. A wreath with the leaves pointing towards a central decoration (medallion?) over a wide band divided into three sections by two vertical grooves is depicted at the lower part of the hat. His head is square. The eyebrows are curving, depicted as thin ridges. The eyes are large and almond-shaped, with thick upper eyelids. The eyeballs are blank. The ears are small and slightly protruding. The nose is long with a wide base. The mouth is small, with full lips. The chin is pointed. The neck is short and wide.

He wears a >Parthian-style< tunic, a chlamys, and >Parthian-style< trousers. The tunic has a wide, round neckline with a decorated border and long sleeves decorated with a band at the cuffs. The tunic has a central, wide band with floral decoration extending downwards. The tunic ends above the knees and has a decorated band with wavy(?) motifs at the hem. The folds of the tunic are indicated by oblique grooves. Over the tunic, he wears a chlamys that falls over the left shoulder and one fold is wrapped around the left elbow with two wide, zigzag-shaped folds falling from under the left forearm. It is fastened at the right shoulder with a round brooch (Colledge classification: i), and is folded over the upper part of the torso. The folds of the chlamys are indicated by curving grooves. He also wears a band belt. It is tied low around the waist. The ends of the belt are fastened to the belt on both sides and are descending from it. Each trouser leg is decorated in the middle with a wide band that extends downwards (visible from above the knees to above the hem). The lower hem of the trousers is decorated with a band. The folds of the trousers are indicated by oblique grooves. He wears closed shoes decorated with a beaded band at the side.

With his right hand, he holds a pinecone. With his left hand, he holds a skyphos. It has a conical foot, a round body, a rectangular rim, and handles. The foot and the body are decorated with oblique incised lines.

A.D. 180–200

296. FRAGMENTS OF BANQUETING RELIEF

DATABASE NUMBER: LebanonPriv003.
LOCATION: Unknown location, private collection (last known location: Baalbek).
CONTEXT: —
ACQUISITION HISTORY: —
MEASUREMENTS: Height: 108 cm. Width: 135 cm. Depth: 33 cm. Height of figure A: 40 cm. Height of figure B: 40 cm. Height of figure C: 40 cm. Height of figure D: 60 cm. Height of figure E: 60 cm. Height of figure F: 60 cm. Height of figure G: 60 cm.
MATERIAL: Limestone, white/yellow.

PRESERVATION: The relief is composed of several adjoining fragments. The sides of the relief are broken off. Portrait A: The lower part of the figure is broken off at the waist. The face and the right arm of the figure are chipped. Portrait B: The lower part of the figure is broken off at the waist. The nose is chipped. Portrait C: The lower part of the figure is broken off at the waist. The nose is chipped. Portrait D: The head is broken off at the base of the neck. The right arm is chipped. Portrait F: The upper part of the head is chipped. Portrait G: A large crack runs along the right side of the face.

TECHNICAL DESCRIPTION: There are traces of red pigment on the object and on the inscriptions.

DATE: A.D. 180–200.

REFERENCES: Abousamra 2015, 217–224 figs. 1–7. Inscription: Abousamra 2015, 219–223 figs. 2–7.

OBJECT DESCRIPTION

The sarcophagus lid is rectangular in shape and depicts four men reclining on a mattress and three men standing behind them. The mattress is decorated with wide bands (details unclear). Curving grooves indicate the texture of the fabric. On the right side there is a fulcrum with a small lion figure with a rosette on its neck and a small medallion. The stretcher of the kline is rendered (details unclear).

INSCRIPTIONS

INSCRIPTION 1
SCRIPT: Palmyrene Aramaic.
LOCATION ON RELIEF: To the right side of the standing figure on the left side, at the height of the head.
TRANSCRIPTION: RM[- - BR?] | MLKW BR BR[H ḤBL].
TRANSLATION: Ram?[- - son of?] Malkû son of his s[on, alas!].

INSCRIPTION 2
SCRIPT: Palmyrene Aramaic.
LOCATION ON RELIEF: To the right side of the central standing figure, at the height of the head.
TRANSCRIPTION: BLʿQB BR | [M]LKW BR BRH | ḤBL.
TRANSLATION: Belʿaqab, son of Malkû, son of his son, alas!

INSCRIPTION 3
SCRIPT: Palmyrene Aramaic.
LOCATION ON RELIEF: To the right of the head of the figure standing on the right side, at the height of the head.
TRANSCRIPTION: ʾ[- - - BR] | ML[KW? - - -].
TRANSLATION: ʾ[- - - son of] Malkû? - - -.

CIS no. —; PAT no. —.

COMMENTS: Inscription 1: L.1: Very uncertain reading of the first name. The M is unclear. L.2: Restoration of the lacuna on the model of the following text.

PORTRAIT A: STANDING MALE

The figure is shown frontally. The arms are bent in front of the torso.

His hair is short and voluminous, arranged in rows of snail-shell locks. His face is triangular. The eyebrows are depicted by curving grooves. The eyes are large. The irises and pupils are indicated by concentric, incised circles. The nose is straight. The mouth is small, with a full lower lip. The chin is narrow. The neck is long and wide.

He wears a tunic and a himation. The tunic has a wide, round neckline. The folds of the tunic are rendered by curving, wide grooves. Over the tunic, he wears a himation. The himation covers most of the body, leaving only the upper part of the chest and the hand free. One end of the himation is wrapped around the right arm, crosses the chest diagonally, and falls over the left shoulder (›arm-sling‹ type).

He holds a narrow, rectangular object with his right hand, perhaps a schedula.

PORTRAIT B: STANDING MALE

The figure is shown frontally. The arms are bent in front of the torso.

His hair is short and voluminous, arranged in rows of crescent-shaped locks. His face is oval. The eyebrows are depicted by curving grooves. The eyes are large and round with thick upper eyelids. The irises are rendered by incised circles and the pupils by punch holes. The ears are small and close to the head. The nose is wide at the base. The mouth is small, with a full lower lip. The chin is square with a cleft. The neck is long and wide.

He wears a tunic and a himation. The tunic has a wide, round neckline. The folds of the tunic are rendered by curving, wide grooves. Over the tunic, he wears a himation. The himation covers most of the body, leaving only the upper part of the chest and the hand free. One end of the himation is wrapped around the right arm, crosses the chest diagonally, and falls over the left shoulder (›arm-sling‹ type).

He holds a narrow, rectangular object with his right hand, perhaps a schedula. With the left hand, he holds the diagonal fold of the himation that crosses the chest.

PORTRAIT C: STANDING MALE

The figure is shown frontally. The arms are bent in front of the torso.

His hair is short and voluminous, arranged in rows of snail-shell locks. His face is oval. The eyebrows are depicted by curving grooves. The eyes are large and round with thick upper eyelids. The irises are rendered by incised circles and the pupils by punch holes. The ears are small and close to the head with the helix, scapha, and the lobe depicted. The nose is wide at the base. The mouth is small, with full lips. The chin is square with a cleft. The neck is long and wide.

He wears a tunic and a himation. The tunic has a wide, round neckline. The folds of the tunic are rendered by curving, wide grooves. Over the tunic, he wears a himation. The himation covers most of the body, leaving the right shoulder, the upper part of the chest, and the hand free. One end of the himation is wrapped around the right arm, crosses the chest diagonally, and falls over the left shoulder (>arm-sling< type).

He holds a narrow, rectangular object with his right hand, perhaps a schedula. With the left hand, he holds the diagonal fold of the himation that crosses the chest.

PORTRAIT D: RECLINING MALE

The figure is shown frontally. The right arm is bent in front of the torso; the left arm is bent and rests along his side.

He wears a tunic and a himation. The tunic has a wide, round neckline and long, tight-fitting sleeves. The folds of the tunic are rendered by curving, wide grooves. Over the tunic, he wears a himation. The himation covers most of the body: It is folded over the left shoulder and arm, and runs across his waist, leaving the right shoulder, the upper part of the chest, and the hand free.

With the right hand, he holds a cup in front of the chest. The left hand rests against the waist.

PORTRAIT E: RECLINING MALE

The figure is shown frontally. The right arm is obscured by the figure right of him; the left arm is bent in front of the torso. The legs are not rendered.

His face is square and fleshy. The eyes are large. The chin is wide. The neck is wide and short.

He wears a tunic and a himation. The tunic has a wide, round neckline. The folds of the tunic are rendered by curving, wide grooves. Over the tunic, he wears a himation. The himation covers most of the body: it is folded over the left shoulder and arm, and runs across his waist, leaving the right shoulder, the upper part of the chest, and the hand free.

With the left hand, he holds a cup in front of the chest.

PORTRAIT F: RECLINING MALE

The figure is shown frontally. The right arm is obscured by the figure right of him; the left arm is bent in front of the torso. The legs are not rendered.

His face is square and fleshy. The neck is wide and long.

He wears a tunic and a himation. The tunic has a wide, round neckline. The folds of the tunic are rendered by curving, wide grooves. Over the tunic, he wears a himation. The himation covers most of the body: it is folded over the left shoulder and arm, and runs across his waist, leaving the right shoulder, the upper part of the chest, and the hand free.

With the left hand, he holds a cup in front of the chest.

PORTRAIT G: RECLINING MALE

The figure is shown frontally. The right arm is obscured by the figure right of him; the left arm is bent in front of the torso. The legs are not rendered.

His face is square and fleshy. The neck is wide and long.

He wears a tunic and a himation. The tunic has a wide, round neckline. The folds of the tunic are rendered by curving, wide grooves. Over the tunic, he wears a himation. The himation covers most of the body: it is folded over the left shoulder and arm, and runs across his waist, leaving the right shoulder, the upper part of the chest, and the hand free.

With the left hand, he holds a cup in front of the chest.

A.D. 220–240

297. FRAGMENTS OF A BANQUETING RELIEF

DATABASE NUMBER: PalmyraUNK024.
LOCATION: Palmyra, unknown location.
CONTEXT: —
ACQUISITION HISTORY: —
MEASUREMENTS: —
MATERIAL: Limestone.
PRESERVATION: The upper right side is broken off. The background of the relief between the figures is broken off. Portrait A: The head and neck of the figure are broken off. Portrait B: The head and neck of the figure are broken off. Portrait C: The head and neck of the figure are broken off.
TECHNICAL DESCRIPTION: —
DATE: A.D. 220–240.
REFERENCES: Anderson – Ousterhout 2016, pl. 52.

OBJECT DESCRIPTION

The sarcophagus lid is rectangular in shape and depicts one seated female and two reclining males on a mattress. Both reclining males rest their left arm on a cushion. Each of the cushions is decorated with a wide band (details unclear) set between beaded bands. The mattress is decorated with an intersecting lozenge pattern with four-petal flowers in the lozenges.

PORTRAIT A: SEATED FEMALE

The figure is shown frontally. The right arm is bent and rests on her right thigh. The left arm is raised to the side. Her legs are bent with the knees rendered under the drapery. Her feet are obscured by the right foot of the reclining figure to her left.

She wears a veil that falls over the shoulders. She appears to wear at least one necklace over the breasts (details unclear).

She wears a tunic and a himation. The tunic has short, wide sleeves. The folds of the tunic are rendered by curving grooves. The ankle-length himation crosses her chest diagonally from the left shoulder to the right side, and covers the left breast, the stomach, the lower torso, and the feet. The folds of the himation are rendered by curving and oblique grooves.

She rests her right hand on her thigh and holds a fold of the veil. Her left arm is bent and raised to the side, at the height of the chest.

PORTRAIT B: RECLINING MALE

The figure is shown in frontal to three-quarter view. The right arm is slightly bent and the right hand rests on his raised right knee. The left arm is bent and held in front of the torso. His right leg is bent and his foot is resting on the mattress. The left leg is bent under the right with the knee pointing forwards. The lower left leg is obscured by the right leg.

He wears a >Parthian-style< tunic, a chlamys, and >Parthian-style< trousers. The tunic has a wide, round neckline (other details unclear) and long, tight-fitting sleeves. At the middle, the tunic has a wide band that extends downwards (other details unclear). The tunic ends above the knees and has a decorated border (details unclear). The folds of the tunic are rendered by curving, wide grooves. He wears a plain band belt across the lower torso. It is knotted at the centre with the ends looped under on either side of the waist. Along the right thigh he has an object with a pointed end, a rectangular main body, and a lateral rectangular: a sheathed dagger. Over the tunic, he wears a chlamys that falls over both shoulders and is wrapped around the left arm. It appears to be fastened at the right shoulder with a brooch (details unclear). A zigzag-shaped fold falls from under the brooch. Two wide, zigzag-shaped folds, separated by a deep groove fall down from under the left arm, across the cushion, and over the mattress. The folds of the chlamys are indicated by narrow, deep grooves. The trousers are visible from above the knee. Each trouser leg is decorated in the middle with a wide band that extends downwards (other details unclear). The folds of the trousers are indicated by wide, curving grooves. The trousers are tucked into his boots. The plain shoelaces are knotted at the centre with a button from where two laces extend downwards.

The right hand is resting on his knee. He appears to be holding an object with his fingertips (details unclear). He holds a skyphos in his left hand (other details unclear).

PORTRAIT C: RECLINING MALE

The figure is shown in frontal to three-quarter view. The right arm is bent in front of the lower torso. The left arm is bent and held to the torso. The legs are extended behind the reclining figure to his right.

He wears a tunic and a himation. The tunic has long, tight-fitting sleeves (other details unclear). Over the tunic, he wears a himation (details unclear). A zigzag-shaped fold falls from under his left arm across the cushion and over the mattress. The folds of the himation are rendered by diagonal, curving grooves.

He holds a small object in his right hand. It is not clear if he holds an object with the left hand. The middle finger of the left hand is extended.

298. FRAGMENT OF A SARCOPHAGUS LID WITH PORTRAIT BUSTS

DATABASE NUMBER: NCG078.
LOCATION: Copenhagen, Ny Carlsberg Glyptotek, inv. no. IN 1148.
CONTEXT: —
ACQUISITION HISTORY: Puttmann in Syria.
MEASUREMENTS: Height: 50 cm. Width: 54 cm. Depth: 27.5 cm. Portrait A: Height of figure: 24 cm. Width of figure: 19 cm. Depth of figure: 8 cm. Height of head: 11.5 cm. Width of head: 10 cm. Portrait B: Height of figure: 24.5 cm. Width of figure: 19 cm. Depth of figure: 8 cm. Height of head: 11.5 cm. Width of head: 10 cm.
MATERIAL: Limestone, white/grey.
PRESERVATION: The left side of the object, the upper side of the sarcophagus, and the lower frame are broken off. Portrait A: The veil is chipped. Portrait B: The nose and small areas on the chest are chipped.
TECHNICAL DESCRIPTION: There are flat chisel marks on the surface of the background decoration. Portrait A: There are flat chisel marks on the veil, face, neck, and clothing. Rasp marks are visible on the veil, neck, and shoulders. Black pigment is visible in the corners of her eyes and in the irises. Portrait B: There are flat chisel marks on his hair, face, neck, and clothing, and rasp marks on the neck and shoulders. Black pigment is visible in the corners of the eyes and pupils.
DATE: A.D. 220–240 (Hvidberg-Hansen – Ploug 1993: A.D. 230–250).
REFERENCES: Colledge 1976, 73. 240 pl. 97; Sadurska 1982, 271 n. 11; Parlasca 1984, 290 fig. 9; Hvidberg-Hansen – Ploug 1993, 136 cat. 90; Ploug 1995, 219 f. cat. 90; Krag 2016, 188 fig. 4; Krag 2018, 53 n. 258; 58 n. 304; 61 n. 332; 62 n. 350; 102 n. 66; 103 n. 74; 399 cat. 872; Raja 2019a, 256–259 cat. 79.

OBJECT DESCRIPTION

The fragment depicts a lateral side of the sarcophagus lid. The top is decorated with a series of diagonal grooves. A beaded band runs across the upper and left side of the relief. The upper and lower borders of the relief are decorated with alternating rectangular and square panels. There is a lozenge inside each rectangular panel. At the upper border, the ends of the lozenges cut into the rectangular frame. At the lower border, the square and rectangular panels share common upper and lateral frames. The lozenges and the square panels are decorated with flowers with four serrated petals. Small floral motifs are placed on the triangles between each lozenge and the rectangular panel around it. The central part of the relief has two clipei, indicated by three concentric, incised circles, carrying a female and a male armless bust. The upper part of the clipei is cut by the upper decorative band, while the lower part cuts into the lower decorative band. There are two triangles between the two clipei, each decorated with a floral motif. A flower and a leaf can be seen at the right of the clipeus with the female bust.

Parlasca 1984 compares it to a piece from Temple Tomb no. 186 (cat. 180b) that was the lateral side of the lid of the sarcophagus, and suggests that it too was the lateral side of a sarcophagus.

PORTRAIT A: ARMLESS FEMALE BUST

The figure is shown frontally. The head is turned slightly to her right.

She wears three headdresses: a headband, a turban, and a veil. The headband is decorated with a central, rectangular panel between two beaded bands. The turban is coiled, with three slightly curving, wide grooves indicating the coiling of the fabric. Over the turban, she wears a heavy veil that falls down behind the head, and over the shoulders. The right end of the veil crosses the chest in a curving fold and falls over the left shoulder. The hair is visible at the sides of the forehead; it is slightly wavy and combed over the sides of the headband. The individual strands of hair are indicated by s-shaped grooves. Her face is square. The eyebrows are rendered by arched grooves that start from the root of the nose. The eyes are small and almond-shaped, with thick upper eyelids. The end of the upper eyelids extends beyond that of the lower eyelids. The eyeballs are blank. The earlobes are visible. The nose is straight and wide. The alae are indicated by incised lines. The mouth is small, with a full lower lip. The chin is pointed. The neck is short and wide. She wears a necklace composed of small, round beads at the base of the neck. Directly below it she wears a plain, hoop necklace with a circular pendant suspended from the centre; the pendant has an incised border and a raised centre.

She wears a tunic with a wide, round neckline.

PORTRAIT B: ARMLESS MALE BUST

The figure is shown frontally. The head is turned slightly to his right.

Cat. 298, Pl. 60

The hair is short, arranged in two rows of flame-shaped locks. His face is oval and fleshy. The eyebrows are indicated by curving, incised lines. The eyes are large and almond-shaped, with thick upper eyelids. The eyeballs are blank. The ears are small and slightly protruding with the helix depicted. The nose is straight and wide. The mouth is wide with thin lips. The chin is round. The neck is short and wide.

He wears a tunic and himation. The tunic has a small, v-shaped neckline and short, wide sleeves. The folds of the tunic are indicated by curving grooves in the area of the chest and oblique ones at the arms. Over the tunic, he wears a himation: one fold crosses the chest diagonally and passes under the folds that cover the left shoulder and arm.

A.D. 240–273

299. FRAGMENT OF A SARCOPHAGUS LID WITH BANQUETING SCENE

DATABASE NUMBER: DGAM009.
LOCATION: Palmyra, Antiquities Department.
CONTEXT: —
ACQUISITION HISTORY: —
MEASUREMENTS: —
MATERIAL: Limestone.
PRESERVATION: Portrait A: Only the lower legs from the knees downward are preserved. Portrait B: Part of the right upper arm is broken off. Portrait C: Well-preserved. Portrait D: The right hand, the left thigh, and the right foot are slightly chipped.
TECHNICAL DESCRIPTION: There are traces of red pigment in the inscription.
DATE: A.D. 240–273.
REFERENCES: Ali 2015, 50 cat. 8; Krag 2018, 42 n. 153. 154; 58 n. 304; 58 n. 311; 62 n. 353; 65 n. 369; 66 n. 382; 66 n. 385; 73 n. 47; 88 n. 193; 88 n. 195; 88 n. 197; 103 n. 73; 385 cat. 827.

OBJECT DESCRIPTION

The relief is rectangular in shape and depicts a seated female, a standing female, a standing male, and a reclining male on a mattress. The reclining male rests against a cushion, decorated with a wide band between two beaded bands (other details unclear). The mattress is decorated with a pattern of lozenges enclosing a four-petal flower.

INSCRIPTION

SCRIPT: Palmyrene Aramaic.
LOCATION ON RELIEF: To the left of the head of the reclining figure.
TRANSCRIPTION: YRḤY BR | ʿTʿQB | - - - -.
TRANSLATION: Yarḥaî, son of ʿAteʿaqab.

RES no. —; CIS no. —; PAT no. —.

PORTRAIT A: SEATED FEMALE

The figure is shown frontally. The legs are bent and spread. The feet of the figure are obscured by the reclining male.

She wears a himation. The himation covers the lower body. The folds of the himation are rendered by oblique grooves.

PORTRAIT B: STANDING FEMALE

The figure is shown frontally. The right arm falls to the side. The left arm is bent and held in front of the chest. The lower body is obscured by the legs of the reclining figure.

Her hair is uncovered. Several strands are brushed back over the temples (other details unclear). Her face is square. The eyebrows are curving. The eyes are almond-shaped (other details unclear). The nose is short and straight. The mouth is small, with full lower lip. The chin is small. The neck is wide and short with two curving grooves. Grooves over the collarbone indicate that she may be wearing a necklace.

She wears a tunic and a veil. The tunic has a round neckline and long, tight-fitting sleeves. The folds of the tunic are indicated by oblique grooves. Over the tunic she wears a veil that falls over the shoulders and chest in a curving fold. The folds of the veil are indicated by oblique grooves.

With the left hand she holds the fold of the veil. Two curving grooves around the left wrist may indicate a bracelet.

PORTRAIT C: STANDING MALE

The figure is shown frontally. The right arm is bent and held in front of the chest. The left arm is bent and held to the side. The lower body is obscured by the reclining figure.

His hair is short and voluminous. It is arranged in curls around the head. His face is square. The eyebrows are curving. The eyes are almond-shaped (other details unclear). The ears are large and protruding. The nose is short. The mouth is small. The chin is prominent. The neck is wide and short.

He wears a tunic and a himation. The tunic has a wide, round neckline. The folds of the tunic are indicated by oblique grooves. Over the tunic he wears a himation. It is wrapped over the right shoulder and arm, crosses the chest diagonally, and covers the left shoulder and arm. The folds of the himation are indicated by oblique grooves.

With the right hand he holds the fold of the himation. The index and the little fingers are extended. The left hand rests on the shoulder of the reclining figure.

PORTRAIT D: RECLINING MALE

The torso of the figure is shown frontally, the left arm and leg are shown in three-quarter view, and the right arm and leg are shown in profile. The right arm is bent and rests on his right leg. The left arm is bent and rests against a cushion. The right leg is bent. The left leg is bent and pushed back under the right leg.

He wears a >Parthian-style< tunic and a himation. The tunic has a wide, round neckline and long, tight-fitting sleeves. The neckline is decorated with a beaded border. A wide band extends downwards from the middle of the neckline. It is decorated with panels with flowers (other details unclear). The cuffs have a wide, decorated band (details unclear), and a beaded band. The folds of the tunic are indicated by oblique grooves. He also wears a plain, band belt. It is knotted at the centre, and the ends are looped over. Over the tunic, he wears a himation. It is wrapped around his left shoulder and arm, falling along his left side and across his waist, covering the legs and ending at the ankles. A zigzag-shaped fold falls from under the left hand. The folds of the himation are rendered by curving grooves. He wears footwear (other details unclear).

His right hand is placed on his raised right knee. With the tips of the thumb and the index finger he holds a small, round object, possibly fruit. With the fingertips of the left hand, he holds a bowl. It is decorated with hollowed-out circles.

SARCOPHAGUS BOXES

A.D. 100–150

300. FRAGMENT OF A SARCOPHAGUS BOX WITH PORTRAIT BUSTS

DATABASE NUMBER: MBA005.
LOCATION: Baalbek, Baalbek Museum, inv. no. unknown.
CONTEXT: —
ACQUISITION HISTORY: In the possession of the district governor (*kaymakam*) of Baalbek in 1885.
MEASUREMENTS: —
MATERIAL: Limestone.
PRESERVATION: The upper right, the left, and right sides side of the relief are broken off. Portrait B: The nose is chipped.
TECHNICAL DESCRIPTION: —

DATE: A.D. 100–150.
REFERENCES: Ingholt Archives, PS 98; CR 1883, 393; Abamelek-Lazarev 1897, 51. 53 cat. 5; Ingholt 1928, 101 PS 98; Colledge 1976, 247. Inscription: Euting 1885, 676–677 cat. 28–30; Pognon 1885, 78 cat. 5; Chabot 1898, 104–105 cat. 4; RES 409.

OBJECT DESCRIPTION
The sarcophagus box is rectangular in shape and depicts three male busts. It has a protruding plinth on the lower part and a projecting moulding at the upper part.

INSCRIPTIONS
INSCRIPTION 1
SCRIPT: Palmyrene Aramaic.
LOCATION ON RELIEF: To the left of the figure on the left side.
TRANSCRIPTION: ḤBL | TYMRṢ[W] | BR ZBDBWL | BRH.
TRANSLATION: Alas, Taîmarṣû, son of Zabdibôl, his son.

INSCRIPTION 2
SCRIPT: Palmyrene Aramaic.
LOCATION ON RELIEF: To the left of the figure in the middle.
TRANSCRIPTION: ḤBL ZBDBWL | BR MLK'L RMY.
TRANSLATION: Alas, Zabdibôl son of Malakêl Ramî.

INSCRIPTION 3
SCRIPT: Palmyrene Aramaic.
LOCATION ON RELIEF: To the left of the figure on the right side.
TRANSCRIPTION: ḤBL MLK'L | ZBDBWL BRH.
TRANSLATION: Alas, Malakêl son of Zabdibôl, his son.

CIS no. 4372; PAT no. 0730.

Cat. 300

PORTRAIT A: MALE BUST

The figure is shown frontally. Both arms are bent and held to the torso.

His hair is short and arranged in two rows of crescent-shaped curls. His face is square. The eyebrows are curving, rendered by thin ridges. The eyes are almond-shaped. The irises are rendered by incised circles and the pupils by punch holes. The nose is long with a straight bridge. Nasolabial lines are indicated. The mouth is wide with thin lips. The chin is round. The neck is long and slender.

He wears a tunic and a himation. The tunic has a small, v-shaped neckline. The folds of the tunic are rendered by curving grooves. Over the tunic, he wears a himation. The himation covers most of the body: it is wrapped around the right shoulder and arm, leaving only the upper part of the torso and the hand free. One end of the himation crosses the chest diagonally and falls over the left shoulder (›arm-sling‹ type). The folds of the himation are indicated by diagonal and curving grooves.

He holds the diagonal fold of the himation with his right hand. On the left hand he holds a rectangular object, possibly a schedula.

PORTRAIT B: MALE BUST

The figure is shown frontally. Both arms are bent and held to the torso.

His hair is short and arranged in two rows of crescent-shaped curls. His face is square. The eyebrows are curving, rendered by thin ridges. The eyes are almond-shaped. The irises are rendered by incised circles and the pupils by punch holes. Nasolabial lines are indicated. The mouth is small, with thin, upper lip and a full, lower lip. The chin is round. The neck is long and slender.

He wears a tunic and a himation. The tunic has a small, v-shaped neckline. The folds of the tunic are rendered by curving grooves. Over the tunic, he wears a himation. The himation covers most of the body: it is wrapped around the right shoulder and arm, leaving only the upper part of the torso and the hand free. One end of the himation crosses the chest diagonally and falls over the left shoulder (›arm-sling‹ type). The folds of the himation are indicated by diagonal and curving grooves.

He holds the diagonal fold of the himation with his right hand. In the left hand, he holds a rectangular object, possibly a schedula.

PORTRAIT C: MALE BUST

The figure is shown frontally. Both arms are bent and held to the torso.

His hair is short and arranged in two rows of crescent-shaped curls. His face is square. The eyebrows are curving, rendered by thin ridges. The eyes are almond-shaped. The irises are rendered by incised circles and the pupils by punch holes. The nose is long with a straight bridge. Nasolabial lines are indicated. The mouth is small, with a thin, upper lip and a full, lower lip. The chin is round. The neck is long and slender.

He wears a tunic and a himation. The tunic has a small, v-shaped neckline. The folds of the tunic are rendered by curving grooves. Over the tunic, he wears a himation. The himation covers most of the body: it is wrapped around the right shoulder and arm, leaving only the upper part of the torso and the hand free. One fold of the himation crosses the chest diagonally and falls over the left shoulder (›arm-sling‹ type). The folds of the himation are indicated by diagonal and curving grooves.

He holds the diagonal fold of the himation with his right hand. On the left hand he holds a rectangular object, possibly a schedula.

301. SARCOPHAGUS BOX WITH PORTRAIT BUSTS

DATABASE NUMBER: PM751.
LOCATION: Palmyra, Palmyra Museum, inv. no. A 1246.
CONTEXT: Secondary context: Found (1957) in later construction in front of column 6 of the south portico of the Great Colonnade.
ACQUISITION HISTORY: —
MEASUREMENTS: Height: 49 cm. Width: 192 cm.
MATERIAL: Limestone, white.
PRESERVATION: The right side is broken off. A large crack runs vertically through the sarcophagus box to the right of portrait A. Another crack runs vertically through portrait D. The heads of the portraits are chipped. The surface of the sarcophagus box is very weathered.
TECHNICAL DESCRIPTION: —
DATE: A.D. 100–150.
REFERENCES: Bounni – Teixidor 1975, 25 f. cat. 26 pl. 6. Inscription: Bounni – Teixidor 1975, 25 f. cat. 26 pl. 6; Krag 2018, 32 n. 63; 87 n. 182; 98 n. 23; 246 cat. 297.

OBJECT DESCRIPTION

The sarcophagus box is rectangular in shape and is rendered as a kline. Four, possibly armless, figures are depicted between the kline legs: a female bust, a male bust, a female bust, and a male bust. The left kline leg is turned. It is several elements, but only the plinth is well-preserved (other details unclear).

INSCRIPTIONS
INSCRIPTION 1
SCRIPT: Palmyrene Aramaic.
LOCATION ON RELIEF: On right side of the box.
TRANSCRIPTION: BT ʿLM D[- - -].
TRANSLATION: House of eternity of - - -.

INSCRIPTION 2
SCRIPT: Palmyrene Aramaic.
LOCATION ON RELIEF: On the base of the box.
TRANSCRIPTION: [- - -]ʾ | BRH DY | LŠMŠ | BNH.
TRANSLATION: - - - the son of Lišamš Bonnah.

INSCRIPTION 3
SCRIPT: Palmyrene Aramaic.
LOCATION ON RELIEF: On the base of the box.
TRANSCRTIPTION: ʿST[WRG' BRH] | DY LŠMŠ | BNH.
TRANSLATION: ʿAstûrgâ the son of Lišamš Bonnah.

INSCRIPTION 4
SCRIPT: Palmyrene Aramaic.
LOCATION ON RELIEF: On the base of the box.
TRANSCRIPTION: [- - -] | BRH DY | LŠMŠ | BNH.
TRANSLATION: - - - the son of Lišamš Bonnah.

INSCRIPTION 5
SCRIPT: Palmyrene Aramaic.
LOCATION ON RELIEF: On the base of the box.
TRANSCRIPTION: Š[- - - BRH] | D[Y] LŠMŠ | BNH.
TRANSLATION: Š - - - the son of Lišamš Bonnah.

INSCRIPTION 6
SCRIPT: Palmyrene Aramaic.
LOCATION ON RELIEF: On the base of the box.
TRANSCRIPTION: MQYMW BRH | DY LŠMŠ | BNH.
TRANSLATION: Moqîmû the son of Lišamš Bonnah.

CIS no. —; PAT no. 1543.

COMMENT: Inscription 5: L.1: Alternatively BRTH >The daughter of<.

PORTRAIT A: FEMALE BUST
The figure is shown frontally.
She wears a veil. It falls over the shoulders and is wrapped around her upper arms. A lock of hair falls downwards on each shoulder.

She wears a tunic and a himation. The tunic has a wide, round neckline. The folds of the tunic are rendered by curving grooves. Over the tunic, she wears a himation. The himation crosses the chest diagonally from the left shoulder to the right side, and covers the left breast. It is fastened at the shoulder with a trapezoidal brooch (Colledge classification: i). The folds of the himation are rendered by vertical and oblique grooves.

PORTRAIT B: MALE BUST
The figure is shown frontally. The right arm is bent and held to the chest. The left arm is held along the body.

He wears a tunic and a himation. The tunic has a wide, round neckline. The folds of the tunic are rendered by curving grooves. Over the tunic, he wears a himation. The himation covers most of the body: it is wrapped around the right shoulder and arm, leaving only the upper part of the chest free. One fold of the himation crosses the chest diagonally and falls over the left shoulder (>arm-sling< type). The folds of the himation are indicated by diagonal grooves.

PORTRAIT C: FEMALE BUST
The figure is shown frontally.
She wears a veil. It falls over the shoulders and is wrapped around her upper arms. A lock of hair falls downwards on each shoulder.

She wears a tunic and a himation. The tunic has a wide, round neckline. The folds of the tunic are rendered by curving grooves. Over the tunic, she wears a himation. The himation crosses the chest diagonally from the left shoulder to the right side, and covers the left breast. It is fastened at the shoulder with a trapezoidal brooch (Colledge classification: i). The folds of the himation are rendered by vertical and oblique grooves.

PORTRAIT D: MALE BUST
The figure is shown frontally. The right arm is bent and held to the chest. The left arm is held along the body.

He wears a tunic and a himation. The tunic has a wide, round neckline. The folds of the tunic are rendered by curving grooves. Over the tunic, he wears a himation. The himation covers most of the body: it is wrapped around the right shoulder and arm, leaving only the upper part of the chest free. One fold of the himation crosses the chest diagonally and falls over the left shoulder (>arm-sling< type). The folds of the himation are indicated by diagonal grooves.

302. FRAGMENTS OF SARCOPHAGUS BOX WITH PORTRAIT BUSTS

DATABASE NUMBER: DGAM062 (302a) + DGAM061 (302b).
LOCATION: Damascus, Directorate-General of Antiquities and Museums, inv. no. unknown.
CONTEXT: —
ACQUISITION HISTORY: Confiscated in Switzerland, and moved to the Musée d'Art et d'Histoire until its return to Syria.
MEASUREMENTS: —
MATERIAL: Limestone.
PRESERVATION: The relief is cut off at the lower edge and middle.
TECHNICAL DESCRIPTION: —
DATE: A.D. 100–150.
REFERENCES: Online: <http://dgam.gov.sy/index.php?d=314&id=2119> (accessed 06.05.2020; link inactive on 06.05.2022).

OBJECT DESCRIPTION
The box is in the shape of a kline with a mattress and has a female and a male bust between the legs. The mattress is decorated with bands and curving grooves indicate the texture of the fabric. The legs are turned. They are composed of a plinth, and above is a torus, a bell-shaped element, a thin torus, a bell-shaped element, an ovolo, and a torus. A lion head is depicted to the right of the female's head. It is shown in frontal view, the ears are thin and point upwards, the mane surrounds the head, and

a ring hangs from its open mouth. A lion head is depicted to the left of the male's head. It is shown in frontal view, the ears are thin and point upwards, the mane surrounds the head, and a ring hangs from its open mouth.

PORTRAIT A

The figure is shown frontally. The arms are bent; the right is held up to the chest and the left is held in front of the torso.

She wears three headdresses: a headband, a turban, and a veil. The headband is worn low on the head (other details unclear). The turban is coiled. Oblique grooves indicate the coiling of the fabric. The veil is heavy. It falls behind the back of her head, over her shoulders and arms. Locks of hair are brushed back over the temples and the edge of the turban, and disappear under the veil (other details unclear). Her face is oval. The eyebrows are curving. The eyes are close-set with thick eyelids (other details unclear). She is wearing earrings (other details unclear). The nose is thin. The cheeks are fleshy. The mouth is small, with thin lips. The chin is round and the neck is wide and long.

She wears a tunic and a himation. The tunic has a wide, round neckline and sleeves. The folds of the tunic are rendered by curving grooves. The tunic crosses the chest diagonally from the left shoulder to the right side (details unclear). It is fastened at the left shoulder with a brooch (details unclear).

The right hand is raised and the index and middle fingers are extended. With the left hand she holds a spindle and distaff (details unclear).

PORTRAIT B

The figure is shown frontally. The arms are bent and held to the torso.

His hair is straight and arranged in two rows of crescent-shaped locks. His face is triangular. The eyebrows are slightly curving. The eyes are wide-set and almond-shaped, with thick upper eyelids. The eyeballs are blank. The ears are large and protruding with the helix, antihelix, and lobe depicted. The nose is straight. The cheeks are fleshy. The mouth is small, with a full lower lip. The chin is pointed. The neck is wide and short.

He wears a tunic and himation. The tunic has a wide, round neckline. The folds of the tunic are rendered by curving grooves. The himation is wrapped around the right shoulder and arm, leaving only part of the chest and the right hand free. One fold of the himation crosses the chest diagonally and falls over the left shoulder (>arm-sling< type), covering the left side of the torso and the arm. The folds of the himation are rendered by oblique grooves.

With his right hand, he lightly holds the fold of the himation that crosses the chest. The right hand rests in front of the torso. The index and middle fingers are extended.

A.D. 150–170

303. SARCOPHAGUS BOX WITH PORTRAIT BUSTS

DATABASE NUMBER: UNK166.
LOCATION: Last known location: >seraji< of Palmyra.
CONTEXT: —
ACQUISITION HISTORY: —
MEASUREMENTS: —
MATERIAL: Limestone.
PRESERVATION: The object is weathered. The left leg of the kline is broken off. Portrait A: The top of the head, the nose, and the chin are chipped. Portrait B: The nose, mouth, and lower part of the face are broken off. Portrait C: The lower left part of the face is broken off. Portrait D: The central part of the face is chipped.
TECHNICAL DESCRIPTION: —
DATE: A.D. 150–170.
REFERENCES: Ingholt Archives, PS 611; Chabot 1922, 111 pl. 20, 4; Kammerer 1929, 310 n. 2 pl. 119, 1; Silver et al. 2018, 67 fig. 4.11; <https://www.loc.gov/item/mpc2010000997/PP/> (15.11.2022).

OBJECT DESCRIPTION

The sarcophagus box is rectangular in shape and is rendered as a kline. Four armless busts in clipei are depicted between the kline legs. Above the kline is a mattress with three wide, decorated bands with floral motifs between beaded bands. There is a fulcrum on the left side of the kline. The stretcher has a rectangular panel on either end, and a smaller, square panel on either side, and in the centre, a long, rectangular panel divided into two horizontal sections. The central stretcher cuts through the uppermost turning of the kline leg. The legs are turned. They are composed of a conical neck, a convex quarter, a reversed bell-shaped element, a torus, a neck, a ball, a torus, a concave quarter, and above the stretcher is a biconical finial. All elements are decorated with a tongue pattern, rendered diagonally on the ball.

PORTRAIT A: ARMLESS MALE BUST

The figure is shown frontally. The head appears large in relation to the body.

The hair is short, voluminous, and slightly wavy, arranged in flame-shaped locks. His face is square. The eyebrows are curving. The eyes are large and round, with thick upper eyelids. The eyeballs are blank. The ears are large and protruding. The nose is wide. The mouth is small, with a full lower lip. The neck is long and wide.

He wears a tunic and a himation. The tunic has a wide, v-shaped neckline and short, wide sleeves. The folds of the tunic are indicated by curving grooves. The himation falls over the left shoulder, with one fold crossing the chest diagonally.

Cat. 303

PORTRAIT B: ARMLESS BUST OF PRIEST

The figure is shown frontally. The head appears large in relation to the body.

He wears a tall, cylindrical, flat-top headdress divided into three sections by two vertical grooves low on the forehead: a Palmyrene priestly hat. A wreath with leaves pointing towards a central decoration is depicted at the lower part of the headdress. His face is square. The eyebrows are low and curving. The eyes are large and round. The eyeballs are blank. The ears are large and protruding with the helix, scapha, and concha depicted. The nose is straight. The neck is long and wide.

He wears a tunic and a chlamys. The tunic has a wide, round neckline and short, wide sleeves. The folds of the tunic are indicated by wide, vertical grooves over the arms. The chlamys covers most of the chest. It is fastened at the right shoulder with a brooch with small, globular elements at the upper side (details unclear). A small, zigzag-shaped fold falls under the brooch.

PORTRAIT C: ARMLESS BUST OF PRIEST

The figure is shown frontally. The head appears large in relation to the body.

He wears a tall, cylindrical, flat-top headdress divided into three sections by two vertical grooves, low on the forehead: a Palmyrene priestly hat. A wreath with leaves pointing towards a central bust is depicted at the lower part of the headdress. His face is square. The eyebrows are low and curving. The eyes are large and round. The eyeballs are blank. The ears are large and protruding with the helix, scapha, and the lobe depicted. The nose is straight. The neck is short and wide.

He wears a tunic and a chlamys. The tunic has a wide, round neckline and short, wide sleeves. The folds of the tunic are indicated by wide, vertical grooves over the arms. The chlamys covers most of the chest. It is fastened at the right shoulder with a brooch (details unclear). A small, zigzag-shaped fold falls under the brooch.

PORTRAIT D: ARMLESS MALE BUST

The figure is shown frontally. The head appears large in relation to the body.

The hair is short, voluminous, and slightly wavy, arranged in flame-shaped locks. His face is square. The eyebrows are curving. The eyes are large and round with thick upper eyelids. The ears are large and protruding. The eyeballs appear blank. The nose is straight and wide. The mouth is small. The neck is short and wide with a horizontal groove.

He wears a tunic and a himation. The tunic has a wide, v-shaped neckline and short, wide sleeves. The folds of the tunic are indicated by curving grooves. The himation falls over the left shoulder, with one fold crossing the chest diagonally.

304. SARCOPHAGUS BOX WITH PORTRAIT BUSTS

DATABASE NUMBER: PM737.
LOCATION: Palmyra, Palmyra Museum, inv. no. B 2722/9159.
CONTEXT: —
ACQUISITION HISTORY: —
MEASUREMENTS: Height: 84 cm. Width: 235 cm.
MATERIAL: Limestone.
PRESERVATION: The right edge of the kline is chipped. Portrait A: The head and headdress are broken off. Portrait B: The head, headdress, and the left arm are broken off. Portrait C: The top of the headdress is chipped. Portrait D: The surface is chipped.
TECHNICAL DESCRIPTION: —
DATE: A.D. 150–170 (al-Asʿad – Gawlikowski 1997: A.D. 150–200).
REFERENCES: al-Asʿad – Gawlikowski 1997, 75 cat. 117 fig. 117. Inscription: Yon 2013, 349 cat. 71.

OBJECT DESCRIPTION

The sarcophagus box is rectangular in shape and is rendered as a kline. Three armless busts of priests are depicted between the legs. Above the kline is a mattress. The mattress has three wide bands decorated with a floral motif. Curving grooves indicate the texture of the fabric. The fulcrum to the left side is decorated with a bust of a priest at the lower part (portrait D). The stretcher of the kline is decorated by a long, central panel, and on either side, there is a smaller, rectangular panel and a square indentation. The legs are turned. They are composed of a plinth, a concave neck, a thin torus, a cyma recta, a reversed concave quarter, a torus, a ball, a torus, and a concave quarter.

INSCRIPTIONS

INSCRIPTION 1
SCRIPT: Palmyrene Aramaic.
LOCATION ON RELIEF: To the left of the head of portrait A.
TRANSCRIPTION: NŠʾ BRH | DY ʿNNY.
TRANSLATION: Nešâ, the son of ʿAnanî.

INSCRIPTION 2
SCRIPT: Palmyrene Aramaic.
LOCATION ON RELIEF: To the left of the head of the central figure.
TRANSCRIPTION: MLLW BRH | DY ʿNNY.
TRANSLATION: Malkû, the son of ʿAnanî.

INSCRIPTION 3
SCRIPT: Palmyrene Aramaic.
LOCATION ON RELIEF: To the left of the head of portrait C.
TRANSCRIPTION: MLʾ BRH | DY ʿNNY.
TRANSLATION: Malê, the son of ʿAnanî.

CIS no. —; PAT no. —.

Cat. 304

PORTRAIT A: ARMLESS BUST OF PRIEST, NEŠÂ

The figure is shown frontally.

He wears a tall, cylindrical flat-top headdress: a Palmyrene priestly hat (visible only in outline). The face is visible only in outline. The neck is short and wide.

He wears a tunic and a chlamys. The tunic has a wide, v-shaped neckline and short, wide sleeves. The folds of the tunic are rendered by oblique grooves in the area of the shoulders and arms. Over the tunic, he wears a chlamys that is folded over the chest. It is fastened at the right shoulder with a circular brooch with an incised border (Colledge classification: h). A zigzag-shaped fold falls under the brooch.

PORTRAIT B: ARMLESS BUST OF PRIEST, MALKÛ

The figure is shown frontally.

He wears a tall, cylindrical headdress (visible only in outline). The face is visible only in outline. The neck is short and wide.

He wears a tunic and a chlamys. The tunic has a wide, v-shaped neckline and short, wide sleeves. The folds of the tunic are rendered by oblique grooves in the area of the shoulders and arms. Over the tunic, he wears a chlamys that is folded over the chest. It is fastened at the right shoulder with a circular brooch with an incised border (Colledge classification: h). A zigzag-shaped fold falls under the brooch.

PORTRAIT C: ARMLESS BUST OF PRIEST, MALÊ

The figure is shown frontally.

He wears a tall, cylindrical flat-top headdress: a Palmyrene priestly hat. A wreath with the leaves pointing towards a central rosette inside a beaded border is depicted at the lower part of the headdress. His face is square and fleshy. The eyebrows are curving. The eyes are almond-shaped. The irises are indicated (details unclear). The ears are slightly protruding. The nose is straight. The mouth is small. The chin is pointed. The neck is short and wide. A v-shaped groove indicates the sternocleidomastoid muscles.

He wears a tunic and a chlamys. The tunic has a wide, v-shaped neckline and short, wide sleeves. The folds of the tunic are rendered by oblique grooves in the area of the shoulders and arms. Over the tunic, he wears a chlamys that is folded over the chest. It is fastened at the right shoulder with a circular brooch with an incised border (Colledge classification: h). A zigzag-shaped fold falls under the brooch.

PORTRAIT D: ARMLESS BUST OF A PRIEST IN FULCRUM

The figure is shown frontally, rendered in a clipeus.

The outline of a tall, cylindrical headdress is visible: a Palmyrene priestly hat.

A row of oblique grooves, possibly indicating a tunic or chlamys is visible at the right shoulder and side.

A.D. 170–200

305. SARCOPHAGUS BOX WITH PORTRAIT BUSTS

DATABASE NUMBER: DGAM006.
LOCATION: Damascus, Directorate-General of Antiquities and Museums, inv. no. unknown.
CONTEXT: —
ACQUISITION HISTORY: Confiscated by authorities in Palmyra, March 2014.
MEASUREMENTS: —
MATERIAL: Limestone.
PRESERVATION: Slightly weathered.
TECHNICAL DESCRIPTION: —
DATE: A.D. 170–200.
REFERENCES: Ali 2011, 51 cat. 8; Ali 2015, 50 cat. 8; Raja 2019e 98. 141. cat. 79.

OBJECT DESCRIPTION

The sarcophagus box is rectangular in shape and rendered as a kline. Four armless busts are depicted between the kline legs: two priests and two females. The kline has a low mattress divided into four sections with curving grooves by three wide bands with vegetal decoration. The fulcrum is decorated with a male bust at the lower part (portrait E). The stretcher is decorated with two square panels framing a rectangular panel on either side of a central rectangular panel with diagonal incised lines that fan out to the left and right from the centre. The legs are turned. They are composed of a cyma reversa, another cyma reversa, a torus, a biconical torus, a neck, and above the stretcher is a biconical finial. The elements appear decorated (details unclear).

PORTRAIT A: ARMLESS FEMALE BUST

The figure is shown frontally with the head turned to the right.

She wears two headdresses: a turban and a veil. The turban is coiled. Horizontal grooves indicate the coiling of the fabric. The veil falls over the neck and shoulders with the right end of the veil folded over the upper torso and falling over the left shoulder. Part of the hair is visible: several strands of hair above the ears are brushed back over the edge of the turban and disappear under the veil. Her face is square and fleshy. The eyebrows are indicated. The eyes are almond-shaped. The eyeballs are blank. The nose is small. The mouth is large. The chin is wide. The neck is short.

She wears a tunic with a wide, round neckline.

PORTRAIT B: ARMLESS BUST OF PRIEST

The figure is shown frontally.

He wears a tall, plain, cylindrical, flat-top headdress divided into three sections by two vertical grooves: a Palmyrene priestly hat. His face is square. The eyebrows are curving, depicted as thin ridges. The eyes are small and almond-shaped. The ears are large and protruding. The nose is long with a wide base. The mouth is wide. The chin is wide. The neck is short.

He wears a tunic and a himation. The tunic has a wide, v-shaped neckline. The folds of the tunic are rendered by curving grooves on the chest and oblique grooves on the shoulders and arms. Over the tunic, he wears a himation that falls over the left shoulder and arm. One fold crosses the chest diagonally. The folds of the himation are depicted with oblique grooves.

PORTRAIT C: ARMLESS FEMALE BUST
The figure is shown frontally.

She wears two headdresses: a turban and a veil. The turban is coiled. Horizontal grooves indicate the coiling of the fabric. The veil falls over the neck and shoulders with the right end of the veil folded over the upper torso and falling over the left shoulder. Part of the hair is visible: several strands of hair above the ears are brushed back over the edge of the turban and disappear under the veil. Her face is square and long. The eyebrows are indicated. The eyes are small and almond-shaped. The nose is small. The mouth is small. The chin is round. The neck is short.

She wears a tunic with a wide, v-shaped neckline.

PORTRAIT D: ARMLESS BUST OF A PRIEST
The figure is shown frontally.

He wears a tall, cylindrical, flat-top headdress divided into three sections by two vertical grooves: a Palmyrene priestly hat. A wreath with the leaves pointing towards a central decoration is depicted at the lower part of the hat. His face is square. The eyebrows are curving, rendered by incised lines. The eyes are small and almond-shaped. The ears are large and protruding. The nose is long and straight. The mouth is small. The chin is wide. The neck is short.

He wears a tunic, a chlamys, and a himation. The tunic has a round neckline. The folds of the tunic are rendered by vertical grooves on the shoulders and arms. Over the tunic, he wears a chlamys that falls over both shoulders and covers most of the chest. It is fastened at the right shoulder with a circular brooch. The folds of the chlamys are indicated by curving grooves. Over the chlamys, he wears a himation. The himation falls over the left shoulder and arm.

PORTRAIT E: ARMLESS MALE BUST IN FULCRUM
The figure is shown frontally.

He has short hair.

He probably wears a tunic and chlamys.

A.D. 200–220

306. SARCOPHAGUS BOX WITH RELIGIOUS SCENE

DATABASE NUMBER: PM604.
LOCATION: Palmyra, Palmyra Museum, inv. no. unknown.
CONTEXT: —
ACQUISITION HISTORY: —
MEASUREMENTS: Height: 92 cm. Width: 227 cm. Depth: 94 cm.
MATERIAL: Limestone.
PRESERVATION: The upper part of the sarcophagus box is broken off. Side A: The uppermost turning of the left kline leg is broken off. Portrait A: The right shoulder is broken off. Portrait B: Part of the headdress and the tip of the nose are broken off. Portrait C: The tip of the left foot is broken off. The surface is slightly weathered. Portrait D: The tip of the nose and the uppermost part of the head are broken off. Portraits E and F: The uppermost part of the heads has broken off. Side B: The uppermost part of the box and the right kline leg are broken off. Portraits G–M: The heads are broken off. Portrait J: A large crack runs horizontally through the upper torso. Side C: The uppermost part of the box is broken off. Portraits N and O: The heads are broken off. Side D: The uppermost part is broken off along with the upper part of the kline legs. Portrait Q: The head is broken off.
TECHNICAL DESCRIPTION: —
DATE: A.D. 200–220 (Rumscheid 2000: A.D. 200–250).
REFERENCES: Rumscheid 2000, 222 f. cat. 271 pl. 64, 2; pl. 65, 1–3; Degeorge 2001, 246; Kaizer 2002, 180 pls. 5. 6; Schmidt-Colinet – al-Asʿad 2007, 276–278 pl. 90; Schmidt-Colinet 2009, 225–227 figs. 9–14; Wielgosz-Rondolino 2016a, 77–79 cat. 17, a–c; Raja 2017a, 220–222. 227 cat. 22; Raja 2017h, 64 f. 77 cat. 22; Krag 2018, 32 n. 63; 49 n. 229; 55 n. 260; 58 n. 304; 59 n. 320; 62 n. 349; 65 n. 371; 73 n. 47; 87 n. 183; 103 n. 73. 74; 398 f. cat. 865; Raja 2019e, 97–99. 113–119 cat. 32.

OBJECT DESCRIPTION
The sarcophagus box is rectangular in shape and is rendered as a kline. There are seventeen figures depicted on all four sides of the box, between the kline legs.

Side A (portraits A–F) depicts a standing male, a standing female, two standing males, a standing female, and a standing male. Between portraits C and D, at the height of their heads, two cylindrical flat-top headdresses, which are divided into three sections by two vertical grooves (Palmyrene priestly hats), are shown on top of a tall, square pillar. Two wreaths with the leaves pointing towards a central oval are depicted at the lower part of each headdress. A folded cloth with the edges falling down the pillar are depicted under each headdress. A square altar with a triangular top with a flame protruding from it, is also depicted between these portraits.

Side B (portraits G–M) depicts seven male figures. Between portraits G and H, a calf is seen depicted frontally. The calf is depicted with crescent-shaped horns over pointy ears. On top of the head and above the eyes, the hair is rendered by thin, incised lines. The eyes are large and the nose is oval. The chest musculature is rendered by v-shaped incisions. The forelegs are thin with the fetlock joints and coffins rendered. An altar is depicted between portraits I and J: it has a two-stepped square base, a thin, rectangular shaft with a straight-edge moulding, and its top is polygonal. A flame is depicted on its top.

Side C (portraits N and O) depicts two male figures standing on a protruding lower edge.

Side D (portraits P and Q) depicts two female figures standing on a protruding lower edge.

The kline has four turned legs. They are composed of a plinth, above is a reversed bell-shaped element, a concave quarter, a thick torus, a reversed concave quarter, a concave quarter, a biconical element, and two elements of opposed concave quarters. All elements are decorated with a tongue pattern.

SIDE A

PORTRAIT A: STANDING MALE

The figure is shown frontally. The arms appear short in relation to the body. The right arm is bent and held to the torso. The left arm is bent and held outwards. The right leg is slightly bent. The legs are set apart and he rests his weight on his left leg.

His hair is arranged in snail-shell curls around the head. The individual locks of hair are indicated by incised lines. His face is oval. The eyebrows are curving, rendered by incised lines starting from the root of the nose. The eyes are close-set and the eyeballs are blank. Only the earlobes are visible under the hair. The nose is straight. The mouth is small, with full lips. The chin is pointed and the neck is wide with two curving grooves.

He wears a tunic and an undergarment. The undergarment is visible in a curving line above the knees, where the edge has fringes. The tunic has a wide, round neckline and short, wide sleeves. On either side of the chest, there are two plain bands extending downwards (clavi). The tunic ends at the knees, revealing part of the undergarment. The folds of the tunic are rendered by curving and oblique grooves. There is an overfold at the waist. He does not wear shoes, and the toes are rendered by incised lines.

The right hand lies on top of the object carried in his left hand. With the upturned palm of his left hand, he holds a rectangular box. It has a rectangular depression on the frontal side. On top of the box lies a large round object, possibly a roughly carved wreath.

PORTRAIT B: STANDING FEMALE

The figure is shown frontally. The arms appear short in relation to the body. The head is turned slightly to the left. The right arm is bent and held to the chest. The left arm is bent and held to the waist. The left leg is slightly bent. The legs are set apart and she rests her weight on the right leg.

She wears two headdresses: a turban and a veil. The turban is coiled and is divided into two layers. Curving grooves indicate the coiling of the fabric. The veil is heavy. It falls over her shoulders, is folded around the arms, and covers the body and thighs. One end of the veil crosses the chest diagonally, falls over the left shoulder, and extends down her left side. A zigzag-shaped fold falls from under her left hand extending downwards. A fold of the veil falls from her left wrist and extends downwards in a diagonal line to her left side. The lower edge is rendered in a curving line above the knees and is pulled back alongside her legs. The folds of the veil are rendered by curving and oblique grooves. The headdresses cover part of the hair: several strands of hair above the ears are pushed back over the edge of the turban and disappear under the veil. Her face is oval. The eyebrows are indicated by curving grooves. The eyes are close-set and round. The eyeballs are blank. Only the earlobes are visible under the hair and she wears dumbbell-shaped earrings (Colledge classification: H). The chin is pointed with a cleft. The neck is wide with two curving grooves. She wears one necklace composed of small, round beads at the base of the neck.

She wears a tunic. The ankle-length tunic has a wide, round neckline. The folds of the tunic are rendered by curving

Cat. 306

Cat. 306

Cat. 306

grooves at the chest and oblique grooves between the legs. She wears shoes.

Her right arm is raised to the chest. She holds the diagonal fold of the veil with her hand. Her left hand lies at the lower right side of her waist, slightly pulling the veil.

PORTRAIT C: STANDING MALE

The figure is shown in three-quarter view, turned slightly to the left. The arms appear short in relation to the body. The right arm is bent and held across the waist. The left arm is bent and held out from the body. The right leg is slightly bent, and the knee is rendered under the drapery. The legs are set apart and he rests his weight on his left leg.

His hair is voluminous and he wears a wreath high on the forehead with the leaves pointing towards a central rosette. His face is oval. The eyebrows are indicated by curving grooves. The eyes are close-set and round with blank eyeballs. Only the earlobes are visible under the hair. The nose is straight. He has a beard that starts from the temples and covers the cheeks and the chin, as well as a moustache that covers the upper lip. The mouth is small. The neck is wide. A v-shaped groove indicates the jugular notch.

He wears a tunic and a toga. The ankle-length tunic has a wide, round neckline and short, wide sleeves. A wide band decorated with vegetal motifs extends downwards on each side of the chest. The folds of the tunic are rendered by curving grooves. Over the tunic, he wears a toga. The toga is folded from his right side and proceeds horizontally across his abdomen (sinus). The fold from his left shoulder is folded under the horizontal one where it proceeds downwards over his thighs and shins (umbo). Another fold falls from under his left wrist and ends in an s-shape at his left ankle. He probably wears boots.

He holds a pitcher in his right hand, directing it towards the altar. The pitcher has a conical foot, a concave body, and a tall neck. His index finger is extended. With the palm of his left hand turned outwards, he holds an oblong object, possibly a book-roll.

PORTRAIT D: STANDING MALE

The figure is shown frontally. The arms and the torso appear short. The right arm is extended away from the body. The left arm is bent and held to the torso. The left leg is slightly bent, and the knee is rendered under the drapery. The legs are set apart and he rests his weight on his right leg.

His hair is arranged in flame-shaped curls around the head. He wears a wreath high on the forehead with the leaves pointing towards a central rosette. His face is oval. The eyebrows are curving, rendered by thin ridges. The eyes are close-set and almond-shaped, with thick upper eyelids. The upper eyelids extend beyond the end of the lower ones. The eyeballs are blank. The ears are small with the helix and scapha depicted. The nose is straight. He has a beard that starts from the temples and covers the cheeks and the chin, as well as a moustache that covers the upper lip. The facial hair is rendered by flame-shaped curls arranged in rows. The moustache is rendered with narrow, oblique, incised lines: they are centred over the philtrum and curve downwards and to the left and right of the face, reaching the beard. The mouth is small. The neck is wide. A v-shaped groove indicates the sternocleidomastoid muscles.

He wears a tunic and a toga. The ankle-length tunic has a wide, v-shaped neckline and short, wide sleeves. A wide band decorated with a vegetal motif extends downwards on the right side of the chest. The edge of the right sleeve is folded under the toga. The folds of the tunic are rendered by curving grooves. Over the tunic, he wears a toga. The toga covers most of the body: it is wrapped around the left shoulder and arm, leaving only the upper part of the chest free. The toga is folded from his right side and proceeds horizontally across his abdomen (sinus). A fold coming from his left shoulder is folded under the horizontal fold (umbo) where it proceeds downwards over his thighs and shins. Another fold falls from under his left wrist and ends in an s-shape at his left ankle. He wears footwear, either boots or sandals.

With his right hand, he holds a pitcher, directing it towards the altar. The pitcher has an ovoid body and a tall neck. With his left hand, he holds an oblong object to his torso, possibly a book-roll. The index and the little finger are extended.

PORTRAIT E: STANDING FEMALE

The figure is shown frontally. The left arm appears short in relation to the body. The right arm is held along the body. The left arm is bent and held to the chest. The right leg is bent, with the knee rendered under the drapery. The legs are set apart and she rests her weight on her left leg.

She wears three headdresses: a headband, a turban, and a veil. The details of the headband are unclear. The turban is coiled and divided into two layers. Curving grooves indicate the coiling of the fabric. The veil is heavy and covers the whole body: it falls over her head and is wrapped around the right shoulder and arm, leaving only the upper part of the chest and hand free. One fold of the veil crosses the chest diagonally and falls over the left shoulder, leaving the lower arm and hand free. It extends downwards at her left side. The folds of the veil are rendered by curving and oblique grooves. She also wears a head-chain. The chain is fastened at the centre of the turban with a larger bezel, and falls to either side of the forehead with strings of round beads. Her face is oval. The eyebrows are curving. The eyes are almond-shaped and slanting. The eyeballs are blank. Only the earlobes are visible under the headdress. She wears dumbbell-shaped earrings (Colledge classification: H). The chin is pointed. The neck is wide. She wears a necklace composed of small, round beads at the base of the neck.

She wears a tunic. The tunic falls to the ankle. It has a wide, v-shaped neckline. The folds of the tunic are rendered by curving grooves at the chest and oblique grooves between the legs. She wears round-toe shoes.

Her right hand is placed at her right thigh, slightly pulling a fold of the veil. The index and the little finger are extended. Her left arm is raised to the chest. She lightly pulls a diagonal

Cat. 306

fold of the veil with her hand. The index and the little finger are extended.

PORTRAIT F: STANDING MALE

The figure is shown in three-quarter view. The arms appear short in relation to the body. The arms are bent. He stands with the legs set slightly apart.

His hair is arranged in curls around the head. His face is oval. The eyebrows are curving and the eyes are close-set. The eyeballs appear blank. The nose is small and straight. The cheeks are fleshy. The mouth is small, with full lips. The chin is round. The neck is wide.

He wears an undergarment and a tunic. The undergarment is visible from above the left knee and diagonally under the right knee. The edge of the undergarment has fringes. The tunic has a small, v-shaped neckline and wide sleeves that cover his upper arms and elbow. There is an overfold at the waist. The folds of the tunic are rendered by curving and oblique grooves. He does not wear shoes. The toes are indicated by incised lines.

He holds a large bowl in his hands. It is filled with small, round objects, possibly fruit.

SIDE B

PORTRAIT G: STANDING MALE

The figure is shown in three-quarter view. The arms appear short in relation to the body. The right arm is bent and held to the chest. The left arm is bent and held out from the body. His legs are set apart and he rests his weight on his bent right leg.

He wears a short himation. It is fastened at the left shoulder by a circular brooch with an incised border (Colledge classification: h). It covers the left side of the chest and the lower body and thighs, leaving the arms and the upper right part of the chest free. An overfold is depicted at the waist. The folds of the himation are rendered by diagonal and curving grooves. He does not wear shoes.

He holds a small dagger in his right hand: it has a round end, a rectangular main body, and a thin ridge indicating the fuller of the blade. He wears an armlet: a plain hoop. With the left hand, he holds the right horn of the calf.

PORTRAIT H: STANDING MALE

The figure is shown in three-quarter view. The arms appear short in relation to the body. The right arm is bent and held to the torso. The left arm is bent and held out from the body. He stands with his legs set slightly apart with the weight resting on the left leg, while the right leg is slightly bent.

He wears an undergarment, a tunic, and a mantle. The scalloped edge of the undergarment is visible at his legs falling in a diagonal line from above the left knee and over the right. The folds of the garment are rendered by oblique grooves. The tunic has a round neckline and short, wide sleeves and ends at his knees. The folds of the tunic are rendered by curving and oblique grooves. Over the tunic, he wears a mantle. It is folded around his left shoulder and arm leaving most of the torso and the hand free. The folds of the chlamys are rendered by vertical and curving grooves. He wears sandals: they have a single strap between the big toe and index toe and are tied around the ankles.

With his right hand, he holds a pitcher. The pitcher has a ring base, an ovoid body with decoration (details unclear) and a tall neck. With the left hand, he holds a patera with a long handle. There is a tondo decoration on the inside of the patera.

PORTRAIT I: STANDING MALE

The figure is shown in three-quarter view. The arms are bent. He stands with his legs set slightly apart with the weight resting on the left leg, while the right leg is slightly bent.

He wears an undergarment and a tunic. The scalloped edge of the undergarment is visible at his legs falling in a diagonal line from above the left knee and over the right. Over this garment, he wears a short-sleeved tunic that proceeds to his thighs. There is an overfold of the tunic. The folds of the tunic are rendered by curving and oblique grooves. He wears sandals.

He holds an octagonal chest with a lid in his hands. The lid is decorated with a panel with a row of lanceolate leaves with incised midribs. On top of the lid lies an oblong object, possibly a diadem with a central oval. The lower part of the chest is divided into three panels. The central square panel is decorated with a flower with four serrated leaves. A beaded band frames the panel. The narrow rectangular panels on either side are decorated with lanceolate leaves in an opposite arrangement on the stem.

PORTRAIT J: STANDING MALE

The figure is shown frontally. The arms appear short in relation to the body. The right arm is bent and held out from the body. The left is bent and held to the torso. He stands with his legs set slightly apart.

He wears a tunic and a toga. The tunic falls to the ankles and has a round neckline. A band extends downwards from his right shoulder: it is decorated with lanceolate leaves in an opposite arrangement on the stem. The folds of the tunic are rendered by curving grooves. Over the tunic, he wears a toga. It is wrapped around his left shoulder and arm. It falls in a thick fold from his shoulder (umbo) and is looped under another fold of the toga that runs across his waist (sinus). A fold of the toga falls downwards from under his left wrist, proceeds across his lower legs, and falls behind his right leg. The folds of the toga are rendered by curving and oblique grooves. He wears sandals.

With the right hand, he holds a patera with a long handle. With his left hand, he holds an oblong object, possibly a book-roll.

PORTRAIT K: STANDING MALE

The figure is shown in three-quarter view. The arms appear short in relation to the body. The arms are bent. He stands with the legs slightly set apart. The left leg is slightly bent, and he is resting on the right leg.

He wears an undergarment, a tunic, and a mantle. The edge of the undergarment is visible at his legs falling in a diagonal line from above the left knee and over the right, and is decorated with a scalloped border. The tunic has short sleeves and ends above the knees. There is an overfold of the tunic at the waist. The folds of the tunic are rendered by curving and oblique grooves. Over the tunic, he wears a mantle. It is folded around his left shoulder and upper arm. From the elbow, it falls downwards along his right side. The folds of the mantle are rendered by oblique and curving grooves. He wears sandals.

He holds a large bowl in his hands. It is filled with small, round objects, possibly fruit.

PORTRAIT L: STANDING MALE

The figure is shown in three-quarter view. The arms appear short in relation to the body. The arms are bent and held to the chest. He stands with his legs apart. The left leg is slightly bent, and he is resting on the right leg.

He wears an undergarment and tunic. The edge of the undergarment is visible at his legs falling in a diagonal line from above the left knee and over the right. The short-sleeved tunic has a small, v-shaped neckline and ends above the knees. He wears a band belt at the waist which creates an overfold of the tunic. The folds of the tunic are rendered by curving and oblique grooves. He wears sandals.

He holds an oblong object in his hands, possibly a jug.

PORTRAIT M: STANDING MALE

The figure is shown in three-quarter view. The arms appear short in relation to the body. The right arm is slightly bent and held out from the body. The left arm is bent and held to the torso. He stands with his legs slightly set apart. The left leg is slightly bent, and he is resting on the right leg.

He wears an undergarment, a tunic, and a mantle. The edge of the undergarment is visible at his legs falling in a diagonal line from above the left knee and over the right. The tunic has a wide, round neckline and wide, long sleeves, and it ends above the knees. There is an overfold of the tunic at the waist. The folds of the tunic are rendered by curving and oblique grooves. Over the tunic, he wears a mantle. It falls in a wide fold from the back and over his left shoulder. A zigzag-shaped fold falls from under his left hand. The folds of the mantle are rendered by vertical grooves. He wears sandals.

With the right hand, he holds a jug. With the left hand, he holds the vertical fold of the mantle. The left index and the little finger are extended.

SIDE C

PORTRAIT N: STANDING MALE

The figure is shown frontally. Both arms are bent and held to the torso. He stands with his legs slightly apart. The right leg is slightly bent, and he is resting on the left leg.

He wears a ›Parthian-style‹ tunic and ›Parthian-style‹ trousers. The tunic has a wide, round neckline decorated with a beaded band and long sleeves. The cuffs of the sleeves have a wide band decorated with flowers. At the middle, the tunic has a wide band extending downwards decorated with vine scrolls with lobed vine leaves. The tunic ends above the knees and has a decorated lower border with four-petal flowers between two lines at the hem. The folds of the tunic are rendered by curving, wide grooves. He wears a plain band belt, knotted at the centre with the ends looped under on either side of the waist. He also wears another band belt that runs diagonally from the right to the left side of the waist. It is knotted at his left side. The trousers are visible from the knees. Each trouser leg has a wide band extending downwards in the middle, decorated with a vegetal pattern. Along his right side, he has an object with a pointed end and a rectangular main body: a sheathed dagger. He wears plain round-toe boots, which cover the lower part of the shins.

He stands with his arms crossed, the right arm under the left.

PORTRAIT O: STANDING MALE

The figure is shown frontally. Both arms are bent and held to the torso. He stands with his legs slightly apart. The left leg is slightly bent, and he is resting on the right leg.

He wears a ›Parthian-style‹ tunic and ›Parthian-style‹ trousers. The tunic has a wide, round neckline decorated with a beaded band and long sleeves. The cuffs of the sleeves have a wide band decorated with flowers. At the middle, the tunic has a wide band extending downwards. It is decorated with floral patterns separated by beaded bands. The tunic ends above the knees and has a decorated lower border with leaves running towards a central rosette. The folds of the tunic are rendered by curving, wide grooves. He wears a plain band belt, knotted at the centre with the ends looped under on either side of the waist. He also wears another band belt that runs diagonally from the right to the left side of the waist. A long sword is depicted at his left side; with a square top and long, rectangular main body. The trousers are visible from the knees. Each trouser leg has a wide band decorated with a vine scroll with lobed vine leaves, extending downwards. He wears plain round-toe boots, which cover the lower part of the shins.

He stands with his arms crossed, the right arm over the left.

SIDE D

PORTRAIT P: STANDING FEMALE

The figure is shown frontally. Her head is turned to her right. Both arms are bent. She stands with her legs apart. The right leg is bent and she rests the weight on the left leg.

Her hair is curly. It is short at the forehead where it is brushed back. On each side of the face, the hair is brushed to the back, covering her ears and reaching the shoulders. Her face is round. The eyebrows are curving and the eyes are close-set. The eyeballs appear blank. The nose is straight and wide at the base. The cheeks are full. The mouth is small, with full lips. The chin is pointed and the neck is wide.

She wears a tunic. It has a round neckline and short, wide sleeves. There is a large overfold at the waist. The tunic ends at the ankles. The folds of the tunic are rendered by oblique and curving grooves. She wears a closed-toe shoe.

She holds a square chest in her hands. With the right hand, she lifts the lid of the chest. Two necklaces are depicted hanging in half-circles from the opening of the chest. The upper necklace is composed of round beads with a drop-shaped pendant suspended from the centre. The lower necklace is composed of alternating square and oval pendants joined by beaded elements. With the left hand, she holds the bottom of the chest.

PORTRAIT Q: STANDING FEMALE

The figure is shown frontally. The right arm is bent and held away from the torso. The left is bent and held to the torso. She stands with her legs apart.

She wears one necklace. It is composed of round beads on a string, worn at the base of the neck.

She wears a tunic. It has a v-shaped neckline and short, wide sleeves. There is a large overfold at the waist. The tunic ends at the feet. The folds of the tunic are rendered by oblique and curving grooves.

With the right hand, she holds a round mirror with a groove along the outer edge. With the left hand, she holds an oblong object with a round upper part, possibly a perfume bottle with a stopper. The thumb, index, and the little finger are extended.

307. SARCOPHAGUS BOX WITH PORTRAIT BUST

DATABASE NUMBER: NMD157.
LOCATION: Damascus, National Museum of Damascus, inv. no. unknown.
CONTEXT: —
ACQUISITION HISTORY: —
MEASUREMENTS: Height: 88 cm. Width: 212 cm. Depth: 90 cm.
MATERIAL: Limestone.
PRESERVATION: The central part of the stretcher, the lower right corner, and the lower left part of the plinth are broken off. Portrait: The priestly hat and the face of the figure are

Cat. 307

broken off. There are several cracks running across the surface of the object.
TECHNICAL DESCRIPTION: The sides and the reverse are partly carved.
DATE: A.D. 200–220.
REFERENCES: Koch 1989, 169 f. pl. 42 c–e.

OBJECT DESCRIPTION

The object is a sarcophagus box in the shape of a kline on a projecting plinth. On top of the kline there is one mattress. It is undecorated and curving grooves indicate the texture of the mattress. A fulcrum is shown on the left side of the kline. The upper part of the fulcrum is decorated with a lion's head in a clipeus, while at the lower part there is an armless bust of a priest inside a clipeus. The central stretcher of the kline is decorated. It is divided by two square panels with a floral motif into three long rectangular panels decorated with vegetal motifs (other details unclear). The kline legs are turned. They are composed of a plinth, above is a concave quarter, a long reversed concave quarter, a concave quarter, a torus, and a reversed concave quarter. The convex finials of the legs are visible over the stretcher. All elements are decorated with a tongue pattern.

PORTRAIT

The figure is shown frontally.
  He wears a tall, cylindrical, flat-top headdress low on the forehead: a Palmyrene priestly hat (visible in outline). He wears a tunic and a chlamys. The tunic has a wide, round neckline and short, wide sleeves. The folds of the tunic are indicated by wide, vertical grooves over the arms. The chlamys covers most of the chest (other details unclear).

308. SARCOPHAGUS BOX WITH PORTRAIT BUSTS

DATABASE NUMBER: PM990.
LOCATION: Palmyra, Palmyra Museum, inv. no. unknown.
CONTEXT: —
ACQUISITION HISTORY: —
MEASUREMENTS: —
MATERIAL: Limestone.
PRESERVATION: The two lower corners of the box are broken off. Portrait A: The priestly hat and the face of the figure are broken off. Portrait B: The face of the figure is broken off. Portrait C: The priestly hat and the face of the figure are broken off.
TECHNICAL DESCRIPTION: —.
DATE: A.D. 200–220.
REFERENCES: <https://virtual-museum-syria.org/palmyra/sarcophagus-with-bases-relief-of-two-priests-and-a-woman/#> (06.05.2022).

OBJECT DESCRIPTION

The object is a sarcophagus box in the shape of a kline on a projecting plinth. On top of the kline there is one mattress. It is decorated with three broad bands with floral motifs (other details unclear) and curving grooves indicate the texture of the mattress. A fulcrum is shown on the left side of the kline.

The upper part of the fulcrum is decorated with an animal head in a clipeus, while at the lower part there is an armless bust of a priest inside a clipeus. The stretcher of the kline has decorated panels (other details unclear). The kline legs are turned. They are composed of a plinth, and above are two conical elements, a torus, a ball, and another conical element. The finials of the legs are visible over the stretcher. All elements are decorated with a tongue pattern. There are three armless portrait busts inside clipei between the legs of the kline: a priest, a female, and another priest. The clipei are composed of three concentric circles.

PORTRAIT A: ARMLESS BUST OF PRIEST

The figure is shown frontally.

He wears low on the forehead a tall, cylindrical, flat-top headdress: a Palmyrene priestly hat (visible only in outline).

He wears a tunic and a chlamys. The folds of the tunic are indicated by wide, oblique grooves over the arms. The chlamys covers most of the chest. It is fastened at the right shoulder with a brooch (details unclear). A small zigzag-shaped fold falls under the brooch.

PORTRAIT B: ARMLESS FEMALE BUST

The figure is shown frontally.

She wears a veil. The veil is heavy. It falls over both shoulders, crosses the chest in a curving fold, and back over the left shoulder.

She wears a tunic (details unclear).

PORTRAIT C: ARMLESS BUST OF PRIEST

The figure is shown frontally.

He wears low on the forehead a tall, cylindrical, flat-top headdress: a Palmyrene priestly hat (visible only in outline).

He wears a tunic and a chlamys. The folds of the tunic are indicated by wide, oblique grooves over the arms. The chlamys covers most of the chest. It is fastened at the right shoulder with a brooch (details unclear). A small zigzag-shaped fold falls under the brooch.

PORTRAIT D: ARMLESS BUST OF PRIEST IN FULCRUM

The outline of an armless figure is recognizable in a clipeus.

He wears a tall, cylindrical, flat-top headdress (visible only in outline): a Palmyrene priestly hat.

He wears a garment with short sleeves (details unclear).

A.D. 200–273

309. SARCOPHAGUS BOX WITH STANDING FIGURES

DATABASE NUMBER: InSitu135.
LOCATION: Palmyra.
CONTEXT: —
ACQUISITION HISTORY: —.
MEASUREMENTS: —
MATERIAL: Limestone.
PRESERVATION: The upper part of all sides of the sarcophagus are broken off. The left and the right corners are broken off. The object is heavily chipped and weathered. Portrait A: The head of the figure is broken off. Portrait B: The head of the figure is broken off. Portrait C: The head of the figure is broken off. Portrait D: The head of the figure is broken off. Portrait E: The head of the figure is broken off.
DATE: A.D. 200–273.
REFERENCES: Silver et al. 2019, 173 fig. 9.5; <https://www.loc.gov/item/mpc2005008585/PP/> (15.11.2022).

OBJECT DESCRIPTION

The sarcophagus box is rectangular in shape and is rendered as a kline. There are five standing figures between the kline legs. The kline legs are turned (details unclear).

PORTRAIT A: STANDING FIGURE

The figure is shown frontally. The arms are bent, the left arm held in front of the torso and the right arm at the waist, below it. The legs are parted.

They wear a garment that covers the body (other details unclear).

PORTRAIT B: STANDING FIGURE

The figure is shown frontally. The arms are bent, the left arm raised with the hand touching or near the right shoulder, and the right arm held in front of the waist. The legs are parted.

They wear a garment that covers the body (other details unclear).

PORTRAIT C: STANDING FIGURE

The figure is shown frontally. The legs are parted.

They wear a garment that covers the body (other details unclear).

PORTRAIT D: STANDING FIGURE

The figure is shown frontally. The right arm is bent and held in front of the waist. The legs are parted.

They wear a garment that covers the body (other details unclear).

PORTRAIT E: STANDING FIGURE

The figure is shown frontally. The legs are parted.

They wear a garment that covers the body (other details unclear).

310. SARCOPHAGUS BOX WITH STANDING FIGURES

DATABASE NUMBER: InSitu147.
LOCATION: Palmyra.
CONTEXT: —
ACQUISITION HISTORY: —.
MEASUREMENTS: —
MATERIAL: Limestone.
PRESERVATION: The lower left side and the lower edge of the relief are broken off. The surface is heavily weathered.
DATE: A.D. 200–273.
REFERENCES: Silver et al. 2019, 173 fig. 9.5; <https://www.loc.gov/item/mpc2005008585/PP/> (15.11.2022).

OBJECT DESCRIPTION

The sarcophagus box is rectangular in shape and is rendered as a kline. The kline has turned legs (the one on the right side is visible). Six standing figures can be seen at the front of the sarcophagus.

PORTRAIT A: STANDING FIGURE
The figure is shown frontally.
They wear a garment that covers the body (other details unclear).

PORTRAIT B: STANDING FIGURE
The figure is shown frontally. The legs are parted.
They wear a garment that covers the body (other details unclear).

PORTRAIT C: STANDING FIGURE
The figure is shown frontally. The legs are parted.
They wear a garment that covers the body (other details unclear).

PORTRAIT D: STANDING FIGURE
The figure is shown frontally. The legs are parted.
They wear a garment that covers the body (other details unclear).

PORTRAIT E: STANDING FIGURE
The figure is shown frontally. The legs are parted.
They wear a garment that covers the body (other details unclear).

PORTRAIT F: STANDING FIGURE
The figure is shown frontally. The legs are parted.
They wear a garment that covers the body (other details unclear).

311. SARCOPHAGUS BOX WITH STANDING FIGURES

DATABASE NUMBER: InSitu148.
LOCATION: Palmyra.
CONTEXT: —
ACQUISITION HISTORY: —.
MEASUREMENTS: —
MATERIAL: Limestone.
PRESERVATION: The left side and the central upper part of the sarcophagus are broken off.
DATE: A.D. 200–273.
REFERENCES: Silver et al. 2019, 173 fig. 9.5; <https://www.loc.gov/item/mpc2005008585/PP/> (15.11.2022).

OBJECT DESCRIPTION

The sarcophagus box is rectangular in shape. There are five standing figures between the kline legs. Five standing figures can be seen at the front of the sarcophagus.

PORTRAIT A: STANDING FIGURE
The figure is shown frontally. The legs are parted.
They wear a garment that covers the body (other details unclear).

PORTRAIT B: STANDING FIGURE
The figure is shown frontally. The legs are parted.
They wear a garment that covers the body (other details unclear).

PORTRAIT C: STANDING FIGURE
The figure is shown frontally. The legs are parted.
They wear a garment that covers the body (other details unclear).

PORTRAIT D: STANDING FIGURE
The figure is shown frontally. The legs are parted.
They wear a garment that covers the body (other details unclear).

PORTRAIT E: STANDING FIGURE
The figure is shown frontally. The legs are parted.
They wear a garment that covers the body (other details unclear).

312. SARCOPHAGUS BOX

DATABASE NUMBER: InSitu167.
LOCATION: Palmyra.
CONTEXT: —
ACQUISITION HISTORY: —.
MEASUREMENTS: —
MATERIAL: Limestone.
PRESERVATION: The surface is heavily weathered.
DATE: A.D. 200–273.
REFERENCES: Silver et al. 2019, 173 fig. 9.5; <https://www.loc.gov/item/mpc2005008585/PP/> (15.11.2022).

OBJECT DESCRIPTION

The object is rectangular. There is evidence of figural decoration on the surface, but it is not possible to determine either the type (standing figures or busts), or the number of figures.

FRAGMENTS FROM LIDS, LID RELIEFS, OR BANQUETING RELIEFS

A.D. 50–100

313. FRAGMENT OF A BANQUETING RELIEF

DATABASE NUMBER: MAH013.
LOCATION: Geneva, Musée d'Art et d'Histoire, inv. no. 013268.
CONTEXT: —
ACQUISITION HISTORY: Donated by Albertus Hotz in 1930.
MEASUREMENTS: Height: 53 cm. Width: 34 cm.
MATERIAL: Limestone, white/yellow.
PRESERVATION: The background is broken off. The figure is broken off below the waist. The tip of the nose, the chin, the right hand, and the edge of the himation are chipped.
TECHNICAL DESCRIPTION: —
DATE: A.D. 50–100 (Chamay – Maier 1989: A.D. 75–100).
REFERENCES: Deonna 1931, 7. 111. 115 cat. 21; Chamay – Maier 1989, 89 cat. 112 pl. 101, 3.

OBJECT DESCRIPTION
The object depicts a reclining male. He reclines on a cushion decorated with a wide decorated band between two beaded bands. The texture is indicated by curving grooves.

PORTRAIT
The head of the figure is shown frontally. The arms are bent in front of the torso.

He has short, voluminous hair arranged in crescent-shaped curls. The individual strands of hair are depicted by curving grooves. His face is square and fleshy. He has a furrow at the forehead. The eyebrows are curving, depicted by thin, incised lines. The eyes are large, round, with thick upper eyelids. The upper eyelids extend beyond the end of the lower ones. The irises and pupils are depicted by concentric, incised circles. The ears are small and protruding with helix, scapha, tragus, and lobe indicated. The nose is thin and straight. The mouth is small, with full lips. The chin is pointed. The neck is short and wide with two curving grooves.

He wears a tunic and a himation. The tunic has a wide, v-shaped neckline and long, tight-fitting sleeves. The folds of the tunic are indicated by wide, curving grooves over the chest and oblique ones over the arms. Over the tunic he wears a himation that is wrapped over the left shoulder and arm, falls along the left side of the torso, and is wrapped around the waist. The folds of the himation are indicated by deep, oblique grooves.

His left hand rests against the side of the cushion. With his right hand he holds a skyphos: it has a conical foot, a wide, conical lower body, a cylindrical upper body, and handles. The index finger is extended.

A.D. 100–150

314. FEMALE FROM BANQUET SCENE

DATABASE NUMBER: UNK066.
LOCATION: Unknown.
CONTEXT: —
ACQUISITION HISTORY: —
MEASUREMENTS: —
MATERIAL: Limestone.
PRESERVATION: The sides of the object are chipped. The surface is weathered. The face of the female figure is heavily fragmented. No facial features are discernible. The right elbow, both hands, and the clothing over the knees are chipped.
TECHNICAL DESCRIPTION: —
DATE: A.D. 100–150.
REFERENCES: Ingholt Archives, Portrait2016_051.

Cat. 313

OBJECT DESCRIPTION

The object depicts a female figure sitting on a chair. The back of the chair is square in shape with a rounded top. The seat of the chair is rendered by a ridge, visible to the left of her left knee.

PORTRAIT

The figure is shown frontally. Both arms are bent and held in front of the torso. She sits with her knees apart. The knees are rendered under the drapery. Her feet face forward. The thighs appear short in relation to the rest of the body, indicating foreshortening.

She wears a veil. It is heavy and falls over both shoulders, covers the arms, and falls down her sides to the height of the lower legs. The folds of the veil are indicated by oblique grooves. A twisted lock of hair falls over her right shoulder. The individual strands of hair are indicated by incised lines.

Cat. 314

She wears a tunic. It has a wide, possibly v-shaped neckline (details unclear). It ends at her feet. The folds of the tunic are rendered by oblique grooves over the torso and by vertical grooves over the legs. She possibly wears shoes (details unclear). Her right hand rests in front of her chest. All the fingers are slightly extended. With the left hand, she pulls a looped fold of the veil across her body. All the fingers are slightly extended.

315. FRAGMENT OF A MALE FIGURE

DATABASE NUMBER: NMD081.
LOCATION: Damascus, Damascus National Museum, inv. no. —
CONTEXT: Secondary context: Found (30.09.1954) in portico C3, near the thirteenth column.
ACQUISITION HISTORY: —
MEASUREMENTS: Height: 35 cm. Width: 18.5 cm. Depth: 12.5 cm.
MATERIAL: Limestone.
PRESERVATION: The head of the figure is broken off at the base of the neck. The lower part of the figure is broken off diagonally at the thighs. The right arm and the attribute are heavily weathered. The left hand and the attribute are chipped.
TECHNICAL DESCRIPTION: The back of the sculpture is partly carved.
DATE: A.D. 100–150.
REFERENCES: Collart 1961, 433, pl. 2; Dunant – Stucky 2000, 102 cat. 70 pl. 21.

OBJECT DESCRIPTION

The object depicts a standing male.

PORTRAIT

The figure is shown frontally. Both arms are bent; the left is held in front of the torso, and the right falls to the side. The legs are slightly parted.

A vertical incision over the middle of the collarbone indicates musculature or the sternocleidomastoid muscles.

He wears a ›Parthian-style‹ tunic, a chlamys, ›Parthian-style‹ trousers, and over-trousers. The tunic has a wide, scalloped neckline and long, tight-fitting sleeves. The lower border is decorated with a beaded band. He wears a plain band belt. The tunic ends at the top of the thighs. The folds of the tunic are rendered by curving grooves. Over the tunic he wears a chlamys. It falls in a curving fold over the chest, and one end covers the left shoulder and arm and falls down, next to the leg. The trouser legs have a wide band extending downwards. Each band is decorated with three rows of diamond-shaped leaves. The folds of the trousers are rendered by curving grooves. He also wears over-trousers. They fall in a curving fold starting from the outer top of the thighs and their upper border is decorated with a beaded band. Their folds are rendered by curving grooves.

316. FRAGMENT OF A BANQUETING RELIEF

DATABASE NUMBER: PM1085.
LOCATION: Palmyra Museum, inv. no. unknown.
CONTEXT: South-west necropolis. Found in 1914 (cf. CIS 4204–4205 with comm.).
ACQUISITION HISTORY: Formerly in the Palmyra Museum.
MEASUREMENTS: Height: 65 cm. Width: 52 cm.
MATERIAL: Limestone.
PRESERVATION: The relief ground is preserved on either side of the figure. The lower part is broken off horizontally through the waist. The left side of the head is broken off. The surface around the left hand, of the nose, of the lips, and of the lower torso is chipped.
TECHNICAL DESCRIPTION: —
DATE: A.D. 100–150.
REFERENCES: Ingholt Archives, PS 124; Ingholt 1928, 104. Inscription: Ingholt Archives, PS 124.

OBJECT DESCRIPTION

The object depicts a reclining male figure. He rests the left arm on a cushion. The cushion is decorated with a band with hollowed-out lozenges. Curving grooves indicate the texture of the fabric.

Cat. 316

INSCRIPTION

SCRIPT: Palmyrene Aramaic.
LOCATION ON RELIEF: Top right corner, on his left side.
TRANSCRIPTION: ṢLMʾ | ʿGʾ | BR | MTNW | ḤBL.
TRANSLATION: Image of ʿOggâ son of Mattanû, alas!

CIS no. 4205; PAT no. 0561, 1755.

COMMENT: The information of PAT for 1755 as in the Museum of Damascus must come from a misunderstanding of Ingholt 1928, 104 for PS 124 (with footnotes 6 and 7).

PORTRAIT: ʿOGGÂ

The figure is shown frontally. The right arm is bent and held along the lower body. The left arm is bent in front of the torso.

His hair is straight. His eyebrows are curving and the eyes are almond-shaped, with thick upper eyelids. The chin is round and the neck is short and wide. A v-shaped depression indicates the jugular notch.

He wears a tunic and a himation. The tunic has a wide, round neckline leaving part of the upper chest bare, and short, wide sleeves. The folds of the tunic are rendered by vertical and curving grooves. Over the tunic, he wears a himation. It is wrapped around his left shoulder and arm, leaving most of the chest free. It proceeds in a curving fold across the waist and falls back under his right hand. The folds of the himation are rendered by vertical and oblique grooves.

At the centre of the torso, a chipped area suggests that he was holding an object in his left hand.

317. FRAGMENT OF A MALE FIGURE

DATABASE NUMBER: UNK043.
LOCATION: Unknown location.
CONTEXT: —
ACQUISITION HISTORY: —
MEASUREMENTS: —
MATERIAL: Limestone.
PRESERVATION: The head and neck are broken off. The right upper arm is chipped and the lower left and right arms are partly broken off. The cup is heavily damaged. The surface is weathered.
TECHNICAL DESCRIPTION: —
DATE: A.D. 100–150.
REFERENCES: Ingholt Archives, IA_NCG_Portrait2016_060.

OBJECT DESCRIPTION

The object depicts a standing male figure.

PORTRAIT

The figure is shown frontally. The arms are bent and held in front of the waist.

He wears a tunic. It has a wide, round neckline and long, tight-fitting sleeves. The folds of the tunic are rendered by

Cat. 317

Cat. 318

curving grooves over the torso, oblique grooves over the arms, and vertical grooves over the legs. He wears a plain band belt, knotted at the centre, that creates a small overfold.

With both hands, he holds a cup. A mass at the top of the cup is either a rim decorated with a beaded band or sculptural indication of the cup's contents. The rim is decorated by a beaded band. The body is ovoid, and the foot is stemmed.

318. FEMALE FIGURE

DATABASE NUMBER: AMI092.
LOCATION: Istanbul, İstanbul Arkeoloji Müzesi, inv. no. 3733/O.M.188.
CONTEXT: —
ACQUISITION HISTORY: —
MEASUREMENTS: Height: 50 cm.
MATERIAL: Limestone.

PRESERVATION: The surface at the right elbow, at the right knee, and the tip of the right foot is chipped. The surface is weathered.
TECHNICAL DESCRIPTION: The facial details are roughly carved.
DATE: A.D. 100–150.

REFERENCES: Ingholt Archives, PS 722; Krag 2018, 28 n. 9; 33 n. 75; 45 n. 183; 47 n. 208; 49 n. 229; 64. 93 n. 242. 244. 245; 238 cat. 272.

OBJECT DESCRIPTION
The object depicts a seated female.

PORTRAIT
The figure is shown frontally. The head is turned slightly to her right. The arms appear short in relation to the body. The right arm is bent and raised to the neck. The left arm is bent and held to the torso. She sits with the legs apart and the knees are rendered under the drapery.

She wears a veil. It is wrapped around her left shoulder and arm, leaving the hand free. The veil continues in a wide fold from under her arm and reaches the ground. On her right side, the veil falls alongside her leg. A wavy lock of hair falls down on each shoulder. Her face is oval. The forehead is high. Only the outline of the eyes is rendered. The ears are partly carved and grooves along the helix may indicate the presence of hoop earrings. The nose appears large. The mouth is small and the chin is pointed. The neck is wide. She wears a necklace composed of small, round beads at the base of the neck.

She wears a tunic and a himation. The tunic has a wide, round neckline and sleeves reaching her elbows. The folds of the tunic are rendered by curving and oblique grooves. The himation crosses the chest diagonally from the left shoulder to the right side and covers the left breast. It is fastened at the left shoulder with a triangular brooch (Colledge classification: c) (other details unclear). The himation ends at the ankles. The folds of the himation are rendered by curving grooves, and oblique grooves between the legs. She wears round-toe shoes with a square incision at the instep.

Her right hand is raised to the neck, lightly pulling the edge of the veil. The index finger is extended. She wears a bracelet on her right wrist. It is composed of twisted wire. The outline of a cup, possibly a skyphos, is visible at her left hand.

319. FRAGMENT OF A FEMALE FIGURE

DATABASE NUMBER: PM665.
LOCATION: Palmyra, Palmyra Museum, inv. no. CD 41.
CONTEXT: Secondary context: Found in well near the Transversal Colonnade.
ACQUISITION HISTORY: —
MEASUREMENTS: Height: 23 cm. Width: 44 cm. Depth: 13 cm.
MATERIAL: Limestone, white.
PRESERVATION: Broken on all sides. Broken diagonally from the right shoulder to the left side, and from the upper right arm to the lower abdomen. The surface at the left side of the torso is weathered.
TECHNICAL DESCRIPTION: —
DATE: A.D. 100–150.
REFERENCES: Michalowski 1966, 66 cat. 16 fig. 74; Krag 2018, 58 n. 304; 103 n. 74; 382 cat. 811.

OBJECT DESCRIPTION
The fragment depicts a female.

PORTRAIT
The figure is shown in three-quarter view. The left arm is bent and raised to the neck.

She wears three necklaces: One composed of a string with round beads, worn at the base of the neck. The necklace below is composed of round and rectangular bezels joined by elements composed of four beads. The necklace below is a loop-in-loop chain with a round central pendant, partly hidden by the himation.

She wears a tunic and a himation. The tunic has a scalloped neckline. The folds of the tunic are rendered by curving grooves.

320. FRAGMENT OF A MALE FIGURE

DATABASE NUMBER: PM845.
LOCATION: Palmyra, Palmyra Museum, inv. no. CD 49.
CONTEXT: Secondary context: Found (23.04.1961) in the late wall near the fallen column.
ACQUISITION HISTORY: —
MEASUREMENTS: Height: 24 cm. Width: 40 cm. Depth: 25 cm.
MATERIAL: Limestone, white.
PRESERVATION: The relief is broken off on all sides. Only part of the torso and right the arm survive.
TECHNICAL DESCRIPTION: —
DATE: A.D. 100–150.
REFERENCES: Michalowski 1963, 156 cat. 50 fig. 207.

OBJECT DESCRIPTION
The object depicts the torso and right arm of a male figure.

PORTRAIT
The figure is shown frontally. The right arm is bent in front of the waist.

He wears a tunic. The tunic has long, tight-fitting sleeves. The folds of the tunic are rendered by curving grooves.

With his right hand he holds a small bowl (other details unclear). The bowl was identified as probably a kantharos by Michalowski (1963).

321. FRAGMENT OF A MALE FIGURE

DATABASE NUMBER: PM664.
LOCATION: Palmyra, Palmyra Museum, inv. no. CD 36.
CONTEXT: Secondary context: Found in the foundations of the south building in front of the Temple of the Standards (Temple des Enseignes), Camp of Diocletian.
ACQUISITION HISTORY: —
MEASUREMENTS: Height: 32 cm. Width: 21 cm. Depth: 19 cm.
MATERIAL: Limestone, grey.
PRESERVATION: The head is broken off at the base of the neck. The right arm of the figure is broken off below the

shoulder. The left side and the lower part of the figure are broken off.
TECHNICAL DESCRIPTION: —
DATE: A.D. 100–150.
REFERENCES: Michalowski 1966, 59 cat. 9 fig. 66.

OBJECT DESCRIPTION
The object depicts a male figure.

PORTRAIT
The figure is shown frontally. His right arm was extended to the right, the left arm was bent and held in front of the waist.

He wears a tunic and, according to Michalowski (1984), a chlamys. The tunic has a wide, v-shaped neckline. The folds of the tunic are rendered by wide curving grooves. Over the tunic Michalowski recognizes a chlamys whose folds fall vertically over the right shoulder. In front of the waist the outline of a wide bowl held by the left hand can be recognized. Michalowski reports that it is in the shape of a kantharos.

322. FRAGMENT OF A MALE FIGURE

DATABASE NUMBER: PM674.
LOCATION: Palmyra, Palmyra Museum, inv. no. CD 21.
CONTEXT: Secondary context: Found (16.05.1959) in the rubble of the Via Pretoria, ten metres away from the Tetrapylon.
ACQUISITION HISTORY: —
MEASUREMENTS: Height: 34 cm. Width: 32 cm.
MATERIAL: Limestone, grey.
PRESERVATION: Only part of the left side of the torso and the left arm and hand of the figure are preserved. The surface is weathered.
TECHNICAL DESCRIPTION: —
DATE: A.D. 100–150.
REFERENCES: Michalowski 1960, 96 cat. 15 fig. 104.

OBJECT DESCRIPTION
The object depicts a male figure. He reclines on a round cushion, part of which is visible to his left.

PORTRAIT
The figure is shown frontally. His right arm was extended to the right, the left arm was bent and held in front of the waist.

He wears a tunic and a himation. The tunic has a wide, v-shaped neckline. The folds of the tunic are rendered by wide curving grooves. Over the tunic he wears a himation that falls over the left shoulder, covering the left arm. The folds of the himation are rendered by oblique grooves. In front of the waist the outline of a wide bowl held by the left hand can be recognized. Michalowski reports that it is in the shape of a kantharos.

A.D. 100–200

323. FRAGMENT OF A STANDING FIGURE

DATABASE NUMBER: PM031.
LOCATION: Palmyra, Palmyra Museum, inv. no. CD 113.
CONTEXT: Secondary: Found (03.05.1961) in front of the Great Gate.
ACQUISITION HISTORY: —
MEASUREMENTS: Height: 30 cm. Width: 17 cm. Depth: 12 cm.
MATERIAL: Limestone, yellow.
PRESERVATION: The background is broken off except for the area around the head and shoulders. The lower part of the figure is broken off diagonally at the upper thighs. The front of the head is broken off. The right arm is broken off below the shoulder.
TECHNICAL DESCRIPTION: —
DATE: A.D. 100–200.

Cat. 323

REFERENCES: Michalowski 1963, 156 f. cat. 51 fig. 208; Pierson 1984, 96 f. fig. 5.

OBJECT DESCRIPTION
The object depicts a standing child.

PORTRAIT
The figure is shown frontally. The right arm falls to the side. The left arm is bent and held in front of the torso.

The child has short hair. The child wears a necklace composed of a string of round beads around the neck, and below that a thick hoop necklace with a medallion suspended by the centre.

The child wears a tunic. The tunic has a wide, round neckline decorated with a series of inverted triangles, and short, wide sleeves. Two sets of strips extend downwards from under the triangles at either side of the neckline, ending in a round decoration. The tunic has an overfold created by a plain band belt worn around the waist. The ends of the belt are looped around it, and fall down to the side. The folds of the tunic are rendered by curving grooves on the body, and oblique ones at the sleeves.

With the left hand, the child holds a bunch of grapes from the stem. The grapes are rendered as small round elements.

A.D. 120–140
324. FRAGMENT OF A BANQUETING RELIEF

DATABASE NUMBER: PM368.
LOCATION: Palmyra, Palmyra Museum, inv. no. unknown.
CONTEXT: Secondary context: Found (16.10.1955) in portico C1 during excavations at Baalshamin temple. Excavation no. 129.
ACQUISITION HISTORY: —
MEASUREMENTS: Height: 24.5 cm. Width: 27 cm. Depth: 15 cm.
MATERIAL: Limestone.
PRESERVATION: The object is broken off on all sides. Only part of the torso and of the left arm are preserved.
TECHNICAL DESCRIPTION: Partly carved.
DATE: A.D. 120–140 (Dunant – Stucky 2000: A.D. 100–150).
REFERENCES: Dunant – Stucky 2000, 113 cat. 122 pl. 29.

OBJECT DESCRIPTION
The object was originally rectangular in shape and depicts a reclining figure. The figure rests on a cushion. Curving grooves indicate the texture of the fabric.

PORTRAIT
The figure is shown in frontal view. His left arm is bent and rests on the cushion.

He wears a tunic and a himation. The tunic has a wide, round neckline. The folds of the tunic are rendered by curving grooves on the chest. Over the tunic, he wears a himation: it falls over his left shoulder and is wrapped around his left arm. It continues under the left arm. The folds of the himation are indicated with vertical grooves.

His left hand holds a skyphos. The skyphos has a conical foot and a plain body. His left index finger and the thumb are extended.

A.D. 130–150
325. FIGURE OF PRIEST

DATABASE NUMBER: BeirutUNK010.
LOCATION: According to Ingholt (1928) it was in the collection of the American University Museum, Beirut.
CONTEXT: —
ACQUISITION HISTORY: —
MEASUREMENTS: —
MATERIAL: Limestone, white/yellow.
PRESERVATION: The lower part of the figure is broken off from the waist down. The right arm is broken off. The surface is chipped, especially in the areas of the headdress, right ear, nose, left index finger, chest, and clothing.

Cat. 325

TECHNICAL DESCRIPTION: —
DATE: A.D. 130–150.
REFERENCES: Ingholt Archives, PS 152; Ingholt 1928, 107; Colledge 1976, 248.

OBJECT DESCRIPTION
The object depicts the upper part of a priest.

PORTRAIT
The figure is shown frontally. The left arm is bent and held at the torso. The left arm appears small in relation to the body.

He wears a tall, plain, cylindrical, flat-top headdress divided into three sections by two vertical grooves: a Palmyrene priestly hat. His face is square. The eyebrows are curving, starting from the root of the nose. The eyes are large, round, and slanting with thick eyelids. The irises and the pupils are indicated by concentric, incised circles. The ears are protruding. The nose is straight. The mouth is wide with thin lips. The chin is square. The neck is wide and long. The chest musculature is indicated by an incised line at the middle of the collarbone.

He wears a tunic and a himation. The tunic has a wide, v-shaped neckline that leaves a part of the upper torso bare. The folds of the tunic are indicated by wide, curving grooves. Over the tunic, he wears a himation that falls over the left shoulder and covers the left arm and side. The himation to the left of the neck is rendered with a thick fold. The folds of the himation are rendered by oblique grooves.

In his left hand, he holds a skyphos: it has a small, cylindrical foot, a hemispherical body with a flat rim, and handles. The lower part of the body is decorated with a tongue pattern. The thumb, index, and the little finger are extended.

326. MALE FIGURE

DATABASE NUMBER: NMD082.
LOCATION: Damascus, National Museum of Damascus, inv. no. I.N. 8.
CONTEXT: —
ACQUISITION HISTORY: —
MEASUREMENTS: Height: 50 cm. Width: 37 cm.
MATERIAL: Limestone, grey.
PRESERVATION: The nose is chipped.
TECHNICAL DESCRIPTION: —
DATE: A.D. 130–150.
REFERENCES: Ingholt Archives, PS 122; Ingholt 1928, 104; el-Chehadeh 1972, 84 n. 53. Inscription: Ingholt 1928, 104.

OBJECT DESCRIPTION
The object depicts a reclining male figure.

Cat. 326

INSCRIPTION
SCRIPT: Palmyrene Aramaic.
LOCATION ON RELIEF: On the body of the skyphos.
TRANSCRIPTION: —
TRANSLATION: —

CIS no. —; PAT no. —.

COMMENT: The inscription is fake.

PORTRAIT
The figure is shown frontally. The right arm is bent and held along his side. The left is bent and held to the torso.

His hair is arranged in two rows of flame-shaped curls around the head. The individual strands of hair are indicated by incised lines. His face is long. There are two furrows along his forehead. The eyebrows are curving, rendered by incised lines starting from the root of the nose. The eyes are close-set and almond-shaped, with thick eyelids. The upper eyelids extend beyond the end of the lower ones. The irises and pupils are indicated by concentric, incised circles. The ears are protruding. The nose is straight with carved nostrils. The mouth is small, with thin lips. The chin is wide and the neck is long with one horizontal groove.

He wears a tunic and a himation. The tunic has a wide, v-shaped neckline and short, wide sleeves. The folds of the tunic are rendered by curving and diagonal grooves. Over the tunic, he wears a himation. It is wrapped around the left shoulder and arm, leaving most of the torso and the hand free. The folds of the himation are indicated by diagonal grooves. He holds a fold of the himation with his right hand.

With his left hand, he holds a skyphos. It has a conical foot and body. The lower body has a tongue pattern and the upper body is decorated with incised lines. The lip is straight with opposing vertical, looped handles. The left thumb and the index finger are extended. The nails are rendered by fine, incised lines.

327. MALE FIGURE

DATABASE NUMBER: PUAM006.
LOCATION: Princeton, Princeton University Art Museum, inv. no. Y1962-92.
CONTEXT: —
ACQUISITION HISTORY: Gift of Elias S. David.
MEASUREMENTS: Height: 53.3 cm. Width: 37.3 cm. Depth: 18.5 cm.
MATERIAL: Limestone, white/yellow.
PRESERVATION: The right side is broken off at the upper right arm to the right lower torso. The surface is weathered. The nose is slightly chipped.
TECHNICAL DESCRIPTION: Tool marks are visible across the whole finished surface.
DATE: A.D. 130–150.
REFERENCES: Ingholt Archives, PS 123; Ingholt 1928, 104; Parlasca 1998, 314 pl. 126, 3; Gawlikowski 2001a, 350. 352 cat. 150; <https://artmuseum.princeton.edu/collections/objects/28889> (06.05.2022).

OBJECT DESCRIPTION
The object depicts a reclining male figure. He rests the left arm against a cushion. The cushion is decorated with a band with a floral motif and set between beaded bands. Curving grooves indicate the texture of the fabric.

PORTRAIT
The figure is shown frontally. The left arm is bent and held in front of the torso.

The hair is arranged in two rows of crescent-shaped curls around the head. The individual locks of hair are rendered by incised lines. His face is oval. There are two furrows along his forehead. The eyes are almond-shaped, with thick upper eyelids. The irises are rendered by incised circles and the pupils by punch holes. The nose is straight with incised nostrils. The ears are large and protruding with the helix, concha, scapha,

Cat. 327

and lobe depicted. The mouth is small, with thin lips. The chin is oval and the neck is long.

He wears a tunic and a himation. The tunic has a wide, v-shaped neckline, which leaves a part of the upper chest bare. The folds of the tunic are rendered by curving and oblique grooves. Over the tunic, he wears a himation. It is wrapped around his left shoulder and arm, leaving most of the chest and the hand free. The folds of the himation are rendered by curving and oblique grooves.

With the left hand, he holds a skyphos. It has a conical foot and body, a straight lip, and small, looped handles. The lower part of the body is decorated with a tongue pattern.

328. BANQUETING RELIEF

DATABASE NUMBER: PM321.
LOCATION: Palmyra, Palmyra Museum, inv. no. unknown.
CONTEXT: —
ACQUISITION HISTORY: —
MEASUREMENTS: Height: 53 cm. Width: 21 cm.
MATERIAL: Limestone.

PRESERVATION: The left side of the object is chipped. The lower left corner is broken off. The protruding plinth is chipped.
TECHNICAL DESCRIPTION: —
DATE: A.D. 130–150.
REFERENCES: Ingholt Archives, PS 646; Tanabe 1986, 34 pl. 274; Krag 2018, 28 n. 9; 33 n. 75; 47 n. 208; 238 cat. 271.

OBJECT DESCRIPTION

The object is rectangular in shape and depicts a female seated in a chair. The chair has a square plain back, which supports the figure up to the height of her head. The seat and legs are undecorated.

PORTRAIT

The figure is shown frontally, with her head turned slightly to the left. The head appears large. The right arm is bent and held to the chest. The left is bent and rests on the left thigh. She sits with her legs apart with the knees visible under the drapery. Both feet rest on a protruding plinth.

She wears three headdresses: a headband, a turban, and a veil. The headband is placed low on the forehead and is divided into horizontal rectangular panels, decorated with a crisscross pattern. The turban is coiled. It is divided into two layers and the ends are looped into each other creating a knot in the middle. Curving grooves indicate the coiling of the fabric. The veil is heavy. It falls over both her shoulders, and is wrapped around her arms. It continues along both sides of the body until the protruding plinth. The headdresses cover part of the hair: several strands of hair above the ears are pushed back over the headband and disappear under the veil. Two thick, wavy locks of hair fall down her neck and chest. The individual strands of hair are indicated by incised lines. Her face is square. The eyebrows are curving. The eyes are large and almond-shaped, with thick eyelids. The upper eyelids extend beyond the end of the lower ones. The irises and pupils are indicated by concentric, incised circles. The ears are rendered with the helix, tragus, concha, scapha, and lobe. She wears earrings shaped like a miniature bunch of grapes (Colledge classification: E). The nose is straight with a wide base. The alae are incised and the nostrils are carved. The mouth is small, with a full lower lip. The chin is pointed. The neck is short and wide.

She wears a tunic and a himation. The tunic has a wide, round neckline decorated with a plain band. The folds of the tunic are rendered by curving grooves on the chest. The himation crosses the chest diagonally from the left shoulder to the right side, and covers the left breast. It is fastened at the shoulder with a trapezoidal brooch with a rosette finial (Colledge classification: b). The himation covers the lower body and legs and ends at the ankles. The folds of the himation are rendered by oblique grooves on the body and thighs, and

Cat. 328

curving grooves on the lower legs. A large fold runs across the knees, and vertical grooves are rendered between the legs. She wears round closed-toe shoes.

She holds two thin rods that end in oval elements in her right hand: reduced versions of spindle and distaff. The right thumb, index, and the middle finger are extended. She rests her left hand on the left thigh and holds a fold of the veil. The thumb and the index finger are extended.

329. FRAGMENT OF A BANQUETING RELIEF

DATABASE NUMBER: NCG128.
LOCATION: Copenhagen, Ny Carlsberg Glyptotek, inv. no. IN 1083.
CONTEXT: —
ACQUISITION HISTORY: Løytved in Syria.
MEASUREMENTS: Height: 31.5 cm. Width: 20.5 cm. Depth: 10.8 cm.
MATERIAL: Limestone, white/yellow.
PRESERVATION: The object is broken off on all four sides, only a small part of the background is preserved to the right of the figure's head. Portrait: The lower part is broken off diagonally from the right upper arm to the left side of the waist. The nose, left shoulder, and left hand are chipped.
TECHNICAL DESCRIPTION: —
DATE: A.D. 130–150 (Hvidberg-Hansen – Ploug 1993: A.D. 150–250).
REFERENCES: Clermont-Ganneau 1886, 15 fig. F; Clermont-Ganneau 1888, 116 fig. 1.F; Simonsen 1889, 44 cat. F.2; Ingholt 1928, 153 PS 520; Champdor 1953, 30; Michałowski 1960, 180 n. 2; Michałowski 1963, 140 n. 31; Hvidberg-Hansen – Ploug 1993, 108 cat. 64; Ploug 1995, 164 f. cat. 64; Raja 2019a, 252 f. cat. 77.

OBJECT DESCRIPTION
The object depicts a boy.

PORTRAIT
The figure is shown in frontal view, with the head turned slightly to the left. The left arm appears short in relation to the body. The left arm is bent and held in front of the chest.

His hair is arranged in three rows of crescent-shaped locks, the directions of the locks are alternating by each row. The individual strands of hair are indicated by incised lines. His face is round. The eyebrows are slightly curving, depicted as incised lines starting at the root of the nose. The eyes are almond-shaped, with thick eyelids. The upper eyelids extend beyond the end of the lower ones. The ears are slightly protruding, and the helix, tragus, scapha, and earlobe are rendered. The nose is short. The mouth is small, with full lips. The chin is oval and fleshy. The neck is short. He wears a necklace composed of a twisted metal band and has an oval pendant with an incised border suspended by a narrow sleeve at the centre.

He wears a tunic. The neckline of the tunic is wide and v-shaped. It has short sleeves, and an overfold at the waist. The folds of the tunic are rendered with vertical and curving grooves.

In his left hand, he holds a bird. The bird is rendered facing to the right. The beak and feathers are indicated with incised lines: on the body of the bird, there is a diamond-shaped pattern, and the tail has long feathers. He wears a bracelet on his left wrist: it has a thick hoop with a ridge running along the middle. His index finger is extended, and the nails are indicated by incised lines.

330. FRAGMENT OF A BANQUETING RELIEF

DATABASE NUMBER: MHCA001.
LOCATION: Massachusetts, Mount Holyoke College Art Museum, inv. no. 1932.2.CO II.
CONTEXT: —
ACQUISITION HISTORY: Purchased with funds from the Nancy Everett Dwight Fund in 1932.
MEASUREMENTS: Height: 60.96 cm. Width: 40.64 cm. Depth: 22.86 cm.
MATERIAL: Limestone, grey.
PRESERVATION: The entire right side and the lower part of the relief are broken off. The left elbow is chipped. The right upper arm and the legs are broken off.
TECHNICAL DESCRIPTION: There are traces of red pigment in the inscription. There are tooth chisel marks on the relief background.
DATE: A.D. 130–150 (Parlasca 1998: A.D. 100–150).

Cat. 329, Pl. 61

SARCOPHAGI WITH NO KNOWN PROVENANCE OR FROM SECONDARY CONTEXTS 659

Cat. 330

REFERENCES: Ingholt Archives, PS 588; Parlasca 1998, 314 pl. 126, 2; Parlasca 2000, 137 pl. 30, b; <https://museums.fivecolleges.edu/detail.php?museum=all&t=objects&type=all&f=&s=palmyra&record=6> (06.05.2022).

OBJECT DESCRIPTION
The object is rectangular in shape and depicts a male. He rests on a cushion. The cushion is folded around itself, indicated by an oval groove and curving grooves on the cushion.

INSCRIPTION
SCRIPT: —
LOCATION ON RELIEF: Right of figure, at the height of face.
TRANSCRIPTION: —
TRANSLATION: —

CIS no: —; PAT no: —.

COMMENT: The inscription is fake.

PORTRAIT
The reclining figure is shown frontally. The arms appear short in relation to the body. The right upper arm is held away from the body; the left arm is bent and rests on the cushion.

His hair is arranged in rows of snail-shell curls around his head. His face is oval, and there is a single furrow along his forehead. The eyebrows are curving, rendered by incised grooves. The eyes are large and almond-shaped, with thick eyelids. The upper eyelids extend beyond the end of the lower ones. The irises and pupils are indicated by concentric, incised circles. The right eye is larger than the left. The ears are large and protruding, with the helix, tragus, concha, scapha, and earlobe depicted. The nose is straight and has a wide, round base with incised alae. The mouth is straight with full lips. The chin is oval and protruding. The neck is long.

He wears a tunic and a himation. The tunic has a wide, v-shaped neckline, and short, loose sleeves. The folds of the tunic are rendered by curving grooves on the chest and oblique grooves on the right sleeve. The himation is folded around his left shoulder and arm, and wrapped around the wrist. From the wrist falls a fold with vertical grooves. A fold of the himation falls along his left side of the body, possibly indicating the himation being wrapped around his waist. The himation has oblique folds on the upper left arm, and vertical folds on the lower left arm.

In his left hand, he holds a skyphos. The skyphos has a conical foot, with the base rendered by a horizontal line. The body is decorated with a tongue pattern. The rim is plain. His index and little finger are extended.

331. FRAGMENT OF A BANQUETING RELIEF

DATABASE NUMBER: DamascusUNK017.
LOCATION: Damascus, unknown location.
CONTEXT: —
ACQUISITION HISTORY: It was in Damascus before 1928.
MEASUREMENTS: —
MATERIAL: Limestone.
PRESERVATION: The lower part of the figure and the right lower arm are broken off. The nose of the figure is chipped. The object is weathered.
TECHNICAL DESCRIPTION: —
DATE: A.D. 130–150.
REFERENCES: Ingholt Archives, PS 121; Ingholt 1928, 104; Colledge 1976, 247.

OBJECT DESCRIPTION
The object depicts a male figure. The figure rests on a cushion. Curving grooves indicate the texture of the fabric.

INSCRIPTION
SCRIPT: Palmyrene Aramaic.
LOCATION: —
TRANSCRIPTION: —

Cat. 331

TRANSLATION: —

CIS no. —; PAT no. —.

COMMENT: The inscription is fake.

PORTRAIT
The figure is shown in frontal view, and the head is turned slightly to the left. The left arm is bent in front of the torso, and rests on the cushion.

His hair is arranged in a single row of s-shaped curls around the head. The individual strands of hair are indicated with incised lines. His face is oval. The eyebrows are curving and depicted as thin ridges starting at the root of the nose. The eyes are large and almond-shaped, with thick eyelids. The irises and pupils are rendered by concentric, incised circles. The ears are large and elongated, set close to the head. The helix, tragus, scapha, and earlobe are depicted. The nose is straight and narrow. The alae are incised and the nostrils are carved. The mouth is small, with a full upper lip. The chin is oval. The neck is long.

He wears a tunic and a himation. The tunic has a wide, v-shaped neckline, revealing the upper part of the chest. Curving grooves on the chest indicate the folds of the tunic. The himation is wrapped around his left shoulder and arm, and oblique grooves indicate the folds of the fabric.

The left hand is in front of the torso, and he holds a cup, possibly a skyphos. It has a conical foot and a concave body, without decoration. The rim is wide and is protruding from the body of the cup. His index finger is extended.

A.D. 150–170

332. FRAGMENT OF A BANQUETING RELIEF

DATABASE NUMBER: AMI091.
LOCATION: Istanbul, İstanbul Arkeoloji Müzesi, inv. no. 3726/O.M.178.
CONTEXT: —
ACQUISITION HISTORY: —
MEASUREMENTS: Height: 68 cm.
MATERIAL: Limestone.
PRESERVATION: The relief is broken on the upper, left, and lower side. Portrait A: The surface is weathered. Portrait B: Broken vertically at the shins. Only the lower part of the legs and feet are preserved.
TECHNICAL DESCRIPTION: There are traces of red pigment in the inscription. There are chisel marks on the surface.
DATE: A.D. 150–170.
REFERENCES: Ingholt Archives, PS 723; Krag 2018, 28 n. 9; 33 n. 75. 77; 44 n. 174. 175; 45 n. 193; 46 n. 194. 195; 47 n. 208; 239 cat. 275. Inscription: Krag 2018, 239 cat. 275.

OBJECT DESCRIPTION
The object is rectangular in shape and depicts a seated female and a reclining male. The figures are resting on a mattress. It is decorated with a wide band with a row of squares set between beaded bands. Vertical and curving grooves indicate the texture of the fabric.

INSCRIPTION
SCRIPT: —
LOCATION ON RELIEF: To the left of the head.
TRANSCRIPTION: —
TRANSLATION: —

CIS no. —; PAT no. —.

COMMENT: The inscription is fake.

PORTRAIT A: SEATED FEMALE
The figure is shown frontally. The head is turned slightly to her left. The arms appear short in relation to the body. The head appears large in relation to the body. The right arm is bent and rests on her right thigh. The left arm is bent and held to the torso. The legs are bent with the knees visible under the drapery. Her left foot is obscured by the reclining figure to her left. The left edge of the stool is visible at her left side.

She wears three headdresses: a headband, a turban, and a veil. The band is placed low on her forehead and is divided into a rectangular panel in the middle and two squares on either side, separated by vertical, beaded lines. The panel in the middle is decorated with a crisscross pattern while the panels on either side are decorated with X-shaped incisions. The turban is coiled. It is divided into two layers and the ends are looped into each other creating a knot in the middle. Curving grooves indicate the coiling of the fabric. The veil is heavy. It falls over her shoulders and is wrapped around her arms, leaving only the hands free. The headdress covers part of the hair: several strands of hair above the ears are pushed back over the headband and the edge of the turban, and disappear under the veil. A wavy lock of hair falls down on each shoulder. Her face is oval. The eyebrows are slanting, rendered as thin ridges. The eyes are large and almond-shaped, with thick upper eyelids. The eyeballs are blank. The nose is straight and wide at the tip. Only the ears are visible under the headdress and she wears earrings shaped like a miniature bunch of grapes (Colledge classification: E). The mouth is small, with a full lower lip. The chin is oval. The neck is wide. She wears a necklace composed of round beads and a central, round pendant with a central, round depression. Three strands, possibly chains, with a round bead are attached to the pendant. The necklace is worn at the base of the neck.

She wears a tunic and a himation. The tunic has a wide, round neckline. The tunic has a slightly curving band running from the right collarbone and across the right breast extending downwards, rendered by incised lines. The tunic covers her legs. The folds of the tunic are rendered by curving grooves and wide, vertical grooves between the legs. The himation crosses the chest diagonally from the left shoulder to the right side and covers the left breast. It is fastened at the left shoulder with a trapezoidal brooch with a feline finial (Colledge classification: a). The himation ends above the knees. The folds of the himation are rendered by curving and oblique grooves.

The right hand lightly holds a fold of the veil. A fold of the veil falls from under her hand along the right leg. With the left hand, she holds a conical object incised with fine wavy lines, with a bowl-shaped tip, and a thick, short staff topped by a polygonal mass with a pattern of crisscrossing, incised lines, and a small cylinder. These are reduced versions of a spindle and a distaff.

PORTRAIT B: RECLINING MALE
The feet are resting on the mattress.

He wears a garment and shoes. The garment is heavy and has a fold falling in a curving line across the ankles. The folds of the garment are rendered by curving grooves. The figure wears sandals. The soles of the sandals are visible on his right foot. The sandals have a lace running across the phalanges and another lace running along the instep. On the left foot, two laces, possibly coming from a knob, are rendered on the middle of the foot. The nails are rendered by fine, incised lines.

Cat. 332

333. FRAGMENT OF A BANQUETING RELIEF

DATABASE NUMBER: NCG112.
LOCATION: Copenhagen, Ny Carlsberg Glyptotek, inv. no. IN 1149.
CONTEXT: —
ACQUISITION HISTORY: Puttmann in Syria.
MEASUREMENTS: Height: 79 cm. Width: 61 cm. Depth: 29 cm. Portrait A: Height of figure: 79 cm. Width of figure: 37 cm. Depth of figure: 24.5 cm. Height of head: 19 cm. Width of head: 15 cm. Depth of head: 18.5.
MATERIAL: Limestone, white/yellow.
PRESERVATION: All sides are broken off. Portrait A: The head has been broken off but was later reattached. The right eyebrow, nose, left cheek, neck, and the clothing at the upper left side of the figure are chipped. Portrait B: Only the right lower arm, right thigh, knee, and part of the right lower leg are preserved.
TECHNICAL DESCRIPTION: Portrait A: The bust is roughly cut on the back. There are tooth chisel and flat chisel marks on the back, and flat chisel marks on the neck.
DATE: A.D. 150–170.
REFERENCES: Ingholt Archives, PS 178; Ingholt 1928, 110; Hvidberg-Hansen – Ploug 1993, 107 cat. 63; Ploug 1995, 162 f. cat. 63; Raja 2019a, 250 f. cat. 76.

OBJECT DESCRIPTION
The object depicts a male figure standing behind a reclining male figure.

PORTRAIT A: STANDING MALE
The figure is shown in three-quarter view, turned to the right. The arms are bent in front of the torso. The lower part of the body is obscured by the reclining figure.

The hair is arranged in three rows of crescent-shaped curls, the direction of which alternates each row. The individual strands of hair are rendered by thin, incised lines. His face is square. The eyebrows are rendered by thin, curving, incised lines that start from the root of the nose. The eyes are large, almond-shaped, and slanting with thick upper eyelids. The ends of the upper eyelids extend beyond that of the lower ones. The irises are indicated by incised circles, the pupils by punch holes. The ears are large and close to the head, with the helix, scapha, and concha depicted. The nose is straight with a wide base. The alae are indicated by incised lines. The mouth is wide, with a full lower lip. The chin is pointed. The neck is short and slender.

He wears a tunic and a himation. The tunic has a wide, v-shaped neckline. The folds of the tunic are indicated by wide, curving grooves. The himation covers most of the body: it is wrapped around the right shoulder and arm, leaving the hand free (>arm-sling< type). A fold of the himation crosses the chest diagonally and falls over the left shoulder, and over the side of the himation that covers the left shoulder and arm. The folds of the himation are indicated by oblique grooves.

With his right hand, he holds the diagonal fold of the himation. The thumb and the index finger are extended. With the left hand, he holds a branch with six elliptical leaves, arranged in two rows of three leaves, in whorled arrangement. The midribs of the leaves are incised. Two round objects, probably berries, project from between the leaves of the upper row. The thumb, index, and the middle finger are extended. The nails are indicated by fine, incised lines.

PORTRAIT B: RECLINING MALE
The right arm and leg are shown in profile. The right leg is bent and raised; the right arm rests against the right leg.

He wears a tunic with long, tight-fitting sleeves and decorated cuffs. The cuff has a wide band with rosettes inside circles framed by two beaded bands. Wide folds over the leg indicate that he probably wore a himation across the lower body and legs.

With his right hand, he holds a branch with long, elliptical leaves with incised midribs in whorled arrangement.

334. FRAGMENT OF A BANQUETING RELIEF

DATABASE NUMBER: MSA001.
LOCATION: Jerusalem, Musée de Sainte Anne, inv. no. unknown.
CONTEXT: —
ACQUISITION HISTORY: —
MEASUREMENTS: —
MATERIAL: Limestone.
PRESERVATION: All sides of the object are broken off. The lower right arm and lower body are broken off. The nose and chin are chipped.
TECHNICAL DESCRIPTION: —
DATE: A.D. 150–170.
REFERENCES: Ingholt 1928, 107 PS 153.

OBJECT DESCRIPTION
The object depicts a reclining priest.

PORTRAIT
The figure is shown frontally. The left arm is bent and held in front of the torso.

He wears a plain, high, cylindrical, flat-top headdress: a Palmyrene priestly hat. His face is oval. The eyebrows are curving, depicted as thin, curving, incised lines starting at the root of the nose. The eyes are large and almond-shaped, with thick eyelids. The irises and pupils are indicated by concentric, incised circles. The ears are large and protruding with the helix, tragus, scapha, and the lobe depicted. The nose is straight and narrow. The alae are indicated by incised lines. The mouth is small, with thin lips. The neck is short and wide.

He wears a tunic and a himation. The tunic has a wide, v-shaped neckline. The folds of the tunic are rendered by curving grooves on the chest and oblique grooves on the right sleeve. Over the tunic, he wears a himation. The himation

Cat. 333, Pl. 62

falls over the left shoulder and is wrapped around the left arm. It continues along the body and appears to be folded across the waist. The folds of the himation are indicated by oblique grooves.

With the left hand, he holds a skyphos. The body is undecorated, and the walls are vertical. It has looped handles. The thumb, index finger, and the little finger are extended.

335. FRAGMENT OF A BANQUETING RELIEF

DATABASE NUMBER: PalmyraUNK010.
LOCATION: Palmyra, unknown location.
CONTEXT: —
ACQUISITION HISTORY: —
MEASUREMENTS: —
MATERIAL: Limestone.
PRESERVATION: All edges are broken off. Portrait A: The head is broken off at the base of the neck. The lower part is broken off at the shins. Portrait B: The right side is broken off at the waist. The right arm is broken off at the wrist.
TECHNICAL DESCRIPTION: —
DATE: A.D. 150–170.
REFERENCES: Ingholt Archives, PS 1152; Krag 2018, 33 n. 75. 77; 44 n. 174; 45 n. 193; 46 n. 194–196; 47 n. 208; 49 n. 229; 65 n. 379; 239 cat. 276.

OBJECT DESCRIPTION
The object depicts a seated female and a reclining male.

PORTRAIT A: SEATED FEMALE
The figure is shown in frontal view. The hands appear large in relation to the body. The right arm is bent and held in front of her torso. The left arm is bent and rests on her left thigh. She sits with the legs apart and the knees are rendered under the drapery.

A large fold falls over her left shoulder and is wrapped around the left arm, possibly part of a veil. She wears three necklaces: The upper necklace is composed of small, round beads and a central, oval bead, worn at the base of the neck. The middle necklace is composed of two strings of small beads, worn at the base of the neck. The lower necklace is composed of large, oval beads, worn below the collarbone.

She wears a tunic and a himation. The tunic has long, tight-fitting sleeves. The tunic has a band of circles with deep incisions, extending down below the right side of the neckline. The folds of the tunic are rendered on the sleeve with horizontal and oblique grooves. A band of oval beads is visible on the right upper arm, possibly an armlet. The himation crosses the chest diagonally from the left shoulder to the right side, and covers the left breast. It is fastened at the shoulder with a brooch with a trapezoidal shape (details unclear). The himation covers the lower body and legs. The folds of the himation are rendered by curving grooves on the torso and at the legs, and vertical grooves between the legs.

Her right hand holds an object with two globular elements with a protruding semicircular element, possibly a flower. The flower has a central bud and two petals on the sides. She wears a bracelet on her right wrist (other details unclear). The left hand rests on the left thigh and holds a fold of clothing, possibly the veil. The left index finger is extended, and a nail is indicated by fine, incised lines.

PORTRAIT B: RECLINING MALE
The figure is shown in frontal view. The right leg is bent and raised; the knee is rendered under the drapery.

He wears a garment and over-trousers. The garment above the knees has a wide, decorated band set between beaded bands at the centre, possibly ›Parthian-style‹ trousers. The over-trousers have a decorated upper border with leaves on a stem, set between two beaded bands. The folds of the over-trousers are rendered by curving grooves.

His right hand rests on the left shoulder of the seated female. The thumb and the index finger are extended, and a nail is indicated by incised lines.

Cat. 335

336. FRAGMENT OF A MALE FIGURE

DATABASE NUMBER: PM436.
LOCATION: Palmyra, Palmyra Museum, inv. no. A 104.
CONTEXT: —
ACQUISITION HISTORY: —
MEASUREMENTS: Height: 33 cm. Width: 23 cm.
MATERIAL: Limestone, white/yellow.
PRESERVATION: The head is broken off at the base of the neck and the lower part is broken off at the waist. Small areas of the clothing, hands, and attribute are chipped.
TECHNICAL DESCRIPTION: —
DATE: A.D. 150–170.
REFERENCES: Ingholt Archives, PS 955; Tanabe 1986, 44 pl. 451.

OBJECT DESCRIPTION
The object depicts the torso of a male.

PORTRAIT
The figure is shown in frontal view. The arms appear short in relation to the body. Both arms are bent to the torso.

His neck is wide with two curving grooves.

He wears a tunic and a himation. The tunic has a wide, round neckline and long, tight-fitting sleeves. The folds of the tunic are rendered by curving and oblique grooves. Over the tunic, he wears a himation. It is wrapped around his left shoulder and arm, leaving most of the upper torso and hand free. One end of the himation crosses the lower torso diagonally. The folds of the himation are rendered by diagonal and oblique grooves.

He holds two styli between his thumb and index fingers of his right hand; they are oblong with wide upper ends and point to his right. With his left hand, he holds the lower part of a tablet. The tablet is rectangular in shape and rendered in three layers. He opens the tablet with the index and ring fingers of his right hand and the little finger is extended. The nails are indicated by fine, incised lines.

337. FRAGMENT OF A MALE FIGURE

DATABASE NUMBER: PM655.
LOCATION: Palmyra, Palmyra Museum, inv. no. CD 37/66.
CONTEXT: Secondary context: Found in room IIb in the Temple of the Standards (Temple des Enseignes), Camp of Diocletian.
ACQUISITION HISTORY: —
MEASUREMENTS: Height: 38 cm. Width: 25 cm. Depth: 17 cm.
MATERIAL: Limestone, white.
PRESERVATION: The relief is broken on all sides. Broken horizontally through the base of the neck and the thighs. The surface of the chest and lower torso is chipped.

Cat. 336

Cat. 337

TECHNICAL DESCRIPTION: —
DATE: A.D. 150–170 (Gawlikowski 1984: A.D. 150–250).
REFERENCES: Gawlikowski 1984, 107 cat. 62 pl. 90, 196.

OBJECT DESCRIPTION
The fragment depicts a male.

PORTRAIT
The figure is shown frontally. The arms are bent and held to the torso.

His neck is slender.

He wears a tunic. It has a small neckline decorated with a beaded band, and long, tight-fitting sleeves. The folds of the tunic are indicated by curving grooves.

He holds an object (details unclear) in his hands.

338. FRAGMENT OF A MALE FIGURE

DATABASE NUMBER: PM914.
LOCATION: Palmyra, Palmyra Museum, inv. no. CD 39.
CONTEXT: Secondary context: Found (22.04.1961) in a later wall a western side of the Tetrapylon in the Camp of Diocletian.
ACQUISITION HISTORY: —
MEASUREMENTS: Height: 31 cm. Width: 49 cm. Depth: 12 cm.
MATERIAL: Limestone, white/grey.
PRESERVATION: The right, upper, and the left side of the object are broken off. The upper body of the figure is broken off at the waist. The surface is weathered and slightly chipped.
TECHNICAL DESCRIPTION: —
DATE: A.D. 150–170.
REFERENCES: Michalowski 1963, 153 cat. 47 fig. 204.

OBJECT DESCRIPTION
The object depicts a reclining male figure. Beneath the figure is a thin mattress (details unclear).

PORTRAIT
The figure is shown in three-quarter view. The right leg is bent, and the left leg rests along the mattress.

He wears a himation. It is wrapped around his waist in a large fold and covers the rest of his legs. The folds of the himation are indicated by curving grooves at the waist and oblique grooves on the legs. The left knee is rendered under the drapery.

339. FRAGMENT OF A MALE FIGURE

DATABASE NUMBER: PM936.
LOCATION: Palmyra, Palmyra Museum, inv. no. B 1817. Excavation number: 3.

Cat. 338

CONTEXT: Secondary context: Found (04.09.1954) in portico C3 at the Sanctuary of Baalshamin.
ACQUISITION HISTORY: —
MEASUREMENTS: Height: 37 cm. Width: 35.5 cm. Depth: 38 cm.
MATERIAL: Limestone.
PRESERVATION: The right, upper, and the left side of the object are broken off. The upper body of the figure is broken off at the below the knees. The surface is chipped.
TECHNICAL DESCRIPTION: The back of the figure is partly carved.
DATE: A.D. 150–170.
REFERENCES: Dunant – Stucky 2000, 98 cat. 50 pl. 18.

OBJECT DESCRIPTION
The object depicts a standing male figure.

PORTRAIT
The figure is shown in a frontal view. He stands with legs parted and the feet are firmly on the ground.

He wears a garment that covers the legs to the ankles, either >Parthian-style< trousers, or over-trousers. The folds of the garment are rendered by wide, curving grooves. He also wears closed-toe shoes.

340. FRAGMENT OF A MALE FIGURE

DATABASE NUMBER: PM937.
LOCATION: Palmyra, Palmyra Museum, inv. no. unknown. Excavation number: 97.
CONTEXT: Secondary context: Found (03.10.1954) in portico C3 at the Sanctuary of Baalshamin.
ACQUISITION HISTORY: —
MEASUREMENTS: Height: 47 cm. Width: 31 cm. Depth: 14 cm.
MATERIAL: Limestone.
PRESERVATION: The right, upper, and the left side of the object are broken off. The upper body of the figure is broken off at the middle of the thighs. The lower part of the figure is broken off above the knees. The upper front part of the fragment and parts of the left leg are broken off. The surface is heavily chipped.
TECHNICAL DESCRIPTION: The back of the figure is partly carved.
DATE: A.D. 150–170.
REFERENCES: Dunant – Stucky 2000, 98 cat. 51 pl. 19.

OBJECT DESCRIPTION
The object depicts a standing male figure.

PORTRAIT
The figure is shown in a frontal view. He stands with legs parted.

He wears a tunic and trousers. The tunic is visible only in outline and ends at the middle of the thighs. He wears trousers. The folds of the trousers are rendered by wide, curving grooves.

341. FRAGMENT OF A MALE FIGURE

DATABASE NUMBER: PM675.
LOCATION: Palmyra, Palmyra Museum, inv. no. CD 55.
CONTEXT: Secondary context: Found (27.05.1959) in the right lateral entry of the Praetorian Gate, Camp of Diocletian.
ACQUISITION HISTORY: —
MEASUREMENTS: Height: 43 cm. Width: 39 cm. Depth: 21 cm.
MATERIAL: Limestone, yellow.
PRESERVATION: The lower part of the figure is broken off. The base of the neck is chipped. The hands, and the folds of the himation that fall over the left shoulder are chipped.
TECHNICAL DESCRIPTION: A round dowel hole (depth: 6 cm) at the base of the neck indicates that the head was separately made and attached to the figure.
DATE: A.D. 150–170.
REFERENCES: Michalowski 1960, 98 cat. 16 fig. 105.

OBJECT DESCRIPTION
The object depicts a male figure.

PORTRAIT
The figure is shown frontally. His arms are bent and held in front of the waist. The lower arms and the hands appear small in relation to the body. He rests his left arm on a round cushion. The cushion is decorated with a wide band (other details unclear).

He wears a tunic and a himation. The tunic has a wide, round neckline. The folds of the tunic are rendered by curving grooves over the torso. Over the tunic he wears a himation. It falls over the shoulders, covering the arms, and is wrapped around the waist. A fold of the himation is wrapped around the left wrist and falls down and over the cushion.

With his left hand he holds the fold of the himation. With his right hand he holds a bowl. It has a wide rim, a conical body, and a small conical foot. It is identified by Michalowski (1960) as a kantharos.

A.D. 150–200

342. FRAGMENT OF A BANQUETING RELIEF

DATABASE NUMBER: UNK048.
LOCATION: —
CONTEXT: —
ACQUISITION HISTORY: —
MEASUREMENTS: —
MATERIAL: Limestone.
PRESERVATION: Only the upper part of the body, the left arm and hand, and a cushion are preserved. The surface is weathered. The left hand and cup are fragmented. Part of the clothing is chipped.
TECHNICAL DESCRIPTION: —
DATE: A.D. 150–200.
REFERENCES: Ingholt Archives, IA_NCG_Portrait2016_013.

OBJECT DESCRIPTION
The object depicts a reclining male figure. The male figure rests his left arm on a cushion. The cushion is decorated with a wide panel with leaves set on a stem, set between plain bands. Oblique grooves indicate the texture of the fabric.

PORTRAIT
The figure is shown frontally to three-quarter view. The left arm is bent and rests on a cushion.

He wears a tunic and a himation. The tunic has a wide v-shaped neckline. The folds of the tunic are indicated by wide, oblique and curving grooves. Over the tunic, he wears a himation. The himation is wrapped around the left shoulder and arm and covers the left side, leaving only the left hand free. The other side of the himation is wrapped around the waist, crosses the torso diagonally, and disappears under the

Cat 342

fold of the himation, falling down from the left shoulder. The fold that extends downwards from the left shoulder ends in a zigzag-shaped fold and a small tassel decorated with fine, wavy, incised lines. The folds of the himation are indicated by wide, oblique grooves.

With his left hand, he holds a cup. The cup has two small, looped handles attached to it at a vertical angle. The rim is indicated by a wide, plain, horizontal ridge, which extends above the handles. The body is ovoid and is decorated with a plain, horizontal band. The foot is stemmed.

343. FRAGMENT OF A BANQUETING RELIEF

DATABASE NUMBER: PM731.
LOCATION: Palmyra, Palmyra Museum, inv. no. B 1883.
CONTEXT: Secondary context: Found (27.09.1955) in portico C3 by column 13 in the Temple of Baalshamin.
ACQUISITION HISTORY: —
MEASUREMENTS: Height: 22 cm. Width: 36 cm. Depth: 20 cm.
MATERIAL: Limestone, white.
PRESERVATION: The head is broken off at the base of the neck. The lower part is broken off at the middle of the torso. The surface of the left hand and of the right shoulder is chipped.
TECHNICAL DESCRIPTION: The back has not been worked.
DATE: A.D. 150–200 (Dunant – Stucky 2000: A.D. 100–200).
REFERENCES: Dunant – Stucky 2000, 102 cat. 69 pl. 21.

OBJECT DESCRIPTION
The object depicts the torso and arms of a male figure.

PORTRAIT
The figure is shown frontally. Both arms are bent and held to the torso.

He wears a ›Parthian-style‹ tunic with a small, round neckline decorated with a beaded band and long, tight-fitting sleeves. The cuffs of the sleeves are decorated with a band with wave pattern and a beaded band. At the middle, the tunic has a wide band decorated with vines extending downwards. The folds of the tunic are rendered by oblique and curving folds.

With both hands, he holds an undecorated circular bowl. The bowl contains round elements, possibly fruit.

344. FRAGMENT OF A FEMALE FIGURE

DATABASE NUMBER: PM1058.
LOCATION: Palmyra, Palmyra Museum, inv. no. CD 110.
CONTEXT: Secondary context: Found (07.05.1962) at the south side of the foundations of the Great Gate.
ACQUISITION HISTORY: —
MEASUREMENTS: Height: 28 cm. Width: 26 cm. Depth: 18 cm.
MATERIAL: Limestone, grey.
PRESERVATION: Only a fragment of the lower part of the figure is preserved: from between the middle of the left lower leg to the middle of the left thigh, part of the lower right leg, and the space between them.
TECHNICAL DESCRIPTION: —
DATE: A.D. 150–200.
REFERENCES: Michalowski 1964, 73 cat. 6 fig. 106.

OBJECT DESCRIPTION
The object depicts a seated female.

PORTRAIT
The figure is shown frontally. The legs are parted.

She wears a chiton and a himation. The chiton has an overfold that falls over the left knee. Over the chiton she wears a himation: a thick fold falls between the legs and over the left knee.

A.D. 170–200

345. FRAGMENT OF A BANQUETING RELIEF

DATABASE NUMBER: UNK224.
LOCATION: Unknown location.
CONTEXT: —

Cat. 345

ACQUISITION HISTORY: —
MEASUREMENTS: —
MATERIAL: Limestone.
PRESERVATION: The fragment is broken off on the right, upper, and left side. The surface above the portrait is chipped. The nose is chipped.
TECHNICAL DESCRIPTION: There are flat chisel marks on the lower protruding plinth.
DATE: A.D. 170–200.
REFERENCES: Ingholt Archives, PS 1146.

OBJECT DESCRIPTION

The object depicts the left upper corner of a sarcophagus box with a fulcrum with an armless male bust. Along the lower border of the fragment is a protruding plinth. To the right of the portrait, part of a cushion is rendered: it is decorated with a wide band with running scrolls and four-petal rosettes, set between two beaded bands. Curving grooves indicate the fabric of the cushion. To the left of the portrait is a depiction of a small figure with wings. Underneath the winged figure is part of a sarcophagus leg, with a single turning decorated with two opposed tongue pattern bands, divided by a narrow, plain band.

PORTRAIT

The figure is shown in frontal view. Only the upper part of the torso and of the arms is shown.

His hair is arranged in a single row of crescent-shaped locks around the head. His face is round. The eyebrows are slightly curving. The eyes are small with thick upper eyelids. The eyeballs appear blank. The ears are large and protruding, and the helix, scapha, and earlobe are depicted. The nose is wide. The mouth is small, with a full lower lip. There are small, curving ›marionette‹ lines. The chin is oval and prominent. The neck is short and wide.

He wears a tunic and a chlamys. The tunic has a wide, round neckline decorated with a plain band. The folds of the tunic are indicated by oblique grooves. The chlamys falls over both shoulders and covers the lower part of the chest. The chlamys is fastened at the right shoulder with a brooch (details unclear). A large fold falls under the brooch in a zigzag shape. The folds of the chlamys are indicated with curving and oblique grooves.

346. FRAGMENTS OF A BANQUETING RELIEF

DATABASE NUMBER: MLP026.
LOCATION: Paris, Musée du Louvre, inv. no. AO 5001.
CONTEXT: —
ACQUISITION HISTORY: Gift from Joseph Reinach in 1880.
MEASUREMENTS: Height: 31 cm. Width: 37 cm. Depth: 13 cm.
MATERIAL: Limestone, yellow.
PRESERVATION: The upper right corner and the right side are broken off. The lower part of the relief and the lower left corner are broken off. Portrait A: The right side is broken off at the neckline. The lower part is broken off at the waist. The lower left arm is broken off. Portrait B: The mouth, the lips, the chin, and the left hand are chipped. Portrait C: The left side is broken off at the upper arm and the lower part is broken off above the waist. The nose, the neck, and the right hand are chipped.
TECHNICAL DESCRIPTION: Restored in 1995 when it was treated and cleaned. There are traces of a modern red pigment on the relief. There are flat chisel marks on the relief background. Portrait A: Traces of red colour in the central decoration on the tunic. Left hand is undercut. Portrait C: Right hand is undercut.
DATE: A.D. 170–200 (Dentzer-Feydy – Teixidor 1993: A.D. 175–225).
REFERENCES: Ingholt Archives, PS 71; Ingholt 1928, 96. 143 f.; Vigneau 1936, 120; Dentzer-Feydy – Teixidor 1993, 205 cat. 203; Krag 2018, 59 n. 316; 62 n. 350; 66 n. 382; 88 n. 193. 195; 375 cat. 786.

Cat. 346

OBJECT DESCRIPTION

The relief is rectangular in shape and depicts a reclining male, a female, and a male. Portraits A and C, the two males, are in the foreground while portrait B is in lower relief between the two figures. Portrait A rests against a round cushion. The cushion is decorated with a wide band extending downwards. The band has four-petal flowers framed by two intersecting vines set between two beaded bands. Curving grooves indicate the texture of the fabric.

PORTRAIT A: RECLINING MALE

The figure is shown frontally. The left arm appears short in relation to the body. It is bent and rests on a cushion.

He wears a ›Parthian-style‹ tunic and a himation. The tunic has a round neckline decorated with a beaded band. There is a vertical, rectangular element to the left side of the neckline. The tunic has a wide band with a floral pattern between two beaded bands extending downwards from the middle of the neckline. The folds of the tunic are rendered by oblique grooves on his chest. Over the tunic, he wears a himation. The himation is folded around his left shoulder and upper arm and follows the left side of his body, possibly indicating the himation being wrapped around his waist. The folds of the himation are indicated with oblique and vertical grooves.

With the upturned palm of the left hand, he holds a bowl with his fingertips. The body of the bowl is decorated with hollowed-out lozenges. Under his left hand the himation appears to continue down over the cushion.

PORTRAIT B: FEMALE FIGURE

The figure is shown in frontal view. The arms appear short in relation to the body. The right arm is bent and held in front of her body; the left is bent and raised to the neck. From the waist down, the figure is obscured by the two figures in the foreground.

She wears three headdresses: a headband, a turban, and a veil. The headband is placed high on her forehead and is decorated with two horizontal rows of squares, rendered by incised lines. The turban is coiled. It is composed of two coiling layers, the folds indicated by horizontal and oblique grooves. The veil is heavy. It falls over the shoulders and is wrapped around her right arm and falls over the back of her left shoulder. Her hair is visible at the sides of her forehead, brushed back over the headband, and disappears under the veil. Incised lines render four locks of hair on each side. Her face is square and the eyebrows curving. The eyes are almond-shaped, with thick upper eyelids that extend beyond the end of the lower ones. The eyeballs are blank. She wears dumbbell-shaped earrings (Colledge classification: H). The nose is straight and pointed and the alae is slightly incised. Her cheeks are fleshy. The mouth is small, with full lips. Her chin is oval and the neck is wide. She wears a necklace: a string of round beads at the base of her neck.

She wears a tunic and a himation. The tunic has a small, v-shaped neckline and a plain band extending downwards at the right side. The folds of the tunic are indicated by curving, horizontal grooves. The himation crosses the chest diagonally from the left shoulder to the right side, and covers the left breast. It is fastened at the shoulder with a plain, circular brooch (Colledge classification: i). The folds are indicated by oblique and curving grooves.

With the right hand, she holds a fold of the veil. The index and the middle finger are extended. The left hand is raised to the height of the neck and she pulls the edge of the veil.

PORTRAIT C: MALE FIGURE

The figure is shown in frontal view. The right arm appears short in relation to the body. The head is large. The right arm is bent and held in front of the chest.

His hair is arranged in five rows of crescent-shaped curls around the head. Each row of curls points in an alternate direction. The individual strands of hair are indicated by incised lines. His face is square. The eyebrows are curving, rendered by incised lines starting from the top of the nose. The eyes are almond-shaped, with thick upper eyelids that extend beyond the end of the lower ones. The irises are indicated by incised circles. The ears are protruding and the helix, scapha, and earlobe are depicted. The nose is straight with a wide base. The alae are incised, and the nostrils are carved. He has a beard that starts from the temples and covers the outer side of the cheeks, the chin, and the upper lip. The facial hair in the beard is rendered by flame-shaped locks with smaller locks of hair depicted with incised lines. The facial hair in the moustache is rendered by vertical, incised lines. The mouth is large with full lips. The chin is wide and the neck long.

He wears a tunic and a himation. The tunic has a wide, v-shaped neckline. The folds of the tunic are rendered by curving grooves. The himation covers most of the upper body: it is wrapped around the right shoulder and arm, leaving only the upper part of the chest and right hand free. The folds of the himation are indicated by deep, vertical grooves.

With the upturned palm of the right hand, he holds a bowl with his fingertips in front of his chest. The body of the bowl is decorated with hollowed-out lozenges. The thumbnail is indicated by fine, incised lines.

347. FRAGMENT OF A BANQUETING RELIEF

DATABASE NUMBER: MET020.
LOCATION: New York, Metropolitan Museum of Art, inv. no. 01.25.5.
CONTEXT: —
ACQUISITION HISTORY: Purchased in 1901 from the antiquities dealer Azeez Khayat.
MEASUREMENTS: Height: 40 cm. Width: 26.5 cm.
MATERIAL: Limestone, yellow.
PRESERVATION: The entire right side is broken off. Portrait A: The left side of the forehead, the left side of the nose, the right side of the chin, and the mouth are chipped. The

left shoulder and the lower right arm are chipped. The left arm and the right hand are broken off. The lower part of the figure is broken off at the waist. Portrait B: Only part of the left shoulder is preserved.

TECHNICAL DESCRIPTION: There are flat chisel marks on the relief ground. The left hand is undercut.

DATE: A.D. 170–200.

REFERENCES: Ingholt Archives, PS 187; Arnold 1905, 110 cat. 7 fig. 7; Chabot 1922, 129 pl. 31.5; Ingholt 1928, 111; Colledge 1976, 249; Albertson 2000, 160 n. 3; Cussini 2018, 96. fig. 8; <https://www.metmuseum.org/art/collection/search/322371?sortBy=Relevance&ft=palmyra&offset=0&rpp=20&pos=7> (06.05.2022). Inscription: Arnold 1905, 110 cat. 7.

OBJECT DESCRIPTION

The object is rectangular in shape and depicts a male. Just right to the figure is a chipped protruding element, possibly a shoulder from an adjacent person.

INSCRIPTION

SCRIPT: Palmyrene Aramaic.
LOCATION ON RELIEF: Right of the figure, in the height of the head.
TRANSCRIPTION: MLKW B[R] | ZB' BR['T]- | H.
TRANSLATION: Malkû, son of Zabdâ Bar'ateh.

CIS no. 4552; PAT no. 0913.

COMMENT: L.2–3: CIS and Ingholt had seen traces of the final H under l. 2. Not very obvious on the available photographs.

PORTRAIT: STANDING MALE, MALKÛ

The figure is shown frontally. The arms appear short in relation to the body. The head appears large. The right arm is slightly bent and follows his body; the left arm is bent and held in front of the chest.

His hair is arranged in a single row of s-shaped curls around his head, all pointing to the left. Individual strands of hair are indicated by incised lines. His face is oval. The eyebrows are slightly curving, rendered by incised grooves starting from the nose. The eyes are large and almond-shaped, with thick eyelids. The irises are indicated by incised circles and the pupils by punch holes. The ears are large and slightly protruding, with the helix, tragus, concha, scapha, and lobe depicted. The left ear is larger than the right. The nose has incised alae and carved nostrils. The mouth is small, with full lips. The chin is oval and fleshy. The neck has two curving grooves.

He wears a >Parthian-style< tunic with long sleeves. The tunic has a round neckline decorated with a beaded band. The folds of the tunic are rendered by curving and oblique grooves on his chest and curving grooves on the sleeves.

With the upturned palm of the left hand, he holds a bowl with the fingertips in front of his chest. The bowl has a plain upper surface, and a horizontal groove runs along the rim. The body of the bowl is decorated with hollowed-out lozenges. Fine, incised lines indicate the nails.

PORTRAIT B: STANDING FIGURE

Part of the left shoulder. Two curving grooves indicate the folds of a garment.

348. FRAGMENT OF A BANQUETING RELIEF

DATABASE NUMBER: UNK084.
LOCATION: Unknown location.
CONTEXT: —
ACQUISITION HISTORY: —
MEASUREMENTS: —
MATERIAL: Limestone.
PRESERVATION: The background is broken off. The figure is broken off at the height of the collarbone.
TECHNICAL DESCRIPTION: The hands are partly carved.
DATE: A.D. 170–200.

Cat. 347

REFERENCES: Ingholt Archives, IA_NCG_Miscellaneous2016_092.

OBJECT DESCRIPTION

The object depicts a seated female and a reclining male. The figures are resting on a mattress decorated with an intersecting lozenge pattern with four-petal flowers in the lozenges. There are round elements where the lozenges intersect.

PORTRAIT A: SEATED FEMALE

The figure is shown frontally. The left arm is bent and raised to the shoulder; the left arm is bent and rests on the thigh. The legs are bent and the knees are rendered under the drapery.

Only the falling folds of the veil are visible. The folds fall over the right shoulder and arm, covering them.

She wears a tunic and a himation. The tunic has a round neckline. The folds of the tunic are indicated by curving grooves. Over the tunic, she wears a himation that falls diagonally across the chest and covers the lower part of the body. It is fastened at the left shoulder with a circular, button-like brooch with an incised border (Colledge classification: h). The folds of the himation are indicated by curving and oblique grooves. She wears closed-toe, plain shoes (only the right one is visible).

With her right hand, she holds the veil at the height of the shoulder. With the left hand, she holds a looped fold of the veil that is folded across the lap. The index finger is extended. She wears bracelets: a thick hoop around each wrist.

PORTRAIT B: RECLINING MALE

His right leg is bent and the right foot rests on the mattress.

He wears a himation. It covers his leg and ends at the ankle. He wears round, closed-toe shoes. The topline of the shoe is below the ankle, and the shoe is tied at the instep with a thin band or cord.

349. FRAGMENT OF A BANQUETING RELIEF

DATABASE NUMBER: AMI085.
LOCATION: Istanbul, İstanbul Arkeoloji Müzesi, inv. no. 3807/O.M. 266.
CONTEXT: —
ACQUISITION HISTORY: —
MEASUREMENTS: Height: 93 cm.
MATERIAL: Limestone, white/grey.
PRESERVATION: The background is broken off. The lower left and right sides of the relief are heavily chipped. A crack runs across the face and several surface cracks run across the body. The tip of the nose is chipped.
TECHNICAL DESCRIPTION: The finish is a little rough in places. Tool marks are visible on the surface of the face, knees, and feet. The space between the right forearm and veil has been carved out. The right arm and the veil are awkwardly carved.
DATE: A.D. 170–200.
REFERENCES: Ingholt Archives, PS 724; Ruxer – Kubczak 1972, 123. 167. 205. 214. 262 cat. 53 pl. 53; Krag 2018, 28 n. 9; 54 n. 262. 263; 58 n. 304; 59 n. 316; 61 n. 335; 62 n. 350. 353; 101 n. 65; 382 cat. 813.

OBJECT DESCRIPTION

The object depicts a seated female. She rests her feet on a thin mattress decorated with flowers.

PORTRAIT

The figure is shown frontally, the head is turned slightly to the left. The right arm is bent and raised to the shoulder; the left arm is bent and rests on the thigh. The legs are bent and the knees are rendered under the drapery.

She wears three headdresses: a headband, a turban, and a veil. The headband is decorated with three square panels, divided by beaded bands. The outer panels are decorated with a crisscross pattern, and the central panel is decorated with a flower with serrated petals. The turban is coiled, with the upper coils twisted at the centre. The coiling of the fabric is indicated

Cat. 348

Cat. 349

by slightly curving grooves. Over the turban, she wears a heavy veil that falls down the back of the head and covers the left shoulder and arm, covers the outer side of the right arm, and falls across her lap and down her left thigh in a zigzag-shaped fold. The hair is visible at the sides of the forehead; it is slightly wavy and combed backwards with individual strands of hair indicated by curving grooves. It covers the lower sides of the headband and turban. Her face is square. The eyebrows are indicated by thin, incised lines that start from the root of the nose. The eyes are small and almond-shaped, with thick upper eyelids. The end of the upper eyelids extends downwards and beyond that of the lower ones. The irises are indicated. The earlobes are visible. She wears earrings with three juxtaposed, round beads (Colledge classification: K). The nose is wide. The mouth is small, with full lips. The chin is pointed. The neck is short and wide with two horizontal grooves. She wears three necklaces. The first, at the base of the neck, is a string of large, round beads. The second, below that, is a hoop running in a zigzag pattern. The third is a wide, loop-in-loop chain with a round pendant with an incised border suspended from the centre by a thick sleeve.

She wears a tunic and a himation. The tunic has a wide, round neckline and sleeves ending at the elbows. The folds of the tunic are indicated by curving grooves. Over the tunic, she wears a himation that falls diagonally across the chest and covers the lower part of the body. It is fastened at the left shoulder with a round brooch with an outer, beaded border (Colledge classification: f). The folds of the himation are indicated by curving and oblique grooves. She wears closed-toe, plain shoes.

With her right hand, she holds the veil at the height of the shoulder. With the left hand, she holds a fold of the veil that is folded across the lap. The index finger is extended. She wears a ring on the little finger of the left hand; it is a thick, wide hoop with a circular bezel.

350. FRAGMENTS OF A BANQUETING RELIEF

DATABASE NUMBER: PM290.
LOCATION: Palmyra, Palmyra Museum, inv. no. CD 109, CD 58, CD 103, CD 148.
CONTEXT: Secondary context: Found (11/21/24.05.1960) at a later wall at the Tetrapylon in the Camp of Diocletian.
ACQUISITION HISTORY: —
MEASUREMENTS: Fragment A: Height: 73 cm. Width: 64 cm. Depth: 22 cm. Fragment B: Height: 47 cm. Width: 23 cm. Depth: 25 cm. Fragment C: Height: 46 cm. Width: 39 cm. Depth: 22 cm. Fragment D: Height: 35 cm. Width: 18 cm. Depth: 24 cm. Fragment E: Height: 51 cm. Width: 25 cm. Depth: 18 cm.
MATERIAL: Limestone, grey.
PRESERVATION: Five fragments. The lower edge of the relief is preserved in the two pieces depicting the mattress. The surface of the attribute and of the left hand is chipped. Only part of the torso, arms, and upper legs is preserved.
TECHNICAL DESCRIPTION: —
DATE: A.D. 170–200.
REFERENCES: Michalowski 1962, 150 f. cat. 21 fig. 165.

OBJECT DESCRIPTION

The object is composed of five fragments, depicting a reclining figure. Beneath the figure is a mattress. The mattress is decorated with an intersecting lozenges pattern with beaded elements at the intersections. At the centre of the lozenges there are four-petal flowers.

PORTRAIT

The figure is shown in three-quarter view. The right lower arm rests on the right knee. The left arm is bent and held to the chest. His right leg is bent and raised.

He wears a ›Parthian-style‹ tunic, chlamys, and ›Parthian-style‹ trousers. The tunic has long, tight-fitting sleeves, and the cuffs are decorated with a band with floral motif. The tunic has a wide band decorated with vegetal motifs set between two beaded bands extending downwards from the middle of the neckline. The tunic ends at the middle of the thighs, and the hem is decorated with a wide band with a floral motif and a beaded band. The folds of the tunic are rendered by oblique grooves. He also wears a plain band belt, knotted in the centre with the end looped under on the side of the waist. Over the tunic, he wears a chlamys that falls over the left shoulder and covers the left part of the chest. One edge of the chlamys has a border with a running scroll and rosettes pattern. One fold of the chlamys falls on the mattress, in two large, zigzag-shaped folds. The folds of the trousers are rendered with vertical and oblique grooves.

The right hand rests on his right knee, and holds an oval object with a diamond-shaped pattern, possibly a pinecone. With the upturned palm of the left hand he holds a bowl (visible in outline).

351. FRAGMENT OF A BANQUETING RELIEF

DATABASE NUMBER: NCG055.
LOCATION: Copenhagen, Ny Carlsberg Glyptotek, inv. no. IN 1082.
CONTEXT: —
ACQUISITION HISTORY: From Løytved in Syria.
MEASUREMENTS: Height: 31 cm. Width: 25 cm. Depth: 33 cm. Height of head: 33 cm.
MATERIAL: Limestone, white/grey.
PRESERVATION: The head is broken off at the base of the neck. The shoulders, upper arms, part of the right foot, and the left foot are broken off. The right hand and the right leg are chipped.
TECHNICAL DESCRIPTION: Modern modifications are visible on the back where a clamp has been attached. There are flat chisel marks on the clothing and rasp marks on the grapes.
DATE: A.D. 170–200 (Hvidberg-Hansen – Ploug 1993: A.D. 135–150).
REFERENCES: Ingholt Archives, PS 866; Simonsen 1889, 44 cat. F 1 pl. 15; Chabot 1922, 120 cat. 35; Ingholt 1926, 140 n. 4; Ingholt 1928, 152 n. 4; Ingholt 1935, 68 n. 53; Colledge 1976, 75. 124. 135. 146. 240 pl. 99; Pierson 1984, 94. 99 n. 114. 115; Hvidberg-Hansen – Ploug 1993, 77 cat. 32; Ploug 1995, 108 f. cat. 32; Koustrup Høj 2017a, 33 fig. 3; Koustrup Høj 2017b, 33 fig. 3; Raja 2019a, 248 cat. 75. Inscription: Schröder 1885, 352; Simonsen 1889, 44 cat. F 1; Chabot 1922, 120 cat. 35; Hvidberg-Hansen – Ploug 1993, 77 cat. 32; Hvidberg-Hansen 1998, 49 cat. 32; Raja 2019a, 248 f. cat. 75.

OBJECT DESCRIPTION
The object depicts a seated child.

INSCRIPTION
SCRIPT: Palmyrene Aramaic.
LOCATION ON RELIEF: On the right shoulder.
TRANSCRIPTION: BRTH.

TRANSLATION: His/her daughter

CIS no. —; PAT no. —.

COMMENT: Not visible on the available photographs. The >letters< resemble meaningless signs and may indicate that the inscription is fake.

PORTRAIT
The figure is shown frontally. The arms are bent in front of the torso. The legs are parted and the right leg crosses over the left one at the ankles.

He wears a tunic, >Parthian-style< trousers, and over-trousers. The tunic has a wide, round neckline and long, tight-fitting sleeves. It reaches to the knees. It is tied at the waist with a band belt. The folds of the tunic are indicated by curving grooves. The trousers are visible from the knees to just below the knees. They are decorated with a wide band with a branch with small, elliptical leaves in alternate arrangement, framed by two beaded borders. Over the trousers, he wears loose-fitting over-trousers that cover the lower legs. The folds of the garments are indicated by curving grooves. He wears closed shoes. Two trapezoidal, incised lines over the surface of the right shoe indicate that they were laced with a band.

He holds three large bunches of grapes with the stems visible with both hands. The right thumb, index, and the middle finger are extended. Nails are indicated by fine lines.

Cat. 351, Pl. 63

352. FRAGMENT OF A BANQUETING RELIEF

DATABASE NUMBER: NMA004.
LOCATION: Aleppo, National Museum of Aleppo, inv. no. unknown.
CONTEXT: —
ACQUISITION HISTORY: —
MEASUREMENTS: —
MATERIAL: Limestone, white/grey.
PRESERVATION: The head is broken off at the base of the neck. The left hand is broken off.
TECHNICAL DESCRIPTION: The bunch of grapes does not appear fully carved.
DATE: A.D. 170–200.
REFERENCES: Ingholt Archives, IA_NCG_Miscellaneous2016_079.

OBJECT DESCRIPTION
The object depicts a seated child.

INSCRIPTION
SCRIPT: —
LOCATION ON RELIEF: On the right leg.
TRANSCRIPTION: —
TRANSLATION: —
CIS no. —; PAT no. —.
COMMENT: The inscription is fake.

PORTRAIT
The figure is shown frontally and sitting down. The right arm is bent in front of the torso. The legs are parted.

The child wears a tunic. The tunic has a wide, round neckline and long, tight-fitting sleeves. It reaches to the ankles. It is tied high at the waist with a thin band belt. The folds of the tunic are indicated by curving grooves. The child wears closed shoes.

The child holds one large bunch of grapes with the right hand. The right index finger is extended.

353. MALE FIGURE

DATABASE NUMBER: UNK176.
LOCATION: Unknown location.
CONTEXT: —
ACQUISITION HISTORY: —
MEASUREMENTS: —
MATERIAL: Limestone.
PRESERVATION: The right arm is broken off.
TECHNICAL DESCRIPTION: —
DATE: A.D. 170–200.
REFERENCES: Ingholt Archives, PS 1395.

OBJECT DESCRIPTION
The object depicts a reclining male. He rests the left arm against a cushion. It is decorated with a band with a vegetal motif, set between beaded bands. Curving grooves indicate the texture of the fabric.

PORTRAIT
The figure is shown frontally, the head is turned slightly to the left. The left arm appears short in relation to the body. The head and the eyes appear large. The left arm is bent and held to the torso.

His hair is arranged in two rows of crescent-shaped curls around the head. The individual locks of hair are rendered by incised lines. His face is oval. There is a furrow along his forehead. The eyebrows are curving, rendered by thin ridges. The eyes are close-set and round with thick upper eyelids. The irises are rendered by incised circles and the pupils by punch holes. The ears are large and protruding with the helix, scapha, and lobe depicted. The nose is straight and wide at the tip with the nostrils carved. The philtrum is rendered. The mouth has a full lower lip. The corners of the mouth are rendered by curving, incised lines. The chin is prominent and round. The neck is wide with two curving grooves and a v-shaped depression indicates the sternocleidomastoid muscles.

He wears a tunic and a himation. The tunic has a wide, v-shaped neckline leaving the uppermost part of the chest free. A vertical groove indicates the musculature of the chest.

Cat. 352

SARCOPHAGI WITH NO KNOWN PROVENANCE OR FROM SECONDARY CONTEXTS

Cat. 353

Cat. 354

The folds of the tunic are rendered by curving and oblique grooves. Over the tunic, he wears a himation. It is wrapped around his left shoulder, leaving most of the chest and the hand free. A wide fold proceeds in a curve from under his left hand and across the lower torso and back at his right side.

He holds a skyphos in his left hand. It has a conical foot and lower body, straight lip, and small, looped handles. The thumb, index, and the little finger are extended.

354. MALE FIGURE

DATABASE NUMBER: AMI032.
LOCATION: Istanbul, İstanbul Arkeoloji Müzesi, inv. no. 3781/O.M.240.
CONTEXT: —
ACQUISITION HISTORY: —
MEASUREMENTS: Height: 83 cm.
MATERIAL: Limestone, grey.
PRESERVATION: The surface is weathered, with multiple minor scratches.
TECHNICAL DESCRIPTION: There are some light rasp marks visible on the cheeks and chin.
DATE: A.D. 170–200.
REFERENCES: Ingholt Archives, PS 125; Ingholt 1928, 104; Colledge 1976, 247.

OBJECT DESCRIPTION
The fragment depicts a reclining male. The figure rests against a round cushion decorated with a wide band (details unclear). Curving grooves indicate the texture of the fabric.

PORTRAIT
The figure is shown frontally. The arms are bent; the right is held at the torso, the left is held along the side.

He has short hair arranged in two alternate rows of crescent-shaped curls. The individual strands of hair are rendered by incised lines. His face is square. The eyebrows are indicated by thin grooves that start from the root of the nose. The eyes are large and round with thick upper eyelids. The irises and the pupils are indicated by concentric, incised circles. The ears are small and slightly protruding with the helix and lobe indicated. The nose is straight. The mouth is small, with full lips. The chin is round. The neck is long and slender.

He wears a tunic and a himation. The tunic has a wide, v-shaped neckline and long, tight-fitting sleeves. The folds of the tunic are indicated by wide, curving grooves over the area of the torso, and curving ones over the arms. Over the tunic, he wears a himation: it is wrapped around the left shoulder and arm, is twisted around the left wrist, and falls across the waist. The folds of the himation are indicated by oblique grooves.

The left hand rests against the cushion. The thumb, index, and the little finger are extended. With the right hand, he holds a skyphos. The cup has a conical foot, inverted, conical lower body, and straight sides at the upper body, round handles, and a thin rim that extends over the two handles. The index, middle, and the little finger are extended. The nails are indicated.

355. MALE FIGURE

DATABASE NUMBER: PM504.
LOCATION: Palmyra, Palmyra Museum, inv. no. unknown.
CONTEXT: Secondary context: Found at the northern wall in the city.
ACQUISITION HISTORY: —
MEASUREMENTS: Height: 44 cm. Width: 73 cm.
MATERIAL: Limestone, white/yellow.
PRESERVATION: The head is broken off at the base of the neck and the feet are broken off. The surface is lightly chipped.
TECHNICAL DESCRIPTION: There are traces of red pigment in the inscription.
DATE: A.D. 170–200 (al-Asʿad et al. 2012: A.D. 150–200).
REFERENCES: al-Asʿad et al. 2012, 168 cat. 13. Inscription: al-Asʿad et al. 2012, 168 cat. 13.

OBJECT DESCRIPTION
The object depicts a reclining male. He lies on a mattress (details unclear) and rests his left arm on two cushions. Curving grooves indicate the texture of the fabric.

INSCRIPTION
SCRIPT: Palmyrene Aramaic.
LOCATION ON RELIEF: On the skyphos.
TRANSCRIPTION: TYMRṢW | BR ʿTʿQB ʾŠGDT | ḤBL.
TRANSLATION: Taîmarṣû, son of ʿAteʿaqab Ašgadat, alas!

CIS no. —; PAT no.—; al-Asʿad et al. 2012, 168 cat. 13.

PORTRAIT: TAÎMARṢÛ
The figure is shown in frontal to three-quarter view. The arms appear short in relation to the body. The right arm is extended, resting on the right knee. The left arm is bent in front of the torso. His right leg is bent. The left leg is bent under the right leg, and the foot is obscured by the right leg.

He wears a >Parthian-style< tunic, a chlamys, >Parthian-style< trousers, and over-trousers. The tunic has a wide, v-shaped neckline and long, tight-fitting sleeves. The cuffs of the sleeves are decorated with a band with a vegetal motif and a beaded band. The tunic ends above the knees and has a decorated lower border with a running scroll with vines and rosettes between beaded bands. The folds of the tunic are rendered by oblique and curving grooves. Over the tunic, he wears a chlamys that falls over both shoulders, and covers the upper part of the chest. One edge of the chlamys has a scalloped border decorated with rosettes between beaded bands, visible on the

Cat. 355

fold across the chest. It is fastened at the right shoulder with a circular brooch with a rosette within (Colledge classification: g). He also wears a band belt across the lower torso knotted at the centre with the ends looped under either side of the waist. The trousers are visible at the knees. Each trouser leg is decorated in the middle with a beaded band on either side of a wide band with a vegetal motif that extend downwards. The over-trousers are visible from under the knee. The upper borders are decorated with a beaded band. The folds of the garments are indicated by wide, curving grooves.

He holds a branch with lanceolate leaves in his right hand. With his left hand, he holds a skyphos. It has a conical foot, the lower part of the body is conical, while the upper part of the body is trapezoidal. The lip is straight and it has small, looped handles. The lower part of the body is decorated with a tongue pattern. The left thumb, index, and the little finger are extended.

356. FRAGMENT OF A MALE FIGURE

DATABASE NUMBER: UNK078.
LOCATION: Unknown location.
CONTEXT: —
ACQUISITION HISTORY: Ingholt saw it at »Cheruau's Museum«.
MEASUREMENTS: —
MATERIAL: Limestone, white/yellow.
PRESERVATION: Broken on all sides. The head is broken off horizontally at the base of the neck and the lower part is broken off through the waist. The right side is broken off. The surface around the left hand and of the attribute is chipped. The surface is weathered.
TECHNICAL DESCRIPTION: —
DATE: A.D. 170–200.
REFERENCES: Ingholt Archives, PS 934.

OBJECT DESCRIPTION
The object depicts a reclining male. The figure rests the left arm against a cushion. It is decorated with a band with a vegetal motif between beaded bands.

PORTRAIT
The figure is shown frontally. The left arm appears short in relation to the body. The left arm is bent in front of the torso.

He wears a tunic and a himation. The tunic has a wide, round neckline. The folds of the tunic are rendered by curving grooves. Over the tunic, he wears a himation. It is wrapped around his left shoulder and arm, leaving most of the chest and the hand free. It proceeds in a curving fold across his lower torso. The folds of the himation are rendered by vertical and curving grooves.

The outline of a cup is visible in his left hand.

Cat. 356

357. FRAGMENT OF A MALE FIGURE

DATABASE NUMBER: BeirutUNK002.
LOCATION: Beirut, unknown location.
CONTEXT: —
ACQUISITION HISTORY: —
MEASUREMENTS: —
MATERIAL: Limestone.
PRESERVATION: Broken in a diagonal line from the right arm to the left shoulder. The surface at the chin and nose is chipped. The surface is weathered.
TECHNICAL DESCRIPTION: —
DATE: A.D. 170–200.
REFERENCES: Ingholt Archives, PS 587.

OBJECT DESCRIPTION
The fragment depicts the head and upper torso of a male figure.

PORTRAIT
The figure is shown frontally. The head appears large.

Cat. 357

Cat. 358

His hair is straight, voluminous, and long, covers the ears, and reaches the neck. The individual strands of hair are rendered by curving, incised lines. His face is oval. The eyebrows are curving. The eyes are close-set (details unclear). The mouth is large with thin lips. The cheeks are fleshy. The neck is long.

He wears a garment, possibly a tunic, with a wide neckline decorated with a beaded band. The folds of the tunic are rendered by vertical and curving grooves.

358. FRAGMENT OF A MALE FIGURE

DATABASE NUMBER: NCG100.
LOCATION: Copenhagen, Ny Carlsberg Glyptotek, inv. no. IN 1125.
CONTEXT: —
ACQUISITION HISTORY: Løytved in Syria.
MEASUREMENTS: Height: 15 cm. Width: 14 cm. Depth: 14 cm. Height of head: 12.5 cm.
MATERIAL: Limestone, white/yellow.
PRESERVATION: All sides are broken off. The lower part of the portrait is broken off at the base of the neck. The hair, the nose, and the chin are chipped. Cracks run across the face and neck.
TECHNICAL DESCRIPTION: Small tooth chisel marks are on the surface of the background. There are flat chisel marks on the face.

DATE: A.D. 170–200 (Ploug 1995: A.D. 230–250).
REFERENCES: Simonsen 1889, 51 cat. G 36 pl. 16; Hvidberg-Hansen – Ploug 1993, 142 cat. 99; Ploug 1995, 231 f. cat. 99; Raja 2019a, 311 cat. 115.

OBJECT DESCRIPTION
The object depicts a male head and a part of the left shoulder. The relief ground is preserved at the left side of the figure's head.

PORTRAIT
The figure is shown frontally. The head is turned to his left.

The hair is arranged in two rows of snail-shell curls. The individual strands of hair are indicated by incised lines. His face is oval. The eyebrows are rendered by thin, curving, incised lines starting from the root of the nose. The eyes are small and almond-shaped, with thick upper eyelids. The end of the upper eyelids extends downwards and beyond that of the lower eyelids. The eyeballs are blank. The nose is short and wide. The alae are indicated by incised lines. The mouth is small, with a full lower lip. The chin is pointed. The neck is short and wide with two curving grooves.

The left shoulder is visible.

359. FRAGMENT OF A FEMALE FIGURE

DATABASE NUMBER: PM683.
LOCATION: Palmyra, Palmyra Museum, inv. no. CD 89.
CONTEXT: Secondary context: Found (17.05.1960) in the northern part of the Tetrapylon in the Camp of Diocletian, in a later wall.
ACQUISITION HISTORY: —
MEASUREMENTS: Height: 46 cm. Width: 40 cm. Depth: 23 cm.
MATERIAL: Limestone, grey.
PRESERVATION: The upper part is broken off at the waist and the lower part is broken off at the ankles.
TECHNICAL DESCRIPTION: —
DATE: A.D. 170–200 (Michalowski: A.D. 100–150).
REFERENCES: Michalowski 1962, 148 f. cat. 19 fig. 163; Krag 2018, 313 cat. 556.

OBJECT DESCRIPTION
The object depicts a seated female.

PORTRAIT
The figure is shown frontally; the legs are bent, and the knees are rendered under the drapery.

She wears a himation. The folds are rendered by oblique, wide grooves.

The right hand of the figure is holding a fold of the himation. A zigzag-shaped fold falls from under the hand.

A.D. 180–200

360. FRAGMENT OF A FEMALE FIGURE

DATABASE NUMBER: NCG044.
LOCATION: Copenhagen, Ny Carlsberg Glyptotek, inv. no. IN 1150.
CONTEXT: —
ACQUISITION HISTORY: Puttmann in Syria.
MEASUREMENTS: Height: 58 cm. Width: 29 cm. Depth: 24 cm. Height of head: 16 cm. Width of head: 12.5 cm.
MATERIAL: Limestone, white/grey.
PRESERVATION: The lower part of the figure is broken off at the waist. The top of the hair and a section at the left strand over the forehead, the nose, the bracelet on the left wrist, and the back of the palm of the left hand are chipped. There are several cracks across the surface.
TECHNICAL DESCRIPTION: She has traces of black pigment in her pupils. The back of the sculpture has been roughly cut.
DATE: A.D. 180–200 (Ploug 1995: A.D. 210–230).
REFERENCES: Ingholt Archives, PS 450; Ingholt 1928, 142; Ingholt 1935, 68 n. 53; Ingholt 1938, 117 n. 11; el-Chehadeh 1972, 90 n. 94; Colledge 1976, 263; Parlasca 1976, 40 n. 45, e; Parlasca 1987b, 108 f. 112 fig. 2; Hvidberg-Hansen – Ploug 1993, 133 cat. 87; Ploug 1995, 212–214 cat. 87; Krag 2016, 188 f. fig. 6; Krag 2018, 42 n. 153. 154; 58 n. 304. 311; 62 n. 350; 73 n. 47. 51; 74 n. 57; 102 n. 66; 103 n. 73; 381 cat. 805; Raja 2019a, 254 f. cat. 78.

Cat. 360, Pl. 64

OBJECT DESCRIPTION
The object depicts a standing female.

PORTRAIT

The figure is shown frontally. The right arm falls to the side; the left arm is bent and raised to the chest.

The hair directly over the forehead is centrally parted and covers most of the ears. The individual strands of hair are rendered by slightly oblique grooves. The rest of the hair is gathered upwards in a series of plaits indicated by vertical grooves with diagonal, incised lines on either side. At the top, the hair is gathered in a coiled bun. She wears a veil at the back of the hair that falls over both shoulders and covers most of the body. The right edge of the veil proceeds across the chest in a curving fold and falls over the left shoulder. Her face is oval and fleshy. The eyebrows are rendered by thin, curving ridges starting from the root of the nose. The eyes are small and almond-shaped, with thick upper eyelids. The end of the upper eyelids extends downwards and beyond that of the lower eyelids. The irises are circular, touching the upper eyelids, and indicated by black pigment. The earlobes are visible, and she wears single large, round beads as earrings (Colledge classification: J). The nose is straight and wide. The mouth is wide with a full lower lip. The chin is round, and she has a double chin. The neck is short and wide with two curving grooves. She wears a plain, thick hoop necklace with a round pendant suspended by a narrow sleeve from the centre.

With the right hand, she holds a fold of the veil. The index finger is extended. With the left hand, she holds a fold of the veil that crosses the chest. The thumb, index, and the little finger are extended. She wears a thick, wide hoop bracelet on the left wrist with an oval bezel, indicating an inlay.

361. FRAGMENT OF A FEMALE FIGURE

DATABASE NUMBER: PM263.
LOCATION: Palmyra, Palmyra Museum, inv. no. CD 51.
CONTEXT: Secondary: Found (1. and 6.05.1962) at the foundations of the wall of the Great Gate in the Camp of Diocletian to the south of the entrance.
ACQUISITION HISTORY: —
MEASUREMENTS: Height: 68 cm. Width: 37 cm. Depth: 26 cm.
MATERIAL: Limestone, white.
PRESERVATION: The background is broken off. The figure is broken into two pieces that have been reattached. The head is broken off at the neck. The right arm is broken off at the shoulder. The left hand is broken off. The right hip and thigh are broken off. Both legs are broken off at the knees.
TECHNICAL DESCRIPTION: —
DATE: A.D. 180–200 (Michalowski 1964: AD 100–130).
REFERENCES: Michalowski 1964, 84 f. cat. 18 fig. 118; Krag 2018, 58 n. 304; 103 n. 74; 382 cat. 807.

OBJECT DESCRIPTION

The object depicts a standing female.

Cat. 361

PORTRAIT

The figure is shown frontally. The left arm is bent and raised in front of the chest.

She wears a veil. The veil covers the body. One end of the veil falls in a curving fold over the chest and falls over the left shoulder. One fold of the veil falls in front of the middle of the chest.

She wears a tunic. The tunic has a short, v-shaped neckline and short sleeves that reach below the elbow.

With the left hand she holds the curving edge of the veil.

362. FRAGMENTS OF A RELIEF

DATABASE NUMBER: PM932.
LOCATION: Palmyra, Palmyra Museum, inv. no. CD 25.
CONTEXT: Secondary context: Found (28.04.1962) west of the ramp of the Great Gate in the Camp of Diocletian.
ACQUISITION HISTORY: —
MEASUREMENTS: Height: 39 cm. Width: 40 cm. Depth: 24 cm.
MATERIAL: Limestone, white.
PRESERVATION: The object is broken off on all four sides. Portrait A: Only the left hand is preserved. Portrait B: The head is broken off at the base of the neck. The lower part of the right arm, the left side of the torso, and the lower part of the body is broken off. The surface at the abdomen is chipped.
TECHNICAL DESCRIPTION: —
DATE: A.D. 180–200.
REFERENCES: Michalowski 1964, 100 cat. 36 fig. 137.

OBJECT DESCRIPTION
The object depicts a standing male figure. On his arm is the hand of a second figure.

PORTRAIT A: FIGURE
The left hand is placed on the arm of the reclining figure.

PORTRAIT B: RECLINING MALE
The figure is shown frontally. The right arm is extended and held away from the body.

He wears a tunic. The tunic has a large, round neckline. It is decorated with a band (clavus) starting from the right side of the neckline and extends downwards. The folds of the tunic are indicated by oblique grooves on the arm and curving grooves on the torso.

The outline of an object is visible in front of the abdomen, possibly from a bowl held with the fingertips.

363. FRAGMENT OF A FEMALE FIGURE

DATABASE NUMBER: PM268.
LOCATION: Palmyra, Palmyra Museum, inv. no. CD 109.
CONTEXT: Secondary context: Found (08.05.1962) at the foundations of the Great Gate in the Camp of Diocletian.
ACQUISITION HISTORY: —
MEASUREMENTS: Height: 26 cm. Width: 39 cm. Depth: 21 cm.
MATERIAL: Limestone, grey.
PRESERVATION: The background is broken off. The head of the figure is broken off at the neck. The figure is broken off below the chest.
TECHNICAL DESCRIPTION: —
DATE: A.D. 180–200.
REFERENCES: Michalowski 1964, 86 cat. 20 fig. 120; Krag 2018, 58 n. 304; 103 n. 74; 382 cat. 810.

OBJECT DESCRIPTION
The object depicts a female figure.

PORTRAIT
The figure is depicted frontally. Her left arm is bent and raised in front of the chest.

She wears a veil. The veil covers the body. It falls in a curving fold across the chest and falls over the left shoulder.

She wears a tunic. The tunic has a round neckline and short sleeves that reach below the elbows.

She wears a thick, plain hoop bracelet on the wrist of the left hand. With the left hand she holds the curving fold of the veil. The index and the little finger are extended.

A.D. 180–240

364. FRAGMENT OF A BANQUETING RELIEF

DATABASE NUMBER: PM933.
LOCATION: Palmyra, Palmyra Museum, inv. no. CD12.
CONTEXT: Secondary context. Found (27.05.1962) at the foundations of the Great Gate of the Camp of Diocletian.
ACQUISITION HISTORY: —
MEASUREMENTS: Height: 14 cm. Width: 35 cm. Depth: 28 cm.
MATERIAL: Limestone, white.
PRESERVATION: The figure is broken off at the neck, lower arms, and lower body.
TECHNICAL DESCRIPTION: —
DATE: A.D. 180–240.
REFERENCES: Michalowski 1964, 102 f. cat. 38 fig. 139.

OBJECT DESCRIPTION
The object depicts the torso of a figure.

PORTRAIT
The figure is depicted turning slightly to its left. The right arm is lowered and crosses the chest.

The figure wears a garment that falls with curving grooves over the body and covers the torso completely, perhaps a himation or mantle.

A.D. 200–220

365. FEMALE FIGURE

DATABASE NUMBER: NCG119.
LOCATION: Copenhagen, Ny Carlsberg Glyptotek, inv. no. IN 1065.
CONTEXT: —
ACQUISITION HISTORY: Løytved in Syria.

Cat. 365, Pl. 65

MEASUREMENTS: Height: 67.5 cm. Width: 35 cm. Depth: 25 cm. Height of head: 17 cm. Width of head: 16.5 cm. Depth of head: 16.5 cm.
MATERIAL: Limestone, white/yellow.
PRESERVATION: The head has been reattached. The nose, right shoulder, and part of the upper arm, the lower right arm above the wrist, and the hand are broken off. The left eyebrow and necklace are chipped.
TECHNICAL DESCRIPTION: The portrait is roughly cut on the back. There are flat chisel marks on the clothing, face, and neck. Black pigment is visible in the corners of the eyes and on the iris. The inscriptions have traces of red pigment.
DATE: A.D. 200–220 (Ploug 1995: A.D. 230–250).
REFERENCES: Ingholt Archives, PS 458; Simonsen 1889, 35 f. cat. D 13 pl. 16; Poulsen 1921, 87 f.; Chabot 1922, 116 f. 120 cat. 34 pl. 30, 3; Ingholt 1928, 143; Mackay 1949, 167 pl. 52, 1; du Mesnil du Buisson 1962, 282; Michalowski 1964, 98 n. 31; Colledge 1976, 76 n. 239; Sadurska 1977, 151 n. 81; Drijvers 1982, 711 f. 720 pl. 2; Parlasca 1988, 217 f. pl. 46, d; Hvidberg-Hansen – Ploug 1993, 135 f. cat. 89; Ploug 1995, 216 f. cat. 89; Sokolowski 2014, 381 f. fig. 14; Krag 2015, 106 fig. 3; Krag 2018, 15 n. 64; 16 n. 73; 25 n. 178; 42 n. 153. 154. 156; 49 n. 229; 53 n. 260; 56 n. 291; 62 n. 350; 73 n. 47; 58 n. 304; 102 n. 66; 103 n. 73; 105 n. 85. 87. 89; 381 cat. 804; Raja 2019a, 262 f. cat. 81; Raja – Yon 2022, 217 f. cat. 35. Inscription: Simonsen 1889, 35 f. cat. D 13 inscription 43; Lidzbarski 1898, 236; Chabot 1922, 116 f. 120 cat. 34; Drijvers 1982, 711 f.; Parlasca 1988, 217 f. pl. 46, d; Hvidberg-Hansen – Ploug 1993, 135 f. cat. 89; Ploug 1995, 216 f. cat. 89; Hvidberg-Hansen 1998, 77 f. cat. 89; Yon 2012, 417 f. cat. 560; Krag 2018, 381 cat. 804; Raja 2019a, 262 f. cat. 81; Raja – Yon 2022, 217 f.

OBJECT DESCRIPTION
The object depicts a standing female.

INSCRIPTIONS
INSCRIPTION 1
SCRIPT: Greek.
LOCATION ON RELIEF: On the right key.
TRANSCRIPTION: ΛΝΥ.
TRANSLATION: —

INSCRIPTION 2
SCRIPT: Palmyrene Aramaic.
LOCATION ON RELIEF: On the middle key.
TRANSCRIPTION: BT ʿLMʾ.
TRANSLATION: House of eternity.

INSCRIPTION 3
SCRIPT: Greek.
LOCATION ON RELIEF: On the left key.
TRANSCRIPTION: ΦΗΕΛΙ.
TRANSLATION: —

CIS no. 4490; PAT no. 0851.

COMMENT: Inscription 1: Could be read as ΑΝΥ and be the date 451 (A.D. 139/140). Inscription 3: Most probably Greek letters written at random. There are several suggestions for how this is to be read (see Yon 2012, 418 cat. 560), one suggestion being Θ(εοῦ) Ἡελί(ου) (Theou Eliou) »Belonging to the Helios«. See also Drijvers 1982; Kaizer 2010; Yon 2018 for discussion of inscribed keys.

PORTRAIT

The figure is shown frontally. The left arm is bent in front of the torso.

The hair is short and wavy, centrally parted, and covers most of the ears. It reaches to the top of the neck. A small, diamond-shaped lock is depicted at the centre of the forehead. The individual strands of hair are rendered by curving grooves. Her face is square and fleshy. The eyebrows are rendered by thin, curving ridges starting from the root of the nose. The eyes are small, almond-shaped, and slanting with thick upper eyelids. The end of the upper eyelids extends downwards and beyond that of the lower eyelids. The irises, touching the upper eyelids, are indicated by incised circles. The earlobes are visible, and she wears earrings with three juxtaposed round beads, suspended from the lobes by a thin element, possibly the hook (Colledge classification: K). The nose is straight and wide. The mouth is small, with full lips. The chin is pointed, and she has a double chin. The neck is long and wide with two curving grooves. She wears a plain, thick hoop necklace at the base of the neck.

She wears a tunic. It has a wide, v-shaped neckline and short, wide sleeves that reach below the elbow. The tunic has an overfold below the waist. The folds of the tunic are indicated by wide, curving grooves over the torso, and oblique grooves over the arms and lower body.

With her left hand, she holds three L-shaped keys. Over her index finger an object in the shape of a loop is depicted, perhaps a form of key holder. Below her palm and between the two keys is a narrow, rectangular object. Each of the keys is inscribed. The thumb and the index finger are extended.

366. FRAGMENT OF A MALE FIGURE

DATABASE NUMBER: PM976.
LOCATION: Unknown.
CONTEXT: —
ACQUISITION HISTORY: —
MEASUREMENTS: —
MATERIAL: Limestone.
PRESERVATION: The head is broken off at the base of the neck and the right and lower part of the body is broken off horizontally at the right shoulder and at the waist. The left hand is fragmented.
TECHNICAL DESCRIPTION: —
DATE: A.D. 200–220.

Cat. 366

REFERENCES: Ingholt Archive PS 908; IA_NCG_Portrait2016_020.

OBJECT DESCRIPTION

The object depicts a reclining male figure. He rests the left arm against a cushion. It is decorated with a band with a running scroll with central rosettes set between beaded bands. Curving grooves indicate the texture of the fabric.

PORTRAIT

The figure is shown frontally. The left arm is bent in front of the torso.

He wears a tunic and a himation. The tunic has a wide, v-shaped neckline. The folds of the tunic are rendered by curving grooves. Over the tunic, he wears a himation. It is folded over his left shoulder and arm, leaving most of the chest and hand free, and is folded around the left wrist. The folds of the himation are rendered by vertical grooves.

He holds a vessel in his left hand (details unclear).

367. FRAGMENT OF A BANQUETING RELIEF

DATABASE NUMBER: UNK050.
LOCATION: Unknown.
CONTEXT: —
ACQUISITION HISTORY: —
MEASUREMENTS: —
MATERIAL: Limestone.
PRESERVATION: Broken on the left side. The head is broken off at the top of the neck. The left lower arm is missing. The bowl and part of the cushion are chipped. Some garment to the left indicates a second figure.
TECHNICAL DESCRIPTION: —
DATE: A.D. 200–220.
REFERENCES: Ingholt Archives, IA_NCG_Portrait2016_020.

OBJECT DESCRIPTION

The object depicts a reclining male figure. He rests the left arm against a cushion with a decorated wide band with a leaf motif set between beaded bands. Curving grooves indicate the texture of the fabric.

PORTRAIT A: RECLINING MALE

The figure is shown frontally. The right arm is bent and held to the torso. The left arm is bent and held to the chest.

The neck is wide with one curving groove.

He wears a tunic and a himation. The tunic has a wide, v-shaped neckline and short, loose sleeves. The folds of the tunic are rendered by curving grooves at the chest and oblique grooves on the sleeve. Over the tunic, he wears a himation. It is wrapped around the left shoulder and arm, leaving most of the upper torso and hand free. It proceeds in a curving fold across the lower torso and falls over the right side. The edge crossing the torso is scalloped. An s-shaped fold falls from under his left hand. The folds of the himation are rendered by oblique and curving grooves.

He holds an oblong object with a diamond pattern, possibly a branch, in his right hand. With the palm of the left hand turned upwards, he holds a wide bowl with his fingertips (details unclear).

368. FRAGMENT OF A BANQUETING SCENE

DATABASE NUMBER: PM292.
LOCATION: Palmyra, Palmyra Museum, inv. no. CD64, CD112.
CONTEXT: Secondary context: Found (12/21.05.1960) in the south-western part of the Tetrapylon in the Camp of Diocletian.
ACQUISITION HISTORY: —
MEASUREMENTS: Height: 35 cm. Width: 33 cm. Depth: 10 cm.
MATERIAL: Limestone, white.
PRESERVATION: Broken on all sides. The head is broken off at the base of the neck. A fragment is broken off from the right arm and the lower part of the tunic. The surface is weathered.
TECHNICAL DESCRIPTION: —
DATE: A.D. 200–220.
REFERENCES: Michalowski 1962, 156 cat. 26 fig. 171.

OBJECT DESCRIPTION

The object depicts the torso and arms of a male figure.

PORTRAIT

The figure is shown frontally. Both arms are bent; the right held to the waist and the left held to the torso.

He wears a tunic and a himation. The tunic has long, tight-fitting sleeves. The folds of the tunic are rendered by curving and oblique grooves. Over the tunic, he wears a himation. It is wrapped around his right shoulder and arm, leaving most of the chest and hand free. One end of the himation crosses the hip diagonally. The folds of the himation are rendered by oblique grooves.

He holds a leaf in his right hand. The contours of the leaves are rendered by incised lines. With his left hand, he pulls a fold of the himation from the opposite side.

Cat. 367

369. FRAGMENT OF A BANQUETING RELIEF

DATABASE NUMBER: PM787.
LOCATION: Palmyra, Palmyra Museum, inv. no. 169, 300, 301, 228.
CONTEXT: Secondary context: Found (05.10.1955) behind portal S1 and (03.10.1955) behind portal C1 at the Temple of Baalshamin.
ACQUISITION HISTORY: —
MEASUREMENTS: Height: 31 cm. Width: 39 cm. Depth: 24 cm.
MATERIAL: Limestone.
PRESERVATION: The object is preserved in four fragments. Only part of the lower torso, part of the upper legs, and the hands are preserved.
TECHNICAL DESCRIPTION: —
DATE: A.D. 200–220 (Dunant – Stucky 2000: A.D. 150–200).
REFERENCES: Dunant – Stucky 2000, 113 cat. 123 pl. 29.

OBJECT DESCRIPTION
The object is composed of four fragments and depicts a reclining figure.

PORTRAIT
The figure is shown in three-quarter view. The right hand rests on the right knee, the left is held in front of the torso. The right leg is bent and raised.

The figure wears a himation. It falls along the left side of the body and is wrapped around the waist. It covers the legs. The folds of the himation are rendered by curving grooves.

The right hand rests on the right knee. Further down the shin, a round object with round elements is depicted: the figure possibly holds a bunch of grapes. The fingers on the right hand are slightly bent. With the left hand, the figure holds a skyphos. The skyphos has a conical foot, and the lower part of the body is decorated with a tongue pattern. A moulded horizontal line is rendered at the middle of the body. The rim is projecting. The left index finger and the thumb are extended.

370. LOCULUS RELIEF WITH MALE

DATABASE NUMBER: UNK234.
LOCATION: Unknown.
CONTEXT: —
ACQUISITION HISTORY: —
MEASUREMENTS: —
MATERIAL: Limestone.
PRESERVATION: Only a small part of the background has been preserved to the right of the head. The head is broken off at the base of the neck. The nose is missing and the mouth is heavily chipped.
TECHNICAL DESCRIPTION: —
DATE: AD 200–240.
REFERENCES: Ingholt Archives, IA_NCG_Portrait2016_097.

Cat. 370

OBJECT DESCRIPTION
The object depicts a male.

PORTRAIT
The figure is shown frontally.

His hair is arranged in two rows of snail-shell curls around his head. The individual strands of hair are indicated by incised lines. His face is round. The eyebrows are curving, rendered by incised lines, and starting from the root of the nose. The eyes are close-set and almond-shaped with thick eyelids. The irises are indicated by incised circles and the pupils by punch holes. Only the earlobes are visible under the hair. The nose is short. He has a beard that starts from the temples and covers the outer side of the cheeks and the chin. The facial hair is rendered by wavy curls arranged in rows. He might also have a bead covering the upper lip (details unclear). The mouth is wide. The chin is round. The neck is wide with two curving grooves.

Cat. 371

OBJECT DESCRIPTION
The object depicts a standing male.

PORTRAIT
The figure is shown frontally. The left arm is bent and held to the torso.

He wears a ›Parthian-style‹ tunic with a small, round neckline. At the middle, the tunic has a wide band with a floral pattern between two beaded bands extending downwards. The folds of the tunic are rendered by curving and oblique grooves.

With his left hand, he is holding the lower part of an animal, possibly a lamb. The fur is indicated by curving, incised lines.

372. FRAGMENT OF A MALE FIGURE

DATABASE NUMBER: UNK056.
LOCATION: —
CONTEXT: —
ACQUISITION HISTORY: —
MEASUREMENTS: —
MATERIAL: Limestone.
PRESERVATION: Only the upper part of the body, right arm and hand, and upper left arm of the figure are preserved. The surface is weathered. The right hand is fragmented. Part of the clothing is chipped.
TECHNICAL DESCRIPTION: —
DATE: A.D. 200–240.
REFERENCES: Ingholt Archives, IA_NCG_Portrait2016_032.

Cat. 372

A.D. 200–240

371. FRAGMENT OF A MALE FIGURE

DATABASE NUMBER: PM591.
LOCATION: Palmyra, Palmyra Museum, inv. no. unknown.
CONTEXT: —
ACQUISITION HISTORY: —
MEASUREMENTS: —
MATERIAL: Limestone.
PRESERVATION: The background is broken off. The head is broken off at the middle of the neck. The right side is broken off diagonally through the right shoulder, and the lower part is broken off at the knees. The left arm and the head of the animal are chipped. The surface is weathered.
TECHNICAL DESCRIPTION: —
DATE: A.D. 200–240.
REFERENCES: Ingholt Archives, PS 1017.

Cat. 373

OBJECT DESCRIPTION
The object depicts a standing male figure.

PORTRAIT
The figure is shown frontally. The right arm is bent and held in front of the torso.

He wears a tunic and a himation. The tunic has a wide v-shaped neckline and short, loose-fitting sleeves. The folds of the tunic are indicated by wide, oblique and curving grooves. Over the tunic, he wears a himation. The himation covers the back of the right arm and shoulder, is wrapped around the waist, crosses the torso diagonally, and passes over the left shoulder. Another fold of the himation extends down from the left shoulder. The folds of the himation are indicated by wide, oblique grooves.

With his right hand, he holds the fold of the himation that extends down from the left shoulder.

373. FRAGMENT OF FIGURE

DATABASE NUMBER: UNK060.
LOCATION: —
CONTEXT: —
ACQUISITION HISTORY: —
MEASUREMENTS: —
MATERIAL: Limestone.
PRESERVATION: Only the lower part of the torso, lower left arm and hand, and upper part of the lower body are preserved. The surface is weathered. Part of the clothing is chipped.
TECHNICAL DESCRIPTION: —
DATE: A.D. 200–240.
REFERENCES: Ingholt Archives, IA_NCG_Portrait2016_032.

OBJECT DESCRIPTION
The object depicts a standing figure of unknown gender.

PORTRAIT
The figure is shown frontally. The left arm is extended and held along the left side.

The figure wears a himation. The himation is wrapped around the torso, lower body, and left arm, leaving only the left hand free. The folds of the himation are indicated by wide, oblique and curving grooves.

374. FRAGMENT OF A BANQUETING RELIEF

DATABASE NUMBER: MBE006.
LOCATION: Beirut, National Museum, inv. no. unknown.
CONTEXT: —
ACQUISITION HISTORY: —
MEASUREMENTS: —
MATERIAL: Limestone.
PRESERVATION: Broken on all sides. Only the lower arm, hand, and part of the leg and knee are preserved.
TECHNICAL DESCRIPTION: —
DATE: A.D. 200–240.
REFERENCES: Ingholt Archives, PS 1080; Ingholt 1938, 99 pl. 36, 3.

OBJECT DESCRIPTION
The object depicts part of a reclining figure.

PORTRAIT
The figure wears a >Parthian-style< tunic and >Parthian-style< trousers. The tunic has long, tight-fitting sleeves. The cuffs of the sleeves are decorated with a running scroll with six-petal rosettes followed by a beaded band. The folds of the tunic are rendered by curving grooves. The trouser leg is decorated with a band extending downwards and decorated with serrated leaves, set between beaded bands. The midribs of the leaves are

Cat. 374

rendered by incised lines. The folds of the trousers are rendered by oblique grooves. Along his thigh, he has an object with a pointed end and a rectangular main body: a sheathed dagger.

He holds a pinecone in his right hand. The contours of the shells are rendered by incised lines. The top of the pinecone has a six-petal rosette. The nails are indicated by fine, curving, incised lines.

A.D. 200–273

375. FRAGMENT OF A FEMALE FIGURE

DATABASE NUMBER: UNK061.
LOCATION: —
CONTEXT: —
ACQUISITION HISTORY: —
MEASUREMENTS: —
MATERIAL: Limestone.
PRESERVATION: Only the torso is preserved. The head, right arm, and right side of the torso, as well as the left hand and lower arm are missing.
TECHNICAL DESCRIPTION: —
DATE: A.D. 200–273.
REFERENCES: IA_NCG_Portrait2016_032Pic1.

OBJECT DESCRIPTION
The fragment depicts a female figure.

PORTRAIT
Her left arm is bent and raised to the shoulder.

Cat. 375

She wears three necklaces. The first is composed of a wide hoop with a central triangular pendant, worn at the base of the neck. The second is composed of alternating round and square pendants with beaded borders linked by beaded elements, worn above the collarbone. The third necklace is composed of a twisted chain with a central teardrop-shaped pendant, worn high on the chest.

She wears a tunic and a himation. The folds of the tunic are rendered by oblique grooves. Over the tunic, she wears a himation. It falls over the left shoulder, crosses the chest diagonally, and runs under the right arm. The folds of the himation are indicated by wide, curving and oblique grooves. It is fastened at the shoulder with a circular brooch with a raised centre (details unclear).

376. FRAGMENT OF A MALE FIGURE

DATABASE NUMBER: UNK095.
LOCATION: Unknown location.
CONTEXT: —
ACQUISITION HISTORY: —
MEASUREMENTS: —
MATERIAL: Limestone.
PRESERVATION: The background is broken off. The upper part of the figure is broken off at the base of the neck. The lower part of the figure is broken off at the waist. The left lower arm is broken off.
TECHNICAL DESCRIPTION: —
DATE: A.D. 200–273.
REFERENCES: Ingholt Archives, PS 923.

OBJECT DESCRIPTION
The object depicts a male bust.

PORTRAIT
The figure is shown frontally. His right arm is bent and held in front of the chest. The left arm falls to the side.

He wears a tunic and a himation. The tunic has a wide v-shaped neckline. The folds of the tunic are rendered by wide, curving grooves. Over the tunic, he wears a himation. The himation is wrapped around the right shoulder and arm, leaving only part of the chest and the right hand free. One fold of the himation crosses the chest diagonally and falls over the left shoulder (>arm-sling< type), covering the left arm. The folds of the himation are indicated by curving grooves under the right wrist and between the left arm and the body, and oblique grooves at the sides of the arms and the body.

With his right hand, he lightly holds the diagonal fold of the himation. The thumb is extended, the other fingers are slightly bent.

377. MALE BUST

DATABASE NUMBER: PM643.
LOCATION: Palmyra, Palmyra Museum, inv. no. CD 58/73.
CONTEXT: Found in later construction in the northern part of the Via Praetoria.
ACQUISITION HISTORY: —
MEASUREMENTS: Height: 23 cm. Width: 27 cm. Depth: 15 cm.
MATERIAL: Limestone, white.
PRESERVATION: Only the torso has been preserved. The neck and arms are chipped.
TECHNICAL DESCRIPTION: —
DATE: A.D. 200–273.
REFERENCES: Gawlikowski 1984, 101 cat. 33 pl. 80, 168.

OBJECT DESCRIPTION
The object is rectangular in shape and depicts an armless male bust. Below the figure, a beaded frame is depicted.

PORTRAIT
The figure is shown frontally. The arms are not depicted. The head is missing.

He wears a tunic and a himation. The tunic has a small round neckline and wide sleeves. The folds of the tunic are rendered by narrow curving grooves. Over the tunic, he wears

Cat. 376

Cat. 377

a himation. The himation is wrapped around the left shoulder and arm. It is fastened with a brooch on his right shoulder. The folds of the himation are rendered by curving grooves over the torso.

378. FRAGMENT OF A FEMALE FIGURE

DATABASE NUMBER: PM623.
LOCATION: Palmyra, Palmyra Museum, inv. no. CD 42.
CONTEXT: Secondary context: Found (24.05.1959) in the rubble of the Via Praetoria to the right of the Gate.
ACQUISITION HISTORY: —
MEASUREMENTS: Height: 23 cm. Width: 28 cm. Depth: 16 cm.
MATERIAL: Limestone, grey.
PRESERVATION: Only a fragment of the right arm is preserved.
TECHNICAL DESCRIPTION: —
DATE: A.D. 200–273.
REFERENCES: Michalowski 1960, 103 cat. 22 fig. 111.

OBJECT DESCRIPTION
The object depicts part of the body of a female figure.

PORTRAIT
The figure is shown frontally. She is seated. The right arm is bent.
She wears a veil and a garment that covers the body. With the right hand she holds the edge of the veil that falls over the knee.
She wears a bracelet on the right wrist (other detail unclear).

379. FRAGMENT OF A BANQUETING RELIEF

DATABASE NUMBER: PM781.
LOCATION: Palmyra, Palmyra Museum, inv. no. CD 76.
CONTEXT: Secondary context: Found (29.04.1961) in the rubble in front of the Great Gate.
ACQUISITION HISTORY: —
MEASUREMENTS: Height: 50 cm. Width: 48 cm. Depth: 15 cm.
MATERIAL: Limestone, white.
PRESERVATION: The relief is broken off on all sides. Part of the foot and the lower leg of the figure, as well as part of the background over the leg and of the mattress under the foot survive.
TECHNICAL DESCRIPTION: —
DATE: A.D. 200–273.
REFERENCES: Michalowski 1963, 163 cat. 57 fig. 214.

OBJECT DESCRIPTION
The object depicts part of the lower leg of a reclining figure. The figure rests on a mattress (other details unclear).

PORTRAIT
The figure is shown in profile. His leg is bent.

Cat. 379

He wears ›Parthian‹ trousers (only part of the leg is visible). The folds of the trouser legs are rendered by curving grooves. He wears boots (only one is visible). The boot is decorated with rosettes inside running scrolls in the body and has a beaded border and a band with a running dog motif over the ankle. It is tied at the ankle with a band fastened with a round buckle.

380. FRAGMENT OF A BANQUETING RELIEF

DATABASE NUMBER: PM846.
LOCATION: Palmyra, Palmyra Museum, inv. no. CD 132.
CONTEXT: Secondary context: Found (08.05.1962) in the foundations of the (later) wall built at the north side of the north wall of the Forum.
ACQUISITION HISTORY: —
MEASUREMENTS: Height: 62 cm. Width: 48 cm. Depth: 25 cm.
MATERIAL: Limestone, grey.
PRESERVATION: The relief is broken off on all sides. Only part of the mattress and the background next to a lower leg survive. The background and the surface of the leg are heavily chipped. The middle of the upper cushion is broken off.
TECHNICAL DESCRIPTION: —
DATE: A.D. 200–273.

REFERENCES: Michalowski 1964, 104 cat. 40 fig. 141.

OBJECT DESCRIPTION

The object depicts the lower leg of a reclining figure. He rests on a mattress decorated with a pattern of intersecting lozenges with four-petal cruciform flowers. A beaded element is at the point where the lozenges intersect. Two round cushions, one on top of the other, are depicted on the right side of the fragment. They are decorated in the middle with a broad band with serrated leaves, set between two beaded bands.

PORTRAIT

The lower leg of the figure is shown in profile (only the outline is visible).

381. FRAGMENT OF A BANQUETING RELIEF

DATABASE NUMBER: PM1021.
LOCATION: Palmyra, Palmyra Museum, inv. no. B 1824.
CONTEXT: Secondary context: Found (13.09.1954) in portico C3, Sanctuary of Baalshamin.
ACQUISITION HISTORY: —
MEASUREMENTS: Height: 25 cm. Width: 17.5 cm. Depth: 15 cm.
MATERIAL: Limestone, white.
PRESERVATION: The relief is broken off on all sides. Only part of the hand and knee of the figure survive.
TECHNICAL DESCRIPTION: —
DATE: A.D. 200–273.
REFERENCES: Dunant – Stucky 2000, 113 cat. 124 pl. 29.

OBJECT DESCRIPTION

The object depicts a reclining figure.

PORTRAIT

The leg of the figure is shown in profile, the hand is shown frontally. His right hand rests on the raised right knee.

He wears >Parthian-style< trousers. The trouser legs are decorated with a band with serrated leaves.

He wears a thick hoop finger ring with an oval bezel on the little finger of the right hand. The nails are indicated by fine incised lines.

382. FRAGMENT OF A BANQUETING RELIEF

DATABASE NUMBER: PM1019.
LOCATION: Palmyra, Palmyra Museum, inv. no. CD 30/73.
CONTEXT: Secondary context: Found in the debris inside the pottery kiln in the central passage of the Via Praetoria.
ACQUISITION HISTORY: —
MEASUREMENTS: Height: 23 cm. Width: 25 cm. Depth: 25 cm.
MATERIAL: Limestone, white.
PRESERVATION: The relief is broken off on all sides. Only part of the waist and thigh of the figure survives in two joining pieces.
TECHNICAL DESCRIPTION: —
DATE: A.D. 200–273.
REFERENCES: Gawlikowski 1984, 109 cat. 71 pl. 92, 204.

Cat. 382

OBJECT DESCRIPTION
The object depicts a reclining figure from a banqueting relief. A fragment of the mattress was found together with the fragments of the figure. The mattress is decorated with an intersecting lozenges pattern with flowers.

PORTRAIT
The figure is shown in three-quarter view.

He wears a ›Parthian-style‹ tunic. The tunic has a broad band between two beaded bands extending downwards. The band is decorated with a running scroll with four-petal flowers. He also wears a thin band belt: the two ends of the belt are looped twice around the belt.

383. FRAGMENT OF A BANQUETING RELIEF

DATABASE NUMBER: PM1017.
LOCATION: Palmyra, Palmyra Museum, inv. no. CD 9/66.
CONTEXT: Secondary context: Found in part II of the Temple of the Standards, Temple des Enseignes, Camp of Diocletian.
ACQUISITION HISTORY: —
MEASUREMENTS: Height: 32 cm. Width: 23 cm. Depth: 10 cm.
MATERIAL: Limestone, white.
PRESERVATION: The relief is broken off on all sides. Only part of the thigh survives.
TECHNICAL DESCRIPTION: —
DATE: A.D. 200–273.
REFERENCES: Gawlikowski 1984, 108 cat. 69 pl. 92, 203.

OBJECT DESCRIPTION
The object depicts the thigh of a standing figure from a banqueting relief.

Cat. 383

PORTRAIT

The figure is shown frontally.

He wears a >Parthian-style< tunic and >Parthian-style< trousers. The tunic is decorated at the hem with a beaded band. The folds of the tunic are rendered by oblique grooves. The trouser legs have a broad band between beaded bands extending downwards in the middle. The band is decorated with a running scroll with alternating rosettes of flowers with round and twisted petals. The folds of the trouser leg are rendered by curving grooves.

384. FRAGMENT OF A BANQUETING RELIEF

DATABASE NUMBER: PM1016.
LOCATION: Palmyra, Palmyra Museum, inv. no. CD 62/73.
CONTEXT: Secondary context: Found in a late wall, at the south side of the east Via Praetoria.
ACQUISITION HISTORY: —
MEASUREMENTS: Height: 19 cm. Width: 35 cm. Depth: 26 cm.
MATERIAL: Limestone, white.
PRESERVATION: The relief is broken off on all sides. Only part of the thigh survives.
TECHNICAL DESCRIPTION: —
DATE: A.D. 200–273.
REFERENCES: Gawlikowski 1984, 108 cat. 68 pl. 92, 202.

OBJECT DESCRIPTION

The object depicts the thigh of a reclining figure from a banqueting relief.

PORTRAIT

The figure is shown frontally.

He wears a >Parthian-style< tunic and >Parthian-style< trousers. The tunic is decorated at the hem with a broad band with an ivy scroll and four-petal flowers. The trouser legs have a broad band between beaded bands extending downwards in the middle. The band is decorated with a running scroll with clusters of grapes. Along the leg he has an object with a rectangular main body, and two lateral triangles: a sheathed dagger. A series of slightly curving grooves at the edge suggest that he may have been wearing over-trousers.

The fragment is identified as the torso of a banqueter in Gawlikowski 1984.

Cat. 384

385. FRAGMENT OF A RELIEF

DATABASE NUMBER: KMW015.
LOCATION: Vienna, Kunsthistorisches Museum, inv. no. ANSA I 1526.
CONTEXT: —
ACQUISITION HISTORY: Dr James C. Samson, 1896.
MEASUREMENTS: Height: 27 cm. Width: 23 cm. Depth: 8.5 cm.
MATERIAL: Limestone, white/yellow.
PRESERVATION: The upper, left, and right side are broken off. The lower left corner is chipped.
TECHNICAL DESCRIPTION: The inscription has traces of red pigment.
DATE: A.D. 200–273.
REFERENCES: Müller 1885, 973 f. cat. 1; Plattner 2010, 176 f. cat. 15 figs. 30–32. Inscription: Müller 1885, 973 cat. 1; Plattner 2010, 176 cat. 15.

OBJECT DESCRIPTION
The object depicts a small part of a figure and a thin mattress.

INSCRIPTION
SCRIPT: Palmyrene Aramaic.
LOCATION ON RELIEF: At the lower part, on the mattress.
TRANSCRIPTION: ṢLM ŠLMLT | BR ZBDʾ ḤB[L].
TRANSLATION: Image of Šalamallat son of Zabdâ, alas!

CIS no. 4351; PAT no. 0709.

PORTRAIT
Fragment, perhaps from a reclining figure.
  Part of a figure's garment. The folds are indicated with oblique, incised lines.

Cat. 385

A.D. 220–240

386. FRAGMENT OF A BANQUETING RELIEF

DATABASE NUMBER: MLP079.
LOCATION: Paris, Musée du Louvre, inv. no. AO 22249.
CONTEXT: —
ACQUISITION HISTORY: Previously in the De Clercq collection. Gift to Louvre from H. de Boisgelin in 1967.
MEASUREMENTS: Height: 72 cm. Width: 34 cm. Depth: 12 cm.
MATERIAL: Limestone, white/grey.
PRESERVATION: The background is preserved only next to the upper arms and under the left elbow of portrait B. Portrait A: Only the left shoulder is preserved. Portrait B: The head is broken off at the base of the neck and the lower part is broken off diagonally from the left thigh to the right knee.
TECHNICAL DESCRIPTION: —
DATE: A.D. 220–240 (Dentzer-Feydy – Teixidor 1993: A.D. 200–273).
REFERENCES: Clermont-Ganneau 1884, 130 cat. 110 pl. 6, B; Seyrig 1937, 17 n. 2; Bossert 1951, 37 cat. 538 fig. 538; Colledge 1976, 79. 134. 145. 155. 211. 240 pl. 108; Dentzer-Feydy – Teixidor 1993, 233 cat. 226; Fowlkes-Childs – Seymour 2019, 164 f. cat. 110.

OBJECT DESCRIPTION

The fragment depicts two standing figures.

PORTRAIT A: STANDING FIGURE

The left arm of a figure is preserved.
The figure wears a garment visible at the left arm. Its folds are indicated with thin, oblique grooves.

PORTRAIT B: STANDING MALE

The figure is shown frontally. The arms are bent; the right is held at the waist, the left is held at the chest.

He wears a ›Parthian-style‹ tunic and ›Parthian-style‹ trousers. The tunic ends at the middle of the thighs. It has a wide, round neckline decorated with a vegetal motif, and long, tight-fitting sleeves. The cuffs of the sleeves are decorated with a wide band with a running dog and a beaded border. The lower hem is decorated with a wide band with four rows of long and narrow leaves. The folds of the tunic are indicated by wide, curving grooves. He wears a thin band belt tied low at the waist with a double knot, with the ends of the belt looped under the sides. The trousers have a wide band that extends downwards along the centre. The band is decorated with tendrils with vine leaves. The folds of the trousers are indicated by oblique grooves.

In his right hand, he holds a wide, hemispherical basket decorated with a crisscross pattern, full of different fruit. Grapes are positioned at the edge of the basket, while on the top there are two types of round fruit, one with a triangular indentation near the top, and one with a circular centre, out of which curving grooves radiate (possibly apples and pomegranates). Over the round fruits, oblong ones can be recognized (Dentzer-Feydy – Teixidor 1993, 233 suggest these are pinecones). In his left hand, he holds a bunch of stems that end in five large, curving, and ovoid objects. The stems are connected to each other with a slightly angular line, indicating leaves, possibly a bunch of leafy vegetables. The index finger is extended.

Cat. 386, Pl. 66

Cat. 387, Pl. 67

387. FEMALE FIGURE

DATABASE NUMBER: NCG038.
LOCATION: Copenhagen, Ny Carlsberg Glyptotek, inv. no. IN 1066.
CONTEXT: —
ACQUISITION HISTORY: Løytved in Syria.
MEASUREMENTS: Height: 57 cm. Width: 35 cm. Depth: 22 cm. Height of head: 14 cm. Width of head: 14 cm. Depth of head: 15.5 cm.
MATERIAL: Limestone, white/grey.
PRESERVATION: The lower part of the figure is broken off at the waist. The nose, right earring, right elbow, and the left lower arm are chipped. A large crack runs across the neck.
TECHNICAL DESCRIPTION: There are traces of black pigment around the eyes. The space between the thumb and index finger has not been cut and the back of the relief is roughly cut.
DATE: A.D. 220–240 (Ploug 1995: A.D. 230–250).
REFERENCES: Ingholt Archives, PS 457; Simonsen 1889, 36 cat. D 14 pl. 16; Poulsen 1921, 87; Chabot 1922, 114 pl. 20, 3; Ingholt 1928, 143; Mackay 1949, 164; Champdor 1953, 86; Colledge 1976, 76 n. 239; Parlasca 1988, 217 n. 22; Hvidberg-Hansen – Ploug 1993, 134 cat. 88; Ploug 1995, 214–216 cat. 88; Krag 2018, 49 n. 229; 53 n. 260; 58 n. 304; 62 n. 350; 102 n. 66; 103 n. 73; 380 f. cat. 803; Raja 2019a, 260 f. cat. 80.

OBJECT DESCRIPTION
The object depicts a standing female.

PORTRAIT
The figure is shown frontally. Her arms are bent in front of the torso.

Her hair is short and wavy. It is centrally parted. The individual strands of hair are indicated by incised lines. Her face is oblong. The eyebrows are slightly arched, indicated by thin grooves starting from the root of the nose. The eyes are large and almond-shaped, with thick upper eyelids. The eyeballs are blank. The end of the upper eyelids extends beyond that of the lower ones. Only the earlobes are visible. She wears earrings with three juxtaposed beads; an upper and lower, round bead and a central, oval bead, and the earrings appear attached at the upper part of the ear (Colledge classification: K). The nose is straight and short. The mouth is small, with a full lower lip. The chin is pointed with a small, hollow circle in the middle. The nose is short and thick with two curving grooves. Below the base of the neck, she wears a plain hoop necklace with a round pendant suspended from the middle.

She wears a tunic with a wide, v-shaped neckline, and short, wide sleeves that reach to the elbows. The tunic is tied at the waist with a thin band belt knotted at the centre. The edges of the belt are looped over the sides of the belt. The folds of the tunic are rendered by curving grooves at the torso and vertical ones at the arms and below the belt.

With both hands raised in front of her chest, she holds a small, rectangular casket with a lid. It has two small, round feet at the bottom. The body is decorated with a medallion at the centre and two garlands composed of small leaves at the sides. The medallion has four half-elliptical, incised lines at each sector and a small, straight, incised line at the centre. The lid is trapezoidal, with a wide, plain band at the bottom. She wears a plain, wide, and thick hoop bracelet on each wrist; the one on the left wrist is wider than the one on the right.

A.D. 240–273

388. FRAGMENT OF A BANQUETING RELIEF

DATABASE NUMBER: RoMou004.
LOCATION: Beirut, Robert Mouawad Private Museum, inv. no. unknown.
CONTEXT: —
ACQUISITION HISTORY: —
MEASUREMENTS: —
MATERIAL: Limestone, white/yellow.
PRESERVATION: The left and the lower side of the object are broken off. Portrait C: Only the right hand, forearm, and part of the knee are preserved.
TECHNICAL DESCRIPTION: Portrait B: There are traces of tool marks on the lower part of the tunic: punch marks on the wide band extending downwards, and tooth chisel marks.
DATE: A.D. 240–273.
REFERENCES: Parlasca 1987b, 108 f. 113 appendix no. 3; Krag 2018, 58 n. 304. 311; 59 n. 325; 65 n. 369; 66 n. 385; 73 n. 47. 51; 74 n. 57; 88 n. 193. 195; 103 n. 73; 380 cat. 802; Raja 2019e, 98. 148 cat. 94.

OBJECT DESCRIPTION
The sarcophagus lid is rectangular in shape and depicts a female and a male priest standing behind a reclining male figure.

PORTRAIT A: FEMALE
The figure is shown frontally. The arms appear small in relation to the body. The right arm is held along the body; the left is bent and held to the neck. The lower part of the body is obscured by the reclining figure.

The hair is centrally parted high on the forehead, and gathered on top of the head, held by a wide fillet. The fillet is decorated with two round beads and two horizontal, incised lines. Two locks of hair are wound spirally from the top of the head and along the side of the head. Four round elements are suspended by thin strands from the fillet. A narrow band with oblique, incised lines joins the lower two round elements at the forehead, making it likely that they indicate head ornaments. Her face is oval. The eyebrows are curving and indicated by ridges. The eyes are small, close-set, and almond-shaped, with thick eyelids. The irises are indicated by incised circles and the pupils by punch holes. The ears are small and close to the head, with the helix, tragus, and the lobe indicated. The nose is narrow and straight. The mouth is small, with thin lips. The chin is pointed. The neck is short and wide with a curving groove.

She wears a tunic and a himation. The tunic has a short, round neckline decorated with a narrow band, and short sleeves, indicated by the naked lower left arm. The folds of the tunic are rendered by wide, curving grooves. Over the tunic, she wears a himation. It covers most of her body, except for the lower left arm and the right hand. One end of the himation falls in a curving fold across the chest. The himation falls over either side of the left elbow, forming a zigzag-shaped fold on the right side of the arm. The folds of the himation are indicated by wide, curving grooves over the torso, and wide, oblique grooves over the arms.

With the right hand, she holds a fold of the himation. The thumb and the index finger are extended. With the raised left hand, she holds a fold of the himation. The thumb and the index finger are extended.

PORTRAIT B: STANDING PRIEST

The figure is shown frontally. The arms appear small in relation to the body. The right arm is bent and held in front of the chest; the left is bent in front of the torso. The lower part of the body is obscured by the reclining figure.

He wears a plain, high, cylindrical, flat-top headdress divided into three sections by two vertical grooves low on

Cat. 388

the forehead: a Palmyrene priestly hat. His face is oval. The eyebrows are curving, depicted as thin, curving ridges. The eyes are small and almond-shaped, with thick eyelids. The irises are indicated by incised circles and the pupils by punch holes. The ears are small and slightly protruding with the helix, tragus, and the lobe depicted. The nose is straight and narrow. Nasolabial lines are indicated by the carving of the planes of the face. The mouth is small, with thin lips. The chin is pointed. The neck is short and wide.

He wears a tunic and a chlamys. The tunic has a wide, round neckline and long, tight-fitting sleeves. The tunic has a wide, plain band extending downwards from the middle of the neckline. The folds of the tunic are rendered by oblique, wide grooves. Over the tunic, he wears a chlamys that falls over both shoulders, and covers most of the chest. It is fastened at the right shoulder with a circular brooch with a beaded border (Colledge classification: f). A round fold falls from under the brooch. The folds of the chlamys are indicated by oblique, deep grooves.

With the upturned palm of his right hand, he holds a circular bowl with a narrow, conical foot with his fingertips. With the left hand, he holds a fold of the chlamys. The index finger is extended. The nails are indicated by fine, incised lines.

PORTRAIT C: RECLINING MALE FIGURE

The right arm is extended to the side, and rests on the right knee.

The figure wears a ›Parthian-style‹ tunic. The tunic has long, tight-fitting sleeves. The cuffs of the sleeves are decorated with a beaded border, followed by a wide band with a pattern of rosettes between lozenges. The hem of the tunic was also decorated (visible under the wrist). A series of raised oblique grooves over the lower arm could indicate that he also wears a himation over the tunic.

389. FRAGMENT OF A BANQUETING RELIEF

DATABASE NUMBER: PM630.
LOCATION: Palmyra, Palmyra Museum, inv. no. unknown.
CONTEXT: —
ACQUISITION HISTORY: —
MEASUREMENTS: —
MATERIAL: Limestone.
PRESERVATION: Broken into two parts that were rejoined. Broken on right side. Portrait A: The right side is broken off vertically from the lower torso. The head is broken off at the base of the neck. The right lower arm and hand are broken off. Portrait B: The head is broken off at the base of the neck. The left hand and the bowl are chipped.
TECHNICAL DESCRIPTION: —
DATE: A.D. 240–273.
REFERENCES: Photo by J. Aliquot.

OBJECT DESCRIPTION

The object is rectangular in shape and depicts two reclining males. The figures are resting on a mattress decorated with an intersecting lozenge pattern with alternating four-petal and six-petal flowers in the lozenges. Both reclining figures rest their left arm on a cushion. The cushions are decorated with a wide band. The right cushion is decorated with a running scroll with central rosettes set between beaded bands. The left cushion is decorated with a lozenge pattern with four-petal flowers in the lozenges. There are round elements where the lozenges intersect. Curving grooves indicate the texture of the fabric.

PORTRAIT A: RECLINING MALE

The figure is shown in frontal view. The left arm is bent and held in front of the torso. The left arm is bent and rests on the cushion.

He wears a ›Parthian-style‹ tunic and a himation. The tunic has a small, round neckline decorated with a band with alternating oval and lozenge elements, and short, wide sleeves. At the middle, the tunic has a wide band with serrated leaves on the stem between beaded bands, extending downwards. The folds of the tunic are rendered by oblique, wide grooves. Over the tunic, he wears a himation. It is wrapped around his left lower arm and proceeds in a wide fold that ends in two s-shaped folds on the mattress. A small fringe is rendered on the edges. The folds of the himation are rendered by wide grooves. He wears a plain band belt, knotted at the centre with the ends looped under on either side of the waist.

He holds a bowl in his right hand (visible in outline). With his left hand, he holds a fold of the veil. The fingers are extended. He also wears a ring on his left little finger with a wide, thick hoop and an oval bezel.

PORTRAIT B: RECLINING MALE

The figure is shown frontally. The left arm is bent and held in front of the torso. The left arm is bent and rests on the cushion.

He wears a tunic and a himation. The tunic has a wide, v-shaped neckline and short, loose sleeves. The folds of the tunic are rendered by oblique and curving, wide grooves. Over the tunic, he wears a himation. It is wrapped around his left arm and proceeds in a wide fold that ends in an s-shaped fold on the mattress. A small fringe is rendered on the edges. The folds of the himation are rendered by wide grooves.

He holds the diagonal fold of the himation with his right hand. The thumb and index finger are extended. The veins on the back of his hand are plastically rendered. With the upturned palm of the left hand, he holds a bowl with his fingertips. The bowl has a flat bottom and slightly curving sides.

Cat. 389, Pl. 68

390. FRAGMENT OF A BANQUETING RELIEF

DATABASE NUMBER: PM658.
LOCATION: Palmyra, Palmyra Museum, inv. no. unknown.
CONTEXT: —
ACQUISITION HISTORY: —
MEASUREMENTS: —
MATERIAL: Limestone.
PRESERVATION: Broken on the right and upper side. Portrait A: Only the left part of the torso and the left upper arm and elbow are preserved. Portrait B: The figure is broken off horizontally above the waist. The lower arms are fragmented. Portrait C: The figure is broken off horizontally through the upper torso. The arms are fragmented. The left foot is broken off.
TECHNICAL DESCRIPTION: —
DATE: A.D. 240–273.
REFERENCES: Photo by J. Aliquot.

OBJECT DESCRIPTION

The object is rectangular in shape and depicts a reclining male and a seated female with a child on her lap. The figures are resting on a mattress decorated with an intersecting lozenge pattern with alternating four-petal and six-petal flowers in the lozenges. It is also decorated with a vertical band with leaves and rosettes set between beaded bands. The reclining male rests the left arm on two cushions; the lower cushion is decorated with a wide band with a leaf motif set between beaded bands and the upper cushion is decorated with a wide band with a running scroll and rosettes set between beaded bands. Curving grooves indicate the texture of the fabric.

PORTRAIT A: RECLINING MALE

The figure is shown in frontal to three-quarter view. The left arm is bent and rests on the cushion.

He wears a tunic and a himation. The folds are indicated by oblique grooves. He wears a plain band belt, knotted at the centre with the ends looped under on either side of the waist.

Cat. 390, Pl. 69

Over the tunic, he wears a himation. It is wrapped around his left arm and falls down in two wide, s-shaped folds from under his left wrist.

PORTRAIT B: SEATED FEMALE

The figure is shown frontally. The right arm appears bent, reaching out to the child on her lap. The left arm rests on her thigh.

She wears two garments, most likely a tunic and a himation. The tunic is visible under the himation that is ending at the ankles, covering parts of the shoes. The folds of the tunic are indicated by vertical grooves and the folds of the himation are indicated by vertical, oblique, and curving folds. She wears plain, round, closed-toe shoes.

PORTRAIT C: SEATED CHILD

The figure is shown frontally. The boy sits on the female's lap.

He wears a ›Parthian-style‹ tunic and ›Parthian-style‹ trousers. The tunic ends at the height of the knees. The hem is decorated with a wide band with a vegetal motif. Each trouser leg is decorated in the middle with a wide band with leaves set between plain bands. The folds of the trousers are rendered by diagonal grooves. The trousers are tucked into his boots. He is wearing plain ankle boots.

The child has a globular object on its lap.

391. FRAGMENT OF A BANQUETING RELIEF

DATABASE NUMBER: PM649.
LOCATION: Palmyra, Palmyra Museum, inv. no. unknown.
CONTEXT: —
ACQUISITION HISTORY: —
MEASUREMENTS: —
MATERIAL: Limestone.
PRESERVATION: Broken on the left and upper side. Portrait A: The figure is broken off at the waist. The upper legs are fragmented. The left elbow appears to be preserved. Portrait B: The figure is broken off diagonally from the right elbow to the left side of the waist. Portrait C: Only the right shank and the left knee are preserved. The knee and the foot are chipped.
TECHNICAL DESCRIPTION: —
DATE: A.D. 240–273.
REFERENCES: Photo by J. Aliquot.

OBJECT DESCRIPTION
The object is rectangular in shape and depicts a seated female, a standing figure, and a reclining male. The figures are resting on a mattress decorated with an intersecting lozenge pattern with four-petal flowers in the lozenges. There are round elements where the lozenges intersect. The seated female sits on two cushions. Curving grooves indicate the texture of the fabric.

PORTRAIT A: SEATED FEMALE
The figure is shown frontally. Her legs are bent with the knees rendered under the drapery. Her feet are obscured by the right foot of the reclining figure to her left.

She wears a garment that falls down her knees and legs. The folds are rendered by curving and oblique grooves.

PORTRAIT B: STANDING GIRL
The figure is shown frontally. The right arm is held along the body.

She wears a tunic and a himation. The tunic has short sleeves. Over the tunic she wears a himation that is wrapped around her lower body. The folds are rendered by curving and oblique grooves.

The right hand rests on her thigh. She holds a fold of the himation. All fingers are extended. She also wears a bracelet on her right wrist.

PORTRAIT C: RECLINING MALE
His right leg is bent and the right foot rests on the mattress. The left leg appears bent under the right.

He wears a himation. It covers his legs and ends at the ankles. He wears round, closed-toe shoes. The topline of the shoe is below the ankle, and the shoe is tied at the instep with a thin band or cord.

Cat. 391, Pl. 70

392. FRAGMENT OF A BANQUETING RELIEF

DATABASE NUMBER: PM379.
LOCATION: Palmyra, Palmyra Museum, inv. no. unknown.
CONTEXT: —
ACQUISITION HISTORY: —
MEASUREMENTS: —
MATERIAL: Limestone.
PRESERVATION: Broken on the right side. The knees, shanks, and feet are missing. The head is broken off at the base of the neck. The right hand is missing. The left arm and hand are chipped.
TECHNICAL DESCRIPTION: —
DATE: A.D. 240–273.
REFERENCES: Photo by J. Aliquot.

OBJECT DESCRIPTION
The sarcophagus lid is rectangular in shape and depicts a reclining male. The figure is resting on a mattress. It is decorated with an intersecting lozenges pattern with four-petal flowers in the lozenges. There are round elements where the lozenges intersect. The reclining male rests the left hand on a cushion. It is decorated with a wide band with vines set between beaded bands. The texture of the fabric of the cushion is indicated by curving grooves.

PORTRAIT
The figure is shown in frontal to three-quarter view. The right arm is bent and held in front of the torso. The left arm is bent and rests on the cushion. His right leg appears to be bent.

He wears a tunic and a himation. The tunic has a wide, round neckline. The folds of the tunic are rendered by curving, wide grooves. Over the tunic, he wears a himation that falls over both shoulders and covers the left part of the chest. The fold coming from the right is wrapped around his left wrist. Two wide folds of the himation fall along his left side where it is further divided into two s-shaped folds. The folds of the himation are indicated by narrow oblique, deep grooves.

With his right hand, he holds an oval object, possibly a bowl (visible in outline). With his left hand, he holds a fold of the himation. The fingers appear to be extended. On the ring finger of the left hand, he wears a thick hoop ring with a round bezel.

Cat. 392, Pl. 71

393. FRAGMENT OF A BANQUETING RELIEF

DATABASE NUMBER: PM437.
LOCATION: Palmyra, Palmyra Museum, inv. no. A 32.
CONTEXT: Secondary context: Justinian's precinct at the north of the Camp of Diocletian.
ACQUISITION HISTORY: —
MEASUREMENTS: —
MATERIAL: Limestone, white/yellow.
PRESERVATION: The left side of the object is broken off. Portrait A: The head is broken off at the base of the neck. The arms, hands, right foot, and parts of the clothing are chipped. Portrait B: Only one foot is preserved. The toes are chipped.
TECHNICAL DESCRIPTION: —
DATE: A.D. 240–273.

Cat. 393

REFERENCES: Ingholt Archives, PS 969; Tanabe 1986, 42 pl. 418; Krag 2018, 28 n. 9; 58 n. 304; 59 n. 320; 62 n. 353; 103 n. 74; 382 cat. 812.

OBJECT DESCRIPTION

The object depicts a seated female and a reclining male. The thin mattress beneath the figures is decorated with an intersecting lozenges pattern with flowers in the lozenges. The female sits on a cushion where the fabric is indicated by curving grooves. Her left foot is obscured by the reclining figure.

PORTRAIT A: SEATED FEMALE

The figure is shown frontally. The right arm appears short in relation to the body. The right arm is bent and held to the chest. The left is bent and held to the lower torso. Her legs are bent and the knees are rendered under the drapery.

She wears a veil. It falls over her shoulders and covers her torso and legs, leaving her right foot free. One fold of the veil falls from the right shoulder, leaving part of the chest free. Another fold of the veil falls from her left shoulder and is wrapped around her lower left arm and wrist. The folds of the veil are rendered by curving, oblique, and vertical grooves. She wears one necklace composed of a string of round beads worn on the neck.

She wears a tunic with a low, round neckline. The folds of the tunic are indicated by curving folds.

The right arm crosses the chest diagonally and she pulls the edge of the veil from the opposite side with her hand. With the left hand, she holds the lower part of the fold of the veil that is wrapped around her left arm.

PORTRAIT B: RECLINING MALE

The leg is shown in profile. The foot rests on the mattress.

He wears >Parthian-style< trousers with a decorated band at the centre (details unclear). The trousers are tucked into his boots. The upper edge of the boot is decorated with a wave pattern. Originating from a plain lace a pattern of vine leaves on stems and encircled rosettes decorates the lower part of the boot.

394. FRAGMENT OF A BANQUETING RELIEF

DATABASE NUMBER: PM291.
LOCATION: Palmyra, Palmyra Museum, inv. no. CD 123.
CONTEXT: Secondary context: Found (24.05.1960) in the foundations of the west corner of the Tetrapylon in the Camp of Diocletian.
ACQUISITION HISTORY: —
MEASUREMENTS: Height: 87 cm. Width: 50 cm. Depth: 37 cm.
MATERIAL: Limestone, yellow.
PRESERVATION: The lower right corner is chipped. Portrait A: The upper part is broken off at the shoulders. The left hand is broken off. The surface is slightly weathered. Portrait B: Only the foot survives.

TECHNICAL DESCRIPTION: There are traces of pigment in the inscription.
DATE: A.D. 240–273.
REFERENCES: Michalowski 1962, 154–156 cat. 25 fig. 170; Gawlikowski 1974b, 352 f. cat. 171; Krag 2018, 28 n. 9; 58 n. 298. 304; 62 n. 353; 63 n. 355; 87 n. 182; 101 n. 54; 383 cat. 816. Inscription: Michalowski 1962, 241–243 cat. 5 figs. 292. 293; Gawlikowski 1974b, 352 f. cat. 171; Krag 2018, 383 cat. 816.

OBJECT DESCRIPTION

The sarcophagus lid depicts a seated female and the foot of a reclining figure. The thin mattress under the figures is decorated with an intersecting lozenges pattern with alternating flowers and rosettes in the lozenges. The mattress is also decorated with a band with a vegetal motif between beaded bands. The female sits on two cushions.

INSCRIPTIONS

INSCRIPTION 1
SCRIPT: Palmyrene Aramaic.
LOCATION ON RELIEF: To the left of the female.
TRANSCRIPTION: ḤGT | BRT | ʿGYL | ʿMR | ḤBL.
TRANSLATION: Ḥaggat, daughter of ʿOgeîl ʿAmar, alas!

INSCRIPTION 2
SCRIPT: Palmyrene Aramaic.
LOCATION ON RELIEF: To the left of the female.
TRANSCRIPTION: [BʿL]TGʾ | [B]RT | [ʾ]BGR | [TY]MRṢW | ḤBL.
TRANSLATION: Baʿaltagâ, daughter of Abgar Taîmarṣû, alas!

CIS no. —; PAT no. 1953.

COMMENT: Inscription 1: Not visible on the photograph.

PORTRAIT A: SEATED FEMALE, ḤAGGAT

The figure is shown frontally. The arms and legs appear short in relation to the body. The right arm is held along the body. The left arm is bent and raised to the chest. Her legs are bent and the knees are rendered under the drapery. Her feet are obscured by the foot of the other figure.

She wears a veil. It falls over her shoulders. One edge of the veil covers her right shoulder and falls down on her right side and over the cushions in a zigzag-shaped fold. From the left shoulder, the veil is wrapped around her upper arm. She wears five necklaces: a string of small, round beads worn at the base of the neck. One composed of a twisted hoop with an oval pendant with an incised border, suspended from the centre by a narrow sleeve, worn at the collarbone. One composed of large, circular bezels joined together by beaded elements with a central, larger oval pendant, worn below the collarbone. The bezels all have incised borders. One composed of small, round beads with a crescent-shaped pendant suspended from the centre by a wide sleeve. The lower necklace worn at the chest is composed of a wide, loop-in-loop chain with a large, oval pendant. The pendant has a beaded border and a raised centre. Three trefoil-shaped pendants are suspended by triangular bars from the pendant.

She wears a tunic and a himation. The tunic has a small, round neckline and short, wide sleeves. The folds of the tunic are indicated by vertical grooves. The ankle-length himation crosses her chest diagonally from the left shoulder to the right side, and covers the lower chest, body, and legs. It is fastened at the left shoulder with a circular brooch with a beaded border (Colledge classification: f). The folds of the himation are rendered by diagonal and curving grooves. The folds between the legs are rendered by curving grooves.

She holds a fold of the veil with her right hand. The nails are rendered by fine, incised lines. She wears a bracelet on her right wrist. It is composed of twisted plain and beaded wires.

PORTRAIT B: RECLINING MALE

Only the foot of a reclining figure survives. The figure wears a shoe with a circular, raised element in the instep. Further details are unclear.

395. FRAGMENT OF A BANQUETING RELIEF

DATABASE NUMBER: Okayama003.
LOCATION: Okayama, Okayama Orient Museum, inv. no. 7-423.
CONTEXT: —
ACQUISITION HISTORY: —
MEASUREMENTS: Height: 66 cm. Width: 59 cm. Depth: 20 cm.
MATERIAL: Limestone, yellow.
PRESERVATION: The head is broken off at the base of the neck, the lower part is broken off vertically through the waist. The lower right arm is broken off. The attribute in front of the chest is chipped.
TECHNICAL DESCRIPTION: Tool marks are visible on the back of the left hand.
DATE: A.D. 240–273.
REFERENCES: <http://www.orientmuseum.jp/Detail_exhibit.php?touroku_no=13160423> (28.06.2018; link inactive on 06.05.2022).

OBJECT DESCRIPTION

The object depicts a reclining male figure. The figure rests on a mattress (details unclear) and the left arm rests on a cushion. The cushion is decorated with a wide band with four-petal flowers in lozenges. At the point where the lozenges join two round leaves are rendered. The band is set between two beaded bands. Curving grooves indicate the texture of the fabric.

PORTRAIT

The figure is shown frontally. The right arm is bent. The left arm is bent and rests at his side.

He wears a ›Parthian-style‹ tunic and a chlamys. The tunic has a wide, round neckline decorated with a row of circles with a small dot within. The tunic has long, tight-fitting sleeves and the cuffs are decorated with a beaded band. At the middle, the tunic has a wide band decorated with a running scroll with rosettes set between beaded bands, extending downwards. The folds of the tunic are rendered by oblique and curving grooves. He wears a plain band belt, knotted at the centre with the ends looped under on either side of the waist. Over the tunic, he wears a chlamys that falls over both shoulders, and covers most of the chest. It is folded around his left wrist. One edge of the chlamys has a border with a running scroll and rosettes pattern and a beaded band, visible on the fold across the chest, the folds falling down the left shoulder, and the two wide, s-shaped folds falling from under his left hand and over the cushion. The chlamys is fastened at the right shoulder with a circular brooch with a beaded outer border (Colledge classification: f). A zigzag-shaped fold falls from under the brooch.

The outline of an object, perhaps a vessel, is visible at the centre of the chest. He possibly would have held the vessel in his right hand. With the left hand, he holds a fold of the chlamys. The index and the middle finger are extended.

396. MALE FIGURE

DATABASE NUMBER: PM586.
LOCATION: Palmyra, Palmyra Museum, inv. no. unknown.
CONTEXT: —
ACQUISITION HISTORY: —
MEASUREMENTS: —
MATERIAL: Limestone, white.
PRESERVATION: The head is broken off at the base of the neck.
The right arm and upper half of the left arm are broken off. The lower part is broken off diagonally at the waist. The surface is weathered.
TECHNICAL DESCRIPTION: —
DATE: A.D. 240–273.
REFERENCES: Ingholt Archives, PS 906.

OBJECT DESCRIPTION
The object depicts the torso of a reclining male.

PORTRAIT
The figure is shown frontally.

He wears a >Parthian-style< tunic and a chlamys. The tunic has a small, round neckline decorated with a band with a geometric pattern of ovals and rectangles. At the middle, the tunic has a wide band extending downwards. It is decorated with a scroll with flowers in squares between beaded bands. The folds of the tunic are rendered by curving, wide grooves. He also wears a band belt across the lower torso. It is composed of oval and rectangular pendants linked together by pins with globular ends. Over the tunic, he wears a chlamys that falls over both shoulders and covers most of the chest. One edge of the chlamys has a scalloped decorated border, visible on the fold across the chest. The chlamys is fastened at the right shoulder with a circular brooch (Colledge classification: i). A zigzag-shaped fold falls under the brooch. The folds of the chlamys are rendered by narrow, deep grooves.

Cat. 396

Cat. 397

397. FRAGMENT OF A BANQUETING RELIEF

DATABASE NUMBER: UNK041.
LOCATION: Unknown location.
CONTEXT: —
ACQUISITION HISTORY: —
MEASUREMENTS: —
MATERIAL: Limestone.
PRESERVATION: Only part of the torso and the arms is preserved.
TECHNICAL DESCRIPTION: —
DATE: A.D. 240–273.
REFERENCES: Ingholt Archives, PS 929; Krag 2018, 58 n. 304; 103 n. 74; 382 cat. 806.

OBJECT DESCRIPTION
The object depicts the torso of a female.

PORTRAIT
The figure is shown in frontal view. The right arm is slightly bent and is held along the body. The left arm is bent and raised to the neck.

She wears a veil. It covers all of the upper body and has an overfold in her left side at the bottom. The folds of the veil are rendered by vertical grooves on the body, and curving grooves on the breasts and sleeves.

398. FRAGMENT OF A FEMALE FIGURE

DATABASE NUMBER: PM734.
LOCATION: Palmyra, Palmyra Museum, inv. no. B 552/1755.
CONTEXT: —
ACQUISITION HISTORY: —
MEASUREMENTS: Height: 43 cm. Width: 31 cm. Depth: 15 cm.
MATERIAL: Limestone, yellow.
PRESERVATION: The upper part is broken off at the neck. The arms are broken off. The lower part is broken off at the waist.
TECHNICAL DESCRIPTION: —
DATE: A.D. 240–273.
REFERENCES: Tanabe 1986, 40 pl. 363; Fortin 1999, 300 cat. 338; Krag 2018, 61 n. 333; 102 n. 69; 362 cat. 745; <https://virtual-museum-syria.org/palmyra/bust-of-a-woman-covered-with-jewelry/> (06.05.2022).

OBJECT DESCRIPTION
The object depicts a female.

PORTRAIT
The figure is shown frontally.

She wears a veil. It falls behind her head and covers her left shoulder.

She wears five necklaces. The first is a necklace composed of round beads and worn at the base of the neck. The second is composed of round and rectangular bezels with an incised border that are linked by beaded elements, worn on the collarbone. She then wears a necklace composed of large round beads with a central crescent-shaped pendant hanging by a narrow sleeve. Below that one, and over the breasts, she wears an interwoven loop-in-loop chain. It has a central oval pendant with a beaded border, from which hang three loop-in-loop chains ending in trefoil pendants. Falling low on her torso she wears a necklace composed of thick round beads with a hollowed-out centre and with two lateral round pendants with beaded borders.

She wears a tunic and a himation. The folds of the tunic are rendered by oblique, wide grooves. Over the tunic she wears a himation that falls diagonally across her torso from her right shoulder. The folds are rendered by oblique grooves.

399. FRAGMENT OF MALE FIGURE

DATABASE NUMBER: UNK051.
LOCATION: —
CONTEXT: —
ACQUISITION HISTORY: —
MEASUREMENTS: —
MATERIAL: Limestone.

Cat. 399

PRESERVATION: Only part of the lower torso and waist are preserved. The surface is weathered. The belt and part of the clothing are fragmented.
TECHNICAL DESCRIPTION: —
DATE: A.D. 240–273.
REFERENCES: Ingholt Archives, IA_NCG_Portrait2016_032.

OBJECT DESCRIPTION
The object depicts a male figure.

PORTRAIT
He wears a ›Parthian-style‹ tunic. The tunic has a wide band decorated with a running scroll pattern with flowers, set between beaded bands, extending downwards at the centre of the tunic. The folds of the tunic are indicated by wide, oblique grooves. He also wears a plain band belt across the lower torso. The belt is knotted at the centre with the ends looped under on either side of the waist.

400. FRAGMENT OF A BANQUETING RELIEF

DATABASE NUMBER: HamburgPriv001.
LOCATION: Hamburg, private collection (last known location).
CONTEXT: —
ACQUISITION HISTORY: —

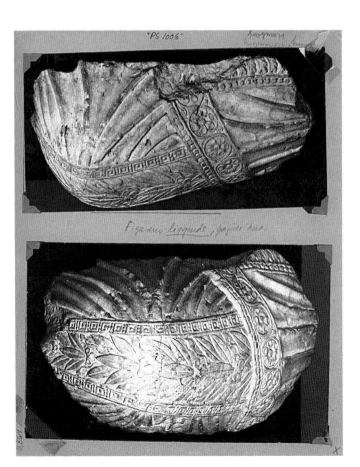

Cat. 400

MEASUREMENTS: —
MATERIAL: Limestone.
PRESERVATION: Only the part of the leg is preserved. There are small chips and cracks on the surface.
TECHNICAL DESCRIPTION: —
DATE: A.D. 240–273.
REFERENCES: Ingholt Archives, PS 864.

OBJECT DESCRIPTION
The object depicts a male from a sarcophagus lid.

PORTRAIT
The figure is shown in profile. The leg is bent.
He wears a ›Parthian-style‹ tunic and trousers. The tunic has a central panel with a vegetal pattern of serrated leaves set between a beaded border. The edge of the tunic is decorated with a border composed of scroll and rosette pattern. A six-petal rosette is set inside each scroll. The tunic ends at the middle of the thigh. The folds of the tunic are indicated by oblique grooves. Under the tunic, he wears trousers. The trousers are decorated with a central panel of acanthus leaves set between a band of squares with a raised centre. Each square is divided by a row of three small beads.

401. FRAGMENT OF A BANQUETING RELIEF

DATABASE NUMBER: PM770.
LOCATION: Palmyra, Palmyra Museum, inv. no. CD 38.
CONTEXT: Secondary context: Found (22.04.1961) at the late wall at the west of the Tetrapylon.
ACQUISITION HISTORY: —
MEASUREMENTS: Height: 30 cm. Width: 45 cm. Depth: 15 cm.
MATERIAL: Limestone, grey.
PRESERVATION: The relief is broken off on all sides. Only part of the left thigh and the knee of the figure survive.
TECHNICAL DESCRIPTION: —
DATE: A.D. 240–273.
REFERENCES: Michalowski 1963, 157 cat. 53 fig. 210.

OBJECT DESCRIPTION
The object depicts part of the lower body of a reclining figure.

PORTRAIT
The figure is shown in profile. His left knee is bent.
He wears a ›Parthian-style‹ tunic and ›Parthian‹ trousers. The tunic falls to the height of the thighs. The tunic is decorated with a broad band extending downwards in the middle, and a broad decorated border at the hem. The band extending downwards is decorated with serrated leaves between two beaded bands. The hem border is decorated with six-petal flowers within a running scroll. The six-petal flowers have round petals that are hollowed out in the centre. The edge is decorated with a beaded band. The folds of the tunic are rendered by oblique grooves. He also wears trousers (only part of the left leg is visible). They are decorated in the middle

with a broad band extending downwards between two beaded bands. The band is decorated with a motif of serrated leaves set opposite against the stem. The folds of the trouser legs are rendered by curving and oblique grooves.

FRAGMENTS FROM BOXES OR BOX RELIEFS

A.D. 100–120

402. FRAGMENT OF A SARCOPHAGUS BOX WITH PORTRAIT

DATABASE NUMBER: BM030.
LOCATION: London, British Museum, inv. no. 125029.
CONTEXT: —
ACQUISITION HISTORY: Donated by Lucy, Lady Howard de Walden, 1895.
MEASUREMENTS: Height: 30.5 cm. Width: 18.5 cm. Depth: 13.5 cm. Height of head: 16 cm.
MATERIAL: Limestone, yellow.
PRESERVATION: All the sides of the relief are broken off, except for the areas immediately next to the head. The lower part of the figure is broken off at the neck. The surface is weathered, and cracks run across the face.
TECHNICAL DESCRIPTION: Tool marks are visible on the cheeks.
DATE: A.D. 100–120 (Ingholt 1928: A.D. 50–150).
REFERENCES: Ingholt Archives, PS 388; Ingholt 1928, 134; Colledge 1976, 257; Krag 2018, 32 n. 63; 55 n. 274; 98 n. 23; 247 cat. 299; <http://www.britishmuseum.org/research/collection_online/collection_object_details.aspx?objectId=468659&partId=1&searchText=palmyra&images=true&page=2> (06.05.2022).

OBJECT DESCRIPTION

The object depicts part of a sarcophagus box. At the upper side, the stretcher of the kline is depicted and it is decorated with a rectangular and a square panel. A female head is rendered under the stretcher.

PORTRAIT

The figure is shown frontally.

She wears three headdresses: a headband, a turban, and a veil. The headband is placed low on the forehead and is decorated with rectangular panels with vegetal motifs divided by beaded bands. The turban is coiled and divided into three layers: the bottom layer is twisted, and the two upper layers are looped into each other creating a knot in the middle. The coiling of the fabric is indicated by oblique and horizontal grooves. Over the turban, she wears a heavy veil. Two separate locks of hair above the ears are combed back under the veil. The individual strands of hair are indicated by curving grooves. Her face is round and fleshy. The eyebrows are curving, indicated by thin grooves. The left eye is larger than the right. The eyes are almond-shaped, with thick eyelids. The irises and the pupils are indicated by concentric, incised circles. The earlobes are visible under the hair. She wears earrings shaped as a miniature bunch of grapes (Colledge classification: E). The nose is thin with a wider base. The mouth is wide with a full lower lip. The chin is square. The neck is wide with one horizontal groove.

Cat. 402

A.D. 150–170

403. FRAGMENT OF A SARCOPHAGUS BOX WITH PORTRAIT BUSTS

DATABASE NUMBER: MLP047.
LOCATION: Paris, Musée du Louvre, inv. no. AO 2630.
CONTEXT: —
ACQUISITION HISTORY: Between 1893 and 1895 from Pusgulian.
MEASUREMENTS: Height: 52 cm. Width: 92 cm. Depth: 27 cm.
MATERIAL: Limestone, yellow.
PRESERVATION: The right side, the upper side, and the left side are broken off. The two lower corners are broken off. Portrait A: The nose is chipped. Portrait B: The nose is chipped.
TECHNICAL DESCRIPTION: There are traces of red pigment in the inscription. The relief was restored in 1999 when the collection was moved to the Sackler Building. There are traces of plaster on the sides of the relief and under the bottom of the plinth. There are marks from a flat chisel on the surface of the background and on the face of the lion. Portrait A: There are marks from a flat chisel on the clothing and from a rasp on the face. Portrait B: There are marks from a flat chisel on the clothing and from a rasp on the face.
DATE: A.D. 150–170 (Dentzer-Feydy – Teixidor 1993: A.D. 150–200).
REFERENCES: Ingholt Archives, PS 854; Bonicatti 1964, 278 pl. 60, 3; Makowski 1985b, 127 n. 23; Dentzer-Feydy – Teixidor 1993, 191 cat. 192; Yon 2002, 261; Stauffer 2010, 211 fig. 5; Krag 2018, 16 n. 73; 32 n. 63; 47 n. 214; 51 n. 241; 87 n. 182; 101 n. 58; 103 n. 74; 106 n. 105. 106; 319 cat. 572; Cussini 2019a, 74 fig. 4. Inscription: Chabot 1922, 123 cat. 32; Dentzer-Feydy – Teixidor 1993, 191 cat. 192; Krag 2018, 319 cat. 572.

OBJECT DESCRIPTION

The object is rectangular in shape and depicts two armless busts: a male and a female. The busts are rendered in clipei, with moulded concentric rings. Between the two busts, an animal head, possibly a lion, is depicted. It has a ring in its mouth and the tongue hanging out. The ears are large and pointed, and on the cheeks there are tufts of fur. A small part of another animal head is visible to the left of the female bust. Underneath the busts there is a protruding plinth.

Cat. 403, Pl. 72

INSCRIPTION

SCRIPT: Palmyrene Aramaic.
LOCATION ON RELIEF: On the front surface of the protruding plinth, on the left side.
TRANSCRIPTION: [- - - BRT - - - ZB]DBWL ṬMS ʾTTH.
TRANSLATION: - - - daughter of - - - Zabdibôl Timaios, his wife.

CIS no. 4410; PAT no. 0770.

COMMENTS: Of all the names ending in BWL, Zabdibôl is the most frequent and the upper part of a letter on the right may well be the top of a D. The female may be the daughter of Zabdibôl himself or of one of his descendants. ṬMS is obviously a Greek name, but note that the usual >suspect< Τίμαιος is rare in the Near East and not very frequent elsewhere.

PORTRAIT A: ARMLESS MALE BUST

The figure is shown frontally.

His hair is arranged in a single row of large, s-shaped curls, and the individual strands of hair are indicated with incised lines. His face is oval. The eyebrows are slightly curving, depicted as thin ridges starting from the root of the nose. The eyes are almond-shaped, with thick eyelids. The irises are indicated by incised circles. The ears are large and protruding. The helix, tragus, scapha, and earlobe are depicted. The nose is straight. The alae are incised, and the nostrils are carved. The mouth has full lips. The chin is oval and prominent. The neck is wide and has two curving grooves.

He wears a tunic and a himation. The tunic has a wide, v-shaped neckline, and the folds of the fabric are rendered as v-shaped grooves on the chest. The himation is wrapped around the left shoulder and arm and crosses the chest diagonally to the right. Another fold of the himation falls from the back and over his left shoulder. The folds of the himation are rendered by vertical and curving grooves.

PORTRAIT B: ARMLESS FEMALE BUST

The figure is shown frontally, and her head is turned slightly to the left.

She wears two headdresses: a turban and a veil. The turban is coiled. It is rendered in a single layer, and oblique grooves indicate the coiling of the fabric. The veil is heavy. It falls over both her shoulders, crosses at the chest in a curving fold, and is wrapped around her arms. Her hair is parted in the centre of the forehead and brushed to the sides. Over the ears, the hair is brushed back under the veil. A single s-shaped lock is depicted at the parting at the centre of the forehead. The individual strands of hair are rendered by incised lines. Her face is oval. The eyebrows are slightly curving, rendered by ridges starting from the root of the nose. The eyes are almond-shaped, with thick eyelids. The upper eyelids extend beyond the edge of the lower ones. The irises are rendered by incised circles. Only the earlobes are visible under the hair. She wears dumbbell-shaped earrings (Colledge classification: H). The nose has a wide base, and the alae are incised. The mouth is small, with thin lips. Small >marionette< lines are rendered. The chin is round and fleshy. The neck is short and wide. There are three curving grooves on the neck. She wears a necklace of small, round beads on a string, at the base of her neck.

She wears a tunic. The neckline of the tunic has a scalloped edge. A few oblique grooves indicate the folds of the tunic.

404. FRAGMENT OF A SARCOPHAGUS BOX WITH PORTRAIT BUSTS

DATABASE NUMBER: BM009.
LOCATION: London, British Museum, inv. no. BM 125017.
CONTEXT: —
ACQUISITION HISTORY: Purchased by J. Shemtob in 1889.
MEASUREMENTS: Height: 45.5 cm. Width: 54.26 cm. Depth: 23.5 cm. Portrait A: Height of figure: 29 cm. Width of figure: 23 cm. Depth of figure: 11.5 cm. Height of head: 13.5 cm. Width of head: 10 cm. Portrait B: Height of figure: 29 cm. Width of figure: 17.5 cm. Depth of figure: 11.5 cm. Height of head: 14 cm. Width of head: 11.5 cm.
MATERIAL: Limestone, grey.
PRESERVATION: The left, upper, and the right sides of the relief are broken off. Portrait A: The surface is lightly weathered. Portrait B: The left side of the figure is broken off at the left shoulder. The nose is chipped.
TECHNICAL DESCRIPTION: Portrait B: The area between the veil and ears has been drilled.
DATE: A.D. 150–170.
REFERENCES: Ingholt Archives, PS 855; Müller 1892, 319 f. cat. 2; Colledge 1976, 249; Krag 2018, 32 n. 63; 47 n. 214; 51 n. 241; 87 n. 182; 89 n. 210; 101 n. 58; 103 n. 74; 319 cat. 573; <http://www.britishmuseum.org/research/collection_online/collection_object_details.aspx?objectId=282724&partId=1&searchText=125017&page=1> (06.05.2022). Inscription: Müller 1892, 320; Krag 2018, 319 cat. 573.

OBJECT DESCRIPTION

The sarcophagus box is rectangular in shape and depicts two busts: a male and a female. The sarcophagus has a projecting plinth at the bottom.

INSCRIPTION

SCRIPT: Palmyrene Aramaic.
LOCATION ON RELIEF: Between the heads.
TRANSCRIPTION: ṢLM | ḤBYBY BR | MLKW | BLY[Dʿ] ḤBL.
TRANSLATION: Image of Ḥabîbî son of Malkû Bolîadaʿ, alas!

CIS no. 4509; PAT no. 0870.

COMMENT: L.4: Restoration of the name CIS 4509.

PORTRAIT A: ARMLESS MALE BUST, ḤABÎBÎ

The figure is shown frontally.

He has short hair arranged in three rows of snail-shell curls. The individual strands of hair are depicted by narrow, curving grooves. His face is oval. The eyebrows are arched, depicted by thin grooves. The eyes are close-set, almond-shaped, and slanting with thick upper eyelids. The end of the upper eyelids extends beyond that of the lower ones. The irises and the pupils are rendered by concentric, incised circles. The ears are small, slightly protruding, with the helix and lobe indicated. The nose is straight and thin. The alae are incised. The mouth is small, with full lips. The chin is pointed. The neck is short and slender.

He wears a tunic and a himation. The tunic has a short, v-shaped neckline. The folds of the tunic are indicated by curving grooves. Over the tunic, he wears a himation. The edge of the himation is visible over the right shoulder and the upper left shoulder. A fold of the himation crosses the chest diagonally and falls over the left shoulder. Its edge is decorated with a pleated band.

Cat. 404

PORTRAIT B: ARMLESS FEMALE BUST
The figure is shown frontally.

She wears three headdresses: a headband, a turban, and a veil. The headband is decorated with three rectangular panels divided by beaded bands. The outer panels are decorated with a crisscross pattern, and the central with a vegetal motif. The turban is coiled. It is rendered in two twisted layers and oblique grooves indicate the coiling of the fabric. Over the turban, she wears a thick veil. It falls down the shoulders. The right side of the veil falls across the chest in a curving fold and over the left shoulder. It is decorated with a woolly fringe. Several strands of hair are combed backwards over the sides of the forehead and the headband. The individual strands of hair are rendered by wavy, incised lines. Her face is oval. The eyebrows are arched, indicated by thin grooves. The eyes are large, close-set, and almond-shaped and slanting, with thick eyelids. The irises and the pupils are indicated by concentric, incised circles. The earlobes are visible under the hair. She wears dumbbell-shaped earrings (Colledge classification: H). The nose is straight with a wide base. The alae are incised. The mouth is small, with full lips. The chin is pointed. The neck is short and slender. She wears a necklace composed of round beads at the base of the neck.

She wears a tunic with a small, scalloped neckline. The folds of the tunic are indicated by wide, curving grooves.

405. SARCOPHAGUS BOX WITH PORTRAIT BUST

DATABASE NUMBER: SUCC002.
LOCATION: Stanford, Stanford University, Cantor Center for the Visual Arts, inv. no. 17201.
CONTEXT: —
ACQUISITION HISTORY: Stanford Family Collections, purchased by Leland Stanford Jr. in 1883 in Europe.
MEASUREMENTS: Height: 44.5 cm. Width: 44.5 cm. Depth: 15 cm.
MATERIAL: Limestone, white/yellow.
PRESERVATION: The object is broken on all sides. The surface of the chin is chipped.
TECHNICAL DESCRIPTION: The background is roughly finished. Tool marks are visible.
DATE: A.D. 150–170 (Parlasca 1990: A.D. 150–200).
REFERENCES: Parlasca 1990, 141 fig. 12; Albertson 2000, 160 n. 2; Krag 2018, 23 n. 160; 32 n. 63; 47 n. 213. 214; 51 n. 241; 87 n. 182; 103 n. 74; 318 f. cat. 570; <http://cantorcollections.stanford.edu/Obj22679?sid=1656&x=13923> (06.05.2022). Inscription: Krag 2018, 318 f. cat. 570.

OBJECT DESCRIPTION
The object shows part of a kline. An armless female bust is depicted between the kline legs. Above the bust, the stretcher of the kline and the mattress is preserved. The mattress has a band decorated with leaves in an opposite arrangement on the stem. Curving grooves indicate the texture of the mattress. The central stretcher is decorated with a rectangular indentation and a square indentation followed by another panel divided into two parts by a horizontal line. The upper part has oblique grooves and the lower has lanceolate leaves in an opposite arrangement. To the left of the figure, part of the kline leg is preserved. The leg is turned, with only part of a calyx-shaped element decorated with a tongue pattern preserved.

INSCRIPTION
SCRIPT: Palmyrene Aramaic.
LOCATION ON RELIEF: To the right of the head.
TRANSCRIPTION: ṢLM[Tʾ DH] | DYʿ[...]
TRANSLATION: Image of - - -.

CIS no. —; PAT no. 1653.

PORTRAIT
The figure is shown frontally.

She wears three headdresses: a headband, a turban, and a veil. The band is placed high on her forehead and is divided into decorated panels separated by vertical, beaded bands. The central panel is decorated with a vegetal motif (details unclear). The turban is coiled. It is divided into two twisting layers with horizontal grooves indicating the coiling of the fabric. The veil is heavy. It falls over her right shoulder and across her chest in a curving fold. At the centre of the chest, the fold falling from the left shoulder is folded under the fold coming from the right. Part of the hair is covered by the headdress: several strands of hair above the ears are pushed back over the headband and the edge of the turban and disappear under the veil. Her face is oval. The eyebrows are curving, rendered as thin ridges. The eyes are almond-shaped, with thick upper eyelids. The upper eyelids extend beyond the ends of the lower ones. The irises are rendered by incised circles. Only the earlobes are visible under the headdress and she wears dumbbell-shaped earrings (Colledge classification: H). The nose is straight with carved nostrils. The chin is small, and the neck is slender.

She wears a tunic with a wide, v-shaped neckline. The folds of the tunic are rendered by curving grooves.

406. FRAGMENT OF A SARCOPHAGUS BOX WITH PORTRAIT BUST

DATABASE NUMBER: VAM006.
LOCATION: Berlin, Vorderasiatisches Museum, inv. no. VA 2989.
CONTEXT: —
ACQUISITION HISTORY: Gift of Moritz Sobernheim 1899.
MEASUREMENTS: Height: 23 cm. Width: 17.5 cm. Depth: 18.5 cm.
MATERIAL: Limestone, white/grey.
PRESERVATION: The relief ground to the left side of the head is preserved. The lower part of the figure is broken off

Cat. 405

Cat. 406

diagonally at the neck and shoulder. The headdress, the nose, and the edge of the veil on the left side are chipped.
TECHNICAL DESCRIPTION: There are traces of red pigment in the inscription.
DATE: A.D. 150–170 (Wartke 1991: A.D. 150–200).
REFERENCES: Ingholt Archives, PS 693; Wartke 1991, 79 f. 92 f. cat. 9 fig. 10; Krag 2018, 32 n. 63; 47 n. 214; 103 n. 74; 320 cat. 576/577; <https://arachne.dainst.org/entity/1198489> (06.05.2022).

OBJECT DESCRIPTION
The object depicts a female. Part of the relief ground is preserved; part of a clipeus is rendered to the left of her head.

INSCRIPTION
SCRIPT: Palmyrene Aramaic.
LOCATION ON RELIEF: To the left of the head.
TRANSCRIPTION: - - -L.
TRANSLATION: —

CIS no. —; PAT no. —.

COMMENT: The translation is presumably [ḤB]L: >Alas!<. There are only traces of letters.

PORTRAIT
The figure is shown frontally.

She wears three headdresses: a headband, a turban, and a veil. The band is placed low on the forehead and is divided into decorated panels separated by vertical grooves. The panels are decorated with an X-shaped incision. The turban is coiled. It is rendered in a twisted layer by oblique grooves. The veil is heavy and falls on both sides of her head. Part of the hair is covered by the headdresses: several strands of hair above the ears are pushed back over the headband and the edge of the turban, and disappear under the veil. Her face is round. The eyebrows are slightly curving, rendered by incised lines starting from the top of the nose. The eyes are close-set, small, and almond-shaped, with thick upper eyelids. The upper eyelids extend beyond the end of the lower ones. The irises are rendered by incised circles and the pupils by punch holes. Only the earlobes are visible and she wears dumbbell-shaped earrings (Colledge classification: H). The cheeks are fleshy, and the mouth is small, with full lips. The chin is prominent and oval. The neck is wide.

She wears a tunic with a small, round neckline. The folds are rendered by curving grooves.

A.D. 150–200

407. FRAGMENT OF A SARCOPHAGUS BOX WITH PORTRAIT BUST

DATABASE NUMBER: FM002.
LOCATION: Cambridge, Fitzwilliam Museum, inv. no. GR.7.1888.
CONTEXT: —
ACQUISITION HISTORY: Bought in 1888 by Professor William Smith-Robertson.
MEASUREMENTS: Height: 50 cm. Width: 38 cm. Depth: 27 cm. Height of figure: 18.5 cm. Width of figure: 12.6 cm. Depth of figure: 14.5 cm.
MATERIAL: Limestone, yellow.
PRESERVATION: The surface is weathered. The edges of the relief are chipped.
TECHNICAL DESCRIPTION: The portrait is roughly finished.
DATE: A.D. 150–200.
REFERENCES: Ingholt Archives, PS 629; Budde – Nicholls 1964, 88 cat. 142 pl. 46; <http://data.fitzmuseum.cam.ac.uk/id/object/66174> (06.05.2022).

OBJECT DESCRIPTION
The object is rectangular in shape and depicts an armless male bust.

Cat. 407

part of the cheeks, the upper lip, and the chin. The facial hair is rendered by depressions (chisel marks). The mouth is small, with a full lower lip. The chin is square. The neck is short and wide. A v-shaped groove indicates the sternocleidomastoid muscles. A vertical line on the chest indicates the chest musculature.

He wears a tunic and a himation. The tunic has a wide, round neckline decorated with a scalloped edge and short loose-fitting sleeves. The folds of the tunic are rendered by narrow, curving grooves. Over the tunic he wears a himation. The himation is wrapped around the left shoulder and covers the left side. One fold crosses the chest diagonally below the right arm and continues underneath the fold covering the left side. The folds of the himation are rendered by oblique, wide grooves over the left side and curving grooves over the chest.

408. SARCOPHAGUS BOX WITH PORTRAIT BUST

DATABASE NUMBER: Sarrafian007.
LOCATION: Last known location: Beirut, Sarrafian (antiques dealer).
CONTEXT: —
ACQUISITION HISTORY: —
MEASUREMENTS: —
MATERIAL: Limestone.
PRESERVATION: The background is broken off on both sides of the bust, except for the areas by her shoulders and beneath the bust.
TECHNICAL DESCRIPTION: —
DATE: A.D. 150–200.
REFERENCES: Ingholt Archives, PS 666.

INSCRIPTION
SCRIPT: Palmyrene Aramaic.
LOCATION ON RELIEF: To the left of the head.
TRANSCRIPTION: —
TRANSLATION: —

COMMENT: Translated as >Zeno (?) son of Idabal. Alas!< in Budde and Nicholls (1964, 88 cat. 142). Possibly a fake inscription.

PORTRAIT
The figure is shown frontally.

His hair is arranged in one row of comma-shaped curls around the head. The individual strands of hair are indicated by incised lines. His face is square. The eyebrows are slightly curving, plastically rendered. The eyes are large and almost round with thick eyelids. The upper eyelids extend beyond the end of the lower ones. The irises are indicated by incised circles. The ears are small with the helix, tragus, concha, and lobe depicted.

The nose is long and straight with a wide base. The alae are incised. He has a beard that starts from the temples, covers

OBJECT DESCRIPTION
The object depicts an armless female bust from a sarcophagus box. Part of the relief ground is visible to the left of her head.

PORTRAIT DESCRIPTION
The figure is shown frontally.

She wears three headdresses: a headband, a turban, and a veil. The headband is placed high on the forehead. The turban is coiled. The veil is heavy and covers her shoulders. The right end of the veil covers the body and is folded across the chest and falls over the left shoulder. The folds of the veil are indicated by oblique grooves. The hair is parted in the centre and brushed back over the ears. The hair covers the sides of the turban and disappears under the veil. Her face is square. The eyebrows are low and curving. The eyes are almond-shaped. Only the earlobes are visible under the hair. She wears dumbbell-shaped earrings (Colledge classification: H). The nose is straight. The mouth is small, with a full lower lip. The chin is round. The neck is long and slender with two curving grooves.

She wears a tunic. The tunic has a small, v-shaped neckline. The folds are indicated by curving grooves.

Cat. 408

Cat. 409

409. FRAGMENT OF A SARCOPHAGUS BOX WITH PORTRAIT BUST

DATABASE NUMBER: UNK002.
LOCATION: Last known location: Beirut, Sarrafian (antiques dealer).
CONTEXT: —
ACQUISITION HISTORY: —
MEASUREMENTS: —
MATERIAL: Limestone.
PRESERVATION: The background is broken off except for a small area to the right of the figure's head. The left and right upper edges of the veil and the right shoulder are broken off. The face is heavily chipped. The clothing over the area of the breasts is chipped.
TECHNICAL DESCRIPTION: —
DATE: A.D. 150–200.
REFERENCES: Ingholt Archives, PS 669.

OBJECT DESCRIPTION

The object depicts an armless female bust from a sarcophagus box.

PORTRAIT DESCRIPTION

The figure is shown frontally.

She wears three headdresses: a headband, a turban, and a veil. The headband is placed high on the forehead and is divided into three panels decorated with a floral motif. The turban is coiled and divided into three layers. The coiling of the fabric is indicated by oblique grooves. Over the turban she wears a heavy veil. The right side of the veil falls down the right shoulder, covers the body, and is folded over the chest, falling over the left shoulder. Two separate locks of hair above the ears are combed back under the veil. The individual strands of hair are indicated by curving grooves. Her face is square. The mouth is small, with full lips. The neck is long and wide.

She wears a necklace composed of round beads at the base of the neck.

She wears a tunic. The folds of the tunic are indicated by curving and oblique grooves.

410. FRAGMENT OF A SARCOPHAGUS BOX WITH PORTRAIT BUST

DATABASE NUMBER: AMI084.
LOCATION: Istanbul, Istanbul Arkeoloji Müzesi, inv. no. 3734/O.M 185.
CONTEXT: —
ACQUISITION HISTORY: Confiscated in Damascus in February 1893.
MEASUREMENTS: Height: 29 cm. Width: 30 cm.
MATERIAL: Limestone, grey.
PRESERVATION: Only the bust is preserved together with a small part of the background next to the left side of the head and the left shoulder. The left side of the veil, the hair, the surface of the head, and part of the clothing over the chest are chipped.
TECHNICAL DESCRIPTION: Tool marks are visible on the surface.
DATE: A.D. 150–200.
REFERENCES: Ingholt Archives, PS 726; Colledge 1976, 264.

Cat. 410

OBJECT DESCRIPTION
The object depicts an armless, female bust.

PORTRAIT
The figure is shown frontally.

She wears two headdresses: a turban and a veil. The turban is coiled. It is composed of three coiling bands, the folds indicated by oblique grooves.

Over the turban, she wears a heavy veil that falls down behind the head, and over the shoulders. The right end of the veil crosses the chest in a curving fold and falls over the left shoulder. The hair is centrally parted, slightly wavy, and combed back under the sides of the turban. The individual strands of hair are indicated by s-shaped grooves. Her face is oval. The eyebrows are curving, rendered by thin ridges. The eyes are large, close-set, and almond-shaped. Only the earlobes are visible under the hair. The chin is heavy. The neck is short and wide with three curving grooves. She wears a beaded necklace composed of small, round beads at the base of the neck.

She wears a tunic with a short, v-shaped neckline. The folds of the tunic are indicated by wide, curving grooves.

411. FRAGMENT OF A SARCOPHAGUS BOX WITH PORTRAIT BUST

DATABASE NUMBER: HDrouot018.
LOCATION: Last known location: Hotel des Ventes de Neuilly sur Seine.
CONTEXT: —
ACQUISITION HISTORY: Offered to the Ny Carlsberg Glyptotek in 1893 by Durighello. Previously in Bertone's collection (possibly acquired during his trip to Palmyra). Sold through Hotel des Ventes de Neuilly-sur-Seine in 1931.
MEASUREMENTS: Height: 44 cm. Width: 45 cm.
MATERIAL: Limestone.
PRESERVATION: The right edge of the relief is chipped. The lower left corner is broken off. The edges of the veil over the forehead and the bridge of the nose are chipped.
TECHNICAL DESCRIPTION: —
DATE: A.D. 150–200.
REFERENCES: Ingholt Archives, PS 384; Ingholt 1928, 133 PS 384; Hotel des Ventes 1931, lot 665; Krag 2018, 47 n. 214; 51 n. 241; 103 n. 74; 106 n. 105; 252 cat. 318.

OBJECT DESCRIPTION
The object is square in shape and depicts an armless female bust.

INSCRIPTION
SCRIPT: Palmyrene Aramaic.
LOCATION ON RELIEF: To the left of the left arm.
TRANSCRIPTION: —
TRANSLATION: —

SARCOPHAGI WITH NO KNOWN PROVENANCE OR FROM SECONDARY CONTEXTS

Cat. 411

CIS no.—; PAT no. —.
COMMENT: The inscription may be falsified.

PORTRAIT
The figure is shown frontally.

She wears two headdresses: a headcloth and a veil. The headcloth is placed high on the forehead and is undecorated. The veil is heavy with a scalloped edge. It falls over the back of the head, over the right shoulder, and falls across the chest and over the left shoulder in a curving fold.

The hair is centrally parted and wavy. The individual strands of hair are indicated by incised lines. Her face is square and fleshy. The eyebrows are arched, rendered by incised lines. The eyes are large, close-set, almond-shaped, with thick upper eyelids. The irises are indicated by incised circles and the pupils by punch holes. Only the earlobes are visible under the hair. She wears dumbbell-shaped earrings (Colledge classification: H). The nose is straight. The mouth is small, with a thin upper, and a full lower lip. The chin is square. The neck is short and thick with a curving groove.

She wears a tunic. The tunic has a wide round neckline. The folds of the tunic are rendered by wide, deep grooves.

412. FRAGMENT OF A SARCOPHAGUS BOX WITH PORTRAIT BUST

DATABASE NUMBER: UNK132.
LOCATION: Unknown location.
CONTEXT: —
ACQUISITION HISTORY: —
MEASUREMENTS: —
MATERIAL: Limestone.
PRESERVATION: Only the bust and part of the background to the right of the figure are preserved. Part of the edges of the veil, and part of the left eyebrow are chipped.
TECHNICAL DESCRIPTION: The ears have no carved details.
DATE: A.D. 150–200.
REFERENCES: Ingholt Archives, PS 672; Krag 2018, 47 n. 214; 48 n. 219; 103 n. 74; 253 cat. 320.

OBJECT DESCRIPTION
The object is rectangular in shape and depicts an armless female bust. The bust is placed inside a clipeus carved in low relief.

INSCRIPTION
SCRIPT: Palmyrene Aramaic.
LOCATION ON RELIEF: To the left of the head.
TRANSCRIPTION: - - - | ḤNYN[ʾ] | ḤBL.
TRANSLATION: - - - Hanînâ, alas!

CIS no. —; PAT no. —.

COMMENT: ḤNYNʾ is a masculine name.

PORTRAIT

The figure is shown frontally.

She wears three headdresses: a headband, a turban, and a veil. The headband is placed low on the forehead and is divided into rectangular panels decorated with vegetal motifs separated by vertical, beaded bands. The turban is divided into four layers and the ends are looped into each other creating a knot in the middle. Curving grooves indicate the coiling of the fabric. The veil is heavy with a scalloped edge. It falls over the back of the head and both shoulders and falls in a curving fold across the chest. The border of the veil has a woollen fringe. Part of the hair is covered by the headdress: several strands of hair above the ears are brushed back over the headband

Cat. 412

and the edge of the turban, and disappear under the veil. The individual strands of hair are indicated by incised lines.

Her face is square. The eyebrows are curving, rendered by incised lines, and starting from the root of the nose. The eyes are close-set and almond-shaped, with thick eyelids. The upper eyelids extend beyond the end of the lower ones. The irises are indicated by incised circles and the pupils by punch holes. Only the earlobes are visible under the hair. She wears dumbbell-shaped earrings (Colledge classification: H). The nose is straight with incised alae. The nostrils are indicated. The mouth is small, with full lips. The chin is square. The neck is short and slender. She wears a string of small, round beads at the base of the neck.

She wears a tunic. The tunic has a small, round neckline. The folds of the tunic are indicated by wide, curving grooves. The photograph of the object was sent to Ingholt in 1930.

413. FRAGMENT OF A SARCOPHAGUS BOX WITH PORTRAIT BUST

DATABASE NUMBER: UNK077.
LOCATION: Unknown location.
CONTEXT: —
ACQUISITION HISTORY: Ingholt saw it at »Cheruau's Museum«.
MEASUREMENTS: —
MATERIAL: Limestone.
PRESERVATION: Only the bust and part of the background behind the shoulders of the figure are preserved.
TECHNICAL DESCRIPTION: —

Cat. 413

DATE: A.D. 150–200.
REFERENCES: Ingholt Archives, PS 933; Krag 2018, 31 n. 54; 47 n. 214; 51 n. 241; 103 n. 74; 215 cat. 183.

OBJECT DESCRIPTION
The object is rectangular in shape and depicts a female bust.

PORTRAIT
The figure is shown frontally.

She wears a tunic and a veil. The veil falls over the upper chest in a curving fold. The curves of the veil are rendered by widely spaced oblique grooves. The tunic has a small, v-shaped neckline. The folds of the tunic are indicated by wide, curving grooves.

A.D. 170–200

414. FRAGMENT OF A SARCOPHAGUS BOX WITH PORTRAIT BUST

DATABASE NUMBER: UPM011.
LOCATION: Philadelphia, University of Pennsylvania Museum of Archaeology and Anthropology, inv. no. B8912.
CONTEXT: —
ACQUISITION HISTORY: —
MEASUREMENTS: Height: 41 cm. Width: 27 cm. Depth: 11 cm.
MATERIAL: Limestone, white.
PRESERVATION: The figure has broken off from the sarcophagus box. The surface around the left part of the forehead, of the left cheek, of the nose, and of the chin is chipped.
TECHNICAL DESCRIPTION: Evidence of tool marks is visible on the face.
DATE: A.D. 170–200 (Romano 2006: A.D. 150–200).
REFERENCES: Ingholt Archives, PS 668; Legrain 1927, 347 cat. 3 fig. 3; Colledge 1976, 261; Romano 2006, 281 f. cat. 130; Krag 2018, 32 n. 63; 47 n. 214; 51 n. 241; 103 n. 74; 320 cat. 575; <https://www.penn.museum/collections/object/58679> (06.05.2022).

OBJECT DESCRIPTION
The object depicts an armless female bust.

PORTRAIT
The figure is shown frontally.

She wears three headdresses: a headband, a turban, and a veil. The band is placed high on the forehead and is divided into rectangular panels separated by vertical, beaded lines. The panels are decorated with four-petal flowers. The centre of the flower petals is rendered by incised lines. The turban is coiled. It is rendered in three twisting layers. Horizontal grooves indicate the texture of the fabric. The veil is heavy with a scalloped edge visible at the right shoulder. It falls from the right shoulder across the chest in a curving fold and back over the left shoulder. Part of the hair is covered by the headdresses:

Cat. 414

ACQUISITION HISTORY: —
MEASUREMENTS: Height: 54 cm. Width: 36 cm. Depth: 32 cm.
MATERIAL: Limestone, yellow.
PRESERVATION: The relief ground is broken on all sides. The lower part of the figure is broken off horizontally through the lower torso. A vertical crack runs from the left eyebrow to the cheek.
TECHNICAL DESCRIPTION: The background is roughly finished.
DATE: A.D. 170–200 (Romano 2006: A.D. 200–273).
REFERENCES: Ingholt Archives, PS 567; Legrain 1927, 348 cat. 6 fig. 6; Ingholt 1935, 72; Romano 2006, 297 f. cat. 142; Heyn 2008, 180 fig. 6, 4; Fowlkes-Childs – Seymour 2019, 164 f. cat. 111; <https://www.penn.museum/collections/object/294156> (06.05.2022). Inscription: Legrain 1927, 348 cat. 6.

OBJECT DESCRIPTION
The object depicts the torso of a standing male. The relief ground is preserved at either side and above him.

INSCRIPTION
SCRIPT: Palmyrene Aramaic.
LOCATION ON RELIEF: To the left and right of the head.

several strands of hair above the ears are pushed back over the headband and the edge of the turban, and disappear under the veil. Her face is square. The eyebrows are curving, rendered by incised lines starting from the root of the nose. The eyes are close-set and almond-shaped, with thick upper eyelids. The upper eyelids extend beyond the end of the lower ones. The irises are rendered by incised circles and the pupils by punch holes. The mouth is large with a full lower lip. The neck is wide. At the base of the neck, a curving line rendered by a series of depressions is visible, possibly a necklace.

She wears a tunic. It has a small, scalloped neckline. The folds of the tunic are rendered by curving grooves.

415. FRAGMENT OF A MALE FIGURE

DATABASE NUMBER: UPM001.
LOCATION: Philadelphia, University of Pennsylvania Museum of Archaeology and Anthropology, inv. no. B 8903.
CONTEXT: —

Cat. 415

TRANSCRIPTION: —
TRANSLATION: —

CIS no. —; PAT no. —.

COMMENTS: According to Legrain (1927) the inscription was added later. The inscription is fake and has no meaning.

PORTRAIT

The figure is shown frontally. The arms appear short in relation to the body. The head is turned slightly to his right. Both arms are bent and held to the torso.

His hair is arranged in three rows of snail-shell curls around the head, covering the ears and reaching the neck. His face is oval. The eyebrows are curving, rendered by thin ridges. The eyes are almond-shaped, with thick upper eyelids. The upper eyelids extend beyond the ends of the lower ones. The pupils are indicated, possibly rendered by punch holes. The nose is straight and wide at the base. The mouth is small, with full lips. The chin is oval and the neck is long with two curving grooves.

He wears a ›Parthian-style‹ tunic. The tunic has a wide, round neckline decorated with a beaded band, and long, tight-fitting sleeves. The cuffs of the sleeves are decorated with a vegetal motif. At the middle, the tunic has a wide band decorated with a running scroll with five-petal rosettes, extending downwards. The folds of the tunic are rendered by vertical and curving grooves.

With the palms of both hands turned upwards, he holds a wide bowl with the fingertips. An object, possibly meat, is placed in the bowl (details unclear).

416. FRAGMENT OF A SARCOPHAGUS BOX WITH PORTRAIT BUST

DATABASE NUMBER: PM624.
LOCATION: Palmyra, Palmyra Museum, inv. no. CD 63.
CONTEXT: Secondary context: Found (02.06.1959) between the two columns of the Transversal Colonnade in front of the right side of the Praetorian Gate.
ACQUISITION HISTORY: —
MEASUREMENTS: Height: 37 cm. Width: 35 cm. Depth: 15 cm.
MATERIAL: Limestone.
PRESERVATION: The upper, right, and the left side of the object are broken off. The relief ground is preserved to the right and under the figure. The upper part of the figure

Cat. 416

is broken off at the base of the neck. The left shoulder is chipped. The surface is weathered.
TECHNICAL DESCRIPTION: —
DATE: A.D. 170–200.
REFERENCES: Ingholt Archives, PS 1348; Michalowski 1960, 98–100 cat. 18 fig. 107; Gawlikowski 1974b, 351 f. cat. 169; Krag 2018, 16 n. 73; 24. 25 n. 163; 32 n. 63; 47 n. 214; 51 n. 241; 87 n. 182; 103 n. 74; 319 cat. 571. Inscription: Michalowski 1960, 212 cat. 7; Gawlikowski 1974b, 351 f. cat. 169; Krag 2018, 319 cat. 571.

OBJECT DESCRIPTION
The object depicts an armless female bust. Under the figure is a protruding plinth.

INSCRIPTION
SCRIPT: Palmyrene Aramaic.
LOCATION ON RELIEF: On the plinth.
TRANSCRIPTION: DKYR MZB[N᾽ - - -].
TRANSLATION: May Mezabbanâ - - - be commemorated.

CIS no. —; PAT no. 1951.

COMMENT: Jean-Baptiste Yon mentions that MZBN᾽ could be the name of the sculptor.

PORTRAIT
The armless bust of a female figure is shown frontally.

She wears one headdress: a veil. It falls across the chest in a curving fold from the right shoulder to the left side. The folds of the veil are rendered by oblique and curving grooves. Part of the hair is visible on the right side of her neck and right shoulder. The hair closest to the neck is rendered with oblique grooves. One s-shaped curl falls downwards on the right shoulder. The neck is wide with one curving groove. She wears a necklace composed of small, round beads at the base of her neck.

She wears a tunic. The tunic has a wide, scalloped neckline. The folds of the tunic are rendered by curving grooves.

417. FRAGMENT OF A SARCOPHAGUS BOX WITH PORTRAIT BUST

DATABASE NUMBER: MLP018.
LOCATION: Paris, Musée du Louvre, inv. no. AO 4450.
CONTEXT: —
ACQUISITION HISTORY: Acquired in 1906 from Ronzevalle.
MEASUREMENTS: Height: 30 cm. Width: 43 cm. Depth: 16 cm.
MATERIAL: Limestone, white/yellow.
PRESERVATION: Only the upper left corner of the box survives.
TECHNICAL DESCRIPTION: There are rasp marks on the fabric of the kline. There are incisions below the portrait indicating letters that cannot be identified. Restored in 1996 when the surface was treated and cleaned.
DATE: A.D. 170–200.
REFERENCES: Ingholt Archives, PS 862; Dentzer-Feydy – Teixidor 1993, 202 cat. 200; Raja 2019e, 98. 138 f. cat 70 fig. 34.

OBJECT DESCRIPTION
The object depicts part of the kline frame and a bust of a priest in the fulcrum. The stretcher is decorated with a single long, rectangular panel with an inscription(?), next to a narrow, incised rectangle. Above the kline stretcher is a single mattress. It has a decorated panel composed of a running scroll and six-petal rosettes motif, framed by beaded bands, a narrow band with running dog, and another beaded band. The fabric of the mattress is indicated by wide, curving grooves. The top of the fulcrum is in the shape of a lion's head: it has wide, round eyes, and an open mouth leaving teeth and tongue visible. The mane is arranged in three rows of crescent-shaped locks that alternate direction each row. At the lower part of the fulcrum

Cat. 417, Pl. 73

there is an armless bust of a priest. The torus finial of the kline leg is visible below the fulcrum.

INSCRIPTION
SCRIPT: Palmyrene Aramaic.
LOCATION ON RELIEF: On the kline stretcher.
TRANSCRIPTION: —
TRANSLATION: —

CIS no. —; PAT no. —.

COMMENT: The inscription is fake.

PORTRAIT
The figure is shown frontally.

He is wearing a plain, cylindrical headdress: a Palmyrene priestly hat. His face is oval. The eyes are large and round. The ears are protruding. The mouth is wide. The chin is round. The neck is short and slender.

He wears a tunic and a chlamys. The tunic has a small, round neckline. The chlamys falls over both shoulders and across the chest. It is fastened at the right shoulder with a circular brooch (Colledge classification: i). The folds of the chlamys are indicated by curving and oblique grooves.

A.D. 180–240

418. FRAGMENT OF A SARCOPHAGUS BOX WITH PORTRAIT BUST

DATABASE NUMBER: UNK225.
LOCATION: Unknown location.
CONTEXT: —
ACQUISITION HISTORY: —
MEASUREMENTS: —
MATERIAL: Limestone.
PRESERVATION: Only part of the stretcher and of the mattress of the kline has been preserved.
TECHNICAL DESCRIPTION: —
DATE: A.D. 180–240.
REFERENCES: Ingholt Archives, PS 1145; Raja 2019e, 98. 139 cat. 72 fig. 36.

OBJECT DESCRIPTION
The object depicts part of a sarcophagus lid in the shape of a kline with a mattress. The mattress has three wide bands: two decorated with a branch of serrated leaves at the sides, and one decorated with rosettes inside a running scroll. Curving grooves indicate the texture of the fabric. There is a fulcrum on the left side of the kline: the middle part is depicted as a

Cat. 418

bunch of branches with serrated leaves. At the lower part, inside a medallion, there is an armless bust of a priest. The stretcher of the kline is decorated with square and rectangular panels on either side of a long, rectangular panel decorated with serrated leaves at the side. The square panels have an incised centre enclosing a flower with four elliptical petals. The rectangular panel has a stepped moulding, and is decorated inside with a running scroll motif.

PORTRAIT

The figure is shown frontally.

He wears a plain, tall, cylindrical, flat-top headdress: a Palmyrene priestly hat. His face is triangular. Facial features are indicated (details unclear).

He wears a tunic and himation. The tunic has a small, round neckline and short, wide sleeves. The folds of the tunic are indicated by curving grooves. The himation covers the left shoulder and arm, and falls diagonally across the chest. The folds of the himation are indicated by wide, curving grooves.

A.D. 200–220

419. FRAGMENT OF A SARCOPHAGUS BOX WITH PORTRAIT BUSTS

DATABASE NUMBER: AMI035.
LOCATION: Istanbul, İstanbul Arkeoloji Müzesi, inv. no. 3787/O.M.246.
CONTEXT: —
ACQUISITION HISTORY: Possibly acquired by the museum in September 1899.
MEASUREMENTS: Height: 44 cm. Width: 91 cm. Depth (field): 17 cm. Portrait A: Height of head: 18 cm. Portrait B: Height of head: 18 cm.
MATERIAL: Limestone, yellow.
PRESERVATION: The background is preserved only around the two busts. There are multiple horizontal cracks across the surface. The lower edge of a rosette at the bottom is broken off. Portrait A: The bust on the headdress, the nose, and part of the mouth are chipped. Portrait B: The upper part of the headdress, the edge of the ears, and the nose are chipped.
TECHNICAL DESCRIPTION: The finish is smooth and no tool marks are visible on the background. Portrait A: Tool marks are visible on the surface of the face. The head leans outwards with no undercutting at the back of the head. Portrait B: Tool marks are visible on the surface of the face. The bust leans outwards and is not cut away at the back of the head.
DATE: A.D. 200–220.
REFERENCES: Ingholt Archives, PS 316; Ingholt 1928, 126; Colledge 1976, 252; Raja 2019e, 98. 142 f. cat. 81 fig. 41.

OBJECT DESCRIPTION

The sarcophagus box is rectangular in shape and depicts two armless busts of priests, each placed inside a clipeus carved in low relief and formed by five concentric grooves. An eight-petal rosette is placed to the right of portrait A, and

Cat. 419

an acanthus-leaves rosette is placed to the right of portrait B, both at the height of the heads. A third rosette is placed at the lower edge of the fragment, between the two clipei.

PORTRAIT A: ARMLESS BUST OF PRIEST
The figure is shown frontally.

He wears a tall, cylindrical, flat-top headdress divided into three sections by two vertical grooves, low on the forehead: a Palmyrene priestly hat. There is a wreath depicted at the lower part of the headdress. It has three rows of long, elliptical leaves pointing towards an armless male bust in a tunic and himation. The midribs of the leaves are incised. It has a horizontal, narrow band at the bottom, suggesting a liner. His face is oval. The eyebrows are curving, rendered by incised lines. The eyes are almond-shaped, with thick eyelids. The upper eyelids extend beyond the end of the lower ones. The irises are indicated by incised circles. The ears are protruding with the helix, tragus, and the lobe depicted. The nose is short with a wide base. The mouth is small, with full lips. The chin is round. The neck is slender and short.

He wears a tunic and a chlamys. The tunic has a small, round neckline. The folds of the tunic are rendered by curving grooves. Over the tunic, he wears a chlamys that falls over both shoulders, and covers most of the torso. It is fastened at the right shoulder with a circular brooch with a rosette within it (Colledge classification: g). A zigzag-shaped fold falls from under the brooch. The folds of the chlamys are indicated by narrow, curving grooves.

PORTRAIT B: ARMLESS BUST OF PRIEST
The figure is shown frontally.

He wears a tall, cylindrical, flat-top headdress divided into three sections by two vertical grooves low on the forehead: a Palmyrene priestly hat. There is a wreath depicted at the lower part of the headdress. It has three rows of long, elliptical leaves pointing towards a circular medallion with a beaded border. The midribs of the leaves are incised. It has a horizontal narrow band at the bottom, suggesting a liner. His face is oval. The eyebrows are curving, rendered by incised lines. The eyes are almond-shaped, with thick eyelids. The upper eyelids extend beyond the end of the lower ones. The irises are indicated by incised circles. The ears are protruding with the helix, tragus, and the lobe depicted. The nose is short with a wide base. The mouth is small, with a full lower lip. The chin is round. The neck is slender and short.

He wears a tunic and a chlamys. The tunic has a small, round neckline. The folds of the tunic are rendered by curving grooves. Over the tunic, he wears a chlamys that falls over both shoulders, and covers most of the torso. It is fastened at the right shoulder with a circular brooch with a rosette within it (Colledge classification: g). A zigzag-shaped fold falls from under the brooch. The folds of the chlamys are indicated by narrow, curving grooves.

420. FRAGMENT OF A SARCOPHAGUS BOX WITH PORTRAIT BUST

DATABASE NUMBER: MAH017.
LOCATION: Geneva, Musée d'Art et d'Histoire, inv. no. 13267.
CONTEXT: —
ACQUISITION HISTORY: Donated by Albertus Hotz, 1930.
MEASUREMENTS: Height: 37 cm. Width: 30 cm.
MATERIAL: Limestone, white/yellow.
PRESERVATION: The background is broken off, except for a part to the left of the head. The surface is weathered. The edges of the veil, the chin, and the curving fold of the veil crossing the chest are chipped. The surface is weathered.
TECHNICAL DESCRIPTION: The lower eyelids are not carved.
DATE: A.D. 200–220 (Deonna 1931: A.D. 200–250).
REFERENCES: Deonna 1931, 7. 111. 115 cat. 20; Chamay – Maier 1989, 91 cat. 116 pl. 102, 3; Krag 2018, 32 n. 63; 53 n. 258; 58 n. 300. 304; 59 n. 323; 62 n. 349. 350; 103 n. 74; 398 cat. 862.

OBJECT DESCRIPTION
The object depicts an armless female bust. To the left of the head, part of a clipeus composed of three concentric incised circles is preserved.

Cat. 420, Pl. 74

PORTRAIT

The head of the figure is shown frontally.

She wears three headdresses: a headband, a turban, and a veil. The headband is decorated with three square panels. The outer ones have a crisscross pattern and the central one a vegetal motif of acanthus leaves. The turban is coiled. It is rendered in three twisting layers, and the upper two are slightly looped into each other at the centre. The coiling of the fabric is indicated by curving and horizontal grooves. Over the turban, she wears a heavy veil that falls down the back of the head, over the right shoulder, across the chest in a curving fold and back over the left shoulder. The hair is visible at the sides of the forehead. It is slightly wavy and combed backwards, with individual strands of hair indicated by s-shaped grooves. It covers the sides of the headband. Her face is oval and fleshy. The eyebrows are rendered by thin, curving ridges that start from the root of the nose. The eyes are small and almond-shaped. The eyeballs are blank. The earlobes are visible, and she wears dumbbell-shaped earrings (Colledge classification: H). The nose is long and wide. The alae are incised. The mouth is small, with full lips. Two small grooves extend downwards from the corners of the mouth. The chin is small and round, with a cleft. She has a double chin. The neck is short and wide. She wears a necklace composed of small, round beads at the base of the neck.

She wears a tunic with a wide, round neckline. The folds of the tunic are indicated by curving grooves.

421. SARCOPHAGUS BOX WITH PORTRAIT BUST

DATABASE NUMBER: Sarrafian005.
LOCATION: Beirut, Sarrafian (antiques dealer) (last known location).
CONTEXT: —
ACQUISITION HISTORY: —
MEASUREMENTS: —
MATERIAL: Limestone.
PRESERVATION: Most of the background is broken off, except for an area to the right of the head. The surface is weathered.
TECHNICAL DESCRIPTION: The surface is smoothly finished.
DATE: A.D. 200–220.
REFERENCES: Ingholt Archives, PS 666; Krag 2018, 32 n. 63; 47 n. 214; 51 n. 241; 103 n. 74; 320 cat. 577.

OBJECT DESCRIPTION

The object depicts an armless female bust. Part of a clipeus is rendered on the relief ground to the right of the figure.

PORTRAIT

The figure is shown frontally.

She wears three headdresses: a headband, a turban, and a veil. The band is placed high on the forehead and is divided into three rectangular, decorated panels separated by vertical,

Cat. 421

beaded bands (details unclear). The turban is rendered in a single twisted layer and oblique grooves indicate the coiling of the fabric. The veil is heavy with a scalloped edge. It falls over the shoulders, and across her chest in a curving fold. Part of the hair is covered by the headdresses: several strands of hair above the ears are pushed back over the headband. Her face is square. The eyebrows are low and curving, rendered by incised lines. The eyes are large and almond-shaped, with thick eyelids. The upper eyelids extend beyond the end of the lower ones. The irises touch the upper eyelids. They are indicated by incised circles and the pupils by punch holes. Only the earlobes are visible under the hair. She wears dumbbell-shaped earrings (Colledge classification: H). The nose is straight with a wide base. The alae are incised and the nostrils are carved. The mouth is small, with full lower lip. The chin is round. The neck is long and slender. She wears a string of round beads at the base of the neck.

She wears a tunic. The tunic has a small, v-shaped neckline. The folds are indicated by curving, wide grooves.

A.D. 200–240

422. FRAGMENT OF A SARCOPHAGUS BOX WITH PORTRAIT BUST

DATABASE NUMBER: UNK222.
LOCATION: Unknown location.
CONTEXT: —
ACQUISITION HISTORY: —
MEASUREMENTS: —
MATERIAL: Limestone.
PRESERVATION: The sides of the object are broken off. The right part of the headdress is broken off. The nose is chipped.
TECHNICAL DESCRIPTION: —
DATE: A.D. 200–240.
REFERENCES: Ingholt Archives, PS 547; Raja 2019e, 98. 139 cat. 71 fig. 35.

OBJECT DESCRIPTION
The object depicts an armless bust of a priest in a clipeus carved in low relief and formed by four concentric grooves. A six-petal rosette is placed at the upper left side of the fragment, and next to the left side of the figure, a small part of a clipeus is preserved.

PORTRAIT
The figure is shown frontally.

He wears a tall, cylindrical, flat-top headdress divided into three sections by two vertical grooves low on the forehead: a Palmyrene priestly hat. A wreath with leaves pointing towards a central medallion is depicted at the lower part of the headdress. His face is square. The eyebrows are low and curving. The eyes are almond-shaped. The eyeballs are blank. The ears are large and protruding. The nose is straight. The neck is long and wide.

He wears a tunic and a chlamys. The tunic has a small, v-shaped neckline. The folds of the tunic are indicated by wide, vertical grooves over the arms. The chlamys covers most of the chest. It is fastened at the right shoulder with a circular brooch (details unclear). A small zigzag-shaped fold falls under the brooch.

423. FRAGMENT OF A SARCOPHAGUS BOX WITH PORTRAIT BUST

DATABASE NUMBER: PM358.
LOCATION: Palmyra, Palmyra Museum, inv. no. B 1913.
CONTEXT: Secondary context: Found (16.10.1955) in the large court during the excavations of the Baalshamin sanctuary. Excavation no. 294.
ACQUISITION HISTORY: —
MEASUREMENTS: Height: 20 cm. Width: 22 cm. Depth: 3 cm.
MATERIAL: Limestone, white/yellow.
PRESERVATION: Part of the relief ground is preserved on either side of the head. The lower part is broken off horizontally at the base of the neck. The headdress, eyebrows, nose, ears, cheeks, mouth, chin, and neck are chipped.
TECHNICAL DESCRIPTION: The portrait appears partly carved.
DATE: A.D. 200–240 (Dunant – Stucky 2000: A.D. 200–273).
REFERENCES: Dunant – Stucky 2000, 112 cat. 117 pl. 28.

OBJECT DESCRIPTION
The object depicts the head of a priest. To the left and right of the Palmyrene priestly hat are three curving grooves, suggesting the portrait was inside a clipeus.

PORTRAIT
The figure is shown frontally.

He is wearing a cylindrical, flat-top headdress that covers his hair (Palmyrene priestly hat). A wreath with the leaves pointing towards a central lozenge-shaped decoration is depicted at the lower part of the headdress. His face is round. The eyebrows are curving, rendered by incised lines starting from the root of the nose. The eyes are close-set and almond-shaped, with thick eyelids. The upper eyelids extend beyond the end of the lower ones. The eyeballs are blank. The ears are large and protruding with the helix, scapha, and concha depicted. The nose is wide at the base and the alae are incised. The mouth is small. The chin is wide and almost double.

Cat. 422

A.D. 200–250

424. FRAGMENT OF A SARCOPHAGUS BOX WITH STANDING FIGURE

DATABASE NUMBER: MLP020.
LOCATION: Paris, Musée du Louvre, inv. no. AO 4084.
CONTEXT: —
ACQUISITION HISTORY: In 1903 by Habra.
MEASUREMENTS: Height: 97 cm. Width: 32.4. Depth: 27 cm. Depth of figure: 14.5 cm.
MATERIAL: Limestone.
PRESERVATION: The side and relief background are chipped. The lower part of the right and left side is broken off. Portrait: The attribute in the right hand is broken off. The attribute in the left hand is chipped at the upper part. Small areas are chipped on the chest.
TECHNICAL DESCRIPTION: Restored in 1997 when the surface was treated and cleaned. Two holes for clams are visible both on the top and bottom of the relief.
DATE: A.D. 200–250.
REFERENCES: Ingholt Archives, PS 566; Rivière 1928, 13; Ingholt 1935, 72 pl. 33, 1; Seyrig 1937, 15 n. 3; 40 n. 3; Bossert 1951, 38. 170 cat. 553; Colledge 1976, 79 fig. 43; Taha 1982, 127 fig. 11; Dentzer-Feydy and Teixidor 1993, 193 cat. 194; Stauffer 2010, 212 fig. 9.

OBJECT DESCRIPTION

The object is rectangular in shape and depicts a male figure standing on a projecting plinth.

PORTRAIT

The figure is shown in frontal view. The head and lower legs appear large in relation to the body. The right arm is held along the side of the body, the left arm is bent and held at the waist. He stands with the legs slightly apart. The feet are pointed to either side and rest on the projecting plinth.

His hair is arranged in two rows of snail-shell curls around the head. His face is oval. The eyebrows are curving. The eyes are large and only indicated by a deep incised curving line at the upper eyelid. The ears are not visible under the hair. The nose is wide. The alae are incised. The mouth is straight with thin lips. The chin is oval. The neck is wide.

He wears a >Parthian-style< tunic and trousers. The tunic has a round neckline, decorated with a beaded band. The tunic has long, loose-fitting sleeves, and the cuffs are decorated with a wide band of a running scroll with a six-petal rosette. At the hem of the sleeve, a beaded band runs. Along the middle of the tunic, runs a vertical band decorated with four-petal flowers with incised midribs, set between two narrow plain bands. The tunic ends at the knees, and the lower border is decorated with a wide band. The band is composed of serrated leaves pointing towards the middle of the tunic, where there is a six-petal rosette. This is set between two narrow bands, and along the lower hem is a beaded band. The folds of the tunic are rendered by curving grooves on the sleeves and vertical grooves on the body. Around his waist, he wears a plain band belt, knotted at the centre with the two ends looped under on either side. The trousers are visible from the knees to the ankles. They are decorated along the centre with a vertical band of leaves set on a stem. The folds of the trousers are rendered by oblique grooves. He wears closed-toe ankle boots, without decoration.

His right hand is at his right thigh, and he holds a plate without decoration. A dagger is depicted next to the hand, along his right side. The left hand is at the waist and holds a large rhyton. The rhyton is decorated with running vines with a bunch of grapes, and at the lower part, in the hand, it is finished with a representation of an animal head with antlers. At the upper part of the rhyton the decoration changes, but details are not visible. On both hands, the nails are indicated by fine, incised lines.

Cat. 424, Pl. 75

A.D. 200–273

425. FRAGMENT OF A SARCOPHAGUS BOX WITH STANDING FIGURES

DATABASE NUMBER: PM1071.
LOCATION: Palmyra, Palmyra Museum, inv. no. unknown.
CONTEXT: —
ACQUISITION HISTORY: —
MEASUREMENTS: —
MATERIAL: Limestone, brown.
PRESERVATION: The object is highly damaged. The faces of both males are missing and large parts of the relief are chipped.
TECHNICAL DESCRIPTION: —
DATE: A.D. 200–273.
REFERENCES: Online: <https://www.gettyimages.dk/detail/news-photo/ancient-artifacts-damaged-and-vandalised-by-the-isis-news-photo/518896966?adppopup=true> (accessed 18.02.2020; link inactive on 06.05.2022).

OBJECT DESCRIPTION

The object is rectangular in shape and depicts two standing males.

PORTRAIT A: STANDING MALE

The figure is shown frontally. Both arms are bent, the left is held to the torso and the left is reaching out. He stands with his legs slightly apart. The left leg is slightly bent, and he is resting on the right leg.

He wears a ›Parthian-style‹ tunic. The tunic has a small, round neckline decorated with a beaded band and long sleeves. The cuffs of the sleeves have a wide decorated band. At the middle, the tunic has a wide plain band extending downwards. The tunic ends above the knees. The folds of the tunic are rendered by vertical and oblique grooves. He wears a plain band belt, knotted at the centre with the ends looped under on either side of the waist. He also wears another band belt that runs diagonally from the right to the left side of the waist. It is knotted at his left side.

PORTRAIT B: STANDING MALE

The figure is shown frontally. Both arms are bent and stretched out. He stands with his legs slightly apart.

He wears a ›Parthian-style‹ tunic. The tunic has a small, round neckline decorated with a beaded band and long sleeves. At the middle, the tunic has a wide plain band extending downwards. The tunic ends above the knees. The folds of the tunic are rendered by vertical grooves. He wears a plain band belt, knotted at the centre with the ends looped under on either side of the waist. He also wears another band belt that runs diagonally from the right to the left side of the waist.

He stands with the arms stretched out, holding an unidentifiable object.

426. FRAGMENT OF A SARCOPHAGUS BOX WITH PORTRAIT BUST

DATABASE NUMBER: PM711.
LOCATION: Palmyra, Palmyra Museum, inv. no. CD 131.
CONTEXT: Secondary context: Found (08.05.1962) in the foundations of the walls between rooms 4 and 3 abutting the wall demarcating the north side of the Forum.
ACQUISITION HISTORY: —
MEASUREMENTS: Height: 69 cm. Width: 80 cm. Depth: 56 cm.
MATERIAL: Limestone, grey.
PRESERVATION: The right and upper side of the object are broken off. The whole surface of the bust is chipped. Only the outline is visible.
TECHNICAL DESCRIPTION: —
DATE: A.D. 200–273.
REFERENCES: Michalowski 1964, 104 cat. 41 fig. 142.

OBJECT DESCRIPTION

The sarcophagus box is rectangular in shape and is rendered as a kline. An armless bust in clipeus is depicted between the kline legs. Part of the left kline leg is preserved and this is turned. It is composed of a plinth, above is a cyma recta, a reversed bell-shaped element, a cyma recta, a reversed concave quarter, a thin torus, and a ball. All elements are decorated with a tongue pattern, rendered diagonally on the ball.

PORTRAIT

The figure wears a garment with a wide, v-shaped neckline.

A.D. 210–230

427. MALE FIGURE

DATABASE NUMBER: PM962.
LOCATION: Palmyra, Palmyra Museum, inv. no. B 9200/2470.
CONTEXT: Secondary context: Mounted on a wall in the house of Sheikh Fayyâḍ at Qaryatein.
ACQUISITION HISTORY: —
MEASUREMENTS: Height: 81 cm. Width: 35 cm.
MATERIAL: Limestone, yellow.
PRESERVATION: The edges of the object are broken off. The surface is weathered. The left eyebrow, the head of the animal, the upper left leg, and the left edge of the tunic are chipped.
TECHNICAL DESCRIPTION: There are traces of black pigment on the eyebrows and the eyes.
DATE: A.D. 210–230.
REFERENCES: Ingholt Archives, PS 562; Uspensky 1902, 120 fig. 19; Chabot 1922, 114 pl. 20.2; Ingholt 1935, 72; Seyrig 1937, 15 n. 3; 43 n. 1; Charles-Gaffiot et al. 2001, 345 cat. 156.

OBJECT DESCRIPTION
The fragment is triangular in shape with a rounded upper end. It depicts a male figure standing on a high projecting plinth.

PORTRAIT
The figure is shown frontally. His arms are bent and held in front of the torso. He stands with the legs slightly apart and the weight is placed on the right leg. The arms appear small in relation to the body.

His hair is voluminous and rendered by rows of snail-shell curls around the head. His face is oval. The eyebrows are arched and rendered by thin grooves. The eyes are large and almond-shaped, with thick eyelids. The irises are rendered by incised circles. The nose is narrow. Nasolabial lines are indicated. The mouth is small, with a thin upper and a full lower lip. An incised line runs down from either corner of the mouth. The chin is pointed. The neck is long and slender with two curving grooves.

He wears a >Parthian-style< tunic and >Parthian-style< trousers. The tunic has a small, round neckline and long, tight-fitting sleeves. The neckline is decorated with a beaded band. The cuffs of the sleeves are decorated with a wide band with a branch of leaves. From the central part of the neckline, a wide band extends downwards decorated with six-petal rosettes. The centre of the petals is hollowed out. The tunic ends at the knees, and along the lower hem of the tunic, another band runs, decorated with six-petal rosettes. The centre of the petals is hollowed out. He wears a plain band belt at his waist. It is knotted in the centre, and the ends are looped under on either side. The folds of the tunic are indicated by oblique grooves on the body and curving grooves on the right arm. The trousers are visible from the knees. They are decorated with a wide band extending downwards at the middle of each leg. The bands are decorated (details unclear). The folds of the trousers are indicated by oblique grooves. He wears closed-toe boots.

With both hands, he holds a tray with an animal. The animal is turned towards the left and is lying on its stomach. A curved horn is visible on the top of the head, the body of the animal is decorated with a scales pattern, and the hooves are indicated. It is a ram.

Cat. 427

428. MALE FIGURE

DATABASE NUMBER: UNK145.
LOCATION: Last known location: Beirut, Ziade private collection.
CONTEXT: —
ACQUISITION HISTORY: —
MEASUREMENTS: —
MATERIAL: Limestone.
PRESERVATION: Broken off on all sides. Portrait: The lower part of the figure is broken off at the waist. The chin is chipped. The left hand is broken off at the elbow, the lower right arm and the hand, as well as the attribute, are chipped.
TECHNICAL DESCRIPTION: —
DATE: A.D. 210–230.
REFERENCES: Ingholt Archives, PS 568; Ingholt 1926, 140 n. 4; Ingholt 1935, 72 n. 79.

OBJECT DESCRIPTION
The object is rectangular in shape and depicts a male bust.

PORTRAIT
The figure is shown frontally. His head is turned slightly to his right. His left arm falls to the side. The right arm is bent and held in front of the torso. The arms appear small in relation to the body.

His hair is rendered by snail-shell curls around the head. His face is square. The eyebrows are curving and rendered by thin ridges. The eyes are large and almond-shaped, with thick eyelids. The end of the upper eyelids extends beyond that of the lower ones. The irises are rendered by incised circles and the pupils by punch holes. The nose is straight. The ears are long and slightly protruding, with the helix, concha, and lobe indicated. The mouth is small, with a thin upper lip and a full lower lip. The chin is square. The neck is short and wide.

He wears a >Parthian-style< tunic. The tunic has a small, round neckline and long, tight-fitting sleeves. The neckline is decorated with a beaded band. From the central part of the neckline, a wide band extends downwards decorated with a branch of serrated leaves in an opposite arrangement.

With his right hand he holds a bowl in front of his lower torso. The bowl has a flat bottom, and slightly curving edges.

Cat. 428

429. FEMALE FIGURE

DATABASE NUMBER: BaronPoche003.
LOCATION: Last known location: Aleppo, Baron Poche private collection.
CONTEXT: —
ACQUISITION HISTORY: —
MEASUREMENTS: Height: 53 cm. Width: 45 cm.
MATERIAL: Limestone.
PRESERVATION: The background is broken off. The lower part of the figure is broken off diagonally at the chest. The edges of the veil are broken off. The left temple, the nose, the chin, and the left hand are chipped.
TECHNICAL DESCRIPTION: The irises are indicated by pigment.
DATE: A.D. 210–230.
REFERENCES: Ingholt Archives, PS 495; Chabot 1897, plate after p. 316 number 10; Ingholt 1928, 149 n. 4; Colledge 1976, 262; Krag 2018, 17 n. 98; 108 n. 125. 127; 102 n. 69; 361 cat. 741.

OBJECT DESCRIPTION
The object depicts a female bust.

PORTRAIT
The figure is shown frontally. Her head is turned slightly to her right. Her left arm is bent and raised.

She wears three headdresses: a headband, a turban, and a veil. The headband is placed low on the forehead (other details unclear). The turban is coiled. It is composed of three coiling bands, the folds indicated by oblique grooves. The veil is heavy. It falls behind the back of the head and over the shoulders. She also wears head ornaments: a head-chain and a central head ornament. The central head ornament runs from under the centre of the veil and towards the forehead. It is composed of three bezels (two oval ones on either side of a rectangular one) joined by beaded elements. The bezels have beaded borders. Three thin rectangular elements ending in round beads hang from the last bezel. Over the head band she wears a headdress chain that is attached under the centre of the turban and runs to the sides disappearing under the veil. It is composed of circular bezels with an incised border joined by beaded elements. Part of the hair is covered by the headdress: several strands of hair above the ears are brushed back over the headband and the edge of the turban, and disappear under the veil. The individual strands of hair are indicated by incised lines.

Her face is round. The eyebrows are indicated by curving grooves. The eyes are close-set, large, round with thick upper eyelids. The irises are indicated by dark pigment. Only the earlobes are visible under the hair. She wears earrings (details unclear). The nose is straight. The philtrum is carved. The mouth is small, with full lips. A small groove runs down from either corner of the mouth. The chin is round. The neck is long and slender with two curving grooves. She wears six necklaces: a string of small, round beads worn at the base of the neck. Below that she wears a necklace composed of round bezels with incised borders and linked by beaded elements,

Cat. 429

and two loop-in-loop chains with a central medallion with an incised border hanging from a thin sleeve. Below that she wears a chain composed of thick rings that crosses the chest, an interwoven loop-in-loop chain, and a chain with thick rings that has a medallion. The medallion has a beaded border and is decorated with the bust of a veiled female.

She wears a tunic and a himation. The tunic is barely visible under the jewellery and the folds of the tunic are indicated by oblique grooves. Over the tunic, she wears a himation. It falls over the left shoulder. It is fastened at the shoulder with a circular brooch that has a polygon whose sides meet in flat ends and whose centre is surrounded by a beaded border (Colledge classification: i). The folds are indicated by oblique, wide grooves.

Her left hand is raised to the height of the shoulder. She wears a wide wristband (other details unclear).

A.D. 220–240

430. FRAGMENT OF A SARCOPHAGUS BOX WITH RELIGIOUS SCENE

DATABASE NUMBER: MLP078.
LOCATION: Paris, Musée du Louvre, inv. no. AO 15556.
CONTEXT: —
ACQUISITION HISTORY: Acquired in 1932. Previously in Laodicea, Didache des Crozes.
MEASUREMENTS: Height: 68.5 cm. Width: 50 cm. Depth: 24 cm. Depth of figure: 6.5 cm. Height of head: 22 cm.
MATERIAL: Limestone, yellow/white.
PRESERVATION: The left and right side and the lower right corner of the relief are broken off. Portrait A: The surface is weathered. The face, the right lower arm, a part of the hand, and a part of the right foot are chipped. Portrait B: The surface of the left side of the face and of the right hand is lightly chipped. Portrait C: Only the right arm and hand are preserved.
TECHNICAL DESCRIPTION: —

Cat. 430, Pl. 76

DATE: A.D. 220–240 (Dentzer-Feydy – Teixidor 1993: A.D. 230–250).
REFERENCES: Ingholt Archives, PS 565; Dussaud 1896, 326 f. fig. 17; Clermont-Ganneau 1903, 156 f.; Mouterde 1926, 315; Dussaud 1932, 149–151; Ingholt 1935, 72; Vigneau 1936, 118; Seyrig 1937, 17 n. 3; 43 n. 1; Bossert 1951, 37 cat. 536 pl. 164; Champdor 1953, fig. 42; Ghirshman 1962, 79 fig. 91; Colledge 1976, 277 n. 245; Dentzer-Feydy – Teixidor 1993, 226 f. cat. 220; Equini Schneider 1993, 114 fig. 23; Seipel 1996, 180 cat. 3. Inscription: Dentzer-Feydy – Teixidor 1993, 226.

OBJECT DESCRIPTION

The sarcophagus box is rectangular in shape and is rendered as a kline. Three standing male figures are depicted. The central stretcher of the kline is decorated with a tongue pattern at the lower half, and a series of medallions, or a running scroll, encircling rosettes or grapes on the upper half (Dentzer-Feydy – Teixidor 1993, 226 write that the decoration of the upper border is a running scroll with grapes). The figures stand on a projecting plinth at the lower border.

INSCRIPTION
SCRIPT: —
LOCATION ON RELIEF: Between the two figures, at the height of the head, and between the legs.
TRANSCRIPTION: —
TRANSLATION: —

CIS no. —; PAT no. —.

COMMENT: There are traces of letters that were probably added in the modern period (Dentzer-Feydy – Teixidor 1993, 226).

PORTRAIT A: STANDING MALE

The figure is shown in a three-quarter view: his body is turned slightly to his right, while the head is turned slightly to the left. Both arms are bent to the left side. The left hand appears large in relation to the body.

His hair is short, reaching to the top of the nape. It is centrally parted, and is straight at the top and curly at the sides, with snail-shell curls arranged in two rows. His face is oval. The eyebrows are curving, depicted by thin grooves. The eyes are almond-shaped and slanting with thick upper eyelids. The ends of the upper eyelids extend beyond that of the lower ones. The irises are indicated by incised circles. The nose is thin and long. The mouth is small, with full lips. The chin is pointed. The neck is short and slender.

He wears a >Parthian-style< tunic and >Parthian-style< trousers. The tunic has a wide, round neckline with a beaded border and tight-fitting, long sleeves. The tunic is decorated at the cuffs with a wide band composed of three rectangular panels with incised borders. A central band extends downwards from the centre of the neckline: it is decorated with a wide band with a vegetal motif between beaded bands. The tunic ends at the knees and the lower hem is decorated with a wide band with squares divided by beaded borders, each square is decorated with a flower (six-petal rosettes and an eight-petal cruciform flower are visible). He wears a thin band belt tied low at the waist with a double knot, with the ends of the belt looped under on either side. Another band belt crosses the lower body diagonally, with a sheathed sword hanging against his left thigh. The folds of the tunic are indicated by narrow, oblique grooves across the body and deep, curving grooves over the arms. The trousers have a band that extends downwards along the centre. The band is decorated with a series of alternating squares and circles with incised borders. He wears ankle-length boots that are higher at the front, and tied with a narrow band across the ankles.

With the right hand, he holds an object that is round at the top and falls down the side of the palm in a narrow band, possibly the reins of a horse or camel. The thumb and the index finger are extended. With the left hand, he holds a sword: the pommel is round and long, the cross-guard is rectangular, and the fuller is indicated by an incised line.

PORTRAIT B: STANDING MALE

The figure is shown in a three-quarter view, turned slightly to the left. The right arm is bent in front of the chest; the left arm is bent to the side. The left hand appears large in relation to the body.

His hair is short, reaching to the middle of the nape. It is centrally parted, and is straight at the top and curly at the sides, with snail-shell curls arranged in two rows. His face is oval. The eyebrows are curving, depicted by thin grooves. The eyes are almond-shaped and slanting with thick upper eyelids. The ends of the upper eyelids extend beyond that of the lower ones. The irises are indicated by incised circles. The nose is thin and short. The mouth is small, with full lips. The chin is pointed. The neck is short and slender with two curving grooves.

He wears a >Parthian-style< tunic and >Parthian-style< trousers. The tunic has a wide, round neckline with a beaded border and tight-fitting, long sleeves. The tunic is decorated at the cuffs with a wide band with a vegetal motif. A central band extends downwards from the centre of the neckline: it is decorated with a wide band with a series of alternating squares and circles with incised borders separated by three beads. The tunic ends at the knees and the lower hem is decorated with a wide band with a vine scroll, a narrow, plain band, and a beaded border. He wears a thin band belt tied low at the waist with a double knot, with the ends of the belt looped under on either side. The folds of the tunic are indicated by narrow, oblique grooves across the body and deep, curving grooves over the arms. The trousers have a band that extends downwards along the centre. The band is decorated with a vegetal motif. He wears ankle-length boots that are higher at the front, and tied with a narrow band across the ankles.

With the right hand, he holds a strap across the right side of his chest, from which a quiver is suspended, visible behind his right shoulder. The thumb and the index finger are extended. With the left hand, he holds a sword: the grip is long, the cross-guard has an incised border, and the fuller is indicated by an incised line.

PORTRAIT C: STANDING MALE

The right arm of the figure is held to the side and upwards.

He wears a >Parthian-style< tunic that has long, tight-fitting sleeves decorated at the cuffs with a wide band with a vegetal motif.

He holds a circular object with a narrow groove near the inner border and a central oval with an incised border, perhaps a schematically rendered wreath.

431. FRAGMENT OF A SARCOPHAGUS BOX WITH PORTRAIT BUST

DATABASE NUMBER: SQatarPriv001.
LOCATION: State of Qatar, private collection.
CONTEXT: —
ACQUISITION HISTORY: Previously in a European private collection, 1982. Sold by Christie's New York, in 2008.
MEASUREMENTS: Height: 47 cm.
MATERIAL: Limestone.
PRESERVATION: Only a part of the box survives. The surface is lightly chipped at the areas of the ears, the neck, and the lower part of the fragment.
TECHNICAL DESCRIPTION: —
DATE: A.D. 220–240.
REFERENCES: Christie's 2008, 9th December, New York, lot 63; Kohlmeyer 2018, 70 cat. 23; <https://www.christies.com/LotFinder/lot_details.aspx?from=salesummary&intObjectID=5157891> (06.05.2022).

OBJECT DESCRIPTION

The sarcophagus box fragment depicts an armless bust of a priest inside a clipeus. It has a plain outer border, a pointed leaf band in the middle, and a beaded band on the inside.

PORTRAIT

The figure is shown frontally.

He wears a tall, cylindrical, flat-top headdress divided into three sections by two vertical grooves: a Palmyrene priestly hat. A wreath with three rows of long, narrow leaves pointing towards a six-petal rosette is depicted at the lower part of the hat. The midribs of the leaves are incised. A narrow horizontal band at the bottom of the hat suggests a liner. His face is oval and fleshy. The eyebrows are arched, rendered by incised lines. The beginning of the eyebrows curves upwards, creating a frowning expression. The eyes are large and almond-shaped, with thick eyelids. The upper eyelids extend beyond the end of the lower ones. The irises are indicated by incised circles and the pupils by punch holes. The ears are large and protruding with the helix, tragus, concha, and scapha depicted. The nose is straight with a wide base. The alae are incised. The mouth is large with full lips. The chin is round. The neck is wide.

He wears a tunic and a chlamys. The tunic has a wide scalloped neckline decorated with a beaded band and loose sleeves. The folds of the tunic are rendered by wide, curving grooves. Over the tunic, he wears a chlamys that falls over both shoulders and covers most of the chest. It is fastened at the right shoulder with a circular brooch (details unclear). The folds of the chlamys are indicated by curving grooves.

432. FRAGMENT OF A SARCOPHAGUS BOX WITH PORTRAIT BUST

DATABASE NUMBER: MLP073.
LOCATION: Paris, Musée du Louvre, inv. no. AO 1010.
CONTEXT: —
ACQUISITION HISTORY: In 1882 from Durighello.
MEASUREMENTS: Height: 22.5 cm. Width: 18 cm. Depth: 11.5 cm. Depth of figure: 6.5 cm. Height of head: 22 cm.
MATERIAL: Limestone, white/yellow.
PRESERVATION: The sides of the relief are broken off, except for two small areas at the left and right side of the neck. The lower part of the figure is broken off at the lower torso. The top of the head and the nose are chipped. The surface is weathered.
TECHNICAL DESCRIPTION: There are traces of black pigment on the hair and the left cheek. There are flat chisel marks on the face, hair, and clothing. The lower eyelids are not carved.
DATE: A.D. 220–240 (Dentzer-Feydy – Teixidor 1993: A.D. 175–225).
REFERENCES: Dentzer-Feydy – Teixidor 1993, 157 cat. 161.

OBJECT DESCRIPTION
The object depicts an armless male bust from a sarcophagus box.

PORTRAIT
The figure is shown frontally.

His hair is short and arranged in two series of snail-shell curls. His face is square and fleshy. The eyebrows are curving, indicated by thin ridges. The eyes are almond-shaped. The eyeballs are blank. The ears are small and protruding. The nose is straight. The mouth is small, with full lips. The chin is round. The neck is short and wide.

He wears a tunic and a himation. The tunic has a small, v-shaped neckline. The folds of the tunic are indicated by deep, curving grooves. Over the tunic, he wears a himation. It is wrapped over the left shoulder; one fold of the himation falls across the chest diagonally from under another end which falls over the left arm.

433. BANQUETING SCENE

DATABASE NUMBER: Sarre002.
LOCATION: Neubabelsberg, Prof. Sarre private collection (last known location).
CONTEXT: —
ACQUISITION HISTORY: Bought by Prof. Sarre from an antiques dealer in Aleppo (the same who sold cat. 84 to Mr Alouf).
MEASUREMENTS: Height: 79 cm (with modern base).
MATERIAL: Limestone.
PRESERVATION: Most of the background is broken off, except for the areas adjacent to the head and lower body. The lower part of the figure is broken off at the thighs. The nose, head of lamb, and lower right hem of the tunic chipped.
TECHNICAL DESCRIPTION: The surface is smoothly finished. The base is modern.
DATE: A.D. 220–240 (Seyrig 1937: A.D. 210–230).
REFERENCES: Ingholt Archives, PS 560; Sarre 1923, 69 f. pl. 3, 2; Ingholt 1935, 72; Seyrig 1937, 16. 19.29 fig. 6; Gawlikowski – Starcky 1985, 131. 133 pl. 18.2.

OBJECT DESCRIPTION
The object depicts a standing male.

NOTE: Seyrig 1937, 41 suggested that it came from the south-west necropolis, tomb no. A120, hypogeum of ʿAtenatan, exedra of Julius Aurelius Maqqaî for stylistic reasons.

Cat. 432

Cat. 433

INSCRIPTION
SCRIPT: Palmyrene Aramaic.
LOCATION ON RELIEF: On the right side of the relief, above the shoulder.
TRANSCRIPTION: —
TRANSLATION: —

CIS no. —; PAT no. —.

COMMENT: The inscription is fake.

PORTRAIT
The figure is shown frontally. His head is turned to the left. His arms are bent in front of the torso.

The hair is short, voluminous, and arranged in three rows of snail-shell curls. His face is oval. The eyebrows are slightly curving, rendered by incised lines. The eyes are large and almond-shaped, with thick upper eyelids that extend beyond the end of the lower eyelids. The eyeballs are blank. The nose is straight. The mouth is small, with full lips. The chin is pointed. The neck is long and slender with three curving grooves.

He wears a ›Parthian-style‹ tunic and ›Parthian-style‹ trousers. The tunic has a wide, round neckline decorated with a beaded border and long, tight-fitting sleeves. The cuffs of the tunic are decorated with a wide band with rosettes. A wide band decorated with a running scroll with six-petal rosettes extends downwards from the centre of the neckline. The lower hem of the tunic is decorated with a wide band with two branches with serrated leaves in opposite arrangement framing a flower with turning, serrated petals. The tunic is tied at the waist with a thin band belt with a double knot. The edges of the belt are looped under on each side. He also wears a sword against the left thigh suspended by a sword belt: the sword has a rectangular grip and cross-guard. The scabbard is long and narrow. Along his right thigh he has an object with a triangular end, a rectangular main body, and lateral semicircles; a sheathed dagger. The trousers are decorated with a wide band with squares with an incised border divided by beaded bands.

In his hands, he holds a lamb turned to the right. The lamb's wool is depicted by circles with a raised circular centre.

Cat. 434

434. MALE FIGURE

DATABASE NUMBER: PM499.
LOCATION: Palmyra, Palmyra Museum, inv. no. B 2741/9201.
CONTEXT: Secondary context: Mounted on a wall in the house of Sheikh Fayyâḍ at Qaryatein.
ACQUISITION HISTORY: —
MEASUREMENTS: Height: 96 cm. Width: 41 cm.
MATERIAL: Limestone.
PRESERVATION: The lower plinth is chipped. The lower left arm is broken off. The nose is chipped.
TECHNICAL DESCRIPTION: —
DATE: A.D. 220–240.
REFERENCES: Ingholt Archives, PS 563; Uspensky 1902, 120 fig. 20; Savignac 1920, 364 fig. 1; Chabot 1922, 114 pl. 20.1; Ingholt 1935, 72; Seyrig 1937, 15 n. 3; 43 n. 1; Charles-Gaffiot et al 2001, 345 cat. 157.

OBJECT DESCRIPTION

The fragment is rectangular in shape with a rounded upper end. It depicts a male figure standing on a high projecting plinth.

PORTRAIT

The figure is shown frontally. His arms are bent and held in front of the torso. He stands with the legs slightly apart and the weight is placed on the left leg. The arms appear small in relation to the body.

His hair is voluminous and rendered by snail-shell curls around the head. His face is square. The eyebrows are curving. The eyes are large and almond-shaped, with thick eyelids. The irises appear indicated (details unclear). The nose is narrow. The mouth is small, with full lips. A line runs down from each corner of the mouth. The chin is pointed. The neck is long and there are two curving grooves.

He wears a >Parthian-style< tunic and >Parthian-style< trousers. The tunic has a small, round neckline and long, tight-fitting sleeves. The neckline is decorated with a beaded band. The cuffs of the sleeves are decorated with a wide band composed of panels with floral motifs. From the central part of the neckline, a wide band extends downwards decorated with alternating six-petal rosettes and four-petal cruciform flowers. The tunic ends at the knees, and along the lower hem of the tunic, another band runs, decorated with two branches of leaves that frame a centrally placed rosette. He wears a plain band belt at his waist. It is knotted in the centre, and the ends are looped under on either side. The folds of the tunic are indicated by oblique grooves on the body and curving grooves on the right arm. The trousers are visible from the knees. They are decorated with a wide band extending downwards at the middle of each leg decorated with a running dog motif. The folds of the trousers are indicated by oblique grooves. He wears closed-toe boots.

With both hands, he holds an animal. The animal is turned towards the left. The body has large, s-shaped locks, and the legs are bent under itself.

435. FRAGMENT OF A SARCOPHAGUS BOX WITH STANDING FIGURE

DATABASE NUMBER: PM693.
LOCATION: Palmyra, Palmyra Museum.
CONTEXT: —
ACQUISITION HISTORY: —
MEASUREMENTS: —
MATERIAL: Limestone.
PRESERVATION: Only the lower part of a standing figure on a projecting plinth and its surrounding background is preserved. The garment over the legs and the lower left leg are chipped.
TECHNICAL DESCRIPTION: —
DATE: A.D. 220–240.
REFERENCES: Seyrig 1937, 22 fig. 14.

OBJECT DESCRIPTION
The object depicts a standing male on a projecting plinth.

PORTRAIT
The figure is shown frontally, with the legs slightly parted and the feet at an angle.

He wears a >Parthian-style< coat, a >Parthian-style< tunic, and >Parthian-style< trousers. The coat falls below the knees and is open at the front. It is decorated with a beaded border. The folds of the coat are rendered by curving grooves. The tunic falls below the knees and has slit sides. The hem has a border decorated with lozenges and beads between and inside the motifs. The folds of the tunic are rendered by oblique grooves. The trousers are decorated with a beaded band extending downwards at the centre of each trouser leg. The trouser legs are inserted into the shoes. He wears round-toe boots that reach up to the ankles.

436. FRAGMENT OF A MALE FIGURE

DATABASE NUMBER: UNK079.
LOCATION: Unknown.
CONTEXT: —
ACQUISITION HISTORY: —
MEASUREMENTS: —
MATERIAL: Limestone.
PRESERVATION: Broken on all sides. The plinth is chipped. The figure is broken off from the middle of the thighs upwards.
TECHNICAL DESCRIPTION: —
DATE: A.D. 220–240.
REFERENCES: Ingholt Archives, IA_NCG_Miscellaneous2016_058.

OBJECT DESCRIPTION
The fragment is rectangular in shape with a rounded upper end. It depicts a male figure standing on a high projecting plinth.

Cat. 436

PORTRAIT
The figure is shown frontally. He stands with the legs slightly apart and with the right foot stepping further back than the left. The left leg is slightly bent with the knee rendered under the drapery.

He wears a >Parthian-style< tunic and >Parthian-style< trousers. At the middle, the tunic has a wide band extending downwards and decorated with serrated leaves and round elements. The tunic ends at the knees and has a decorated border with lanceolate leaves pointing towards a central rosette at the hem. The folds of the tunic are rendered by vertical grooves. He wears a plain band belt, knotted at the centre with the ends looped under on either side of the waist. At the middle, each trouser leg has a band extending downwards and decorated with a running dog motif. The folds of the trousers are rendered by shallow, diagonal grooves. The trousers are tucked into his high boots.

437. FRAGMENT OF A SARCOPHAGUS BOX WITH STANDING FIGURES

DATABASE NUMBER: PM1069.
LOCATION: Palmyra, Palmyra Museum, inv. no. unknown.
CONTEXT: —
ACQUISITION HISTORY: —
MEASUREMENTS: —
MATERIAL: Limestone, white.
PRESERVATION: The chins of both males and the right foot of the left male are chipped. The surface of the chest of the left male is weathered.

TECHNICAL DESCRIPTION: —
DATE: A.D. 220–240.
REFERENCES: Online: <https://pbase.com/bmcmorrow/image/79213643> (06.05.2022).

OBJECT DESCRIPTION

The object is rectangular in shape and depicts two standing males. Between them, a table with a figured leg is shown. Two cups are placed on the table. To the right of the scene, a kantharos is depicted. To the left of the scene, a table leg in the form of a griffin is depicted.

PORTRAIT A: STANDING MALE

The figure is shown frontally. Both arms are bent and held to the torso. He stands with his legs slightly apart. The right leg is slightly bent, and he is resting on the left leg.

He wears a >Parthian-style< tunic and >Parthian-style< trousers. The tunic has a wide, round neckline decorated with a beaded band and long sleeves. The cuffs of the sleeves have a wide decorated band. At the middle, the tunic has a wide decorated band extending downwards. The tunic ends above the knees and has a plain lower border. The folds of the tunic are rendered by curving, wide grooves. He wears a plain band belt, knotted at the centre with the ends looped under on either side of the waist. He also wears another band belt that runs diagonally from the right to the left side of the waist. It is knotted at his left side. The trousers are visible from the knees. Each trouser leg has a wide band extending downwards in the middle, decorated with a pattern. Along his right side, he has an object with a pointed end and a rectangular main body: a sheathed dagger. He wears plain round-toe boots, which cover the lower part of the shins.

He stands with his arms crossed, the left arm under the right.

PORTRAIT B: STANDING MALE

The figure is shown frontally. Both arms are bent and held to the torso. He stands with his legs slightly apart. The left leg is slightly bent, and he is resting on the right leg.

He wears a >Parthian-style< tunic and >Parthian-style< trousers. The tunic has a wide, round neckline decorated with a beaded band and long sleeves. The cuffs of the sleeves have a wide decorated band. At the middle, the tunic has a wide band extending downwards. It is decorated with floral patterns. The tunic ends above the knees and has a decorated lower border. The folds of the tunic are rendered by curving, wide grooves. He wears a plain band belt, knotted at the centre with the ends looped under on either side of the waist. He also wears another band belt that runs diagonally from the right to the left side of the waist. A long sword is depicted at his left side; with a square top and long, rectangular main body. A dagger is depicted at his right side. The trousers are visible from the knees. Each trouser leg has a wide band decorated with a vine scroll with lobed vine leaves, extending downwards. He wears plain round-toe boots, which cover the lower part of the shins.

He stands with his arms crossed, the left arm under the right.

A.D. 240–273

438. FRAGMENT OF A SARCOPHAGUS BOX WITH PORTRAIT BUST

DATABASE NUMBER: MLP019.
LOCATION: Paris, Musée du Louvre, inv. no. AO 5000.
CONTEXT: —
ACQUISITION HISTORY: Gift from Joseph Reinach in 1880.
MEASUREMENTS: Height: 27 cm. Width: 23 cm. Depth: 12 cm. Depth of figure: 8.5 cm.
MATERIAL: Limestone, white/yellow.
PRESERVATION: Only a fragment of a kline is preserved and the head of a priest. The background has been removed. The surface is chipped, especially at the areas of the headdress, the nose, mouth, ears, and chin. The head is broken off at the top of the neck.
TECHNICAL DESCRIPTION: There are traces of red in the inscription. There are rasp traces on the fabric of the kline. Restored in 1995 when it was treated and cleaned. There are traces of black pigment in the contours of the eyes and eyebrows. There are rasp marks on the headdress and on the face.
DATE: A.D. 240–273 (Dentzer-Feydy – Teixidor 1993: A.D. 200–273).
REFERENCES: Ingholt Archives, PS 323; Legrain 1886, 26 cat. 18; Ingholt 1928, 126; Colledge 1976, 252; Dentzer-Feydy – Teixidor 1993, 204 cat. 202. Inscription: Legrain 1886, 26

Cat. 438

cat. 18; Chabot 1922, 123 cat. 27; Dentzer-Feydy – Teixidor 1993, 204 cat. 202.

OBJECT DESCRIPTION
The fragment depicts part of a kline stretcher and the head of a priest.

INSCRIPTION
SCRIPT: Palmyrene Aramaic.
LOCATION ON RELIEF: On the frame of the kline.
TRANSCRIPTION: MLK' BR - - -.
TRANSLATION: Malkâ son of - - -.

CIS no. 4377; PAT no. 0736.

PORTRAIT
The figure is shown frontally.

He wears a tall, cylindrical, flat-top headdress divided into three sections by two vertical grooves: a Palmyrene priestly hat. A wreath is depicted at the lower part of the hat. It has three rows of leaves pointing towards a medallion with the bust of a male figure with a tunic and chlamys. The midribs of the leaves are incised. A narrow, horizontal band at the bottom of the hat suggests a liner. His face is oval and fleshy. The eyebrows are curving, rendered by thin grooves. The eyes are large, almond-shaped, and slanting, with thick upper eyelids. The irises are rendered as incised circles with traces of black pigment and the pupils are rendered by black pigment. The irises touch the upper eyelids. The ears are small with the helix, scapha, tragus, and concha depicted. The mouth is medium-sized, with full lips. The chin is wide.

439. FRAGMENTS OF A MALE FIGURE

DATABASE NUMBER: UNK233.
LOCATION: Unknown location.
CONTEXT: —
ACQUISITION HISTORY: —
MEASUREMENTS: —
MATERIAL: Limestone.
PRESERVATION: The head is broken off horizontally through the base of the neck and the lower part is broken off through the shins. The right upper arm and left lower arm are broken off. The surface of the right lower arm and left leg is chipped. The surface is weathered.
TECHNICAL DESCRIPTION: —
DATE: A.D. 240–273.
REFERENCES: Ingholt Archives, PS 1279.

OBJECT DESCRIPTION
The object depicts a standing male. The figure appears to be standing on a protruding plinth.

PORTRAIT
The figure is shown frontally. The outline of his right arm is visible; it is bent and held to the torso. He stands with the legs set apart.

He wears a ›Parthian-style‹ tunic and ›Parthian-style‹ trousers. It has a small, round neckline decorated with a beaded band. At the middle, the tunic has a wide band extending downwards and decorated with serrated leaves in an opposite arrangement on the stem. The midribs of the leaves are rendered by incised lines. The tunic ends above the knees and has a border decorated with a running scroll with rosettes followed by a beaded band. The folds of the tunic are rendered by oblique and curving grooves. He wears a plain band belt, knotted at the centre with the ends looped under on either

Cat. 439

side of the waist. He also wears trousers. Each trouser leg has a decorated band extending downwards (details unclear). The upper edge of a boot is visible above the ankles at his right leg.

The outline of a bowl is visible at the centre of the torso (details unclear). Next to his left shoulder is the outline of a cylindrical object, possibly a rhyton. The object is decorated with spirals in relief (details unclear).

440. FRAGMENT OF A MALE FIGURE

DATABASE NUMBER: PM430.
LOCATION: Palmyra, Palmyra Museum, inv. no. unknown.
CONTEXT: —
ACQUISITION HISTORY: —
MEASUREMENTS: Height: 84 cm. Width: 48 cm.
MATERIAL: Limestone, white/yellow.
PRESERVATION: The right, lower, and upper side are broken off. The head of the figure is broken at the base of the neck and the lower part is broken off at the shins. The surface of the right hand is chipped.
TECHNICAL DESCRIPTION: —
DATE: A.D. 240–273.
REFERENCES: Ingholt Archives, PS 569; Tanabe 1986, 44 pl. 456.

OBJECT DESCRIPTION

The object depicts a standing male. The relief ground is preserved at either side of the figure.

PORTRAIT

The figure is seen in frontal view. The arms appear short in relation to the body. The right arm is bent and held to the torso. The left arm is bent and held away from the torso. The weight is placed on his left leg.

He wears a ›Parthian-style‹ tunic and ›Parthian-style‹ trousers. The tunic has a small, round neckline decorated with a beaded band and long, tight-fitting sleeves. The cuffs of the sleeves are decorated with a band of leaves. At the middle, the tunic has a wide band decorated with a vine scroll between beaded bands extending downwards. The tunic ends at the knees and has a decorated lower border with leaves pointing towards a central six-petal rosette. The folds of the tunic are rendered by oblique and curving grooves. He wears a plain band belt, knotted at the centre with the ends looped under on either side of the waist. Another plain belt runs diagonally across the waist. A sword is attached at his left side. The pommel is narrow and elongated and the hilt is long and convex. The cross-guard is rendered by a curving line. He also wears trousers. Each trouser leg is decorated in the middle with a band with leaves. The folds are indicated by vertical grooves.

With the upturned palm of his right hand, he holds a wide bowl with his fingertips. With his palm turned outwards, he holds the upper lace of a garland in his left hand. The garland is oblong and composed of lanceolate leaves fastened to two thick strips of fabric.

Cat. 440

441. MALE FIGURE

DATABASE NUMBER: PM434.
LOCATION: Palmyra, Palmyra Museum, inv. no. unknown.
CONTEXT: —
ACQUISITION HISTORY: —
MEASUREMENTS: Height: 50 cm. Width: 24 cm.
MATERIAL: Limestone, white/yellow.
PRESERVATION: The head of the figure is broken at the base of the neck and the lower part is broken off at the knees. The left hand is broken off. The object in the left hand and the right hand with the object are heavily chipped. Cracks run across the surface.
TECHNICAL DESCRIPTION: —

DATE: A.D. 240–273.
REFERENCES: Tanabe 1986, 44 pl. 445.

OBJECT DESCRIPTION
The object depicts a standing male.

PORTRAIT
The figure is seen in frontal view. The left arm is bent and held to the torso. The right arm falls to the side. He stands with the legs parted.

He wears two ›Parthian-style‹ tunics, a chlamys, and ›Parthian-style‹ trousers. The inner tunic has a round neckline decorated with a beaded band. The second tunic has a wider, round neckline decorated with a beaded band and long, tight-fitting sleeves. At the middle, the tunic has a wide band extending downwards and set between beaded bands. It is decorated with intersecting lozenges. Inside the lozenges there are cruciform, four-petal flowers. The central vein of the petals is incised, and there is a small round element between each petal. The tunic ends at the middle of the thighs and has a decorated lower border with hollowed-out squares with a round element in the middle, separated by beaded bands. The folds of the tunic are rendered by oblique and curving grooves. He wears a plain band belt, knotted at the centre with the ends looped under on either side of the waist. Over the tunic he wears a chlamys. It has a scalloped border decorated with a beaded band. It falls across the chest in a curving fold and one part is wrapped around the left arm and falls down in two zigzag-shaped folds. It is fastened at the right shoulder with a circular brooch enclosing a polygon with curved sides meeting in a flat end (Colledge classification: i). A small zigzag-shaped fold falls from under the brooch. He also wears trousers. The folds are indicated by curving grooves.

With the upturned palm of his left hand, he holds a wide bowl (visible in outline). With his right hand he holds an object (unclear, heavily damaged).

442. FRAGMENT OF A MALE FIGURE

DATABASE NUMBER: VAM017.
LOCATION: Berlin, Vorderasiatisches Museum, inv. no. VA 2209.
CONTEXT: —
ACQUISITION HISTORY: Gift of Louis Simon, 1887.
MEASUREMENTS: Height: 15.5 cm. Width: 19.5 cm. Depth: 8 cm.
MATERIAL: Limestone, white/grey.
PRESERVATION: Broken on all sides. Only part of the right arm, torso, and the headdress are preserved.
TECHNICAL DESCRIPTION: —
DATE: A.D. 240–273.
REFERENCES: Wartke 1991, 87. 95 cat. 18 fig. 21; Raja 2017a, 220. 227 cat. 23; Raja 2017c, 64 f. 77 cat. 23; Raja 2019e, 97 f. 123 f. cat. 39; <https://arachne.uni-koeln.de/item/objekt/214771> (06.05.2022).

OBJECT DESCRIPTION
The object depicts a standing figure.

PORTRAIT
The right arm is bent and held to the torso.

The figure wears a ›Parthian-style‹ tunic. The tunic has long, tight-fitting sleeves and the cuffs are decorated with a running scroll with six-petal rosettes. The folds of the garment are rendered by vertical grooves.

The figure holds a high, cylindrical, flat-top headdress divided into three sections by two vertical grooves: a Palmyrene priestly hat. A wreath with the leaves pointing towards a central oval is depicted at the lower part of the headdress. The midribs of the leaves are incised. A horizontal groove under the headdress suggests a liner. A garment falls from under the headdress in two volute-shaped folds. The folds of the garment are rendered by curving grooves. He also holds a branch: it has serrated leaves.

443. FRAGMENT OF A SARCOPHAGUS BOX WITH PORTRAIT BUST

DATABASE NUMBER: UNK223.
LOCATION: Unknown location.
CONTEXT: —
ACQUISITION HISTORY: —
MEASUREMENTS: —
MATERIAL: Limestone.
PRESERVATION: Only the left part of the kline is preserved. The head and headdress of the figure are chipped.
TECHNICAL DESCRIPTION: —
DATE: A.D. 240–273.
REFERENCES: Ingholt Archives, PS 1149; Raja 2019e, 98. 140 cat. 75 fig. 37.

OBJECT DESCRIPTION
The object depicts part of a kline with a mattress. The texture of the mattress is rendered by curving grooves. There is a fulcrum on the left side of the kline. The upper part of the fulcrum carries the bust of a horse. The reins of the horse are depicted on the horse's forehead and side of the head. At the central part of the fulcrum, there is a reclining male figure, and at the lower part, inside a medallion, there is the bust of a priest. The stretcher of the kline is decorated with a square and a rectangular panel. The square has an incised centre enclosing a flower with eight petals: four elliptical ones in the foreground, and four in the background, whose ends are visible. The rectangular panel has a stepped moulding, and is decorated inside with a running scroll motif and circles between the waves.

PORTRAIT A: ARMLESS BUST OF A PRIEST
The figure is shown frontally.

SARCOPHAGI WITH NO KNOWN PROVENANCE OR FROM SECONDARY CONTEXTS

Cat. 442

Cat. 443, Pl. 77

He wears a cylindrical, flat-top headdress: a Palmyrene priestly hat (visible only in outline). The neck is long and wide.

He wears a tunic and a chlamys. The tunic has a wide, round neckline and short, wide sleeves. The folds of the tunic are indicated by wide, curving grooves over the chest. The chlamys covers most of the chest. It is fastened at the right shoulder with a plain, circular brooch (Colledge classification: i). A small, zigzag-shaped fold falls under the brooch.

PORTRAIT B: RECLINING MALE

The figure's torso is shown frontally, the head and arms in a three-quarter view, and the legs in profile. The arms are bent; the right held to the side perhaps falling between the legs, the left raised to the left cheek. The legs are bent, with parted knees and the feet touching.

The figure wears a himation that covers the legs completely. The folds of the himation are depicted by curving grooves.

444. SARCOPHAGUS BOX FRAGMENT WITH PORTRAIT BUST AND RECLINING FIGURE

DATABASE NUMBER: PM949.
LOCATION: Palmyra, Palmyra Museum, inv. no. CD27/66.
CONTEXT: Secondary context: Found in the chapel of the Temple of the Standards (Temple des Enseignes), Camp of Diocletian.
ACQUISITION HISTORY: —
MEASUREMENTS: Height: 19 cm. Width: 30 cm. Depth: 28 cm.
MATERIAL: Limestone, white.
PRESERVATION: Only the upper left corner of the kline is preserved.
TECHNICAL DESCRIPTION: —
DATE: A.D. 240–273.
REFERENCES: Gawlikowski 1984, 109 cat. 74 pl. 93, 205.

OBJECT DESCRIPTION

The object depicts the upper left corner of a kline. At the upper side a mattress is depicted: the surviving part is undecorated with the texture and material of the mattress depicted by curving grooves. At the lower part the stretcher of the kline is depicted: it has a rectangular panel decorated with a running dog pattern.

PORTRAIT A: ARMLESS MALE BUST

The figure is depicted frontally.
He wears a tunic. The tunic has an angular neckline. The folds of the tunic are rendered by angular grooves.

PORTRAIT B: RECLINING MALE FIGURE

The head, torso, and upper legs of the figure are depicted frontally. The arms and the lower legs are depicted in three quarter-view. The feet of the figure are obscured by the armless bust to his right. The right arm is bent and raised next to the head, while the left arm is bent in front of the torso. The legs are bent, with the left leg crossing under the right one.

He wears a tunic and a himation. The folds of the tunic are rendered by oblique grooves (details unclear). The himation is wrapped around the waist and covers the legs of the figure. The folds of the himation are rendered by curving grooves. With the left hand he holds a drinking bowl in front of the chest, possibly a skyphos.

205
Cat. 444

Sarcophagi Reliefs

SARCOPHAGI

A.D. 220–240

445. COMPLETE SARCOPHAGUS RELIEF WITH BANQUETING SCENE AND PORTRAIT BUSTS

DATABASE NUMBER: NMD111 (445a) + NMD112 (445b).
LOCATION: Damascus, National Museum of Damascus, inv. no. B 7405, B 7406.
CONTEXT: —
ACQUISITION HISTORY: —
MEASUREMENTS: 445a: Height: 155 cm. Width: 126 cm. Depth: 28 cm. 445b: —
MATERIAL: Limestone, white/yellow.
PRESERVATION: 445a: On the right side of the sarcophagus lid there is a large crack running diagonally, separating portrait A from the rest of the relief. It has been reassembled at the museum. There are many scratches on the surface. Portrait A: The right foot is broken off and there is a crack in the turban. Portrait B: Small areas of the head and of the clothing are chipped. Portrait C: The nose is chipped. Portrait D: The chin and the right toes are chipped. 445b: The upper right corner of the sarcophagus box has broken off. There are several cracks on the surface. Portrait F: The nose, the left eye, and the right eyebrow are chipped. Portrait G: The nose is chipped and there is damage on his left eye and forehead.
TECHNICAL DESCRIPTION: 445a: The background is roughly cut with visible tool marks. There are traces of red pigment on the jewellery. There are traces of colour in the inscriptions. 445b: The limestone above the heads of the figures is not worked, possibly for stabilization. The lower part of the box is roughly cut with indication of tools marks.
DATE: A.D. 220–240.
REFERENCES: 445a: al-Asʿad 1993, 298 f. cat. 238; Sartre-Fauriat – Sartre 2008, 111; Kaizer 2010, 26 fig. 3; Krag – Raja 2017, 199 n. 24; 204 n. 72. 73; 205 n. 75. 76; 208 n. 99; 209 n. 100; 210 n. 109. 110; 219 cat. 33; Krag 2018, 28 n. 9; 32 n. 63; 53 n. 258. 259; 58 n. 308; 59 n. 323. 325; 61 n. 332; 62 n. 349. 350. 353. 359; 63 n. 355; 65 n. 377; 66 n. 382; 87 n. 182. 185; 88 n. 193. 195. 197; 89 n. 206; 101 n. 63. 64; 103 n. 74; 108 n. 125; 388 cat. 83; Raja 2019e, 98. 146 f. cat. 90. 445b: al-Asʿad 1993, 298 f. cat. 238; Krag 2018, 28 n. 9; 32 n. 63; 53 n. 258. 259; 58 n. 300; 59 n. 323. 325; 61 n. 332; 62 n. 349. 350. 353. 359; 63 n. 355; 65 n. 377; 66 n. 382; 87 n. 182. 185; 88 n. 193. 195. 197; 89 n. 206; 101 n. 63. 64; 103 n. 74; 108 n. 125; 388 cat. 838; Raja 2019e, 98. 146 f. cat. 90. Inscription: Yon 2013, 343 cat. 34; Krag – Raja 2017, 199 n. 24; 204 n. 72. 73; 205 n. 75. 76; 208 n. 99; 209 n. 100; 210 n. 109. 110; 219 cat. 33; Krag 2018, 388 cat. 838.

OBJECT DESCRIPTION

The sarcophagus lid is rectangular in shape and depicts a seated female, two standing males, and a reclining priest. Beneath the figures is a mattress decorated with an intersecting lozenges pattern. The female sits on two large cushions. Curving grooves indicate the texture of the fabric. The reclining figure rests the left arm on a cushion with a wide band decorated with a vine scroll set between beaded bands. Curving grooves indicate the texture of the fabric. Two animal heads protrude from the lower left corner of the mattress. The sarcophagus relief box is rendered as a kline. Three busts are depicted inside clipei between the kline legs: a male, a female, and a priest. Above the kline is a mattress. The mattress is decorated with three bands. The central band is decorated with serrated leaves in an opposite arrangement on the stem, set between beaded bands. The bands on either side are decorated with a running scroll with rosettes. Curving grooves indicate the texture of the mattress. The left side of the kline is decorated with a fulcrum with a six-petal rosette and a protruding branch with lanceolate leaves. The central stretcher of the kline is decorated. The wide, central panel is divided into two sections by a horizontal line. The upper section is decorated with a row of oblique grooves. The lower section is decorated with a tongue pattern. On either side are two rectangular, plain indentations. On each side of these, there are two square and undecorated indentations. The stretcher cuts through the uppermost trapezoidal turning of the kline legs. The legs of the kline are turned. They are composed of a plinth, above is a cyma recta, a reversed bell-shaped element, a concave quarter, a scotia, a ball, a torus, a concave quarter, and above the stretcher is a biconical finial. All elements are decorated with a tongue pattern, rendered diagonally on the ball, and divisions between elements are indicated by horizontal raised ridges.

INSCRIPTIONS ON 445A

INSCRIPTION 1
SCRIPT: Palmyrene Aramaic.
LOCATION ON RELIEF: To the left of the seated female, at the height of the head.
TRANSCRIPTION: MRTY ʾTT | [T]YBWL.
TRANSLATION: Martî, wife of Taîbbôl.

INSCRIPTION 2
SCRIPT: Palmyrene Aramaic.
LOCATION ON RELIEF: To the right of the reclining figure, at the height of the head.
TRANSCRIPTION: TYBWL BR | YDYʿY TYBWL | QRDʾ.

Cat. 445a, Pl. 78

TRANSLATION: Taîbbôl, son of Yidîʿaî Taîbbôl Qirdâ.

CIS no. —; PAT no. —.

COMMENT: Inscription 1: Dotted reš.

SARCOPHAGUS LID

PORTRAIT A: SEATED FEMALE, MARTÎ

The figure is shown in three-quarter view. The right arm is bent and rests on her thigh. The left arm is raised to the neck. Her legs are bent with the knees rendered under the drapery. Her left foot is obscured by the reclining male to her left.

She wears three headdresses: a headband, a turban, and a veil. The headband is placed high on her forehead and is divided into rectangular decorated panels separated by vertical bands. The central panel is decorated with a four-petal flower. The details of the outer panels are unclear. The turban is coiled. It is rendered in three layers with horizontal and oblique grooves indicating the coiling of the fabric. The veil is heavy. It falls over her shoulders. One fold of the veil covers her right shoulder and falls down her right side, over the cushions, and along her right leg in a zigzag-shaped fold. From the left shoulder, the veil is wrapped around her upper arm. She also wears a head-chain that is attached under the centre of the turban and runs to the sides disappearing under the veil. It is composed of circular pendants joined by beaded elements. Part of the hair is covered by the headdress. Several strands of hair above the ears are pushed back over the edge of the headband and disappear under the veil. The individual locks of hair are rendered by incised lines. Her face is long. Her eyebrows are slightly curving, rendered by incised lines and starting from the root of the nose. The eyes are close-set and almond-shaped, with thick upper eyelids. The upper eyelids extend beyond the end of the lower ones. The irises are indicated by incised circles. Only the earlobes are visible under the hair and she is wearing earrings with three juxtaposed beads; a central, small, round bead and larger, round beads at each side (Colledge classification: K). Her nose is straight with carved alae. The mouth is large with a full upper lip. The cheeks are fleshy, and the chin is round and almost double. The neck is wide. She wears four necklaces. One with a string of small, round beads worn at the base of the neck. The second, worn high on the chest, is composed of a plain chain with a pendant with an incised border suspended from the centre by a narrow sleeve. The third, worn at the centre of the chest, is composed of large, oval beads with a circular pendant with an incised border suspended from the centre by a narrow sleeve. The lower necklace, worn at the chest is composed of a wide, loop-in-loop chain with a round pendant with an incised border suspended from the centre by a narrow sleeve.

She wears a tunic and a himation. The tunic has short, wide sleeves and a small, v-shaped neckline. The folds of the tunic are indicated by curving and oblique grooves. The himation falls to the ankles. It crosses her chest diagonally from the left shoulder to the right side, and covers the left breast, body, and legs. It is fastened at the left shoulder with a circular brooch with an outer beaded border (Colledge classification: f). The folds of the himation are rendered by diagonal and curving grooves. The folds between the legs are rendered by curving grooves.

She rests her right hand on her thigh where she holds a fold of the veil. The index finger is extended. The left hand is raised to the height of the neck, and she is lightly pulling a fold of the veil. She is wearing a ring on her left little finger; a thick hoop with a circular bezel. She also wears a plain hoop bracelet around her left wrist.

PORTRAIT B: STANDING MALE

The figure is shown frontally. The right arm appears disproportioned in relation to the body. The right arm is held along the body; the left is bent and held to the torso. His legs are obscured by the reclining figure to his left.

His hair is arranged in two rows of snail-shell curls around the head. His face is oval. The eyebrows are rendered by incised lines, starting from the root of the nose. The eyes are close-set and almond-shaped, with thick eyelids. The pupils are indicated by incised circles. The ears are placed low on the head and are large and protruding with the helix and concha depicted. The nose is thin with carved alae. The mouth is large with full lips. A vertical groove is rendered at the corners of the mouth. The cheeks are fleshy, and the chin is prominent and round. The neck is long.

He wears a tunic and a himation. The tunic has a small, v-shaped neckline and short, wide sleeves. The folds of the tunic are rendered by oblique and curving grooves. Over the tunic, he wears a himation. It falls over his left shoulder and is folded around his arm, leaving the upper part of the body and the hand free. One end of the himation crosses the waist in a curving fold. The folds of the himation are rendered by diagonal and curving grooves.

With his left hand, he holds a fold of the himation. The index finger is extended.

PORTRAIT C: STANDING MALE

The figure is shown frontally. The right hand appears large in relation to the body. The right arm is bent and held to the torso. The left arm is bent and held out from the body. The legs are obscured by the reclining figure to his left.

His hair is arranged in two rows of snail-shell curls around the head. His face is oval. The eyebrows are slightly curving, rendered by incised lines starting from the root of the nose. The eyes are close-set and almond-shaped, with thick eyelids. The upper eyelids extend beyond the end of the lower ones. The pupils are indicated by incised circles. The nose is large with carved nostrils. The ears are placed low on the head and they are large and protruding with the helix, scapha, and lobe depicted. The mouth is small, with full lips. The cheeks appear hollow, and the chin is round and double. The neck is short and wide.

He wears a tunic and a himation. The tunic has a small, v-shaped neckline. The folds of the tunic are rendered by curving grooves. Over the tunic, he wears a himation. It is wrapped around his right shoulder and arm, leaving the upper part of the chest and the hand free. One fold of the himation crosses the chest diagonally and falls over the left shoulder (›arm-sling‹ type). The folds of the himation are rendered by diagonal and curving grooves.

He holds the diagonal fold of the himation with his right hand. The left hand rests on the right shoulder of the reclining figure.

PORTRAIT D: RECLINING PRIEST, TAÎBBÔL

The figure is shown in frontal to three-quarter view. The head appears short in relation to the body. The hands appear large in relation to the body. The right arm is extended and rests on his right raised knee. The left arm is bent and held to the torso. His right leg is bent, and his foot is resting on the mattress. The left is bent under the right leg with the knee pointing forwards. The lower left leg is obscured by the right leg.

He wears a high, cylindrical, flat-top headdress divided into three sections by two vertical grooves: a Palmyrene priestly hat. A wreath with the leaves pointing towards a central oval decoration is depicted at the lower part of the hat. The midribs of the leaves are incised. His face is oblong. The eyebrows are slightly curving, rendered by incised lines starting from the root of the nose. His eyes are close-set and almond-shaped, with thick upper eyelids. The irises are indicated by incised circles. The ears are large and protruding with the helix, scapha, anti-helix, and the lobe depicted. His nose is straight with carved alae. The mouth is small, with thick lips. The chin is round, and the neck is long.

He wears a ›Parthian-style‹ tunic and a chlamys. The tunic has a small, round neckline decorated with a band with alternating squares and rhombi with central round elements. The tunic has long, slightly loose sleeves and the cuffs of the sleeves are decorated with a band with a running scroll with six-petal rosettes. At the middle, the tunic has a wide band with serrated leaves in an opposite arrangement on the stem, set between beaded bands extending downwards. The tunic ends above the knees and has a decorated lower border with four-petal flowers in lozenges. The folds of the tunic are rendered by oblique and curving, wide grooves. Over the tunic, he wears a chlamys that falls over the shoulders and is wrapped around his left arm, leaving the hand free. The

Cat. 445b, Pl. 79

edge of the chlamys, visible across the chest has a scalloped border. It is fastened at the right shoulder with a circular brooch with an outer beaded border (Colledge classification: f). A zigzag-shaped fold falls from the brooch. A wide fold of the chlamys falls onto the cushion and the mattress. It divides into two zigzag-shaped folds. The folds of the chlamys are rendered by narrow, deep grooves. He also wears a plain band belt across the lower torso. It is knotted at the centre with the ends looped under on either side of the waist. Along the right thigh he has an object with a round end, a rectangular main body, and a semicircular lateral element: a sheathed dagger. He also wears trousers that are visible from above the knees. Each trouser leg is decorated in the middle with a wide band with leaves on a stem extending downwards. The trousers are tucked into his plain boots. The folds of the garment are indicated by wide, curving grooves.

The right hand is resting on the right knee. He holds a skyphos in his left hand. It has a conical foot and lower body, decorated with a tongue pattern. The body of the skyphos is decorated with leaves in an opposite arrangement on the stem, pointing towards a central element. The thumb, index, and the little finger are extended. The nails are indicated by fine, incised lines.

SARCOPHAGUS BOX

PORTRAIT E: ARMLESS MALE BUST

The figure is shown frontally, rendered in a clipeus. The head is turned slightly to his right.

His hair is arranged in rows of s-shaped curls around the head. The individual locks of hair are indicated by incised lines. His face is oval. The eyebrows are curving. The eyes are almond-shaped, with thick eyelids. The eyeballs are blank. The ears are large. The nose is straight and wide at the base with the alae carved. The mouth is small, with full lips. The chin is wide and double. The neck is wide.

He wears a tunic and a himation. The tunic has a wide, v-shaped neckline. The folds of the tunic are rendered by oblique and curving grooves. Over the tunic, he wears a himation. It is folded over his left shoulder in a vertical fold. Another fold comes from his right lower side, crosses the chest in a curving fold, and is folded under the vertical fold. The folds of the himation are rendered by diagonal and vertical grooves.

PORTRAIT F: ARMLESS FEMALE BUST

The figure is shown frontally, rendered in a clipeus. The figure is tilted slightly to the left.

She wears three headdresses: a headband, a turban, and a veil. The headband is placed high on her forehead and is divided into rectangular decorated panels separated by vertical, plain bands. The central panel is decorated with a four-petal flower. The outer panels have a geometric design. The turban is coiled. It is rendered in three twisting layers with horizontal and oblique grooves indicating the coiling of the fabric. The veil is heavy. It falls over her right shoulder and proceeds in a curving fold across the chest and over the left shoulder. Part of the hair is covered by the headdresses. Several strands of hair above the ears are pushed back over the edge of the headband and disappear under the veil. Her face is oblong. Her eyebrows are curving, rendered as thin ridges. The eyes are close-set and almond-shaped, with thick upper eyelids. The eyeballs are blank. Only the earlobes are visible under the hair and she is wearing dumbbell-shaped earrings (Colledge classification: H). The nose is short, and the alae are incised. The mouth is small, with full lips. The chin is wide. The neck is wide with two curving grooves.

She wears a tunic with a wide, round neckline. The folds of the tunic are indicated by curving grooves.

PORTRAIT G: ARMLESS BUST OF A PRIEST

The figure is shown frontally, rendered in a clipeus. The head is turned slightly to his right.

He wears a high, cylindrical, flat-top headdress divided into three sections by two vertical grooves: a Palmyrene priestly hat. A wreath with the leaves pointing towards a central oval is depicted at the lower part of the headdress. His face is oval. The eyebrows are slightly curving, rendered by incised lines. The eyes are almond-shaped, with thick upper eyelids. The eyeballs are blank. The ears are large and protruding with the helix and lobe depicted. The mouth is small, with thin lips. The chin is wide, and the neck is long.

He wears a tunic and a chlamys. The tunic has a small, scalloped neckline. The folds are rendered by curving grooves. The chlamys is folded from behind and over his left shoulder, and proceeds across the chest in a curving fold. It is fastened at the right shoulder with a circular brooch with an incised border (Colledge classification: h).

A.D. 240–273

446. FRAGMENT OF A COMPLETE SARCOPHAGUS RELIEF WITH BANQUETING SCENE

DATABASE NUMBER: UNK246.
LOCATION: Unknown location.
CONTEXT: —
ACQUISITION HISTORY: Reported to be in a private collection.
MEASUREMENTS: —
MATERIAL: Limestone.
PRESERVATION: The right side of the sarcophagus is broken off. The surface of the tall vessel depicted to the left on the box is chipped. Portrait A: The right side of the figure is broken off from the right side of the neck and vertically through the torso. Portrait B: The surface at the face, centre of the chest, and the left arm is chipped. Portrait C: The surface of the nose, of the mouth, and of the chin is chipped.
TECHNICAL DESCRIPTION: —
DATE: A.D. 240–273.
REFERENCES: Colledge 1976a, 63. 74. 77. 132. 155. 157. 240 pl. 105; Raja – Yon 2022, 190–192 cat. 14. Inscription: Yon 2012, 416 cat. 557; Raja – Yon 2022, 190 f.

OBJECT DESCRIPTION

The relief is rectangular in shape and depicts three reclining male figures. Beneath these figures is a kline and a mattress. The mattress is decorated with a wide band with leaves on a stem. Curving grooves indicate the texture of the fabric. Beneath the mattress is the central stretcher of the kline. The central part in the middle is divided into two sections by a horizontal line. The upper section is decorated with a sequence of oblique grooves. The lower section is decorated with lanceolate leaves pointing towards a central oval element. All three figures rest their left arm on a cushion: the cushion to the right is decorated with a band with flowers separated by beaded bands. The flowers have incised petals in the middle. The central cushion is decorated with a band with leaves in an opposite arrangement on a stem. The left cushion is decorated with a band with flowers separated by beaded bands. Curving grooves indicate the texture of the fabric on the cushions. The left side of the kline is decorated with a rectangular indentation flanked by two square ones. The legs are turned. They are composed of a plinth, above is a convex quarter, a reversed bell-shaped element, a convex quarter, a reversed concave quarter, a torus, a ball, a bell-shaped element, and above the stretcher is a biconical finial. All elements are decorated with a tongue pattern, rendered diagonally on the ball. Between the legs, a three-legged dining table, a tall jug, and a vessel with tall handles are depicted. The table is circular in shape and has three curved legs connected by stretchers. The top of the leg has an animal head rendered in profile. On top of the table, there are one crescent-shaped object, perhaps a rhyton, and two bowls, one with a conical foot and body decorated with a beaded band, and one with a conical and undecorated body.

Cat. 446

To the left of the table stands a tall, undecorated jug with a conical body, a convex neck, and a narrow, straight handle. The outline of a tall vessel to the left of the jug is recognizable. The foot is conical and decorated with a tongue pattern. The handles are tall and have small loops where they are fastened to the lip.

INSCRIPTIONS
INSCRIPTION 1
SCRIPT: Greek.
LOCATION ON RELIEF: Upper right corner on the relief background.
TRANSCRIPTION: Ἀλέξαν | δρος.
TRANSLATION: Alexandros.

INSCRIPTION 2
SCRIPT: Greek.
LOCATION ON RELIEF: Central on the relief background.
TRANSCRIPTION: Κλήμης.
TRANSLATION: Clemens.

CIS no. —; PAT no. —.

PORTRAIT A: RECLINING MALE
The figure is shown frontally. The left arm is bent and held to the torso.

He wears a tunic with a wide, round neckline and long, tight-fitting sleeves. The cuffs of the sleeves are decorated with a band with a pattern of serrated leaves. The folds of the tunic are rendered by oblique and curving grooves.

He holds a skyphos in his left hand. It has a conical foot and a straight body. The thumb and the little finger are extended.

PORTRAIT B: RECLINING MALE, ALEXANDROS
The figure is shown in frontal to three-quarter view. The right arm is extended behind the reclining figure to his right. The left arm is bent and held to the torso. His legs are extended behind the reclining figure to his right.

His hair is straight and brushed to each side of the head. The facial features are unclear. The eyes are almond-shaped, with thick upper eyelids. The irises are indicated by incised circles, the pupils by punch holes. The ears are small and protruding with the helix depicted. His neck is wide. A v-shaped depression indicates the jugular notch.

He wears a tunic and a chlamys. The tunic has a wide, round neckline. The folds of the tunic are rendered by vertical and curving grooves. An object is depicted extending downwards at his lower body. It has a circular element at the top followed by a square and oval element, and a triangular element at the end. Over the tunic, he wears a chlamys. It falls over the shoulders and left arm, and covers most of the chest. One edge of the chlamys has fringes, visible at the curving line across his torso. A wide fold falls from under his left hand, across the cushion, and onto the mattress. The chlamys is fastened at the right shoulder with a circular brooch with an incised border (Colledge classification: h). The folds of the chlamys are rendered by vertical and oblique grooves.

At the centre of his chest, the outline of a vessel is recognizable.

PORTRAIT C: RECLINING MALE, CLEMENS
The figure is shown in frontal to three-quarter view. The right arm is bent and held to the waist. The left arm is bent and held to the chest. His legs are extended behind the reclining figure to his right.

His hair is straight and brushed to each side of the head. His face is oval. The eyebrows are curving. The eyes are close-set and almond-shaped, with thick upper eyelids. The irises are indicated by incised circles. The ears are large and protruding with the helix depicted. He has a beard that starts from the temples and covers the lower part of the cheeks. The facial hair is rendered by incised lines. The neck is short and wide.

He wears a tunic and a himation. The tunic has a wide, round neckline and short, wide sleeves. The tunic has a plain band on the right side of the chest, extending downwards (clavus). The folds of the tunic are rendered by curving and oblique grooves. Over the tunic, he wears a himation. It is wrapped around his left shoulder and arm, leaving most of the chest and the hand free. The himation continues in a curving fold across his waist and falls back at his left side. A wide fold falls from under his left arm, across the cushion and onto the mattress. The folds of the himation are rendered by vertical and curving grooves.

With the right hand, he holds a lanceolate leaf between his extended thumb and index finger. The midrib of the leaf is rendered by an incised line. With the upturned palm of the left hand, he holds a bowl with his fingertips.

SARCOPHAGUS BOX

A.D. 240–273

447. SARCOPHAGUS BOX RELIEF WITH TRADE SCENE

DATABASE NUMBER: PM328.
LOCATION: Palmyra, Palmyra Museum, inv. no. 2093/7431.
CONTEXT: Secondary: Found at the south-west area of the Tetrapylon in the Camp of Diocletian (12.05.1960). Excavation no. CD 66.
ACQUISITION HISTORY: —
MEASUREMENTS: Height: 75 cm. Width: 115 cm. Depth: 12 cm.
MATERIAL: Limestone.
PRESERVATION: The upper left corner has broken off. A large crack runs vertically through the stretcher and the left side of portrait A. The upper right corner is chipped. The lower right side has been restored. Portrait A: The left side of the face has broken off. The surface of the head is weathered. The right shoulder is chipped. Portrait B: The lower left leg has broken off. The surface of the head is slightly weathered.
TECHNICAL DESCRIPTION: —
DATE: A.D. 240–273.
REFERENCES: Michalowski 1962, 143–147 cat. 16 figs. 158–160; Colledge 1976, 133. 160 pl. 143; Taha 1982, 123 f. fig. 8; Schmidt-Colinet 1992, vol. II, pl. 69, d; Equini Schneider 1993, 126 fig. 31; Wielgosz 1997, 70 pl. 2, 2; Stoneman 1999, 48 pl. 19; Yon 2002, 101 fig. 26; Sartre-Fauriat – Sartre 2008, 84; Smith 2013, 74 fig. 3.7; Gawlikowski 2016b, 21. 23 fig. 5; Seland 2016, 21. 69 fig. 2; Seland 2017, 107 f. fig. 2; Silver et al. 2018, 23 fig. 2.18; <https://virtual-museum-syria.org/palmyra/a-war-camel-with-two-armed-men/> (06.05.2022).

OBJECT DESCRIPTION

The sarcophagus is rectangular in shape and depicts a camel and two standing male figures. Above these figures is the central stretcher of the kline depicted. The central part is divided into two sections by a horizontal line. The upper section is decorated with oblique lines and a figure on the left side, possibly an animal. The lower part is decorated with a tongue pattern. On the left side, the stretcher is decorated with a rectangular

Cat. 447

plain indentation followed by a square inlay with a four-petal flower within. The kline leg is turned. It is composed of a tall plinth, above is a conical neck, a long conical quarter, a quarter, two opposed quarters, and a torus. The camel is rendered in profile. The camel has an oblong head with the eye and ear rendered. The neck is slender and curving, the body is oval and oblong. The legs are slender, and the hooves are rendered by incised lines. The tail of the camel is curling upwards and the hairs are rendered by incised lines. The camel is equipped with a tall saddle covered by a woollen skin, possibly sheep, indicated by small, incised lines. The head of a sheep hangs on the cover, seen frontally. On the front of the saddle is a short fabric in the form of an embroidered carpet surrounded by a beaded band from which three tufts descend. Underneath the saddle is an embroidered cloth decorated with beads in squares surrounded by a beaded band. The saddle is attached to the camel by three lanyards which form a single band on the belly. The lanyards are covered at the top of the saddle by the skin. A rectangular bag is attached to the saddle cloth by three straps. On the hip of the camel is a round shield decorated with nails attached by a strap connected to the saddle. A cylindrical object, possibly a quiver, is attached to the saddle. A saddlebag is rendered below the belly by fine, incised lines. Between the portraits is a wreath with the leaves pointing towards a central oval depicted. A piece of cloth falls from under the wreath.

PORTRAIT A: STANDING MALE

The figure is shown frontally. The legs and left arm appear short in relation to the body. The right arm is slightly bent and held along the torso. The left arm is slightly bent and held out from the body. He stands with the legs slightly apart.

His hair is arranged in rows of snail-shell curls around the head, covering the ears and reaching the neck. His face is long. The neck is short.

He wears a >Parthian-style< tunic and >Parthian-style< trousers. The tunic has a small, round neckline decorated with a beaded band, and long sleeves. The cuffs of the sleeves are decorated with a vegetal motif. At the middle, the tunic has a wide band extending downwards. The band is decorated with four-petal flowers separated by horizontal, beaded lines. The tunic ends at the knees and has a decorated lower border with lanceolate leaves in an opposite arrangement at the hem. The folds of the tunic are rendered by curving and oblique grooves. He also wears a plain band belt, knotted at the centre with the ends looped under on either side of the waist. The trousers are tucked into his boots. Each trouser leg is decorated in the middle with a band with square and oval elements extending downwards. The folds of the garments are indicated by oblique grooves. The boots are rounded.

He holds the reins with the right hand. The thumb and the index finger are extended. With the palm turned outwards, he holds a spear in his left hand. The spear has a long shaft and the centre of the spear-head is rendered by incised lines.

PORTRAIT B: STANDING MALE

The figure is shown frontally. The arms appear short in relation to the body. The head is turned slightly to his left. The right arm is held along the body. The left arm is bent and held to the torso. He stands with the legs slightly apart. The left leg is slightly bent and he rests the weight on his right leg.

His hair is arranged in crescent-shaped curls around the head. The face is oval. The eyebrows are curving, depicted as thin ridges. The eyes are close-set and almond-shaped, with thick upper eyelids. The ears are protruding with the helix and lobes depicted. The nose is straight. He has a beard that starts from the temples and covers parts of the cheeks, the upper lip, and the chin. The facial hair is rendered by oblique, incised lines. The mouth is small, with thin lips. The neck is wide.

He wears a >Parthian-style< tunic and >Parthian-style< trousers. The tunic has a wide, round neckline decorated with a beaded band, and long sleeves. The cuffs of the sleeves are decorated (details unclear). At the middle, the tunic has a wide band decorated with a running scroll with rosettes extending downwards. The tunic ends at the knees and has a decorated lower border with round and square elements and a four-petal flower at the centre at the hem. The folds of the tunic are rendered by curving and oblique grooves. He also wears a plain band belt, knotted at the centre with the ends looped under on either side of the waist. Another belt runs in a diagonal line from the right to the left side. It is fastened by a round button with a lace hanging from it. The trousers are tucked into his boots. Each trouser leg is decorated in the middle with a band with oval elements extending downwards. The folds of the garments are indicated by oblique grooves.

He holds an oblong object in his right hand, possibly a pinecone. The thumb and the index finger are extended. With his left hand he holds the shaft of a long sword. The sword has a small, round pommel rendered above the hand. The index finger is extended.

FRAGMENTS FROM BOXES, BOX RELIEFS, OR BANQUETING RELIEFS

A.D. 100–120

448. FRAGMENT OF A SARCOPHAGUS BOX RELIEF WITH PORTRAIT BUST

DATABASE NUMBER: PM251.
LOCATION: Palmyra, Palmyra Museum, inv. no. CD 46.
CONTEXT: Secondary context: Found (01.05.1962) in the extension to the south of the colonnade to the west of the Great Gate in the Camp of Diocletian.
ACQUISITION HISTORY: —
MEASUREMENTS: Height: 39 cm. Width: 40 cm. Depth: 24 cm.
MATERIAL: Limestone, white.
PRESERVATION: A part of the mattress and the right leg of the kline from a sarcophagus box is preserved. It is broken

vertically on the left side. The nose, the chin, and the right hand of the female bust are chipped.

TECHNICAL DESCRIPTION: —
DATE: A.D. 100–120 (Wielgosz 1997: A.D. 100–150).
REFERENCES: Michalowski 1964, 27. 98–100 cat. 34 fig. 135; Tanabe 1986, 43 fig. 429; Wielgosz 1997, 73 pl. 6, 2; Krag 2018, 32 n. 63; 39 n. 129; 44 n. 171. 173; 45 n. 193; 46 n. 194. 195; 98 n. 23; 115 n. 63; 246 cat. 296.

OBJECT DESCRIPTION

The sarcophagus box is rectangular in shape and renders part of a kline. A female figure is depicted between the kline legs. The mattress of the kline is decorated with a wide band with a running scroll with rosettes between beaded bands. Curving grooves indicate the texture of the fabric. The central stretcher of the kline is decorated with a rectangular indentation on the right side. Next to it is a square inlay or appliqué with a floral motif. The kline leg is turned. It is composed of a plinth, above is a conical neck, a bell-shaped element, a neck, a small torus, a larger torus, a neck, a ball, a neck, a bell-shaped element, and above the stretcher is a torus finial.

PORTRAIT

The figure is shown frontally. The head is turned to her right. The arms appear short in relation to the body. The arms are bent to the chest.

She wears three headdresses: a headband, a turban, and a veil. The band is placed low on the forehead and is divided into rectangular decorated panels by vertical, beaded bands. The central panel has a vegetal motif. The outer panels are decorated with an X-shaped incision. The turban is rendered in two straight layers separated by a thin, horizontal ridge. The veil is heavy and falls over the shoulders. It is wrapped around her left arm and falls over the back of her right shoulder. The veil covers most of the hair; a thick, wavy lock of hair falls down onto her left neck and shoulder. The individual strands of hair are rendered by incised lines. Her face is oval. The eyebrows are depicted as thin ridges. The eyes are wide-set and almond-shaped, with thick eyelids. The irises are indicated by incised circles and the pupils by punch holes. Only the earlobes are visible and she wears earrings shaped like a miniature bunch of grapes (Colledge classification: E). The mouth is small, with full lips. The chin is small and the neck is wide with two horizontal grooves.

She wears a tunic and a himation. The tunic has a wide, round neckline decorated with a beaded band and long, loose sleeves. The folds of the tunic are indicated by curving grooves. The himation crosses the chest diagonally and is fastened at the left shoulder with a trapezoidal brooch with a rosette finial (Colledge classification: b). The body of the brooch is decorated with a floral motif. The folds of the himation are indicated by oblique grooves.

Her right hand is raised to the chest and turned so the palm is towards the viewer. Her left hand holds a fold of the himation.

Cat. 448

A.D. 100–150

449. FRAGMENT OF A SARCOPHAGUS BOX WITH PORTRAIT BUST

DATABASE NUMBER: DGAM037.
LOCATION: Damascus, Directorate-General of Antiquities and Museums.
CONTEXT: —
ACQUISITION HISTORY: Confiscated by the Department of Antiquities in Palmyra August 2014.
MEASUREMENTS: —
MATERIAL: Limestone, white/yellow.
PRESERVATION: The upper and lower right corners, the lower side, and the lower left side of the relief are broken off. The right eye, the nose, and the folds of the veil near the collarbone are chipped.
TECHNICAL DESCRIPTION: —
DATE: A.D. 100–150.
REFERENCES: <http://www.dgam.gov.sy/index.php?d=239&id=1206> (accessed 04.06.2019; link inactive on 06.05.2022).

OBJECT DESCRIPTION
The object is rectangular in shape and depicts an armless female bust.

PORTRAIT
The figure is shown frontally.

She wears three headdresses: a headband, a turban, and a veil. The headband is placed low on the forehead and is divided into rectangular, decorated panels separated by vertical, beaded bands. The central panel has a cruciform flower with serrated petals. The outer panels have a geometric design (other details unclear). The turban is composed of a coiled band. The folds are indicated by oblique grooves. The veil is heavy with a scalloped edge. It falls down over the back of the head and the shoulders. The right end of the veil crosses the chest in a curving fold and falls over the left shoulder. Part of the hair is covered by the headdress: several strands of hair above the ears are brushed back over the headband and the edge of the turban, and disappear under the veil. Two thick, wavy locks of hair fall down her neck and shoulders. The individual strands of hair are indicated by incised lines. Her face is square. The eyebrows are curving, rendered by thin ridges. The eyes are large, almond-shaped, with thick eyelids. The eyeballs are blank. Only half of the ears are visible under the hair. The helix, scapha, and concha are depicted. She wears earrings shaped like a miniature bunch of grapes (Colledge classification: E). The nose is straight. The mouth is wide, with a thin upper, and a full lower lip. The chin is pointed. The neck is short and wide with two curving grooves.

She wears a tunic. It has a wide, scalloped neckline. The folds of the tunic are indicated by wide, curving grooves.

A.D. 120–140

450. FRAGMENT OF A SARCOPHAGUS BOX RELIEF WITH PORTRAIT BUST

DATABASE NUMBER: PM344.
LOCATION: Palmyra, Palmyra Museum, inv. no. B 1842.
CONTEXT: Secondary context: Found (28.09.1954) to the south of the temple during the excavations at the Baalshamin sanctuary. Excavation no. 68.
ACQUISITION HISTORY: —
MEASUREMENTS: Height: 31 cm. Width: 43 cm. Depth: 12.5 cm.
MATERIAL: Limestone, white/yellow.
PRESERVATION: All four sides of the object are broken off. The surface is weathered. Several cracks run across the portrait. The upper part of the portrait is broken off at the base of the neck. The left side of the chest and the surface of the himation are chipped.
TECHNICAL DESCRIPTION: —
DATE: A.D. 120–140 (Dunant – Stucky 2000: A.D. 100–150).
REFERENCES: Dunant – Stucky 2000, 108 cat. 102 pl. 26.

OBJECT DESCRIPTION
The object depicts an armless male bust.

PORTRAIT
The figure is shown frontally.

He wears a tunic and a himation. The tunic has a small, round neckline. The folds of the tunic are rendered by curving, wide grooves. Over the tunic, he wears a himation. It is wrapped around the right shoulder and arm, leaving the left and central part of the chest free. One end of the himation crosses the chest in a wide curve and falls over the left shoulder and arm. The folds of the himation are indicated by narrow, curving grooves over the chest and oblique grooves over the left arm.

Fragments from either Sarcophagus Lids or Boxes

SARCOPHAGUS FRAGMENTS

A.D. 100–150

451. FRAGMENT OF A MALE FIGURE

DATABASE NUMBER: PM1028.
LOCATION: Palmyra, Palmyra Museum, inv. no. CD 19.
CONTEXT: Secondary context: Found (15.05.1959) on the Via Praetoria, in the rubble, halfway between the column with the console and the Tetrapylon.
ACQUISITION HISTORY: —
MEASUREMENTS: Height: 8 cm. Width: 21 cm.
MATERIAL: Limestone, grey.
PRESERVATION: Only part of the upper torso of the figure is preserved.
TECHNICAL DESCRIPTION: —
DATE: A.D. 100–150.
REFERENCES: Michalowski 1960, 109 cat. 29 fig. 118.

OBJECT DESCRIPTION
The object depicts a male figure.

PORTRAIT
The figure is shown frontally.
He wears a tunic and chlamys. The folds of the tunic are rendered by oblique grooves over the left shoulder. The chlamys falls in a wide curving fold across the chest. The folds of the chlamys are rendered by wide, curving grooves.

A.D. 150–200

452. FRAGMENT OF A RELIEF

DATABASE NUMBER: PM752.
LOCATION: Palmyra, Palmyra Museum, inv. no. CD 12.
CONTEXT: Secondary context: Found (09.05.1959) on the Via Praetoria, behind the Gate.
ACQUISITION HISTORY: —
MEASUREMENTS: Height: 20 cm. Width: 22 cm. Depth: 9.5 cm.
MATERIAL: Limestone, grey.
PRESERVATION: The relief is broken off on all sides. Portrait A: The upper part of the figure is broken off at the waist. The right part of the figure, as well as the feet below the ankles are broken off. Portrait B: The upper part of the figure is broken off at the waist. The left arm, part of the left leg, and the feet of the figure are broken off.
TECHNICAL DESCRIPTION: —
DATE: A.D. 150–200.
REFERENCES: Michalowski 1960, 114 cat. 37 fig. 126.

OBJECT DESCRIPTION
The object depicts two standing figures. Probably fragment of a sarcophagus box. According to Michalowski (1960) there are traces of a palm branch between the two figures.

PORTRAIT A: STANDING FIGURE
The figure is shown in a three-quarter view. He stands turned towards his left.
The figure is dressed, but only the belt is visible (Michalowski 1960).

PORTRAIT B: STANDING FIGURE
The figure is shown in a three-quarter view. He stands with legs parted and turned towards his left. His right hand falls to the side.
He wears a tunic. The tunic has long, tight-fitting sleeves and ends at the height of the knees. A vertical groove at the waist indicates that the tunic was probably belted, or had an overfold. The folds of the tunic are rendered by oblique grooves at the right arm, and curving grooves over the body and legs.

Cat. 452

453. FRAGMENT OF A MALE FIGURE

DATABASE NUMBER: PM703.
LOCATION: Palmyra, Palmyra Museum, inv. no. CD 31.
CONTEXT: Secondary context: Found (30.04.1962) at the west of the Great Gate in the Camp of Diocletian, to the north of the main entrance.
ACQUISITION HISTORY: —
MEASUREMENTS: Height: 21.5 cm. Width: 14 cm. Depth: 13 cm.
MATERIAL: Limestone, white.
PRESERVATION: The background of the relief, the head, the right side and lower part of the torso, and the right hand are broken off. Part of the tunic is chipped. The portrait is slightly weathered.
TECHNICAL DESCRIPTION: —
DATE: A.D. 150–200.
REFERENCES: Michalowski 1964, 71 cat. 3 fig. 103.

OBJECT DESCRIPTION
The object depicts a male figure.

PORTRAIT
The figure is shown in three-quarter view towards his left. His right arm is partly bent and held in front of the torso.

The neck is short with two curving grooves.

He wears a tunic and a himation. The tunic has a small round neckline and short, loose-fitting sleeves. The folds of the tunic are rendered by wide, curving grooves over the chest and oblique grooves over the right shoulder, upper arm, and lower torso. Over the tunic, he wears a himation. The himation is wrapped behind the right shoulder and arm, leaving most of the upper torso, the right shoulder, and the right arm free. One fold of the himation crosses the chest diagonally. The folds of the himation are indicated by oblique and curving grooves.

454. FRAGMENT OF A MALE FIGURE

DATABASE NUMBER: PM705.
LOCATION: Palmyra, Palmyra Museum, inv. no. CD 49.
CONTEXT: Secondary context: Found (01.05.1962) in the foundations of the wall delimiting the south side of the Forum, to the west of the Great Gate, Camp of Diocletian.
ACQUISITION HISTORY: —
MEASUREMENTS: Height: 33 cm. Width: 31 cm. Depth: 23 cm.
MATERIAL: Limestone, white.
PRESERVATION: The head, the right side, and the lower part of the figure are broken off. The left edge of the relief is broken off.
TECHNICAL DESCRIPTION: —
DATE: A.D. 150–200.
REFERENCES: Michalowski 1964, 77 cat. 9 fig. 109.

OBJECT DESCRIPTION
The object depicts a male figure.

PORTRAIT
The figure is shown frontally. His left arm is bent and held in front of the waist. The hand appears large in relation to the body.

He wears a tunic (no details visible) and a himation. The himation covers the left side of the body and the arm. A fold of the himation crosses the chest diagonally and falls over the left shoulder. This fold is decorated with a scalloped band. The folds of the himation are rendered by oblique grooves.

In his left hand he holds a bowl: the rim is decorated with boucrania supporting a garland (of palm leaves, according to Michalowski 1964), and a band of alternating five-petal rosettes and medallions with an incised border. The foot is visible under the fingers. The thumb touches the edge of the rim, the other fingers are extended. The nails are rendered by fine, incised lines. He wears a thick hoop ring with a round bezel on the little finger.

455. FRAGMENT OF A MALE FIGURE

DATABASE NUMBER: PM993.
LOCATION: Palmyra, Palmyra Museum.
CONTEXT: Secondary context: Found (13.10.1954) in portico C4, Sanctuary of Baalshamin. Excavation number: 152.
ACQUISITION HISTORY: —
MEASUREMENTS: Height: 22 cm. Width: 14 cm. Depth: 9.5 cm.
MATERIAL: Limestone.
PRESERVATION: The head, the left side, the right arm from above the elbow, the lower right part of the chest, and the lower part of the figure are broken off.
TECHNICAL DESCRIPTION: —
DATE: A.D. 150–200.
REFERENCES: Dunant — Stucky 2000, 103 cat. 74 pl. 21.

OBJECT DESCRIPTION
The object depicts a male figure.

PORTRAIT
The figure is shown frontally. His right arm falls to the side.

He wears a tunic. The tunic has a wide round neckline decorated with a band with alternating squares and lozenges with incised borders. The folds of the tunic are rendered by oblique grooves. A wide band crosses the right shoulder and side of the chest, possibly a baldrick.

456. FRAGMENT OF A MALE FIGURE

DATABASE NUMBER: PM990.
LOCATION: Palmyra, Palmyra Museum.
CONTEXT: Secondary context: Found (08.09.1954) in portico C1, Sanctuary of Baalshamin. Excavation number: 304.
ACQUISITION HISTORY: —
MEASUREMENTS: Height: 16.5 cm. Width: 10 cm. Depth: 14 cm.

MATERIAL: Limestone.
PRESERVATION: Only the foot on its base is preserved.
TECHNICAL DESCRIPTION: —
DATE: A.D. 150–200.
REFERENCES: Dunant — Stucky 2000, 100 cat. 63 pl. 19.

OBJECT DESCRIPTION
The object depicts the right foot of a male figure.

PORTRAIT
The foot is shown in profile. He wears a soft boot.

457. FRAGMENT OF A SARCOPHAGUS WITH PORTRAIT BUST

DATABASE NUMBER: UPM015.
LOCATION: Philadelphia, University of Pennsylvania Museum of Archaeology and Anthropology, inv. no. B9186.
CONTEXT: —
ACQUISITION HISTORY: —
MEASUREMENTS: Height: 11.5 cm. Width: 10.5 cm.
MATERIAL: Limestone.
PRESERVATION: All sides are broken off. The figure is weathered and the nose is chipped.
TECHNICAL DESCRIPTION: The eyelids are not carved.
DATE: A.D. 150–200 (Legrain 1927: A.D. 175–225).
REFERENCES: Ingholt Archives, PS 858; Legrain 1927, 350 cat. 14 fig. 14.

OBJECT DESCRIPTION
The object depicts an armless bust of a male from a sarcophagus box. The figure is rendered in a medallion with a tongue pattern decoration. The outer border of the medallion appears to be part of a running scroll.

PORTRAIT
The figure is shown frontally.

His hair is rendered in three rows of circular curls around the head. His face is oval. The eyebrows are curving. The eyes are large and there is no depiction of eyelids. The eyeballs are blank. The nose is short, and the base of the nose is wide. The mouth is small. The chin is oval. The neck is wide.

He wears a tunic and a himation. The tunic has a wide, v-shaped neckline. The folds of the tunic are rendered by curving grooves. The himation falls over the left shoulder, across the chest and under the right arm. The folds of the himation are indicated by oblique grooves.

Cat. 457

Cat. 458

A.D. 180–200

458. FRAGMENT OF A MALE FIGURE

DATABASE NUMBER: PM657.
LOCATION: Palmyra, Palmyra Museum, inv. no. CD 33/66.
CONTEXT: Secondary context: Found in later wall in the eastern part of the Via Praetoria.
ACQUISITION HISTORY: —
MEASUREMENTS: Height: 40 cm. Width: 60 cm. Depth: 15 cm.
MATERIAL: Limestone, white.
PRESERVATION: Broken on all sides. Broken diagonally from the right side of the neck and at the left shoulder. Broken horizontally at the thighs. The surface at the lower arm and central part of the torso is chipped.
TECHNICAL DESCRIPTION: —
DATE: A.D. 180–200.
REFERENCES: Gawlikowski 1984, 108 cat. 65 pl. 91, 199.

OBJECT DESCRIPTION
Fragment depicting a male figure.

PORTRAIT
The figure is shown frontally. The arms are bent and held in front of the torso.

He wears a >Parthian-style< tunic. The tunic has a round neckline decorated with a beaded band. The tunic has a wide band decorated with five-petal rosettes rendered within circles extending downwards from the middle of the neckline. The folds of the tunic are rendered by oblique and curving grooves. He also wears a plain band belt, knotted at the centre with the ends looped under on either side of the waist.

An outline of an object is visible at the centre of the torso (details unclear).

459. FRAGMENT OF A MALE FIGURE

DATABASE NUMBER: PM942.
LOCATION: Palmyra, Palmyra Museum, inv. no. B1919.
CONTEXT: Secondary context: Found (22.09.1956) at the north-east of the large courtyard of the Sanctuary of Baalshamin. Excavation no. 329.
ACQUISITION HISTORY: —
MEASUREMENTS: Height: 25 cm. Width: 17.5 cm. Depth: 15 cm.
MATERIAL: Limestone.
PRESERVATION: The upper part of the figure is broken off at the waist and the lower part at the legs above the knees.
TECHNICAL DESCRIPTION: —
DATE: A.D. 180–200.
REFERENCES: Dunant – Stucky 2000, 113 cat. 125 pl. 29, 125.

OBJECT DESCRIPTION
The object depicts a standing male figure.

PORTRAIT
The figure is depicted frontally.

He wears a >Parthian-style< tunic and >Parthian-style< trousers. The tunic has a central band extending downwards; it is decorated with a running scroll with rosettes and leaves. The border of the tunic is decorated with a band with a branch of leaves. The folds of the tunic are rendered by oblique grooves. He also wears trousers. Each trouser leg has a band extending downwards decorated with a running dog pattern.

A.D. 200–220

460. FRAGMENT OF A MALE FIGURE

DATABASE NUMBER: PM750.
LOCATION: Palmyra, Palmyra Museum, inv. no. A 82.
CONTEXT: —
ACQUISITION HISTORY: —
MEASUREMENTS: —
MATERIAL: Limestone.

Cat. 460

PRESERVATION: Broken on all sides. The upper part of the figure is broken off horizontally from the right to the left shoulder and the lower part is broken off through the shins. The surface of the right hand and of the vessel is chipped.
TECHNICAL DESCRIPTION: —
DATE: A.D. 200–220.
REFERENCES: Ingholt Archives, PS 920; Tanabe 1986, 44 pl. 454.

OBJECT DESCRIPTION
The object depicts a standing male.

PORTRAIT
The figure is shown frontally. The right arm is bent and held to the torso. He stands with the legs slightly apart. He rests his weight on the right leg, and the left leg is slightly bent.

He wears an undergarment and a tunic. The edge of the undergarment is visible at his legs falling in a diagonal line from above the left knee and over the right. The edge is tasselled. The folds of the garment are rendered by oblique grooves. He wears a tunic over the undergarment. It has long, wide sleeves. On either side of the neckline, wide, plain bands extend downwards (clavi). The tunic ends at the knees. There is an overfold of the tunic at the waist. The folds of the tunic are rendered by diagonal and curving grooves.

With the right hand, he holds the right handle of a decorated amphora. It has a wide mouth and tall handles. The neck is decorated with plastically rendered s-shapes, indicated by curving grooves. The body of the vessel is decorated with a pattern of hollowed-out lozenges.

461. FRAGMENT OF A RELIEF

DATABASE NUMBER: PM697.
LOCATION: Palmyra, Palmyra Museum, inv. no. CD 90.
CONTEXT: Secondary context: Found (30.04.1961) near the steps to the Great Gate.
ACQUISITION HISTORY: —
MEASUREMENTS: Height: 42 cm. Width: 57 cm. Depth: 20 cm.
MATERIAL: Limestone, white.
PRESERVATION: The object is broken on all sides. Portrait A: Only the right hand is preserved. Portrait B: The upper part of the figure is broken off at the base of the neck. The

Cat. 461

upper part of the left arm is broken off. The lower part of the figure is broken off at the waist.
TECHNICAL DESCRIPTION: —
DATE: A.D. 200–220 (Michalowski 1963: A.D. 50–150).
REFERENCES: Michalowski 1963, 156 cat. 49 fig. 206.

OBJECT DESCRIPTION
The object is square in shape and depicts a standing male. The relief background is preserved on the right and left side of the figure. To the right of the figure is part of a hand from another portrait. The hand is clenched.

PORTRAIT A: FIGURE
The figure holds an object in the left hand (details unclear).

PORTRAIT B: MALE FIGURE, POSSIBLY STANDING
The figure is shown in three-quarter view. The right arm appears short in relation to the body. The right arm is bent and held at the right side of the chest. The lower left arm is held at the left side of the waist.

He wears a tunic. The tunic is decorated with two wide, plain bands (clavi) extending downwards from either side of the neckline, and has an overfold, indicating a belt. The folds of the tunic are rendered by oblique and vertical grooves.

The right hand is held at the side of the chest, and the figure holds a pitcher. The pitcher has a conical foot, and the lower part of the body is decorated with grooves.

A.D. 200–240

462. FRAGMENT OF A MALE FIGURE
DATABASE NUMBER: UNK231.
LOCATION: Unknown location.
CONTEXT: —
ACQUISITION HISTORY: —
MEASUREMENTS: —
MATERIAL: Limestone.
PRESERVATION: The head is broken off horizontally at the neck and the lower part is broken off at the lower torso. The right hand and the left arm and side are chipped. The surface is weathered.
TECHNICAL DESCRIPTION: —
DATE: A.D. 200–240.
REFERENCES: Ingholt Archives, PS 1150; Raja 2019e, 97–99. 113 cat. 31 fig. 22.

OBJECT DESCRIPTION
The object depicts a standing male. A small part of the relief ground is preserved on either side of the figure's neck.

Cat. 462

PORTRAIT

The figure is shown frontally. The right arm is bent and held to the torso.

The neck is slender.

He wears a ›Parthian-style‹ tunic with a small, round neckline decorated with a beaded band, and long, tight-fitting sleeves. The cuffs of the sleeves are decorated with four-petal flowers separated by vertical, beaded bands. The midribs of the leaves are rendered by incised lines. At the middle, the tunic has a wide band extending downwards and decorated with a vine scroll, set between beaded bands. The folds of the tunic are rendered by vertical and curving grooves.

He holds a high cylindrical flat-top headdress in his hands: a Palmyrene priestly hat. The hat is divided into two sections by a vertical groove. A wreath with the leaves pointing towards a central oval is depicted at the middle of the hat. Three oblique and shallow grooves, possibly from a garment, are visible under the hat.

463. FRAGMENT OF A MALE FIGURE

DATABASE NUMBER: PM635.
LOCATION: Palmyra, Palmyra Museum, inv. no. CD 32/66.
CONTEXT: Secondary context: Found in later wall in the eastern part of the Via Praetoria.
ACQUISITION HISTORY: —
MEASUREMENTS: Height: 40 cm. Width: 24 cm. Depth: 17 cm.
MATERIAL: Limestone, white.
PRESERVATION: Broken on all sides. Broken horizontally at the upper part of the head. Broken diagonally on the right side of the face and from the right shoulder to the left side. The surface of the face is chipped. The surface is weathered.
TECHNICAL DESCRIPTION: The relief ground is roughly carved.
DATE: A.D. 200–240.
REFERENCES: Gawlikowski 1984, 99 f. cat. 23 pl. 76, 160.

OBJECT DESCRIPTION

The object depicts a male figure.

PORTRAIT

The figure is shown frontally. The left arm is bent.

The hair is arranged in snail-shell curls around the head, covering the ears and reaching to the shoulders. The individual strands of hair are indicated by incised lines. The outline of the head is visible, and his face is long. The neck is short and narrow.

He wears a ›Parthian-style‹ tunic. The tunic has a wide, round neckline decorated with a beaded band and long, tight-fitting sleeves. The folds of the tunic are rendered by oblique and curving grooves.

Cat. 463

A.D. 200–273

464. FRAGMENT OF A RELIEF

DATABASE NUMBER: DGAM013.
LOCATION: Palmyra, Department of Antiquities.
CONTEXT: —
ACQUISITION HISTORY: Confiscated and surrendered to the Department of Antiquities in Palmyra.
MEASUREMENTS: —
MATERIAL: Limestone.
PRESERVATION: Only the torso of the figure is preserved.
TECHNICAL DESCRIPTION: —
DATE: A.D. 200–273.
REFERENCES: Ali 2015, 50 cat. 9 fig. 70; Krag 2018, 45 n. 183; 49 n. 229; 53 n. 260; 58 n. 304; 93 n. 242. 245; 103 n. 73; 382 cat. 808.

NOTE: The figure has been identified as female by Krag (2018).

OBJECT DESCRIPTION
The object depicts a standing figure.

PORTRAIT
The figure is shown frontally. The arms are bent and held in front of the chest.

The figure wears a tunic. The tunic has a wide neckline and short, loose sleeves. The folds of the tunic are indicated by vertical grooves over the arms and oblique grooves over the torso.

With both hands the figure holds a bowl in front of the chest. The bowl is decorated with a pattern of lozenges and is filled with various objects in different shapes, possibly fruit.

465. FRAGMENT OF A MALE FIGURE

DATABASE NUMBER: PM764.
LOCATION: Palmyra, Palmyra Museum, inv. no. CD 99.
CONTEXT: Secondary context: Found (18.05.1960) in the east part of the Tetrapylon.
ACQUISITION HISTORY: —
MEASUREMENTS: Height: 16 cm. Width: 20 cm. Depth: 19 cm.
MATERIAL: Limestone, grey.
PRESERVATION: The relief is broken off on all sides. The upper part of the figure is broken off at the thighs. The lower part of the figure is broken off diagonally above the knees.
TECHNICAL DESCRIPTION: —
DATE: A.D. 200–273.
REFERENCES: Michalowski 1962, 154 cat. 24 fig. 169.

OBJECT DESCRIPTION
The object depicts part of the lower body of a standing figure.

PORTRAIT
The figure is shown in a three-quarter view. He stands with his legs parted and turned towards his left.

He wears a ›Parthian-style‹ tunic and ›Parthian‹ trousers. The tunic falls to the height of the thighs. The tunic is decorated with a broad band extending downwards in the middle, and a broad decorated border at the hem. The band extending downwards is decorated with flowers and lozenges (other details unclear) between two beaded bands. The hem border is decorated with alternating six-petal and eight-petal flowers within a running scroll. The six-petal flowers have round petals with a hollowed-out centre, and the eight-petal flowers have elliptical-shaped petals. The edge is decorated with a beaded band. The side edge of the tunic is slit and decorated with a beaded band. He also wears trousers. They are decorated in the middle with a broad band extending downwards between two beaded bands. The band is decorated with a motif of leaves set opposite against the stem.

466. FRAGMENT OF A FEMALE BUST

DATABASE NUMBER: UNK003.
LOCATION: Last known location: Palmyra, D'Andurain collection.
CONTEXT: —
ACQUISITION HISTORY: —
MEASUREMENTS: Height: 44 cm. Width: 32 cm.
MATERIAL: Limestone.
PRESERVATION: The background is preserved only around the head and right shoulder of the figure. The lower part of the figure is broken off diagonally at the upper chest. The left shoulder is broken off. The lower part of the face is broken off. The surface of the upper face is chipped.
TECHNICAL DESCRIPTION: —
DATE: A.D. 200–273.
REFERENCES: Ingholt Archives, PS 942–943; Krag 2018, 170 cat. 25.

OBJECT DESCRIPTION
The fragment depicts the head of a female figure.

PORTRAIT
The figure is shown frontally.

She wears two headdresses: a turban and a veil. The turban is placed low on the forehead. It is composed of three coiling bands, the folds indicated by oblique grooves. The veil falls behind the head and over the right shoulder. Two thick, wavy

Cat. 466

locks of hair fall down her neck and shoulders. The individual strands of hair are indicated by incised lines. Her face is round. The eyes are large and round, with thick upper eyelids. The ears are large and protruding with the helix carved. She wears large, crescent-shaped earrings (Colledge classification: C). The neck is wide.

She wears a tunic. The tunic has a wide round neckline and sleeves.

467. FRAGMENT OF A FEMALE FIGURE

DATABASE NUMBER: PM.
LOCATION: Palmyra, Palmyra Museum, inv. no. CD 10/68.
CONTEXT: Secondary context: A late wall in the Temple of the Standards (Temple des Enseignes), Camp of Diocletian.
ACQUISITION HISTORY: —
MEASUREMENTS: Height: 32 cm. Width: 32 cm. Depth: 13 cm.
MATERIAL: Limestone, white.
PRESERVATION: The relief is broken on all four sides. The face is broken off. The surface is heavily weathered and chipped.

TECHNICAL DESCRIPTION: —
DATE: A.D. 200–273.
REFERENCES: Myśliwiec 1974, 85. 94 fig. 2; Gawlikowski 1984, 104 f. cat. 47 pl. 84, 182; Krag 2018, 31 n. 54; 47 n. 214; 51 n. 241; 103 n. 74; 214 cat. 177.

OBJECT DESCRIPTION
The object is rectangular in shape and depicts an armless female bust in clipeus composed of concentric, incised circles.

PORTRAIT
The figure is shown frontally.

She wears a veil. It is heavy, falls over the back of the head and over both shoulders and is loosely wrapped around the torso, disappearing behind the left shoulder. Two thick, wavy locks of hair fall down her neck and shoulders. She appears to wear earrings (details unclear). The chin is wide. The neck is short and wide.

She wears a tunic. The tunic has a wide, round neckline with a scalloped edge. The folds of the tunic are indicated by curving grooves.

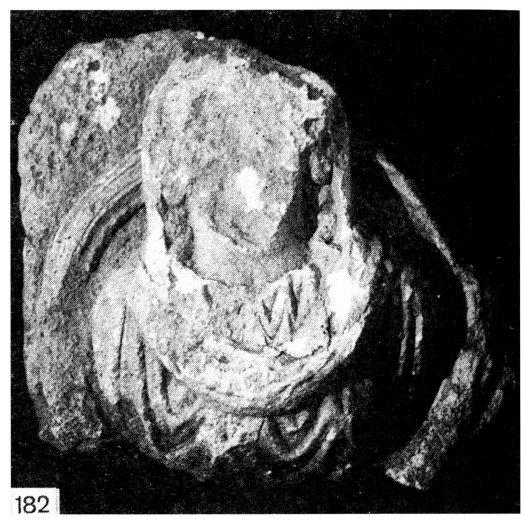

Cat. 467

A.D. 210–230

468. FRAGMENT OF A BANQUETING RELIEF

DATABASE NUMBER: UNK045.
LOCATION: Last known location: Brussels, Deryver collection.
CONTEXT: —
ACQUISITION HISTORY: —
MEASUREMENTS: —
MATERIAL: Limestone.
PRESERVATION: The relief is broken off at the height of the waist of the figure. The lower part of the figure is missing. The lower arms of the figure are partly broken off.
TECHNICAL DESCRIPTION: —
DATE: A.D. 210–230.
REFERENCES: Ingholt Archives, IA_NCG_Portrait2016_088.

OBJECT DESCRIPTION

The object is rectangular in shape and depicts a male bust.

PORTRAIT

The figure is shown frontally. His head is turned slightly to his right. Both arms are bent and held in front of the torso. The lower arms appear small in relation to the body.

His hair is rendered by snail-shell curls around the head. His face is oval-shaped. The eyebrows are arched and rendered by thin ridges. The eyes are large and almond-shaped, with thick eyelids. The end of the upper eyelids extends beyond that of the lower ones. The irises are rendered by incised circles and the pupils by punch holes. The ears are long and slightly protruding, with the helix, concha, and lobe indicated. The nose is straight. The alae are carved. The mouth is small, with a thin upper lip and a full lower lip. The chin is pointed. The neck is short and wide.

He wears a ›Parthian-style‹ tunic. The tunic has a small, round neckline and long, tight-fitting sleeves. The neckline is decorated with a beaded band. From the central part of the neckline, a wide band extends downwards decorated with a branch of serrated leaves in an opposite arrangement.

With both hands, he holds a bowl in front of his lower torso. The mouth is rectangular, and the lip is indicated by a horizontal, incised line. The body is round and undecorated.

Cat. 468

A.D. 220–240

469. MALE FIGURE

DATABASE NUMBER: MLP031.
LOCATION: Paris, Musée du Louvre, inv. no. AO 18174.
CONTEXT: —
ACQUISITION HISTORY: In 1935 by Seyrig.
MEASUREMENTS: Height: 45 cm. Width: 37 cm. Depth: 18 cm.
MATERIAL: Limestone, white/yellow.
PRESERVATION: All four sides of the relief are broken off. The upper part of the head is broken off. The left eye, nose, and the clothing are chipped.
TECHNICAL DESCRIPTION: There are tooth chisel marks on the surface of the background. The relief was restored in 1995 when the surface was polished and restored. There is modern red pigment in the inscription and on the figure.
DATE: A.D. 220–240.
REFERENCES: Rostovtzeff 1932, 152 pl. XXIII, 3; Colledge 1976, 62. 69. 124. 138 f. 145. 151. 154. 216. 240 f. 246. 252 pl. 82; Parlasca 1982b, 12 n. 98; Dentzer-Feydy – Teixidor 1993, 228 cat. 221; Sokolowski 2014, 379. 384. 388 fig. 7; Kaizer 2017, 35 f.; Raja – Yon 2022, 218 f. cat. 36. Inscription: Parlasca 1982b, 12 n. 98; Dentzer-Feydy – Teixidor 1993, 228 cat. 221; Yon 2012, 417 cat. 559; Kaizer 2017, 35 f; Raja – Yon 2022, 218 f.

OBJECT DESCRIPTION
The object depicts a standing male. The relief ground is preserved at either side of the figure.

NOTE: Rostovtzeff 1932, pl. XXIII, 3 shows the figure with hair; according to Dentzer-Feydy – Teixidor 1993, 228 cat. 221 the top of the head with the hair was lost.

INSCRIPTION
SCRIPT: Greek.
LOCATION ON RELIEF: On the writing tablet.
TRANSCRIPTION: ΩΨ | ΧΦ | Υ̣.
TRANSLATION: —

CIS no. —; PAT no. —.

COMMENT: In reverse, end of the Greek alphabet.

PORTRAIT
The figure is shown frontally. The head is turned towards the left. The arms are bent in front of the torso.

The hair is short and straight. The individual strands of hair are indicated by thin, incised lines. His face is square. The eyebrows are curving, depicted by thick ridges. The eyes are small and almond-shaped, with thick upper eyelids. The eyeballs are blank. The ears are small and slightly protruding

Cat. 469

with helix, scapha, and concha indicated. The nose has a wide base. The alae are indicated by incised lines. The mouth is small, with full lips. The chin is pointed. The neck is long and slender with two curving grooves. He wears a thick, plain hoop necklace with a round pendant with an incised border suspended from the centre by a narrow sleeve.

He wears a tunic and a chlamys. The tunic has a wide, round neckline and long, tight-fitting sleeves. The cuff of the right sleeve is decorated with a series of narrow triangles. The folds of the tunic are indicated by curving grooves over the arms. Over the tunic, he wears a chlamys that falls over both shoulders, and covers the chest. The edge of the chlamys that falls across the upper part of the chest has a woolly fringe. The chlamys is fastened at the right shoulder with a round brooch with an incised border and a circle at the centre indicated by red pigment (Colledge classification: h). The folds of the chlamys are indicated by curving grooves.

With his right hand, he holds a writing stylus. He wears a bracelet with twisted plain wires on the right wrist. With his left hand, he holds an open writing tablet with four horizontal grooves. He wears a bracelet with a thick, plain hoop on the left wrist.

470. FRAGMENT OF A MALE FIGURE

DATABASE NUMBER: PM656.
LOCATION: Palmyra, Palmyra Museum, inv. no. CD 11/66.
CONTEXT: Secondary context: Found in Temple of the Standards (Temple des Enseignes), Camp of Diocletian.
ACQUISITION HISTORY: —
MEASUREMENTS: Height: 40 cm. Width: 20 cm. Depth: 9 cm.
MATERIAL: Limestone, white.
PRESERVATION: Broken on all sides. Broken diagonally from the right side of the neck to the left shoulder and the thighs. The surface of the right lower arm and hand is chipped.
TECHNICAL DESCRIPTION: —
DATE: A.D. 220–240.
REFERENCES: Gawlikowski 1984, 107 f. cat. 63 pl. 90, 197.

OBJECT DESCRIPTION
Fragment depicting a male figure.

PORTRAIT
The figure is shown frontally. The arms are bent and held to the torso.

He wears a ›Parthian-style‹ tunic. The tunic has a small, round neckline decorated with a beaded band, and long sleeves. The cuffs of the sleeves are decorated with a floral motif. The tunic has two beaded bands framing a wide band decorated with four-petal serrated flowers each separated by horizontal, beaded bands extending downwards from the middle of the neckline. The folds of the tunic are rendered by oblique and curving grooves. The centre of the flower petals is indicated by incised lines. He also wears a plain band belt, knotted at the centre with the ends looped under on either side of the waist.

He stands with his arms crossed, the right hand over the left.

471. FRAGMENT OF A MALE FIGURE

DATABASE NUMBER: PM717.
LOCATION: Palmyra, Palmyra Museum, inv. no. CD 80.
CONTEXT: Secondary context: Found in a later Arabic wall south of the Pretorian Road between the portico and the Tetrapylon.
ACQUISITION HISTORY: —
MEASUREMENTS: Height: 56 cm. Width: 26 cm. Depth: 17 cm.
MATERIAL: Limestone, grey.
PRESERVATION: The upper part is broken off diagonally from the left shoulder to below the right shoulder; the lower part is broken off diagonally at the legs. The surface of the animal and of the hand are chipped.
TECHNICAL DESCRIPTION: —
DATE: A.D. 220–240.
REFERENCES: Michalowski 1962, 153 cat. 23 fig. 167.

OBJECT DESCRIPTION
The object depicts a standing male.

PORTRAIT
The figure is shown frontally. Both arms are bent and held to the torso.

He is wearing a tunic with long, tight-fitting sleeves. The folds of the tunic are rendered by curving grooves. He also wears a band belt across the lower torso. It is knotted at the centre with the ends looped under on either side of the waist.

He holds an animal, possibly a goat or a lamb, in his hands.

Cat. 470

472. FRAGMENT OF A MALE FIGURE

DATABASE NUMBER: PM718.
LOCATION: Palmyra, Palmyra Museum, inv. no. CD 59.
CONTEXT: Secondary context: Found in a later Arabic wall south of the Pretorian Road between the portico and the Tetrapylon, in the Camp of Diocletian.
ACQUISITION HISTORY: —
MEASUREMENTS: Height: 35 cm. Width: 26 cm. Depth: 19 cm.
MATERIAL: Limestone, grey.
PRESERVATION: The head is broken off at the neck and diagonally at the left shoulder. The lower part is broken off at the waist. The right hand is chipped. The surface is weathered.
TECHNICAL DESCRIPTION: —
DATE: A.D. 220–240.
REFERENCES: Michalowski 1962, 153 cat. 23 fig. 168.

OBJECT DESCRIPTION
The object depicts a standing male.

PORTRAIT
The figure is shown frontally. The right arm is bent and held to the chest.

He wears a ›Parthian-style‹ tunic with a small, round neckline decorated with a plain band, and long, tight-fitting sleeves. The folds of the tunic are rendered by curving and oblique grooves.

He holds the right handle of a decorated amphora. It has a wide mouth decorated with a beaded band and tall handles. The neck is decorated with oblique grooves. The body of the vessel is decorated with a pattern of inverted circles.

A.D. 240–273

473. FRAGMENT OF A MALE FIGURE

DATABASE NUMBER: PM915.
LOCATION: Palmyra, Palmyra Museum, inv. no. A83.
CONTEXT: —
ACQUISITION HISTORY: —
MEASUREMENTS: —
MATERIAL: Limestone.
PRESERVATION: The relief ground is broken on all sides. The lower part of the figure is broken off horizontally at the thighs. The surface of the face is chipped.
TECHNICAL DESCRIPTION: —
DATE: A.D. 240–273.
REFERENCES: Ingholt Archives, PS 921; Tanabe 1986, 44 pl. 455.

OBJECT DESCRIPTION
The object depicts a standing male.

PORTRAIT
The figure is shown frontally. The head is turned to his right. The right arm is bent and held to the torso. The left arm is bent and held out from the body.

His hair is arranged in rows of snail-shell curls that reach his neck. His neck is slender with two horizontal grooves.

He wears a tunic and a himation. The tunic has a wide, v-shaped neckline and long, loose sleeves. An overfold is depicted in a curving line across the waist. The folds of the tunic are rendered by vertical and curving grooves. Over the tunic, he wears a himation. It is wrapped around his left shoulder and arm and proceeds downwards in a wide fold. The folds of the himation are rendered by vertical and curving grooves.

He holds a garland of two sections in his hands. His right hand is clenched around a part of the garland. The garland proceeds in a curve across his torso to his left side, where he holds the other lace fastened to the next section of the garland that extends downwards alongside his left leg. The garlands are composed of leaves pointing towards a central rosette.

Cat. 473

474. FRAGMENT OF A MALE FIGURE

DATABASE NUMBER: PM651.
LOCATION: Palmyra, Palmyra Museum, inv. no. CD 20/66.
CONTEXT: Secondary context: Found in room IIb in the Temple of the Standards (Temple des Enseignes), Camp of Diocletian.
ACQUISITION HISTORY: —
MEASUREMENTS: Height: 32 cm. Width: 20 cm. Depth: 11 cm.
MATERIAL: Limestone, white.
PRESERVATION: Only the torso is preserved of the portrait. The surface of the lower part of the torso is chipped.
TECHNICAL DESCRIPTION: —
DATE: A.D. 240–273.
REFERENCES: Gawlikowski 1984, 106 cat. 56 pl. 87, 190.

OBJECT DESCRIPTION
The object is rectangular in shape and depicts the torso of a figure, possibly a male. The relief is framed by an outer plain band, and an inner frame with leaf-and-dart moulding. The midribs of the leaves are indicated by incised lines.

PORTRAIT
The figure is shown in frontal view.
He wears a tunic and a chlamys. The tunic has a round neckline decorated with a beaded band. The chlamys falls over both shoulders and is fastened at the right shoulder with a circular brooch with an incised circle (Colledge classification: h). The folds of the chlamys are rendered by curving grooves.

475. FRAGMENT OF A MALE FIGURE

DATABASE NUMBER: PM935.
LOCATION: Palmyra, Palmyra Museum, inv. no. CD12/66.
CONTEXT: Secondary context. Found in part of the Temple of the Standards (Temple des Enseignes), Camp of Diocletian.
ACQUISITION HISTORY: —
MEASUREMENTS: Height: 35 cm. Width: 26 cm. Depth: 6 cm.
MATERIAL: Limestone, white.
PRESERVATION: The figure is broken off at the upper part of the torso and the legs below the knees. The surface in the area of the right knee is chipped.
TECHNICAL DESCRIPTION: —
DATE: A.D. 240–273.
REFERENCES: Gawlikowski 1984, 108 cat. 64 pl. 90, 198.

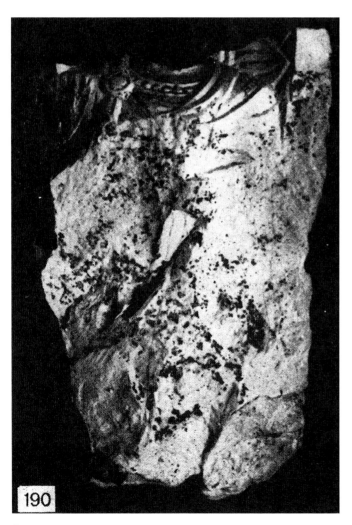

Cat. 474

Cat. 475

OBJECT DESCRIPTION
The object depicts a standing male.

PORTRAIT
The figure is depicted frontally.

He wears a ›Parthian-style‹ tunic. The tunic has a central band extending downwards; it is decorated with a running scroll with ivy leaves. At the end of the band there is a panel decorated with a scales pattern. He wears a plain band belt, knotted at the centre with the ends looped under on either side of the waist.

476. FRAGMENT OF A SARCOPHAGUS WITH PORTRAIT BUST

DATABASE NUMBER: MFA004.
LOCATION: Boston, Museum of Fine Arts, inv. no. 10.73.
CONTEXT: —
ACQUISITION HISTORY: Gift of the Estate of Dana Estes 1910.
MEASUREMENTS: Height: 21.5 cm.
MATERIAL: Limestone, white/grey.
PRESERVATION: Broken on all sides. The surface is weathered.
TECHNICAL DESCRIPTION: —
DATE: A.D. 240–273 (Comstock – Vermeule 1976: A.D. 200–273).
REFERENCES: Caskey 1910, 60; Bates 1911, 432 f.; Comstock – Vermeule 1976, 260 cat. 407; Albertson 2000, 160 n. 7; <https://www.mfa.org/collections/object/fragment-of-funerary-sarcophagus-relief-151401> (06.05.2022).

OBJECT DESCRIPTION
The object depicts part of a kline. There is an armless bust of a male rendered. Oblique grooves are rendered on the relief ground around the portrait, possibly indicating the texture of a mattress. Below the figure there is a projecting plinth with two rectangular panels, separated by a vertical groove.

INSCRIPTION
SCRIPT: —
LOCATION ON RELIEF: Inside the panel on the projecting plinth.
TRANSCRIPTION: —
TRANSLATION: —

CIS no. —; PAT no. —.

COMMENT: The inscription is fake.

PORTRAIT DESCRIPTION
The figure is shown frontally.

His hair is rendered in three rows of round curls, which cover his ears. His face is oval. The eyes are close-set and almond-shaped. The eyeballs are blank. The nose is large and narrow. The mouth is rendered as a thin, horizontal line. The neck is long.

Cat. 476

He wears a tunic and a chlamys. The tunic has a wide, round neckline. The folds of the tunic are rendered by curving grooves. Over the tunic, he wears a chlamys that falls over both shoulders, and covers most of the chest. The wide fold visible across the chest is decorated with a beaded line. It is fastened at the right shoulder with a circular brooch with an incised border (Colledge classification: h). A wide triangular fold falls from under the brooch. The folds of the chlamys are indicated by oblique grooves.

Possible Sarcophagus Fragments

A.D. 100–150

477. MALE FIGURE

DATABASE NUMBER: NMD092.
LOCATION: Damascus, National Museum of Damascus, inv. no. 6795.
CONTEXT: —
ACQUISITION HISTORY: —
MEASUREMENTS: Height: 88 cm.
MATERIAL: Limestone, grey.
PRESERVATION: The right arm of the figure is broken off. The nose and part of the upper lip are chipped.
TECHNICAL DESCRIPTION: The back is partly carved.
DATE: A.D. 100–150.
REFERENCES: Ingholt Archives, PS 865; Ingholt 1935, 68 f. pl. 29.2; Seyrig 1937, 10 n. 5; Abdul-Hak and Abdul-Hak 1951, 30–31 cat. 5 pl. 17.2a; Tanabe 1986, 43 fig. 443.

OBJECT DESCRIPTION
The object depicts a standing male.

PORTRAIT
The figure is shown frontally. His left arm is bent in front of the waist and the right arm falls to the side, with the hand touching the thigh. The legs are parted with the feet planted firmly on the ground.

His hair is voluminous, with crescent-shaped curls arranged in two rows over the forehead, and a single row over the temples. His face is square. He has a single, horizontal groove along the forehead. The eyebrows are curving, rendered by thin ridges that start from the root of the nose. The eyes are large, round, with thick eyelids. The irises and the pupils are indicated by concentric, incised circles. The ears are large and protruding with the helix, scapha, and lobe depicted. The nose is straight with a wide base. The mouth is small, with full lips. The chin is round. The neck is long and wide.

He wears a >Parthian-style< tunic, a chlamys, >Parthian-style< trousers, and over-trousers. The tunic has a wide scalloped neckline, long sleeves, and falls to the middle of the thighs. The hem of the tunic is decorated with a thin band with squares with incised borders divided by small, beaded bands. The folds of the tunic are rendered by wide curving grooves. He wears a narrow band belt knotted at the centre, with the ends of the band looped over the sides. The ends of the bands have short tassels or fringes, indicated by a series of short, incised lines. The band belt creates an overfold. Over the tunic he wears a chlamys. The chlamys has a scalloped edge, decorated with a beaded band. It falls in a curving fold across the chest, covers the left shoulder and arm, and falls

Cat. 477

down along the body until below the knees. It is fastened at the right shoulder with a circular brooch with a beaded outer border (Colledge classification: f). The folds of the chlamys are rendered by oblique grooves. Under the tunic he wears ›Parthian-style‹ trousers. Each trouser leg has a wide band with a vine scroll with bunches of grapes extending downwards and set between beaded bands. Over the trousers he wears over-trousers. They cover the outer upper part of the thighs and fall in a curve to the knees, covering the lower legs. They are decorated with a beaded band at the upper edge. The folds of the over-trousers are rendered by wide, curving grooves. He wears closed-toe shoes with a pointed end.

In his left hand he holds a thin, trapezoidal object, a schedula. His thumb, the index, and the middle finger are extended. In the little finger he wears a wide hoop ring with a round bezel. In the right hand he holds several branches with long, narrow leaves (only the leaves are visible). All the fingers are extended.

A.D. 150–170

478. FRAGMENT OF A FEMALE FIGURE

DATABASE NUMBER: UAG007.
LOCATION: New Haven, Yale University Art Gallery, inv. no. 1957.7.6.
CONTEXT: —
ACQUISITION HISTORY: Gift of Mr and Mrs Fred Olsen.
MEASUREMENTS: Height: 31.9 cm. Width: 20.32 cm.
MATERIAL: Limestone, white/yellow.
PRESERVATION: The lower part of the figure is broken off diagonally from the upper right arm and under the right breast. A crack runs from the mouth to the left shoulder. The surface of the mouth and of the left cheek is chipped.
TECHNICAL DESCRIPTION: There are flat chisel marks on the veil, the neck, the earring, and on the face.
DATE: A.D. 150–170.
REFERENCES: Krag 2018, 32 n. 63; 47 n. 214; 51 n. 241; 103 n. 74; 319 cat. 574; <https://artgallery.yale.edu/collections/objects/7104> (06.05.2022).

OBJECT DESCRIPTION
The object depicts an armless female bust.

PORTRAIT
The figure is shown frontally.

She wears three headdresses: a headband, a turban, and veil. The headband is placed high on the forehead and is divided into rectangular, undecorated panels separated by vertical grooves. The turban is coiled. It is rendered in one twisted layer, with horizontal and oblique grooves indicating the coiling of the fabric. The veil is heavy with a scalloped edge. It falls across the chest in a curving fold and back over the left shoulder. Part of the hair is covered by the headdresses:

Cat. 478

several strands of hair above the ears are pushed back over the headband and the edge of the turban and disappear under the veil. Her face is oval. The eyebrows are curving, rendered by incised lines starting from the root of the nose. The eyes are close-set and almond-shaped, with thick upper eyelids. The upper eyelids extend beyond the end of the lower ones. The irises are rendered by incised circles. Only the earlobes are visible under the headdress and she wears dumbbell-shaped earrings (Colledge classification: H). The nose is large with carved nostrils. The cheeks are fleshy, and the mouth is small, with thin lips. The chin is round and almost double. The neck is wide.

She wears a tunic with a small, scalloped neckline. The folds of the tunic are rendered by curving grooves.

A.D. 200–220

479. MALE FIGURE

DATABASE NUMBER: PM226.
LOCATION: Palmyra, Palmyra Museum, inv. no. CD 18/77.
CONTEXT: Secondary context: A late wall in the Temple of the Standards (Temple des Enseignes), Camp of Diocletian.

Cat. 479

ACQUISITION HISTORY: —
MEASUREMENTS: Height: 45 cm. Width: 18 cm. Depth: 10 cm.
MATERIAL: Limestone, white.
PRESERVATION: The head is broken off at the base of the neck, and the lower part of the figure is broken off at the knees. The hands are broken off.
TECHNICAL DESCRIPTION: —
DATE: A.D. 200–220.
REFERENCES: Gawlikowski 1984, 101 f. cat. 35 pl. 81, 170; Tanabe 1986, 44 pls. 446. 447; Parlasca 2001a, 341 cat. 137; Liberati 2002, 119 cat. 145.

OBJECT DESCRIPTION
The object depicts a standing male.

PORTRAIT
The figure is shown frontally. The arms appear short in relation to the body. The right arm is bent and held to the chest. The left is slightly bent. The legs are set apart and he rests his weight on the right leg, resulting in a slight s-curve.

He wears a necklace composed of rectangular bezels with central inlays separated by vertical, beaded elements.

He wears a ›Parthian-style‹ tunic, a chlamys, and ›Parthian-style‹ trousers. The tunic has long, tight-fitting sleeves. The tunic ends above the knees. The cuffs of the sleeves are decorated with a beaded band. The folds of the tunic are rendered by curving and diagonal wide grooves. He wears a plain band belt, knotted at the centre. Another belt runs diagonally from the right to his left side. A wide lace runs downwards at the left thigh and is fastened to the belt strap with a circular button. The belts are fastened to a broad, long, rectangular sheath hanging vertically at his left side. The sheath is adorned with an animal skin, possibly leopard, placed vertically as a harness attachment. It is likely a quiver. Over the tunic, he wears a chlamys that falls over both shoulders, and covers the upper chest and upper left arm and falls downwards at his left side in a wide, s-shaped fold that ends in a tassel. A zigzag-shaped fold falls from the right shoulder. Each trouser leg is decorated in the middle with a wide band with a vegetal motif, extending downwards. The folds of the trousers are rendered by curving grooves.

480. MALE FIGURE

DATABASE NUMBER: PM435.
LOCATION: Palmyra, Palmyra Museum, inv. no. unknown.
CONTEXT: —
ACQUISITION HISTORY: —
MEASUREMENTS: Height: 32 cm. Width: 16 cm.
MATERIAL: Limestone, white/yellow.
PRESERVATION: The head is broken off at the base of the neck, and the lower part is broken off at the knees. The right arm is broken off. The left elbow and lower part of clothing are chipped.
TECHNICAL DESCRIPTION: —
DATE: A.D. 200–220.
REFERENCES: Ingholt Archives, PS 1035; Tanabe 1986, 44 pl. 450; Krag 2018, 71 n. 23. 26. 28. 32; 72 n. 43. 45; 75 n. 62. 65; 77 n. 80; 78 n. 88. 89; 79 n. 98; 95 n. 2; 187 cat. 83.

OBJECT DESCRIPTION
The object depicts a standing male.

PORTRAIT
The male figure is seen frontally. The left arm appears short in relation to the body. The left arm is bent and held to the torso.

POSSIBLE SARCOPHAGUS FRAGMENTS

Cat. 480

He wears a tunic and a himation. The tunic is sleeveless and has a wide, round neckline that is slit in the middle, and the upper edges of the fabric are turned. The borders of the sleeves are decorated with a beaded band. Another beaded band runs vertically across the upper chest. The folds of the tunic are rendered by curving and oblique grooves. Over the tunic, he wears a himation. It falls over his shoulders and across his chest in a wide, curving fold with a scalloped edge. Another thick fold runs across his waist. The folds of the himation are rendered by curving and oblique grooves.

With his left hand, he holds two rectangular objects, possibly two schedulae. At the upper and lower end of the book-roll is an X-shaped incision. The thumb, index, and little fingers are extended. The nails are indicated by fine, incised lines.

481. MALE FIGURE

DATABASE NUMBER: PM369.
LOCATION: Palmyra, Palmyra Museum, inv. no. B 1827.
CONTEXT: Secondary context: Found (15.09.1954) at portico C3 during the excavations of the Baalshamin temple.
ACQUISITION HISTORY: —
MEASUREMENTS: Height: 29 cm. Width: 12.5 cm. Depth: 7.5 cm.
MATERIAL: Limestone, white/yellow.
PRESERVATION: The head is broken off at the base of the neck and the lower part is broken off at the ankles. The figure is very weathered and areas of the hands, of the attributes, and of the clothing are chipped.
TECHNICAL DESCRIPTION: —
DATE: A.D. 200–220.
REFERENCES: Dunant – Stucky 2000, 106 cat. 87 pl. 25.

OBJECT DESCRIPTION
The object depicts a standing male.

PORTRAIT
The male figure is seen standing in frontal view. The left arm appears short in relation to the body. The right arm is held along the body. The left arm is bent and held to the torso. The legs are slightly set apart and the weight is placed on the left leg. He wears a tunic and a himation. The tunic has a wide, v-shaped neckline and short, wide sleeves. The folds of the tunic are rendered by curving and oblique grooves. Over the tunic, he wears a himation. It is wrapped around his left shoulder and arm, leaving only part of the chest free. One end of the himation crosses the chest diagonally. Another end of the himation falls vertically from the left shoulder. The folds of the himation are rendered by diagonal and oblique grooves. He holds a jug in his right hand. The body is convex and the rim oval. He holds the jug by the handle. The outline of an object is visible in the left hand, perhaps a small branch.

482. FRAGMENT OF A MALE FIGURE

DATABASE NUMBER: UNK232.
LOCATION: Unknown location.
CONTEXT: —
ACQUISITION HISTORY: —
MEASUREMENTS: —
MATERIAL: Limestone.
PRESERVATION: The head is broken off horizontally at the base of the neck and the lower part is broken off at the shins. The right arm is broken off. The surface of the hands and of the left arm is chipped. The surface is weathered.
TECHNICAL DESCRIPTION: —
DATE: A.D. 200–220.
REFERENCES: Ingholt Archives, PS 1151; Colledge 1976, 76 fig. 42.

Cat. 482

OBJECT DESCRIPTION
The object depicts a standing male.

PORTRAIT
The figure is shown frontally. He stands with the legs set apart. The left leg is slightly bent with the knee visible under the drapery.

He wears an undergarment and a tunic. The undergarment is visible running in slight curve from left knee to the right shin. The garment has a fringed border. Over the undergarment, he wears a tunic. It has a small, v-shaped neckline and short, wide sleeves. An overfold is rendered at the waist. The tunic ends at the knees. The folds of the tunic are rendered by curving grooves.

He holds a flute in his hands. It is composed of six tubes that gradually become smaller. They are fastened together by two horizontal bands.

483. FRAGMENT OF A MALE FIGURE

DATABASE NUMBER: PM710.
LOCATION: Palmyra, Palmyra Museum, inv. no. CD 52.
CONTEXT: Secondary context: Found (01.05.1962) in the foundation of the Great Gate in the Camp of Diocletian.
ACQUISITION HISTORY: —
MEASUREMENTS: Height: 23 cm. Width: 24 cm. Depth: 23 cm.
MATERIAL: Limestone, white.
PRESERVATION: The upper part is broken off diagonally from the right shoulder to the left and the lower part is broken off at the lower torso. Broken vertically at the right arm.
TECHNICAL DESCRIPTION: —
DATE: A.D. 200–220.
REFERENCES: Michalowski 1964, 102 cat. 37 fig. 138.

OBJECT DESCRIPTION
The object depicts part of the torso and arm of a male figure.

PORTRAIT
The figure is shown frontally. The left arm is slightly bent and held in front of the body.

He wears a tunic and a himation. The folds of the tunic are rendered by curving grooves. Over the tunic, he wears a himation. It is wrapped around his left shoulder and arm leaving the chest and the hand free. The edge of the himation has a fringe, indicated by curving grooves.

The left hand is clenched (details unclear).

484. FRAGMENT OF A MALE FIGURE

DATABASE NUMBER: PM684.
LOCATION: Palmyra, Palmyra Museum, inv. no. CD 132.
CONTEXT: Secondary context: Found (24.05.1960) in the north-eastern part of the Tetrapylon in the Camp of Diocletian.
ACQUISITION HISTORY: —
MEASUREMENTS: Height: 20 cm. Width: 45 cm.
MATERIAL: Limestone, yellow.
PRESERVATION: Broken diagonally from the left shoulder to the right side and vertically under the chest. Only the central part of the torso is preserved.
TECHNICAL DESCRIPTION: —
DATE: A.D. 200–220.
REFERENCES: Michalowski 1962, 150 cat. 20 fig. 164.

OBJECT DESCRIPTION
The object depicts part of a male figure.

PORTRAIT
The figure is wearing a >Parthian-style< tunic. On either side of the neckline is a band decorated with four-petal flowers inside lozenges. The midribs of the leaves are rendered by incised lines. The folds of the tunic are rendered by wide, curving grooves.

POSSIBLE SARCOPHAGUS FRAGMENTS

Cat. 485

485. FEMALE FIGURE

DATABASE NUMBER: NMD113.
LOCATION: Damascus, National Museum of Damascus, inv. no. unknown.
CONTEXT: —
ACQUISITION HISTORY: —
MEASUREMENTS: —
MATERIAL: Limestone, grey/white.
PRESERVATION: The relief ground is broken off but is visible as very rough sides towards the back of the figure. There are many small breaks in the stone. Her right side is badly damaged; the right side of her face, her right arm, and the lower part of her legs including her feet are broken off.
TECHNICAL DESCRIPTION: —
DATE: A.D. 200–220.
REFERENCES: Krag 2018, 28 n. 9; 48 n. 217; 103 n. 74; 313 cat. 554.

OBJECT DESCRIPTION
The object depicts a standing female.

PORTRAIT
The figure is shown frontally. The right arm is bent and held to the shoulder. The left arm is held along the body. The left leg is rendered under the drapery.

She wears a veil. It is heavy with a scalloped edge. It falls back over both her shoulders. Part of the hair is covered by the headdress; the hair is centrally parted and brushed away on each side of the forehead. Several strands of hair above the ears are pushed back and disappear under the veil. The individual strands of hair are rendered by incised lines. Her face is round. Her eyebrows are depicted as thin ridges. The eyes are close-set and almond-shaped, with thick upper eyelids that extend beyond the lower ones. Only the earlobes are visible under the hair and she wears large, circular beads suspended from the ear by a thin element, possibly the hook (Colledge classification: B). The cheeks are fleshy. The mouth is small, with a thin upper lip and a full lower lip. The chin is pointed and almost double. The neck is wide.

She wears a tunic and a himation. The tunic has short sleeves and is visible from the waist where it proceeds to her ankles. The folds are indicated by diagonal grooves. Over the tunic she wears a himation. It is wrapped over her shoulders and is wrapped around the left arm. From the right shoulder, it falls diagonally across her lower body in a thick fold. The folds of the himation are rendered by curving and oblique grooves.

Her right hand is raised to the shoulder where she holds a fold of the himation. At the left thigh, she holds a fold of the himation with her left hand.

A.D. 200–273
---

486. FRAGMENT OF A FEMALE FIGURE

DATABASE NUMBER: DGAM021.
LOCATION: Damascus, Directorate-General of Antiquities and Museums, inv. no. unknown.
CONTEXT: —
ACQUISITION HISTORY: Confiscated by the Department of Antiquities in Palmyra 30th March 2014.
MEASUREMENTS: —
MATERIAL: Limestone, white.
PRESERVATION: The background, the head and neck, and the lower part of the relief are broken off.
TECHNICAL DESCRIPTION: —

DATE: A.D. 200–273.
REFERENCES: <http://www.dgam.gov.sy/index.php?d=239&id=1200> (22.05.2019; link inactive on 06.05.2022).

OBJECT DESCRIPTION
The object is rectangular in shape and depicts a female bust.

PORTRAIT
The figure is shown frontally. Her left arm is bent and raised to the height of the shoulder. The arm appears small in relation to the body.

She wears one necklace: a plain necklace with a circular pendant suspended from the centre worn below the collarbone.

She wears a tunic and a veil. The tunic has a wide round neckline (details unclear). Over the tunic, she wears a veil, which is wrapped around the entire upper torso from the right to the left. The folds of the veil are indicated by wide, curving grooves.

With the left hand, she holds a fold of the himation. The fingers are partly extended.

Cat. 487

487. MALE FIGURE

DATABASE NUMBER: PM728.
LOCATION: Palmyra, Palmyra Museum, inv. no. CD 243/65.
CONTEXT: Secondary context: Found in the northern part of the Temple of the Standards (Temple des Enseignes), Camp of Diocletian.
ACQUISITION HISTORY: —
MEASUREMENTS: Height: 20 cm. Width: 27 cm. Depth: 10 cm.
MATERIAL: Limestone, white.
PRESERVATION: Broken on all sides. Only a small part of the torso is preserved.
TECHNICAL DESCRIPTION: —
DATE: A.D. 200–273.
REFERENCES: Gawlikowski 1984, 108 cat. 66 pl. 91, 201.

OBJECT DESCRIPTION
The object depicts part of the torso of a male figure.

PORTRAIT
He wears a ›Parthian-style‹ tunic. At the middle, the tunic has a band decorated with serrated leaves in an opposite arrangement, extending downwards. The folds of the tunic are rendered by oblique grooves.

A.D. 220–240

488. FRAGMENT OF A MALE FIGURE

DATABASE NUMBER: VAM018.
LOCATION: Berlin, Vorderasiatisches Museum, inv. no. VA2017.
CONTEXT: —
ACQUISITION HISTORY: Gift of Louis Simon, 1887.
MEASUREMENTS: Height: 18.5 cm. Width: 13 cm. Depth: 10 cm.
MATERIAL: Limestone, white/grey.
PRESERVATION: The upper part of the figure is broken off at the upper and right side of the torso, and the lower part of the figure is broken off at the knees. The hands holding the rhyton are broken off from the rest of the fragment.
TECHNICAL DESCRIPTION: —
DATE: A.D. 220–240.
REFERENCES: Wartke 1991, 84 cat. 17 figs. 19. 20.

OBJECT DESCRIPTION
The object depicts a standing male.

PORTRAIT
The figure is shown frontally. The arms are bent in front of the torso.

He wears a tunic. It has long sleeves. The folds of the tunic are indicated by wide, curving ridges. A diagonal, coiled fabric at the lower waist may indicate that the tunic had an overfold. A fold of another item of clothing falls along and under his

Cat. 488

left arm, possibly from a chlamys. Wartke (1991, 84) suggests that he wears a himation.

With both hands, he holds a rhyton against the chest. The vessel has a wide, conical body decorated with oblique grooves, a beaded band between the body and the base, and a base shaped like the head of a horned animal, perhaps a gazelle.

Heads from Sarcophagi

PRIEST HEADS

1–10 CM

A.D. 100–150

---

489. FRAGMENT OF A HEAD OF A PRIEST

DATABASE NUMBER: PM969.
LOCATION: Palmyra, Palmyra Museum, inv. no. CD 40.
CONTEXT: Secondary context: Camp of Diocletian. Found in the rubble to the left of the column with the console.
ACQUISITION HISTORY: —
MEASUREMENTS: Height: 10 cm. Width: 13 cm. Depth: 6 cm.
MATERIAL: Limestone, grey.
PRESERVATION: Only the hat and part of the forehead are preserved. The surface is weathered. There is a small drill hole on the forehead.
TECHNICAL DESCRIPTION: —
DATE: A.D. 100–150.
REFERENCES: Michalowski 1960, 86 cat. 4 fig. 93.

OBJECT DESCRIPTION
The object depicts a priest.

PORTRAIT
The figure is shown frontally.
He wears a tall, cylindrical, flat-top headdress divided into three sections by two vertical grooves: a Palmyrene priestly hat. A wreath with three rows of leaves pointing towards a six-petal rosette is depicted at the lower part of the hat. A narrow, horizontal band at the bottom of the hat suggests a liner.

11–20 CM

A.D. 100–150

---

490. HEAD OF A PRIEST

DATABASE NUMBER: PM301.
LOCATION: Palmyra, Palmyra Museum, inv. no. CD 39.
CONTEXT: Secondary context: Found (14.05.1960) in the south-western part of the Tetrapylon in the Camp of Diocletian.
ACQUISITION HISTORY: —
MEASUREMENTS: Height: 15.5 cm. Width: 9.5 cm. Depth: 11.5 cm.
MATERIAL: Limestone, white.

PRESERVATION: The lower part of the portrait is broken off at the neck. The central and left part of the Palmyrene priestly hat are broken off. A crack runs horizontally across the top of the headdress. The surface is weathered and chipped.
TECHNICAL DESCRIPTION: —
DATE: A.D. 100–150.
REFERENCES: Michalowski 1962, 168 cat. 37 figs. 183. 184.

OBJECT DESCRIPTION
The fragment depicts a priest.

PORTRAIT
The figure is shown frontally.

He wears a tall, cylindrical, flat-top headdress: a Palmyrene priestly hat. A wreath with three rows of small, elliptical leaves is depicted at the lower part of the hat. A horizontal line at the bottom of the hat suggests a liner. His face is round and fleshy. The eyebrows are depicted by low, curving grooves. The eyes are large and round with thick eyelids. The irises and the pupils are indicated by concentric, incised circles. The ears are large and protruding, with helix, scapha, and concha depicted. The nose is large, straight, and wide. The mouth is small, with thin lips. The chin is pointed. The neck is short and wide.

Cat. 491

A.D. 150–170

491. HEAD OF A PRIEST

DATABASE NUMBER: PM206.
LOCATION: Palmyra, Palmyra Museum, inv. no. CD 21/73.
CONTEXT: Secondary context: Found in the foundation of the stylobate to the Praetorian Gate in the Temple of the Standards (Temple des Enseignes), Camp of Diocletian.
ACQUISITION HISTORY: —
MEASUREMENTS: Height: 18 cm. Width: 11 cm. Depth: 18 cm.
MATERIAL: Limestone, white.
PRESERVATION: The head is broken off at the neck with a small part of the background at the right side of the head preserved.
TECHNICAL DESCRIPTION: —
DATE: A.D. 150–170.
REFERENCES: Gawlikowski 1984, 98 cat. 16 pl. 74, 155.

OBJECT DESCRIPTION
The object depicts a priest.

PORTRAIT
The figure is shown frontally. The head is turned slightly to his left.

He wears a tall, cylindrical, flat-top headdress divided into three sections by two vertical grooves: a Palmyrene priestly hat. A wreath with three rows of leaves pointing towards a medallion with an incised border, indicating an inlay, is depicted at the lower part of the hat. A narrow, horizontal band at the bottom of the hat suggests a liner. His face is square and fleshy. The eyebrows are curving, rendered by incised lines. The eyes are small and almond-shaped, with thick upper eyelids. The eyeballs are blank. The ears are small and protruding with the helix and concha depicted. The nose is narrow and long. The mouth is small, with thin lips. The chin is pointed. The neck is wide.

A.D. 170–200

492. HEAD OF A PRIEST

DATABASE NUMBER: PM005.
LOCATION: Palmyra, Palmyra Museum, inv. no. CD 109.
CONTEXT: Secondary context: Found (03.05.1961) at the staircase of the Great Gate in the Camp of Diocletian.
ACQUISITION HISTORY: —
MEASUREMENTS: Height: 20 cm. Width: 12 cm. Depth: 15 cm.
MATERIAL: Limestone, grey.
PRESERVATION: The lower part of the figure is broken off at the base of the neck. The upper part of the Palmyrene priestly hat is broken off. A crack runs along the left side of his mouth.
TECHNICAL DESCRIPTION: —

HEADS FROM SARCOPHAGI

Cat. 492

The eyes are almond-shaped, with thin eyelids. The end of the upper eyelids extends beyond that of the lower ones. The eyeballs are blank. The ears are small, slightly protruding with the helix, concha, and tragus depicted. The nose is straight. The mouth is small, with a full lower lip. The chin is round. The neck has two curving grooves.

A.D. 200–240

493. HEAD OF A PRIEST

DATABASE NUMBER: DamascusUNK009.
LOCATION: Damascus, unknown location.
CONTEXT: —
ACQUISITION HISTORY: —
MEASUREMENTS: Height: 17 cm.
MATERIAL: Limestone, white/yellow.
PRESERVATION: The lower part of the figure is broken off at the top of the neck. The top of the Palmyrene priestly hat is broken off.
TECHNICAL DESCRIPTION: The lower eyelids are uncarved.
DATE: A.D. 200–240.
REFERENCES: Ingholt Archives, PS 949.

DATE: A.D. 170–200.
REFERENCES: Michalowski 1963, 117 cat. 8 fig. 165.

OBJECT DESCRIPTION

The fragment depicts a priest.

PORTRAIT

The figure is shown frontally. The head is slightly turned to his right.

He wears a tall, cylindrical, flat-top headdress divided into three sections by two vertical grooves low on the forehead: a Palmyrene priestly hat. A band that has an angular cross-section and a groove running across the middle, with a medallion (?) with an armless, male bust is depicted at the lower part of the hat. A horizontal, incised line at the bottom of the hat suggests a liner. His face is oval. The eyebrows are low and curving, rendered by incised lines starting from the root of the nose.

Cat. 493

Cat. 494, Pl. 80

OBJECT DESCRIPTION
The fragment depicts a priest.

PORTRAIT
The figure is shown frontally.

He wears a cylindrical headdress divided into three sections by two vertical grooves: a Palmyrene priestly hat. A wreath is depicted at the lower part of the hat. It has three rows of leaves, elliptical at the centre and narrow at the sides, pointing towards a central oval. His face is oval. The eyebrows are depicted by curving ridges. The eyes are large, deep-set, and almond-shaped, with thick upper eyelids. The end of the upper eyelids extends beyond that of the lower ones. The eyeballs are blank. The ears are large and protruding with the helix, concha, and scapha depicted. The nose is short with a wide base. The mouth is small, with full lips. The chin is pointed.

A.D. 200–273

494. HEAD OF A PRIEST

DATABASE NUMBER: NCG098.
LOCATION: Copenhagen, Ny Carlsberg Glyptotek, inv. no. IN 1108.
CONTEXT: —
ACQUISITION HISTORY: Løytved in Syria.
MEASUREMENTS: Height: 15.8 cm. Width: 7.3 cm. Depth: 8.3 cm.
MATERIAL: Limestone, white/yellow.
PRESERVATION: The lower part of the portrait is broken off at the neck. The upper part of the Palmyrene priestly hat is broken off.
TECHNICAL DESCRIPTION: The head is partly carved and the eyes, mouth, ears, eyebrows, and wreath have not been carved. The head is roughly cut on the back. There are marks of flat chisel work on the headdress, face, and neck.
DATE: A.D. 200–273 (Ploug 1995: A.D. 200–250).
REFERENCES: Simonsen 1889, 49 cat. G 19 pl. 13; Colledge 1976, 252; Hvidberg-Hansen – Ploug 1993, 149 cat. 112; Ploug 1995, 242 cat. 112; Raja 2019a, 278 cat. 92.

OBJECT DESCRIPTION
The fragment depicts the head of a priest.

PORTRAIT
The figure is shown frontally.

He wears a high, cylindrical flat-top headdress: a Palmyrene priestly hat. A wide band is depicted at the lower part of the headdress (in the place of a wreath). His face is oval. The eyebrows, eyes, and nose are roughly carved. The ears are small and slightly protruding. The neck is short and slender.

A.D. 220–240

495. HEAD OF A PRIEST

DATABASE NUMBER: NCG050.
LOCATION: Copenhagen, Ny Carlsberg Glyptotek, inv. no. IN 1123.
CONTEXT: —
ACQUISITION HISTORY: Løytved in Syria.
MEASUREMENTS: Height: 13.5 cm; Width: 8 cm; Depth: 9 cm.
MATERIAL: Limestone, white/grey.

HEADS FROM SARCOPHAGI 787

Cat. 495

PRESERVATION: The lower part of the figure is broken off at the neck. The lower part of the front of the face and the top of the Palmyrene priestly hat are broken off. The surface is chipped in the areas of the forehead, the nose, the mouth, and the chin. Cracks are running through the face. There are brown impressions in the stone.

TECHNICAL DESCRIPTION: The head is roughly cut on the back with flat chisel marks on the face, ears, and neck.

DATE: A.D. 220–240 (Ploug 1995: A.D. 230–250).

REFERENCES: Ingholt Archives, PS 310; Simonsen 1889, 51 cat. G 34 pl. 16; Ingholt 1928, 126; Ingholt 1934, 33 n. 14; Colledge 1976, 252; Hvidberg-Hansen – Ploug 1993, 148 cat. 110; Ploug 1995, 241 cat. 110; Raja 2019a, 299 cat. 107.

OBJECT DESCRIPTION
The fragment depicts the head of a male figure.

PORTRAIT
The figure is shown frontally, head turning towards his left.

He wears a tall, cylindrical, flat-top headdress divided into three sections by two vertical grooves low on the forehead: a Palmyrene priestly hat. A wreath with three rows of pointed leaves pointing towards an undecorated medallion is depicted at the lower part of the hat. The midribs of the leaves are incised. The wreath reaches to the middle of the hat at the sides; it is continued by a wide band (metallic tube for inserting the leaves?). A narrow, horizontal band at the bottom of the hat suggests a liner. His face is fleshy. The eyebrows are depicted by incised lines that curve upwards over the top of the bridge of the nose and follow a low curve over the eyes. The eyes are small and almond-shaped, with heavy upper eyelids. The end of the upper eyelids extends beyond that of the lower ones. The eyeballs are blank. The ears are small and protruding with the helix, scapha, and concha depicted. The neck is wide and short.

496. FRAGMENT OF A HEAD OF A PRIEST

DATABASE NUMBER: Medelhavsmuseet001.
LOCATION: Stockholm, Medelhavsmuseet, inv. no. 4163, 09879D/ MM 1978:026.
CONTEXT: —
ACQUISITION HISTORY: Purchased in Palmyra by Professor Herman N. Almkvist at some point during the 19th cent. Donated by Lison Almkvist, 1978.
MEASUREMENTS: Height: 16.3 cm. Width: 15.5 cm. Depth: 17.3 cm.
MATERIAL: Limestone, white/yellow.
PRESERVATION: The lower part of the figure is broken off at the height of the mouth. The upper part of the Palmyrene priestly hat, the left ear, and most of the bridge of the nose are broken off. There are cracks running across the surface.
TECHNICAL DESCRIPTION: —
DATE: A.D. 220–240.
REFERENCES: <https://collections.smvk.se/carlotta-mhm/web/object/3908604>; <https://collections.smvk.se/carlotta-mhm/web/object/3923644>; <https://collections.smvk.se/carlotta-mhm/web/object/3102354> (06.05.2022).

OBJECT DESCRIPTION
The fragment depicts the head of a priest.

PORTRAIT
He wears a tall, cylindrical headdress divided into three sections by two vertical grooves: a Palmyrene priestly hat. A wreath is depicted at the lower part of the hat. It has three rows of leaves (elliptical at the centre and narrow at the sides), pointing towards a medallion. The medallion has the armless bust of a male figure with short hair wearing a tunic

Cat. 496

and chlamys. The midribs of the leaves are incised. A narrow, horizontal band at the bottom of the hat suggests a liner. His face is oval and fleshy. The eyebrows are curving, rendered by thin ridges. The eyes are large and almond-shaped, with thick upper eyelids. The irises are rendered by incised arches that touch the upper eyelids. The ears are thick and protruding with the helix, scapha, concha, and lobe depicted. The nose is wide. The mouth is small, with full lips.

497. FRAGMENT OF A HEAD OF A PRIEST

DATABASE NUMBER: PM207.
LOCATION: Palmyra, Palmyra Museum, inv. no. CD 27/73.
CONTEXT: Secondary context: Late wall in the Temple of Standards (Temple des Enseignes), Camp of Diocletian. Found in the north-east part of the temple.
ACQUISITION HISTORY: —
MEASUREMENTS: Height: 13 cm. Width: 9 cm. Depth: 6 cm.
MATERIAL: Limestone, white.
PRESERVATION: The head is broken off at the top of the root of the neck. Most of the headdress, the right side of the face, the tip of the nose, the ears, the left cheek, left side of the mouth, and part of the chin are broken off.
TECHNICAL DESCRIPTION: —
DATE: A.D. 220–240.
REFERENCES: Gawlikowski 1984, 98 f. cat. 17 pl. 75, 156.

Cat. 497

OBJECT DESCRIPTION
The object depicts a priest.

PORTRAIT
The figure is shown frontally. The head is turned to his right.

He wears a headdress: a Palmyrene priestly hat (?). A narrow horizontal band at the bottom of the hat suggests a liner. His face is oval and fleshy. The eyebrows are curving, rendered by incised lines. The eyes are large and almond-shaped, with thick upper eyelids. The upper eyelids extend beyond the end of the lower ones. The irises are indicated by incised circles and the pupils by punch holes. The irises touch the upper eyelids. The nose is narrow and straight. The mouth is small, with full lips. The chin is round.

498. HEAD OF A PRIEST

DATABASE NUMBER: NCG105.
LOCATION: Copenhagen, Ny Carlsberg Glyptotek, inv. no. IN 1116.
CONTEXT: —
ACQUISITION HISTORY: Løytved in Syria.
MEASUREMENTS: Height: 15 cm. Width: 9.3 cm. Depth: 7.7 cm.
MATERIAL: Limestone, white/yellow.
PRESERVATION: The lower part of the figure is broken off at the base of the neck. The upper half of the head is broken off: most of the front part of the Palmyrene priestly hat, the forehead, the right eye, and the nose are broken off.
TECHNICAL DESCRIPTION: The head is roughly cut on the back. There are flat chisel marks on the surface of the face. A dark impression is visible at the left temple.
DATE: A.D. 220–240 (Ploug 1995: A.D. 230–250).
REFERENCES: Simonsen 1889, 50 cat. G 27 pl. 16; Hvidberg-Hansen – Ploug 1993, 147 cat. 109; Ploug 1995, 240 cat. 109; Raja 2019a 312 cat. 116.

OBJECT DESCRIPTION
The fragment depicts the head of a priest.

PORTRAIT
The figure is shown frontally. The head is turned downwards and to the left.

He wears a high, cylindrical flat-top headdress low on the forehead: a Palmyrene priestly hat. A wreath with three rows of long, elliptical (?) leaves is depicted at the lower part of the headdress (visible at the sides of the hat). The midribs of the leaves are incised. His face is oval. The eyebrows are indicated by low, curving grooves. The eyes are small, almond-shaped, and slanting with thick upper eyelids. The lower eyelids are indicated by curving, incised lines. The end of the upper eyelids extends beyond that of the lower ones. The eyeballs are blank. The ears are small and protruding with the helix, scapha, and concha depicted. The mouth is small, with a full lower lip. The chin is pointed. The neck is slender.

Cat. 498

499. HEAD OF A PRIEST

DATABASE NUMBER: NCG096.
LOCATION: Copenhagen, Ny Carlsberg Glyptotek, inv. no. IN 1024.
CONTEXT: —
ACQUISITION HISTORY: Løytved in Syria.
MEASUREMENTS: Height: 19.5 cm. Width: 11.5 cm. Depth: 8 cm.
MATERIAL: Limestone, white/yellow.
PRESERVATION: The lower part of the figure is broken off at the neck. The surface is chipped at the areas of the Palmyrene priestly hat, ears, nose, and chin.
TECHNICAL DESCRIPTION: The head is roughly cut on the back and top. There are marks of flat chisel work on the headdress and the face. The wreath is partly carved.
DATE: A.D. 220–240 (Ploug 1995: A.D. 230–250).
REFERENCES: Simonsen 1889, 7 f. cat. A 1 pl. 1; Ingholt 1934, 34; Ingholt – Starcky 1951, 171; Hvidberg-Hansen – Ploug 1993, 148 cat. 111; Ploug 1995, 241 f. cat. 111; Raja 2019a, 307 cat. 112.

OBJECT DESCRIPTION
The fragment depicts the head of a priest.

PORTRAIT
The figure is shown frontally.

He wears a tall, cylindrical, flat-top headdress divided into three sections by two vertical grooves low on the forehead: a Palmyrene priestly hat. A wreath with three rows of long, elliptical (?) leaves pointing towards a central oval is depicted at the lower part of the hat. His face is oval. The eyebrows are indicated by low curving grooves. The eyes are small and almond-shaped, with thick upper eyelids. The end of the upper eyelids extends beyond that of the lower ones. The eyeballs are blank. The ears are small and protruding with the helix and concha depicted. The nose is short and thin. The alae are indicated by incised lines. The mouth is small, with a full lower lip. The chin is pointed with a cleft and he has a double chin. The neck is slender.

A.D. 240–273

500. FRAGMENT OF A HEAD OF A PRIEST

DATABASE NUMBER: PM006.
LOCATION: Palmyra, Palmyra Museum, inv. no. CD 8.
CONTEXT: Secondary context: Found (16.04.1961) at late wall to the north-east of the Tetrapylon in the Camp of Diocletian.
ACQUISITION HISTORY: —
MEASUREMENTS: Height: 20 cm. Width: 16.5 cm. Depth: 7 cm.
MATERIAL: Limestone, white.
PRESERVATION: The head is broken off at the mouth. The right side of the face is broken off. The upper part of the headdress, the nose, and the left cheek are chipped.
TECHNICAL DESCRIPTION: —
DATE: A.D. 240–273.
REFERENCES: Michalowski 1963, 118 f. cat. 9 fig. 166.

OBJECT DESCRIPTION
The object depicts a priest.

PORTRAIT
The figure is shown frontally.

He wears a tall, cylindrical, flat-top headdress divided into three sections by two vertical grooves: a Palmyrene priestly hat. A wreath with three rows of small leaves pointing towards a medallion with an incised border and an armless bust of a male figure is depicted at the lower part of the hat. A narrow, horizontal band at the bottom of the hat suggests a liner. The eyebrows are curving, plastically rendered with oblique, incised lines, indicating individual hair. The eyes are almond-shaped,

Cat. 499

with thick eyelids. The irises are indicated by incised circles and the pupils by punch holes. The irises touch the upper eyelids. The nose is straight with a wide base.

21–30 CM

A.D. 120–140

501. HEAD OF A PRIEST

DATABASE NUMBER: SHM012.
LOCATION: St Petersburg, State Hermitage Museum, inv. no. ДВ-3925.
CONTEXT: —
ACQUISITION HISTORY: Entered the State Hermitage Museum in 1927; transferred from the Museum of Anthropology and Ethnography of the Academy of Sciences.
MEASUREMENTS: Height: 26 cm.
MATERIAL: Limestone, yellow.
PRESERVATION: The lower part of the portrait is broken off at the neck. The tip of the nose and the left cheek are broken off. The surface is lightly chipped and weathered.

Cat. 501

TECHNICAL DESCRIPTION: —
DATE: A.D. 120–140.
REFERENCES: <https://www.hermitagemuseum.org/wps/portal/hermitage/digital-collection/25.+archaeological+artifacts/86598> (06.05.2022).

OBJECT DESCRIPTION
The fragment depicts a priest.

PORTRAIT
The figure is shown frontally.

He wears a tall, cylindrical, flat-top headdress divided into three sections by two vertical grooves low on the forehead: a Palmyrene priestly hat. A narrow, horizontal band at the bottom of the hat suggests a liner. His face is fleshy. A furrow is depicted over the middle of the forehead. The eyebrows are indicated by curving ridges. The eyes are large and round with thick eyelids. The irises and the pupils are indicated by concentric, incised circles. The irises touch the upper eyelids. The ears are small and protruding with the helix, anti-helix, and lobe indicated. The nose is thin and straight. Nasolabial lines are indicated by the carving of the planes of the face. The mouth is small, with full lips. The neck is wide with two curving grooves.

502. HEAD OF A PRIEST

DATABASE NUMBER: PM237.
LOCATION: Palmyra, Palmyra Museum, inv. no. CD 102.
CONTEXT: Secondary context: Camp of Diocletian. Found in the foundations of a wall in the southern part of the Forum.
ACQUISITION HISTORY: —
MEASUREMENTS: Height: 21 cm. Width: 16 cm. Depth: 18 cm.
MATERIAL: Limestone, white.
PRESERVATION: The head is broken off at the neck. The top and bottom part of the headdress, the left eyebrow, the nose, and the right cheek are chipped.
TECHNICAL DESCRIPTION: —
DATE: A.D. 120–140.
REFERENCES: Michalowski 1964, 68 f. cat. 1 fig. 100; Kaspar 1969–1970, 284. 287 fig. 8; Bäärnhielm 1988, 24 fig. 11.

OBJECT DESCRIPTION
The object depicts a priest.

PORTRAIT
The figure is shown frontally.

He wears a tall, cylindrical, flat-top headdress divided into three sections by two vertical grooves: a Palmyrene priestly hat. A wreath with three rows of elliptical leaves pointing towards an armless bust of a male figure is depicted at the lower part of the hat. The figure has short hair and wears a tunic and chlamys. His face is round. The eyebrows are curving, rendered as thin ridges. The eyes are large, almond-shaped, and slanting with thick eyelids. The upper eyelids extend beyond the end of the lower ones. The irises and the pupils are indicated by concentric, incised circles. The irises touch the upper eyelids. The ears are large and protruding with the helix and lobe depicted. The nose has a wide base. Nasolabial lines are indicated. The mouth is small, with thin lips. The chin is round. The neck is wide.

A.D. 130–150

503. HEAD OF A PRIEST

DATABASE NUMBER: WAM002.
LOCATION: Baltimore, Walters Art Museum, inv. no. 22.475.
CONTEXT: —
ACQUISITION HISTORY: Gift of Mr Arthur Houghton in 2008.
MEASUREMENTS: Height: 24 cm. Width: 11 cm. Depth: 13 cm.
MATERIAL: Limestone.
PRESERVATION: The lower part of the portrait is broken off at the neck. The top and central part of the Palmyrene priestly hat, the right ear, and the tip of the nose are broken off. The surface of the Palmyrene priestly hat is weathered.
TECHNICAL DESCRIPTION: The left ear appears partly carved.
DATE: A.D. 130–150.
REFERENCES: <https://art.thewalters.org/detail/76362/funerary-portrait-of-a-priest-from-palmyra/> (06.05.2022).

OBJECT DESCRIPTION
The fragment depicts a priest.

PORTRAIT
The figure is shown frontally.

He wears a tall, cylindrical, flat-top headdress divided into three sections by two vertical grooves low on the forehead: a Palmyrene priestly hat. A wreath with three rows of small leaves pointing towards a central decoration is depicted at the lower part of the headdress. A narrow, horizontal band at the bottom of the headdress suggests a liner. His face is square. The eyebrows are low and curving, depicted by thin grooves. The eyes are large and almond-shaped, with thick eyelids. The end of the upper eyelids extends beyond that of the lower ones. The irises are indicated by incised circles and the pupils by punch holes. The irises touch the upper eyelids. The ears are large and protruding with helix, scapha, and concha depicted. The nose is thin and straight. The alae are indicated by the carving of the planes of the face. The mouth is small, with full lips. The chin is round, and he has a double chin. The neck is slender.

Cat. 503

A.D. 170–200

504. HEAD OF A PRIEST

DATABASE NUMBER: NCG081.
LOCATION: Copenhagen, Ny Carlsberg Glyptotek, inv. no. IN 1162.
CONTEXT: —
ACQUISITION HISTORY: Puttmann in Syria.
MEASUREMENTS: Height: 26 cm. Width: 17.5 cm. Depth: 21.5 cm. Height of head: 23.5 cm. Width of head: 17.5 cm. Depth of head: 21.5 cm.
MATERIAL: Limestone, white/yellow.

HEADS FROM SARCOPHAGI 793

Cat. 504

PRESERVATION: The lower part of the figure is broken off at the neck. The surface is lightly chipped, especially at the Palmyrene priestly hat, nose, and mouth.
TECHNICAL DESCRIPTION: The head is roughly cut on the back. There are rasp marks on the Palmyrene priestly hat, face, and neck, and flat chisel marks on the back of the ears. There are traces of iron on the back of the head.
DATE: A.D. 170–200 (Ploug 1995: A.D. 150–170).

REFERENCES: Ingholt Archives, PS 324; Ingholt 1928, 126; Ingholt 1934, 34 n. 15; Colledge 1976, 252; Hvidberg-Hansen – Ploug 1993, 109 cat. 66; Ploug 1995, 167 cat. 66; Raja 2019a, 273 cat. 89.

OBJECT DESCRIPTION
The fragment depicts a priest.

PORTRAIT
The figure is shown frontally. The head is slightly turned to his right.

He wears a tall, cylindrical, flat-top headdress divided into three sections by two vertical grooves low on the forehead: a Palmyrene priestly hat. A wreath is depicted at the lower part of the hat. It has three rows of small, elliptical (?) leaves pointing towards an armless bust. The bust shows a male figure with short hair wearing a tunic and chlamys. The midribs of the leaves are incised. His face is round and fleshy. The eyebrows are depicted as thin, low curving ridges. The eyes are large and almond-shaped, with thick eyelids. The upper eyelids are heavy. The end of the upper eyelids extends beyond that of the lower ones. The irises are indicated by incised circles and they touch the upper eyelids. The ears are small and slightly protruding with the helix, tragus, concha, and scapha depicted. The nose is straight with a wide base. The alae are indicated by incised lines. The mouth is medium-sized, with thin lips. The chin is square, and he has a double chin. The neck is wide.

A.D. 200–220

505. HEAD OF A PRIEST

DATABASE NUMBER: NCG091.
LOCATION: Copenhagen, Ny Carlsberg Glyptotek, inv. no. IN 1101.
CONTEXT: —
ACQUISITION HISTORY: Løytved in Syria.
MEASUREMENTS: Height: 23.5 cm. Width: 13 cm. Depth: 17.5 cm.
MATERIAL: Limestone, white/yellow.
PRESERVATION: The lower part of the figure is broken off at the base of the neck. The surface is chipped at the areas of the wreath on the Palmyrene priestly hat, left cheek, tip of nose, and ears.
TECHNICAL DESCRIPTION: The head is roughly cut on the back. There are flat chisel marks on the face and the back of the ears, and rasp marks on the Palmyrene priestly hat, ears, and neck. The bust on the Palmyrene priestly hat is not fully carved.
DATE: A.D. 200–220 (Ploug 1995: A.D. 210–230).
REFERENCES: Ingholt Archives, PS 325; Simonsen 1889, 48 cat. G 12 pl. 13; Ingholt 1928, 126 n. 15; Colledge 1976, 252; Hvidberg-Hansen – Ploug 1993, 146 cat. 106; Ploug 1995, 238 cat. 106; Raja 2019a, 284 cat. 98.

Cat. 05

OBJECT DESCRIPTION
The fragment depicts the head of a priest.

PORTRAIT
The figure is shown frontally. The head is turned to his left.

He wears a tall, cylindrical, flat-top headdress divided into three sections by two vertical grooves low on the forehead: a Palmyrene priestly hat. A wreath is depicted at the lower part of the hat. It has three rows of long, elliptical (?) leaves pointing towards the armless bust of a male figure with short hair. The wreath of leaves reaches to the middle of the hat at the sides; it is continued by a wide band. On the left side of the hat the band is plain, but on the right side, it is decorated with oblique grooves that have three round protrusions at the point of joining with the wreath (metallic tube for inserting the leaves? Wrapped ribbon?). His face is oval and fleshy. The eyebrows are indicated by low curving grooves. The eyes are large, almond-shaped, and slanting with thin eyelids. The lower eyelids are indicated by curving, incised lines. The upper eyelids extend beyond the end of the lower ones. The eyeballs are blank. The ears are small and slightly protruding, with the helix, scapha, concha, and tragus depicted. The nose is thin. The alae are indicated by incised lines, and the nostrils are carved. The mouth is small, with full lips. The chin is round and he has a double chin. The neck is short and wide.

506. HEAD OF A PRIEST

DATABASE NUMBER: PM210.
LOCATION: Palmyra, Palmyra Museum, inv. no. CD 63/73.
CONTEXT: Secondary context: Late wall in the Temple of Standards (Temple des Enseignes), Camp of Diocletian. Found in the east part of the temple.
ACQUISITION HISTORY: —
MEASUREMENTS: Height: 28 cm. Width: 18 cm. Depth: 23 cm.
MATERIAL: Limestone, white.
PRESERVATION: The head is broken off at the neck. The surface heavily weathered. The face and the top of the headdress are broken off.
TECHNICAL DESCRIPTION: —
DATE: A.D. 200–220.
REFERENCES: Gawlikowski 1984, 99 cat. 21 pl. 76, 158.

OBJECT DESCRIPTION
The object depicts a priest.

PORTRAIT
The figure is shown frontally.

He wears a cylindrical, flat-top headdress divided into three sections by two vertical grooves: a Palmyrene priestly hat. A wreath with three rows of leaves pointing towards an armless bust of a male figure is depicted at the lower part of the hat. His face is round and fleshy. The eyes are large and round. The mouth is small, with full lips. The chin is round.

HEADS FROM SARCOPHAGI

Cat. 506

A.D. 220–240

507. HEAD OF A PRIEST

DATABASE NUMBER: SHM014.
LOCATION: St Petersburg, State Hermitage Museum, inv. no. ДВ-8846.
CONTEXT: —
ACQUISITION HISTORY: Transferred to the Hermitage from the Russian Archaeological Institute in Constantinople.
MEASUREMENTS: Height: 21 cm.
MATERIAL: Limestone, yellow.
PRESERVATION: The lower part of the figure is broken off at the neck. The bridge of the nose and the mouth are weathered.
TECHNICAL DESCRIPTION: There are traces of red pigment on the Palmyrene priestly hat above his left ear.
DATE: A.D. 220–240.
REFERENCES: <https://www.hermitagemuseum.org/wps/portal/hermitage/digital-collection/25.+archaeological+artifacts/162834> (06.05.2022).

OBJECT DESCRIPTION
The fragment depicts the head of a priest.

PORTRAIT
He wears a tall, cylindrical, flat-top headdress divided into three sections by two vertical grooves low on the forehead: a Palmyrene priestly hat. A wreath with three rows of narrow, elliptical leaves pointing towards a six-petal rosette is depicted at the lower part of the hat. Two small, round objects (berries?) are depicted on either side of the central leaf of each row. The midribs of the leaves are incised. A narrow horizontal band at the bottom of the hat suggests a liner. His face is oval. The eyebrows are curving and plastically rendered with small, oblique, incised lines indicating individual hairs. The eyes are almond-shaped and slanting with thick upper eyelids. The irises touch the upper eyelids and are indicated by incised semicircles. The nose is wide. The alae are indicated by incised lines. The mouth is small, with a full lower lip. The neck is wide.

Cat. 507, Pl. 81

508. HEAD OF A PRIEST

DATABASE NUMBER: NCG082.
LOCATION: Copenhagen, Ny Carlsberg Glyptotek, inv. no. IN 1124.
CONTEXT: —
ACQUISITION HISTORY: Løytved in Syria.
MEASUREMENTS: Height: 23 cm. Width: 18 cm. Depth: 21 cm.
MATERIAL: Limestone, white/yellow.
PRESERVATION: The lower part of the figure is broken off at the lower right part of the face. The top of the Palmyrene priestly hat and the tip of the nose are broken off. The surface is lightly chipped in the areas of the headdress, the eyebrows, the nose, the ears, and the left cheek.
TECHNICAL DESCRIPTION: The head is roughly cut on the back. There are rasp marks on the sides of the Palmyrene priestly hat, the head, and the ears, and flat chisel marks on the head and behind the ears. Black pigment is preserved on his iris.
DATE: A.D. 220–240 (Ploug 1995: A.D. 230).
REFERENCES: Ingholt Archives, PS 322; Simonsen 1889, 51 cat. G 35 pl. 16; Ingholt 1928, 126; Ingholt 1934, 34 n. 16; Colledge 1976, 252; Hvidberg-Hansen – Ploug 1993, 145 cat. 104; Ploug 1995, 236 cat. 104; Raja 2019a, 296–297 cat. 105.

OBJECT DESCRIPTION
The fragment depicts the head of a priest.

PORTRAIT
He wears a tall, cylindrical, flat-top headdress divided into three sections by two vertical grooves low on the forehead: a Palmyrene priestly hat. A wreath is depicted at the lower part of the hat. It has three rows of serrated leaves pointing towards the armless bust of a male figure. The figure has short hair, small eyes, straight nose, and a wide mouth with full lips, and wears a tunic and chlamys. The midribs of the leaves are incised. The wreath of leaves reaches to the middle of the hat at the sides; it is continued by a wide band (metallic tube for inserting the leaves?). A narrow, horizontal band under the hat suggests a liner. His face is wide and fleshy. The eyebrows are depicted as thin, arched ridges. The eyes are large and almond-shaped, with thick upper eyelids. The end of the upper eyelids extends beyond that of the lower ones. The irises are indicated by incised arches that touch the upper eyelids, and the pupils by punch holes. The ears are small and slightly protruding with the helix, tragus, concha, and scapha depicted. The nose is wide. The alae are indicated by incised lines. The nostrils are drilled. The mouth is small, with full, slightly parted lips.

509. HEAD OF A PRIEST

DATABASE NUMBER: DamascusUNK015.
LOCATION: Damascus, unknown location.
CONTEXT: —
ACQUISITION HISTORY: —
MEASUREMENTS: Height: 23 cm.
MATERIAL: Limestone, white/yellow.
PRESERVATION: The lower part of the figure is broken off at the neck. The head of the bust on the wreath, the nose, and the right ear are broken off. The surface is chipped, especially in the areas of the headdress and the neck.
TECHNICAL DESCRIPTION: —
DATE: A.D. 220–240.
REFERENCES: Ingholt Archives, PS 950.

Cat. 508

Cat. 509

510. HEAD OF A PRIEST

DATABASE NUMBER: NCG056.
LOCATION: Copenhagen, Ny Carlsberg Glyptotek, inv. no. IN 1112.
CONTEXT: —
ACQUISITION HISTORY: Løytved in Syria.
MEASUREMENTS: Height: 24 cm. Width: 15.5 cm. Depth: 18.5 cm.
MATERIAL: Limestone, white/grey.

OBJECT DESCRIPTION
The fragment depicts the head of a priest.

PORTRAIT
The figure is shown frontally.

He wears a tall, cylindrical, flat-top headdress divided into three sections by two vertical grooves: a Palmyrene priestly hat. A wreath is depicted at the lower part of the hat. It has three rows of leaves pointing towards a medallion with the armless bust of a male figure in tunic and chlamys (?). His face is square. The eyebrows are depicted by curving grooves. The eyes are small, deep-set, and almond-shaped, with thick eyelids. The upper eyelids extend beyond the end of the lower ones. The eyeballs are blank. The ears are large and protruding with the helix, concha, and scapha depicted. Nasolabial lines are depicted with curving grooves. The mouth is small, with a full lower lip. A groove extends downwards from either corner of the mouth (›marionette‹ lines). The chin is pointed. The neck is wide.

Cat. 510

PRESERVATION: The lower part of the figure is broken off at the neck. The surface of the Palmyrene priestly hat and ears is chipped. Cracks are running through the face.
TECHNICAL DESCRIPTION: The head is roughly cut on the back. There are marks of rasp work on the face, neck, and the Palmyrene priestly hat, and of flat chisel work on the headdress and ears. There is mortar on the back of the head.
DATE: A.D. 220–240 (Ploug 1995: A.D. 210–230).
REFERENCES: Ingholt Archives, PS 315; Simonsen 1889, 49 cat. G 23 pl. 24; Ingholt 1928, 126; Ingholt 1934, 33 n. 14; Champdor 1953, 87; Michalowski 1960, 85; Colledge 1976, 252; Hvidberg-Hansen – Ploug 1993, 145 cat. 105; Ploug 1995, 237 cat. 105; Raja 2018b, 247 fig. 11; Raja 2019a, 281 cat. 95.

OBJECT DESCRIPTION
The fragment depicts the head of a priest.

PORTRAIT
The figure is shown frontally, head turning towards his right.
He wears low on the forehead a tall, cylindrical, flat-top headdress divided into three sections by two vertical grooves: a Palmyrene priestly hat. A wreath is depicted at the lower part of the hat. It has three rows of serrated leaves pointing towards a central oval with a beaded band border and an indication of a central inlay. The midribs of the leaves are incised. The wreath of leaves reaches to the middle of the headdress at the sides; it is continued by a wide band (metallic tube for inserting the leaves?). A narrow, horizontal band at the bottom of the hat suggests a liner. His face is oval and fleshy. The eyebrows are depicted by curving, incised lines. The eyes are large and almond-shaped, with thick eyelids. The end of the upper eyelids extends beyond that of the lower ones. The irises are rendered by incised circles. The ears are small and protruding with the helix, scapha, antiscapha, concha, and tragus depicted. The nose is long and straight with a wide base. The nostrils are drilled. Nasolabial lines are indicated by the modelling of the planes of the face. The mouth is small, with full lips. The neck is wide and long with two curving grooves.

511. HEAD OF A PRIEST

DATABASE NUMBER: NCG086.
LOCATION: Copenhagen, Ny Carlsberg Glyptotek, inv. no. IN 1122.
CONTEXT: —
ACQUISITION HISTORY: Løytved in Syria.
MEASUREMENTS: Height: 27 cm. Width: 17 cm. Depth: 17.5 cm.
MATERIAL: Limestone, white/yellow.
PRESERVATION: The lower part of the figure is broken off at the neck. The nose is broken off; the surface is chipped at the areas of the headdress, of the wreath, of the eyebrows, of the left eye, of the cheeks, and chin.
TECHNICAL DESCRIPTION: The head is roughly cut on the back. Rasp marks are visible on the face.

Cat. 511

DATE: A.D. 220–240 (Ploug 1995: A.D. 230–250).
REFERENCES: Ingholt Archives, PS 308; Simonsen 1889, 51 cat. G 33 pl. 16; Ingholt 1928, 126; Ingholt 1934, 33 n. 14;

Colledge 1976, 252; Hvidberg-Hansen – Ploug 1993, 147 cat. 108; Ploug 1995, 239 f. cat. 108; Raja 2019a, 304 f. cat. 110.

OBJECT DESCRIPTION
The fragment depicts the head of a priest.

PORTRAIT
The figure is shown frontally. The head is slightly turned to his right.

He wears a tall, cylindrical, flat-top headdress divided into three sections by two vertical grooves low on the forehead: a Palmyrene priestly hat. A wreath is depicted at the lower part of the hat. It has three rows of elliptical (?) leaves pointing towards a central oval with an incised border indicating an inlay. Two round objects (berries?) are depicted between the leaves pointing directly at the oval. The wreath of leaves reaches to the middle of the hat at the sides; it is continued by a wide band that has three round protrusions at the point of joining with the wreath (metallic tube for inserting the leaves?). The midribs of the leaves are incised. A narrow, horizontal band under the bottom of the hat suggests a liner. His face is oval and fleshy. The eyebrows are plastically rendered with oblique lines indicating individual hairs. The eyes are large, almond-shaped, and slanting with thick eyelids. The upper eyelids extend beyond the end of the lower ones. The irises are indicated by incised circles that touch the upper eyelids, and the pupils by punch holes. The ears are small and protruding with the helix, tragus, concha, and scapha depicted. The alae are indicated by incised lines. Nasolabial lines are indicated by the modelling of the planes of the face. The mouth is small, with full lips. The chin is square. The neck is wide.

512. HEAD OF A PRIEST

DATABASE NUMBER: SHM013.
LOCATION: St Petersburg, State Hermitage Museum, inv. no. ДВ-3926.
CONTEXT: —
ACQUISITION HISTORY: Entered the State Hermitage Museum in 1927; transferred from the Museum of Anthropology and Ethnography of the Academy of Sciences.
MEASUREMENTS: Height: 23 cm.
MATERIAL: Limestone, yellow.
PRESERVATION: The lower part of the portrait is broken off at the neck. The Palmyrene priestly hat and the nose are lightly chipped.
TECHNICAL DESCRIPTION: There are traces of red pigment on the Palmyrene priestly hat above his left ear.
DATE: A.D. 220–240.
REFERENCES: <https://www.hermitagemuseum.org/wps/portal/hermitage/digital-collection/25.+archaeological+artifacts/86599> (06.05.2022).

OBJECT DESCRIPTION
The fragment depicts the head of a priest.

PORTRAIT
The head is turned towards his right.

He wears a tall, cylindrical, flat-top headdress divided into three sections by two vertical grooves low on the forehead: a Palmyrene priestly hat. A wreath is depicted at the lower part of the hat. It has three rows of narrow leaves pointing towards a central oval with an incised oval at the centre, indicating an inlay. The midribs of the leaves are incised. A narrow, horizontal band at the bottom of the hat suggests a liner. His face is oval. The eyebrows are indicated by low, curving ridges. The eyes are almond-shaped, with thick upper eyelids. The eyeballs are blank. The ears are small with the helix, anti-helix, and lobe indicated. The nose is thin and straight. The alae are indicated by carved grooves. The philtrum is carved. The mouth is small, with a full lower lip. The neck is wide. A v-shaped groove indicates the sternocleidomastoid muscles.

A.D. 240–273

513. HEAD OF A PRIEST

DATABASE NUMBER: NCG088.
LOCATION: Copenhagen, Ny Carlsberg Glyptotek, inv. no. IN 1117.
CONTEXT: —
ACQUISITION HISTORY: Puttmann in Syria.
MEASUREMENTS: Height: 23 cm. Width: 14.5 cm. Depth: 16 cm.
MATERIAL: Limestone, white/yellow.
PRESERVATION: The lower part of the figure is broken off at the neck. The surface is chipped at the areas of the headdress, of the wreath, of the eyebrows, of the nose, and the chin.
TECHNICAL DESCRIPTION: The back of the head is roughly cut. There are rasp marks on the neck and face and flat chisel marks on the neck. The irises were indicated by inlays.
DATE: A.D. 240–273 (Ploug 1995: A.D. 230–250).
REFERENCES: Ingholt Archives, PS 309; Simonsen 1889, 50 cat. G 28 pl. 16; Ingholt 1928, 126; Ingholt 1934, 33 n. 14; Colledge 1976, 252; Hvidberg-Hansen – Ploug 1993, 146 cat. 107; Ploug 1995, 238 f. cat. 107; Raja 2018a, 250b fig. 18; Raja 2019a, 308 f. cat. 113.

OBJECT DESCRIPTION
The fragment depicts the head of a priest.

PORTRAIT
The figure is shown frontally. The head is turned to his left.

He wears a tall, cylindrical, flat-top headdress divided into three sections by two vertical grooves low on the forehead: a Palmyrene priestly hat. A wreath is depicted at the lower part of the hat. It has three rows of long, elliptical (?) leaves pointing towards a central oval with an incised border indicating an

Cat. 513

inlay. Two round objects (berries?) are depicted between the leaves pointing directly at the oval. The wreath of leaves reaches to the middle of the headdress at the sides; it is continued by a wide band that has three round protrusions at the point of joining with the wreath (metallic tube for inserting the leaves?). The midribs of the leaves are incised. A narrow, horizontal band under the bottom of the hat suggests a liner. His face is oval and fleshy. The eyebrows are indicated by low curving grooves. The eyes are small, almond-shaped, and slanting, with thin eyelids. The upper eyelids extend beyond the end of the lower ones. The irises were indicated by circular inlays that touched the upper eyelids. The ears are small and protruding with the helix, and concha depicted. The nose is thin. The alae are indicated by incised lines, and the nostrils are carved. Nasolabial lines are indicated by the modelling of the planes of the face. The mouth is small, with full lips. Two small lines are indicated at the corners of the mouth through sculpting. The chin is pointed. The neck is wide with two curving grooves.

514. HEAD OF A PRIEST

DATABASE NUMBER: PM357.
LOCATION: Palmyra, Palmyra Museum, inv. no. B 1889.
CONTEXT: Secondary context: Found (05.10.1955) in the southern part of the south court during the excavations of the Baalshamin sanctuary.
ACQUISITION HISTORY: —
MEASUREMENTS: Height: 25 cm. Width: 19 cm. Depth: 19 cm.
MATERIAL: Limestone, white/grey.
PRESERVATION: The lower part of the portrait is broken off at the neck, with a small part of the background preserved. The surface is heavily chipped, especially in the areas of the Palmyrene priestly hat, the forehead, the eyebrows, the eyes, the nose, the cheeks, the mouth, the chin, and the ears.
TECHNICAL DESCRIPTION: —
DATE: A.D. 240–273.
REFERENCES: Dunant – Stucky 2000, 111 cat. 115 pl. 28.

OBJECT DESCRIPTION
The fragment depicts the head of a priest.

PORTRAIT
The figure is shown frontally. The head is turned slightly to his left.
He wears a tall, cylindrical, flat-top headdress divided into three sections by two vertical grooves: a Palmyrene priestly hat. A wreath is depicted at the lower part of the hat. It has three rows of small, narrow, elliptical leaves pointing towards a five-petal rosette. Two small, round objects (berries?) are depicted on either side of each leaf of the central row. The midribs of the leaves are incised. A horizontal, incised line at the bottom of the hat indicates a liner. His face is square and fleshy. The eyebrows are indicated by curving grooves. The eyes are deep-set and almond-shaped. The ears are small and slightly protruding, with helix, scapha, concha, and tragus depicted. The neck is wide.

515. HEAD OF A PRIEST

DATABASE NUMBER: UPM010.
LOCATION: Philadelphia, University of Pennsylvania Museum of Archaeology and Anthropology, inv. no. 89-22-5.
CONTEXT: —

ACQUISITION HISTORY: —
MEASUREMENTS: Height: 23.4 cm. Width: 14.3 cm. Depth: 7.9 cm.
MATERIAL: Limestone.
PRESERVATION: The head is broken off at the neck. The upper part of the headdress is broken off. The headdress and the nose are chipped. Large cracks run diagonally across the face.
TECHNICAL DESCRIPTION: —
DATE: A.D. 240–273.
REFERENCES: Romano 2006, 293 cat. 138; <https://www.penn.museum/collections/object/106645> (05.07.2022).

OBJECT DESCRIPTION
The fragment depicts the head of a male figure.

PORTRAIT
He wears a plain, cylindrical headdress divided into three sections by two vertical grooves that covers his hair and most of his forehead. A horizontal groove just below the headdress possibly indicates a liner. His face is oval. The eyebrows are curving and rendered by incised lines. The eyes are large and almond-shaped, with thick eyelids. The irises and pupils are indicated by concentric, incised circles. The earlobes are visible. The nose is long and narrow with a pointed end. The alae are incised, and the nostrils are carved. The mouth is small, with thin lips. The chin is oval.

31–40 CM

A.D. 170–200

516. HEAD OF A PRIEST

DATABASE NUMBER: PM036.
LOCATION: Palmyra, Palmyra Museum, inv. no. CD 52.
CONTEXT: Secondary context: Found (27.05.1959) at the ground level in the right side of the Praetorian Gate in the Camp of Diocletian.
ACQUISITION HISTORY: —
MEASUREMENTS: Height: 31 cm. Width: 15.5 cm. Depth: 23 cm.
MATERIAL: Limestone, grey.
PRESERVATION: The lower part of the figure is broken off at the top of the neck. The top and most of the right side of the Palmyrene priestly hat, and the nose are broken off. The surface is heavily weathered and cracks run across the face.
TECHNICAL DESCRIPTION: —
DATE: A.D. 170–200.
REFERENCES: Michalowski 1960, 84 cat. 2 figs. 90. 91.

OBJECT DESCRIPTION
The fragment depicts a priest.

PORTRAIT
He wears low on the forehead a tall, cylindrical headdress divided into three sections by two vertical grooves: a Palmyrene priestly hat. A wreath is depicted at the lower part of the hat. It has three rows of leaves pointing towards a medallion with the armless bust of a figure. The figure wears a chlamys that falls in a wide, curving fold across the chest. A narrow, horizontal band at the bottom of the hat suggests a liner. His face is oval. The eyebrows are low and curving, rendered by ridges that start from the root of the nose. The eyes are large and almond-shaped, with thick upper eyelids. The irises are rendered by incised circles that touch the upper eyelids. The ears are small, with the helix, scapha, and concha depicted. The nose has a wide base. The mouth is small and down-turned, with a full lower lip. The chin is round.

517. HEAD OF A PRIEST

DATABASE NUMBER: MV005.
LOCATION: Rome, Musei Vaticani, inv. no. VII 66/1600.
CONTEXT: —
ACQUISITION HISTORY: Donated to the museum by Federico Zeri.
MEASUREMENTS: Height: 34 cm. Width: 25 cm. Height of Palmyrene priestly hat: 14 cm. Width of Palmyrene priestly hat: 22 cm. Height of bust on Palmyrene priestly hat: 6 cm. Width of bust on Palmyrene priestly hat: 4.5 cm.
MATERIAL: Limestone, white/yellow.
PRESERVATION: The lower part of the figure is broken off at the neck. The surface is chipped in the areas of the Palmyrene priestly hat, ears, nose, and neck.
TECHNICAL DESCRIPTION: There are flat chisel marks and rasp marks on the face, neck, and the Palmyrene priestly hat. The head is roughly cut on the back.
DATE: A.D. 170–200.
REFERENCES: Nigro 2002, 40 cat. 35; Krag et al. 2019, 23. 30. 34. 60–63 cat. 5 fig. 2.

OBJECT DESCRIPTION
The fragment depicts a priest.

PORTRAIT
The figure is shown frontally. The head is slightly turned to his right.

He wears a tall, cylindrical, flat-top headdress divided into three sections by two vertical grooves low on the forehead: a Palmyrene priestly hat. A wreath is depicted at the lower part of the hat. It has three rows of elliptical leaves pointing towards a medallion with a beaded border. The medallion frames the armless bust of a male figure with short, straight hair in a tunic and himation. The small figure is beardless, with small eyes, a straight nose with a wide base, and a small mouth with full lips. There are two small, round objects (berries?) on either side of the central leaves next to the medallion. The midribs of the

Cat. 517

leaves are incised. A narrow, horizontal band underneath the hat suggests a liner. His face is oval and fleshy. The eyebrows are plastically rendered, arched, thicker near the bridge of the nose, and thinner at the end. A triangular, incised line is carved between the eyebrows, indicating a frowning expression. The eyes are large, wide-set, and almond-shaped, with thick upper eyelids. The end of the upper eyelids extends beyond that of the lower eyelids. The eyeballs are blank. The ears are large and protruding with the helix, tragus, concha, scapha, and large lobes depicted. The nose is thick and straight with the alae indicated both by fine, incised lines and by the modelling of the planes of the face. The mouth is small, with full lips. The chin is pointed and almost double. The neck is wide with a v-shaped groove indicating the sternocleidomastoid muscles.

518. HEAD OF A PRIEST

DATABASE NUMBER: MLP074.
LOCATION: Paris, Musée du Louvre, inv. no. AO 5003.
CONTEXT: —
ACQUISITION HISTORY: Donated by Vogüé.
MEASUREMENTS: Height: 35 cm. Width: 18 cm. Depth: 23 cm.
MATERIAL: Limestone, white/yellow.
PRESERVATION: The lower part of the figure is broken off at the neck. The surface is weathered and chipped, especially at the areas of the headdress, the face, and the neck. Cracks run across the head and headdress.
TECHNICAL DESCRIPTION: The sculpture was restored in 1997. It is possible that it is a sculpture in the round. Traces of graphite have been found in the pupils and the surface has been treated and cleaned.
DATE: A.D. 170–200 (Dentzer-Feydy – Teixidor 1993: A.D. 180–220).

Cat. 518

REFERENCES: Ingholt Archives PS 317; Ingholt 1928, 126; Colledge 1976, 252; Dentzer-Feydy – Teixidor 1993, 207 cat. 205.

OBJECT DESCRIPTION

The fragment depicts the head of a priest.

PORTRAIT

The figure is shown frontally.

He wears a tall, cylindrical, flat-top headdress divided into three sections by two vertical grooves: a Palmyrene priestly hat. A wreath is depicted at the lower part of the hat. It has three rows of lanceolate leaves at the sides, and elliptical leaves at the centre, pointing towards the armless bust of a male figure with short hair, wearing a tunic and himation. The figure has eyes, nose, and mouth indicated by incisions. The midribs of the leaves are incised. A narrow, horizontal band at the bottom of the hat suggests a liner. His face is oval and fleshy. There are two upwards-pointing grooves at the forehead. The eyebrows are depicted as curving ridges, with oblique, incised lines denoting individual hairs. The eyes are large and almond-shaped, with thick eyelids. The irises are indicated by incised arches. The ears are long and close to the head, with the helix, scapha, and concha depicted. The nose is long with a round tip. Nasolabial lines are indicated. The mouth is small, with full lips. The chin is round. The neck is wide.

519. HEAD OF A PRIEST

DATABASE NUMBER: MV001.
LOCATION: Rome, Musei Vaticani, inv. no. 56599.
CONTEXT: —
ACQUISITION HISTORY: Donated to the museum in June 2000 by Federico Zeri.
MEASUREMENTS: Height: 38 cm. Width: 23 cm. Depth: 22 cm.
MATERIAL: Limestone, white/yellow.
PRESERVATION: The lower part of the figure is broken off at the neck. Most of the nose and the chin are broken off. The surface is chipped in the areas of the Palmyrene priestly hat, eyebrows, ears, cheeks, and neck.
TECHNICAL DESCRIPTION: There are flat chisel marks and rasp marks on the Palmyrene priestly hat and face. The head is roughly cut on the back. There are drill holes in the ears.
DATE: A.D. 170–200 (Ciliberto 2017: A.D. 150–200).
REFERENCES: Callieri 1986, 232–234 cat. 5 fig. 66, 2; Kingley 2002, 4; Nigro 2002, 41 cat. 37; Cappozzo 2017, 101 cat. 7; Krag et al. 2019, 23. 30. 34. 36–39 cat. 1.

OBJECT DESCRIPTION

The fragment depicts a priest.

PORTRAIT

The figure is shown frontally.

He wears low on the forehead a cylindrical, flat-top headdress divided into three sections by two vertical grooves: a Palmyrene priestly hat. A wreath is depicted at the lower part of the hat. It has three rows of serrated leaves pointing towards an armless bust. The bust shows a male figure with short hair in a tunic and himation. The midribs of the leaves are incised. His face is oval and fleshy. The eyebrows are curving, rendered by an incised groove starting from the root of the nose. The eyes are close-set and almond-shaped, with thick upper eyelids. The lower eyelid is rendered by an incised groove. The irises are indicated by incised circles that touch the upper eyelids. The ears are small and protruding with the helix, tragus, concha, scapha, and lobe depicted. The ears are not symmetrically placed on the head: the left ear is positioned lower than the right one. The nose has a wide base. The mouth is small, with a full lower lip. The neck is wide.

Cat. 519

A.D. 220–240

520. HEAD OF A PRIEST

DATABASE NUMBER: NCG016.
LOCATION: Copenhagen, Ny Carlsberg Glyptotek, inv. no. IN 1151.
CONTEXT: —
ACQUISITION HISTORY: Løytved in Syria.
MEASUREMENTS: Height: 35.5 cm. Width: 21.5 cm. Depth: 18.5 cm.
MATERIAL: Limestone, white/grey.
PRESERVATION: The lower part of the figure is broken off at the neck. The surface is chipped, especially at the areas of the Palmyrene priestly hat, the eyebrows, the nose, the left ear, and the cheek. Several small cracks run across the face.
TECHNICAL DESCRIPTION: The head is roughly cut on the back.
DATE: A.D. 220–240 (Ploug 1995: A.D. 190–210).
REFERENCES: Ingholt Archives, PS 321; Ingholt 1928, 126; Colledge 1976, 144 n. 536; 252; Ingholt 1976, 115 n. 67; Parlasca 1985, 351 pl. 147; Equini Schneider 1992b, 128–130 fig. 10; Hvidberg-Hansen – Ploug 1993, 144 cat. 103; Ploug 1995, 234–236 cat. 103; Raja 2018b, 252 f. fig. 20; Raja 2019a, 276 f. cat. 91.

OBJECT DESCRIPTION
The object depicts a priest.

PORTRAIT
The figure is shown frontally, head turning slightly towards his left.

He wears a tall, cylindrical, flat-top headdress divided into three sections by two vertical grooves: a Palmyrene priestly hat. A wreath is depicted at the lower part of the hat. It has three rows of pointed leaves pointing towards a round medallion with incised borders and two small loops at the sides. The medallion carries the armless bust of a young male with short, voluminous hair, carved eyebrows, large eyes, wide nose, and full mouth, wearing a tunic with a wide, v-shaped neckline and a himation over the left shoulder. The midribs of the leaves are incised. The wreath of leaves reaches to the middle of the headdress at the sides; it is continued by a wide band with oblique grooves that has three circular protrusions at the point of joining with the wreath (metallic tube for inserting the leaves? wrapped ribbon?). A narrow, horizontal band at the bottom of the hat suggests a liner. His face is square and fleshy. The eyebrows are depicted as wide, arched ridges created by the carving of the planes of the face. Two vertical, incised lines at the root of the nose indicate frown lines. The eyes are small, deep-set, and almond-shaped, with thick and heavy upper eyelids. The end of the upper eyelids extends beyond that of

Cat. 520, Pl. 82

the lower ones. The irises are indicated by punch holes. The ears are large and protruding with the helix, scapha, and concha depicted. The lobe is long. The nose is short with a wide base. Nasolabial lines are indicated by incised lines and the carving of the planes of the face. The mouth is small, with full lips. The chin is square and wide. The neck is wide. A v-shaped groove indicates the sternocleidomastoid muscles.

521. HEAD OF PRIEST

DATABASE NUMBER: PM300.
LOCATION: Palmyra, Palmyra Museum, inv. no. CD 103, B 2088/7425.
CONTEXT: Secondary context: Found in later wall near column I in the Camp of Diocletian.
ACQUISITION HISTORY: —
MEASUREMENTS: Height: 35 cm. Width: 18 cm. Depth: 24 cm.
MATERIAL: Limestone, white.
PRESERVATION: The head is broken off at the neck. The surface is weathered and lightly chipped. The nose and tip of the chin are broken off.
TECHNICAL DESCRIPTION: The upper part of the headdress has been restored. The central bust of the wreath is unfinished.
DATE: A.D. 220–240 (Charles-Gaffiot et al. 2001: A.D. 150–200).
REFERENCES: Michalowski 1962, 165–167 cat. 36 fig. 182; Gawlikowski 1966, 75. 77 fig. 2; Kaspar 1969–1970, 292 fig. 11; Charles-Gaffiot et al. 2001, 256. 343 cat. 147; Equini Schneider 2002, 33 cat. 23.

OBJECT DESCRIPTION
The object depicts a priest.

PORTRAIT
The figure is shown frontally.

He wears a tall, cylindrical, flat-top headdress divided into three sections by two vertical grooves: a Palmyrene priestly hat. A wreath with three rows of serrated leaves pointing towards an armless bust of a male figure is depicted at the lower part of the hat. The figure has short hair and wears a tunic and chlamys. A narrow, horizontal band at the bottom of the hat suggests a liner. His face is oval. The eyebrows are curving, depicted by incised lines. The eyebrows curve upwards at the root of the nose, creating a frowning expression. The eyes are large, deep-set, and almond-shaped, with thick upper eyelids. The lower eyelids are indicated by incised lines. The end of the upper eyelids extends beyond the end of the lower ones. The irises that touch the upper eyelids are indicated by incised circles. The ears are large and protruding with the helix, scapha, tragus, and concha depicted. The nose is long with a wide base with drilled nostrils. Nasolabial lines are indicated. The mouth is small, with full lips. The chin is round. The neck is short and wide.

A.D. 240–273

522. HEAD OF PRIEST

DATABASE NUMBER: FDES001.
LOCATION: Fondazione Dino ed Ernesta Santarelli (private collection).
CONTEXT: —
ACQUISITION HISTORY: —
MEASUREMENTS: Height: 35.5 cm. Depth: 24.5 cm.
MATERIAL: Limestone, white/yellow.
PRESERVATION: The head is broken off at the base of the neck. The bridge and tip of the nose is broken off. The headdress, the ears, and chin are chipped.
TECHNICAL DESCRIPTION: There are traces of red pigment on the headdress and the wreath. Rasp marks are visible on the face and headdress; flat chisel marks are visible on the wreath, bust on the wreath, and the eyes. The back of the head is roughly cut.
DATE: A.D. 240–273.
REFERENCES: Papini 2016, 146–150 cat. 35.

OBJECT DESCRIPTION
The object depicts a priest.

PORTRAIT
The figure is shown frontally. The head is turned slightly to his left.

He wears a tall, cylindrical, flat-top headdress divided into three sections by two vertical grooves: a Palmyrene priestly hat. A wreath with three rows of small, elliptical leaves pointing towards a medallion with a beaded border with an armless bust of a male figure is depicted at the lower part of the hat. The figure has short hair and wears a tunic and chlamys fastened at the right shoulder with a circular(?) brooch. The facial features of the figure are indicated. The midribs of the leaves are incised. A narrow, horizontal band at the bottom of the hat suggests a liner. His face is oval. The eyebrows are plastically rendered with oblique, incised lines indicating individual hairs. The eyes are large and deep-set, almond-shaped, with thick upper eyelids. The upper eyelids extend beyond the end of the lower ones. The irises are rendered by incised circles and the pupils by punch holes. The irises touch the upper eyelids. The ears are large with the helix, scapha, concha, tragus, and lobe depicted. The nose is straight. The mouth is small, with full lips. The chin is square. The neck is short and wide.

523. HEAD OF A PRIEST

DATABASE NUMBER: PM356.
LOCATION: Palmyra, Palmyra Museum, inv. no. B 1874.
CONTEXT: Secondary context: Found (07.09.1955) in portico C1 during excavations at the Baalshamin temple.
ACQUISITION HISTORY: —
MEASUREMENTS: Height: 34 cm. Width: 20 cm. Depth: 22 cm.
MATERIAL: Limestone, white/grey.
PRESERVATION: The lower part of the figure is broken off at the neck. The surface is heavily chipped, especially in the areas of the Palmyrene priestly hat, the ears, and the face.
TECHNICAL DESCRIPTION: The irises are drilled.
DATE: A.D. 240–273.
REFERENCES: Dunant – Stucky 2000, 111 cat. 114 pl. 28.

OBJECT DESCRIPTION
The fragment depicts the head of a priest.

PORTRAIT
The figure is shown frontally. The head is turned slightly to his left.

He wears a tall, cylindrical, flat-top headdress divided into three sections by two vertical grooves: a Palmyrene priestly hat. A wreath is depicted at the lower part of the hat. It has three rows of long, narrow, serrated leaves pointing towards a medallion with the armless bust of a figure in a chlamys. The midribs of the leaves are incised. A narrow, horizontal band at the bottom of the hat indicates a liner. His face is oval. The eyebrows are indicated by curving grooves. The eyes are almond-shaped, with thick upper eyelids. The upper eyelids extend downwards and beyond the end of the lower ones. The irises are indicated by large drill holes that touch the upper eyelids. The chin is square.

524. HEAD OF A PRIEST

DATABASE NUMBER: MLP040.
LOCATION: Paris, Musée du Louvre, inv. no. AO 2065.
CONTEXT: —
ACQUISITION HISTORY: Acquired in 1890 by Nemher.
MEASUREMENTS: Height: 38 cm. Width: 21 cm. Depth: 26 cm.
MATERIAL: Limestone, white/yellow.
PRESERVATION: The lower part of the figure is broken off at the neck. The surface is chipped, especially at the areas of the headdress, the forehead, the left eye, the left cheek, the mouth, the chin, and the neck.
TECHNICAL DESCRIPTION: There are traces of black pigment in the iris of the eyes. There are rasp marks on the face and neck. Flat chisel marks are visible on the wreath and both ears. The nostrils are drilled. The head is roughly cut on the back.
DATE: A.D. 240–273 (Dentzer-Feydy – Teixidor 1993: A.D. 150–250).
REFERENCES: Ingholt Archives, PS 318; Ingholt 1928, 126; Colledge 1976, 252; Dentzer-Feydy – Teixidor 1993, 174 cat. 176.

OBJECT DESCRIPTION
The fragment depicts the head of a priest.

PORTRAIT
The figure is shown frontally, head turning towards his left.

He wears a tall, cylindrical, flat-top headdress divided into three sections by two vertical grooves: a Palmyrene priestly hat.

Cat. 524, Pl. 83

A wreath is depicted at the lower part of the hat. It has three rows of serrated leaves pointing towards an armless bust. The bust shows a male figure with short hair, wearing a tunic and chlamys. The bust figure has tousled hair, and the eyes, nose, and mouth are indicated by incisions. The midribs of the leaves are incised. A narrow, horizontal band at the bottom of the hat suggests a liner. His face is oval. The eyebrows are plastically rendered with oblique, incised lines denoting individual hairs. The eyes are large, deep-set, and almond-shaped, with thick eyelids. The end of the upper eyelids extends beyond that of the lower ones. The lower eyelids are indicated by grooves. The eyeballs are blank. The ears are small and protruding with the helix, scapha, concha, and tragus depicted. The nose is long with a wide base. The nostrils are drilled. The philtrum is carved. The mouth is small, with a full lower lip. The chin is square. The neck is wide with vertical grooves indicating the sternocleidomastoid muscles and a slight protrusion between them indicating the Adam's apple.

NO MEASUREMENTS

A.D. 50–150

525. HEAD OF PRIEST

DATABASE NUMBER: PM785.
LOCATION: Palmyra, Palmyra Museum, inv. no. A 134.
CONTEXT: —
ACQUISITION HISTORY: —
MEASUREMENTS: —
MATERIAL: Limestone.
PRESERVATION: The head is broken off at the neck. The surface is weathered and chipped. The ears and nose are broken off.
TECHNICAL DESCRIPTION: —
DATE: A.D. 50–100.
REFERENCES: Ingholt Archives, PS 938.

OBJECT DESCRIPTION
The object depicts a priest.

PORTRAIT
The head is turned slightly to his left.

He wears a tall, cylindrical, flat-top headdress divided into three sections by two vertical grooves: a Palmyrene priestly hat. His face is oval. The eyes are almond-shaped and slanting with thick upper eyelids. The upper eyelids extend beyond the end of the lower ones (details unclear). The nose is short and wide. The mouth is small, with full lips. The chin is round and pointed. The neck is wide.

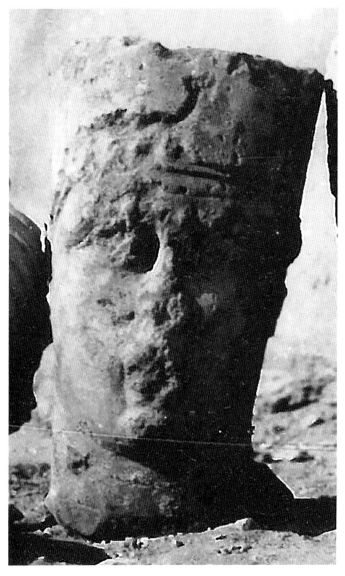

Cat. 525

A.D. 200–220

526. HEAD OF A PRIEST

DATABASE NUMBER: TWM001.
LOCATION: Newcastle-upon-Tyne, Great North Museum, inv. no. NEWGM: 809.
CONTEXT: —
ACQUISITION HISTORY: Noted to be in the auction house Spink and Son, London in 1928. Now in the Shefton collection of the Great North Museum.
MEASUREMENTS: —
MATERIAL: Limestone, white/yellow.
PRESERVATION: The lower part of the figure is broken off at the neck. There are multiple surface chips, especially at the top of the Palmyrene priestly hat and the left cheek.

TECHNICAL DESCRIPTION: The finish is rough. The backs of the ears are uncarved. Tool marks are visible on the face and the Palmyrene priestly hat. The lower eyelids are not carved.
DATE: A.D. 200–220.
REFERENCES: Ingholt Archives, PS 311A; Ingholt 1928, 126; Colledge 1976, 252.

OBJECT DESCRIPTION
The fragment depicts the head of a priest.

PORTRAIT
The figure is shown frontally.

He wears a tall, cylindrical, flat-top headdress divided into three sections by two vertical grooves, low on the forehead: a Palmyrene priestly hat. A wreath is depicted at the lower part of the hat. It has three rows of elliptical leaves pointing towards a medallion with an incised circle at the centre, indicating an inlay. At the sides, the wreath projects out of a tubular band. His face is oval. The eyebrows are rendered by low, curving grooves. The eyes are small and almond-shaped, with thin eyelids. The eyeballs are blank. The ears are of unequal size, the right smaller than the left, and protruding with helix, scapha, and tragus depicted. The nose is straight and short with a wide base. The nostrils are carved. The mouth is small, with a full lower lip. The chin is round. The neck is slender with a curving groove.

A.D. 220–240

527. HEAD OF A PRIEST

DATABASE NUMBER: BeirutPriv002.
LOCATION: Beirut, private collection.
CONTEXT: —
ACQUISITION HISTORY: —
MEASUREMENTS: —
MATERIAL: Limestone.
PRESERVATION: The lower part of the portrait is broken off at the neck. The area of the priestly hat, the eyebrows, the nose, and the chin is chipped.
TECHNICAL DESCRIPTION: —
DATE: A.D. 220–240.
REFERENCES: Ingholt Archives, PS 328; Ingholt 1928, 126 n. 15; Colledge 1976, 252.

OBJECT DESCRIPTION
The fragment depicts a priest.

PORTRAIT
The head turns slightly to its left.

He wears a tall, cylindrical, flat-top headdress divided into three sections by two vertical grooves: a Palmyrene priestly hat. A wreath is depicted at the lower part of the hat. It has three rows of long, narrow leaves pointing towards an armless bust. The bust shows a male figure with short hair and wearing a chlamys that falls in a curving fold over the chest. A horizontal band at the bottom of the hat suggests a liner. His face is square. The eyebrows are plastically rendered with oblique, incised lines indicating individual hairs. The eyes are almond-shaped, with thick upper eyelids. The upper eyelids extend beyond the end of the lower ones. The irises are indicated by incised circles. The ears are small and protruding with the helix and concha depicted. The nose is straight. The mouth is small, with full lips. The chin is pointed. The neck is wide. A v-shaped groove indicates the sternocleidomastoid muscles.

Cat. 526

Cat. 527

528. HEAD OF PRIEST

DATABASE NUMBER: CrébierPriv001.
LOCATION: Lyon, private collection.
CONTEXT: —
ACQUISITION HISTORY: Acquired in Palmyra by an aviation officer. In 1926 it was in the possession of the painter Paul-Louis Crébier in Lyon.
MEASUREMENTS: —
MATERIAL: Limestone, white/yellow.
PRESERVATION: The head is broken off at the neck. The surface is weathered. The left ear is broken off.
TECHNICAL DESCRIPTION: Tool marks are visible on the face and neck.
DATE: A.D. 220–240 (Ingholt: A.D. 200–273).
REFERENCES: Ingholt Archives, PS 319; Ingholt 1928, 126 PS 316; Colledge 1976, 252.

Cat. 528

Cat. 528

OBJECT DESCRIPTION
The object depicts a priest.

PORTRAIT
The head is turned slightly to his left.

He wears a tall, cylindrical, flat-top headdress divided into three sections by two vertical grooves: a Palmyrene priestly hat. A wreath with three rows of serrated leaves pointing towards an armless bust of a male figure is depicted at the lower part of the hat. The figure has short hair and wears a tunic and chlamys fastened on the shoulder with a brooch. The facial features of the figure are indicated. The midribs of the leaves are incised. His face is oval. The eyebrows are curving, rendered by thin ridges. The eyes are almond-shaped and slanting with thick upper eyelids. The upper eyelids extend beyond the end of the lower ones. The irises are indicated by incised circles. The irises touch the upper eyelids. The ear is large and protruding with the helix, concha, scapha, and lobe depicted. The nose is straight. The mouth is small, with a full lower lip. The corners of the mouth curve downwards. The chin is round. The neck is slender.

529. HEAD OF A PRIEST

DATABASE NUMBER: Beirutpriv003.
LOCATION: Beirut, private collection.
CONTEXT: —
ACQUISITION HISTORY: —
MEASUREMENTS: —
MATERIAL: Limestone.
PRESERVATION: The lower part of the figure is broken off at the base of the neck. The surface is chipped, especially in the areas of the top of the Palmyrene priestly hat, the wreath, the right eyebrow, the cheek, and the chin. The tip of the nose is broken off.
TECHNICAL DESCRIPTION: There are traces of black pigment in the eyes.
DATE: A.D. 220–240.
REFERENCES: Ingholt Archives, PS 313; Ingholt 1928, 126; Colledge 1976, 252.

OBJECT DESCRIPTION
The fragment depicts a priest.

PORTRAIT
The figure is shown frontally. The head is turned slightly to his left.

He wears a tall, cylindrical, flat-top headdress divided into three sections by two vertical grooves: a Palmyrene priestly hat. A wreath is depicted at the lower part of the hat. It has three rows of small, elliptical leaves pointing towards an oval decoration with an incised border. A narrow, horizontal band at the bottom of the hat suggests a liner. His face is round and plump. The eyebrows are arched, rendered by incised lines.

Cat. 529

The eyes are deep-set, almond-shaped, and slanting with thick upper eyelids. The irises are indicated by incised arches that touch the upper eyelids. The ears are large with the helix, anti-helix, and lobe depicted. The nose is wide. The mouth is small, with a full lower lip. The chin is wide and pointed. The neck is wide and has three curving grooves.

530. HEAD OF A PRIEST

DATABASE NUMBER: MBE015.
LOCATION: Beirut, American University Museum, inv. no. unknown.
CONTEXT: —
ACQUISITION HISTORY: —
MEASUREMENTS: —
MATERIAL: Limestone.
PRESERVATION: The lower part of the figure is broken off at the neck. The head of the bust on the headdress and the nose are broken off. The surface is chipped, especially in

the areas of the left top of the headdress, the right eyebrow, the ear, the chin, the neck.
TECHNICAL DESCRIPTION: —
DATE: A.D. 220–240.
REFERENCES: Ingholt Archives, PS 327; Ingholt 1928, 126 n. 15; Colledge 1976, 252.

OBJECT DESCRIPTION
Head of a priest.

PORTRAIT
The figure is shown frontally.

He wears a tall, cylindrical, flat-top headdress divided into three sections by two vertical grooves: a Palmyrene priestly hat. A wreath is depicted at the lower part of the hat. It has three rows of serrated leaves pointing towards an armless bust. The bust shows a male figure wearing a tunic and chlamys. The chlamys falls in a curving fold over the chest and is fastened at the right shoulder with a circular brooch (other details unclear). A small, zigzag-shaped fold falls from under the brooch. The midribs of the leaves are incised. A narrow, horizontal band at the bottom of the hat suggests a liner. His face is oval and fleshy. There is a small furrow at the centre of the forehead. The eyebrows start from the root of the nose. They are slightly curving and plastically rendered with oblique, incised lines indicating individual hairs. The eyes are almond-shaped. The eyeballs are blank. The ears are small and protruding with the helix and lobe depicted. The mouth is large with a full lower lip. The chin is pointed. The Adam's apple is indicated by a protrusion at the top of the neck.

A.D. 240–273

531. HEAD OF A PRIEST

DATABASE NUMBER: PM828.
LOCATION: Palmyra, Palmyra Museum, inv. no. unknown.
CONTEXT: —
ACQUISITION HISTORY: —
MEASUREMENTS: —
MATERIAL: Limestone, white/yellow.
PRESERVATION: The head is broken off at the neck. The left side of the headdress is broken off.
TECHNICAL DESCRIPTION: —
DATE: A.D. 240–273.
REFERENCES: Silver et al. 2018, 72 fig. 4, 23; <https://www.alamy.com/stock-photo-head-man-carrying-the-priests-cylindrical-coiffeure-2-cent-palmyra-55355602.html> (06.05.2022).

OBJECT DESCRIPTION
The object depicts a priest.

PORTRAIT
The figure is shown frontally. The head is turned slightly to his right.

He wears a tall, cylindrical flat-top headdress divided into three sections by two vertical grooves low on the forehead: a Palmyrene priestly hat. A wreath with three rows of small, elliptical leaves pointing towards a medallion is depicted at the lower part of the hat. The medallion has a beaded border with a bust of a short-haired, beardless figure in tunic and himation. A horizontal band under the bottom of the hat indicates a liner. His face is triangular. The eyebrows are plastically rendered with oblique incised lines, indicating individual hairs. The eyes are small and almond-shaped, with thick upper eyelids. The lower eyelids are carved and indicated by incised lines. The irises that touch the upper eyelids are indicated by incised circles and the pupils by punch holes. The ears are large and slightly protruding with helix, antihelix, scapha, and lobe indicated. The nose is long and straight. The alae are indicated by incised lines. The mouth is wide with a full lower lip. The chin is pointed. The neck is short and slender.

Cat. 530

MALE HEADS

1–10 CM

A.D. 200–240

532. MALE HEAD

DATABASE NUMBER: PM305.
LOCATION: Palmyra, Palmyra Museum, inv. no. CD 134.
CONTEXT: Secondary context: Found (24.05.1960) on the north-eastern side of the Tetrapylon in the Camp of Diocletian.
ACQUISITION HISTORY: —
MEASUREMENTS: Height: 8 cm. Width: 17 cm. Depth: 13.5 cm.
MATERIAL: Limestone, yellow.
PRESERVATION: The lower part of the figure is broken off at the base of the neck. The left and right upper side of the head are broken off. The surface of the nose, of the upper lip, and of the chin is chipped.
TECHNICAL DESCRIPTION: —
DATE: A.D. 200–240.
REFERENCES: Michalowski 1962, 171 f. cat. 42 fig. 189.

OBJECT DESCRIPTION
The fragment depicts the head of a male figure.

PORTRAIT
The head is turned slightly upwards.

His hair is arranged in rows of snail-shaped curls around the head, covering the ears and reaching the shoulders. The individual strands of hair are indicated by incised lines. His face is square. The eyebrows are rendered by incised lines. The eyes are close-set and almond-shaped, with thick upper eyelids. The eyeballs are blank. The mouth is small, and the chin is wide. The neck is wide.

A.D. 200–273

533. MALE HEAD

DATABASE NUMBER: PUAM003.
LOCATION: Princeton, Princeton University Art Museum, inv. no. y1930.447.
CONTEXT: —
ACQUISITION HISTORY: —
MEASUREMENTS: Height: 8.6 cm. Width: 7.5 cm. Depth: 8.8 cm.
MATERIAL: Limestone, white/grey.
PRESERVATION: The lower part of the figure is broken off at the base of the neck. The background is preserved only to the left and right of the head. The upper part of the head and the nose are broken off.
TECHNICAL DESCRIPTION: Tool marks are visible on the surface of the face.
DATE: A.D. 200–273.
REFERENCES: Gawlikowski 2001b, 363 cat. 158; Wenning 2001, 313 n. 1; <https://artmuseum.princeton.edu/collections/objects/19704> (06.05.2022).

OBJECT DESCRIPTION
The fragment depicts the head of a male figure.

PORTRAIT
The head is shown frontally.

His hair is arranged in two rows of snail-shaped curls around the head. The individual strands of hair are indicated by incised lines. The eyebrows are rendered by incised lines. The eyes are almond-shaped, with thick upper eyelids. The end of the upper eyelids extends beyond that of the lower ones. The irises are indicated (details unclear). He has a beard that starts from the temples, covers part of the cheeks, the upper lip, and the chin. The facial hair is indicated by oblique incised lines in two rows. The mouth is small.

Cat. 533

HEADS FROM SARCOPHAGI 813

534. MALE HEAD

DATABASE NUMBER: UPM005.
LOCATION: Philadelphia, University of Pennsylvania Museum of Archaeology and Anthropology, inv. no. B 8908.
CONTEXT: —
ACQUISITION HISTORY: Collected for the museum by Rev. John Punnett Peters during his expedition to Nippur in 1889–1890.
MEASUREMENTS: Height: 9.8 cm. Width: 9.5 cm. Depth: 8 cm.
MATERIAL: Limestone.
PRESERVATION: The head is broken off at the neck. The chin is broken off.
TECHNICAL DESCRIPTION: —
DATE: A.D. 200–273.
REFERENCES: Ingholt Archives, PS 634; Legrain 1927, 350 cat. 12 fig. 12; Romano 2006, 299 cat. 143; <https://www.penn.museum/collections/object/222625> (06.05.2022).

OBJECT DESCRIPTION
The fragment depicts the head of a male figure.

PORTRAIT
His hair is rendered by flame-shaped locks around the head. He has a high receding hairline. His face is square in shape. The eyebrows are indicated by curving ridges. The eyes are large and almond-shaped and are partly uncarved. The ears are small and protruding and the scapha and earlobe are indicated. The nose has a flat bridge, and the alae and nostrils are carved. He has a beard. It starts at the temples, covers the outer side of the cheeks, the chin, and the upper lip. The facial hair is rendered by flame-shaped locks. The mouth is large with accentuated lips.

535. MALE HEAD

DATABASE NUMBER: UPM006.
LOCATION: Philadelphia, University of Pennsylvania Museum of Archaeology and Anthropology, inv. no. B9189.
CONTEXT: —
ACQUISITION HISTORY: Collected for the museum by Rev. John Punnett Peters during his expedition to Nippur in 1889–1890.

Cat. 534

Cat. 535

MEASUREMENTS: Height: 9.5 cm. Width: 9.8 cm. Depth: 10 cm.
MATERIAL: Limestone.
PRESERVATION: The head is broken off at the neck.
TECHNICAL DESCRIPTION: —
DATE: A.D. 200–273.
REFERENCES: Ingholt Archives, PS 614; Legrain 1927, 350 cat. 13 fig. 13; Romano 2006, 301 cat. 145; <https://www.penn.museum/collections/object/261882> (06.05.2022).

OBJECT DESCRIPTION
The fragment depicts the head of a male figure.

PORTRAIT
His hair is arranged in two rows of snail-shell curls around his head. His face is round. The eyebrows are indicated by curving ridges. The eyes are large and almond-shaped, and partly carved. The ears are small and protruding with the helix, scapha, and earlobe. The nose is narrow and short with the alae incised and the nostrils carved. The mouth is small, with thin upper and full lower lip.

11–20 CM

A.D. 140–160

536. MALE HEAD

DATABASE NUMBER: PM299.
LOCATION: Palmyra, Palmyra Museum, inv. no. CD 87.
CONTEXT: Secondary context: Found (17.05.1960) in the south part of the Tetrapylon in the Camp of Diocletian.
ACQUISITION HISTORY: —
MEASUREMENTS: Height: 12 cm. Width: 7 cm.
MATERIAL: Limestone, grey.
PRESERVATION: The lower part of the figure is broken off at the neck. The left side of the neck is broken off. The face is heavily chipped and weathered.
TECHNICAL DESCRIPTION: —
DATE: A.D. 140–160.
REFERENCES: Michalowski 1962, 165 f. cat. 35 figs. 180–181.

OBJECT DESCRIPTION
The fragment depicts the head of a male figure.

PORTRAIT
The hair is arranged in at least two alternating rows of s-shaped curls around his head. His face is square. The eyebrows are slightly curving. The eyes are small and almond-shaped (other details unclear). The neck is wide.

A.D. 150–170

537. MALE HEAD

DATABASE NUMBER: NMD042.
LOCATION: Damascus, National Museum of Damascus, inv. no. C18.
CONTEXT: —
ACQUISITION HISTORY: —
MEASUREMENTS: Height: 16 cm.
MATERIAL: Limestone, yellow.
PRESERVATION: The lower part of the figure is broken off at the neck. The left side of the neck is broken off. The nose is chipped.
TECHNICAL DESCRIPTION: —
DATE: A.D. 150–170.
REFERENCES: Ingholt Archives, PS 823; Abdul-Hak – Abdul-Hak 1951, 43 f. cat. 42; Parlasca 1969–1970, 179 fig. 10; Colledge 1976, 251; Ingholt 1976, 118 pl. 5, 4; Al-Ush et al. 1980, 123; Tanabe 1986, 45 cat. 458; Equini Schneider 1992b, 123 f. fig. 7; Parlasca 2001c, 336 cat. 99; Equini Schneider 2002, 31 cat. 19.

Cat. 537

OBJECT DESCRIPTION
The fragment depicts the head of a male figure.

PORTRAIT
The hair is arranged in four rows of flame-shaped curls around his head. Every second curl in the row above the forehead ends in a snail-shell curl. The individual strands of hair are indicated by incised lines. His face is oval. The eyebrows are slightly curving and have an incised middle line with individual strands of hair rendered plastically on either side. The eyes are large and almond-shaped, with thick eyelids. The upper eyelids extend beyond the end of the lower ones. The irises are indicated by incised circles and the pupils by punch holes. The ears are large and protruding and the helix, scapha, and earlobes are depicted. The nose is straight. The alae are incised. He has a beard: it starts at the temples, covers the outer side of the cheeks, the chin, and the upper lip. The facial hair is rendered by flame-shaped curls in the beard and incised, vertical lines above the upper lip. The individual strands of hair are indicated by incised lines. The mouth is small, with full lips. The chin is square.

538. MALE HEAD

DATABASE NUMBER: PUAM002.
LOCATION: Princeton, Princeton University Art Museum, inv. no. y1930.441.
CONTEXT: —
ACQUISITION HISTORY: —
MEASUREMENTS: Height: 15 cm. Width: 11.3 cm. Depth: 16.5 cm.
MATERIAL: Limestone, white/grey.
PRESERVATION: The lower part of the figure is broken off at the neck. The right upper side of the face has broken off. The top of the head, the nose, the lower lip, and chin are chipped.
TECHNICAL DESCRIPTION: —
DATE: A.D. 150–170.
REFERENCES: Wenning 2001, 313 n. 1; Gawlikowski 2001c, 359 cat. 156; <https://artmuseum.princeton.edu/collections/objects/19694> (06.05.2022).

OBJECT DESCRIPTION
The fragment depicts the head of a male figure.

PORTRAIT
The figure is shown frontally.
The hair is arranged in snail-shell curls around the head, covering the ears and reaching the upper neck. The individual strands of hair are rendered by incised lines. His face is oval. The eyebrows are curving, rendered by incised lines starting from the root of the nose. The eyes are almond-shaped, with thick upper eyelids. The upper eyelids extend beyond the ends of the lower ones. The eyeballs are blank. The nose is large. The mouth is small, with a thin upper lip. The neck is slender.

Cat. 538

539. MALE HEAD

DATABASE NUMBER: MCH002.
LOCATION: Oslo, Museum of Cultural History, inv. no. C40815.
CONTEXT: —
ACQUISITION HISTORY: —
MEASUREMENTS: Height: 16 cm. Width: 15 cm. Depth: 12 cm.
MATERIAL: Limestone, yellow.
PRESERVATION: The lower part of the figure is broken off at the base of the neck. Cracks run across the head. There is brown/green discoloration on some of the cracks.
TECHNICAL DESCRIPTION: —
DATE: A.D. 150–170.
REFERENCES: <https://www.unimus.no/portal/#/things/57d2600b-4b86-425f-8ee8-5ae4387a8e50> (06.05.2022).

OBJECT DESCRIPTION
The fragment depicts the head of a male figure.

Cat. 539

Cat. 540

PORTRAIT

His hair is arranged in two rows of snail-shell curls around the head. The individual strands of hair are indicated by incised lines. His face is square. The eyebrows are curving and indicated by incised lines. The eyes are almond-shaped, with thick upper eyelids. The end of the upper eyelids extends beyond that of the lower ones. The irises are indicated by incised circles and the pupils by punch holes. The nose is short and straight. The alae are incised. The mouth is small, with full lips, and he has ›marionette‹ lines. The chin is square. The neck is wide and has two curving grooves.

540. MALE HEAD

DATABASE NUMBER: PM013.
LOCATION: Palmyra, Palmyra Museum, inv. no. CD 45.
CONTEXT: Secondary context: Found (23.04.1961) at the later wall near the tilted column in the Camp of Diocletian.
ACQUISITION HISTORY: —
MEASUREMENTS: Height: 18 cm. Width: 15 cm. Depth: 8 cm.
MATERIAL: Limestone.
PRESERVATION: The lower part of the figure is broken off at the top of the neck. The hair, the nose, and the chin are chipped.

TECHNICAL DESCRIPTION: —
DATE: A.D. 150–170.
REFERENCES: Michalowski 1963, 126 cat. 17 fig. 174.

OBJECT DESCRIPTION

The fragment depicts the head of a male figure.

PORTRAIT

The hair is arranged in three rows of snail-shell curls around the head. The individual strands of hair are indicated by incised lines. His face is oval. The eyebrows are curving, rendered by narrow ridges starting from the root of the nose. The eyes are large and almond-shaped, with thick eyelids. The irises are rendered by incised circles and the pupils by punch holes. The nose is straight. The alae are incised, and the nostrils are carved. The mouth is small, and the lips are full. The chin is oval and fleshy.

541. MALE HEAD

DATABASE NUMBER: PM348.
LOCATION: Palmyra, Palmyra Museum, inv. no. B 1917.
CONTEXT: Secondary context: Found (19.09.1956) in the west corner of the hypogeum below the Baalshamin temple.

ACQUISITION HISTORY: —
MEASUREMENTS: Height: 18 cm. Width: 11.5 cm. Depth: 13 cm.
MATERIAL: Limestone.
PRESERVATION: The lower part of the figure is broken off at the base of the neck. It is badly weathered. The right cheek and the right side of the chin are broken off. The nose and the right eye are chipped.
TECHNICAL DESCRIPTION: —
DATE: A.D. 150–170.
REFERENCES: Dunant – Stucky 2000, 109 cat. 105 pl. 26.

OBJECT DESCRIPTION
The fragment depicts the head of a male figure.

PORTRAIT
The head is turned slightly to the right.

His hair is rendered in crescent-shaped curls around the head. The individual strands of hair are indicated by incised lines. His face is diamond-shaped. The eyebrows are curving and rendered with incised lines starting at the root of the nose. The eyes are almond-shaped, with a thick upper eyelid. The end of the upper eyelids extends beyond that of the lower ones. The eyeballs are blank. The ears are protruding and the helix, scapha, tragus, and earlobe are depicted. The nose bridge is narrow. The neck is long.

A.D. 150–200

542. MALE HEAD

DATABASE NUMBER: PM353.
LOCATION: Palmyra, Palmyra Museum, inv. no. unknown.
CONTEXT: Secondary context: Found (13.09.1955) behind portico C1 during excavations at Baalshamin temple.
ACQUISITION HISTORY: —
MEASUREMENTS: Height: 19 cm. Width: 18 cm. Depth: 17 cm.
MATERIAL: Limestone.
PRESERVATION: The lower part of the figure is broken off at the top of the neck. The head is heavily chipped.
TECHNICAL DESCRIPTION: —
DATE: A.D. 150–200.
REFERENCES: Dunant – Stucky 2000, 110 cat. 110 pl. 27.

OBJECT DESCRIPTION
The fragment depicts the head of a male figure.

PORTRAIT
The hair is arranged in two rows of crescent-shaped curls. Individual strands of hair are indicated by incised lines. His face is oval. The eyebrows are curving. The eyes are large and almond-shaped, with thick upper eyelids. The root of the nose is narrow.

Cat. 543

543. MALE HEAD

DATABASE NUMBER: PM208.
LOCATION: Palmyra, Palmyra Museum, inv. no. CD 42/73.
CONTEXT: Secondary context: Found in a later building at the north side of the Via Praetoria.
ACQUISITION HISTORY: —
MEASUREMENTS: Height: 16 cm. Width: 15 cm. Depth: 9 cm.
MATERIAL: Limestone.
PRESERVATION: The lower part of the figure is broken off at the top of the neck. The nose, the mouth, and the chin are chipped.
TECHNICAL DESCRIPTION: The object is partly carved. The lower eyelids are not carved.
DATE: A.D. 150–200.
REFERENCES: Gawlikowski 1984, 99 cat. 19 pl. 75, 157.

OBJECT DESCRIPTION
The fragment depicts the head of a male figure.

PORTRAIT
The hair is rendered as a thick cap, without incised locks of hair. The hair appears partly carved. His face is oval. The eyebrows are curving. The eyes are large and almond-shaped, with thick upper eyelids. The eyeballs are blank. The ears are protruding, and the tail of the helix, tragus, and earlobe are depicted.

544. MALE HEAD

DATABASE NUMBER: UPM014.
LOCATION: Philadelphia, University of Pennsylvania Museum of Archaeology and Anthropology, inv. no. B9187.
CONTEXT: —
ACQUISITION HISTORY: —
MEASUREMENTS: Height: 18 cm. Width: 14 cm. Depth: 14 cm.
MATERIAL: Limestone.
PRESERVATION: The lower part of the figure is broken off at the base of the neck. The hair over the forehead and the tip of the nose are chipped.
TECHNICAL DESCRIPTION: The ears are partly carved.
DATE: A.D. 150–200.
REFERENCES: Ingholt Archives, PS 642; Legrain 1927, 342. 350 cat. 11 fig. 11; Romano 2006, 291 f. cat. 137.

OBJECT DESCRIPTION
The fragment depicts the head of a male figure.

PORTRAIT
The hair is arranged in two rows of alternating, crescent-shaped curls. The individual strands of hair are indicated by incised lines. The face is square. The eyebrows are curving, rendered by grooves starting from the root of the nose. The eyes are large and almond-shaped, with thick upper eyelids. The irises are indicated by incised circles and the pupils by punch holes. The ears are protruding with only the helix carved. The nose is straight. The mouth is small, with full lips. The neck is short and wide.

Cat. 544

HEADS FROM SARCOPHAGI 819

Cat. 545

545. MALE HEAD

DATABASE NUMBER: PM199.
LOCATION: Palmyra, Palmyra Museum, inv. no. CD 248/65.
CONTEXT: Secondary context: Found outside of the Temple of the Standards (Temple des Enseignes), Camp of Diocletian.
ACQUISITION HISTORY: —
MEASUREMENTS: Height: 18 cm. Width: 15 cm. Depth: 13 cm.
MATERIAL: Limestone, white.
PRESERVATION: The background of the relief is broken off except next to the lower left of the face and the upper right of the head. The figure is broken off at the top of the neck. The hair and the forehead are heavily chipped. The ears, nose, and part of the left cheek are broken off.
TECHNICAL DESCRIPTION: —
DATE: A.D. 150–200.
REFERENCES: Gawlikowski 1984, 96 cat. 7 pl. 72, 145.

OBJECT DESCRIPTION
The object depicts a male head.

PORTRAIT
The figure is shown frontally.
  His hair is voluminous, arranged in two rows of flame shaped curls around the head. The individual strands of hair are indicated by incised lines. His face is triangular. The eyes are almond-shaped, with thick eyelids. The nose has a wide base. The mouth is small, with a thin upper and a full lower lip. The chin is round.

546. FRAGMENT OF A MALE HEAD

DATABASE NUMBER: PM352.
LOCATION: Palmyra, Palmyra Museum, inv. no. B 1872.
CONTEXT: Secondary context: Found (07.09.1955) in portico C1 during excavations at Baalshamin temple.
ACQUISITION HISTORY: —
MEASUREMENTS: Height: 12 cm. Width: 10 cm. Depth: 12 cm.
MATERIAL: Limestone, white/yellow.
PRESERVATION: The lower part of the figure is broken off at the middle of the head. The top of the head, the right, and the central part of the face, including the ears, are chipped.
TECHNICAL DESCRIPTION: —
DATE: A.D. 150–200.
REFERENCES: Dunant – Stucky 2000, 110 cat. 109 pl. 27.

OBJECT DESCRIPTION
The fragment depicts the head of a male figure.

PORTRAIT
The hair is arranged in two alternating rows of crescent-shaped curls. Individual strands of hair are indicated by incised lines. His face is oval. The eyebrows are curving. The eyes are large and almond-shaped, with thick upper eyelids. The irises are indicated by incised circles.

547. MALE HEAD

DATABASE NUMBER: AMI064.
LOCATION: Istanbul, İstanbul Arkeoloji Müzesi, inv. no. 3731/O.M.182.
CONTEXT: —
ACQUISITION HISTORY: —
MEASUREMENTS: Height: 20 cm.
MATERIAL: Limestone, white.
PRESERVATION: The lower part of the figure is broken off at the base of the neck. The surface is weathered.
TECHNICAL DESCRIPTION: There are traces of black pigment in the outline of the eyes and the outlines of the irises.
DATE: A.D. 150–200.
REFERENCES: Ingholt Archives, PS 718.

OBJECT DESCRIPTION
The fragment depicts the head of a male figure.

PORTRAIT
The hair is arranged in two rows of alternating, crescent-shaped curls around the head, reaching the neck. The individual strands of hair are rendered by incised lines. His face is square. The eyebrows are curving, rendered by incised lines starting from the root of the nose. The eyes are close-set and almond-shaped, with thick, upper eyelids. The upper eyelids extend beyond the end of the lower ones. The irises are rendered by incised circles and the pupils by punch holes. The ears are large and

Cat. 547

Cat. 548

protruding, with the helix, scapha, and lobe depicted. The cheeks are fleshy. The mouth is small, with a full lower lip. The chin is oval. The neck is wide.

A.D. 170–200

548. MALE HEAD

DATABASE NUMBER: MCH003.
LOCATION: Oslo, Museum of Cultural History, inv. no. C40816.
CONTEXT: —
ACQUISITION HISTORY: —
MEASUREMENTS: Height: 18.5 cm. Width: 16 cm. Depth: 21 cm.
MATERIAL: Limestone, yellow.
PRESERVATION: The lower part of the figure is broken off at the base of the neck. The left eye, the nose, and the mouth are chipped.
TECHNICAL DESCRIPTION: —
DATE: A.D. 170–200.
REFERENCES: <https://www.unimus.no/portal/#/things/c4d3a0ef-4653-44fd-bf3f-6f41c06a992d> (06.05.2022).

OBJECT DESCRIPTION
The fragment depicts the head of a male figure.

PORTRAIT
The figure is shown frontally. The head turns sharply to his right and downwards.

His hair is arranged in three rows of snail-shell curls around the head. The individual strands of hair are indicated by incised lines. His face is diamond-shaped. The eyebrows are slightly curving and are rendered by narrow ridges. The eyes are small and almond-shaped, with thick upper eyelids. The end of the upper eyelids extends beyond that of the lower ones. The eyeballs are blank. The nose is short with a wide base. The alae are incised. The mouth is small, with a full lower lip. The chin is oval. The neck is short and has three curving grooves.

HEADS FROM SARCOPHAGI 821

Cat. 549

A.D. 200–220

549. MALE HEAD

DATABASE NUMBER: PM194.
LOCATION: Palmyra, Palmyra Museum, inv. no. CD 1/65.
CONTEXT: Secondary context: Found at the northern part of the Temple of the Standards (Temple des Enseignes), Camp of Diocletian.
ACQUISITION HISTORY: —
MEASUREMENTS: Height: 19.5 cm. Width: 16 cm. Depth: 8 cm.
MATERIAL: Limestone.
PRESERVATION: The lower part of the figure is broken off at the base of the neck. The left ear is chipped.
TECHNICAL DESCRIPTION: The lower eyelids are not carved.
DATE: A.D. 200–220.
REFERENCES: Gawlikowski 1984, 95 cat. 1 pl. 70, 139.

OBJECT DESCRIPTION
The fragment depicts the head of a male figure.

PORTRAIT
His hair is arranged in three rows of snail-shell curls around the head. The individual strands of hair are indicated by incised lines. His face is round. The eyebrows are slightly curving. The eyes are almond-shaped, with thick upper eyelids. The eyeballs are blank. The ears are partly visible under the hair: the tail of the helix, tragus, and earlobe is depicted. The nose is straight and pointed. The alae are incised, and the nostrils are carved. The mouth is small, with a full lower lip. The chin is oval. The neck has a wide, curving groove.

550. MALE HEAD

DATABASE NUMBER: NCG051.
LOCATION: Copenhagen, Ny Carlsberg Glyptotek, inv. no. IN 1128.
CONTEXT: —
ACQUISITION HISTORY: Løytved in Syria.
MEASUREMENTS: Height: 13 cm. Width: 9 cm. Depth: 11.5 cm.
MATERIAL: Limestone, white/grey.

Cat. 550

PRESERVATION: The lower part of the figure is broken off at the base of the neck. The hair, right cheek, and the tip of the nose are chipped. Cracks run across the surface.
TECHNICAL DESCRIPTION: The head is roughly cut on the back. There are traces of black pigment in the corners of his eyes. Flat chisel marks and rasp marks are visible on his neck, face, and hair.
DATE: A.D. 200–220 (Ploug 1995: A.D. 230–250).
REFERENCES: Simonsen 1889, 52 cat. G 39 pl. 16; Hvidberg-Hansen – Ploug 1993, 143 cat. 101; Ploug 1995, 233 cat. 101; Raja 2019a, 300 f. cat. 108.

OBJECT DESCRIPTION
The fragment depicts the head of a male figure.

PORTRAIT
The figure is shown frontally.

The hair is short and arranged in three rows of crescent-shaped curls. The individual strands of hair are rendered by incised lines. His face is oval. The eyebrows are rendered by low, curving grooves. The eyes are large, almond-shaped, and slanting, with thick upper eyelids. The end of the upper eyelids extends beyond that of the lower ones. The irises are circular and indicated by pigment. The ears are small and close to the head with helix, scapha, and concha depicted. The nose is straight. The nostrils are drilled. The mouth is small, with a full lower lip. The neck is long and slender with two curving grooves.

551. MALE HEAD

DATABASE NUMBER: PM252.
LOCATION: Palmyra, Palmyra Museum, inv. no. CD 68.
CONTEXT: Secondary context: Found (02.05.1962) in the south foundation wall of the forum in the Camp of Diocletian.
ACQUISITION HISTORY: —
MEASUREMENTS: Height: 15.5 cm. Width: 12 cm. Depth: 16 cm.
MATERIAL: Limestone.
PRESERVATION: The lower part of the figure is broken off at the base of the neck. The surface is weathered. The left eye, the nose, and the mouth are chipped.
TECHNICAL DESCRIPTION: —
DATE: A.D. 200–220.
REFERENCES: Michalowski 1964, 100 f. cat. 35 fig. 136.

OBJECT DESCRIPTION
The fragment depicts the head of a male figure.

PORTRAIT
The figure is depicted frontally.

The hair is arranged in three rows of snail-shell curls around the head. The individual locks of hair are rendered by incised lines. His face is round. The eyebrows are curving, and they are indicated by incised lines starting at the root of the nose. The eyes are large and almond-shaped, with thick eyelids. The eyeballs are blank. The nose is wide, and the alae are incised. The nostrils are carved. The mouth is small. The chin is pointed. The neck is short and wide.

552. MALE HEAD

DATABASE NUMBER: NCG052.
LOCATION: Copenhagen, Ny Carlsberg Glyptotek, inv. no. IN 1131.
CONTEXT: —
ACQUISITION HISTORY: Løytved in Syria.
MEASUREMENTS: Height: 16 cm. Width: 11 cm. Depth: 11.5 cm. Height of head: 12 cm.
MATERIAL: Limestone, white/grey.
PRESERVATION: The lower part of the figure is broken off at the base of the neck. The hair, left side of the face, and the tip of the nose are chipped.
TECHNICAL DESCRIPTION: The head is roughly cut on the back. There are rasp marks on the face, on the neck, and hair. There are flat chisel marks on the nose, hair, neck, and ears.

Cat. 552

DATE: A.D. 200–220 (Ploug 1995: A.D. 210–230).
REFERENCES: Simonsen 1889, 52 cat. G 42 pl. 16; Hvidberg-Hansen – Ploug 1993, 140 cat. 96; Ploug 1995, 226 f. cat. 96; Raja 2019a, 280 cat. 94.

OBJECT DESCRIPTION
The fragment depicts the head of a male figure.

PORTRAIT
The figure is shown frontally, and the head turns to his left.

The hair is short and arranged in three rows of snail-shell curls. The individual strands of hair are rendered by incised lines. His face is oval. The eyebrows are rendered by low, curving grooves. The eyes are large, almond-shaped, and slanting with thick upper eyelids. The end of the upper eyelids extends beyond that of the lower ones. The irises are indicated by incised circles. The ears are small and close to the head with helix and scapha depicted. The nose is straight. The mouth is small, with a full lower lip. The neck is long and slender.

553. MALE HEAD

DATABASE NUMBER: BM010.
LOCATION: London, British Museum, inv. no. 125059.
CONTEXT: —
ACQUISITION HISTORY: Purchased in 1885 from Levi Bros.
MEASUREMENTS: Height: 20.5 cm. Width: 16.5 cm. Depth: 11.5 cm.
MATERIAL: Limestone, yellow.
PRESERVATION: The lower part of the figure is broken off at the base of the neck. The chin is broken off. The hair, the right eyebrow, and the nose are chipped.
TECHNICAL DESCRIPTION: —
DATE: A.D. 200–220.
REFERENCES: Ingholt Archives, PS 579; <http://www.britishmuseum.org/research/collection_online/collection_object_details.aspx?objectId=468663&partId=1&searchText=125059&page=1.> (06.05.2022).

OBJECT DESCRIPTION
The fragment depicts the head of a male figure.

PORTRAIT
The head is turned slightly to his left.

The hair is arranged in two rows of snail-shell curls around the head, covering the ears and reaching the neck. His face is oblong. The eyebrows are curving, rendered by incised lines starting from the root of the nose. The eyes are large and almond-shaped, with thick upper eyelids. The irises are rendered by incised circles. The upper eyelids extend beyond the ends of the lower ones. The nose is large with the alae carved. The mouth is large with a full lower lip. The corners of the mouth are accentuated by an oblique groove. The neck is slender.

Cat. 553

A.D. 200–230

554. MALE HEAD

DATABASE NUMBER: MLP058.
LOCATION: Paris, Musée du Louvre, inv. no. AO 6213.
CONTEXT: —
ACQUISITION HISTORY: Acquired in 1912 by Ms Hanin. On loan to the Musées Royaux in Brussels.
MEASUREMENTS: Height: 16 cm. Width: 15 cm.
MATERIAL: Limestone, white/yellow.
PRESERVATION: Broken off at the base of the neck. The left eyebrow and the chin are chipped. Several cracks run across the face.
TECHNICAL DESCRIPTION: There are flat chisel marks on the hair, face, and the neck. The head is roughly cut on the back.
DATE: A.D. 200–230.
REFERENCES: Colledge 1976, 252; Dentzer-Feydy – Teixidor 1993, 219 cat. 215.

OBJECT DESCRIPTION
The object depicts a male figure.

Cat. 554

Cat. 555, Pl. 84

PORTRAIT

The figure is shown frontally.

The hair is short and voluminous, arranged in two rows of snail-shell curls. The individual strands of hair are indicated by incised lines. His face is oval. The eyebrows are rendered by thin, curving, incised lines that start from the root of the nose. The eyes are small and almond-shaped, with thick upper eyelids. The eyeballs are blank. The nose is straight. The alae are carved. The philtrum is carved. The mouth is small, with full lips. The chin is pointed. The neck is slender with two curving grooves.

555. MALE HEAD

DATABASE NUMBER: MWM001.
LOCATION: Würzburg, Martin von Wagner Museum, inv. no. HA 1305.
CONTEXT: —
ACQUISITION HISTORY: —
MEASUREMENTS: Height: 13 cm. Width: 12.5 cm. Depth: 14 cm.
MATERIAL: Limestone, white/yellow.
PRESERVATION: Broken off at the base of the neck. Several cracks run across the face.
TECHNICAL DESCRIPTION: Tool marks are visible on the surface of the face.
DATE: A.D. 200–230.
REFERENCES: —

OBJECT DESCRIPTION

The object depicts a male figure.

PORTRAIT

The figure is shown frontally.

The hair is short and voluminous, arranged in three rows of snail-shell curls. The individual strands of hair are indicated by incised lines. His face is round. The eyebrows are rendered by thin, curving, incised lines that start from the root of the nose. The eyes are small and almond-shaped, with thick upper eyelids. The end of the upper eyelids extends beyond that of the lower ones. The irises are indicated by incised circles. The nose is straight. The alae are carved. The philtrum is carved. The mouth is small, with full lips. Two grooves are carved at the corners of the mouth. The chin is pointed. The neck is slender with one curving groove.

A.D. 200–240

556. MALE HEAD

DATABASE NUMBER: PM196.
LOCATION: Palmyra, Palmyra Museum, inv. no. CD 58/65.
CONTEXT: Secondary context: Found in the northern part of the Temple of the Standards (Temple des Enseignes), Camp of Diocletian.
ACQUISITION HISTORY: —
MEASUREMENTS: Height: 19 cm. Width: 20 cm. Depth: 14 cm.
MATERIAL: Limestone, white.
PRESERVATION: A part of the object background is preserved to the right of the head of the figure. The head is broken off at the neck. The nose and chin are chipped.

TECHNICAL DESCRIPTION: —
DATE: A.D. 200–240.
REFERENCES: Gawlikowski 1984, 96 cat. 4 pl. 71, 142.

OBJECT DESCRIPTION
The object depicts a male.

PORTRAIT
The figure is shown frontally.

His hair is voluminous and arranged in two rows of snail-shell curls around his head. The individual strands of hair are indicated by incised lines. His face is diamond-shaped. The eyebrows are curving and indicated by incised lines. The eyes are almond-shaped and slanting with thick eyelids. The upper eyelids extend beyond the end of the lower ones. The irises are indicated (details unclear). The nose is short, and the alae are incised. The nostrils appear carved. The mouth is small, with thin lips. The chin is pointed and prominent. The neck is short.

Cat. 556

A.D. 200–273

557. MALE HEAD

DATABASE NUMBER: BM041.
LOCATION: London, British Museum, inv. no. 2003,0521.1.
CONTEXT: —
ACQUISITION HISTORY: Donated by Mrs E. Ralphs in 2003. According to the British Museum, an »old paper adhering to the neck states, ›found near a tomb at Palmyra (›Tadmor in the Wilderness‹) in 1942‹«.
MEASUREMENTS: Height: 11 cm. Width: 9 cm. Depth: 12 cm.
MATERIAL: Limestone, white/yellow.
PRESERVATION: The lower part of the figure is broken off at the base of the neck. The surface is heavily weathered.
TECHNICAL DESCRIPTION: The head is roughly cut on the back.
DATE: A.D. 200–273.
REFERENCES: <http://www.britishmuseum.org/research/collection_online/collection_object_details.aspx?objectId=1434996&partId=1&place=35414&object=20526&page=1> (05.05.2022).

OBJECT DESCRIPTION
The fragment depicts the head of a male figure.

PORTRAIT
The hair is arranged in two rows of crescent-shaped curls around the head. The individual strands of hair are rendered by incised lines. His face is oval. The eyebrows are curving, rendered by thin ridges. The eyes are almond-shaped, with thick upper eyelids. The eyeballs are blank. The ears are small and close to the head, with the helix, scapha, and tragus depicted. The nose is thin. The mouth is small, with full, lower lip. The chin is pointed. The neck is slender.

558. MALE HEAD

DATABASE NUMBER: BM006.
LOCATION: London, British Museum, inv. no. BM 125058,A.
CONTEXT: —
ACQUISITION HISTORY: Purchased in 1889.
MEASUREMENTS: Height: 16.5 cm. Width: 9.5 cm. Depth: 10.5 cm.
MATERIAL: Limestone, yellow.
PRESERVATION: The lower part of the figure is broken off at the base of the neck. The surface is weathered and chipped.

Cat. 557

Cat. 558

TECHNICAL DESCRIPTION: There are traces of red pigment on the hair and pupils of the eyes.
DATE: A.D. 200–273.
REFERENCES: Long 2016, 136 fig. 1.

OBJECT DESCRIPTION
The fragment depicts the head of a male figure.

PORTRAIT
The hair is arranged in two rows of alternating, crescent-shaped curls around the head, reaching the neck. The individual strands of hair are rendered by incised lines. His face is round. The eyebrows are curving, rendered by thin ridges. The eyes are close-set, round, with thick eyelids. The end of the upper eyelids extends beyond that of the lower ones. The irises were rendered by colour (traces of pigment remain). The ears are large and protruding with the helix, scapha, and tragus depicted. The cheeks are fleshy, and the mouth is small, with thin lips. The chin is pointed, and he has a double chin. The neck is short and wide.

There are traces of clothing on the right side of the neck, perhaps from a himation.

559. MALE HEAD

DATABASE NUMBER: UPM007.
LOCATION: Philadelphia, University of Pennsylvania Museum of Archaeology and Anthropology, inv. no. B9188.
CONTEXT: —
ACQUISITION HISTORY: Collected for the museum by Rev. John Punnett Peters during his expedition to Nippur in 1889–1890.
MEASUREMENTS: Height: 15.5 cm. Width: 14.8 cm. Depth: 14.5 cm.
MATERIAL: Limestone.
PRESERVATION: The head is broken off at the neck. Small cracks run across the forehead.
TECHNICAL DESCRIPTION: —
DATE: A.D. 200–273.
REFERENCES: Ingholt Archives, PS 613; Legrain 1927, 349 cat. 10 fig. 10; Romano 2006, 300 cat. 144; <https://www.penn.museum/collections/object/218806> (06.05.2022).

OBJECT DESCRIPTION
The fragment depicts the head of a male figure.

PORTRAIT
His hair is arranged in three rows of snail-shell curls around the head. The individual strands of hair are indicated by incised lines. His face is rectangular. The eyebrows are curving, rendered by incised lines. The eyes are large, almond-shaped, and slanting with thick upper eyelids. The upper eyelids extend beyond the end of the eye. The irises are indicated by incised circles and the pupils by punch holes. The ears are protruding

Cat. 559

and the helix, scapha, and earlobe are indicated. The nose is large and wide. The alae are incised, and the nostrils are carved. The mouth is small, with a thin lower lip. The chin is oval and fleshy. The neck is slender.

A.D. 210–230

560. MALE HEAD

DATABASE NUMBER: NCG104.
LOCATION: Copenhagen, Ny Carlsberg Glyptotek, inv. no. IN 1163.
CONTEXT: —
ACQUISITION HISTORY: —
MEASUREMENTS: Height: 19.5 cm. Width: 18.5 cm. Depth: 21 cm. Height of head: 17 cm.
MATERIAL: Limestone, white/yellow.
PRESERVATION: Broken off at the upper part of the neck. The tip of the nose is broken off. The eyebrows and left cheek are chipped. Several cracks run across the face.

Cat. 560

TECHNICAL DESCRIPTION: The head is roughly cut on the back. There are flat chisel marks on the hair and face. There are traces of red pigment on the hair.
DATE: A.D. 210–230.
REFERENCES: Ingholt Archives; Hvidberg-Hansen – Ploug 1993, 140 cat. 95; Ploug 1995, 225 f. cat. 95; Raja 2019a, 285 cat. 99.

OBJECT DESCRIPTION
The object depicts a male figure.

PORTRAIT
The figure is shown frontally.
  The hair is short and voluminous, arranged in three rows of snail-shell curls. The individual strands of hair are indicated by incised lines. His face is round. The eyebrows are rendered by thin, curving, incised lines that start from the root of the nose. The eyes are small, almond-shaped, and slanting with thick upper eyelids. The end of the upper eyelids extends beyond that of the lower ones. The irises, that touch the upper eyelids, are indicated by incised circles and the pupils by punch holes. The nose is straight and wide. The alae are indicated by incised lines. The nostrils are carved. The mouth is small, with full lips. The chin is pointed. The neck is wide and has one curving groove.

A.D. 220–240

561. MALE HEAD

DATABASE NUMBER: NCG097.
LOCATION: Copenhagen, Ny Carlsberg Glyptotek, inv. no. IN 1130.
CONTEXT: —
ACQUISITION HISTORY: Løytved in Syria.
MEASUREMENTS: Height: 16.5 cm. Width: 10 cm. Depth: 10.5 cm.
MATERIAL: Limestone, yellow.
PRESERVATION: The lower part of the figure is broken off at the base of the neck. The lower part of the forehead, the nose, and part of the neck are chipped.
TECHNICAL DESCRIPTION: The head is roughly cut on the back and there are cracks in the stone. There are rasp marks and flat chisel marks on the hair and face.
DATE: A.D. 220–240 (Ploug 1995: A.D. 230–250).

Cat. 561

REFERENCES: Simonsen 1889, 52 cat. G 41 pl. 16; Hvidberg-Hansen – Ploug 1993, 144 cat. 102; Ploug 1995, 234 cat. 102; Raja 2019a, 310 cat. 114.

OBJECT DESCRIPTION
The fragment depicts the head of a male figure.

PORTRAIT
His hair is arranged with flame-shaped curls around his head in an unruly manner. He has a slightly receding hairline. The individual strands of hair are indicated by incised lines. His face is oval. The eyebrows are curving and rendered by narrow ridges starting from the root of the nose. The eyes are almond-shaped, with thick upper eyelids. The upper eyelids extend beyond the corner of the eye. The irises are indicated with incised circles. The ears are small and the tail of the helix, the scapha, and earlobe are depicted. The nose is wide. The alae are incised. The mouth is straight with a full lower lip. The chin is oval and prominent. The neck is long.

562. MALE HEAD

DATABASE NUMBER: PM249.
LOCATION: Palmyra, Palmyra Museum, inv. no. CD 77.
CONTEXT: Secondary context: Found in the foundations of the wall of the Great Gate in the Camp of Diocletian.
ACQUISITION HISTORY: —
MEASUREMENTS: Height: 19 cm. Width: 17 cm. Depth: 18 cm.
MATERIAL: Limestone, white.
PRESERVATION: The lower part of the figure is broken at the base of the neck. The nose has broken off.
TECHNICAL DESCRIPTION: —
DATE: A.D. 220–240.
REFERENCES: Ingholt Archives, PS 1402; Michalowski 1964, 91. 98 cat. 32 figs. 124. 133.

OBJECT DESCRIPTION
The object depicts the head of a male figure.
The object was found together with the objects cat. 531, cat. 584, cat. 585, cat. 586, cat. 611, cat. 612, cat. 613, cat. 614, cat. 615. According to Michalowski (1964, 91) they come from the same sarcophagus.

PORTRAIT
His hair is arranged in s-shaped curls brushed towards his forehead. The individual strands of hair are indicated by incised lines. His face is oval. There are two lightly curving furrows along his forehead. The eyebrows are curving, rendered by incised lines starting from the root of the nose. The eyes are close-set and almond-shaped, with thick upper eyelids. The upper eyelids extend beyond the end of the lower ones. The irises are indicated by incised circles and the pupils by punch holes. The ears are protruding with the helix, scapha, and lobe depicted. He has a beard that starts from the temples and covers the cheeks and the chin, as well as the philtrum and upper lip. The facial hair is rendered by curving, incised lines on the upper lip and two rows of oblique lines on the cheeks and chin. The mouth is wide with a full lower lip. The chin is wide, and the neck is wide.

563. MALE HEAD

DATABASE NUMBER: PM250.
LOCATION: Palmyra, Palmyra Museum, inv. no. CD 78.
CONTEXT: Secondary context: Found in the foundations of the wall of the Great Gate in the Camp of Diocletian.
ACQUISITION HISTORY: —
MEASUREMENTS: Height: 19 cm. Width: 14 cm. Depth: 17 cm.
MATERIAL: Limestone, white.
PRESERVATION: The lower part of the figure is broken off at the base of the neck. The right eye and the nose are chipped. There are cracks running across the face.
TECHNICAL DESCRIPTION: —
DATE: A.D. 220–240.
REFERENCES: Michalowski 1964, 91. 98 cat. 33 figs. 124. 134.

OBJECT DESCRIPTION
The object depicts the head of a male figure.
The object was found together with the objects cat. 530, cat. 584, cat. 585, cat. 586, cat. 611, cat. 612, cat. 613, cat. 614, cat. 615. According to Michalowski (1964, 91) they come from the same sarcophagus.

PORTRAIT
The hair is arranged in snail-shell curls around the head. The individual strands of hair are indicated by incised lines. His face is oval. The eyebrows are curving and rendered by incised lines starting at the root of the nose. The eyes are small and almond-shaped, with thick eyelids. A deep groove depicts the upper eyelid as very thick. The irises are indicated by incised circles and the pupils by punch holes. The ears are protruding and the helix, scapha, tragus, and earlobe are depicted. The nose is wide. The alae are incised. The mouth is small, with a full lower lip. The chin is oval and fleshy. The neck is short.

564. MALE HEAD

DATABASE NUMBER: KMW014.
LOCATION: Vienna, Kunsthistorisches Museum, inv. no. ANSA I 608.
CONTEXT: —
ACQUISITION HISTORY: Gift of Crown Prince Archduke Rudolf in 1885.
MEASUREMENTS: Height: 20 cm. Width: 16 cm. Depth: 10.5 cm.
MATERIAL: Limestone, yellow.

PRESERVATION: The lower part of the figure is broken off at the top of the neck. Part of the hair over the centre of the forehead is broken off.
TECHNICAL DESCRIPTION: The head is partly carved: the face is not carved.
DATE: A.D. 220–240.
REFERENCES: Plattner 2010, 176 cat. 14 fig. 29; <https://www.khm.at/de/object/976e5a7c9f/> (06.05.2022).

OBJECT DESCRIPTION
The fragment depicts the head of a male figure.

PORTRAIT
His hair is arranged in two rows of snail-shell curls. The individual strands of hair are rendered by incised lines. His face is oval. The eyebrows are curving. The eyes are not carved. The nose is straight. The mouth is small.

565. MALE HEAD

DATABASE NUMBER: NCG099.
LOCATION: Copenhagen, Ny Carlsberg Glyptotek, inv. no. IN 1126.
CONTEXT: —
ACQUISITION HISTORY: Acquired by Løytved in Syria.
MEASUREMENTS: Height: 15 cm. Width: 14 cm. Depth: 14 cm. Height of head: 12.5 cm.
MATERIAL: Limestone, white/yellow.
PRESERVATION: Broken off at the middle of the neck. The hair, forehead, and tip of the nose are chipped.
TECHNICAL DESCRIPTION: The back of the head is roughly cut and flat. Small tooth chisel marks are visible on the back. Flat chisel marks are on the hair and face.
DATE: A.D. 220–240.
REFERENCES: Simonsen 1889, 51 cat. G.37 pl. 16; Hvidberg-Hansen – Ploug 1993, 142 cat. 98; Raja 2019a, 298 cat. 106.

OBJECT DESCRIPTION
The object depicts a male figure.

PORTRAIT
The head is turned downwards and to his left.

The hair is short and voluminous, arranged in three rows of snail-shell curls. The individual strands of hair are indicated by incised lines. His face is oval. The eyebrows are rendered by thin, curving incised lines that start from the root of the nose. The eyes are small and almond-shaped, with thick upper eyelids. The end of the upper eyelids extends downwards and beyond that of the lower eyelids. The eyeballs are blank. The nose is straight. The alae are indicated by incised lines. The mouth is small, with a full lower lip. The chin is pointed. The neck is slender.

Cat. 565, Pl. 85

566. MALE HEAD

DATABASE NUMBER: UNK167.
LOCATION: Unknown location.
CONTEXT: —
ACQUISITION HISTORY: —
MEASUREMENTS: Height: 20.32 cm.
MATERIAL: Limestone.
PRESERVATION: The lower part of the figure is broken off at the base of the neck. The nose is chipped.
TECHNICAL DESCRIPTION: —
DATE: A.D. 220–240.
REFERENCES: Ingholt Archives, PS 622.

OBJECT DESCRIPTION
The fragment depicts the head of a male figure.

PORTRAIT
His hair is rendered in three rows of snail-shell curls around the head. The individual strands of hair are indicated by incised lines. His face is oval. The eyebrows are curving and plastically rendered with oblique, incised lines indicating individual hairs. The eyes are almond-shaped, with a thick upper eyelid. The end of the upper eyelids extends beyond that of the lower ones. The eyeballs are blank. The ears are protruding and the helix, scapha, tragus, and earlobe are depicted. The nose is

Cat. 566

Cat 567

wide. He has a beard: it starts at the temples and covers the outer side of the cheeks, the chin, and the upper lip. The facial hair is rendered by snail-shell curls in the beard and vertical, incised lines on the moustache. The mouth is small, with a full lower lip. The chin is oval. The neck has a curving groove.

A.D. 230–250

567. MALE HEAD

DATABASE NUMBER: IMJ001.
LOCATION: Last known location: Paris (?).
CONTEXT: —
ACQUISITION HISTORY: —
MEASUREMENTS: Height: 15 cm.
MATERIAL: Limestone.
PRESERVATION: The lower part of the figure is broken off at the neck. The nose and the chin are broken off. The left eye, the cheek, and the neck are chipped. There are cracks running across the face.
TECHNICAL DESCRIPTION: —
DATE: A.D. 230–250.
REFERENCES: Ingholt Archives, PS 578; <https://www.imj.org.il/en/collections/506853> (06.05.22).

OBJECT DESCRIPTION
The object depicts a male head.

PORTRAIT
The figure is shown frontally.

His hair is voluminous and rendered by rows of snail-shell curls around the head. His face is square. The eyebrows are curving and rendered by thin grooves. The eyes are large and almond-shaped, with thick eyelids. The eyeballs appear blank. The ears are not visible. The nose is straight. The mouth is small, with full lips. The chin is pointed. The neck is wide with one curving groove.

1–30 CM

A.D. 130–150

568. MALE HEAD

DATABASE NUMBER: PM205.
LOCATION: Palmyra, Palmyra Museum, inv. no. CD 20/73.
CONTEXT: Secondary context: Found at the surface of the threshold of the Praetorian Gate in the Camp of Diocletian.
ACQUISITION HISTORY: —

Cat. 568

MEASUREMENTS: Height: 25 cm. Width: 23 cm. Depth: 18 cm.
MATERIAL: Limestone.
PRESERVATION: The lower part of the figure is broken off at the base of the neck. The nose and part of the right cheek are broken off. The left ear and the right cheek are chipped.
TECHNICAL DESCRIPTION: —
DATE: A.D. 130–150.
REFERENCES: Gawlikowski 1984, 98 cat. 15 pls. 74, 153. 154.

OBJECT DESCRIPTION
The fragment depicts the head of a male figure.

PORTRAIT
His hair is arranged in four rows of crescent-shaped curls around the head. The individual locks of hair are indicated by incised lines. His face is round. There are two horizontal lines in the forehead. The eyebrows are slightly curving. The eyes are large and almond-shaped, with thick eyelids. The irises are indicated with incised arches. The ears are large and the helix, tragus, scapha, and earlobe are depicted. The mouth is small, with full lips. The chin is oval. The neck is long.

569. MALE HEAD

DATABASE NUMBER: RosPriv001.
LOCATION: Unknown location.
CONTEXT: —
ACQUISITION HISTORY: Formerly in the collection of Dr M. Ros, Zürich. Sold in E. Brummer, Art dealer in Paris.
MEASUREMENTS: Height: 26.5 cm. Depth: 12.5 cm. Head height: 22.7 cm.
MATERIAL: Limestone, white.
PRESERVATION: The lower part of the figure is broken off at the neck. Broken vertically at the back of the head.
TECHNICAL DESCRIPTION: —
DATE: A.D. 130–150.
REFERENCES: Ingholt Archives, PS 581; Kaspar 1969–1970, 283–287 cat. A figs. 1–4; Jucker – Willers 1983, 245 cat. 108.

OBJECT DESCRIPTION
The fragment depicts the head of a male figure.

PORTRAIT
His hair is voluminous and rendered by snail-shell curls arranged in four rows around the head. The individual locks of hair are rendered by curving, incised lines. His face is square. There are two long, curving lines on his forehead (>furrows<). The eyebrows are curving and rendered by thin ridges. The eyes

Cat. 569

are large and almond-shaped, with thick eyelids. The upper eyelids extend beyond the end of the lower ones. The irises are rendered by incised circles and the pupils by punch holes. The ears are completely covered by the hair. The nose is straight with incised alae. The nasolabial lines are indicated. The mouth is wide with thin lips. The chin is round and pointed. The neck is wide.

A.D. 150–170

570. MALE HEAD

DATABASE NUMBER: UNK075.
LOCATION: Unknown location.
CONTEXT: —
ACQUISITION HISTORY: Formerly in the D'Andurain Collection.
MEASUREMENTS: Height: 26 cm.
MATERIAL: Limestone.
PRESERVATION: The lower part of the figure is broken off at the base of the neck. The nose is chipped.
TECHNICAL DESCRIPTION: —

Cat. 570

DATE: A.D. 150–170.
REFERENCES: Ingholt Archives, PS 945.

OBJECT DESCRIPTION
The fragment depicts the head of a male figure.

PORTRAIT
The figure is shown frontally.
His hair is rendered in three rows of snail-shell curls around the head. The individual strands of hair are indicated by incised lines. His face is rectangular. The eyebrows are curving and rendered by incised lines starting from the root of the nose. The eyes are almond-shaped, with thick upper eyelids. The eyeballs are blank. The ears are large and protruding and the helix, scapha, tragus, and earlobe are depicted. The nose is wide. The alae are incised. The mouth is small, with thin lips. The chin is pointed. The neck is long. A v-shaped groove indicates the sternocleidomastoid muscles.

A.D. 150–200

571. MALE HEAD

DATABASE NUMBER: BM031.
LOCATION: London, British Museum, inv. no. BM 125026.
CONTEXT: —
ACQUISITION HISTORY: Donated by Lady Howard de Walden in 1895.
MEASUREMENTS: Height: 29 cm. Width: 23 cm. Depth: 16.5 cm.
MATERIAL: Limestone, white/yellow.
PRESERVATION: The head is broken off at the neck. The upper left part of the hair is broken off. The nose is chipped.
TECHNICAL DESCRIPTION: —
DATE: A.D. 150–200.
REFERENCES: Ingholt Archives, PS 233; Ingholt 1928, 117 PS 233; Colledge 1976, 249.

OBJECT DESCRIPTION
The object depicts a male.

PORTRAIT
His hair is arranged in a single row of long, s-shaped curls brushed from the top of the head towards the forehead. The individual strands of hair are indicated by incised lines. His face is oval. The eyebrows are curving and indicated by thin ridges. The eyes are large and almond-shaped, with thick eyelids. The irises are indicated by incised circles. The ears are small and protruding with the helix, scapha, and earlobe indicated. The nose is narrow. The alae are incised, and the nostrils are carved. On either side of the nose, there is a curving groove. The mouth is small, with thin lips. The chin is oval. The neck is long and slender with two curving lines.

Cat. 571

Cat. 572

572. FRAGMENT OF A MALE HEAD

DATABASE NUMBER: PM197.
LOCATION: Palmyra, Palmyra Museum, inv. no. CD 77/65.
CONTEXT: Secondary context: Found in a late wall blocking room IVa in the Temple of the Standards (Temple des Enseignes), Camp of Diocletian.
ACQUISITION HISTORY: —
MEASUREMENTS: Height: 30 cm. Width: 25 cm. Depth: 14 cm.
MATERIAL: Limestone.
PRESERVATION: The lower part of the figure is broken off at the neck. The right side of the face is broken off.
TECHNICAL DESCRIPTION: —
DATE: A.D. 150–200.
REFERENCES: Gawlikowski 1984, 96 cat. 5 pl. 71, 143.

OBJECT DESCRIPTION
The fragment depicts the head of a male figure.

PORTRAIT
The figure is depicted frontally.
  His hair is arranged in three rows of snail-shell curls around the head. The eyebrows are curving and plastically rendered with incised lines starting at the root of the nose. The eyes are large, almond-shaped, and slanting, with thick upper eyelids. The end of the upper eyelids extends beyond that of the lower ones. The irises are indicated by incised circles and the pupils by punch holes. The cheeks are fleshy.

573. MALE HEAD

DATABASE NUMBER: RISD001.
LOCATION: Providence, Rhode Island School of Design, inv. no. 71.167.
CONTEXT: —
ACQUISITION HISTORY: —

MEASUREMENTS: Height at back: 21.7 cm. Height from top of head to chin: 14.8 cm. Height (max): 23.4 cm. Width: 14.6 cm. Depth: 15.7 cm.
MATERIAL: Limestone, white/yellow.
PRESERVATION: The head is broken off at the top of the neck. The edge of the veil is chipped. The surface of the hair, the eyes, the nose, the mouth, and the chin are chipped. The surface is weathered.
TECHNICAL DESCRIPTION: —
DATE: A.D. 150–200.
REFERENCES: Ingholt Archives, PS 615; Sotheby's New York 1971, 5th November lot 173; <https://risdmuseum.org/art-design/collection/head-man-71167?return=%2Fart-design%2Fcollection%3Fsearch_api_fulltext%3Dsyria%26op%3D> (06.05.2022).

OBJECT DESCRIPTION
The fragment depicts the head of a male figure.

PORTRAIT
His hair is arranged in a single row of long, wavy locks brushed from the top of the head towards the forehead. The individual strands of hair are indicated by incised lines. His face is diamond-shaped. The eyebrows are plastically rendered with oblique incised lines indicating the individual hairs. The eyes are almond-shaped and slightly slanting with thick eyelids. The upper eyelids extend a bit further than the end of the lower ones. The irises are indicated by incised circles. The ears are protruding and the helix, scapha, tragus, and earlobe are rendered. The nose has a wide base. The alae are incised, and the nostrils are carved. He has a beard. It starts at the temple, covers the cheeks, the chin, and the upper lip. The facial hair is indicated by s-shaped locks. The mouth is small. The chin is oval.

A.D. 170–200
574. MALE HEAD

DATABASE NUMBER: SMB001.
LOCATION: Berlin, Staatliche Museen zu Berlin, inv. no. VA 3101 (last known location). The location of the object is unknown since 1945.
CONTEXT: —

Cat. 573

Cat. 574, Pl. 86

ACQUISITION HISTORY: Moritz Sobernheim, 1901.
MEASUREMENTS: Height: 24 cm.
MATERIAL: Limestone, white/grey.
PRESERVATION: The lower part of the figure is broken off horizontally at the base of the neck. The upper right part of the headdress and hair is chipped.
TECHNICAL DESCRIPTION: Tool marks are visible on the surface of the face, eyes, and headdress.
DATE: A.D. 170–200.
REFERENCES: Ingholt Archives, PS 573; Wartke 1991, 69. 84 f. cat. 16 figs. 17–18.

OBJECT DESCRIPTION
The object depicts a male head.

PORTRAIT
The figure is shown frontally.

He wears a headdress that is pulled from the base of the neck and over the head, covering part of the hair. The headdress has a pointed end, which is bent forward at the top of the head. At the middle, and at the edges, the headdress has a beaded band. His hair is arranged in snail-shell curls around the head. One row is visible at the forehead and two rows on each side of the head, covering the ears. The individual strands of hair are rendered by incised lines. His face is oval. The eyebrows are curving, rendered by incised lines, starting from the root of the nose. The eyes are almond-shaped, with thick upper eyelids. The upper eyelids extend beyond the ends of the lower ones. The irises are indicated by incised circles. The nose is wide with carved nostrils. The cheeks are fleshy, and the mouth is small, with a full lower lip. The chin is small, and the neck is wide with two curving grooves.

A.D. 180–200

575. MALE HEAD

DATABASE NUMBER: VAM016.
LOCATION: Berlin, Vorderasiatisches Museum, inv. no. VA 3102.
CONTEXT: —
ACQUISITION HISTORY: Moritz Soberheim, 1901.
MEASUREMENTS: Height: 22 cm. Width: 18.5 cm. Depth: 25 cm.
MATERIAL: Limestone, white/grey.
PRESERVATION: The lower part of the figure is broken off at the collarbone. A small crack runs across the lower part of the face.
TECHNICAL DESCRIPTION: —
DATE: A.D. 180–200.
REFERENCES: Ingholt Archives, PS 576; Wartke 1991, 84 cat. 15 fig. 16.

OBJECT DESCRIPTION
The fragment depicts the head of a male figure.

Cat. 575, Pl. 87

PORTRAIT
The figure is shown frontally.

His hair is arranged in two rows of snail-shell curls around the head, covering the ears and reaching the neck. The individual strands of hair are rendered by incised lines. His face is oval. The eyebrows are curving, rendered by incised lines starting from the root of the nose. The eyes are almond-shaped, with thick upper eyelids. The upper eyelids extend beyond the end of the lower ones. The irises are rendered by incised circles. The nose is large with carved nostrils. The mouth is small, with a curving upper lip and a full lower lip. The chin is oval. The neck is wide with two curving grooves.

There are traces of a garment on either side of the neck.

A.D. 200–220

576. MALE HEAD

DATABASE NUMBER: MLP072.
LOCATION: Paris, Musée du Louvre, inv. no. AO 26433.
CONTEXT: —

Cat. 576, Pl. 88

ACQUISITION HISTORY: Acquired in 1883.
MEASUREMENTS: Height: 22 cm. Width: 15 cm. Depth: 17 cm.
MATERIAL: Limestone, yellow.
PRESERVATION: The lower part of the figure is broken off at the base of the neck. The nose, the chin, and the lower part of the neck are chipped.
TECHNICAL DESCRIPTION: Restored in 1987. The surface was sandblasted (Powder ROXAL 29). It was restored again in 1997 and 1999. The head is roughly cut on the back.
DATE: A.D. 200–220 (Dentzer-Feydy – Teixidor 1993: A.D. 175–225).
REFERENCES: Dentzer-Feydy – Teixidor 1993, 242 cat. 235.

OBJECT DESCRIPTION
The fragment depicts the head of a male figure.

PORTRAIT
His hair is rendered in snail-shell curls around the head. The individual strands of hair are indicated by incised lines. He has a slightly receding hairline. His face is oval. The eyebrows are curving and are rendered as narrow ridges. The eyes are large and almond-shaped, with thick upper eyelids. The end of the upper eyelids extends beyond that of the lower ones.

The eyeballs are blank. The ears are small and the helix, tragus, and earlobes are depicted. The nose is straight, and the alae are incised. He has a nasolabial fold on each side of the nose. He has a beard: it starts at the temples and runs along the jawline. He also has a moustache. The facial hair is rendered by vertical and oblique, incised lines. The mouth is small, with thin lips. At each corner of the mouth is a ›marionette‹ line. The chin is pointed. The neck is long and has two curving grooves.

577. MALE HEAD

DATABASE NUMBER: NCG084.
LOCATION: Copenhagen, Ny Carlsberg Glyptotek, inv. no. IN 1105.
CONTEXT: —
ACQUISITION HISTORY: Løytved in Syria.
MEASUREMENTS: Height: 21.5 cm. Width of head: 16.5 cm. Depth of head: 19.5 cm.
MATERIAL: Limestone, white/yellow.
PRESERVATION: The lower part of the figure is broken off at the base of the neck. A few locks of hair on the left side of the head and the tip of the nose are broken off. The eyebrows and cheeks are chipped. The surface is weathered.

Cat. 577, Pl. 89

TECHNICAL DESCRIPTION: The head is roughly cut on the back. There are rasp marks on the neck and flat chisel marks on the cheeks and the back of the ears.
DATE: A.D. 200–220 (Ploug 1995: A.D. 210–230).
REFERENCES: Simonsen 1889, 48 cat. G 16 pl. 13; Colledge 1976, 253; Hvidberg-Hansen – Ploug 1993, 139 cat. 93; Ploug 1995, 224 cat. 93; Raja 2019a, 282 cat. 96.

OBJECT DESCRIPTION
The fragment depicts the head of a male figure.

PORTRAIT
The figure is shown frontally. His head is turned to his right.

The hair is short and arranged in four rows of snail-shell curls. The individual strands of hair are rendered by incised lines. His face is oval. The eyebrows are indicated by curving grooves that start from the root of the nose. The beginnings of the eyebrows curve upwards, creating a frowning expression. The eyes are small, close-set, almond-shaped, and slanting with thick upper eyelids. The end of the upper eyelids extends beyond that of the lower ones. The irises are rendered by incised circles and touch the upper eyelids. The ears are small and close to the head, with helix, scapha, and tragus depicted. The nose is straight and wide. He has a beard that starts from the temples, covers the cheeks and the chin, as well as a moustache that covers the upper lip. The facial hair is rendered by small, s-shaped curls arranged in rows. The moustache is rendered by oblique lines centred over the philtrum that curve downwards and to the left and right of the face. The mouth is small, with full lips. The neck is wide.

Cat. 578

578. MALE HEAD

DATABASE NUMBER: PM008.
LOCATION: Palmyra, Palmyra Museum, inv. no. 108.
CONTEXT: Secondary context: Found (02.05.1961) in the rubble in front of the northern foundation wall of the Great Gate.
ACQUISITION HISTORY: —
MEASUREMENTS: Height: 22 cm. Width: 19 cm. Depth: 15 cm.
MATERIAL: Limestone.
PRESERVATION: The lower part of the figure is broken off at the neck. The mouth is chipped.
TECHNICAL DESCRIPTION: —
DATE: A.D. 200–220.
REFERENCES: Michalowski 1963, 119 f. cat. 11 fig. 168.

OBJECT DESCRIPTION
The fragment depicts the head of a male figure.

PORTRAIT
The figure is depicted frontally.

His hair is arranged in two rows of snail-shell curls around the head. The individual strands of hair are indicated by incised lines. His face is oval. The eyebrows are curving and are rendered with fine, incised lines starting at the root of the nose. The eyes are almond-shaped, with thick upper eyelids. The eyeballs are blank. The nose is straight and pointed. The alae are incised, and the nostrils are carved. The mouth is small, with a full lower lip. The chin is pointed. The neck has two curving grooves.

A.D. 200–250

579. MALE HEAD

DATABASE NUMBER: PM412.
LOCATION: Palmyra, Palmyra Museum, inv. no. 457/1660.
CONTEXT: —
ACQUISITION HISTORY: —
MEASUREMENTS: Height: 21 cm.
MATERIAL: Limestone.
PRESERVATION: The head is broken off at the neck. The upper part of the headdress is chipped. The nose is chipped.
TECHNICAL DESCRIPTION: —
DATE: A.D. 200–250.
REFERENCES: Ingholt Archives, PS 1060; Colledge 1976, 140. 253 pl. 142; Tanabe 1986, 44 pl. 460; Gawlikowski – Starcky 1985, fig. 9; Degeorge 2001, 229; Degeorge 2002, 189.

HEADS FROM SARCOPHAGI 839

Cat. 579

OBJECT DESCRIPTION
The object depicts a male head.

PORTRAIT
His hair is arranged in differently sized snail-shell curls around the head. The individual strands of hair are indicated by incised lines. He wears a plain headband with three medallions above the forehead. An armless bust is rendered inside each medallion: they wear a himation fastened at the right shoulder with a circular brooch (details unclear). His face is oval. The eyebrows are plastically rendered with an incised line indicating the centre of the eyebrow and small, oblique lines indicating the individual hairs. The eyes are small and almond-shaped, with thick eyelids. The irises are indicated by incised circles. The ears are long and protruding with the helix, scapha, and earlobe indicated. The alae are incised. He has a beard. It starts at the temples, covers the outer side of the cheeks and the chin. The facial hair is indicated by small snail-shell curls. He also has a moustache rendered by oblique lines and ending in small snail-shell curls on either side. The mouth is small, with thin lips. The chin is oval.

A.D. 200–273

580. MALE HEAD

DATABASE NUMBER: PM304.
LOCATION: Palmyra, Palmyra Museum, inv. no. CD 133.
CONTEXT: Secondary context: Found (24.05.1960) between the columns lying on the north–south axis of the Tetrapylon in the Camp of Diocletian.
ACQUISITION HISTORY: —
MEASUREMENTS: Height: 24.5 cm. Width: 15.5 cm. Depth: 17 cm.
MATERIAL: Limestone.
PRESERVATION: The lower part of the figure is broken off at the collarbone. The left and the lower part of face are broken off.
TECHNICAL DESCRIPTION: The lower eyelids are not carved.
DATE: A.D. 200–273.
REFERENCES: Michalowski 1962, 171 f. cat. 41 fig. 188.

OBJECT DESCRIPTION
The fragment depicts the head of a male figure.

PORTRAIT
His hair is rendered with flame-shaped curls around the head. The individual strands of hair are indicated by incised lines. His face is oval. The eyebrows are curving and plastically rendered. The eyes are large and almond-shaped. The eyeballs are blank. The ears are depicted with the helix, scapha, tragus, and earlobe. He has a beard: it starts at the temples and covers the outer side of the cheeks and the chin. The facial hair is rendered by flame-shaped curls. The neck is wide.

A.D. 220–240

581. MALE HEAD

DATABASE NUMBER: KMB002.
LOCATION: Budapest, Museum of Fine Arts, inv. no. 8430.
CONTEXT: —
ACQUISITION HISTORY: Transferred from the Hungarian National Museum in 1943.
MEASUREMENTS: Height: 26.5 cm. Width: 19 cm. Depth: 22 cm.
MATERIAL: Limestone, white/yellow.
PRESERVATION: The lower part of the figure is broken off horizontally at the base of the neck. The surface around the right eye is slightly chipped. There are cracks running across the face.
TECHNICAL DESCRIPTION: —
DATE: A.D. 220–240.
REFERENCES: Ingholt Archives, PS 238; Ingholt 1928, 117; Colledge 1976, 251; Ingholt 1976, 118 n. 84.

Cat. 581

OBJECT DESCRIPTION
The fragment depicts the head of a male figure.

PORTRAIT
The figure is shown frontally, with his head turned towards his left.

His hair is arranged in s-shaped curls around the head. The individual locks of hair are rendered by drill lines at the forehead and incised lines on each side of the head. His face is round. There are two furrows along his forehead. The eyebrows are curving and plastically rendered with curving, incised lines indicating individual hairs. The eyes are large and almond-shaped, with thick eyelids. The upper eyelids extend beyond the ends of the lower ones. The irises are rendered by incised circles and the pupils by punch holes. The ears are large and protruding with the helix, scapha, tragus, and lobes depicted. The nose is large with the alae carved and the nostrils rendered by drill holes. He has a beard that starts from the temples and covers the cheeks, philtrum, and chin. The facial hair is rendered by small, flame-shaped curls arranged in rows. The mouth is small and slightly open with full lips. The chin is round, and the neck is wide.

582. MALE HEAD

DATABASE NUMBER: PM289.
LOCATION: Palmyra, Palmyra Museum, inv. no. CD 1.
CONTEXT: Secondary context: Found (24.05.1964) at the winding south of the Temple of Standards, Camp of Diocletian, under block TE 34.
ACQUISITION HISTORY: —
MEASUREMENTS: Height: 23 cm. Width: 19 cm. Depth: 21 cm.
MATERIAL: Limestone, white.
PRESERVATION: The lower part of the figure is broken off at the top of the neck. The surface is chipped and weathered.
TECHNICAL DESCRIPTION: —
DATE: A.D. 220–240.
REFERENCES: Michalowski 1966, 180 f. cat. 2 figs. 231–232.

OBJECT DESCRIPTION
The object depicts a male head.

PORTRAIT
The figure is shown frontally.

His hair is arranged in rows of comma-shaped curls around the head. He has a receding hairline. The individual strands of hair are indicated by incised lines. His face is triangular. The eyebrows are curving. The eyes are wide-set, almond-shaped, with thick upper eyelids. The upper eyelids extend beyond the end of the lower ones. The irises are indicated by incised circles. The ears are large, close to the head, with the helix and lobe carved. The nose is straight with a wide base. Nasolabial lines are indicated. He has a beard that starts from the temples, covers the outer side of the cheeks and the chin, as well as a moustache that covers the upper lip. The facial hair is rendered by small, flame-shaped curls arranged in rows. The mouth is small, with full lips. The neck is wide.

583. MALE HEAD

DATABASE NUMBER: KMW013.
LOCATION: Vienna, Kunsthistorisches Museum, inv. no. ANSA I 610.
CONTEXT: —
ACQUISITION HISTORY: Gift of Crown Prince Archduke Rudolf in 1885.
MEASUREMENTS: Height: 23 cm. Width: 15.5 cm. Depth: 17.5 cm.
MATERIAL: Limestone, white.
PRESERVATION: The lower part of the figure is broken off at the base of the neck.
TECHNICAL DESCRIPTION: The eyes and ears are partly carved. The lower eyelids are not carved.
DATE: A.D. 220–240.

HEADS FROM SARCOPHAGI 841

Cat. 583, Pl. 90

REFERENCES: Plattner 2010, 175 cat. 13 figs. 27. 28; <https://www.khm.at/de/object/bd571c082a/> (06.05.2022).

OBJECT DESCRIPTION
The fragment depicts the head of a male figure.

PORTRAIT
The hair is rendered by snail-shell curls around the head. The individual strands of hair are indicated by incised lines. His face is oval. The eyebrows are curving. The upper eyelids are indicated by a horizontal, curving groove. The eyeballs are blank. The ears are protruding and the helix, tragus, scapha, and earlobe are depicted. The nose is straight with a wide base. The alae are incised. The mouth is small, with full lips. The chin is oval and fleshy. The neck is long.

A.D. 230–250

584. MALE HEAD

DATABASE NUMBER: NCG111.
LOCATION: Copenhagen, Ny Carlsberg Glyptotek, inv. no. IN 1097.
CONTEXT: —
ACQUISITION HISTORY: Acquired by Løytved in Syria.
MEASUREMENTS: Height: 23.5 cm. Width: 15 cm. Depth: 15 cm. Height of head: 18.5 cm.
MATERIAL: Limestone, white/yellow.
PRESERVATION: Broken off at the base of the neck. The headdress, forehead, and left eyebrow are chipped.
TECHNICAL DESCRIPTION: The head is roughly cut on the back and there are tooth chisel marks. Rasp marks are visible on the face and flat chisel marks on the headdress, hair, and grooves on the neck. The lower part of the eyes is not carved.
DATE: A.D. 230–250.

Cat. 584, Pl. 91

REFERENCES: Simonsen 1889, 47 cat. G.8 pl. 12; Seyrig 1937, 25 f. pl. 3.2; Colledge 1976, 252; Taha 1982, 121 fig. 5 top right; Hvidberg-Hansen – Ploug 1993, 149 cat. 113; Ploug 1995, 243 cat. 113; Raja 2019a, 313 cat. 117.

OBJECT DESCRIPTION
The object depicts a male figure.

PORTRAIT
The figure is shown frontally.

The hair is short and voluminous and centrally parted. It is arranged in two rows of snail-shell curls, reaching to the nape. He wears a conical headdress decorated with beaded bands: one beaded band extends downwards from the centre, and another runs across the bottom of the headdress. Curving grooves indicate the folds of the headdress. His face is square. The eyebrows are rendered by thin, curving, incised lines that start from the root of the nose. The eyes are almond-shaped, of unequal size, and the left is placed lower than the right. The eyeballs are blank. The nose is straight with a wide base. The alae are indicated by incised lines and the carving of the planes of the face. The mouth is small, with full lips. The chin is square with a cleft and he has a double chin. The neck is wide with two curving grooves.

A.D. 240–273

585. MALE HEAD

DATABASE NUMBER: PM259.
LOCATION: Palmyra, Palmyra Museum, inv. no. CD 134.
CONTEXT: Secondary context: Found (10.05.1962) in the eastern foundations of the Great Gate in the Camp of Diocletian.
ACQUISITION HISTORY: —
MEASUREMENTS: Height: 26 cm. Width: 18 cm. Depth: 20 cm.
MATERIAL: Limestone, white.
PRESERVATION: The lower part of the figure is broken off at the base of the neck. The nose and the right cheek are chipped.
TECHNICAL DESCRIPTION: —
DATE: A.D. 240–273.
REFERENCES: Michalowski 1964, 80 cat. 14 fig. 114; Colledge 1976, 253; Equini Schneider 1992b, 130–132 fig. 12; Equini Schneider 1993, 137 fig. 38.

OBJECT DESCRIPTION
The fragment depicts the head of a male figure.

PORTRAIT
The figure is shown frontally. The head is slightly turned to his left.

He wears a headband high on his head: it is decorated with two horizontal, incised lines and a central oval medallion, with incised border. His hair is rendered underneath the band

Cat. 585

by crescent-shaped curls. The individual strands of hair are indicated by incised lines. His face is square. There are three horizontal grooves on the forehead. The eyebrows are curving and plastically rendered with oblique, incised lines indicating individual hairs. The eyes are almond-shaped, with thick upper eyelids. The end of the upper eyelids extends beyond that of the lower ones. A curving groove is depicted underneath the eyes. The pupils are depicted by small, round depressions (details unclear). The ears are small and protruding and the helix, scapha, tragus, and earlobe are depicted. The nose is narrow and pointed. The alae are incised, and the nostrils are carved. There is a nasolabial fold on each side of the nose. He has a beard: it starts at the temples and covers the outer side of the cheeks, the chin, and the upper lip. The facial hair is rendered by comma-shaped curls in the beard, and vertical, incised lines on the moustache. The mouth is small, with a full lower lip. The chin is oval. The neck has a protrusion indicating the Adam's apple.

31–40 CM

A.D. 100–150

586. MALE HEAD

DATABASE NUMBER: AMI009.
LOCATION: Istanbul, İstanbul Arkeoloji Müzesi, inv. no. 3720/O.M.170.

Cat. 586

CONTEXT: —
ACQUISITION HISTORY: —
MEASUREMENTS: Height: 34 cm. Width: 20 cm.
MATERIAL: Limestone.
PRESERVATION: The lower part of the figure is broken off at the neck. The nose is broken off. The ears and neck are chipped.
TECHNICAL DESCRIPTION: —
DATE: A.D. 100–150.
REFERENCES: Ingholt Archives, PS 133; Musée Impérial Ottoman 1895, 70 cat. 170; Ingholt 1928, 105.

OBJECT DESCRIPTION
The object depicts a male head.

PORTRAIT
The figure is shown frontally.

His hair is arranged in two rows of s-shaped curls alternating direction in each row. The individual strands of hair are rendered by incised lines. The eyebrows are curving and rendered by thin ridges. The eyes are large and almond-shaped, with thick upper eyelids. The irises and the pupils are indicated by concentric circles. The ears are close to the head. The nose is wide. The mouth is small, with full lips. The chin is square with a cleft. The neck is wide.

A.D. 140–160

587. MALE HEAD

DATABASE NUMBER: PM277.
LOCATION: Palmyra, Palmyra Museum, inv. no. CD 20.
CONTEXT: Secondary context: Found in the foundations of the south platform in front of the Temple of the Standards (Temple des Enseignes), Camp of Diocletian.
ACQUISITION HISTORY: —
MEASUREMENTS: Height: 35 cm. Depth: 15.5 cm.
MATERIAL: Limestone.
PRESERVATION: The lower part of the figure is broken off at the base of the neck. The nose is chipped.
TECHNICAL DESCRIPTION: —
DATE: A.D. 140–160.
REFERENCES: Michalowski 1966, 56 f. cat. 7 figs. 63. 64.

OBJECT DESCRIPTION
The fragment depicts the head of a male figure.

PORTRAIT
His hair is rendered by wide curls arranged in an unruly manner around the head. The individual strands of hair are indicated by incised lines. His face is oval. The eyebrows are curving rendered by incised lines starting at the root of the nose. The eyes are large and almond-shaped, with thick eyelids. The irises and pupils are rendered by concentric, incised circles. The ears are protruding and the helix, scapha, tragus, and earlobe are depicted. The nose is narrow. The alae are incised. The mouth is large with thin lips. The chin is oval. The neck is long.

A.D. 150–200

588. MALE HEAD

DATABASE NUMBER: PM012.
LOCATION: Palmyra, Palmyra Museum, inv. no. CD 6.
CONTEXT: Secondary context: Found (16.04.1961) in a late wall east of the Tetrapylon in the Camp of Diocletian.
ACQUISITION HISTORY: —
MEASUREMENTS: Height: 33 cm. Width: 22 cm. Depth: 25 cm.
MATERIAL: Limestone, white.
PRESERVATION: The head is broken off at the top of the neck. The top of the head is broken off. The ears are broken off. The nose is chipped.
TECHNICAL DESCRIPTION: —
DATE: A.D. 150–200.
REFERENCES: Michalowski 1963, 125 cat. 16 fig. 173.

OBJECT DESCRIPTION
The object depicts a male figure.

PORTRAIT

His hair is arranged in three rows of snail-shell curls around his head. The individual strands of hair are indicated by incised lines. His face is oval. The eyebrows are curving and plastically rendered with oblique grooves indicating the individual hairs. The eyes are large and almond-shaped, with thick eyelids. The irises are indicated by incised circles and the pupils by punch holes. The nose has a wide base. The alae are incised, and the nostrils are carved. He has a beard. It covers the outer sides of the cheeks, the chin, and the upper lip. The facial hair is indicated by vertical and oblique, small, incised lines. His mouth is small with full lips. The chin is rectangular and fleshy.

589. MALE HEAD

DATABASE NUMBER: PM296.
LOCATION: Palmyra, Palmyra Museum, inv. no. CD 119.
CONTEXT: Secondary context: Camp of Diocletian. Found in the north-western part of the Tetrapylon.
ACQUISITION HISTORY: —
MEASUREMENTS: Height: 34 cm. Width: 18 cm. Depth: 25 cm.
MATERIAL: Limestone, white.
PRESERVATION: The head is broken off at the base of the neck. The surface is very weathered. The facial features are unclear. The nose and mouth are broken off.
TECHNICAL DESCRIPTION: —
DATE: A.D. 150–200.
REFERENCES: Michalowski 1962, 163 f. cat. 32 fig. 177.

OBJECT DESCRIPTION

The object depicts a male.

PORTRAIT

The figure is shown frontally. The head is turned slightly to the right.

His hair is arranged in one row of snail-shell curls. He wears a wreath with two rows of narrow, pointed leaves pointing towards an armless bust of a male figure (?) high on the head. The face is rectangular. The eyebrows are curving, rendered by incised lines, and starting from the root of the nose. The eyes are large with thick eyelids. The ears are protruding with the helix, concha, and lobe depicted. The chin is square. The neck is slender.

A.D. 200–273

590. MALE HEAD

DATABASE NUMBER: NMD017.
LOCATION: Damascus, National Museum of Damascus, inv. no. C 1519/3332.
CONTEXT: —
ACQUISITION HISTORY: Found in 1931 in Palmyra.

Cat. 590

MEASUREMENTS: Height: 33 cm.
MATERIAL: Limestone, white/yellow.
PRESERVATION: The head is broken off at the neck. There are several cracks on the face and neck. The nose is broken off and the mouth is chipped.
TECHNICAL DESCRIPTION: The head is roughly finished on the back.
DATE: A.D. 200–273.
REFERENCES: Tanabe 1986, 44 cat. 459; Equini Schneider 1992b, 130–132 fig. 11; Equini Schneider 1993, 137 fig. 37; Charles-Gaffiot et al. 2001, 317 cat. 7; Equini Schneider 2002, 24 cat. 6.

OBJECT DESCRIPTION

The object depicts a male.

PORTRAIT

The figure is shown frontally.

His hair is arranged in two rows of comma-shaped curls around the head. The individual strands of hair are indicated by incised lines. He wears a wreath with three rows of pointed leaves pointing towards an oval with a plain band high on the head. The midribs of the leaves are incised. His face is rectangular. There is a horizontal line across his forehead. The eyebrows are plastically rendered with oblique, incised lines indicating individual hairs. The eyes are almond-shaped and slanting with thick upper eyelids. The irises are indicated by incised circles. The right ear is protruding with the helix, concha, scapha, and lobe depicted. He has a beard that starts from the temples and covers part of the cheeks, the upper lip, and the chin. The facial hair is rendered by flame-shaped curls arranged in rows and by oblique, incised lines on the upper lip. The chin is square. The neck is wide.

A.D. 240–273

591. MALE HEAD

DATABASE NUMBER: PM258.
LOCATION: Palmyra, Palmyra Museum, inv. no. CD 48.
CONTEXT: Secondary context: Found (01.05.1962) in the foundations of a wall in the southern part of the forum in the Camp of Diocletian.
ACQUISITION HISTORY: —
MEASUREMENTS: Height: 31 cm. Width: 22 cm. Depth: 33.5 cm.
MATERIAL: Limestone.
PRESERVATION: The lower part of the figure is broken off at the base of the neck. The central part of the hair and the nose are chipped.
TECHNICAL DESCRIPTION: —
DATE: A.D. 240–273.
REFERENCES: Ingholt Archives, PS 1404; Michalowski 1964, 80 cat. 13 fig. 113.

OBJECT DESCRIPTION
The fragment depicts the head of a male figure.

PORTRAIT
His hair is arranged with crescent-shaped curls in an unruly manner around the head. He has a receding hairline. The individual strands of hair are indicated by incised lines. His face is oval. He has three furrows on the forehead. The eyebrows are slightly curving and plastically rendered with oblique, incised lines indicating individual hairs. The eyes are almond-shaped, with thick upper eyelids. The end of the upper eyelids extends beyond that of the lower ones. The eyeballs are blank. The ears are depicted with the tail of the helix, scapha, tragus, and earlobe. The nose is straight and narrow. The alae are incised. He has a nasolabial fold on each side of the nose. He has a beard: it starts at the temples and covers the outer side of the cheeks, the chin, and the upper lip. The facial hair is rendered by small curls, which have alternating directions and vertical, incised lines on the upper lip. Beneath the lower lip, there are two sets of three small locks of hair. The mouth is large with full lips. The chin is oval.

Cat. 591

592. MALE HEAD

DATABASE NUMBER: NCG023.
LOCATION: Copenhagen, Ny Carlsberg Glyptotek, inv. no. IN 1145.
CONTEXT: —
ACQUISITION HISTORY: Puttmann in Syria.
MEASUREMENTS: Height: 33 cm. Width: 26 cm. Depth: 33 cm. Height of head: 37 cm.
MATERIAL: Limestone, white/grey.
PRESERVATION: The lower part of the figure is broken off at the base of the neck. The tip of the nose is broken off. The hair, right eye, right cheek, and mouth are chipped. Cracks run across the surface.
TECHNICAL DESCRIPTION: The head is roughly cut on the back.
DATE: A.D. 240–273 (Ploug 1995: A.D. 210–230).
REFERENCES: Ingholt Archives, PS 243; Ingholt 1928, 118 n. 4; Colledge 1976, 91 n. 305; 144 n. 537; Parlasca 1984, 283; Parlasca 1985, 346 n. 20; Hvidberg-Hansen – Ploug

Cat. 592

1993, 138 cat. 92; Ploug 1995, cat. 222 f. cat. 92; Raja 2019a, 279 cat. 93.

OBJECT DESCRIPTION
The fragment depicts the head of a male figure. Perhaps from an honorific statue.

PORTRAIT
The figure is shown frontally. The head is turned towards his left.

The hair is short and arranged in four rows of snail-shell curls. The individual strands of hair are rendered by incised lines. His face is square. There are two furrows along his forehead. The eyebrows are plastically rendered with oblique, incised lines on either side of a low, curving ridge. The eyes are wide-set, almond-shaped, and slanting with thick upper eyelids. The end of the upper eyelids extends beyond that of the lower ones. The irises are rendered by incised circles and the pupils by punch holes. The ears are small and close to the head with helix, concha, and large earlobes depicted. The nose is straight and wide. The nostrils are drilled. He has a beard that starts from the temples, covers the cheeks and the chin, as well as a moustache that covers the upper lip. The facial hair is rendered by small, flame-shaped curls arranged in rows. The moustache is rendered with s-shaped curls: they are centred over the philtrum and curve downwards and to the left and right of the face. The mouth is small, with a full lower lip. The neck is long and wide with a curving groove.

41–50 CM

A.D. 240–273
---

593. MALE HEAD

DATABASE NUMBER: NCG021.
LOCATION: Copenhagen, Ny Carlsberg Glyptotek, inv. no. IN 1121.
CONTEXT: —
ACQUISITION HISTORY: Løytved in Syria.
MEASUREMENTS: Height: 42 cm. Width: 29.5 cm. Depth: 31 cm.
MATERIAL: Limestone, white/grey.
PRESERVATION: The lower part of the figure is broken off at the base of the neck. The tip and base of the nose is broken off. The wreath, left upper lip, and mouth are

Cat. 593, Pl. 92

chipped. Cracks run across the surface, especially at the left side of the face.
TECHNICAL DESCRIPTION: There were inlays in the eyes, now missing. The head is roughly cut on the back.
DATE: A.D. 240–273 (Ploug 1995: A.D. 230–250).
REFERENCES: Ingholt Archives, PS 241; Simonsen 1889, 50 f. cat. G 32 pl. 16; Poulsen 1921, 83 f. fig. 10; Chabot 1922, 63 f.; Ingholt 1928, 118; Ingholt 1934, 35 n. 34; Champdor 1953, 123; Michalowski 1962, 163 n. 72; Colledge 1976, 91 n. 305; 113. 120 n. 396; 125. 140. 142. 144 n. 536. 537; 240 pl. 123; Ingholt 1976, 115 pl. 3, 1. 2; Parlasca 1984, 283; Parlasca 1985, 346; Parlasca 1988, 221 pl. 48, d; Equini Schneider 1992b, 126–128 fig. 8; Equini Schneider 1993, 132 fig. 33; Hvidberg-Hansen – Ploug 1993, 141 cat. 97; Ploug 1995, 227–230 cat. 97; Albertson 2000, 166 n. 32; Yon 2002, 132 fig. 34; Raja 2019a, 302 f. cat. 109.

OBJECT DESCRIPTION

The fragment depicts the head of a male figure. Albertson (2000, 166) claims that the head is either from a sarcophagus or an honorific statue.

PORTRAIT

The figure is shown frontally.

He wears a wreath composed of three rows of serrated leaves: short ones at the centre and longer ones at the sides. The leaves point towards a medallion with an armless male bust. The figure wears a tunic with a wide, round neckline and a chlamys fastened at the right shoulder with a round brooch (other details unclear). The hair is short and arranged in flame-shaped locks at the sides; two snail-shell curls framing a crescent-shaped lock are depicted over the centre of the forehead. His face is oval. There are three furrows along his forehead. The eyebrows are plastically rendered with oblique, incised lines over a low, curving groove. The eyes are close-set, almond-shaped, and slanting with thick eyelids. The eyelashes are indicated as a series of oblique, incised lines along the upper and lower eyelids. The irises were depicted by circular inlays. The ears are small and close to the head with helix, scapha, tragus, concha, and large earlobes depicted. The nose is straight. The nostrils are drilled. He has a beard that starts from the temples, covers the outer side of the cheeks and the chin, as well as a moustache that covers the upper lip. The facial hair is rendered by small, flame-shaped curls arranged in rows. The moustache is rendered with oblique, incised lines: they are centred over the philtrum and curve downwards and to the left and right of the face. The mouth is small, with a full lower lip. The neck is long and slender with two curving grooves.

NO MEASUREMENTS

A.D. 50–150

594. MALE HEAD

DATABASE NUMBER: GSC001.
LOCATION: Paris, George Salles Collection, inv. no. unknown.
CONTEXT: —
ACQUISITION HISTORY: —
MEASUREMENTS: —
MATERIAL: Limestone.
PRESERVATION: The head is broken off at the neck. The nose is slightly chipped.
TECHNICAL DESCRIPTION: —
DATE: A.D. 50–150.
REFERENCES: Ingholt Archives, PS 1087.

OBJECT DESCRIPTION

The object depicts a male.

PORTRAIT

His hair is arranged in a single row of crescent-shaped curls around his head. The individual strands of hair are indicated by incised lines. His face is diamond-shaped. The eyebrows are curving and are indicated by ridges. The eyes are large and almost round with thick eyelids. The irises and the pupils are indicated by concentric, incised circles. The ears are large

Cat. 594

and protruding with the scapha, concha, tragus, and earlobe rendered. The nose is large and wide. The alae are incised, and the nostrils are indicated. The mouth is small, with full lips. The chin is prominent and pointed. The neck has a curving groove.

A.D. 100–150

595. MALE HEAD

DATABASE NUMBER: DamascusUNK005.
LOCATION: Damascus, unknown location.
CONTEXT: —
ACQUISITION HISTORY: —
MEASUREMENTS: —
MATERIAL: Limestone.
PRESERVATION: The head is broken off at the neck. The back of the head is broken off. The surface is weathered.

TECHNICAL DESCRIPTION: —
DATE: A.D. 100–150.
REFERENCES: Ingholt Archives, PS 1159.

OBJECT DESCRIPTION
The object depicts a male figure.

PORTRAIT
His hair is arranged in two rows of snail-shell curls around his head. The individual strands of hair are indicated by incised lines. His face is oval. The eyebrows are curving and are indicated by incised lines. The eyes are large and almond-shaped, with thick eyelids. The upper eyelids extend slightly beyond the end of the lower ones. The irises and the pupils are indicated by concentric, incised circles. The ears are small and the helix, scapha, concha, and earlobe are rendered. The nose is short. The alae and nostrils are carved. The mouth is small, with thin lips. The chin is prominent and oval. The neck is slender.

Cat. 595

Cat. 596

596. MALE HEAD

DATABASE NUMBER: DamascusUNK004.
LOCATION: Damascus, unknown location.
CONTEXT: —
ACQUISITION HISTORY: —
MEASUREMENTS: —
MATERIAL: Limestone.
PRESERVATION: The head is broken off at the neck. A small area above the left eyebrow and on the tip of the nose is chipped.
TECHNICAL DESCRIPTION: —
DATE: A.D. 100–150.
REFERENCES: Ingholt Archives, PS 1158.

OBJECT DESCRIPTION
The object depicts a male figure.

PORTRAIT
His hair is arranged in three rows of snail-shell curls around his head. The individual strands of hair are indicated by incised lines. His face is triangular. The eyebrows are curving, indicated by thin ridges. The eyes are large and almond-shaped, with thick eyelids. The irises and pupils are indicated by concentric, incised circles. The ears are small and the helix, scapha, tragus, and earlobe are rendered. The nose is straight with a wide base. The alae and nostrils are carved. The mouth is wide with thin lips. The chin is square and prominent. The neck is slender.

A.D. 150–200

597. FRAGMENT OF A MALE HEAD

DATABASE NUMBER: PM371.
LOCATION: Palmyra, Palmyra Museum, inv. no. B 1935. Excavation number: 339.
CONTEXT: Secondary context: Found (01.10.1956) north of the great court at Baalshamin temple.
ACQUISITION HISTORY: —
MEASUREMENTS: Height: 7.5 cm. Width: 6 cm. Depth: 2 cm.
MATERIAL: Limestone.
PRESERVATION: The lower part of the figure is broken off at the middle of the head.
TECHNICAL DESCRIPTION: —
DATE: A.D. 150–200.
REFERENCES: Dunant – Stucky 2000, 116 cat. 142 pl. 30.

OBJECT DESCRIPTION
The fragment depicts the head of a male figure.

PORTRAIT
He wears a headdress. Curving grooves indicate that it is a cap made of a soft material that covers the hair. It is decorated with a beaded band along the centre that runs to the back of the headdress, and a beaded band across the lower border. There is a six-petal rosette where the two bands intersect over the centre of the forehead.

The hair is centrally parted. It is wavy, and the strands end in snail-shaped locks over the temples. The eyebrows are rendered by thin ridges. The eyes are almond-shaped, with thick eyelids. The irises are indicated by incised lines.

598. FRAGMENT OF A MALE HEAD

DATABASE NUMBER: PM934.
LOCATION: Palmyra, Palmyra Museum, inv. no. CD 45/66.
CONTEXT: Secondary context: Found in later wall in the western part of the Via Praetoria.
ACQUISITION HISTORY: —
MEASUREMENTS: Height: 13 cm. Width: 12 cm. Depth: 6 cm.
MATERIAL: Limestone, white/yellow.
PRESERVATION: Only the left part of the face of the figure is preserved. The ear and eyebrow are slightly chipped.
TECHNICAL DESCRIPTION: —
DATE: A.D. 150–200.
REFERENCES: Gawlikowski 1984, 97 cat. 11 pl. 73, 149.

OBJECT DESCRIPTION
The object depicts the left side of a male head.

PORTRAIT
His hair is arranged in two rows of crescent-shaped locks. The individual strands of hair are indicated by incised lines. The

Cat. 598

eyebrows are rendered by curving, incised lines starting from the root of the nose. The eye is large, almond-shaped, and slanting with heavy eyelids. The upper eyelid extends beyond the end of the lower one. The iris and pupil are indicated by concentric, incised circles. The eyes are large and protruding. The helix, scapha, tragus, and lobe are depicted.

A.D. 170–200

599. MALE HEAD

DATABASE NUMBER: AleppoPriv002.
LOCATION: Aleppo, private collection.
CONTEXT: —
ACQUISITION HISTORY: —
MEASUREMENTS: —
MATERIAL: Limestone, white.
PRESERVATION: The lower part of the figure is broken off horizontally at the base of the neck. The nose has been reattached.
TECHNICAL DESCRIPTION: —
DATE: A.D. 170–200.
REFERENCES: Ingholt Archives, PS 240; Ingholt 1928, 118; Colledge 1976, 251.

OBJECT DESCRIPTION
Head of male figure.

PORTRAIT
His hair is arranged in flame-shaped locks around the head. The individual strands of hair are rendered by incised lines. He wears a wreath with the leaves pointing towards a central four-petal flower. The midribs of the leaves are rendered by incised lines. His face is oval. The eyebrows are curving, rendered by thin ridges. The eyes are almond-shaped, with thick upper eyelids. The end of the upper eyelids extends beyond that of the lower ones. The irises are rendered by incised circles and the pupils by punch holes. The helix, anti-helix, and earlobe are depicted. The nose is large with the alae carved. He has a beard that starts from the temples and covers the lower part of the cheeks, the upper lip, and the chin. The facial hair is rendered by flame-shaped curls arranged in rows. The individual strands of hair are rendered by curving, incised lines. The mouth is large with full lips. The neck is wide with two curving grooves.

A.D. 180–200

600. MALE HEAD

DATABASE NUMBER: UNK068.
LOCATION: Palmyra, Palmyra Museum, inv. no. unknown.
CONTEXT: —
ACQUISITION HISTORY: —
MEASUREMENTS: —
MATERIAL: Limestone.
PRESERVATION: The head is broken off at the chin.
TECHNICAL DESCRIPTION: —

Cat. 599

Cat. 600

DATE: A.D. 180–200.
REFERENCES: Ingholt Archives, A_NCG_Portrait2016_058.

OBJECT DESCRIPTION
The object depicts a male figure from a banquet scene.

PORTRAIT: MALE HEAD
His hair is rendered in three rows of snail-shell curls around the head. The individual strands of hair are indicated by incised lines. The face is oval. The eyes are almond-shaped, with thick upper eyelids and indicated lower eyelids. The end of the upper eyelids extends beyond that of the lower ones. The irises are indicated by incised circles. The ears are completely covered by the hair. The nose is narrow with indicated nostrils. The mouth is small, with full lips.

A.D. 180–240

601. FRAGMENT OF A MALE HEAD

DATABASE NUMBER: PM930.
LOCATION: Palmyra, Palmyra Museum, inv. no. CD 25.
CONTEXT: Secondary context: Found (19.04.1961) in a later wall in the north-western part of the Tetrapylon in the Camp of Diocletian.
ACQUISITION HISTORY: —
MEASUREMENTS: Height: 12 cm. Width: 17 cm. Depth: 10 cm.
MATERIAL: Limestone, white.
PRESERVATION: The lower part of the figure is broken off at the height of the eyes. The surface is heavily chipped and weathered.
TECHNICAL DESCRIPTION: —
DATE: A.D. 180–240.
REFERENCES: Michalowski 1963, 124 cat. 15 fig. 172.

OBJECT DESCRIPTION
The object depicts the upper part of a male head.

PORTRAIT
The hair is arranged in an unruly manner, rendered with comma-shaped locks. The individual strands of hair are indicated by incised lines. The eyebrows are indicated by curving ridges. The upper eyelids appear heavy.

A.D. 200–220

602. MALE HEAD

DATABASE NUMBER: UNK070.
LOCATION: Palmyra, Palmyra Museum, inv. no. unknown.
CONTEXT: —
ACQUISITION HISTORY: —

Cat. 602

MEASUREMENTS: —
MATERIAL: Limestone.
PRESERVATION: The head is broken off at the base of the neck.
TECHNICAL DESCRIPTION: —
DATE: A.D. 200–220.
REFERENCES: Ingholt Archives, IA_NCG_Portrait2016_058.

OBJECT DESCRIPTION
The object depicts a male figure from a banquet scene.

PORTRAIT: MALE HEAD
His hair is rendered in two rows of snail-shell curls around the head. The individual strands of hair are indicated by incised lines. The face is oval. The eyes are almond-shaped, with thick upper eyelids and indicated lower eyelids. The eyeballs appear blank. The ears are completely covered by the hair. The nose is wide with indicated alae and nostrils. The mouth is small, with full lips.

603. MALE HEAD

DATABASE NUMBER: UNK165.
LOCATION: Unknown location.
CONTEXT: —
ACQUISITION HISTORY: In the Tsiade collection in December 1928.
MEASUREMENTS: —
MATERIAL: Limestone.
PRESERVATION: The lower part of the figure is broken off at the base of the neck. The surface of the nose is chipped.

Cat. 603

and earlobe are depicted. The nose bridge is narrow. He has a beard: it starts at the temples and covers the outer side of the cheeks and the chin. He also has a moustache. The facial hair is rendered by dense comma-shaped curls in the beard and horizontal, incised lines in the moustache. The mouth is small, with full lips. The chin is square. The neck is long.

A.D. 200–240

604. MALE HEAD

DATABASE NUMBER: UNK053.
LOCATION: —
CONTEXT: —
ACQUISITION HISTORY: —
MEASUREMENTS: —
MATERIAL: Limestone.
PRESERVATION: The head is broken off at the base of the neck. The tip of the nose is chipped.
TECHNICAL DESCRIPTION: —
DATE: A.D. 200–240.
REFERENCES: Ingholt Archives, IA_NCG_Portrait2016_037.

TECHNICAL DESCRIPTION: —
DATE: A.D. 200–220.
REFERENCES: Ingholt Archives, PS 635.

OBJECT DESCRIPTION
The fragment depicts the head of a male figure.

PORTRAIT
His hair is rendered in two rows of snail-shell curls around the head. The individual strands of hair are indicated by incised lines. His face is oval. The eyebrows are curving and plastically rendered with oblique, incised lines indicating individual hairs. The eyes are almond-shaped, with thick upper eyelids. The end of the upper eyelids extends beyond that of the lower ones. The irises are indicated by incised circles and the pupils with punch holes. The ears are small and the helix, scapha,

Cat. 604

OBJECT DESCRIPTION
The object depicts a male.

PORTRAIT
The hair is short and arranged in rows of snail-shell curls. His face is square. The eyebrows are curving and rendered by incised lines. The eyes are almond-shaped, with thick eyelids. The end of the upper eyelids extends beyond that of the lower ones. The irises are indicated by incised circles and touch the upper eyelids. The ears are large and protruding with the helix, antihelix, scapha, and lobe depicted. The nose is long and wide. The mouth is wide with thin lips. The neck is wide.

A.D. 220–240

605. FRAGMENT OF A MALE HEAD

DATABASE NUMBER: PM634.
LOCATION: Palmyra, Palmyra Museum, inv. no. CD 2/65.
CONTEXT: Secondary context: Found in the northern part of the Temple of the Standards (Temple des Enseignes), Camp of Diocletian.
ACQUISITION HISTORY: —
MEASUREMENTS: Height: 8 cm. Width: 15.5 cm. Depth: 9.5 cm.
MATERIAL: Limestone, white.
PRESERVATION: The upper and lower part of the head is broken off. Only the forehead, eyes, and upper part of the nose are preserved.
TECHNICAL DESCRIPTION: —
DATE: A.D. 220–240.
REFERENCES: Gawlikowski 1984, 95 cat. 2 pl. 70, 140.

OBJECT DESCRIPTION
The object depicts a male head.

PORTRAIT
His hair is voluminous and curly (details unclear). The eyebrows are curving. The eyes are large and partly carved.

Cat. 605

A.D. 230–250

606. MALE HEAD

DATABASE NUMBER: UNK101.
LOCATION: Unknown location.
CONTEXT: —
ACQUISITION HISTORY: —
MEASUREMENTS: —
MATERIAL: Limestone.
PRESERVATION: The lower part of the figure is broken off at the neck. The left side of the head, including the ear and temple, and the tip of the nose are broken off.
TECHNICAL DESCRIPTION: The eyes are partly carved.
DATE: A.D. 230–250.
REFERENCES: Ingholt Archives, PS 585.

OBJECT DESCRIPTION

The object depicts a male head.

PORTRAIT

The figure is shown frontally.

His hair is voluminous and rendered by rows of snail-shell curls around the head. His face is square. The eyebrows are curving and rendered by thin grooves. The eyes are large and almond-shaped, with thick eyelids. The eyeballs are blank. The ears are not visible. The nose is straight. The alae are carved. The mouth is small, with full lips. The chin is pointed. The neck is wide with one curving groove.

FEMALE HEADS

1–10 CM

A.D. 150–200

607. FEMALE HEAD

DATABASE NUMBER: PM215.
LOCATION: Palmyra, Palmyra Museum, inv. no. CD 34/66.
CONTEXT: Secondary context: Found in square IIb in the Temple of the Standards (Temple des Enseignes), Camp of Diocletian.
ACQUISITION HISTORY: —
MEASUREMENTS: Height: 9 cm. Width: 8 cm. Depth: 4 cm.
MATERIAL: Limestone.
PRESERVATION: The lower part of the figure is broken off at the base of the neck. The nose, the mouth, and the chin are chipped.

Cat. 606

Cat. 607

TECHNICAL DESCRIPTION: —
DATE: A.D. 150–200.
REFERENCES: Gawlikowski 1984, 102 cat. 37 pl. 81, 172.

OBJECT DESCRIPTION
The fragment depicts a female head. Part of the relief background is preserved at the right side of the head.

PORTRAIT
The figure is shown frontally.

The hair is parted in the centre and brushed to the sides in wavy strands. The individual locks of hair are rendered by incised lines. Her face is oval. The eyes are almond-shaped, with thick upper eyelids. According to Gawlikowski (1984) she wears earrings composed of two juxtaposed round beads (Colledge classification: L). The neck is wide.

11–20 CM

A.D. 100–150
---

608. FEMALE HEAD

DATABASE NUMBER: Sotheby's006.
LOCATION: Last known: Sotheby's, New York.
CONTEXT: —
ACQUISITION HISTORY: Previously in Museum of Fine Arts Boston, inv. 10.72, gift of the Estate of Dana Estes in 1910.
MEASUREMENTS: Height: 16 cm.
MATERIAL: Limestone.
PRESERVATION: All sides of the object are broken off. The figure is broken off below the neck. The centre of the nose is chipped.
TECHNICAL DESCRIPTION: —
DATE: A.D. 100–150 (Comstock – Vermeule 1976: A.D. 150).
REFERENCES: Ingholt Archives, PS 489; Ingholt 1928, 148 n. 8 PS 489; Colledge 1976, 257; Comstock – Vermeule 1976, 259 cat. 405; Sotheby's, 17th December 1997, lot 399; Krag 2018, 215 cat. 184.

OBJECT DESCRIPTION
The object depicts a female head.

PORTRAIT
The figure wears one headdress: a veil. The veil is heavy and falls to the back of her head. The hair is wavy and centrally parted. Three locks of hair are brushed back over the ears. The individual strands of hair are indicated by incised lines. The face is square. The eyebrows are indicated by curving grooves starting from the root of the nose. The eyes are almond-shaped, with thick eyelids. The irises and the pupils are indicated by concentric, incised circles. The ears are indicated (details unclear). She wears earrings composed of a triangular element with three hanging bars (Colledge classification: L). The nose

Cat. 608

is narrow and straight. The philtrum is carved. The mouth is large with thin lips. The chin is pointed.

609. FEMALE HEAD

DATABASE NUMBER: MAH015.
LOCATION: Geneva, Musée d'Art et d'Histoire, inv. no. 17658.
CONTEXT: —
ACQUISITION HISTORY: Gift from Laurent Rehfous in 1941.
MEASUREMENTS: Height: 18 cm. Width: 14.6 cm.
MATERIAL: Limestone, white/yellow.
PRESERVATION: The head is broken off at the top of the neck. The nose is chipped.
TECHNICAL DESCRIPTION: —
DATE: A.D. 100–150.
REFERENCES: Chamay – Maier 1989, 90 f. cat. 114 pl. 102, 1; Krag 2018, 17 n. 98; 211 cat. 166.

OBJECT DESCRIPTION
The fragment depicts the head of a female figure.

Cat. 609

PORTRAIT

She wears three headdresses: a headband, a turban, and a veil. The headband is placed low on the forehead and is divided into panels separated by beaded bands. The central panel is rectangular and decorated with a vegetal motif, while the panels on either side are square and decorated with large, asterisk-shaped incisions. The outermost panels appear undecorated (details unclear). The turban is coiled. It is divided into three layers where the two upper layers are looped into each other creating a knot in the middle. Curving grooves indicate the coiling of the fabric. The veil is heavy, and the edge is scalloped. Her hair is visible on either side of the head. Three locks above each ear are brushed back over the sides of the headband and disappear under the veil. The individual strands of hair are indicated by incised lines. The face is rectangular. The eyebrows are curving and indicated by incised lines. The eyes are almond-shaped, with thick upper eyelids. The irises are indicated by incised circles and the pupils are drilled. The earlobes are visible under the hair and she wears earrings, depicted as horizontal bars decorated with two upper volutes, and two strands with a bead attached descending from the volutes (Colledge classification: F). The nose is short, and the alae are incised. The mouth is small, with thin lips. The chin is oval and fleshy.

A.D. 130–150

610. FEMALE HEAD

DATABASE NUMBER: Sotheby's021.
LOCATION: Last known: Sotheby's, New York.
CONTEXT: —
ACQUISITION HISTORY: Previously at Boston, Museum of Fine Arts, inv. no. 10.75, gift of the Estate of Dana Estes.
MEASUREMENTS: Height: 20.5 cm.
MATERIAL: Limestone.
PRESERVATION: All sides of the object are broken off. The centre of the headdress, the nose, and the chin are chipped.
TECHNICAL DESCRIPTION: —
DATE: A.D. 130–150 (Comstock – Vermeule 1976: A.D. 120–150).
REFERENCES: Ingholt Archive, PS 658; Caskey 1910, 60; Comstock – Vermeule 1976, 257 cat. 400; Krag 2018, 41 n. 145. 146; 208 cat. 152.

OBJECT DESCRIPTION

The object depicts a female head.

PORTRAIT

The figure wears three headdresses: a headband, a turban, and a veil. The headband is placed low on the forehead and is decorated with rectangular, vertical panels separated by beaded bands. The panels are decorated with a vegetal motif.

Cat. 610

The turban is coiled. It is rendered in three layers and the coiling of the fabric are indicated by curving grooves. The veil is heavy. Her face is square. The eyebrows are indicated by curving ridges. The eyes are almond-shaped, with thick eyelids. The irises and the pupils are indicated by concentric, incised circles. The nose is narrow and straight. The philtrum is indicated by a wide groove. The mouth is small, and the lips are thin. The chin is oval.

A.D. 150–200

611. FEMALE HEAD

DATABASE NUMBER: GML002.
LOCATION: Los Angeles, J. Paul Getty Museum, inv. no. 81. AA.170.
CONTEXT: —
ACQUISITION HISTORY: In 1981 at Astarte Gallery, London. Acquired by Robert Blaugrund and donated by him to the museum in 1981.
MEASUREMENTS: Height: 16.5 cm.
MATERIAL: Limestone.
PRESERVATION: Only the head and part of the relief background are preserved. The surface is lightly chipped.
TECHNICAL DESCRIPTION: —

Cat. 611

DATE: A.D. 150–200.
REFERENCES: Parlasca 1987b, 107–109 fig. 1a-b; Parlasca 1990, 141 f. fig. 14; Koch – Wight 1988, 108 f. cat. 40; Krag 2018, 55 n. 275; 73 n. 47. 51; 299 cat. 496.

OBJECT DESCRIPTION
The object depicts the head of a female.

PORTRAIT
The figure is shown frontally.

Her hair is rendered by vertical rows combed upwards and gathered in a circular bun on the top of the head (so-called ›Faustina hair-style‹). The bun is braided and tied up with a fillet. Several wavy locks of hair start from the middle of the forehead and run to the ears. The individual strands of hair are indicated by incised lines.

Her face is round. The eyebrows are arched, rendered by ridges with an incised line running along the middle, and starting from the root of the nose. The eyes are wide-set, almond-shaped, and slanting with thick eyelids. The upper eyelids extend beyond the end of the lower ones. The irises are indicated by incised circles and the pupils by punch holes. The ears are small and close to the head, with the helix, fossa, concha, scapha, tragus, and lobe depicted. She wears dumbbell-shaped earrings (Colledge classification: H). The nose is straight with a wide base. The alae are carved. The mouth is small, with full lips. The chin is small and round. The neck is wide, with a curving groove.

612. FRAGMENT OF A FEMALE HEAD

DATABASE NUMBER: PM926.
LOCATION: Palmyra, Palmyra Museum, inv. no. CD 104.
CONTEXT: Secondary context: Found (18.05.1960) in a later wall of colonnade 1.
ACQUISITION HISTORY: —
MEASUREMENTS: Height: 12.5 cm. Width: 15 cm.
MATERIAL: Limestone, white/grey.
PRESERVATION: All sides of the object are broken off, only a small part of the head is preserved. The veil on the right side is slightly chipped, the central part of the turban is broken off.
TECHNICAL DESCRIPTION: —
DATE: A.D. 150–200.
REFERENCES: Michalowski 1962, 178 cat. 48 fig. 195.

OBJECT DESCRIPTION
The object depicts the upper part of a female head.

PORTRAIT
She wears three headdresses: a headband, a turban, and a veil. The headband is divided into rectangular, horizontal panels divided by a thin, plain, vertical band. The turban is coiled. It is rendered in two layers. The coiling layers are indicated by

incised, curving grooves. The veil is heavy. The hair is brushed from the centre of the forehead to the sides in a wavy manner. It is pulled back over the ears, over the corner of the headband and turban, and disappears under the veil. The individual locks of hair are indicated by wavy, incised lines.

613. FRAGMENT OF A FEMALE HEAD

DATABASE NUMBER: PM927.
LOCATION: Palmyra, Palmyra Museum, inv. no. CD 117.
CONTEXT: Secondary context: Found (22.05.1960) in the north-western side of the Tetrapylon in the Camp of Diocletian.
ACQUISITION HISTORY: —
MEASUREMENTS: Height: 13.5 cm. Width: 6 cm.
MATERIAL: Limestone, white.
PRESERVATION: The object is broken off at the upper, right, and lower side. The central part of the object is chipped.
TECHNICAL DESCRIPTION: —
DATE: A.D. 150–200.
REFERENCES: Michalowski 1962, 180 cat. 51 fig. 198.

OBJECT DESCRIPTION
The object depicts the left part of a female head.

PORTRAIT
She wears a veil and a turban. The veil falls along the left side of her face. The veil is heavy. The turban is coiled. Part of the hair is visible: it is pushed back under the veil. Individual locks of hair are indicated by incised lines.

A.D. 170–200

614. FEMALE HEAD

DATABASE NUMBER: NCG061.
LOCATION: Copenhagen, Ny Carlsberg Glyptotek, inv. no. IN 1109.
CONTEXT: —
ACQUISITION HISTORY: Løytved in Syria.
MEASUREMENTS: Height: 14 cm. Width: 11.5 cm. Depth: 8.5 cm. Height of head: 12 cm. Width of head: 11.5 cm. Depth of head: 8.5 cm.
MATERIAL: Limestone, white/grey.
PRESERVATION: The lower part of the figure is broken off at the base of the neck. The nose is broken off. The veil is chipped.
TECHNICAL DESCRIPTION: The head is roughly cut on the back and on the outside of the veil. There are flat chisel marks on the face, on the earrings, and the headdresses, and tooth chisel marks on the sides of the veil.
DATE: A.D. 170–200 (Ploug 1995: A.D. 230).
REFERENCES: Simonsen 1889, 49 cat. G 20 pl. 14; Colledge 1976, 264; Hvidberg-Hansen – Ploug 1993, 153 cat. 121; Ploug 1995, 251 cat. 121; Krag 2018, 56 n. 291; 369 cat. 769; Raja 2019a, 316 f. cat. 119.

OBJECT DESCRIPTION
The fragment depicts the head of a female figure.

PORTRAIT
The figure is shown frontally. The head is turned slightly to her right.

She wears three headdresses: a headband, a turban, and a veil. The headband is placed high on the forehead. It is decorated with three square panels separated by beaded borders. The central panel has a vegetal motif, and the two side panels have four-petal rosettes. The turban is coiled: curving and oblique grooves indicate the coiling of the fabric. Over the turban, she wears a heavy veil that falls down the sides of the head. The hair is visible at the sides of the forehead; it is slightly wavy and combed backwards, with individual strands of hair indicated by curving grooves. It covers the sides of the headband and the turban. A small, s-shaped lock of hair is depicted at the centre of the forehead. Her face is oval and fleshy. The eyebrows are rendered by thin, arched grooves starting from the root of the nose. The eyes are small and almond-shaped, with thick upper eyelids. The end of the upper eyelids extends beyond

Cat. 614

that of the lower eyelids. The eyeballs are blank. The earlobes are visible under the hair and she wears earrings composed of three juxtaposed beads: two large, round ones on either side of a small, biconical one (Colledge classification: L). The nose is long and wide. The philtrum is carved. The mouth is small, with full lips. The chin is round. She has a double chin. The neck is long and slender with two curving grooves.

A.D. 180–240

615. FRAGMENT OF A FEMALE HEAD

DATABASE NUMBER: PM931.
LOCATION: Palmyra, Palmyra Museum, inv. no. CD 47.
CONTEXT: Secondary context: Found (23.04.1960) on the Via Praetoria.
ACQUISITION HISTORY: —
MEASUREMENTS: Height: 12 cm. Width: 12 cm. Depth: 5 cm.
MATERIAL: Limestone, white.
PRESERVATION: The lower part of the figure is broken off on all sides. The central part of the headdresses is broken off. The left side of the turban and the eyes are chipped.
TECHNICAL DESCRIPTION: —
DATE: A.D. 180–240.
REFERENCES: Michalowski 1963, 142 cat. 35 fig. 192.

OBJECT DESCRIPTION
The object depicts the upper part of a female head.

PORTRAIT
She wears three headdresses: a headband, a turban, and a veil. The headband is placed high on the forehead and is decorated with horizontal, plain, rectangular panels divided by vertical plain bands. The turban is coiled and rendered in three layers. The coiling of the fabric is indicated by curving grooves. The veil is heavy, and the edge is scalloped, visible at the top of the head. The hair is brushed to the side and over the corner of the headband. It disappears under the turban and veil. Individual strands of hair are indicated by wavy, incised lines. The eyebrows are rendered by incised, curving lines starting from the root of the nose. The eyes are large and almond-shaped. The upper eyelids are heavy.

A.D. 210–230

616. FEMALE HEAD

DATABASE NUMBER: NCG102.
LOCATION: Copenhagen, Ny Carlsberg Glyptotek, inv. no. IN 1110.
CONTEXT: —
ACQUISITION HISTORY: Acquired by Løytved in Syria.
MEASUREMENTS: Height: 19.5 cm. Width: 16.5 cm. Depth: 18 cm. Height of head: 18 cm.
MATERIAL: Limestone, white/yellow.
PRESERVATION: Broken off at the base of the neck. The right side and the lower left side of the veil are broken off. Several cracks run across the face.
TECHNICAL DESCRIPTION: The head is roughly cut on the back. Drill holes are visible along the edge of the veil on top of the head. There are rasp marks on the face, and tooth chisel marks on the back of the head. Flat chisel marks are visible on the veil, hair, and jewellery.
DATE: A.D. 210–230.
REFERENCES: Simonsen 1889, 49 cat. G.21 pl. 14; Colledge 1976, 264; el-Chehadeh 1972, 90 n. 89; 91; Hvidberg-Hansen – Ploug 1993, 152 cat. 118; Ploug 1995, 248 cat. 118; Krag 2018, 59 n. 325; 108 n. 125. 127; 344 cat. 665; Charles-Gaffiot et al. 2001, 329 cat. 65 fig. 65; Raja 2019a, 290 f. cat. 102.

OBJECT DESCRIPTION
The object depicts a female figure.

PORTRAIT
The head is slightly turned to her left.

She wears three headdresses: a headband, a turban, and a veil. The headband is decorated with square panels with floral motifs between beaded bands. The turban is coiled, with curving grooves indicating the coiling of the fabric. Over the

Cat. 616, Pl. 93

headband she wears a heavy veil with a scalloped edge that falls down the back of the head. She also wears head ornaments: a central head ornament and a head-chain. The central head ornament is fastened under the centre of the veil and runs to the forehead. It is composed of an upper circular bezel with a beaded border and a rectangular bezel with a beaded border underneath. The two bezels are linked by beaded elements. Three narrow, rectangular beads with round ends are suspended from the square bezel. The head-chain is fastened under the central head ornament and runs to either side of the face. It is composed of round elements with incised borders, linked by small, beaded elements. The hair is visible at the sides of the forehead; it is slightly wavy and combed back over the lower sides of the headband and the turban. The individual strands of hair are indicated by s-shaped, incised lines. Her face is oval and fleshy. The eyebrows are rendered by thin, curving, incised lines that almost meet as they start from the root of the nose. The eyes are large and almond-shaped, with thick upper eyelids. The end of the upper eyelids extends downwards and beyond that of the lower eyelids. The eyeballs are blank. The earlobes are visible, and she wears dumbbell-shaped earrings (Colledge classification: H). The nose is long and wide. The alae are indicated by the carving of the planes of the face and accentuated by incised lines. The philtrum is carved. The mouth is small, with full lips. The chin is pointed with a cleft. The neck is wide with two curving grooves.

A.D. 220–240

617. FEMALE HEAD

DATABASE NUMBER: KMW010.
LOCATION: Vienna, Kunsthistorisches Museum, inv. no. ANSA I 1520.
CONTEXT: —
ACQUISITION HISTORY: Dr James C. Samson, 1896.
MEASUREMENTS: Height: 17 cm. Width: 13.8 cm. Depth: 13.5 cm.
MATERIAL: Limestone, white.
PRESERVATION: The lower part of the figure is broken off at the base of the neck. The nose has been broken off and reattached. Parts of the edge of the veil on the right side are broken off. The upper part of the headdress is chipped. There are small chips and cracks across the surface.
TECHNICAL DESCRIPTION: —
DATE: A.D. 220–240.
REFERENCES: Masner 1893, 132 cat. 1576; Colledge 1976, 261; Plattner 2010, 172 cat. 10 figs. 22. 23; Krag 2018, 106 n. 104; 295 cat. 480; <https://www.khm.at/de/object/61e437816d/> (06.05.2022).

OBJECT DESCRIPTION
The fragment depicts the head of a female figure.

PORTRAIT
She wears two headdresses: a diadem and a veil. The diadem is placed high on her head. It is semicircular and along the border runs a beaded band. The veil is heavy. The hair is parted at the centre of the forehead and brushed to the sides. Above the ears, several locks of hair are brushed back over the corners of the diadem. A single diamond-shaped lock falls to her forehead at the parting. The individual strands of hair are indicated with incised lines. His face is diamond-shaped. The right eyebrow is arched, the left eyebrow is curving; they are indicated by narrow ridges starting at the root of the nose. The eyes are almond-shaped, with heavy eyelids. The upper eyelids extend beyond the end of the lower ones. The irises are indicated with incised circles, the pupils by punch holes. The irises touch the upper eyelids. She wears earrings composed of three juxtaposed beads: two round ones on either side of a biconical one (Colledge classification: L). The nose is short with a round tip. The alae are incised, and the nostrils are carved. The cheeks are fleshy. The mouth is small, with full and accentuated lips. The chin is small and round with a small depression. The neck is short.

Cat. 617

618. FEMALE HEAD

DATABASE NUMBER: PM245.
LOCATION: Palmyra, Palmyra Museum, inv. no. CD 73.
CONTEXT: Secondary context: Found in the foundations of the wall of the Great Gate in the Camp of Diocletian.
ACQUISITION HISTORY: —
MEASUREMENTS: Height: 18 cm. Width: 14 cm. Depth: 19 cm.
MATERIAL: Limestone, white.
PRESERVATION: The lower part of the figure is broken off at the base of the neck. The nose and the left cheek are broken off. Cracks run across the face.
TECHNICAL DESCRIPTION: —
DATE: A.D. 220–240.
REFERENCES: Michalowski 1964, 91. 97 f. cat. 29 figs. 124. 130; Krag 2018, 73 n. 47; 311 cat. 542.

OBJECT DESCRIPTION

The object depicts a female head.
The object was found together with the objects cat. 530, cat. 531, cat. 585, cat. 586, cat. 611, cat. 612, cat. 613, cat. 614, cat. 615. According to Michalowski (1964, 91) they come from the same sarcophagus.

PORTRAIT

The figure is shown frontally.

Her face is square. The hair is parted at the centre of her forehead and covers the upper part of her ears. The individual strands of hair are rendered by incised lines. A diamond-shaped lock of hair is rendered in the middle of the forehead extending downwards. The eyebrows are curving, rendered by incised lines starting from the root of the nose. The eyes are deep-set and almond-shaped, with thick upper eyelids. The end of the upper eyelids extends beyond that of the lower ones. The irises are indicated by incised circles and they touch the upper eyelids. The earlobes are visible under the hair. She wears earrings with three juxtaposed beads: two round ones on either side of a biconical one (Colledge classification: L). The cheeks are fleshy. The mouth is small, with a full lower lip. The chin is pointed. The neck is short and wide.

619. FEMALE HEAD

DATABASE NUMBER: PM247.
LOCATION: Palmyra, Palmyra Museum, inv. no. CD 75.
CONTEXT: Secondary context: Found in the foundations of the wall of the Great Gate in the Camp of Diocletian.
ACQUISITION HISTORY: —
MEASUREMENTS: Height: 20 cm. Width: 14 cm. Depth: 18 cm.
MATERIAL: Limestone, white.
PRESERVATION: The lower part of the figure is broken off horizontally at the base of the neck. The surface at the nose is chipped.
TECHNICAL DESCRIPTION: —
DATE: A.D. 220–240.
REFERENCES: Michalowski 1964, 91. 97 f. cat. 30 figs. 124. 131; Gawlikowski 1987, 288 fig. 2; Krag 2018, 73 n. 47; 310 cat. 537.

OBJECT DESCRIPTION

The object depicts a female head.
The object was found together with the objects cat. 530, cat. 531, cat. 584, cat. 586, cat. 611, cat. 612, cat. 613, cat. 614, cat. 615. According to Michalowski (1964, 91) they come from the same sarcophagus.

PORTRAIT

The figure is shown frontally.
Her face is oval. The hair is parted at the centre of her forehead and covers the ears. The individual strands of hair are rendered by incised lines. A thin lock of hair is rendered in the middle of the forehead extending downwards. The eyebrows are curving, rendered by incised lines starting from the root of the nose. The eyes are close-set and almond-shaped, with thick upper eyelids. The upper eyelids extend beyond the end of the lower ones. The irises are indicated by incised circles and the pupils by punch holes. Only the earlobes are visible under the hair. She wears earrings with three juxtaposed round beads (Colledge classification: K). The cheeks are fleshy. The mouth is small, with a full upper lip. The chin is round with a cleft and the neck is slender.

620. FEMALE HEAD

DATABASE NUMBER: PM248.
LOCATION: Palmyra, Palmyra Museum, inv. no. CD 76.
CONTEXT: Secondary context: Found in the foundations of the wall of the Great Gate in the Camp of Diocletian.
ACQUISITION HISTORY: —
MEASUREMENTS: Height: 20 cm. Width: 14 cm. Depth: 18 cm.
MATERIAL: Limestone, white.
PRESERVATION: The lower part of the figure is broken off at the base of the neck. The surface of the nose is chipped. The upper right side, the left cheek, and the chin are chipped. There are cracks running across the lower part of the face.
TECHNICAL DESCRIPTION: —
DATE: A.D. 220–240.
REFERENCES: Michalowski 1964, 91. 97 f. cat. 31 figs. 124. 132; Krag 2018, 55 n. 274; 73 n. 47; 311 cat. 540.

OBJECT DESCRIPTION

The object depicts a female head.
The object was found together with the objects cat. 530, cat. 531, cat. 584, cat. 585, cat. 611, cat. 612, cat. 613, cat. 614, cat. 615. According to Michalowski (1964, 91) they come from the same sarcophagus.

PORTRAIT

The figure is shown frontally.

Her face is oval. The hair is parted at the centre of her forehead and covers the upper part of her ears. The individual strands of hair are rendered by incised lines. A crescent-shaped lock of hair is rendered in the middle of the forehead extending downwards. The eyebrows are curving, rendered by incised lines starting from the root of the nose. The eyes are close-set and almond-shaped, with heavy upper eyelids. The end of the upper eyelids extends beyond that of the lower ones. The irises are indicated by incised semicircles and they touch the upper eyelids. Only the earlobes are visible under the hair. She wears earrings with three juxtaposed round beads (Colledge classification: K). The cheeks are fleshy, and the mouth is small, with a full lower lip. The chin is round with a cleft.

621. FEMALE HEAD

DATABASE NUMBER: BMC001.
LOCATION: Pennsylvania, Bryn Mawr College, inv. no. S-88.
CONTEXT: —
ACQUISITION HISTORY: Gift from Jean Beck Dalzell.
MEASUREMENTS: Height: 14.5 cm. Width: 11.5 cm. Depth: 10.8 cm.
MATERIAL: Limestone, yellow.

Cat. 621

PRESERVATION: The lower left part of the figure is broken off at the clavicle, and the lower right part at the neck. The lower right side of the veil and the nose are broken off. The edge of the veil, the right eye, the left cheek, and the chin are chipped. The surface is weathered.
TECHNICAL DESCRIPTION: —
DATE: A.D. 220–240.
REFERENCES: Ingholt Archives, PS 924; Howarth 1969, 441–446 pl. 123, 1–4; Hansen – Croll 2010, 11; Krag 2018, 106 n. 105; 368 cat. 763.

OBJECT DESCRIPTION
The fragment depicts the head of a female figure.

PORTRAIT
The figure is shown frontally.

She wears two headdresses: a turban and a veil. The turban is coiled. It is rendered in two twisted layers. A curving groove indicates the coiling of the fabric. The veil is heavy and has a scalloped edge. It falls downwards on each side of the head. Her hair is centrally parted and brushed away on each side of the forehead. At the centre of the forehead, a small, crescent-shaped curl extends downwards. Part of the hair is covered by the headdress. Several strands of hair on each side of the head and above the earlobes are pushed back over the edge of the turban and disappear under the veil. A narrow, curving lock of hair is shown on each cheek. Her face is oval. The eyebrows are curving, rendered by thin ridges. The eyes are almond-shaped, with thick upper eyelids. The end of the upper eyelids extends beyond that of the lower ones. Only the earlobes are visible, and she is wearing dumbbell-shaped earrings (Colledge classification: H). The mouth is small and slightly open, and the lips are full. The cheeks are fleshy, and the chin is round. The neck is wide with two curving grooves.

At the base of the neck, she wears a necklace composed of small, round beads.

622. FEMALE HEAD

DATABASE NUMBER: NCG106.
LOCATION: Copenhagen, Ny Carlsberg Glyptotek, inv. no. IN 1090.
CONTEXT: —
ACQUISITION HISTORY: Acquired by Løytved in Syria.
MEASUREMENTS: Height: 20.5 cm. Width: 11 cm. Depth: 14.5 cm. Height of head: 20 cm.
MATERIAL: Limestone, white/yellow.
PRESERVATION: Broken off at the middle of the neck. The back of the head, the hair, tip of the nose, ears, chin, and neck are chipped. Cracks run on the surface.
TECHNICAL DESCRIPTION: The back of the head is roughly cut. There are rasp marks on the face and flat chisel marks on the sides of the neck. On the top is a hole for a clamp,

HEADS FROM SARCOPHAGI

Cat. 622, Pl. 94

Width: 2.5; Depth: 3. The hollows at the three bezels of the hair jewellery indicate the presence of inlays (now lost).
DATE: A.D. 220–240.
REFERENCES: Simonsen 1889, 46 cat. G.1 pl. 11; Ingholt 1928, 143 PS 455; Ingholt 1935, 68 n. 53; Mackay 1949, 171. 179 n. 2 pl. 60.2; Bossert 1951, 37 cat. 537 pl. 165; Eydoux 1964, 268. 282 fig. 297; el-Chehadeh 1972, 90 n. 93; Colledge 1976, 261; Parlasca 1976, 40 n. 45i; Parlasca 1987b, 114 appendix cat. 17 fig. 7; Hvidberg-Hansen – Ploug 1993, 110 f. cat. 67; Ploug 1995, 167–170 cat. 67; Krag 2018, 17 n. 98; 73 n. 17. 51; 108 n. 125; 299 cat. 495; Raja 2019a, 274 f. cat. 90.

OBJECT DESCRIPTION
The object depicts a female figure.

PORTRAIT
The head is slightly turned to her left.

The hair directly over the forehead is centrally parted and tucked behind the ears. A small, wavy lock is depicted over each temple. The locks over the ears continue towards the back of the head, where the hair is gathered close to the head. The rest of the hair is gathered upwards; the strands are indicated by vertical grooves with s-shaped, incised lines that radiate from the centre of the head. At the top the hair is plaited and gathered in a coiled bun kept in place by a thick ribbon that is wrapped around the plaits at regular intervals. The individual strands of hair are rendered by slightly oblique grooves.

She wears a central head ornament. It falls from the top of her head, at the bun, and down to the forehead. It is composed of three bezels linked by beaded elements. The upper bezel is square, containing a diamond-shaped decoration with an incised border around a diamond-shaped, hollowed centre. An oval bezel is at the centre, with an incised border around a circular, hollowed centre. Lowest, just above the forehead, is a rectangular bezel. This is decorated with a band along the borders decorated with oblique grooves and with an oval, incised centre that is hollowed out. Seven thin, rectangular beads with round ends are suspended from the lower side of the rectangular bezel. Her face is oval and fleshy. The eyebrows are rendered by thin, curving ridges that start from the root of the nose. The eyes are small, almond-shaped, and slanting with thick upper eyelids. The end of the upper eyelids extends beyond that of the lower eyelids. The irises, that touch the upper eyelids, are indicated by incised circles and the pupils by punch holes. The ears are visible, with helix, scapha, and concha carved. She wears two pairs of dumbbell-shaped earrings, one pair hanging from the top of the helix, another from the lobes (Colledge classification: H). The nose is straight and wide. The alae are indicated by the carving of the planes of the face. The philtrum is carved. The mouth is small, with full lips. The chin is pointed. The neck is slender.

A.D. 240–273

623. FEMALE HEAD

DATABASE NUMBER: Okayama002.
LOCATION: Okayama, Okayama Orient Museum, inv. no. 098-2474.
CONTEXT: —
ACQUISITION HISTORY: —
MEASUREMENTS: Height: 19 cm. Width: 20 cm. Depth: 20 cm.
MATERIAL: Limestone, grey.
PRESERVATION: The lower part of the figure is broken off at the base of the neck. The upper left part of the veil has broken off. The edges of the veil, the left side of the nose, and the upper lip are chipped.
TECHNICAL DESCRIPTION: Tool marks are visible, particularly on the forehead and veil on the right side of the head.
DATE: A.D. 240–273.
REFERENCES: Krag 2018, 350 cat. 695.

OBJECT DESCRIPTION
The object depicts a female head.

PORTRAIT

The head is shown frontally.

She wears two headdresses: a headband and a veil. The band is placed high on the forehead and is divided into decorated panels separated by beaded bands. The central panel has a flower with four serrated petals. The veins of the petals are rendered by incised lines. The lateral panels have a crisscross pattern. The veil is heavy with a scalloped edge. It falls from the top of the head and downwards on each side of the face. Part of the hair is covered by the headdress: several strands of hair above the ears are pushed back over the headband and disappear under the veil. Her face is oval. The eyebrows are curving, rendered by thin ridges. The eyes are almond-shaped, with thick upper eyelids. The end of the upper eyelids extends beyond that of the lower ones. The irises are rendered by incised circles and the pupils by punch holes. The nose is straight. Only the earlobes are visible under the hair. She wears earrings composed of three juxtaposed beads: two small, round ones on either side of a teardrop-shaped bead (Colledge classification: L). The mouth is small, with a full lower lip. The chin is round. The neck is slender.

624. FEMALE HEAD

DATABASE NUMBER: UPM012.
LOCATION: Philadelphia, University of Pennsylvania Museum of Archaeology and Anthropology, inv. no. B8910.
CONTEXT: —
ACQUISITION HISTORY: Collected in Palmyra by Rev. John Punnett Peters during the expedition to Nippur in 1889–1890.
MEASUREMENTS: Height: 20.5 cm. Width: 18.5 cm. Depth: 12 cm.
MATERIAL: Limestone, yellow.
PRESERVATION: The lower part of the figure is broken off at the top of the neck. The left side of the forehead, the eyebrows, and the nose are chipped.
TECHNICAL DESCRIPTION: —
DATE: A.D. 240–273.
REFERENCES: Ingholt Archives, PS 502; Legrain 1927, 348 cat. 7 fig. 7; Ingholt 1928, 150; Colledge 1976, 264; Romano 2006, 288 f. cat. 135; Krag 2018, 106 n. 101; 108 n. 125. 127; 344 cat. 669; <https://www.penn.museum/collections/object/271619> (06.05.2022).

OBJECT DESCRIPTION

The fragment depicts the head of a female figure.

PORTRAIT

The figure is shown frontally.

She wears two headdresses: a headband and a veil. The headband is placed high on her forehead: it is wide and divided into two registers. The lower register is undecorated. The upper register is decorated with crisscrossing, beaded bands surrounding six-petal flowers. The petals have a circular depression at the centre. Over the band, she wears two head ornaments: a central one that extends downwards from the middle of the top of the head from under the veil and a head-chain. The central ornament is composed of three bezels, possibly an oval one at the top, a rectangular one in the middle, and an oval one at the bottom. All bezels have beaded borders and are linked by beaded elements. The head-chain is attached to the oval bezel of the central head ornament and runs to the sides disappearing under the veil. It is composed of circular bezels with incised borders linked by beaded elements. The veil is heavy, and the edge is scalloped. Part of the hair is covered by the headdress: several strands of hair at the sides are brushed back under the head-chain, over the headband, and disappear under the veil. The individual strands of hair are indicated by incised lines. Her face is oval. The eyebrows are curving. The eyes are large and almond-shaped. The upper eyelids are indicated by an incised line. The eyeballs are blank. She wears earrings composed of three juxtaposed, round beads (Colledge classification: K). The base of the nose is wide. The mouth is small, with full lips. The chin is oval.

Cat. 624

625. FEMALE HEAD

DATABASE NUMBER: BeirutPriv001.
LOCATION: Beirut, private collection.
CONTEXT: —
ACQUISITION HISTORY: —
MEASUREMENTS: Height: 20 cm.
MATERIAL: Limestone.
PRESERVATION: The head is broken off at the neck. The edge of the veil is chipped. The nose and the chin are chipped. Small cracks run horizontally across the forehead and chin.
TECHNICAL DESCRIPTION: —
DATE: A.D. 240–273.
REFERENCES: Ingholt Archives, PS 503; Ingholt 1928, 150 PS 503; Colledge 1976, 264; Krag 2018, 106 n. 101; 108 n. 125; 342 cat. 658.

OBJECT DESCRIPTION
The fragment depicts the head of a female figure.

PORTRAIT
She wears two headdresses: a headband and a veil. The headband is divided into two registers: the lower is decorated with vertical beaded bands. The upper is decorated with an intersecting lozenges pattern created by beaded bands. Both outer lozenges contain a six-petal rosette. The veil is heavy with a scalloped edge. She also wears head ornaments. She wears a central head ornament over the headband. It is fastened under the centre of the veil and runs vertically to the forehead. It is composed of a rectangular bezel and an oval bezel, both with outer beaded borders. The bezels are joined by a beaded element. Four thin, rectangular elements ending in round beads are suspended beneath the oval bezel. She also wears a head-chain. It is fastened under the central head ornament and runs to either side of the head. It is composed of circular bezels with incised borders joined with beaded elements. The hair is visible on either side of the head: it is brushed over the headband and under the head-chain and disappears under the veil. The individual strands of hair are indicated by wavy, incised lines. Her face is oval. The eyebrows are curving and rendered by incised lines. The eyes are large, almond-shaped, and slightly slanting with thick upper eyelids. The irises are indicated by incised circles. She wears earrings with two juxtaposed beads: an upper narrow element and a lower circular element (Colledge classification: L). The nose has a curving bridge. The alae are incised, and the nostrils are carved. The mouth is small, with a full lower lip. The chin is oval and fleshy. The neck has a curving groove.

21–30 CM

A.D. 100–150
---

626. FEMALE HEAD

DATABASE NUMBER: MAH016.
LOCATION: Geneva, Musée d'Art et d'Histoire, inv. no. 017659.
CONTEXT: —
ACQUISITION HISTORY: Gift from Laurent Rehfous in 1941.
MEASUREMENTS: Height: 22.5 cm. Width: 15 cm.
MATERIAL: Limestone, white/yellow.
PRESERVATION: The head is broken off at the top of the neck. The edge of the veil, the headband, the forehead, the left eye, the left cheek, and the nose are chipped.
TECHNICAL DESCRIPTION: —
DATE: A.D. 100–150.
REFERENCES: Chamay – Maier 1989, 91 cat. 115 pl. 102, 2; Krag 2018, 17 n. 98; 211 cat. 167.

OBJECT DESCRIPTION
The fragment depicts the head of a female figure.

PORTRAIT
She wears three headdresses: a headband, a turban, and a veil. The headband is placed low on the forehead and is divided into rectangular panels: three long and wide panels alternating with three short and narrow ones. The turban is coiled. It is divided into three layers where the two upper layers are looped into each other creating a knot in the middle. Curving grooves indicate the coiling of the fabric. The veil is heavy, and the edge is scalloped. Her hair is visible on either side of the head. Two

Cat. 625

Cat. 626

CONTEXT: Secondary context: Found (29.04.1961) behind the wall of the north side of the Great Gate.
ACQUISITION HISTORY: —
MEASUREMENTS: Height: 23 cm. Width: 17 cm. Depth: 26 cm.
MATERIAL: Limestone, grey.
PRESERVATION: The lower part of the figure is broken off at the neck. Part of the hair over the left temple is broken off. The top right of the hair and the surface of the face are chipped.
TECHNICAL DESCRIPTION: —
DATE: A.D. 100–150 (Michalowski 1963: A.D. 175–225).
REFERENCES: Michalowski 1963, 166 cat. 62 fig. 220; Tanabe 1986, 45 pl. 465.

OBJECT DESCRIPTION
The object depicts a female head.

PORTRAIT
The figure is shown frontally.

Her hair is centrally parted over the forehead, and four thick locks of hair are brushed back over the temples and the ears. The hair is divided into thick locks only, indicated by curving grooves. Her face is square. The eyebrows are indicated by thin curving grooves. The eyes are close-set, large, round, locks above each ear are brushed back over the sides of the headband and disappear under the veil. The individual strands of hair are indicated by incised lines. The face is rectangular. The eyebrows are curving and indicated by incised lines. The eyes are almond-shaped, with thick upper eyelids. The irises are indicated by incised circles and the pupils are drilled. The earlobes are visible under the hair and she wears earrings, depicted as horizontal bars decorated with two upper volutes, and two strands with a bead attached descending from the volutes (Colledge classification: F). The nose is short, and the alae are incised. The mouth is small, with thin lips. A line descends from either corner of the mouth downwards. The chin is oval and fleshy. The neck is short and slender.

627. FEMALE HEAD

DATABASE NUMBER: PM032.
LOCATION: Palmyra, Palmyra Museum, inv. no. CD 72.

Cat. 627

with thick eyelids. The irises and the pupils are indicated by concentric, incised circles. The ears are covered by the hair. She wears earrings: single, round beads (Colledge classification: J). The nose is straight. The mouth is small. The chin is round. The neck is long and slender.

628. FEMALE HEAD

DATABASE NUMBER: PM311.
LOCATION: Palmyra, Palmyra Museum, inv. no. CD 90.
CONTEXT: Secondary context: Found (17.05.1960) incorporated into the Arabic wall between the portico and the Tetrapylon.
ACQUISITION HISTORY: —
MEASUREMENTS: Height: 30 cm. Width: 17 cm. Depth: 18 cm.
MATERIAL: Limestone, yellow.
PRESERVATION: The background is broken off. The lower part of the figure is broken off at the neck. The edges of the veil are broken off. The surface is heavily chipped.
TECHNICAL DESCRIPTION: —
DATE: A.D. 100–150.
REFERENCES: Michalowski 1962, 178 cat. 49 fig. 196; Krag 2018, 207 cat. 150.

OBJECT DESCRIPTION
The object depicts a female head.

PORTRAIT
The figure is shown frontally.
She wears three headdresses: a headband, a turban, and a veil. The headband is placed low on the forehead (other details unclear). The veil falls over the back of the head. The face is round (other details unclear). She wears earrings (details unclear).

A.D. 150–170

629. FEMALE HEAD

DATABASE NUMBER: UPM009.
LOCATION: Philadelphia, University of Pennsylvania Museum of Archaeology and Anthropology, inv. no. B8909.
CONTEXT: —
ACQUISITION HISTORY: Collected in Palmyra by Rev. John Punnett Peters during the expedition to Nippur in 1889–1890.
MEASUREMENTS: Height: 21 cm. Width: 17.5 cm. Depth: 12 cm.
MATERIAL: Limestone, yellow.
PRESERVATION: The lower part of the figure is broken off at the upper part of the neck. The surface of the upper part of the headdress is chipped. There are several cracks running across the face.
TECHNICAL DESCRIPTION: —
DATE: A.D. 150–170.
REFERENCES: Ingholt Archives, PS 697; Legrain 1927, 349 cat. 8 fig. 8; Colledge 1976, 261; Romano 2006, 287 cat. 134; Krag 2018, 106 n. 105; 294 cat. 473; <https://www.penn.museum/collections/object/271618> (06.07.2022).

OBJECT DESCRIPTION
The object depicts the head of a female figure.

PORTRAIT
She wears three headdresses: a headband, a turban, and a veil. The headband is placed low on the forehead and is divided into three panels separated by narrow, beaded bands. The central panel is rectangular and decorated with leaves on a stem, the two lateral panels are square and decorated with four-petal flowers. The headband has a horizontal, narrow band at the lower border. The turban is coiled. It is composed of a single layer and the coiling of the fabric is indicated by curving, incised lines. The veil is heavy. Only part of the hair is visible under the headdress: locks of hair above the ears are brushed back over the headband and disappear under the veil. The individual strands of hair are indicated by incised lines. Her face is round. The eyebrows are curving and depicted by incised lines starting at the root of the nose. The eyes are almond-shaped, with thick upper eyelids. The end of the upper eyelids extends beyond that of the lower ones. The irises are indicated by incised circles and the pupils by punch holes. She wears a dumbbell-shaped earring on the left ear (Colledge classification: H). The nose bridge is narrow, the base is wide. The alae are incised. The mouth is small, with a full lower lip. The chin is round.

630. FEMALE HEAD

DATABASE NUMBER: UPM008.
LOCATION: Philadelphia, University of Pennsylvania Museum of Archaeology and Anthropology, inv. no. B8911.
CONTEXT: —
ACQUISITION HISTORY: Collected in Palmyra by Rev. John Punnett Peters during the expedition to Nippur in 1889–1890.
MEASUREMENTS: Height: 22.5 cm. Width: 18 cm. Depth: 15 cm.
MATERIAL: Limestone, yellow.
PRESERVATION: The lower part of the figure is broken off at the base of the neck. The nose is chipped.
TECHNICAL DESCRIPTION: —
DATE: A.D. 150–170.
REFERENCES: Ingholt Archives, PS 691; Legrain 1927, 349 cat. 9 fig. 9; Colledge 1976, 261; Romano 2006, 286 cat. 133; Krag 2018, 99 n. 36; 263 cat. 359; <https://www.penn.museum/collections/object/293902> (06.05.2022).

OBJECT DESCRIPTION
The object depicts the head of a female figure.

Cat. 630

PORTRAIT

She wears three headdresses: a headband, a turban, and a veil. The headband is placed low on the forehead and is divided into three rectangular panels separated by four vertical, incised lines. The turban is coiled. It is composed of a single layer and the coiling of the fabric is indicated by curving, incised lines. The veil is heavy, and the edge is scalloped. Part of the hair is covered by the headdress: several strands of hair at the ears are pushed back over the headband and disappear under the veil. The individual strands of hair are indicated by incised lines. Her face is oval. The eyebrows are curving and depicted by incised lines starting at the root of the nose. The eyes are almond-shaped, with thick upper eyelids. The end of the upper eyelids extends beyond that of the lower edge of the eye. The irises are indicated by incised circles and the pupils by punch holes. The ears are not visible under the hair and she wears dumbbell-shaped earrings (Colledge classification: H). The nose is wide. The alae are incised, and the nostrils are carved. The mouth is small, with full lips. The chin is square. The neck is long.

631. FEMALE HEAD

DATABASE NUMBER: PM306.
LOCATION: Palmyra, Palmyra Museum, inv. no. CD 88.
CONTEXT: Secondary context: Found (17.05.1960) in a later wall of the northern part of the Tetrapylon in the Camp of Diocletian.
ACQUISITION HISTORY: —
MEASUREMENTS: Height: 25 cm. Width: 20 cm. Depth: 18 cm.
MATERIAL: Limestone.
PRESERVATION: The lower part of the figure is broken off at the base of the neck. The sides of the veil, the eyes, the nose, the mouth, and the chin are chipped.
TECHNICAL DESCRIPTION: —
DATE: A.D. 150–170.
REFERENCES: Michalowski 1962, 176 cat. 46 fig. 193; Krag 2018, 292 cat. 466.

OBJECT DESCRIPTION

The object depicts the head of a female figure.

PORTRAIT

She wears three headdresses: a headband, a turban, and a veil. The headband is divided into three panels separated by beaded bands. The central panel is decorated with a vegetal motif; the two panels on either side are decorated with four-petal rosettes.

Cat. 631

The turban is coiled. It is composed of three layers; the upper two are looped into each other creating a knot in the middle. Curving grooves indicate the coiling of the fabric. The veil is heavy, and an edge of the veil is scalloped. Part of the hair is covered by the headdress: several strands of hair above the ears are pushed back over the headband and corners of the turban and disappear under the veil. The individual locks of hair are indicated by incised lines. Her face is oval. The eyebrows are curving and depicted by incised lines starting at the root of the nose. The eyes are almond-shaped, with thick eyelids. The end of the upper eyelids extends beyond that of the lower ones. The irises are indicated by incised circles and the pupils by punch holes. Below the right ear, a single round element is rendered, possibly earrings with a single ball (Colledge classification: J). The nose is wide. The mouth is small, with full lips. The chin is oval and prominent. The neck is wide.

A.D. 150–200

632. FEMALE HEAD

DATABASE NUMBER: HJM001.
LOCATION: New York, Herbert F. Johnson Museum of Art, Cornell University, inv. no. 72.021.
CONTEXT: —
ACQUISITION HISTORY: —
MEASUREMENTS: 29.85 cm.
MATERIAL: Limestone.
PRESERVATION: Only the head of the figure is preserved. The edges of the veil are broken off.
TECHNICAL DESCRIPTION: There are rasp marks on the face, flat chisel marks on the face and neck, and drill marks at the nostrils and the pendants on both sides of the head and the earrings.
DATE: A.D. 150–200.
REFERENCES: Kuniholm et al. 2010, 43 fig. 14; Krag 2018, 290 cat. 455; <https://emuseum.cornell.edu/view/objects/asitem/items$0040:8954> (06.05.2022).

OBJECT DESCRIPTION
The object depicts a female.

PORTRAIT
The figure is shown frontally. Her head is turned slightly to her left.

She wears three headdresses: a headband, a turban, and a veil. The headband is placed low on the forehead and is divided into decorated panels separated by vertical, beaded bands. The central panel is rectangular and has a vegetal motif. The outer panels are square and have a cruciform, four-petal flower inside a diamond, while the space between the sides of the diamond and the rectangle have dots. The turban is coiled. It is rendered in three layers: the lower is twisting, with oblique grooves indicating the coiling of the fabric. The upper two

Cat. 632, Pl. 95

have the ends looped into each other creating a knot in the middle. Curving and oblique grooves indicate the coiling of the fabric. The veil is heavy. It falls over the back of her head. She also wears head ornaments: two pendants placed on the edges of the turban: they are composed of a round bead, a diamond-shaped bead, and a thin bar, from which a round bead is suspended. Part of the hair is covered by the headdress: several strands of hair above the ears are brushed back over the headband and the edge of the turban and disappear under the veil. The individual strands of hair are indicated by incised lines. Her face is oval. The eyebrows are curving, rendered by incised lines, and starting from the root of the nose. The eyes are almond-shaped, with thick upper eyelids. The upper eyelids extend beyond the end of the lower ones. The irises are indicated by incised circles and the pupils by a semicircular incised line. Only the earlobes are visible under the hair. She wears earrings, depicted as horizontal bars decorated with two upper volutes, and two bars with a bead attached descending from the volutes (Colledge classification: F). The nose is straight. The alae are incised, and the nostrils are drilled. The philtrum is carved. The mouth is small, with thin, parted lips. There is a small depression under the centre of the lower lip. The chin is pointed, and she has a double chin. The neck is short and wide with three curving grooves. She wears a string of small, round beads around the base of the neck.

633. FEMALE HEAD

DATABASE NUMBER: PM441.
LOCATION: Palmyra, Palmyra Museum, inv. no. B 2790/9279.
CONTEXT: Secondary context: Found near the north rampart of Palmyra.
ACQUISITION HISTORY: —
MEASUREMENTS: Height: 27 cm. Width: 23 cm.
MATERIAL: Limestone, yellow.
PRESERVATION: The lower part of the figure is broken off at the base of the neck. The right side of the veil is broken off. The left eyebrow, the nose, and the chin are chipped.
TECHNICAL DESCRIPTION: —
DATE: A.D. 150–200.
REFERENCES: Charles-Gaffiot et al. 2001, 336 cat. 98; Equini Schneider 2002, 31, no. 18; Krag 2018, 48 n. 217; 73 n. 47 n. 51; 74 n. 57; 300 f. cat. 500.

OBJECT DESCRIPTION
The fragment depicts the head of a female figure.

PORTRAIT
The figure is shown frontally.

She wears one headdress: a veil. The veil is heavy and falls behind the back of her head. The lower part of the hair is centrally parted and brushed back at either side of the forehead. The remaining hair is combed to the top of the head and arranged in plaits that are gathered in a twisted bun, held in place with a ribbon, the so-called Faustina hairstyle. A small diamond-shaped lock of hair falls on the middle of the forehead. The individual strands of hair are indicated by incised, curving lines. Her face is square. The eyebrows are indicated by thin, arched grooves. The eyes are close-set, almond-shaped, and slanting. The upper eyelids extend beyond the end of the lower ones. The irises are indicated by incised circles and the pupils by punch holes. The ears are protruding with the helix and scapha carved. She wears two pairs of dumbbell-shaped earrings (Colledge classification: H), one at the upper part of the ears, and one at the lobes. The nose is straight with a wide base. Nasolabial lines are indicated by the carving of the planes of the face. The philtrum is carved. The mouth is small, with a thin upper lip and a full lower lip. A deep groove between the lips gives the impression of a slightly parted mouth, and the ends of the groove descend from either corner of the mouth. The neck is long and slender with two curving grooves.

634. FEMALE HEAD

DATABASE NUMBER: SHM010.
LOCATION: St Petersburg, State Hermitage Museum, inv. no. ДВ-8848.
CONTEXT: —
ACQUISITION HISTORY: Transferred from the Museum of Anthropology and Ethnography of the Academy of Sciences to the museum in 1927.
MEASUREMENTS: Height: 23 cm. Width: 20 cm. Depth: 18 cm.
MATERIAL: Limestone, white/yellow.
PRESERVATION: The lower part of the figure is broken off at the base of the neck. The edges of the veil are broken off. The turban, the eyebrows, the right eye, the nose, and the chin are chipped.
TECHNICAL DESCRIPTION: —
DATE: A.D. 150–200.
REFERENCES: Ingholt Archives, PS 692; Abamelek-Lazarev 1897, pl. 17; Charles-Gaffiot et al. 2001, 338 cat. 124; Krag 2018, 270 cat. 386.

OBJECT DESCRIPTION
The fragment depicts the head of a female figure.

PORTRAIT
The figure is shown frontally.

She wears three headdresses: a headband, a turban, and a veil. The headband is divided into decorated panels separated by vertical, beaded bands. The central panel has a motif of serrated leaves, possibly acanthus leaves. The outer panels have a cruciform flower with serrated petals. The turban is coiled. It is composed of three coiling bands, the folds indicated by oblique grooves. The veil is heavy. It falls behind her head.

Cat. 634

Part of the hair is covered by the headdress: several strands of hair above the ears are brushed back over the headband and the edge of the turban and disappear under the veil. The individual strands of hair are indicated by incised lines. Her face is oval. The eyebrows are indicated by thin, curving ridges. The eyes are large, almond-shaped, with thick eyelids. The upper eyelids extend beyond the end of the lower ones. The irises are indicated by concentric, incised circles and the pupils by punch holes. Only the earlobes are visible under the hair. She wears large circular earrings (Colledge classification: B). The nose is thin and straight. The alae are carved. The mouth is small, with thin upper and full lower lip. The chin is pointed. The neck is slender.

A.D. 175–225

635. FEMALE HEAD

DATABASE NUMBER: Burrell001.
LOCATION: Glasgow, the Burrell Collection, inv. no. 19.57.
CONTEXT: —
ACQUISITION HISTORY: Donated by Sir William and Lady Burrell to the City of Glasgow in 1944.
MEASUREMENTS: Height: 25.6 cm. Width: 23 cm. Depth: 19.4 cm.
MATERIAL: Limestone.
PRESERVATION: The background is broken off. The lower part of the figure is broken off at the neck. The left edge of the veil is broken off. The left eyebrow is chipped. The tip of the nose, part of the left cheek, and the chin are broken off.
TECHNICAL DESCRIPTION: The volutes and the area between the hanging elements of the earrings have been drilled.
DATE: A.D. 175–225.
REFERENCES: Ingholt Archives, PS 688; Hôtel des Ventes de Neuilly-sur-Seine 1931, 44 cat. 654; Krag 2018, 289 cat. 454; <http://collections.glasgowmuseums.com/mwebcgi/mweb?request=record;id=34871;type=101> (06.05.2022).

OBJECT DESCRIPTION
The object depicts a female head.

PORTRAIT
The figure is shown frontally.

She wears three headdresses: a headband, a turban, and a veil. The headband is placed low on the forehead and is divided into square, decorated panels separated by vertical, beaded bands. The central panel has a flower with eight petals and four serrated leaves. The following panels have a small branch with serrated leaves, and the outer panels have a geometric crisscross design. The turban is divided into three layers. The lower is a coiling band, and the upper two are coiled and looped into each other creating a knot in the middle. Curving grooves indicate the coiling of the fabric. The veil is heavy. It falls over the back of the head. Part of the hair is covered

Cat. 635

by the headdress: several strands of hair above the ears are brushed back over the headband and the edge of the turban and disappear under the veil. Her face is diamond-shaped. The eyebrows are indicated by curving grooves that start from the root of the nose. The eyes are large, almond-shaped, with thick upper eyelids. The upper eyelids extend beyond the end of the lower ones. The irises are indicated by incised circles and the pupils by punch holes. Only the earlobes are visible under the hair. She wears earrings, depicted as horizontal bars decorated with two upper volutes, and two strands with a bead attached descending from the volutes (Colledge classification: F). The nose is straight. The nostrils are drilled. The mouth is small, with thin lips. The chin is round. The neck is wide with two curving grooves.

A.D. 180–200

636. FEMALE HEAD

DATABASE NUMBER: PM214.
LOCATION: Palmyra, Palmyra Museum, inv. no. CD 25/66.
CONTEXT: Secondary context: Found in a later wall in the Temple of the Standards (Temple des Enseignes), Camp of Diocletian.
ACQUISITION HISTORY: —
MEASUREMENTS: Height: 26 cm. Width: 23 cm. Depth: 19 cm.
MATERIAL: Limestone.

Cat. 636

incised lines. Her face is oval. The eyebrows are slightly curving and are rendered by narrow ridges starting at the root of the nose. The eyes are almond-shaped, with thick eyelids. The end of the upper eyelids extends beyond the outer corner of the eyes. The irises are indicated by incised circles and the pupils by punch holes. She wears earrings composed of two beads (Colledge classification: L). The nose is narrow. The mouth is small, with full lips. The chin is oval. The neck is short.

A.D. 200–220

637. FEMALE HEAD

DATABASE NUMBER: NCG107.
LOCATION: Copenhagen, Ny Carlsberg Glyptotek, inv. no. IN 1132.
CONTEXT: —
ACQUISITION HISTORY: Løytved in Syria.
MEASUREMENTS: Height: 22 cm. Width: 16 cm. Depth: 12 cm.
MATERIAL: Limestone, yellow.
PRESERVATION: The lower part of the figure is broken off at the base of the neck. The lower part of the veil is broken off. The edge of the veil is chipped.

PRESERVATION: The lower part of the figure is broken off at the middle of the neck. The veil is chipped. The nose and mouth are chipped.
TECHNICAL DESCRIPTION: —
DATE: A.D. 180–200.
REFERENCES: Gawlikowski 1984, 102 cat. 36 pl. 81, 171; Krag 2018, 326 cat. 598.

OBJECT DESCRIPTION
The fragment depicts the head of a female figure.

PORTRAIT
The figure is shown frontally.
  She wears three headdresses: a headband, a turban, and a veil. The headband is placed low on the forehead, and is divided into panels separated by beaded bands. The panels are decorated with vegetal motifs (details unclear). She also wears a head-chain: it is fastened under the headband and runs to either side of the head and disappears under the veil. The chain is composed of large, circular bezels joined by beaded elements. The turban is coiled. It is divided into three layers and the two upper layers are looped into each other, creating a knot in the middle. The coiling of the turban is depicted with oblique and horizontal grooves. The veil is heavy with a scalloped edge. Only part of the hair is visible under the headdress: several locks of hair above the ears are brushed back over the headband and edge of the turban and disappear under the veil. The individual strands of hair are indicated by

Cat. 637

TECHNICAL DESCRIPTION: The head is roughly cut on the back and there are many cracks in the stone. Rasp marks are visible on the face and the eyes. The lower parts of the eyes are not carved.
DATE: A.D. 200–220 (Hvidberg-Hansen – Ploug 1993: A.D. 210–230).
REFERENCES: Simonsen 1889, 52 cat. G 43 pl. 16; Hvidberg-Hansen – Ploug 1993, 151 cat. 116; Ploug 1995, 246 cat. 116; Krag 2018, 344 cat. 667; Raja 2019a, 292 f. cat. 103.

OBJECT DESCRIPTION
The fragment depicts the head of a female figure.

PORTRAIT
The figure is shown frontally.

She wears three headdresses: a headband, a turban, and a veil. The headband is divided into three square, plain panels, separated by narrow bands. Along the lower border runs a narrow, plain band. The turban is coiled. It is divided into two layers and the ends are looped into each other creating a knot in the middle. Curving grooves indicate the coiling of the fabric. The veil is heavy. Part of the hair is covered by the headdress: several strands of hair above the ears are pushed back over the headband and corners of the turban and disappear under the veil. Her face is oval. The eyebrows are curving. The eyes are almond-shaped, with the upper eyelids indicated by a curving groove. The eyeballs are blank. She wears earrings composed of three juxtaposed round beads (Colledge classification: K). The nose is wide and straight, and the alae are incised. The mouth is small, with full lips. The chin is pointed. The neck is slender.

A.D. 200–273

638. FEMALE HEAD

DATABASE NUMBER: MLP070.
LOCATION: Paris, Musée du Louvre, inv. no. AO 6212.
CONTEXT: —
ACQUISITION HISTORY: Acquired in 1912 by Ms Hanin.
MEASUREMENTS: Height: 27 cm. Width: 17 cm. Depth: 24 cm.
MATERIAL: Limestone, white/yellow.
PRESERVATION: The figure is broken off below the neck. The edges of the veil are broken off. The upper part of the head, the right eyebrow, the tip of the nose, and the chin are chipped. Several cracks run through the face.
TECHNICAL DESCRIPTION: There are drill holes along the edge of the veil. There are flat chisel marks on the face and veil, and on the neck.
DATE: A.D. 200–273.
REFERENCES: Colledge 1976, 264; Dentzer-Feydy – Teixidor 1993, 218 cat. 214; Krag 2018, 108 n. 125. 127; 343 cat. 662.

OBJECT DESCRIPTION
The object depicts a female figure.

PORTRAIT
The figure is shown in a slight three-quarter view, with the head turned upwards and to her left.

She wears three headdresses: a headband, a turban, and a veil. The headband is decorated with a crisscross pattern and has a lower, beaded border. The turban is coiled with curving grooves indicating the coiling of the fabric. Over the turban she wears a heavy veil with a scalloped edge that falls down the back of the head. She also wears head ornaments: a central head ornament and a head-chain. The central head ornament is fastened under the centre of the veil and runs to the forehead. It is composed of two rectangular bezels with a beaded border linked by beaded elements. Four narrow, rectangular elements with round ends (perhaps indicating chains with beads) are suspended from the lower rectangular bezel. The head-chain is fastened under the upper head ornament and runs to either side of the face. It is composed of round elements with incised borders, linked by small, beaded elements. The hair is visible at the sides of the forehead; it is slightly wavy and combed back over the side of the headband and turban and disappears under the veil. The individual strands of hair are indicated by s-shaped, incised lines. Her face is square. The eyebrows are

Cat. 638

rendered by thin, curving, incised lines that start from the root of the nose. The eyes are large, almond-shaped, and slanting with thick upper eyelids. The end of the upper eyelids extends downwards and beyond that of the lower eyelids. The eyeballs are blank. The earlobes are visible, and she wears earrings composed of three juxtaposed beads: a round bead on either side of a biconical one (Colledge classification: K). The nose is long with a wide base. The alae are carved. The mouth is small, with full lips. The chin is pointed. The neck is long and slender with two curving grooves.

639. FEMALE HEAD

DATABASE NUMBER: APM001.
LOCATION: Amsterdam, Allard Pierson Museum, inv. no. 8176.
CONTEXT: —
ACQUISITION HISTORY: Acquired from the art dealer Van Lier in Amsterdam.
MEASUREMENTS: Height: 21.1 cm. Width: 18.2 cm. Depth: 19.1 cm. Height of head: 16 cm.
MATERIAL: Limestone, grey.
PRESERVATION: The lower part of the figure is broken off at the middle of the neck. The nose is broken off. The hair on the left side of the face is chipped.
TECHNICAL DESCRIPTION: —
DATE: A.D. 200–273.
REFERENCES: Moormann 2000, 112 f. cat. 136 pl. 60, a. b.

OBJECT DESCRIPTION
The object depicts a female head.

PORTRAIT
The figure is shown frontally.
She has wavy hair that is centrally parted. The hair is combed back and covers most of the ears. Two triangular locks of hair are depicted along each temple. The individual strands of hair are rendered by curving grooves. She wears dumbbell-shaped jewellery in the hair, above and to the side of each ear. Her face is square and fleshy. The eyebrows are curving, indicated by thin, incised lines starting from the root of the nose. The eyes are small, almond-shaped, and slanting with thick upper eyelids. The end of the upper eyelids extends downwards and beyond that of the lower eyelids. The irises, that touch the upper eyelids, are indicated by incised circles. The earlobes are visible, and she wears earrings in the shape of three juxtaposed round beads (Colledge classification: K). The nose has a wide base. The mouth is small, with full lips. The chin is pointed with a cleft. The neck is short and wide with two curving grooves.

640. FEMALE HEAD

DATABASE NUMBER: PM034.
LOCATION: Palmyra, Palmyra Museum, inv. no. CD 71.
CONTEXT: Secondary context: Found (29.04.1961) behind the Great Gate at the north side of the Camp of Diocletian.
ACQUISITION HISTORY: —
MEASUREMENTS: Height: 27 cm. Width: 15 cm. Depth: 14 cm.
MATERIAL: Limestone, white.
PRESERVATION: The lower part of the figure is broken off at the middle of the clavicle.
TECHNICAL DESCRIPTION: The head is partly carved. The eyes, the ears, the nose, and the lower part of face are not carved.
DATE: A.D. 200–273.
REFERENCES: Michalowski 1963, 168 f. cat. 63 fig. 221; Krag 2018, 73 n. 47; 310 cat. 533.

OBJECT DESCRIPTION
The fragment depicts the head of a female figure.

PORTRAIT
The figure is shown frontally.
The hair is parted in the centre of the forehead and brushed to either side. Above the ears, several locks of hair are brushed back. Her face is oval. There is a slightly curving groove on the forehead. The nose is wide. The neck is wide.

641. FEMALE HEAD

DATABASE NUMBER: PM043.
LOCATION: Palmyra, Palmyra Museum, inv. no. CD 20.
CONTEXT: Secondary context: Found (15.05.1959) in rubble at the Via Praetoria in the Camp of Diocletian.
ACQUISITION HISTORY: —
MEASUREMENTS: Height: 24.5 cm. Width: 20 cm. Depth: 13 cm.
MATERIAL: Limestone.
PRESERVATION: The lower part of the figure is broken off at the base of the neck. The crown of the head and the entire face are chipped.
TECHNICAL DESCRIPTION: —
DATE: A.D. 200–273.
REFERENCES: Michalowski 1960, 91 f. cat. 9 fig. 98; Krag 2018, 73 n. 47; 310 cat. 534.

OBJECT DESCRIPTION
The fragment depicts the head of a female figure.

PORTRAIT
The figure is shown frontally.
The hair is parted in the centre of the forehead and brushed to either side. At the sides of the head, the hair is brushed to the back in large locks. The individual strands of hair are rendered by incised lines. The neck is wide.

642. FEMALE HEAD

DATABASE NUMBER: JAM003.
LOCATION: Omaha, Joslyn Art Museum, inv. no. 1952.32.
CONTEXT: —
ACQUISITION HISTORY: Acquired by the museum from the collection of Giuseppe De Ciccio, in Naples, Italy, 21st February 1952.
MEASUREMENTS: Height: 23.495 cm.
MATERIAL: Limestone.
PRESERVATION: The head is broken off at the middle of the neck. The nose and the right eyebrow are chipped.
TECHNICAL DESCRIPTION: —
DATE: A.D. 200–273.
REFERENCES: Finlayson 1998, pl. 85.

OBJECT DESCRIPTION
The object depicts a female.

PORTRAIT
The figure is shown frontally.
She wears three headdresses: a headband, a turban, and a veil. The headband is placed high on the forehead and is divided into a central rectangular panel and flanked by two horizontal rows of squares. The central panel is decorated with two flowers enclosed by a beaded band running along the edge of the panel. The flowers have eight serrated petals each. The turban is coiled. Curving grooves indicate the coiling of the fabric. The veil is heavy with a scalloped edge (details unclear). She also wears head ornaments: a head-chain. Under the headband, she wears a headdress chain that is attached at either end of the central panel and runs to the sides disappearing under the veil. It is composed of circular bezels joined by elements composed of a bead on either side of a link. Part of the hair is covered by the headdress: several strands of hair above the ears are brushed back over the headband and the edge of the turban and disappear under the veil. The individual strands of hair are indicated by incised lines. Her face is long. The eyes are almond-shaped, with thick upper eyelids. The upper eyelids extend beyond the end of the lower ones. The eyes appear to be blank (details unclear). Only the earlobes are visible under the hair. She wears earrings composed of a large triangular bead and a small, round bead (Colledge classification: L). The nose is long. The mouth is small, with full lips. The chin is pointed.

643. FRAGMENT OF A FEMALE HEAD

DATABASE NUMBER: PM686.
LOCATION: Palmyra, Palmyra Museum, inv. no. CD 83.
CONTEXT: Secondary context: Found (16.05.1960) in rubble near the Praetorian Gate, in the Camp of Diocletian.
ACQUISITION HISTORY: —
MEASUREMENTS: Height: 21 cm. Width: 16 cm. Depth: 9 cm.
MATERIAL: Limestone.
PRESERVATION: The lower part of the figure is broken off at the neck. The crown of the head and most of the face are broken off. The surface is heavily weathered and chipped.
TECHNICAL DESCRIPTION: —
DATE: A.D. 200–273.
REFERENCES: Michalowski 1962, 182 cat. 52 fig. 199; Krag 2018, 73 n. 47; 309 f. cat. 531.

OBJECT DESCRIPTION
The object depicts the head of a female figure.

PORTRAIT
Individual strands of hair are rendered by incised lines, brushed to the back of her head (details unclear). The face is chipped off.

A.D. 210–230

644. FEMALE HEAD

DATABASE NUMBER: NCG059.
LOCATION: Copenhagen, Ny Carlsberg Glyptotek, inv. no. IN 1102.
CONTEXT: —
ACQUISITION HISTORY: Acquired by Løytved in Syria.
MEASUREMENTS: Height: 30.5 cm. Width: 27.5 cm. Depth: 23 cm.

Cat. 644

MATERIAL: Limestone, white/grey.
PRESERVATION: Broken off below the base of the neck. The edges of the veil, the tip of the nose, and the chin are chipped. There are several cracks across the face.
TECHNICAL DESCRIPTION: The head is roughly cut on the back. There are flat chisel marks and rasp marks on the face and rasp marks on the neck and inside of the veil. The lower eyes and eyelids are not carved.
DATE: A.D. 210–230.
REFERENCES: Ingholt Archives, PS 501; Simonsen 1889, 48 cat. G.13 pl. 13; Ingholt 1928, 142 n. 4; 150 PS 501; Ingholt 1934, 35 n. 37; Mackay 1949, 171. 179 n. 1; pl. 60.3; el-Chehadeh 1972, 90 n. 88; Colledge 1976, 62. 72. 124. 138. 141. 144. 150 f. 240 f. 264. pl. 90; Sadurska 1977, 149 n. 78; Gawlikowski 1984, 95 cat. 1; Equini Schneider 1993, 135 f. fig. 36; Hvidberg-Hansen – Ploug 1993, 150 cat. 114; Ploug 1995, 244 f. cat. 114; Koustrup Høj 2017a, 35 fig. 4; Koustrup Høj 2017b, 35 fig. 4; Krag 2018, 106 n. 101; 108 n. 125. 127; 343 cat. 664; Raja 2019a, 286 f. cat. 100.

OBJECT DESCRIPTION
The object depicts a female figure.

PORTRAIT
The head is turned slightly to the left.

She wears two headdresses: a headcloth and a veil. The headcloth is placed low on the forehead. It is divided into two zones: one over the forehead, and one over the rest of the head. The lower zone is decorated with squares with possibly floral decoration between beaded bands. The upper zone is decorated with lozenges created by beaded bands. Each lozenge contains a six-petal rosette, while serrated leaves are placed on either side of the lozenges. Over the headcloth she wears a heavy veil with a scalloped edge that falls down the back of the head. She also wears head ornaments: a central head ornament and a head-chain. The central head ornament is fastened under the centre of the veil and runs to the forehead. It is composed of an upper oval bezel with a beaded border and a square bezel with a beaded border underneath. The two bezels are linked by beaded elements. Three narrow, rectangular beads with round ends are suspended from the square bezel. The head-chain is fastened under the central head ornament and runs to either side of the face. It is composed of round elements with incised borders, linked by small, beaded elements. The hair is visible at the sides of the forehead; it is slightly wavy and combed back over the sides of the headcloth. The individual strands of hair are indicated by s-shaped, incised lines. Her face is oval. The eyebrows are rendered by thin, curving ridges that start from the root of the nose. The eyes are almond-shaped, with thin upper eyelids. The end of the upper eyelids extends beyond that of the lower eyelids. The eyeballs are blank. The earlobes are visible, and she wears dumbbell-shaped earrings (Colledge classification: H). The nose is long and wide. The alae are indicated by incised lines. The mouth is small, with full lips. The chin is small and round with a cleft. She has a double chin. The neck is short and slender with two curving grooves.

A.D. 220–240

645. FEMALE HEAD

DATABASE NUMBER: PM309.
LOCATION: Palmyra, Palmyra Museum, inv. no. CD 116.
CONTEXT: Secondary context: Found (22.05.1960) on the north-western side of the Tetrapylon in the Camp of Diocletian.
ACQUISITION HISTORY: —
MEASUREMENTS: Height: 22 cm. Width: 17 cm. Depth: 18 cm.
MATERIAL: Limestone.
PRESERVATION: The lower part of the figure is broken off at the base of the neck. The nose and chin are chipped.
TECHNICAL DESCRIPTION: There are several drill holes between the veil and the turban and hair, as well as between the earrings and the face.
DATE: A.D. 220–240.
REFERENCES: Michalowski 1962, 175 f. cat. 45 fig. 192; Gawlikowski 1987, 289 cat. 5; Bäärnhielm 1988, 24 fig. 10; Krag 2018, 292 cat. 465; <https://collections.smvk.se/carlotta-mhm/web/object/3909086> (06.07.2022).

OBJECT DESCRIPTION
The fragment depicts the head of a female figure.

Cat. 645

PORTRAIT

She wears two headdresses: a turban and a veil. The turban is coiled and composed of a single layer. Curving grooves indicate the coiling of the fabric. The veil is heavy and the edge is scalloped. The hair is parted in the centre of the forehead and is brushed to the sides in a waving manner. At the sides, the hair is brushed back under the veil. A single s-shaped lock is rendered at the parting of the hair. The individual locks of hair are indicated by incised lines. Her face is round. The eyebrows are curving and depicted by incised lines starting at the root of the nose. The eyes are almond-shaped, with thick eyelids. The end of the upper eyelids extends beyond that of the lower ones. The irises are indicated by incised circles and the pupils by punch holes. She wears earrings composed of two round beads on either side of a biconical bead (Colledge classification: L). The cheeks are fleshy. The nose is short and wide. The alae are incised, and the nostrils are drilled. The mouth is straight with full lips. The neck has two curving grooves, and the flesh between them is bulging out.

646. FEMALE HEAD

DATABASE NUMBER: PM246.
LOCATION: Palmyra, Palmyra Museum, inv. no. CD 74.
CONTEXT: Secondary context: Found in the foundations of the wall of the Great Gate in the Camp of Diocletian.
ACQUISITION HISTORY: —
MEASUREMENTS: Height: 22 cm. Width: 16 cm. Depth: 23 cm.
PRESERVATION: The lower part of the figure is broken off at the base of the neck. The left side of the forehead, the left eye, and the right side of the nose are chipped. Cracks run across the face.
TECHNICAL DESCRIPTION: —
DATE: A.D. 220–240.
REFERENCES: Michalowski 1964, 91. 97 f. cat. 28 figs. 124. 129; Krag 2018, 73 n. 47; 310 cat. 536.

OBJECT DESCRIPTION

The object depicts a female head.
The object was found together with the objects cat. 530, cat. 531, cat. 584, cat. 585, cat. 586, cat. 612, cat. 613, cat. 614, cat. 615. According to Michalowski (1964, 91) they come from the same sarcophagus.

PORTRAIT

The figure is shown frontally.
Her face is oval. The hair is parted at the centre of her forehead, rendered in three rows, and covers the upper part of her ears. The individual strands of hair are rendered by incised lines. A crescent-shaped lock of hair is rendered in the middle of the forehead extending downwards. The eyebrows are curving, rendered by incised lines starting from the root of the nose. The eyes are close-set and almond-shaped, with thick upper eyelids. The upper eyelids extend beyond the end of the lower ones. The irises are indicated by incised circles. Only the earlobes are visible under the hair. She wears earrings with three juxtaposed round beads (Colledge classification: K). The cheeks are fleshy. The mouth is small, with a full upper lip. The chin is round with a small, round depression in the middle. The neck is wide.

647. FEMALE HEAD

DATABASE NUMBER: PM243.
LOCATION: Palmyra, Palmyra Museum, inv. no. CD 71.
CONTEXT: Secondary context: Found in the foundations of the wall of the Great Gate in the Camp of Diocletian.
ACQUISITION HISTORY: —
MEASUREMENTS: Height: 24 cm. Width: 20 cm. Depth: 24 cm.
MATERIAL: Limestone, white.
PRESERVATION: The lower part of the figure is broken off at the base of the neck. The surface around the centre of the top of the head, the forehead, and the left eye is broken off. The tip of the nose has broken off. The left side of the neck is chipped.
TECHNICAL DESCRIPTION: —
DATE: A.D. 220–240.
REFERENCES: Michalowski 1964, 91 f. 97 f. cat. 25 figs. 124. 126; Krag 2018, 73 n. 47; 310 cat. 538.

OBJECT DESCRIPTION

The object depicts a female head.
The object was found together with the objects cat. 530, cat. 531, cat. 584, cat. 585, cat. 586, cat. 611, cat. 613, cat. 614, cat. 615. According to Michalowski (1964, 91) they come from the same sarcophagus.

PORTRAIT

The figure is shown frontally. The head is slightly tilted to the right.
Her face is oval. The hair is parted at the centre of her forehead, rendered in five rows, and covers the upper part of her ears. The individual strands of hair are rendered by incised lines. A narrow lock of hair is rendered at the temples on each side of the face. The eyebrows are curving, rendered by incised lines starting from the root of the nose. The eyes are close-set and almond-shaped, with thick upper eyelids. The right eye curves downwards. The end of the upper eyelids extends beyond that of the lower ones. The irises are indicated by incised circles and the pupils by punch holes. The irises touch the upper eyelids. Only the earlobes are visible under the hair. She wears earrings with three juxtaposed round beads (Colledge classification: K). The mouth is small, with a full lower lip. The chin is pointed with a cleft and the neck is slender.

648. FEMALE HEAD

DATABASE NUMBER: PM244.
LOCATION: Palmyra, Palmyra Museum, inv. no. B 2173/7657.
CONTEXT: Secondary context: Found in the foundations of the wall of the Great Gate in the Camp of Diocletian.
ACQUISITION HISTORY: —
MEASUREMENTS: Height: 25 cm. Width: 19 cm. Depth: 21.5 cm.
MATERIAL: Limestone, white.
PRESERVATION: The lower part of the figure is broken off at the base of the neck. The left side of the top of the head and the lower lip are chipped.
TECHNICAL DESCRIPTION: —
DATE: A.D. 220–240.
REFERENCES: Michalowski 1964, 91. 97 f. cat. 26 figs. 124. 127; Charles-Gaffiot et al. 2001, 312. 367 cat. 253; Equini Schneider 2002, 35 fig. 25; Krag 2018, 73 n. 47; 311 cat. 539.

OBJECT DESCRIPTION
The object depicts a female head.
The object was found together with the objects cat. 530, cat. 531, cat. 584, cat. 585, cat. 586, cat. 611, cat. 612, cat. 614, cat. 615. According to Michalowski (1964, 91) they come from the same sarcophagus.

PORTRAIT
The figure is shown frontally.
Her face is oval. The hair is parted at the centre of her forehead, rendered in four rows, and covers the upper part of her ears. The individual strands of hair are rendered by incised lines. A crescent-shaped lock of hair is rendered in the middle of the forehead extending downwards. The eyebrows are curving, rendered by incised lines starting from the root of the nose. The eyes are close-set and almond-shaped, with thick upper eyelids. The end of the upper eyelids extends beyond that of the lower ones. The irises are indicated by incised circles and the pupils by punch holes. The irises touch the upper eyelids. Only the earlobes are visible under the hair. She wears earrings with three juxtaposed beads: two round ones on either side of a biconical one (Colledge classification: L). The nose is straight and the nostrils large. The cheeks are fleshy. The mouth is small, with a full upper lip. The chin is round, and the neck is wide.

649. FEMALE HEAD

DATABASE NUMBER: PM241.
LOCATION: Palmyra, Palmyra Museum, inv. no. 2170/7654.
CONTEXT: Secondary context: Found in the foundations of the wall of the Great Gate in the Camp of Diocletian.
ACQUISITION HISTORY: —
MEASUREMENTS: Height: 30 cm. Width: 22 cm. Depth: 25 cm.
MATERIAL: Limestone, white.
PRESERVATION: The lower part of the figure is broken off at the base of the neck.
TECHNICAL DESCRIPTION: —
DATE: A.D. 220–240.
REFERENCES: Michalowski 1963, 85 fig. 7; Michalowski 1964, 90. 97 cat. 24 fig. 125; Tanabe 1986, 45 pl. 464; al-As'ad 1993, 306 f. cat. 246; Krag 2018, 73 n. 47; 311 cat. 543.

OBJECT DESCRIPTION
The object depicts a female head.
The object was found together with the objects cat. 530, cat. 531, cat. 584, cat. 585, cat. 586, cat. 611, cat. 612, cat. 613, cat. 615. According to Michalowski (1964, 91) they come from the same sarcophagus.

PORTRAIT
The figure is shown frontally.
Her face is oval. The hair is straight, parted at the centre of her forehead, and covers the upper part of her ears. The individual strands of hair are rendered by incised lines. A narrow lock of hair is rendered at the temples on either side of the face. The eyebrows are curving, rendered by incised lines starting from the root of the nose. The eyes are close-set, almond-shaped, and slanting, with thick upper eyelids. The end of the upper eyelids extends beyond that of the lower ones. The irises are indicated by incised circles and they touch the upper eyelids. Only the earlobes are visible under the hair and she wears earrings with three juxtaposed beads: two round ones on either side of a biconical one (Colledge classification: L). The cheeks are fleshy. The nose is straight. The alae are carved. The mouth is small, with full lips. The chin is square, and the neck is slender.

650. FEMALE HEAD

DATABASE NUMBER: PM242.
LOCATION: Palmyra, Palmyra Museum, inv. no. CD70.
CONTEXT: Secondary context: Found in the foundations of the wall of the Great Gate in the Camp of Diocletian.
ACQUISITION HISTORY: —
MEASUREMENTS: Height: 30 cm. Width: 21 cm. Depth: 25 cm.
MATERIAL: Limestone, white.
PRESERVATION: The lower part of the figure is broken off at the base of the neck. The surface of the nose and right eyebrow is chipped.
TECHNICAL DESCRIPTION: —
DATE: A.D. 220–240.
REFERENCES: Michalowski 1964, 91. 97 f. cat. 27 figs. 124. 128; Krag 2018, 73 n. 47; 311 cat. 541.

OBJECT DESCRIPTION
The object depicts a female head.
The object was found together with the objects cat. 530, cat. 531, cat. 584, cat. 585, cat. 586, cat. 611, cat. 612, cat. 613, cat. 614.

According to Michalowski (1964, 91) they come from the same sarcophagus.

PORTRAIT

The figure is shown frontally.

Her face is oval. The hair is parted at the centre of her forehead, rendered in three rows, and covers the upper part of her ears. The individual strands of hair are rendered by incised lines. A drop-shaped, twisted lock of hair is rendered in the middle of the forehead extending downwards. A narrow lock of hair is rendered at the temples on either side of the face. The eyebrows are curving, rendered by incised lines starting from the root of the nose. The eyes are close-set and almond-shaped, with thick upper eyelids. The end of the upper eyelids extends beyond that of the lower ones. The irises are indicated by incised circles and the pupils by punch holes. The irises touch the upper eyelids. Only the earlobes are visible under the hair and she wears earrings with three juxtaposed beads: two round ones on either side of a biconical one (Colledge classification: L). The cheeks are fleshy. The mouth is small, with a full lower lip. The chin is pointed, and the neck is slender.

651. FEMALE HEAD

DATABASE NUMBER: Boisgirard001.
LOCATION: Last known location: Boisgirard auction house.
CONTEXT: —
ACQUISITION HISTORY: It was acquired by Mr Josef Müller, the father of Monique Barbier-Mueller (wife of the late Mr Jean Paul Barbier-Mueller), before 1940. In the collection of the Barbier-Mueller Museum, until it was sold by the family in 2007.
MEASUREMENTS: Height: 27.5 cm. Width: 22.9.
MATERIAL: Limestone, yellow/grey.
PRESERVATION: Only the head and neck are preserved.
TECHNICAL DESCRIPTION: —
DATE: A.D. 220–240.
REFERENCES: Ingholt Archives, PS 706; Jucker 1967, 96 cat. 243 pl. 34; Kaspar 1969–1970, 299–304 figs. 15–17; Jucker and Willers 1983, 249 cat. 112; Zimmermann 1991, 118 f. cat. 47.

OBJECT DESCRIPTION

The object depicts a female head.

PORTRAIT

The figure is shown frontally.

She wears three headdresses: a headband, a turban, and a veil. The headband is placed high on the forehead and has a thin band underneath. It is divided into three decorated square panels separated by vertical, beaded bands. The central panel has three serrated leaves. The outer panels have flowers with four serrated petals. The turban is coiled. It is divided into three layers and the ends of the two upper layers are looped into each other creating a knot in the middle. The lower layer

Cat. 651

is rendered as a coiling band. Curving grooves indicate the coiling of the fabric. The veil is heavy with a scalloped edge. It falls over the back of the head. Part of the hair is covered by the headdress: several strands of hair above the ears are brushed back over the headband and the edge of the turban and disappear under the veil. The individual strands of hair are indicated by incised lines. Her face is oval. The eyebrows are curving, rendered by incised lines, and starting from the root of the nose. The eyes are close-set, almond-shaped, and slanting, with thick eyelids. The upper eyelids extend beyond the end of the lower ones. The irises are indicated by incised circles and the pupils by punch holes. Only the earlobes are visible under the hair. She wears earrings (details unclear). The nose is straight. The alae are incised, and the nostrils carved. The philtrum is carved. The mouth is small, with thin upper and full lower lip. The chin is pointed. The neck is slender.

652. FRAGMENT OF A FEMALE HEAD

DATABASE NUMBER: PM345.
LOCATION: Palmyra, Palmyra Museum, inv. no. B 1886.
CONTEXT: Secondary context: Found (01.10.1955) in the large court during the excavations of the Baalshamin sanctuary.
ACQUISITION HISTORY: —
MEASUREMENTS: Height: 29 cm. Width: 26 cm. Depth: 22 cm.

MATERIAL: Limestone.
PRESERVATION: The lower part of the figure is broken off at the top of the neck. The crown of the head and the face are broken off.
TECHNICAL DESCRIPTION: —
DATE: A.D. 220–240.
REFERENCES: Dunant – Stucky 2000, 116 cat. 141 pl. 30; Krag 2018, 284 cat. 434.

OBJECT DESCRIPTION
The object depicts the head of a female figure.

PORTRAIT
She wears three headdresses: a headband, a turban, and a veil. The headband is decorated with five rectangular panels separated by beaded bands. The central panel is decorated with a vegetal motif. The remaining panels on either side are decorated with a crisscross pattern. She also wears a head-chain over the headband: it is attached under the centre of the turban and runs to both sides disappearing under the veil. It is composed of circular bezels with an incised border, linked by beaded elements. The turban is coiled. It is composed of three layers and the two upper layers are looped into each other, creating a knot in the middle. Curving grooves on the two upper layers and oblique grooves on the lower layer indicate the coiling of the fabric. The veil is heavy and has a scalloped edge. Only part of the hair is visible under the headdress: locks of hair above the ears are brushed back over the headband and disappear under the veil. The individual strands of hair are indicated by incised lines. Traces of an earring are visible on the right earlobe.

A.D. 240–273

653. FEMALE HEAD

DATABASE NUMBER: VAM004.
LOCATION: Berlin, Vorderasiatisches Museum, inv. no. VA 3099.
CONTEXT: —
ACQUISITION HISTORY: Gift from Moritz Sobernheim, in 1901.
MEASUREMENTS: Height: 21 cm. Width: 16.5 cm. Depth: 19.5 cm. Height of head: 18.5 cm.
MATERIAL: Limestone, white/grey.
PRESERVATION: The lower part of the figure is broken off across the neck. A crack runs across the face and mouth. There is damage to the right.
TECHNICAL DESCRIPTION: The finish is quite smooth with light tool marks visible. The nostrils are drilled.
DATE: A.D. 240–273 (Wartke 1991: A.D. 200–250).
REFERENCES: Ingholt Archives, PS 504; Ingholt 1928, 150; Colledge 1976, 264; Wartke 1991, 79 cat. 8 fig. 9; Krag 2018, 106 n. 101; 108 n. 125. 127; 344 cat. 668; <https://arachne.uni-koeln.de/item/objekt/214759> (06.05.2022).

OBJECT DESCRIPTION
The fragment depicts the head of a female figure.

PORTRAIT
The figure is shown frontally. The head is turned slightly to the left.
She wears two headdresses: a headband and a veil. She also wears head ornaments. The headband is divided into two registers: the lower is decorated with rectangular panels separated by beaded bands. The upper is decorated with lozenges created by beaded bands. Each lozenge contains a six-petal rosette with serrated petals. Over the headband, she wears head ornaments: a chain composed of circular bezels with incised borders is attached to a central head ornament fastened under the veil, and runs to either side of the head, disappearing under the edges of the veil. The central head ornament extends downwards over the middle of the forehead. It is composed of a rectangular and an oval bezel, both with a beaded border, joined by a beaded element. Four thin, rectangular elements, probably indicating chains, ending in large, round beads are suspended from the lower edge of the oval bezel and fall over the centre of the forehead. Over the headband, she wears a heavy veil with a scalloped edge that falls down the back of the head. The hair is visible at the sides of the forehead; it is

Cat. 653

slightly wavy and combed backwards with individual strands of hair indicated by s-shaped grooves. It covers the sides of the lower register of the headband. Her face is square. The eyebrows are rendered by thin, curving grooves that start from the root of the nose. The eyes are almond-shaped, with thick upper eyelids. The end of the upper eyelids extends beyond that of the lower eyelids. The irises, that touch the upper eyelids, are indicated by incised circles. She wears earrings composed of three juxtaposed beads: two biconical ones on either side of a round one (Colledge classification: L). The nose is long with a wide base. The alae are indicated by incised lines. The nostrils are drilled. The mouth is small, with full lips. The chin is pointed. She has a double chin. The neck is long and slender with two curving grooves.

654. FEMALE HEAD

DATABASE NUMBER: PM440.
LOCATION: Palmyra, Palmyra Museum, inv. no. B 2770/9254.
CONTEXT: Secondary context: Found (1980) at the northern city wall.
ACQUISITION HISTORY: —
MEASUREMENTS: Height: 23 cm.
MATERIAL: Limestone, yellow.
PRESERVATION: The lower part of the figure is broken off at the base of the neck. The veil, the left eye, and the nose are chipped. Cracks run across the left side of the face and the neck.
TECHNICAL DESCRIPTION: There are traces of black pigment in the eyes and eyebrows.
DATE: A.D. 240–273 (Equini Schneider 2002: A.D. 200–273).
REFERENCES: Charles-Gaffiot et al. 2001, 329 cat. 66; Equini Schneider 2002, 32 cat. 20; Krag 2018, 17 n. 98; 351 cat. 699.

OBJECT DESCRIPTION
The fragment depicts the head of a female figure.

PORTRAIT
The figure is shown frontally.

She wears three headdresses: a headband, a turban, and a veil. The headband is placed high on the forehead. It is decorated with three panels separated by beaded bands. The central panel is decorated with a flower with four serrated petals. The veins of the petals are indicated by incised lines. The lateral panels are decorated with a crisscross pattern. Along the lower border runs a horizontal band. She also wears a head-chain over the headband: it is attached under the centre of the turban and runs to both sides disappearing under the veil. It is composed of circular bezels with an incised border joined by beaded elements. The turban is coiled. It is composed of a single layer and curving grooves indicate the coiling of the fabric. The veil is heavy. Only part of the hair is visible under the headdress: locks of hair above the ears are brushed back over the headband and disappear under the veil. The individual strands of hair are indicated by incised lines. Her face is oval. The eyebrows are curving and depicted by incised lines starting at the root of the nose. The eyes are almond-shaped, with thick upper eyelids. The irises are indicated by deep, circular depressions. She wears earrings composed of three juxtaposed beads: two round ones on either side of a biconical one (Colledge classification: L). The nose is narrow. The alae are incised, and the nostrils carved. The mouth is small, with full lips. The chin is pointed with a small round depression in the middle. The neck is long.

655. FEMALE HEAD

DATABASE NUMBER: NCG057.
LOCATION: Copenhagen, Ny Carlsberg Glyptotek, inv. no. IN 1104.
CONTEXT: —
ACQUISITION HISTORY: Løytved in Syria.
MEASUREMENTS: Height: 24 cm. Width: 21 cm. Depth: 24 cm.
MATERIAL: Limestone, white/grey.
PRESERVATION: The lower part of the figure is broken off at the base of the neck. The edges of the veil, the right eyebrow, nose, chin, and the head-chain and pendants on the right side of the head are chipped. There are several cracks across the face.
TECHNICAL DESCRIPTION: The head is roughly cut on the back. There are flat chisel marks on her veil and face and marks from rasps on her face and neck. Pick chisel marks are visible on the sides of the veil.
DATE: A.D. 240–273 (Hvidberg-Hansen – Ploug 1993: A.D. 230).
REFERENCES: Ingholt Archives, PS 507; Simonsen 1889, 48 cat. G 15 pl. 13; Ingholt 1928, 150; Colledge 1976, 264; el-Chehadeh 1972, 90 n. 90; Hvidberg-Hansen – Ploug 1993, 151 cat. 117; Ploug 1995, 247 cat. 117; Krag 2018, 106 n. 101; 108 n. 125; 352 cat. 712; Raja 2019a, 314 f. cat. 118.

OBJECT DESCRIPTION
The fragment depicts the head of a female figure.

PORTRAIT
The figure is shown frontally. The head is turned slightly to the left.

She wears two headdresses: a headband and a veil. The headdress is placed low on the forehead. It is divided into two registers. The lower register is decorated with a beaded band at the bottom, and squares with possibly floral decoration above. The upper register is decorated with lozenges created by beaded bands. Each lozenge contains a flower: there is a flower with five serrated petals and two six-petal rosettes on the right side of the headband, and a flower with four serrated petals and a four-petal rosette on the left side of the headband. Over the headband, she wears head jewellery: a central head ornament placed under the veil and over the middle of the head that extends downwards, and a head-chain. The central

Cat. 655

ornament is composed of a square and an oval bezel, both with beaded borders, linked by a beaded element. Three narrow, rectangular bars ending in round beads are suspended from the lower edge of the oval bezel. A chain composed of circular bezels with incised borders linked by beaded elements, runs from the central beaded element linking the two bezels of the central ornament, to either side of the head. Over the headband, she wears a heavy veil with a scalloped edge that falls down the back of the head. The hair is visible at the sides of the forehead; it is slightly wavy and combed backwards with the individual strands of hair indicated by s-shaped grooves. It covers the sides of the head cloth. Her face is oval and fleshy. The eyebrows are rendered by thin, arched ridges that start from the root of the nose. The eyes are large and almond-shaped, with thick upper eyelids. The end of the upper eyelids extends downwards and beyond that of the lower eyelids. The eyeballs are blank. The earlobes are visible, and she wears earrings composed of three juxtaposed beads: two large, round ones on either side of a biconical one (Colledge classification: H). The nose is long and wide. The alae are carved. The philtrum is carved. The mouth is small, with full lips. The chin is small and round with a cleft. She has a double chin. The neck is long and slender with two curving grooves.

656. FEMALE HEAD

DATABASE NUMBER: MGG003.
LOCATION: Grenoble, Museum of Grenoble, inv. no. 1580.
CONTEXT: —
ACQUISITION HISTORY: Gift from Léon de Beylié in 1907.
MEASUREMENTS: Height: 27 cm. Width: 20 cm. Depth: 18 cm.
MATERIAL: Limestone, yellow.
PRESERVATION: The lower part of the figure is broken off at the base of the neck. The veil, the lower part of the hair, the right eye, the nose, and the surface of the neck are chipped. There are cracks running across the face.
TECHNICAL DESCRIPTION: —
DATE: A.D. 240–273.
REFERENCES: Ingholt Archives, PS 698; Krag 2018, 17 n. 98; 351 cat. 701.

OBJECT DESCRIPTION
The fragment depicts the head of a female figure.

PORTRAIT
The figure is shown frontally.
She wears three headdresses: a headband, a turban, and a veil. The headband is located high on the forehead and is divided into three square panels, separated by beaded bands. The central panel is decorated with a four-petal flower, with the veins of the petals indicated by incised lines. The lateral

Cat. 656

panels are decorated with a crisscross pattern. She also wears a head-chain that is attached under the centre of the turban and runs to the sides disappearing under the veil. It is composed of circular bezels with an incised border joined by beaded elements. The turban is coiled. It is composed of three coiling bands; the upper two layers are looped into each other, creating a knot in the centre. The folds are indicated by curving grooves. The veil is heavy. Part of the hair is covered by the headdress: several strands of hair above the ears are pushed back over the headband and disappear under the veil. Her face is round. The eyebrows are curving and rendered by incised lines. The eyes are almond-shaped, with thick upper eyelids. The end of the upper eyelids extends beyond that of the lower ones. The irises are indicated by deep, circular depressions. She wears earrings composed of two juxtaposed round beads (Colledge classification: L). The nose is wide. The mouth is small, with a full lower lip. The chin is pointed. The neck has three curving grooves.

657. FEMALE HEAD

DATABASE NUMBER: PM312.
LOCATION: Palmyra, Palmyra Museum, inv. no. CD 120.
CONTEXT: Secondary context: Found (23.05.2018) in the north-western part of the Tetrapylon in the Camp of Diocletian.
ACQUISITION HISTORY: —
MEASUREMENTS: Height: 29 cm. Width: 22 cm. Depth: 24 cm.
MATERIAL: Limestone.
PRESERVATION: The lower part of the figure is broken off at the top of the neck. The edge of the veil, the left eye, the nose, the lower side of the face, and the chin are chipped.
TECHNICAL DESCRIPTION: —
DATE: A.D. 240–273.
REFERENCES: Michalowski 1962, 180 f. cat. 50 fig. 197; Krag 2018, 108 n. 125; 351 cat. 703.

OBJECT DESCRIPTION
The fragment depicts the head of a female figure.

PORTRAIT
She wears three headdresses: a headband, a turban, and a veil. The headband (details unclear) is placed high on the forehead. She wears a head-chain over the headband: it is attached under the centre of the turban and runs to both sides disappearing under the veil. It is composed of circular bezels joined by beaded elements. A head ornament is fastened under the veil, at the centre of the head, and extends downwards over the middle of the forehead. It is composed of an oval and a square bezel, both with a beaded border, joined by a beaded element. There are three round beads suspended from the lower edge of the square bezel. The turban is coiled. It is composed of a single layer and curving grooves indicate the coiling of the fabric. The veil is heavy, and the edge is scalloped. Only part

Cat. 657

of the hair is visible under the headdress: locks of hair above the ears are brushed back over the headband and disappear under the veil. A thick, wavy lock falls down onto her right shoulder. The individual strands of hair are indicated by incised lines. Her face is oval. The eyebrows are curving and depicted by incised lines starting at the root of the nose. The eyes are almond-shaped, with thick upper eyelids. The irises are indicated by incised circles and the pupils by punch holes. She wears dumbbell-shaped earrings (Colledge classification: H). The nose is narrow. The mouth is small, with a full lower lip.

658. FEMALE HEAD

DATABASE NUMBER: PM041.
LOCATION: Palmyra, Palmyra Museum, inv. no. CD 26.
CONTEXT: Secondary context: Found (17.05.1959) in the rubble in the middle of the Via Praetoria in the Camp of Diocletian.
ACQUISITION HISTORY: —
MEASUREMENTS: Height: 29 cm. Width: 23 cm.
MATERIAL: Limestone.
PRESERVATION: The lower part of the figure is broken off at the base of the neck. The veil, the eyes, the nose, the mouth, and the chin are chipped.

TECHNICAL DESCRIPTION: —
DATE: A.D. 240–273.
REFERENCES: Michalowski 1960, 88–90 cat. 7 fig. 96; Krag 2018, 351 cat. 705.

OBJECT DESCRIPTION
The fragment depicts the head of a female figure.

PORTRAIT
The figure is shown frontally.

She wears three headdresses: a headband, a turban, and a veil. The headband is placed low on the forehead and is wide. It is divided into three panels separated by vertical, beaded bands. The central panel is decorated with serrated leaves set on a stem with the midribs of the leaves indicated by incised lines. The two lateral panels are decorated with a crisscross pattern. There is a beaded band at the lower border of the headband. She also wears a head-chain: it is attached under the centre of the turban and runs to the sides disappearing under the hair. It is composed of circular bezels with an incised border joined by beaded elements. The turban is coiled. It is composed of three layers; the two upper layers are looped into each other, creating a knot in the middle. Horizontal grooves indicate the coiling of the turban. The veil is heavy, and the edge is scalloped. Part of the hair is covered by the headdress: several strands of hair above the ears are pushed back over the headband and head-chain and disappear under the veil. The individual strands of hair are indicated by incised lines. Her face is oval. The eyebrows are straight and rendered by narrow ridges starting at the root of the nose. The eyes are large and almond-shaped, with thick upper eyelids (details unclear). Round elements are depicted under the hair, possibly large circular earrings (Colledge classification: B). The lips are full. The chin is oval and fleshy. The neck is long and has three curving grooves.

31–40 CM

A.D. 50–150

659. FEMALE HEAD

DATABASE NUMBER: PM040.
LOCATION: Palmyra, Palmyra Museum, inv. no. CD 32.
CONTEXT: Secondary context: Found (09.05.1959) in the ninth compartment to the right of the Via Praetoria, Camp of Diocletian.
ACQUISITION HISTORY: —
MEASUREMENTS: Height: 35 cm. Width: 21 cm. Depth: 17 cm.
MATERIAL: Limestone.
PRESERVATION: The lower part of the figure is broken off at the base of the neck. The upper left part of the head, and the areas of the left eye, the nose, and the chin are broken off.
TECHNICAL DESCRIPTION: —

DATE: A.D. 50–150.
REFERENCES: Michalowski 1960, 87 f. cat. 6 fig. 95; Krag 2018, 178 cat. 48.

OBJECT DESCRIPTION
The fragment depicts a female head.

PORTRAIT
The figure is shown frontally.

She wears three headdresses: a headband, a turban, and a veil. The headband is placed low on the forehead and divided into panels separated by beaded bands (details unclear). The turban is coiled. The coiling of the turban is rendered by curving grooves. The veil is heavy. Her face is square. The eyebrows are curving and are rendered by thin ridges. The eyes are large and round with thick eyelids. The eyeballs appear blank. She wears several hoop earrings along the helix (Colledge classification: A). The neck is long and slender with two curving grooves.

A.D. 150–200

660. FEMALE HEAD

DATABASE NUMBER: MLP001.
LOCATION: Paris, Musée du Louvre, inv. no. AO 1002.
CONTEXT: —
ACQUISITION HISTORY: Bought from Durighello in 1882.
MEASUREMENTS: Height: 33 cm. Width: 23 cm. Depth: 14.5 cm.
MATERIAL: Limestone.
PRESERVATION: The lower part of the figure is broken off diagonally at the neck. The edges of the veil and the chin are broken off. The central part of the upper part of the head and the nose are chipped. Cracks running at the upper part of the head.
TECHNICAL DESCRIPTION: There are traces of black pigment in the eyes. The head was restored in 1987 and was sandblasted. The head is roughly cut on the back and there are rasp marks on the face and drill holes in the earrings.
DATE: A.D. 150–200.
REFERENCES: Colledge 1976, 264; Dentzer-Feydy – Teixidor 1993, 156 cat. 160; Krag 2018, 101 n. 58; 252 cat. 316.

OBJECT DESCRIPTION
The fragment depicts a female head.

PORTRAIT
The head faces frontally.

She wears three headdresses: a headband, a turban, and a veil. The headband is placed low on the forehead and divided into five panels separated by vertical, beaded bands. The central panel is rectangular and is decorated with leaves on a stem. The panels on either side are square, decorated with a crisscross pattern. The turban is coiled. The coiling of the turban is rendered by oblique grooves. The veil is heavy.

Cat. 660

She also wears head ornaments: a head-chain and pendants. The head-chain is fastened under the turban and runs to either side of the face. It is composed of round bezels with incised borders linked by beaded elements. She also wears diamond-shaped pendants with hanging, rectangular elements at the hair, next to the temples. Only part of the hair is visible under the headdress: several locks above the ears are brushed back over the headband and disappear under the veil. The individual strands of hair are indicated by fine, incised lines. Her face is oval. The eyebrows are curving and are rendered by thin ridges starting at the root of the nose. The eyes are large and almond-shaped, with thick, upper eyelids. The irises are depicted by incised circles. Only the earlobes are visible under the hair. She wears earrings. They are composed of three thin, rectangular elements ending in round beads, that hang from a bar (Colledge classification: G). The nose is straight and wide. The alae are indicated by grooves. The mouth is small, with full lips. The chin is round. The neck is long with three curving grooves. She wears a necklace composed of small, round beads at the middle of the neck.

A.D. 170–200

661. FEMALE HEAD

DATABASE NUMBER: PM219.
LOCATION: Palmyra, Palmyra Museum, inv. no. CD 7/77.
CONTEXT: Secondary context: Found in a later wall in the Temple of the Standards (Temple des Enseignes), Camp of Diocletian.
ACQUISITION HISTORY: —
MEASUREMENTS: Height: 36 cm. Width: 27 cm. Depth: 30 cm.
MATERIAL: Limestone.
PRESERVATION: The lower part of the figure is broken off at the base of the neck. The surface of the face is lightly chipped.
TECHNICAL DESCRIPTION: —
DATE: A.D. 170–200.
REFERENCES: Gawlikowski 1984, 103 cat. 42 pl. 83, 177; Krag 2018, 275 cat. 403.

OBJECT DESCRIPTION
The fragment depicts a female head.

Cat. 661

PORTRAIT

The head is turned slightly to the left.

She wears three headdresses: a headband, a turban, and a veil. The headband is placed high on the forehead and divided into three panels separated by vertical, beaded bands. The central panel is rectangular and is decorated with leaves on a stem. The panels on either side are square and decorated, possibly with a floral motif (details unclear). The turban is coiled. It is composed of three layers and the two upper layers are looped into each other, creating a knot in the middle. The coiling of the turban is rendered by horizontal grooves. The veil is heavy. Only part of the hair is visible under the headdress: several locks above the ears are brushed back over the headband and disappear under the veil. The individual strands of hair are indicated by fine, incised lines. Her face is square. There is a single horizontal groove on the forehead. The eyebrows are curving and are rendered by incised lines starting at the root of the nose. The eyes are small and almond-shaped, with the indication of upper eyelids. The irises are depicted by incised circles, the pupils by punch holes. The ears are not visible under the hair and she wears earrings composed of two round beads on either side of a biconical bead (Colledge classification: L). The nose is straight and wide. The mouth is small, with thin lips. The chin is square and fleshy. The neck is short.

A.D. 175–225

662. FEMALE HEAD

DATABASE NUMBER: MR001.
LOCATION: Paris, Musée Rodin, inv. no. Co.00440.
CONTEXT: —
ACQUISITION HISTORY: Acquired by Rodin before autumn 1900. Donated in 1916.
MEASUREMENTS: Height: 32 cm. Width: 21.4 cm. Depth: 22.2 cm.
MATERIAL: Limestone.
PRESERVATION: The background is broken off. The lower part of the figure is broken off at the neck. The edges of the veil are broken off. The left side of the forehead and the hair, the eyebrow, the nose, the left cheek, and the area of the upper lip are chipped.
TECHNICAL DESCRIPTION: —
DATE: A.D. 175–225.
REFERENCES: Schnapp et al. 2008, 199 cat. 124; <https://collections.musee-rodin.fr/fr/museum/rodin/portrait-d-une-femme-voilee/Co.00440?q=palmyre&position=0> (06.05.2022).

OBJECT DESCRIPTION

The object depicts a female head.

PORTRAIT

The figure is shown frontally.

She wears two headdresses: a turban and a veil. The turban is composed of one coiling band, with its folds indicated by oblique grooves. The veil is heavy with a scalloped edge. It falls over the back of the head. The hair is centrally parted and brushed back over the ears. Two crescent-shaped locks of hair, one placed opposite the other, fall under the parting over the centre of the forehead. One small, curving lock of hair falls over each ear and the temple. Her face is oval and fleshy. The eyebrows are indicated by curving grooves. The eyes are wide-set, almond-shaped, with thick upper eyelids. The upper eyelids extend beyond the end of the lower ones. The irises are indicated by incised circles and the pupils by incised semicircles. Only the earlobes are visible under the hair. She wears dumbbell-shaped earrings (Colledge classification: H). The nose is narrow with a wide base. The alae are carved. The mouth is small, with a full lower lip. The chin is round. The neck is wide.

A.D. 200–220

663. FEMALE HEAD

DATABASE NUMBER: UAG001.
LOCATION: New Haven, Yale University Art Gallery, inv. no. 1931.135.
CONTEXT: —
ACQUISITION HISTORY: Gift of Vicountess d'Andurain.
MEASUREMENTS: Height: 31 cm. Width: 23 cm. Depth: 28 cm. Depth (of field): 9 cm.
MATERIAL: Limestone, white/yellow.
PRESERVATION: The background is preserved only around the head of the figure. The lower part of the figure is broken off below the base of the neck. Part of the nose is broken off. The edge of the veil, the mouth, and the neck are chipped off.
TECHNICAL DESCRIPTION: —
DATE: A.D. 200–220.
REFERENCES: Brody – Hoffman 2011, 375 cat. 74 pl. 74; Krag 2018, 59 n. 325; 76 n. 67; 77 n. 79; 353 cat. 714; <https://artgallery.yale.edu/collections/objects/4726> (06.05.2022).

OBJECT DESCRIPTION

The fragment depicts the head of a female figure.

PORTRAIT

The figure is shown frontally.

She wears three headdresses: a headband, a turban, and a veil. The headband is placed high on the forehead and is divided into rectangular, decorated panels separated by vertical, beaded bands. The central panel has a motif of a stem with elliptical leaves on opposite arrangement. The outer panels have a cruciform flower. The turban is composed of several coiling bands. The folds are indicated by oblique grooves. The veil is heavy with a scalloped edge. It falls over the back

Cat. 663

PRESERVATION: The lower part of the figure is broken off at the base of the neck. The nose and the chin are chipped. There are cracks running along the face.
TECHNICAL DESCRIPTION: —
DATE: A.D. 200–273.
REFERENCES: Gawlikowski 1984, 103 cat. 41 pl. 82, 176; Krag 2018, 73 n. 47; 310 cat. 535.

OBJECT DESCRIPTION
The fragment depicts the head of a female figure.

PORTRAIT
The figure is shown frontally.

The hair is parted in the centre and brushed to the sides. Above the ears, the hair is brushed back in large locks. The individual strands of hair are indicated by incised lines. Her face is square. The eyebrows are slightly curving and are indicated by incised lines starting at the root of the nose. The eyes are small and almond-shaped, with thick upper eyelids. The end of the upper eyelids extends beyond that of the lower ones. The irises are indicated by incised circles and the pupils by punch holes. The earlobes are visible under the hair and she wears dumbbell-shaped earrings (Colledge classification: H). The nose is wide. The alae are incised, and the nostrils are carved. The mouth is small, with thin lips. The chin is square. The neck is long.

of her head and the shoulders. Part of the hair is covered by the headdress: several strands of hair above the ears are brushed back over the headband and the edge of the turban and disappear under the veil. The individual strands of hair are indicated by incised lines. Her face is oval. The eyebrows are indicated by arched grooves that start from the root of the nose. The eyes are close-set, almond-shaped, with thick eyelids. The eyeballs are blank. Only the earlobes are visible under the hair. The nose is straight with a wide base, with incised alae. The mouth is small, with full lips. The chin is pointed. The neck is short and wide with three curving grooves.

A.D. 200–273

664. FEMALE HEAD

DATABASE NUMBER: PM217.
LOCATION: Palmyra, Palmyra Museum, inv. no. CD 6/77.
CONTEXT: Secondary context: Found on the surface against the south-eastern wall of the forum in the Temple of the Standards (Temple des Enseignes), Camp of Diocletian.
ACQUISITION HISTORY: —
MEASUREMENTS: Height: 31 cm. Width: 24 cm. Depth: 27 cm.
MATERIAL: Limestone.

Cat. 664

665. FEMALE HEAD

DATABASE NUMBER: PM026.
LOCATION: Palmyra, Palmyra Museum, inv. no. CD 23.
CONTEXT: Secondary context: Found (19.05.1961) a late wall to the east of the Tetrapylon, Camp of Diocletian.
ACQUISITION HISTORY: —
MEASUREMENTS: Height: 33 cm. Width: 37 cm. Depth: 21 cm.
MATERIAL: Limestone, grey.
PRESERVATION: The lower part of the figure is broken off at the collarbone. The edges of the veil and the lower part of the face are broken off.
TECHNICAL DESCRIPTION: —
DATE: A.D. 200–273 (Michalowski 1963: A.D. 175–225).
REFERENCES: Michalowski 1963, 143 cat. 36 fig. 193; Krag 2018, 352 cat. 710.

OBJECT DESCRIPTION
The object depicts a female head.

PORTRAIT
The figure is shown frontally.

She wears three headdresses: a headband, a turban, and a veil. The headband is placed low on the forehead and is divided into three rectangular decorated panels separated by vertical, beaded bands. The central panel has a flower with four petals. The outer panels have a geometric crisscross design. The turban is composed of coiling bands, the folds indicated by oblique grooves. The veil is heavy. It falls over the back of the head and her shoulders. She also wears head ornaments: a head-chain. The head-chain is attached under the left and right edges of the headband, runs across the sides of the forehead, and disappears under the veil. Part of the hair is covered by the headdress: several strands of hair above the ears are brushed back over the headband and disappear under the veil. The individual strands of hair are indicated by incised lines. Her face is long. The eyebrows are indicated by curving grooves. The eyes are almond-shaped. The irises are indicated by incised circles and the pupils by punch holes.

Only the earlobes are visible under the hair. She wears dumbbell-shaped earrings (Colledge classification: H). The neck is short and slender with a curving groove. She wears two necklaces: a string of round beads worn at the base of the neck and a loop-in-loop chain below that.

A.D. 230–250

666. FEMALE HEAD

DATABASE NUMBER: NCG093.
LOCATION: Copenhagen, Ny Carlsberg Glyptotek, inv. no. IN 1091.
CONTEXT: —
ACQUISITION HISTORY: Acquired by Løytved in Syria.
MEASUREMENTS: Height: 31 cm. Width: 25.5 cm. Depth: 23 cm. Height of head: 26 cm.
MATERIAL: Limestone, white/yellow.
PRESERVATION: Broken off below the neck. The upper and right edges of the veil are broken off. The left eyebrow, left cheek, and the tip of the nose are chipped.
TECHNICAL DESCRIPTION: The head is roughly cut on the back and there are many cracks in the stone. There are marks from a drill along the veil on the top of the head and the nostrils are drilled. There are flat chisel marks on the inside of the veil.
DATE: A.D. 230–250.
REFERENCES: Simonsen 1889, 46 cat. G.2 pl. 12; el-Chehadeh 1972, 90 n. 86; Colledge 1976, 264; Hvidberg-Hansen – Ploug 1993, 154 cat. 122; Ploug 1995, 252 cat. 122; Krag 2017a, 38 f. fig. 4; Krag 2017b, 38 f. fig. 4; Krag 2018, 108 n. 125. 127; 342 cat. 660; Raja 2019a, 318 f. cat. 120.

OBJECT DESCRIPTION
The object depicts a female figure.

PORTRAIT
The figure is shown frontally.

She wears three headdresses: a headband, a turban, and a veil. Only the edges of the headband are visible, and the headband is decorated. The turban is coiled with curving and oblique grooves indicating the coiling of the fabric. The

Cat. 666

central coils of the turban are twisted into each other. Over the turban she wears a heavy veil with a scalloped edge that falls down the back of the head. She also wears head ornaments: a central head ornament and a head-chain. The central head ornament is fastened under the centre of the veil and runs to the forehead. It is composed of an upper rectangular bezel with a beaded border, a central oval bezel with a beaded border, and a rectangular bezel with a beaded border. The bezels are linked by beaded elements. Four narrow, rectangular beads with round ends are suspended from the lowest rectangular bezel. The head-chain is fastened under the central head ornament and runs to either side of the face. It is composed of round elements with incised borders, linked by small, beaded elements. The hair is visible at the sides of the forehead; it is slightly wavy and combed back over the side of the headband and turban and disappears under the veil. The individual strands of hair are indicated by s-shaped, incised lines. Her face is oblong. The eyebrows are rendered by thin, curving, incised lines that start from the root of the nose. The eyes are large and almond-shaped, with thin upper eyelids. The end of the upper eyelids extends downwards and beyond that of the lower eyelids. The irises, that touch the upper eyelids, are indicated by incised circles and the pupils by punch holes. The earlobes are visible, and she wears dumbbell-shaped earrings (Colledge classification: H). The nose is long with a wide base. The alae are indicated by incised lines. The nostrils are drilled. The philtrum is carved. The mouth is small, with full lips. The chin is pointed. The neck is short and slender with a curving groove.

A.D. 240–273

667. FEMALE HEAD

DATABASE NUMBER: MAH001.
LOCATION: Geneva, Musée d'Art et d'Histoire, inv. no. 12703.
CONTEXT: —
ACQUISITION HISTORY: Purchased from Henri Dufour 1928.
MEASUREMENTS: Height: 31 cm. Width: 23 cm.
MATERIAL: Limestone.
PRESERVATION: The lower part of the figure is broken off at the base of the neck. The bridge of the nose is broken off. The edges of the veil, the mouth, and the chin are chipped.
TECHNICAL DESCRIPTION: There are drill holes between the turban and the veil. The nostrils are drilled.
DATE: A.D. 240–273 (Chamay – Maier 1989: A.D. 200–250).
REFERENCES: Deonna 1929, 7–14; 213 cat. 1 fig. 2; Deonna 1931, 114 cat. 17; Sollberger 1950, 2 fig. 3; Chamay – Maier 1989, 96 cat. 123 pl. 104, 2; Krag 2018, 17 n. 96; 42 n. 153. 156; 59 n. 325; 108 n. 125; 110 n. 141; 342 cat. 656.

OBJECT DESCRIPTION
The fragment depicts the head of a female figure.

PORTRAIT
The figure is shown frontally, with the head slightly tilted to her left.

She wears three headdresses: a headband, a turban, and a veil. The headband is placed high on her forehead and is decorated with square panels with a crisscross pattern divided by beaded bands. Over the band, she wears a head-chain that is attached under the centre of the turban and runs to the sides disappearing under the veil. It is composed of circular bezels with an incised border joined by beaded elements. Another head ornament is fastened under the veil, at the centre of the head, and extends downwards over the middle of the forehead. It is composed of an oval and a rectangular bezel, both with beaded borders that are joined by a beaded element. Five thin, rectangular elements, perhaps indicating chains, ending in large, round beads are suspended from the lower edge of the rectangular bezel and fall over the centre of the forehead. The turban is coiled, and the coiling is indicated by horizontal, curving grooves. The veil is heavy with a scalloped edge. Part of the hair is covered by the headdress: several strands of hair at the sides are brushed back under the head-chain, over the headband and corners of the turban, and disappear under the veil. The individual strands of hair are indicated by incised lines. Her face is oval. The eyebrows are arched. The eyes are small and almond-shaped, with thick upper eyelids. The end of

Cat. 667

the upper eyelids extends beyond that of the lower ones. The irises and pupils are rendered with concentric, incised circles. She wears earrings with a single ball (Colledge classification: J). The base of the nose is wide. The alae are incised, and the nostrils drilled. The mouth is small, with full lips. The chin is oval. The neck has two curving grooves.

NO MEASUREMENTS

A.D. 100–120

668. FEMALE HEAD

DATABASE NUMBER: ParisPriv004.
LOCATION: Paris, private collection, inv. no. unknown.
CONTEXT: —
ACQUISITION HISTORY: Bought at the Parisian art market.
MEASUREMENTS: —
MATERIAL: Limestone.
PRESERVATION: The lower part of the figure is broken off at the top of the neck. The central part of the headdresses, the nose, and the chin are chipped. The object is weathered.
TECHNICAL DESCRIPTION: —
DATE: A.D. 100–120 (Charles-Gaffiot et al. 2001: A.D. 100–150).
REFERENCES: Charles-Gaffiot et al. 2001, 329 cat. 67.

OBJECT DESCRIPTION
The object depicts a female head.

PORTRAIT
The figure wears three headdresses: a headband, a turban, and a veil. The headband is placed low on the forehead and is divided into plain, rectangular, vertical panels separated by plain bands. The turban is coiled. It is rendered in three layers, two of them are looped into each other creating a fold in the centre. The coiling of the fabric is indicated by curving grooves. The veil is heavy. Only part of the hair is visible under the headdresses: several locks above the ears are brushed back over the corners of the headband and turban and disappear under the veil. The individual strands of hair are indicated by incised lines. Her face is rectangular. The eyebrows are indicated by soft, curving ridges. The eyes are large and almond-shaped, with thick upper eyelids. The irises and the pupils are indicated by concentric, incised circles. The nose is short and wide, and the alae are incised. The mouth is small, with full lips. The chin is oval.

A.D. 150–170

669. FRAGMENT OF A FEMALE HEAD

DATABASE NUMBER: UNK160.
LOCATION: Unknown location.
CONTEXT: —
ACQUISITION HISTORY: Found in Palmyra in 1917. Formerly in Watzinger Collection (private collection), Karlsruhe.
MEASUREMENTS: —
MATERIAL: Limestone.
PRESERVATION: The lower part of the figure is broken off at the chin. The veil and the chin are chipped.
TECHNICAL DESCRIPTION: —
DATE: A.D. 150–170.
REFERENCES: Ingholt Archives, PS 704; Krag 2018, 293 cat. 472.

OBJECT DESCRIPTION
The object depicts the head of a female figure.

PORTRAIT
She wears three headdresses: a headband, a turban, and a veil. The headband is placed low on the forehead and is divided into three rectangular panels separated by narrow, beaded bands. The central panel is decorated with a floral motif and the two lateral panels are decorated with a crisscross pattern. She also wears a head-chain: it is attached under the centre of the headband and runs to both sides disappearing under the veil. It is composed of circular bezels joined by beaded

Cat. 669

elements. The turban is coiled. It is composed of two layers and the ends are looped into each other, creating a knot in the middle. Curving grooves indicate the coiling of the fabric. The veil is heavy and has a scalloped edge. Only part of the hair is visible under the headdress: locks of hair above the ears are brushed back over the headband and corners of the turban and disappear under the veil. The individual strands of hair are indicated by incised lines. Her face is oval. The eyebrows are curving and depicted by incised lines starting at the root of the nose. The eyes are almond-shaped, with thick eyelids. The end of the upper eyelids extends beyond that of the lower ones. The irises are indicated by incised circles and the pupils by punch holes. The ears are not visible under the hair. The nose is wide. The alae are incised. The mouth is small, with full lips.

670. FEMALE HEAD

DATABASE NUMBER: PA003.
LOCATION: Damascus, Palais d'Azem, inv. no. unknown.
CONTEXT: —
ACQUISITION HISTORY: —
MEASUREMENTS: —
MATERIAL: Limestone.

PRESERVATION: The head is broken off at the top of the neck. The edge of the veil is chipped. The surface of the hair, the eyes, the nose, the mouth, and the chin is chipped. The surface is weathered.
TECHNICAL DESCRIPTION: —
DATE: A.D. 150–170.
REFERENCES: Ingholt Archives, PS 696; Krag 2018, 270 cat. 381.

OBJECT DESCRIPTION
The fragment depicts the head of a female figure.

PORTRAIT
She wears three headdresses: a headband, a turban, and a veil. The headband is placed low on the forehead and divided into square panels separated by beaded bands. The central panel is decorated with serrated leaves with incised midribs, and with small tendrils between the leaves. The panels on either side are decorated with a lozenges pattern with round beads in each lozenge. The turban is coiled. It is divided into three layers and the two upper layers are looped into each other creating a knot in the middle. Curving grooves indicate the coiling of the fabric. The veil is heavy. Her hair is visible under the headdresses. It is parted in the centre and brushed in a wavy manner back over the sides of the headband and the turban and disappears under the veil. The individual strands of hair are indicated by incised lines. Her face is oval. The eyebrows are curving, rendered by incised lines. The eyes are large and almond-shaped, with thick upper eyelids. The irises are indicated by incised circles and the pupils by punch holes. The earlobes are visible under the hair and she wears earrings with juxtaposed beads (details unclear). The mouth is small.

A.D. 150–200

671. FEMALE HEAD

DATABASE NUMBER: UNK144.
LOCATION: Palmyra or Damascus.
CONTEXT: —
ACQUISITION HISTORY: —
MEASUREMENTS: —
MATERIAL: Limestone.
PRESERVATION: The lower part of the figure is broken off at the base of the neck. The right side and the lower left side of the veil are broken off. The upper part of the veil, the turban, the left eyebrow, the nose, the chin, and the neck are chipped.
TECHNICAL DESCRIPTION: There are round holes in the place of the irises, indicating the presence of inlays.
DATE: A.D. 150–200.
REFERENCES: Ingholt Archives, PS 1085; Krag 2018, 17 n. 98; 276 cat. 408.

Cat. 670

892 CATALOGUE

Cat. 671

A.D. 150–273

672. FEMALE HEAD

DATABASE NUMBER: UNK064.
LOCATION: Unknown.
CONTEXT: —
ACQUISITION HISTORY: —
MEASUREMENTS: —
MATERIAL: Limestone.
PRESERVATION: The head is broken off at the base of the neck. The nose is broken off. The surface of the face is very weathered and chipped. The veil is chipped.
TECHNICAL DESCRIPTION: —
DATE: A.D. 150–273.
REFERENCES: Ingholt Archives, IA_NCG_Portrait2016_058_f_3.

OBJECT DESCRIPTION
The object depicts a female.

PORTRAIT
She wears two headdresses: a headband and a veil. The headband is placed high on the forehead. It is possibly decorated (details unclear). The veil is heavy and falls on either side of her head. Her face is oval. The eyebrows are curving, depicted as thin ridges. The eyes are almond-shaped with thick upper eyelids (details unclear). The irises are indicated by incised circles and the pupils by punch holes (details unclear). The nose is straight (details unclear). The mouth is small (details unclear). The chin is round. The neck is long.

OBJECT DESCRIPTION
The fragment depicts the head of a female figure.

PORTRAIT
The figure is shown frontally. The neck is turned slightly to her left.

She wears two headdresses: a turban and a veil. The turban is coiled: oblique grooves indicate the coiling of the fabric. Over the turban, she wears a heavy veil with a scalloped edge that falls down the sides of the head. The hair is visible from below the turban and is centrally parted. It is slightly wavy, with individual strands of hair indicated by curving grooves. Her face is oval. The eyebrows are rendered by thin ridges starting from the root of the nose. The eyes are almond-shaped, with thick upper eyelids. The end of the upper eyelids extends beyond that of the lower eyelids. There are round holes in the place of the irises, indicating the presence of inlays. The ears are large and slightly protruding. The helix, scapha, fossa triangularis, concha, and lobe are carved. The nose is straight. The mouth is small, with full lips. The chin is round. The neck is long and slender.

Cat. 672

A.D. 200–220

673. FEMALE HEAD

DATABASE NUMBER: AMI090.
LOCATION: Istanbul, İstanbul Arkeoloji Müzesi, inv. no. 3812.
CONTEXT: —
ACQUISITION HISTORY: —
MEASUREMENTS: —
MATERIAL: Limestone, yellow.
PRESERVATION: The lower part of the figure is broken off at the base of the neck. The surface at the lower part of the hair and headdress is chipped. There are cracks running across the lower part of the face.
TECHNICAL DESCRIPTION: —
DATE: A.D. 200–220.
REFERENCES: Ingholt Archives, PS 728; Krag 2018, 344 cat. 666.

OBJECT DESCRIPTION

The fragment depicts the head of a female figure.

PORTRAIT

The figure is shown frontally.

She wears two headdresses: a headband and a turban. The headband is placed high on the forehead and is divided into panels separated by vertical, beaded bands. The central panel is rectangular and is decorated with an incised triangle. Over the band, she wears a head-chain that is attached under the centre of the turban and runs to the sides disappearing behind and above the ears. It is composed of circular bezels with an incised border joined by beaded elements. The turban is coiled. It is rendered in two twisted layers. Two horizontal grooves indicate the coiling of the fabric. Part of the hair is covered by the headdress: several strands of hair above the ears are pushed back over the headband and the edge of the turban. Her face is oval. The eyebrows are curving, rendered by incised lines starting from the root of the nose. The eyes are almond-shaped, with thick upper eyelids. The end of the upper eyelids extends beyond that of the lower ones. The eyeballs are blank. Only the earlobes are visible under the hair. She wears earrings with three juxtaposed balls (Colledge classification: K). The nose is large with the alae carved. The philtrum is carved. The mouth is large with a thin upper lip. An oblique groove is rendered on either side of the mouth. The chin is round with a round depression and the neck is slender with two wide, curving grooves. She wears a necklace composed of small, round beads at the base of the neck.

A.D. 200–273

674. FRAGMENTS OF A FEMALE HEAD

DATABASE NUMBER: UNK054.
LOCATION: —
CONTEXT: —
ACQUISITION HISTORY: —
MEASUREMENTS: —
MATERIAL: Limestone.
PRESERVATION: The head is broken off at the base of the neck. Only a small part of the left shoulder and hand have been preserved. It is broken in three pieces; two larger ones of each side of the face and a smaller piece from the top of the head.
TECHNICAL DESCRIPTION: —
DATE: A.D. 200–273.
REFERENCES: Ingholt Archives, IA_NCG_Portrait2016_037.

OBJECT DESCRIPTION

The object depicts a female figure.

PORTRAIT

She wears two headdresses: a veil and a turban. The veil that falls on either side of her head. The turban is coiled (details unclear). The hair is centrally parted and arranged in rows that are brushed back over the ears and disappear under the veil. Incised lines indicate the individual strands of hair. The face is round and fleshy. The eyebrows are curving. The upper eyelids appear thick. Only the earlobes are visible under the hair. She wears dumbbell-shaped earrings (Colledge classification: H). The neck is slender and long.

Cat. 673

Cat. 674

Cat. 675

She wears a tunic.
With her right hand, she holds the edge of the veil.

675. FEMALE HEAD

DATABASE NUMBER: HomsPriv001.
LOCATION: Homs, private collection.
CONTEXT: —
ACQUISITION HISTORY: —
MEASUREMENTS: —
MATERIAL: Limestone.
PRESERVATION: The head is broken off at the neck. The edge of the veil is chipped. The chin is chipped.
TECHNICAL DESCRIPTION: —
DATE: A.D. 200–273.
REFERENCES: Ingholt Archives, PS 500; Ingholt 1928, 150 PS 500; Colledge 1976, 264.

OBJECT DESCRIPTION
The fragment depicts the head of a female figure.

PORTRAIT
The figure is shown frontally.
She wears two headdresses: a headband and a veil. The headband is divided into two registers. The lower register is decorated with three square panels separated by beaded bands. The central panel is decorated with a four-petal rosette with serrated leaves, and the panels on either side of the head are decorated with a vegetal motif. The upper register is decorated by an intersecting lozenges pattern created by beaded bands. The upper and lower lozenges are decorated with serrated leaves. The central lozenge contains a six-petal rosette with depressions in the petals, while the lozenges on either side contain a four-petal rosette with serrated leaves. The midribs of all the leaves are incised. The veil is heavy with a scalloped edge. Her hair is visible on either side of the head where it is brushed over the sides of the headband and disappears under the veil. The individual strands of hair are indicated by incised lines. Her face is oval. The eyebrows are curving, rendered by incised lines. The eyes are large, almond-shaped, and slanting with thick, upper eyelids. The upper eyelids extend beyond the end of the corners of the eyes. The irises are indicated by incised circles. She wears earrings composed of a biconical element (details unclear). The nose is wide with a wide base. The alae are incised, and the nostrils are carved. The mouth is small, with full lips. The chin is small and fleshy.

A.D. 220–240

676. FEMALE HEAD

DATABASE NUMBER: UNK163.
LOCATION: Unknown location.
CONTEXT: —

ACQUISITION HISTORY: —
MEASUREMENTS: —
MATERIAL: Limestone.
PRESERVATION: The lower part of the figure is broken off at the neck. The upper part of the head is broken off. The bridge of the nose is chipped.
TECHNICAL DESCRIPTION: —
DATE: A.D. 220–240.
REFERENCES: Ingholt Archives, PS 699; Krag 2018, 294 cat. 475.

OBJECT DESCRIPTION
The fragment depicts the head of a female figure.

PORTRAIT
The figure is shown frontally.

She wears three headdresses: a headband, a turban, and a veil. The headband is placed low on the forehead and is divided into five rectangular panels separated by vertical, beaded bands. The central panel is decorated with a floral motif. The two adjacent panels are decorated with leaves on a stem and the two outer panels are decorated with a crisscross pattern. She also wears a head-chain. The chain is attached under the centre of the headband and runs to both sides disappearing under the veil. It is composed of circular bezels with an incised border linked by beaded elements. The turban is coiled. It is composed of a single layer and the coiling of the fabric is indicated by horizontal, incised lines. The veil is heavy. Only part of the hair is visible under the headdress: locks of hair above the ears are brushed back over the headband and turban and disappear under the veil. The individual strands of hair are indicated by incised lines. Her face is oval. The eyebrows are slightly curving and depicted by incised lines starting at the root of the nose. The eyes are large and almond-shaped, with thick upper eyelids. The irises are indicated by incised circles and the pupils by punch holes. She wears dumbbell-shaped earrings (Colledge classification: H). The nose is wide. The alae are incised. The mouth is small, with full lips. The chin is square.

677. FEMALE HEAD

DATABASE NUMBER: BluntPriv001.
LOCATION: London, collection of Anthony Blunt (dir. of Courtauld Institute), inv. no. unknown.
CONTEXT: —
ACQUISITION HISTORY: —
MEASUREMENTS: —
MATERIAL: Limestone.
PRESERVATION: The lower part of the figure is broken off at the base of the neck. A large crack runs from the hair, over the cheek, and to the chin. The chin is chipped.

Cat. 676

Cat. 677

TECHNICAL DESCRIPTION: There are flat chisel marks on the face.
DATE: A.D. 220–240.
REFERENCES: Ingholt Archives, PS 1336.

OBJECT DESCRIPTION
The fragment depicts the head of a female figure. A small part of a background is preserved on both sides.

PORTRAIT
The figure is shown frontally.

The hair at either side of the forehead is brushed back. The remaining hair is combed to the top of the head, where it is gathered in a twisted bun, the so-called Faustina hairstyle. The individual strands of hair are indicated by incised, curving lines. She wears two head ornaments. The first is composed of an oval and a rectangular bezel, both with incised borders, linked by a beaded element. Three round beads are suspended from the lower edge of the rectangular bezel. A head-chain is attached on either side of the rectangular bezel: it is composed of round bezels with incised borders linked by beaded elements and runs to the sides of the head. Her face is oval. Her eyebrows are curving. The eyes are large and rendered by a curving, incised line at the upper eyelid. The eyeballs are blank. The ears are not visible under the hair and she wears earrings with three juxtaposed beads: two round beads on either side of a biconical one (Colledge classification: L). The nose is long and narrow. The alae are incised. The mouth is small, with a full lower lip. The chin is pointed. The neck is short.

Cat. 678

678. FEMALE HEAD

DATABASE NUMBER: AMI096.
LOCATION: Istanbul, İstanbul Arkeoloji Müzesi, inv. no. unknown.
CONTEXT: —
ACQUISITION HISTORY: —
MEASUREMENTS: —
MATERIAL: Limestone.
PRESERVATION: The lower part of the figure is broken off at the base of the neck. The upper part of the head, and the veil on either side of the head and neck are broken off.
TECHNICAL DESCRIPTION: —
DATE: A.D. 220–240.
REFERENCES: Ingholt Archives, PS 727; Krag 2018, 369 cat. 765.

OBJECT DESCRIPTION
The fragment depicts the head of a female figure.

PORTRAIT
The figure is shown frontally.

She wears three headdresses: a headband, a turban, and a veil. The headband is placed low on the forehead and is divided into rectangular, decorated panels separated by vertical, beaded bands. The central panel has a cruciform flower with four petals. The outer panels have a six-petal rosette. The turban is coiled. It is divided into two layers and the ends are looped into each other creating a knot in the middle. Curving grooves indicate the coiling of the fabric. The veil is heavy. It falls behind the head. Part of the hair is covered by the headdress: several strands of hair above the ears are brushed back over the headband and disappear under the veil. The individual strands of hair are indicated by incised lines. Her face is square. The eyebrows are indicated by thin, curving ridges. The eyes are close-set and almond-shaped. The right eye is placed lower than the left on the face. The eyelids and irises are not indicated. The pupils are indicated by punch holes. Only the earlobes are visible under the hair. She wears earrings with three juxtaposed beads: two round beads on either side of a biconical one (Colledge classification: L). The nose is straight with a wide base. The mouth is wide with full lips. The chin is square with a cleft. The neck is wide.

679. FEMALE HEAD

DATABASE NUMBER: UNK161.
LOCATION: Unknown location.
CONTEXT: —

HEADS FROM SARCOPHAGI 897

Cat. 679

strands of hair are indicated by incised lines. Her face is oval. The eyebrows are curving. The eyes are almond-shaped, with thick upper eyelids. The eyeballs are blank. She wears earrings composed of three juxtaposed balls (Colledge classification: H). The nose is wide. The alae are incised, and the nostrils carved. The mouth is small, with a full lower lip. The chin is oval. The neck is wide and has two curving grooves.

680. FEMALE HEAD

DATABASE NUMBER: UNK142.
LOCATION: Unknown location.
CONTEXT: —
ACQUISITION HISTORY: —
MEASUREMENTS: —
MATERIAL: Limestone.
PRESERVATION: The lower part of the figure is broken off at the base of the neck. The surface of the forehead, nose, and mouth is chipped.
TECHNICAL DESCRIPTION: —
DATE: A.D. 220–240.
REFERENCES: Ingholt Archives, PS 701; Krag 2018, 351 cat. 702.

OBJECT DESCRIPTION
The fragment depicts the head of a female figure.

ACQUISITION HISTORY: —
MEASUREMENTS: —
MATERIAL: Limestone.
PRESERVATION: The lower part of the figure is broken off at the middle of the neck. The chin is chipped.
TECHNICAL DESCRIPTION: —
DATE: A.D. 220–240.
REFERENCES: Ingholt Archives, PS 702; Krag 2018, 369 cat. 766.

OBJECT DESCRIPTION
The fragment depicts the head of a female figure.

PORTRAIT
The figure is shown frontally.
She wears three headdresses: a headband, a turban, and a veil. The headband is placed low on the forehead and is decorated with vertical, beaded bands. She also wears a head-chain that is attached under the centre of the turban and runs to the sides disappearing under the veil. It is composed of circular bezels joined by beaded elements. The turban is coiled. It is divided into three layers and the two upper layers are looped into each other, creating a knot in the middle. Curving grooves indicate the coiling of the fabric. The veil is heavy, and the edge is scalloped. Only part of the hair is visible under the headdress: locks of hair above the ears are brushed back over the headband and disappear under the veil. The individual

Cat. 680

PORTRAIT

The figure is shown frontally.

She wears three headdresses: a headband, a turban, and a veil. The headband is placed high on the forehead and is divided into three rectangular panels separated by vertical, beaded bands. The central panel is decorated with leaves on a stem. The two lateral panels are decorated with a floral motif. She also wears a head-chain: it is attached under the centre of the headband and runs to both sides of the head disappearing under the veil. It is composed of circular bezels linked by beaded elements. The turban is coiled. It is composed of three layers and the two upper layers are looped into each other, creating a knot in the middle. Curving grooves indicate the coiling of the fabric. The veil is heavy, and the edge is scalloped. Only part of the hair is visible under the headdress: locks of hair above the ears are brushed back over the headband and corners of the turban and disappear under the veil. The individual strands of hair are indicated by incised lines. Her face is oval. The eyebrows are curving. The eyes are almond-shaped, with thick eyelids. The end of the upper eyelids extends beyond that of the lower ones. The pupils are indicated by punch holes (details unclear). The earlobes are visible under the hair and she wears dumbbell-shaped earrings (Colledge classification: H). The mouth is small, with a full lower lip. The chin is round. The neck is long and has two curving grooves.

A.D. 240–273

681. FEMALE HEAD

DATABASE NUMBER: MET018.
LOCATION: New York, Metropolitan Museum of Art, inv. no. 65.77.
CONTEXT: —
ACQUISITION HISTORY: A gift of Harry Jones in 1965.
MEASUREMENTS: —
MATERIAL: Limestone, yellow.
PRESERVATION: The lower part of the figure is broken off at the base of the neck. The lower part of the veil is broken off. The nose is chipped.
TECHNICAL DESCRIPTION: —
DATE: A.D. 240–273.
REFERENCES: Krag 2018, 369 cat. 768; <https://www.metmuseum.org/art/collection/search/255206> (06.05.2022).

OBJECT DESCRIPTION

The fragment depicts the head of a female figure.

PORTRAIT

The head is turned slightly to the left.

She wears two headdresses: a turban and a veil. The turban is coiled. It is rendered in a single layer and curving grooves indicate the coiling. The veil is heavy. The hair is parted in the centre of the forehead and brushed to either side. Above

Cat. 681

the ears, the hair is brushed back under the turban and veil. The individual locks of hair are rendered by incised lines. Her face is rectangular. The eyebrows are curving and indicated by incised lines. The eyes are almond-shaped, with thick upper eyelids. The end of the upper eyelids extends beyond the end of the lower ones. The irises are depicted by deep, circular depressions (possibly for the insertion of inlays). She wears earrings composed of three juxtaposed beads: two round ones on either side of a biconical one (Colledge classification: L). The nose is wide, and the alae are incised. The mouth is small, with full lips. The chin is pointed and prominent. The neck has two wide curving grooves.

682. FEMALE HEAD

DATABASE NUMBER: Tsiade002.
LOCATION: Beirut, private collection of Dr Tsiade, inv. no. unknown.
CONTEXT: —
ACQUISITION HISTORY: —

Cat. 682

MEASUREMENTS: —
MATERIAL: Limestone.
PRESERVATION: The lower part of the figure is broken off at the middle of the neck. Part of the headdress and the nose are chipped.
TECHNICAL DESCRIPTION: —
DATE: A.D. 240–273.
REFERENCES: Ingholt Archives, PS 707; Krag 2018, 352 cat. 707.

OBJECT DESCRIPTION
The fragment depicts the head of a female figure.

PORTRAIT
The figure is shown frontally.
  She wears three headdresses: a headband, a turban, and a veil. The headband is placed low on the forehead and is very wide. It is decorated with a central, rectangular panel with leaves on a stem. On either side of that, the band is decorated with vertical, narrow bands and beaded bands. Along the lower border runs a horizontal band. She also wears a head-chain over the headband: it is attached under the centre of the turban and runs to both sides disappearing under the veil. It is composed of circular bezels joined by beaded elements. The turban is coiled. It is composed of a single layer and curving grooves indicate the coiling of the fabric. The veil is heavy. Only part of the hair is visible under the headdress: locks of hair above the ears are brushed back over the headband and disappear under the veil. She wears pendants in her hair, located on either side of the head ornament. They are composed of a rhomboid bezel with an incised border, a vertical bar, and an oval bead. The individual strands of hair are indicated by incised lines. Her face is oval. The eyebrows are curving and depicted by narrow ridges starting at the root of the nose. The eyes are almond-shaped, with thick eyelids. The irises are indicated by incised circles and the pupils by punch holes. She wears earrings composed of a round bead, a vertical bar, and a rhomboid element (Colledge classification: L). The nose is narrow. The alae are incised. The mouth is small, with full lips. The chin is oval. The neck has two curving grooves.
  Fingers are rendered at the side of the left cheek.

683. FEMALE HEAD

DATABASE NUMBER: AUB025.
LOCATION: Beirut, American University Museum, inv. no. 2741.
CONTEXT: —
ACQUISITION HISTORY: Acquired by G. E. Post in 1890 at Palmyra.
MEASUREMENTS: —
MATERIAL: Limestone.
PRESERVATION: The lower part of the figure is broken off horizontally at the base of the neck. A crack runs from the right side of the forehead to her left cheek. The lower left side of the headdress is chipped.
TECHNICAL DESCRIPTION: There are traces of a black pigment in the irises and along the outline of the eyeballs.
DATE: A.D. 240–273.
REFERENCES: Ingholt Archives, PS 694; Post 1891, 37 figs. on page 36 f.; Krag 2018, 106 n. 98; 330 cat. 613.

OBJECT DESCRIPTION
The fragment depicts the head of a female figure.

PORTRAIT
The figure is shown frontally.
  She wears three headdresses: a headband, a turban, and a veil. The band is placed low on her forehead and is divided into square, decorated panels separated by beaded bands. The central panel has serrated leaves in an opposite arrangement on the stem. The outer panels have a star with eight beams and a round element between each beam. The turban is coiled. It is rendered in three twisted layers with the ends looped into each other, creating a knot in the middle. Curving grooves indicate the texture of the fabric. The veil is thick and has a scalloped edge. Part of the hair is covered by the headdress: several strands of hair above the ears are pushed back over

Cat. 683

the headband and the edge of the turban and disappear under the veil. Her face is oval. The eyebrows are curving, rendered by incised lines. The eyes are large, almond-shaped, with thick upper eyelids. The irises are rendered by incised arches and touch the upper eyelids. Only the earlobes are visible under the hair and she is wearing dumbbell-shaped earrings (Colledge classification: H). The nose is large with the alae and the nostrils carved. The philtrum is rendered. The mouth is small, with full lips. The chin is round. The neck is wide, with two curving grooves. She wears a necklace composed of small, round beads worn at the base of the neck.

Banqueting Reliefs

FOUNDER RELIEFS

A.D. 170–200

684. FOUNDER BANQUETING RELIEF

DATABASE NUMBER: PM320.
LOCATION: Palmyra, Palmyra Museum, inv. no. A 3.
CONTEXT: —
ACQUISITION HISTORY: —
MEASUREMENTS: Height: 64 cm. Width: 90 cm.
MATERIAL: Limestone.
PRESERVATION: The upper part of the relief is broken off. The surface is weathered. Portrait A: The head is broken off. The legs are chipped. The surface is weathered. Portrait B: The head is broken off. The surface is weathered. Portrait C: The head is broken off. The surface is weathered. Portrait D: The upper part of the head of the figure is broken off. The right foot is broken off. The surface is weathered, especially at the head and upper torso.
TECHNICAL DESCRIPTION: —
DATE: A.D. 170–200.
REFERENCES: Ingholt Archives, PS 1032; Will 1951, 89 fig. 11; Colledge 1976, 66 n. 194; Tanabe 1986, 42 pl. 416.

OBJECT DESCRIPTION
The object is rectangular in shape with an arched top. It depicts a male figure reclining in the foreground and three standing male figures depicted in the background. The reclining figure rests against a round cushion decorated with a wide band with four-petal rosettes, framed by beaded borders. The texture and fabric of the cushion are indicated by curving grooves.

PORTRAIT A: STANDING MALE
The figure is shown frontally. The arms are bent in front of the torso. The left foot and leg are obscured by the reclining figure.

He wears a tunic and a himation. The tunic has a wide, round neckline. Over the tunic, he wears a himation: it is wrapped around the right shoulder and arm, leaving part of the upper chest and the hand free, crosses the chest diagonally, and covers the left shoulder and arm, as well as the lower body (>arm-sling< type). A fold of the himation falls over the left wrist and down the left leg.

With his right hand, he holds the diagonal fold of the himation. With his left hand, he holds a rectangular object, perhaps a schedula.

PORTRAIT B: STANDING MALE
The figure is shown frontally. The arms are bent in front of the waist. The lower body is obscured by the reclining figure.

He wears a tunic and a himation. The tunic has a wide, round neckline. Over the tunic, he wears a himation: it is wrapped around the right shoulder and arm, leaving part of the upper chest and the hand free, crosses the chest diagonally, and covers the left shoulder and arm, as well as the lower body (›arm-sling‹ type). A fold of the himation falls over the left wrist and down the left leg.

With his right hand, he holds the diagonal fold of the himation. He holds an object in the left hand (details unclear).

PORTRAIT C: STANDING MALE

The figure is shown frontally. The arms are bent in front of the torso. The lower body is obscured by the reclining figure.

He wears a tunic and a himation. The himation crosses the chest diagonally, and covers the left shoulder and arm, as well as the lower body (›arm-sling‹ type).

With his right hand, he holds the diagonal fold of the himation. He holds an object in the left hand (details unclear).

PORTRAIT D: RECLINING MALE

The figure's torso is shown frontally. The arms and right leg are shown in profile. The right arm is bent and held to the side, the left arm is bent in front of the torso. The left upper leg is shown frontally, the left lower leg is shown in three-quarter view, foreshortened. The right leg is raised with the foot resting on the mattress, the left leg is bent and crossing under the right leg. The left foot is obscured by the right leg.

He wears a ›Parthian-style‹ tunic, a chlamys, ›Parthian-style‹ trousers, and over-trousers. The tunic has a wide, round neckline and long, tight-fitting sleeves. The cuffs of the sleeves are decorated with a wide band (details unclear). The lower hem of the tunic is decorated with a wide band with a running scroll. The folds of the tunic are rendered by curving grooves. Over the tunic, he wears a chlamys: it is folded over the chest and falls over the left arm in a wide fold. One end of the chlamys that crosses the chest is decorated with a wide band with a series of squares with a hollowed centre. It is fastened at the right shoulder with a circular brooch with an incised border (Colledge classification: h). A small, zigzag-shaped fold falls under the brooch. He wears a thin band belt tied low at the waist, knotted in the centre with each end looped under on either side of the waist. He wears trousers: they are decorated with a wide band with a crisscross pattern framed by beaded borders extending downwards. Over the lower legs, he also wears loose over-trousers.

His right hand rests on his right knee. He holds a skyphos with a conical foot and an ovoid body separated by the foot by a narrow band in his left hand.

Cat. 684

BANQUETING RELIEFS

A.D. 150–170

685. BANQUETING RELIEF

DATABASE NUMBER: ParisPriv002.
LOCATION: Paris, private collection, inv. no. unknown.
CONTEXT: —
ACQUISITION HISTORY: —
MEASUREMENTS: Height: 50 cm. Width: 70 cm.
MATERIAL: Limestone, grey.
PRESERVATION: The upper left corner and the left side of the relief are broken off.
TECHNICAL DESCRIPTION: There are chisel marks on the relief ground.
DATE: A.D. 150–170 (Parlasca 1984: A.D. 150–200).
REFERENCES: Parlasca 1984, 289 fig. 6; Krag 2018, 28 n. 9; 33 n. 77. 82; 46 n. 198; 66 n. 382; 87 n. 182; 88 n. 193. 195. 197; 98 n. 28; 314 cat. 559. Inscription: Parlasca 1984, 289; Krag 2018, 314 cat. 559.

OBJECT DESCRIPTION

The relief is rectangular in shape and depicts a kline with a seated female, a standing female, a standing male, and a reclining male resting on a mattress. The mattress is decorated with three wide bands. The central band is decorated with a running scroll with rosettes set between beaded bands. The two bands on either side are decorated with lanceolate leaves in an opposite arrangement on the stem and set between beaded bands. Oblique and curving grooves indicate the texture of the fabric. The reclining male rests against two cushions. The upper cushion is decorated with a wide band with lanceolate leaves, set between beaded bands. The lower cushion has a band decorated with a running scroll with rosettes, set between beaded bands. On the left side of the kline a fulcrum is shown. It is decorated with a small armless bust of a male rendered in a clipeus (portrait E). Beneath the mattress is a kline. The central stretcher of the kline is decorated with a rectangular panel on each side followed by a smaller, rectangular panel. The kline legs are short and turned. They are composed of a plinth, above is a torus, a convex quarter, a thin torus, and a long cylindrical element.

INSCRIPTION

SCRIPT: Palmyrene Aramaic.
LOCATION ON RELIEF: Between the reclining male and the two individuals.
TRANSCRIPTION: ZBYD' BR [- - -] | ZBYD'.
TRANSLATION: Zebîdâ son of - - - Zebîdâ.

CIS no. —; PAT no. —.

PORTRAIT A: SEATED FEMALE

The figure is shown frontally. The body appears short. The right arm is bent and held to the chest. The left arm is bent and rests on the left leg. The legs are bent with the knees visible under the drapery. She rests her feet on the mattress.

She wears three headdresses: a headband, a turban, and a veil. The band is placed low on the forehead and is composed of a row of beads. The turban is coiled: two horizontal grooves indicate the coiling of the fabric. The veil is heavy. It is wrapped around her right shoulder and falls downwards to her ankles. It is also wrapped around her left shoulder, arm, and wrist where it continues along her left side and to the ankles. Her face is round. The eyebrows are curving. The eyes are close-set and round with thick upper eyelids (details unclear). Only the earlobes are visible under the headdress and she wears earrings (details unclear). The nose is large and the cheeks are fleshy. The mouth is small, with a full lower lip. The chin is round and the neck is wide.

She wears a tunic and a himation. The tunic has a wide, v-shaped neckline and short sleeves. The folds of the tunic are rendered by oblique grooves. The himation crosses the chest diagonally from the left shoulder to the right side, covers the chest and the body, and falls to her ankles. The folds of the himation are rendered by oblique and curving grooves.

She lightly holds the upper edge of the himation with her right hand. She holds a large fold of the himation with her left hand.

PORTRAIT B: STANDING FEMALE

The figure is shown frontally. The right arm is bent and held to the lower torso. The left arm is bent and held to the abdomen. She stands with the legs set slightly apart. The right leg is slightly bent with the knee visible under the drapery. Her feet are obscured by the reclining figure to her left.

The hair is short and arranged in s-shaped locks brushed from the top of the head and down the forehead and covering the ears. The individual locks of hair are rendered by curving grooves. Her face is oval. The eyebrows are curving. The eyes are close-set and almond-shaped (other details unclear). The nose is small and the cheeks are fleshy. The mouth is small, with full lips and the chin is oval. The neck is wide. She wears a necklace composed of large, round beads over the collarbone.

She wears a tunic. The tunic falls to the ankles. It has a wide, round neckline and long, tight-fitting sleeves. The folds of the tunic are rendered by oblique and curving grooves.

She holds a branch with lanceolate leaves in her right hand. With the left hand she holds a bird.

PORTRAIT C: STANDING MALE

The figure is shown frontally. The right arm is bent and held to the chest. The left arm is bent and held out from the body. The left leg and the lower right leg are obscured by the reclining figure to his left.

His hair is short and arranged in flame-shaped locks around the head. The individual locks of hair are rendered by curving, incised lines. His face is square. The eyebrows are curving. The eyes are close-set and round with thick upper eyelids (details unclear). The nose is small. The ears are large and protruding with the helix depicted. The mouth is small, with full lips. The chin is round and the neck is long.

He wears a tunic. The tunic has a wide, v-shaped neckline and short, wide sleeves. The tunic has an overfold across the lower abdomen, possibly created by a belt. The folds of the tunic are rendered by oblique and curving grooves.

With the right hand, he holds a bunch of grapes. The left hand is placed on the right knee of the reclining figure.

PORTRAIT D: RECLINING MALE

The figure is shown in three-quarter view. The right arm is slightly bent and rests on his right leg. The left arm is bent and rests against two cushions. The right leg is bent and the foot is resting on top of the left foot. The left leg is slightly bent and extended. The left foot is resting on the mattress.

His hair is arranged in s-shaped curls around the head. The individual locks of hair are rendered by curving, incised lines. His face is square. The eyebrows are curving, rendered as thin ridges. The eyes are close-set and almond-shaped. The upper eyelids extend beyond the end of the lower ones. The irises and pupils are indicated by concentric, incised circles. The nose is narrow. The ears are large and protruding with the helix, concha, and scapha depicted. The cheeks are fleshy. The mouth is small, with thin lips. The chin is round and the neck is wide with two curving grooves.

He wears a tunic and a himation. The tunic has a wide, v-shaped neckline, leaving part of the upper chest bare. Two grooves indicate the jugular notch. The tunic has short, wide sleeves. The folds of the tunic are rendered by curving and oblique grooves. Over the tunic, he wears a himation. It is wrapped around his left shoulder and arm, falling along his left side and across his waist, covering the legs and ending at the ankles. An s-shaped fold falls from under the left hand. The folds of the himation are rendered by curving and oblique grooves. He wears footwear, possibly a sandal, which only covers his wrists, indicated by a v-shaped groove. The nails are rendered by fine, incised lines.

His right hand is placed on his raised right knee on top of the hand of the standing male to his right. With the left hand, he holds a skyphos. It has a conical foot and body and small, looped handles. The lower body is decorated with a fluting. The thumb, index, and little finger are extended.

PORTRAIT E: ARMLESS BUST OF A MALE IN THE FULCRUM

The figure is shown frontally, rendered in a medallion.

His face is oval.

He wears a tunic and a himation. The folds of the tunic are rendered by curving grooves. The himation covers most of the body: it is wrapped around the right shoulder and arm, leaving only part of the upper torso and the hand free. One fold of the himation crosses the chest diagonally and falls over the left shoulder (>arm-sling< type). With his right hand, he holds lightly the fold of the himation.

A.D. 150–200

686. FRAGMENT OF A RELIEF

DATABASE NUMBER: UNK065.
LOCATION: —
CONTEXT: —
ACQUISITION HISTORY: —
MEASUREMENTS: —
MATERIAL: Limestone.
PRESERVATION: The left and lower side of the relief are broken off. The upper side is very fragmented. The right side is chipped. The surface is weathered. The head and the left and right foot are broken off. The left arm and hand and left knee are fragmented. Part of the clothing is chipped.
TECHNICAL DESCRIPTION: —
DATE: A.D. 150–200.
REFERENCES: Ingholt Archives, A_NCG_Portrait2016_032.

OBJECT DESCRIPTION

The object was originally rectangular in shape and depicts a seated female figure. The upper side of the relief is decorated with a cavetto moulding.

PORTRAIT

The figure is shown frontally. The right arm is bent and rests on her raised right knee, while the left arm is bent and raised to the height of the head. The right arm appears large in relation to the body.

She wears a veil. The veil is heavy. It falls over the back of the head and over both shoulders, covers the upper arms, and falls onto her lap, ending in a zigzag-shaped fold. The folds of the veil are indicated by oblique grooves. She possibly wears a necklace composed of a string of round beads at the base of the neck (details unclear).

She wears a tunic and a himation. The tunic has a small v-shaped neckline and short sleeves. The folds of the tunic are indicated by wide, oblique and curving grooves. Over the tunic, she wears a himation. It falls over the left shoulder, crosses the chest diagonally, and runs under the right arm. The himation ends at the shins. The folds of the himation are indicated by vertical and wide, oblique grooves. It is fastened at the shoulder with a brooch (details unclear).

With her right hand, she holds a fold of the veil in her lap. The thumb, index, and middle finger are extended. With her left hand, she lightly holds the edge of the veil.

Cat. 686

Cat. 687

A.D. 170–200

687. BANQUETING RELIEF

DATABASE NUMBER: AMI086.
LOCATION: Istanbul, İstanbul Arkeoloji Müzesi, inv. no. 3788.
CONTEXT: —
ACQUISITION HISTORY: —
MEASUREMENTS: Height: 53 cm.
MATERIAL: Limestone, yellow.
PRESERVATION: Broken on all sides. Portrait A: Broken diagonally from the left shoulder to the right side. The surface of the left upper arm and of the right leg is chipped. Portrait B: The tip of the foot is broken off. The surface of the nose, of the left arm, of the right hand, of the left leg, and of the lower torso is chipped.
TECHNICAL DESCRIPTION: —
DATE: A.D. 170–200.
REFERENCES: Ingholt Archives, PS 720; Anderson – Ousterhout 2016, pl. 12.

OBJECT DESCRIPTION

The relief is square in shape and depicts a seated figure and a reclining male.

PORTRAIT A: SEATED FEMALE

The figure is shown frontally. The left arm is bent and raised to the chest. The right leg and the left foot are obscured by the reclining figure to her left.

The figure wears two garments, possibly a tunic and a himation. The first garment, possibly the tunic, is visible at the chest. The folds are rendered by curving and oblique grooves. The other garment, possibly a himation, is fastened at the left shoulder by a circular brooch with an indication of a central inlay (Colledge classification: i). The garment covers most of the chest, the left arm, and the right leg. The folds of the garment are rendered by oblique and curving grooves.

PORTRAIT B: RECLINING MALE

The figure is shown in frontal to three-quarter view. The right arm appears short in relation to the body. The head appears large in relation to the body. The right arm is bent and he rests his hand on his raised right knee. The right leg is bent with the foot resting on the ground of the relief. The left leg is bent and extends under the right leg. The left lower leg is obscured by the right leg.

His hair is arranged in snail-shell curls around the head reaching the neck. His face is round. The eyebrows are curving, rendered as thin ridges. The eyes are almond-shaped, with thick upper eyelids. The upper eyelids extend beyond the end of the lower ones. The irises are rendered by incised circles. The ears are large with the helix depicted. He has a beard that starts from the temples and covers his cheeks, upper lip, and chin. The facial hair is rendered by incised circles. The mouth is small, with a full lower lip and the chin is oval. The neck is wide.

He wears a ›Parthian-style‹ tunic and a chlamys. The tunic has a wide, round neckline decorated with a beaded band and long, tight-fitting sleeves. The tunic has a band decorated with serrated leaves in an opposite arrangement on the stem extending downwards from the middle of the neckline. The tunic ends above the knees and has a beaded band at the hem. The folds of the tunic are rendered by oblique and curving grooves. He also wears a chlamys that is only visible at his right shoulder, where it is fastened with a circular brooch with an incised circle (Colledge classification: h). He wears a plain band belt, knotted at the centre with the ends looped under on either side of the waist. Along his right thigh he has an object with a triangular lower end, a rectangular main body, a lateral angular protrusion, and a triangular upper end: a sheathed dagger. He also wears trousers. In the middle, each trouser leg has a band with possibly a vegetal motif extending downwards. The folds of the garment are rendered by oblique grooves. The trousers are tucked into his boots. The upper edge of the boots has a beaded band followed by a lace that is fastened with a round knob above the ankles.

The outline of a circular object, possibly a bowl, is recognizable at the centre of his chest.

A.D. 180–200

688. BANQUETING RELIEF

DATABASE NUMBER: AMI082.
LOCATION: Istanbul, İstanbul Arkeoloji Müzesi, inv. no. 231.
CONTEXT: —
ACQUISITION HISTORY: Entered the museum in 1882.
MEASUREMENTS: Height: 32 cm. Width: 36 cm.
MATERIAL: Limestone, grey.
PRESERVATION: The tip of the right foot is broken off. The surface at the top of the head is chipped. A crack runs horizontally at the base of the neck. The surface is weathered.
TECHNICAL DESCRIPTION: There are traces of red pigment on the relief ground above the right arm of the figure.
DATE: A.D. 180–200.
REFERENCES: Ingholt Archives, PS 719; Ingholt 1935, 70 n. 67 pl. 32, 1; Seyrig 1937, 15 n. 3.

OBJECT DESCRIPTION

The relief is rectangular in shape and depicts a reclining male figure. Beneath the figure is a mattress. The texture and fabric of the mattress are indicated by wide, curving grooves. He rests against a round cushion. It is decorated with a plain, wide band extending downwards.

PORTRAIT

The figure is shown in frontal to three-quarter view. The arms and legs appear short in relation to the body. The right arm is slightly bent and rests on his right leg. The left arm is bent and rests against the cushion. The right leg is bent with the

Cat. 688

foot resting on the mattress. The left leg is bent under the right with the knee pointing outwards. The left foot is obscured by the right leg.

His hair is arranged in thick, curly locks around the head. His face is round. There is a furrow in the forehead. The eyebrows are curving, and the eyes are almond-shaped, with thick upper eyelids. The irises are carved. The helixes of the ears are depicted. The nose is straight with the alae incised. He has a beard that starts from the temples and covers the lower part of the cheeks, the upper lip, and the chin. The facial hair is rendered by oblique grooves. The mouth is small, with a full lower lip. The neck is short.

He wears a ›Parthian-style‹ tunic, a chlamys, and ›Parthian-style‹ trousers. The tunic has a wide, round neckline, leaving part of the upper chest bare, and long, tight-fitting sleeves. The cuffs of the sleeves are decorated with concentric circles in relief. The tunic has a plain band extending downwards from the middle of the neckline. The tunic ends above the knees and has a plain band at the hem. The tunic has a slit at the right side with a button-like element at the top. The folds of the tunic are rendered by curving and oblique grooves. Over the tunic, he wears a chlamys. It falls over the shoulders and is folded around his left wrist. A wide fold falls from under the wrist, across the cushion and the mattress. The lower end of the fold is divided into two s-shaped edges. One edge of the chlamys has a scalloped border, visible on the fold across the chest. The chlamys is fastened at the right shoulder with an oval brooch with an incised border, possibly indicating a central inlay (Colledge classification: i). The folds of the chlamys are rendered by curving and oblique grooves. He wears a plain band belt, knotted at the centre with the ends looped under on either side of the waist. Along his right thigh he has an object with a rectangular body and two curving lateral protrusions: a sheathed dagger. He also wears trousers. Each trouser leg is decorated in the middle with a narrow, plain band extending downwards. The trousers are tucked into his boots. The folds of the garment are rendered by curving grooves. The plain boots have an upper edge decorated with two horizontal grooves.

He rests his right hand on his right, raised knee. With the upturned palm of the left hand, he holds a round bowl.

A.D. 200–220

689. BANQUETING RELIEF

DATABASE NUMBER: FM004.
LOCATION: Cambridge, Fitzwilliam Museum, inv. no. GR.6.1888.
CONTEXT: —
ACQUISITION HISTORY: Purchased in 1888.
MEASUREMENTS: Height: 51.5 cm. Width: 81.5 cm. Depth: 8.5 cm. Portrait A: Height: 40.7 cm. Width: 15.7 cm. Depth: 8 cm. Head height: 9.5. Head width: 7 cm. Portrait B: Height: 35.5 cm. Width: 13.5 cm. Head height: 8.5 cm. Head width: 7.5 cm. Portrait C: Height: 20 cm Width: 13 cm. Head height: 8.5 cm. Head width: 7.5 cm. Portrait D: Height: 45 cm. Width: 67.5 cm. Depth: 8.5 cm. Head height: 14.5 cm. Head width: 16.7 cm. Head depth: 7.5 cm.
MATERIAL: Limestone.
PRESERVATION: The relief ground between Portraits C and D is broken off. The lower right corner is chipped. Portrait A: The nose and the mouth are chipped. Portrait D: The chin is chipped. The surface of the left hand and of the left knee is chipped.
TECHNICAL DESCRIPTION: —
DATE: A.D. 200–220 (Budde – Nicholls 1964: A.D. 200–273).
REFERENCES: Ingholt Archives, PS 847; Ingholt 1935, 70 pl. 31, 3; Budde – Nicholls 1964, 87 f. cat. 141 pl. 46; Scrase 2005, 204; Krag – Raja 2017, 199 n. 23–25; 201 n. 28. 29; 203 n. 43. 47. 48. 50. 51; 214 cat. 5 fig. 2; Krag 2018, 28 n. 9; 62 n. 353; 65 n. 369. 377; 66 n. 385; 87 n. 182. 185; 88 n. 190. 193. 195. 89 n. 205–207. 210; 104 n. 83; 379 f. cat. 799. Inscription: Budde – Nicholls 1964, 88; Krag 2018, 379 f. cat. 799.

OBJECT DESCRIPTION
The relief is rectangular in shape and depicts a seated female, two standing males, and a reclining male. Beneath these figures is a mattress. It is decorated by an intersecting lozenges pattern with four-petal flowers at the centre. The female sits on two cushions. Curving grooves indicate the texture of the fabric. The reclining male rests on a large, round cushion. The texture of the fabric is indicated by wide, curving grooves.

INSCRIPTIONS
INSCRIPTION 1
SCRIPT: Palmyrene Aramaic.
LOCATION ON RELIEF: Between seated female and standing male, at the height of their heads.
TRANSCRIPTION: ṢLMT TMʾ | BRT WHBL[T] | ʾTTH.
TRANSLATION: Image of Tammê, daughter of Wahballat, his wife.

INSCRIPTION 2
SCRIPT: Palmyrene Aramaic.
LOCATION ON RELIEF: Between two standing males, at the height of their heads.
TRANSCRIPTION: ṢL<M> WHBY | BRH | ṢLM MLKʾL | BRH.
TRANSLATION: Image of Wahbaî, his son. Image of Malakêl, his son.

INSCRIPTION 3
SCRIPT: Palmyrene Aramaic.
LOCATION ON RELIEF: Between standing male and reclining male, at the height of their heads.
TRANSCRIPTION: Ṣ[LM - - -] | BR [- - -] | SRB? [- - -].
TRANSLATION: Image of - - - son of - - -.

CIS no. —; PAT no. —.

COMMENTS: Inscription 2: L.1: M has been forgotten by the stone-cutter. Inscription 3: Visible with difficulty on the available pictures. L.1: Reading Budde – Nicholls 1964, 88.

PORTRAIT A: SEATED FEMALE
The figure is shown in frontal view. The head is slightly turned to the left. The heads appear large. The arms appear short in relation to the body. The right arm is bent and rests on her lap. The left arm is bent and raised to the neck. She sits with her legs apart and the knees are visible under the drapery. The right foot is resting on the mattress; the left is obscured by the reclining figure to her left.

She wears three headdresses: a headband, a turban, and a veil. The headband is placed high on the forehead (details unclear). The turban is coiled. It is rendered in one twisted layer with horizontal and oblique grooves indicating the coiling of the fabric. The veil is heavy. It falls over her shoulders and in a wide fold around her right arm. Part of the hair is covered by the headdress: several strands of hair above the ears are brushed back over the headband and disappear under the veil. The individual strands of hair are indicated by incised lines. Her face is square. The eyebrows are curving. The eyes are almond-shaped, with thick upper eyelids. The eyeballs are possibly blank. At her ears and further along the neck, round objects are depicted, possibly earrings. The nose is short and straight. The cheeks are fleshy and the mouth is small, with a full lower lip. The chin is prominent and oval. The neck is short and wide. She wears a necklace composed of a string of large, round beads at the base of her neck.

She wears a tunic and a himation. The tunic has a wide, v-shaped neckline and short, loose sleeves. The folds of the tunic are rendered by curving grooves on the chest and vertical grooves under the right shoulder. The himation crosses the chest diagonally from the left shoulder to the right side, and covers the left breast. It is fastened at the left shoulder with a trapezoidal brooch with a rosette finial (Colledge classification: b). The main body of the brooch is divided into two sections with incised borders and decorated with possibly a vegetal motif. The himation covers the lower body and legs and ends at the ankles. The folds of the himation are rendered by vertical grooves on the body and upper legs, and curving and oblique grooves on the lower legs. She wears a round shoe.

She rests her right hand on her lap and is holding a fold of the veil. A long fold falls from under her hand, along her right thigh and down her right side. The right thumb is extended.

The left hand is raised to the neck and she lightly pulls the edge of the veil.

PORTRAIT B: STANDING MALE

The figure is in frontal view. The arms appear short in relation to the body. The head appears large. The right arm is bent and held in front of the chest. The left arm is bent and held in front of the right side of the body. The lower legs are obscured by the reclining figure to his left.

His hair is arranged in at least two rows of flame-shaped curls around the head. Incised lines indicate the individual locks of hair. His face is square. The eyebrows are curving, rendered by incised grooves starting from the root of the nose. The eyes are large and almond-shaped, with thick upper eyelids. The irises are indicated by round depressions. The ears are large; the left ear is larger than the right. The helix, tragus, concha, and lobe are depicted. The nose is wide and short with incised alae and slightly carved nostrils. The mouth is small. The chin is round and protruding. The neck is wide.

He wears a tunic and a himation. The tunic has a wide, v-shaped neckline. The folds of the tunic are rendered by curving and vertical grooves. Over the tunic, he wears a himation: it is wrapped around the arms, and covers most of the body, leaving only part of the upper torso and hands free. One fold of the himation crosses the chest diagonally and falls in front

Cat. 689, Pl. 96

of the left shoulder. The folds of the himation are indicated by oblique and curving grooves.

With his right hand, he holds the diagonal fold of the himation. The right thumb and the index finger are extended. With his left hand, he holds the vertical fold of the himation. The left thumb and the index finger are extended.

PORTRAIT C: STANDING MALE

The figure is shown in frontal view. The arms appear short in relation to the body. The head appears large. The right arm is bent and held in front of the chest. The left arm is bent and held in front of the right side of the body. The legs are obscured by the reclining figure to his left.

His hair is arranged in a single row of comma-shaped curls around the head. The individual locks of hair are indicated by incised lines. His face is oval. The eyebrows are curving, rendered by incised grooves starting from the root of the nose. The eyes are large and almond-shaped, with thick upper eyelids. The irises are indicated by incised circles, the pupils are indicated by punch holes. The ears are protruding, the left ear more than the right. Helix, tragus, concha, and lobe are depicted. The nose is short with a wide base. The alae are incised and the nostrils slightly carved. The mouth is small, with a full lower lip. The chin is oval and protruding. The neck is wide and short.

He wears a tunic and a himation. The tunic has a wide, v-shaped neckline. The folds of the tunic are rendered by curving grooves. Over the tunic, he wears a himation: it is wrapped around the arms, and covers most of the body, leaving only part of the upper torso and hands free. One fold of the himation crosses the chest diagonally and falls over the left shoulder (>arm-sling< type). The folds of the himation are indicated by oblique and curving grooves.

With his right hand, he holds the diagonal fold of the himation. The right thumb and the index finger are extended. With his left hand, he appears to grab the himation. The left thumb and the index finger are extended.

PORTRAIT D: RECLINING MALE

The body is shown in frontal view. The head is turned to the left. The head appears large. The arms appear short in relation to the body. The right arm is bent and rests on his raised right knee; the left arm is bent and rests on a cushion. His right leg is bent. The left leg is bent under the right, with the knee visible under the drapery as pointing forwards. His left lower leg is obscured by the right leg and the himation.

His hair is curly, with individual locks of hair plastically rendered. His face is square. The forehead is prominent and the eyebrows are curving. The eyes are almond-shaped, with thick upper eyelids. The upper eyelids extend beyond the end of the lower ones. The eyeballs are possibly blank. The ears are protruding and the helix, concha, scapha, and lobe are depicted. The nose is straight and wide with incised alae. He has a beard that starts from under his ears and covers the outer part of the cheeks, the chin, and the upper lip. The facial hair is depicted with plastically rendered curls. The mouth is small, with a full lower lip. The chin is square. The neck is wide and short.

He wears a >Parthian-style< tunic, a himation, and >Parthian-style< trousers. The tunic has a round neckline decorated with a beaded band. The tunic has long, tight-fitting sleeves. The cuffs are decorated with a band of lozenges with floral motifs at their centre. The tunic has a wide band decorated with leaves on a stem extending downwards from the middle of the neckline. The folds of the tunic are depicted by vertical grooves on the arm and curving grooves on the body. He wears a plain band belt with a single loop visible. The himation is folded around his left arm and wrapped around the left wrist. It falls along the left side of his body and is wrapped across the waist. It covers the lower body and legs until the middle of the shins. A folded edge of the himation falls from under the left hand onto the mattress in two large, zigzag-shaped folds. The folds of the himation are rendered by flat, oblique grooves. The trousers are visible from the shins to the ankles (details unclear). He wears closed ankle boots with the sole indicated by a horizontal, incised line. It is decorated with a beaded band along the arch of the foot and floral incisions on the lower part.

He rests his right hand on his right knee. The nails on the right hand are indicated with fine, incised lines. The outline of a bowl is visible in his left hand. With the upturned palm of the left hand, he holds a bowl with his fingertips.

690. BANQUETING RELIEF

DATABASE NUMBER: BNU004.
LOCATION: Strasbourg, University Library (Bibliothèque Nationale Universitaire).
CONTEXT: —
ACQUISITION HISTORY: Previously in the private collection of Prof. Euting. Euting donated his collection in his will to the Strasbourg University Library.
MEASUREMENTS: Height: 36 cm. Width: 48 cm.
MATERIAL: Limestone.
PRESERVATION: The upper right corner, the lower left corner, and the lower side of the relief are broken off. Portrait A: The head is broken off from the nose upwards. The mouth, the right hand, and the left knee are chipped. Portrait B: The surface of the middle part of the torso is weathered. The surface of the left thigh and of the right foot are chipped.
TECHNICAL DESCRIPTION: —
DATE: A.D. 200–220 (Chabot 1922: A.D. 200–273).
REFERENCES: Ingholt Archives, PS 72; Chabot 1922, 131 pl. 27, 12; Ingholt 1928, 96; Krag 2018, 28 n. 9; 62 n. 353; 65 n. 369; 66 n. 385; 379 cat. 798. Inscription: Chabot 1922, 131; Krag 2018, 379 cat. 798.

OBJECT DESCRIPTION

The object is rectangular in shape and depicts a seated female and a reclining male. Beneath the figures is a mattress. It is decorated with two wide bands with a crisscross pattern. Curving grooves indicate the texture of the fabric. The male rests against a round cushion. The cushion is decorated with a wide band with a running scroll and vine leaves. Curving grooves indicate the texture of the fabric.

INSCRIPTION
SCRIPT: Palmyrene Aramaic.
LOCATION ON RELIEF: Between the heads of the figures.
TRANSCRIPTION: [M]L[W]Kʾ.
TRANSLATION: Malôkâʾ.

CIS no. 4619; PAT no. 0980.

PORTRAIT A: SEATED FEMALE
The figure is shown in frontal view, the head is turned slightly to the left. The arms and head appear large in relation to the body. The right arm is bent and rests on her right thigh. The left arm is bent and raised to the neck. She sits with the legs apart with the knees visible under the drapery. The right foot rests on the mattress; the left foot is obscured by the reclining figure to her left.

She wears a veil. The veil is heavy and falls over the shoulders. It is wrapped around her right arm and falls back over her upper left arm. Her face is round. The earlobes are visible. The mouth is small. The chin is oval. Her neck is wide and short.

She wears a tunic and a himation. The tunic has a small, v-shaped neckline and short, loose sleeves. The folds of the tunic are indicated by v-shaped grooves on her chest. The himation crosses the chest diagonally from the left shoulder to the right side and covers the left breast. It is fastened at the shoulder with a circular brooch with an incised circle (Colledge classification: h). The himation covers the lower body and legs and ends at the ankles. The folds of the himation are rendered by oblique grooves on her body and legs. She wears a pointed shoe.

Her right hand rests on the right thigh and she holds a fold of the veil. The thumb and the index finger are extended. The left hand is raised to the height of the neck and she pulls the edge of the veil. The left index finger is extended.

PORTRAIT B: RECLINING MALE
The figure is shown in frontal view. His head and hands appear large. The right arm is extended and rests on his raised right

Cat. 690

knee; the left arm is bent and rests against a cushion. His right leg is bent. The left leg is bent under the right leg, with the knee pointing forwards. The left foot is obscured by the right leg and the himation.

His hair is arranged in flame-shaped curls in an unruly manner. Individual strands of hair are indicated by incised lines. His face is round. The eyebrows are curving and rendered as thin ridges. The eyes are large and almond-shaped. The upper eyelids are thick and extend beyond the end of the lower ones. The irises and pupils are indicated by concentric, incised circles. The ears are protruding with the helix, scapha, and lobe depicted. The nose is wide and pointed. The alae are incised, and the nostrils indicated. He has a beard: it starts at the temples and covers the outer side of the cheeks and the chin. The facial hair is rendered by small, crescent-shaped curls; incised lines indicate the individual strands of hair. The mouth is small with full lips. The chin is square. The neck is wide and short.

He wears a ›Parthian-style‹ tunic, a himation, and ›Parthian-style‹ trousers. The tunic has a round neckline decorated with a band of alternating incised squares and lozenges. The tunic has long sleeves, and the cuffs are decorated with a band with a vegetal motif. The tunic has a band, decorated possibly with a geometric pattern, extending downwards from the middle of the neckline. The folds of the tunic are rendered by oblique grooves. He also wears a plain band belt, knotted at the centre with the ends looped under on each side of the waist. Over the tunic, he wears a himation: it falls over his left shoulder and upper arm, along the left side of his body, and is wrapped around his waist. A fold of the himation falls under his left arm onto the cushion and mattress and ends in two zigzag-shaped folds. The himation ends at the middle of the shins. The folds of the himation are rendered by vertical grooves on his shoulder, and curving grooves on the lower body. The trousers are visible only on the lower part of the shins. The folds of the trousers are indicated by oblique grooves. He wears shoes: a thin shoelace is knotted with a bow at the ankle.

He rests his right hand on the right knee, holding an oblong oval object with a scale pattern, possibly a pinecone. With the upturned palm of the left hand, he holds a bowl with his fingertips. The bowl is decorated with hollowed-out lozenges with a raised dot in the centre. Horizontal, incised lines indicate the rim and base.

A.D. 220–240

691. BANQUETING RELIEF

DATABASE NUMBER: UPM013.
LOCATION: Pennsylvania, University of Pennsylvania Museum of Archaeology and Anthropology, inv. no. B8902.
CONTEXT: —
ACQUISITION HISTORY: —
MEASUREMENTS: Height: 45.5 cm. Width: 57 cm. Depth: 12 cm.
MATERIAL: Limestone, yellow.
PRESERVATION: The upper right corner is broken off. The surface of the right side and of the lower left corner is chipped.
TECHNICAL DESCRIPTION: —
DATE: A.D. 220–240 (Legrain 1927: A.D. 200–273).
REFERENCES: Ingholt Archives, PS 262; Legrain 1927, 348 cat. 5 fig. 5; Ingholt 1928, 120; Ingholt 1935, 70 pl. 32, 2; Seyrig 1937, 15 n. 3; Bossert 1951, 39 cat. 557 pl. 557; Danti 2001, 37 fig. 4; White et al. 2002, 86 cat. 126; Romano 2006, 295–297 cat. 141; Heyn 2008, 175. 179 fig. 6, 3; Long 2017, 78 f. fig. 9; Fowlkes-Childs – Seymour 2019, 164 f. cat. 109; <https://www.penn.museum/collections/object/189545> (06.05.2022). Inscription: Legrain 1927, 348 cat. 5; Romano 2006, 297 cat. 141.

OBJECT DESCRIPTION

The object is rectangular in shape and depicts two standing males and a reclining male. Behind the reclining figure a cloth is depicted. It is hanging from two six-petal rosettes at the height of the cheeks. A branch of palm leaves projects upwards and inwards from each rosette. The midribs of the leaves are incised. The folds of the cloth are indicated by curving and vertical grooves. Beneath the figures is a mattress: it is decorated with two plain, wide bands, and curving grooves indicate the texture of the fabric. The reclining male rests against a cushion. The cushion is decorated with a vertical band decorated with a stylized running scroll and rosettes. Curving grooves indicate the texture of the fabric.

INSCRIPTION

SCRIPT: Palmyrene Aramaic.
LOCATION ON RELIEF: Between the two standing figures.
TRANSCRIPTION: MLKW BR | MQYMW ḤBL.
TRANSLATION: Malkû, son of Moqîmû, alas!

CIS no. —; PAT no. 1772.

COMMENT: Vertical inscription.

PORTRAIT A: STANDING MALE

The figure is shown in three-quarter view, the head turned slightly to the left. The head and hands appear large. The legs appear small in relation to the body. The right arm is bent and held in front of the torso. The left arm is bent and held to the left. He stands with the right foot on the mattress; the left foot is obscured by the reclining figure to his left.

His hair is arranged in two rows of snail-shell curls around the head. Individual strands of hair are indicated by incised lines. His face is oval. The eyebrows are curving. The eyes are almond-shaped, with thick upper eyelids. The eyeballs are blank. The nose is straight, with a pointed end. The alae are incised, and the nostrils are indicated. The mouth is small, with thin lips. The chin is oval and prominent. The neck is short and has two horizontal grooves.

He wears a ›Parthian-style‹ tunic and ›Parthian-style‹ trousers. The tunic has a round neckline decorated with two plain bands. The tunic has long sleeves. The cuffs are decorated with a beaded band. The tunic has a beaded band extending downwards from the middle of the neckline. The tunic ends at the knees, and the lower border is decorated with a beaded band. The tunic is slit on the right side. The folds of the tunic are rendered by vertical and oblique grooves. A large fold across the waist indicates a belt. Along his right thigh he has an object with a rectangular main body and a lateral curving protrusion: a sheathed dagger. Each trouser leg is decorated at the middle with a beaded band extending downwards. The folds of the trousers are indicated by oblique grooves. He wears closed-toe shoes.

With the upturned palm of the left hand, he holds a bowl. The body of the bowl is decorated with a crisscross pattern, and the rim is indicated with a horizontal, incised line. In the left hand, he holds a ladle. The fingernails are indicated with incised lines.

PORTRAIT B: STANDING MALE

The figure is shown in three-quarter view, the head in frontal view. The head and hands appear large. The right arm is bent and held across the chest. The lower torso and legs are obscured by the reclining figure to the left.

His hair is arranged in two rows of snail-shell curls around the head. Individual strands of hair are indicated by incised lines. His face is oval. The eyebrows are curving. The eyes are almond-shaped, with thick upper eyelids. The eyeballs are blank. The nose bridge is narrow, and the base is wide. The alae are incised, and the nostrils are carved. The mouth is small, with full lips. The chin is pointed and prominent. The neck is wide and has two horizontal grooves.

He wears a ›Parthian-style‹ tunic. The tunic has a round neckline decorated with a beaded band. The tunic has long sleeves, and the cuffs are decorated with a beaded band. The tunic has a beaded band extending downwards from the middle of the neckline. The folds of the tunic are rendered by vertical grooves on the body and curving grooves on the sleeve.

Cat. 691

With his right hand, he holds an amphora by the handle; the left hand supports the base. The body of the amphora is decorated with hollowed-out lozenges, the neck by a tongue pattern. The handles are curling at the end attached to the body.

PORTRAIT C: RECLINING MALE, MALKÛ

The figure is shown in three-quarter view; the head is turned slightly to the left. His head and arms appear large in relation to the body. The right arm is extended and rests on the right knee. The left arm is bent in front of the chest and rests on a cushion. His right leg is bent and the right foot rests on the mattress. The left leg is bent under the right leg.

His hair is arranged in two rows of crescent-shaped curls around his head. His face is oval. The eyebrows are curving. The eyes are almond-shaped, with the upper eyelids indicated. The eyeballs are blank. The ears are large and protruding, and the helix, scapha, tragus, and earlobe are indicated. The nose is wide, and the alae are incised. The mouth is small, with a full lower lip. The chin is oval. The neck has two curving grooves.

He wears a >Parthian-style< tunic, a chlamys, and >Parthian-style< trousers. The tunic has a round neckline decorated with a beaded band. It has long sleeves, and the cuffs are decorated with a band of alternating incised squares and circles. The tunic is decorated with a band of lanceolate leaves extending downwards from the middle of the neckline. The tunic ends above the knees and the hem is decorated with a running scroll. The tunic is slit on the right side. The folds are rendered by vertical grooves on the sleeves and oblique grooves on the body. He also wears a plain band belt, knotted at the centre with the ends looped under on each side of the waist. Over the tunic, he wears a chlamys: it falls over both his shoulders and covers the left arm. It continues along the left side of the body, and ends at the mattress in two large, zigzag-shaped folds. It is fastened at the right shoulder with a circular brooch decorated with two concentric circles (Colledge classification: h), and a small fold falls underneath the brooch. The folds of the chlamys are rendered by curving grooves. The trousers are decorated with a band at the middle of each trouser leg extending downwards: the band is decorated with a crisscross pattern. The folds of the trousers are rendered by curving grooves. Along his right thigh he has an object with a rectangular main body and two lateral curving protrusions: a sheathed dagger. He wears ankle boots. A lace is knotted around the ankle and fastened to the shoe around the heel. Above the ankle is a strap with a circular attachment. The shaft is decorated with a beaded band.

His right hand rests on the right knee, and holds a round object with a small incised circle, possibly fruit. With the upturned palm of the left hand he holds a bowl with the fingertips in front of the chest. The body of the bowl is decorated with hollowed-out circles. The base and rim of the bowl are indicated with horizontal, incised lines. The fingernails are depicted with incised lines.

692. BANQUETING RELIEF

DATABASE NUMBER: MLP013.
LOCATION: Paris, Musée du Louvre, inv. no. AO 2000.
CONTEXT: —
ACQUISITION HISTORY: Bought by the Louvre Museum from the art dealer Naoum Mitri in 1890.
MEASUREMENTS: Height: 46 cm. Width: 56 cm. Depth: 21 cm. Portrait A: Height: 37 cm. Width: 13.5 cm. Depth: 9 cm. Head height: 8 cm. Head width: 7 cm. Head depth: 5 cm. Portrait B: Height: 37 cm. Width: 51 cm. Depth: 9 cm. Head height: 8 cm. Head width: 7 cm. Head depth: 5 cm.
MATERIAL: Limestone, white/yellow.
PRESERVATION: The right upper corner and the upper edge are chipped. Portrait A: The upper part of the veil is chipped. Portrait B: The forehead is chipped. The left thumb is broken off.
TECHNICAL DESCRIPTION: Restored in 1999 when the surface was treated and cleaned. There is mortar on the upper edge of the relief. There are traces of a red pigment in the inscription. There are tooth chisel marks on the relief background. Portrait A: Left arm is undercut. Traces of red colour on brooch. Portrait B: Traces of red colour on the forehead.
DATE: A.D. 220–240 (Chabot 1922: A.D. 200–250).
REFERENCES: Ingholt Archives, PS 73; Chabot 1922, 122 cat. 11 pl. 32, 12; Ingholt 1928, 96; Bossert 1930, 259. 398. 409 f. fig. 3; Seyrig 1937, 15 n. 3; Bossert 1951, 39 cat. 556 pl. 556; Colledge 1976, 62. 73 f. 129. 133 f. 136. 144. 148. 151. 153. 211. 216 pl. 61; Caubet 1990, 84 cat. 35; Dentzer-Feydy – Teixidor 1993, 172 cat. 175; Parlasca 1998, 315 pl. 127, 1; Long 2017, 72. 78 fig. 1; Krag 2018, 16 n. 73. 75; 28 n. 9; 39 n. 122; 45 n. 193; 46 n. 194. 196; 54 n. 262; 58 n. 301. 304–306; 59 n. 325; 62 n. 350. 353; 65 n. 377; 66 n. 385. 389; 67 n. 5; 87 n. 182. 185; 89 n. 204. 206. 210; 379 cat. 797; Krag 2019, 52 fig. 4; <https://collections.louvre.fr/ark:/53355/cl010127798> (06.05.2022). Inscription: Bossert 1951, 39 cat. 556; Caubet 1990, 84 cat. 35; Dentzer-Feydy – Teixidor 1993, 172; Krag 2018, 379 cat. 797.

OBJECT DESCRIPTION

The relief is rectangular in shape and depicts a seated female and a reclining male. Beneath these figures is a mattress. It is decorated with three bands. The central band is decorated with lozenges with beads in the corners and central vegetal motifs. It is set between beaded bands. The bands on either side are decorated with lanceolate leaves in an opposite arrangement on the stem. Curving grooves indicate the texture of the fabric. The female sits on two round cushions. Curving grooves indicate the texture of the fabric. The male rests against two cushions. Both cushions are decorated with a band with lanceolate leaves in an opposite arrangement on the stem. Curving grooves indicate the texture of the fabric.

INSCRIPTION

SCRIPT: Palmyrene Aramaic.

LOCATION ON RELIEF: Between the heads of the figures framed by an incised tabula ansata.

TRANSCRIPTION: ṢLM MLKW BR ḤGGW BR | MLKW QŠYŠʾ DY | DYRʾ ḤBL WHDYRʾ | ʾTTH ḤBL.

TRANSLATION: Image of Malkû, son of Ḥagegû, son of Malkû the elder of the community, alas! And Hadîrâ his wife, alas!

CIS no. 4501; PAT no. 0862.

PORTRAIT A: SEATED FEMALE, HADÎRÂ

The figure is shown in frontal view. The hands appear large in relation to the body. The right arm is bent and rests on her right thigh. The left arm is bent and raised to the neck. She sits on two cushions. She sits with the legs apart with the knees visible under the drapery. The right foot is resting on the mattress. The left foot is obscured by the reclining figure to her left.

She wears three headdresses: a headband, a turban, and a veil. The headband is placed high on her forehead and is decorated with four vertical grooves on each side of the band. The turban is coiled. It is composed of three coiling layers; the folds are indicated by oblique and horizontal grooves. The veil is heavy, with a scalloped edge at the top. It falls over the shoulders and is wrapped around her right arm. It falls behind her upper left arm. Her hair is parted at the centre of the forehead and brushed back over the headband and disappears under the veil. Incised lines render the individual locks of hair. A single straight lock of hair is depicted at the centre of her forehead, with individual hair strands rendered by incised lines. Her face is square and the eyebrows slightly curving. The eyes are almond-shaped, with thick upper eyelids. The eyeballs are blank. She wears earrings composed of three juxtaposed beads: two round ones on either side of a biconical one (Colledge classification: K). The nose is short with incised alae. The mouth is straight with a full lower lip. The chin is prominent and pointed. Her neck is wide with

Cat. 692

two curving grooves. She wears a necklace: a string of round beads at the base of her neck.

She wears a tunic and a himation. The tunic has a small, v-shaped neckline and long, tight-fitting sleeves. The cuffs of the sleeves are decorated with a beaded border. The folds of the tunic are indicated by curving grooves on her chest and left sleeve. The himation crosses the chest diagonally from the left shoulder to the right side and covers the left breast. It is fastened at the shoulder with a circular brooch decorated with two concentric circles (Colledge classification: h). The himation covers the lower body and legs and ends at the ankles. The folds of the himation are rendered by oblique grooves on her body and from the left knee and down, and curving grooves between the legs. A large fold falls diagonally from the left knee to the back. She wears a sandal with a plain strap fastened between her big and index toe.

Her right hand rests on the right thigh and holds the fold of the veil. The index finger is extended. The left hand is raised to the neck and she pulls the edge of the veil. She wears a wide hoop bracelet with a bell pendant attached by a narrow sleeve.

PORTRAIT B: RECLINING MALE, MALKÛ
The figure is shown in frontal view and the head is turned slightly to his left. The arms appear short in relation to the body. His head is large. The right arm is bent and rests on his raised right knee; the left arm rests on two cushions. His right leg is bent. The left leg is bent under the right leg, with the knee pointing forwards. The left foot is obscured by the right leg.

His hair is arranged in three rows of flame-shaped curls around his head, with individual strands of hair indicated by incised lines. His head is oval. The eyebrows are curving and meet in a pointed groove above the nose. The eyes are almond-shaped, with thick upper eyelids. The eyeballs are blank. His ears are protruding with helix, tragus, and earlobe depicted. The nose is straight with two small frowns at the root. The nose is pointed, and the alae are incised. He has a beard that starts from the temples, covers the outer side of the cheeks, the upper lip, and the chin. The facial hair is rendered with flame-shaped curls arranged in rows. Individual strands of hair are indicated with incised lines. The mouth is small, with full lips. His chin and neck are wide, and a v-shaped depression indicates the sternocleidomastoid muscles.

He wears a ›Parthian-style‹ tunic, a chlamys, and ›Parthian-style‹ trousers. The tunic has a round neckline decorated with a beaded band between two narrow bands. The tunic has long sleeves, and the cuffs of the sleeves are decorated with three beaded bands. The tunic has a wide band with vegetal motif between two beaded bands extending downwards from the middle of the neckline. The tunic ends above the knees and has a decorated border with vegetal motif and a beaded band between two lines at the hem. The folds of the tunic are rendered by vertical grooves on the sleeves and oblong grooves on the body. Over the tunic, he wears a chlamys that falls over the right shoulder and left upper arm and covers the left side of the chest. It falls over his left arm and along his body and ends in two zigzag-shaped folds on the mattress.

One edge of the chlamys has a scalloped border, visible on the fold across the chest. It is fastened at the right shoulder with a circular brooch with two concentric, incised circles (Colledge classification: h). A zigzag-shaped fold falls from under the brooch. The folds of the chlamys are indicated by horizontal grooves. He also wears a band belt across the lower torso. The belt has an undecorated strap in the middle and a decorated strap with a beaded band at the sides. The belt is knotted in the centre with a bow. The trousers are visible from above the knee. Each trouser leg is decorated in the middle with a wide band with vegetal motifs extending downwards. The folds of the trousers are indicated by wide, curving grooves. Along his right thigh he has an object with a round end, a curving main body, and a lateral, trapezoidal protrusion: a sheathed dagger. He wears boots, which are decorated with three bands at the shaft. The upper band is beaded, the central band is decorated with a zigzag pattern, and the lower band is plain, but with an incised loop falling down the boot.

He rests his right hand on his right knee, holding an oblong object with diamond pattern, possibly a pinecone. With the upturned palm of the left hand, he holds a bowl with the fingertips. The bowl is circular and has horizontal, incised lines on the rim and base. The body is decorated with hollowed-out circles.

693. BANQUETING RELIEF

DATABASE NUMBER: MLP023.
LOCATION: Paris, Musée du Louvre, inv. no. AO 2093.
CONTEXT: —
ACQUISITION HISTORY: Bought by the Louvre Museum from the art dealer Naoum Mitri in 1890.
MEASUREMENTS: Height: 43 cm. Width: 63 cm. Depth: 18 cm.
MATERIAL: Limestone, yellow.
PRESERVATION: The top, right, and left side of the object are chipped. The lower central part of the mattress is chipped. Portrait A: Her left knee is chipped.
TECHNICAL DESCRIPTION: Flat chisel marks are visible on the relief background. There are traces of red pigment in the inscription. Portrait A: The left arm is undercut.
DATE: A.D. 220–240 (Chabot 1922: A.D. 200–250).
REFERENCES: Ingholt Archives, PS 74; Chabot 1922, 122 cat. 12 pl. 32, 13; Ingholt 1928, 96. 145 f.; Vigneau 1936, 118; Seyrig 1937, 25 n. 1 fig. 17; Colledge 1976, 62 f. 73 f. 124. 129. 136. 148. 155. 211. 216 f. 240 f. pl. 62; Taha 1982, 127 fig. 12; Dentzer-Feydy – Teixidor 1993, 178 cat. 180; Plattner 2010, 167 n. 50; Cussini 2016a, 140 n. 7; Krag – Raja 2017, 199 n. 23–25; 201 n. 28; 202. 203 n. 44. 47. 48; 213 cat. 4 fig. 5; Krag 2018, 16 n. 73; 28 n. 9; 39 n. 122; 54 n. 262; 59 n. 325–326; 61 n. 336; 62 n. 350. 353; 65 n. 377; 66 n. 385. 387; 87 n. 182. 185; 89 n. 207. 210; 378 f. cat. 796; Krag 2019, 52 fig. 5. Inscription: Chabot 1922, 122 cat. 12; Dentzer-Feydy – Teixidor 1993, 178 cat. 180; Krag 2018, 378 f. cat. 796.

OBJECT DESCRIPTION

The relief is rectangular in shape and depicts a seated female and a reclining male. Beneath these figures is a mattress. It is decorated with three bands. The right and central bands are decorated with vegetal motifs set between two beaded bands. The left band has serrated leaves in opposite arrangement on the stem, set between two beaded bands. Curving grooves indicate the texture of the fabric. The female sits on two cushions, where curving grooves indicate the texture of the fabric. The male rests against a round cushion. The cushion is decorated with a band with a vegetal motif, possibly lanceolate leaves, set between two beaded bands. Curving grooves indicate the texture of the fabric.

INSCRIPTION

SCRIPT: Palmyrene Aramaic.
LOCATION ON RELIEF: Between the figures framed by an incised tabula ansata.
TRANSCRIPTION: ṢLM TYMʾ BR MLKW BR | ḤGGW ḤBL WHDYRʾ | ʾMH ḤBL.
TRANSLATION: Image of Taîmê, son of Malkû, son of Ḥagegû, alas! And of Hadîrâ, his mother. Alas!

CIS no. 4502; PAT no. 0863.

PORTRAIT A: SEATED FEMALE, HADÎRÂ

The figure is shown frontally, with her head turned slightly to her left. The hands appear large, while the legs appear short in relation to the body. The right arm is bent and rests on her right thigh. The left arm is bent and raised to the height of the neck. She sits with the legs apart with the knees visible under the drapery. The right foot rests on the mattress; the left foot is obscured by the figure to her left.

She wears three headdresses: a headband, a turban, and a veil. The headband is placed high on her forehead and is divided into three horizontal, rectangular panels. The central panel is decorated with a vegetal motif, the outer two panels with horizontal, incised lines. They are separated by two vertical, plain bands. The turban is coiled. It is composed of two coiling layers, the folds indicated by horizontal and oblique grooves. The veil is heavy. It falls behind her head and back, over her shoulders, and the upper arms. It continues under her lower right arm. Her hair is parted at the centre of the forehead, brushed back over the headband and turban, and disappears under the veil. The individual locks of hair are rendered by

Cat. 693

incised curving lines. Her face is oval and the eyebrows slightly curving. The eyes are small and almond-shaped, with thick upper eyelids that extend beyond the end of the lower ones. The eyeballs are blank. Only the earlobes are visible under the hair and she wears dumbbell-shaped earrings (Colledge classification: H). The nose is short and pointed, and the alae are incised. Her mouth is small with full lips. The chin is pointed. Her neck is wide with a curving groove. She wears two necklaces: a string of large, round beads at the base of her neck, and under her collarbone she wears a loop-in-loop chain with two crescent-shaped terminals on either side of an oval pendant with an incised border and a central, round depression. Four chains ending in round beads are suspended from the pendant.

She wears a tunic and a himation. The tunic has a small, v-shaped neckline and short, loose sleeves that reach to the elbow. The folds of the tunic are indicated by vertical grooves. The himation crosses the chest diagonally from the left shoulder to the right side, and covers the left breast. It is fastened at the shoulder with a circular brooch with an incised circle (Colledge classification: h). The himation covers the lower body and legs and ends at the ankles. A large fold falls on the mattress between her feet. The folds of the himation are rendered by oblique and curving grooves. She wears a round-toe shoe.

Her right hand rests on the right thigh and holds the fold of the veil. A folded edge of the veil falls from her hand. The thumb and the index finger are extended. The left hand is raised to the neck and she pulls a fold of the veil. She wears a thin hoop bracelet on her left wrist with two incised, vertical lines.

PORTRAIT B: RECLINING MALE, TAÎMÊ

The torso and the left leg of the figure are shown in frontal view, the right leg in profile, the head turned to his left. The arms appear short in relation to the body. His head is large. The right arm is bent and held in front of his chest; the left arm is bent and rests on a cushion. His right leg is bent and raised. The left leg is bent under the right leg, with the knee pointing forward, visible under the drapery, and the lower left leg is obscured by the right leg.

His hair is arranged in three rows of flame-shaped curls around his head, with individual strands of hair indicated by incised lines. His head is oval and the eyebrows are slightly curving. The eyes are almond-shaped, with a thick upper eyelid. The ears are protruding and the tail of the helix, scapha, and earlobe are depicted. His nose is short and pointed with a wide base and the alae are incised. He has a beard that starts from the temples and covers the cheeks but not the chin. He has a moustache that covers the upper lip and does not reach the beard. The facial hair in the beard is rendered with flame-shaped locks arranged in rows, with individual strands of hair indicated with incised lines. The hair in the moustache is rendered with curving locks of hair. The mouth is small, with full lips. His chin is pointed and the neck is wide with two wide, curving grooves. The jugular notch is depicted with an incised vertical line at the neckline.

He wears a tunic, a himation, and >Parthian-style< trousers. The tunic has a small, round neckline and the folds of the tunic are indicated by curving grooves. Over the tunic, he wears a himation. The himation covers most of the body: it is wrapped around the right shoulder and arm, leaving only the upper part of the chest and the hands free. One fold of the himation crosses the chest diagonally and falls over the left shoulder (variation of >arm-sling< type). It is folded around his left wrist, falls over the cushion and mattress, and ends in two zigzag-shaped folds. The himation ends at the middle of the shins with a scalloped edge that is folded up. The folds of the himation are rendered by curving grooves. The trousers are only visible on the right leg, and are decorated in the middle with a wide band of vegetal motifs and a beaded band extending downwards. The folds of the trousers are indicated with curving grooves. He wears boots. The shaft of the boot is decorated with three bands: the uppermost a beaded band, the central a band with a zigzag pattern, and the lowest a plain band with an incised, oval shape with two s-shaped strings falling down. A lace is knotted in the centre and fastened to the boot around the heel and ankle. The sole of the boot is indicated by a horizontal, incised line.

With the upturned palm of the right hand, he holds a bowl with his fingertips. The bowl has a horizontal, incised line at the rim, the body decorated with hollowed-out circles, and a horizontal, incised line indicates the base. His left hand lightly holds the fold of the himation, and the thumb, index, and the middle finger are extended.

694. BANQUETING RELIEF

DATABASE NUMBER: BM004.
LOCATION: London, British Museum, inv. no. 132614.
CONTEXT: —
ACQUISITION HISTORY: Previously in Bertone's collection, sold through Hotel des Ventes de Neuilly-sur-Seine in 1931. Then, in 1959, it was donated to the museum by David Nash (WAA deposit book entry 1249).
MEASUREMENTS: Height: 40.64 cm. Width: 43.18 cm. Depth: 19.05 cm.
MATERIAL: Limestone, yellow.
PRESERVATION: The upper edge of the relief is chipped on the left corner. The central part of the mattress is chipped. Portrait A: The surface of the right lower leg, of the left knee, and of the lower part of the right hand is chipped. Portrait B: The surface of the left hand, of the attribute, and of the lower leg are chipped.
TECHNICAL DESCRIPTION: —
DATE: A.D. 220–240 (Davies 2017: A.D. 200–273).
REFERENCES: Hôtel des Ventes de Neuilly-sur-Seine 1931, 43 cat. 648; Ingholt Archives, PS 849; Parlasca 2005, 141 n. 28; Long 2016, 143 fig. 6; Davies 2017, 33 fig. 10; Krag 2018, 28 n. 9; 39 n. 122; 59 n. 325; 62 n. 353; 106 n. 105; 378 cat. 793; <http://www.britishmuseum.org/research/

collection_online/collection_object_details.aspx?objectId=282710&partId=1&searchText=palmyra+bust&page=1> (06.05.2022). Inscription: Krag 2018, 378 cat. 793.

OBJECT DESCRIPTION
The relief is rectangular in shape and depicts a seated female and a reclining male. Beneath these figures is a mattress. It is decorated with three bands. The central band is decorated with four-petal flowers separated by horizontal, beaded bands. The petals of the flowers are incised in the middle. The bands on either side are decorated with serrated leaves in an opposite arrangement on the stem. Vertical and curving grooves indicate the texture of the fabric. The female sits on two cushions. Curving grooves indicate the texture of the fabric. The male figure rests on a round cushion. The cushion is decorated with a single band with individual squares separated by narrow, horizontal bands. Curving grooves indicate the texture of the fabric.

INSCRIPTION
SCRIPT: Palmyrene Aramaic.
LOCATION ON RELIEF: Between the heads.
TRANSCRIPTION: —
TRANSLATION: —

CIS no. —; PAT no. —.

COMMENT: The inscription is fake.

PORTRAIT A: SEATED FEMALE
The figure is shown in frontal to three-quarter view. The head is turned slightly to her left. The arms appear short in relation

Cat. 694, Pl. 97

to the body. The head appears large. The right arm is bent and rests on her right thigh. The left arm is bent and raised to the neck. She sits with the legs apart with the knees visible under the drapery. The right foot is resting on the mattress. The left foot is obscured by the reclining figure to her left.

She wears two headdresses: a turban and a veil. The turban is coiled. It is divided into two layers and the ends are looped into each other creating a knot in the middle. Curving grooves indicate the coiling of the fabric. The veil is heavy. It falls over her shoulders. It falls in a wide fold around her upper right arm and proceeds under her right lower arm. Her hair is parted at the centre of the forehead and is brushed to the sides. The locks of hair on each side of the head, covering most of the ears, are brushed back and disappear under the veil. The individual locks of hair are rendered by incised lines. Her face is square. The eyebrows are curving. The eyes are almond-shaped, with thick upper eyelids. The eyeballs are blank. The nose is short and wide with incised alae. Only the earlobes are visible and she wears earrings with two juxtaposed balls (Colledge classification: K). The cheeks are fleshy, and the mouth is large with a full lower lip. The chin is oval and the neck is wide.

She wears a tunic and a himation. The tunic has a wide, round neckline and short, loose sleeves. The folds of the tunic are rendered by curving and oblique grooves. The himation crosses the chest diagonally from the left shoulder to the right side, and covers the left breast. It is fastened at the shoulder with a plain, circular brooch (Colledge classification: i). The himation covers the lower body and legs and ends at the ankles. The folds of the himation are rendered by vertical, curving and oblique grooves. She wears a round-toe shoe.

She rests her right hand on the right thigh and is holding a fold of the veil. A fold of the veil falls from under her hand. The thumb and the index finger are extended. The left hand is raised to the neck and she lightly pulls the fold of the veil.

PORTRAIT B: RECLINING MALE

The body is shown frontally, and the head is turned to his left. The arms appear short in relation to the body. The head is large. The right arm is bent and rests on his raised right knee; the left arm rests against a cushion. His right leg is bent. The left leg is slightly bent, with the knee rendered pointing forwards; the left foot is resting on the mattress. The right lower leg is obscured by the left leg and the himation.

His hair is arranged in three rows of snail-shell curls around the head. His face is oval. The eyebrows are slightly curving. The eyes are almond-shaped, with thick upper eyelids. The lower eyelids are indicated by incised lines. The eyeballs are blank. His ears are slightly protruding with the helix shown. The nose is straight with incised alae. He has a beard that starts from the temples, covers the outer side of the cheeks, the upper lip, and the chin. The facial hair is rendered by vertical and oblique, incised lines. The mouth is large with a full lower lip. The chin is round and the neck is wide.

He wears a ›Parthian-style‹ tunic and a himation. The tunic has a round neckline decorated with a beaded band and long, tight-fitting sleeves. The cuffs of the sleeves are decorated with a band with vegetal motifs, possibly lanceolate leaves. The tunic has a wide band decorated with lanceolate leaves in an opposite arrangement on the stem extending downwards from the middle of the neckline. The folds of the tunic are rendered by oblique grooves on the sleeves and curving grooves on the torso. He wears a plain band belt, knotted at the centre with the ends looped under either side of the waist. Over the tunic, he wears a himation. It is folded around his left upper arm and falls along the left side of his torso where it is folded over the tunic, across his waist and legs. One end of the himation is falling from under his left arm, over the cushion and mattress, ending in a zigzag-shaped fold. The folds of the himation are rendered by diagonally curving grooves. He wears either shoes or boots (details unclear).

He rests his right hand on his right knee, holding an oblong object with diamond pattern, possibly a pinecone. The outline of a bowl is visible in his left hand. With the upturned palm of the left hand, he holds a bowl (visible in outline) with his fingertips.

695. FRAGMENT OF A BANQUETING RELIEF

DATABASE NUMBER: NCG110.
LOCATION: Copenhagen, Ny Carlsberg Glyptotek, inv. no. IN 1157.
CONTEXT: —
ACQUISITION HISTORY: Puttmann in Syria.
MEASUREMENTS: Height: 19.5 cm. Width: 18 cm. Depth: 10 cm. Field depth: 4 cm.
MATERIAL: Limestone, yellow.
PRESERVATION: The left side and the lower part are broken off diagonally. The upper and right side are chipped. The left arm and the legs are broken off.
TECHNICAL DESCRIPTION: There are flat chisel marks on her hair, face, and clothing.
DATE: A.D. 220–240 (Hvidberg-Hansen – Ploug 1993: A.D. 230–250).
REFERENCES: Hvidberg-Hansen – Ploug 1993, 137 no. 91; Ploug 1995, 220 f. cat. 91; Krag 2018, 49 n. 229; 53 n. 260; 65, 73 n. 47; 103 n. 73; 375 cat. 787; Raja 2019a, 244 f. cat. 74.

OBJECT DESCRIPTION

The object was originally rectangular in shape. It depicts a standing female. A plastically rendered circular object is visible left of the figure on the relief background.

PORTRAIT

The body is shown in three-quarter view, the head in frontal view. The head appears large. The right arm appears small in relation to the body. The right arm is bent and held in front of the torso.

The hair is parted at the centre and brushed back to the neck. The individual locks of hair are rendered by wavy, incised lines. Her face is oval. The eyebrows are curving. The eyes are

Cat. 695, Pl. 98

round and the eyelids are depicted. The eyeballs are blank. The nose is short and wide. The alae are incised. The mouth is small, with full lips. The chin is square and prominent. The neck is long. She wears a necklace: a string of large, round beads worn at the base of the neck.

She wears a tunic. The tunic has a wide, round neckline, and long, loose sleeves. The folds of the tunic are rendered by v-shaped grooves on the chest and curving grooves on the sleeve.

With the right hand, she holds a short staff with a circular cross-section.

Cat. 696

696. FRAGMENT OF A BANQUETING RELIEF

DATABASE NUMBER: PM202.
LOCATION: Palmyra, Palmyra Museum, inv. no. CD 24/66.
CONTEXT: Secondary context: Found in later wall at the south side of the east part of the Via Praetoria.
ACQUISITION HISTORY: —
MEASUREMENTS: Height: 25 cm. Width: 40 cm. Depth: 18 cm.
MATERIAL: Limestone, white.
PRESERVATION: The background is broken off except for the area around the head and the left shoulder. The hair, right eyebrow, the nose, and the right cheek are chipped.
TECHNICAL DESCRIPTION: —
DATE: A.D. 220–240.
REFERENCES: Gawlikowski 1984, 97 cat. 10 pl. 73, 148.

OBJECT DESCRIPTION
The object depicts a male head.

PORTRAIT
The figure is shown in a three-quarter view. His head is turned to his left.

His hair is voluminous, arranged in three rows of snail-shell curls around the head. The individual strands of hair are indicated by incised lines.

His face is oval. The eyebrows are curving, rendered by incised lines, and starting from the root of the nose. The eyes are wide-set, almond-shaped, with thick, upper eyelids. The pupils are indicated by punch holes. Only the earlobes are visible under the hair. The nose is straight, with a wide base. The mouth is wide with full lips. The neck is short and wide.

The left shoulder is preserved (no other details visible).

697. FRAGMENT OF A MALE FIGURE

DATABASE NUMBER: PM654.
LOCATION: Palmyra, Palmyra Museum, inv. no. CD6/66.
CONTEXT: Secondary context: Found in the Temple of the Standards (Temple des Enseignes), Camp of Diocletian.
ACQUISITION HISTORY: —
MEASUREMENTS: Height: 14 cm. Width: 28 cm. Depth: 6 cm.
MATERIAL: Limestone, white.
PRESERVATION: Broken on all sides. Broken horizontally at the base of the neck, diagonally at the left upper arm, and horizontally at the abdomen. The surface of the right lower arm and chest is chipped.
TECHNICAL DESCRIPTION: —
DATE: A.D. 220–240.
REFERENCES: Gawlikowski 1984, 107 cat. 61 pl. 90, 195.

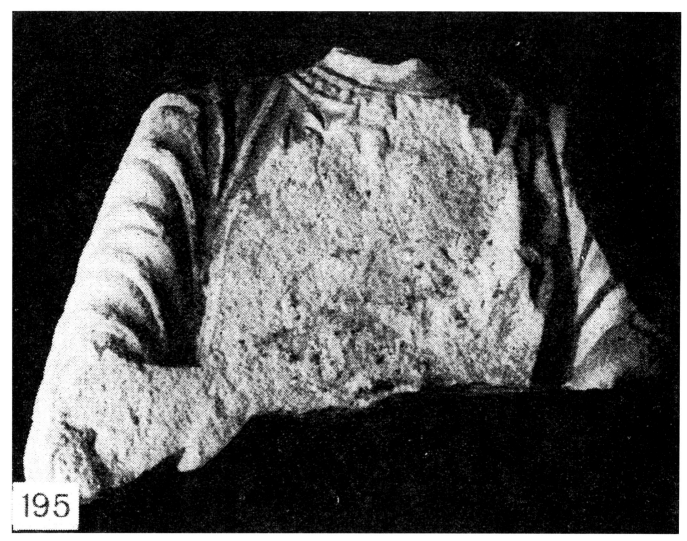

Cat. 697

OBJECT DESCRIPTION
Fragment depicting a male torso, possibly from a banquet relief.

PORTRAIT
The figure is shown frontally. The right arm is bent and held to the torso.

He wears a tunic. The tunic has a small, round neckline decorated with a beaded band, and long, tight-fitting sleeves. The folds of the tunic are rendered by curving and oblique grooves.

698. FRAGMENT OF A MALE FIGURE

DATABASE NUMBER: PM727.
LOCATION: Palmyra, Palmyra Museum, inv. no. CD 243/65.
CONTEXT: Secondary context: Found in the northern part of the Temple of the Standards (Temple des Enseignes), Camp of Diocletian.
ACQUISITION HISTORY: —
MEASUREMENTS: Height: 13 cm. Width: 17 cm. Depth: 10 cm.
MATERIAL: Limestone, white.
PRESERVATION: Broken on all sides. The upper part is broken off horizontally from the upper right to the upper left shoulder and the lower part is broken off at the torso. Broken diagonally from the left shoulder to the left side. The surface of the right hand is chipped. The surface is weathered.
TECHNICAL DESCRIPTION: —
DATE: A.D. 220–240.
REFERENCES: Gawlikowski 1984, 108 cat. 66 pl. 91, 200.

OBJECT DESCRIPTION
The fragment depicts the torso of a male figure.

PORTRAIT
The figure is shown reclining. The right arm is bent and held to the torso.

Cat. 698

He wears a ›Parthian-style‹ tunic with long, tight-fitting sleeves. At the middle, the tunic has a band decorated with serrated leaves in an opposite arrangement, extending downwards. The folds of the tunic are rendered by curving and oblique grooves.

699. FRAGMENT OF A BANQUETING RELIEF

DATABASE NUMBER: PM1070.
LOCATION: Palmyra, Palmyra Museum, inv. no. unknown.
CONTEXT: —
ACQUISITION HISTORY: —
MEASUREMENTS: Height: 21 cm. Width: 42 cm.
MATERIAL: Limestone.
PRESERVATION: Only part of the right side of the figure is preserved: part of the lower torso, the lower right arm and hand, the right thigh.
TECHNICAL DESCRIPTION: —
DATE: A.D. 220–240.
REFERENCES: Tanabe 1986, 44 pl. 444.

OBJECT DESCRIPTION
The fragment depicts a reclining male.

PORTRAIT
He is depicted in a profile view.

He wears a ›Parthian-style‹ tunic, ›Parthian-style‹ trousers, and over-trousers. The tunic has long and tight-fitting sleeves. The cuffs are decorated with a vegetal motif framed by two beaded bands. The tunic has a decorated lower border with a beaded band under a band with alternating four-petal flowers and diamonds with a bead at their centre. The folds of the tunic are indicated by widely spaced narrow grooves. It is tied at the waist with a plain band belt that was probably tied with a central knot; the ends of the belt are looped under on either side of the waist. The trousers are visible from under the tunic, and each trouser leg is decorated in the middle with a wide band with running scroll and leaves or flower buds, framed by two beaded bands. The folds of the trousers are indicated by wide grooves. The over-trousers are decorated with a beaded band at the border.

His right hand is resting against his thigh. He holds a sprig of wide, pointed leaves.

A.D. 240–273

700. BANQUETING RELIEF

DATABASE NUMBER: MSR001.
LOCATION: Toulouse, Musée Saint-Raymond, inv. no. 2003.2.1.
CONTEXT: —
ACQUISITION HISTORY: Acquired in June 2003, previously in a collection in Lebanon.
MEASUREMENTS: Height: 29 cm. Width: 49 cm. Depth: 29 cm.
MATERIAL: Limestone, yellow.
PRESERVATION: The upper left and right corners are broken off. A large v-shaped crack runs down the right arm and leg. The surface is chipped and weathered, especially in the upper chest area.
TECHNICAL DESCRIPTION: There are tooth chisel marks on the surface of the background. Tool marks are visible on the surface of the face.
DATE: A.D. 240–273 (Balty 2010: A.D. 200–273).
REFERENCES: Balty 2010, 25 f. fig. 2; Raja 2019e, 98. 126 cat. 49; <https://saintraymond.toulouse.fr/Relief-funeraire_a681.html> (06.05.2022).

OBJECT DESCRIPTION

The object is rectangular in shape and depicts a reclining priest on the left side of the relief. He reclines on a low mattress decorated with a pattern of intersecting lozenges with six-petal rosettes, and leans against a round cushion. The surface of the cushion is indicated by curving grooves and is decorated with a narrow band with a beaded border next to a wide band with a vegetal motif. On the right side of the relief is a square pedestal decorated with a six-petal rosette. On the pedestal, there is a two-handled amphora: the foot and neck of the vase are decorated with horizontal lines, while the body has a pattern of hollowed-out lozenges with three horizontal lines at the shoulder of the vase.

PORTRAIT

The figure is full-length, with his upper body depicted frontally, and the head turned slightly to his right. The arms and right leg are depicted in profile; the left leg is depicted frontally. His left arm is bent in front of the middle of the chest, and his right arm is extended. He is reclining with his left leg bent under the right leg, leaving only the thigh and knee visible, and the right leg bent. His left ankle is obscured by the right leg.

He wears a tall, cylindrical, flat-top headdress divided into three sections by two vertical grooves: a Palmyrene priestly hat.

Cat. 700, Pl. 99

A wreath is depicted at the lower part of the headdress. It has three rows of leaves pointing towards a central oval decoration.

The head is oval. The eyes are round, with thick eyelids. The eyeballs are blank. The ears are small, with helix, scapha, and lobe depicted. The nose is straight with a wide base. The mouth is small, with full lips. The chin is round. The neck is short and wide.

He wears a ›Parthian-style‹ tunic, a chlamys, and ›Parthian-style‹ trousers. The tunic has long, tight-fitting sleeves with cuffs decorated with a border with a chevron pattern, and a central, wide band with vegetal decoration extending downwards. The slashed sides have decorated borders, while the hem has a border of chevron design. Drapery is indicated by curved, oblique, and short, pointed grooves. Over the left thigh he has an object with a rectangular body and two lateral angular protrusions: a sheathed dagger. The chlamys falls over both shoulders, falls in a curving fold over the upper chest, and covers the left upper arm. Two wide, zigzag-shaped folds fall from under the left forearm onto the cushion and the mattress, where the decorated border is visible. A thin band belt is tied low around the waist. The ends of the belt are fastened to the belt on both sides and are descending from it. Each trouser leg is decorated in the middle with a wide band with a vegetal motif extending downwards (visible from above the knees to above the hem). They are tucked into soft, closed-toe ankle boots decorated with a floral design. There is a cuff or band with a central detail at the ankle.

His right hand rests on his knee. With his left hand, he holds a skyphos with a conical foot, a decorated body divided into a trapezoid and a cylindrical section, a rectangular rim, and two handles. The foot is decorated with oblique, incised lines. The body is decorated with a vegetal motif. The thumb, index, and the little finger of the left hand are extended.

BANQUETING RELIEFS WITH FRAME

A.D. 150–200

701. FRAGMENT OF A BANQUETING RELIEF

DATABASE NUMBER: PM225.
LOCATION: Palmyra, Palmyra Museum, inv. no. CD 49/73.
CONTEXT: Secondary context: A late pavement north of the Via Praetoria, to the east.
ACQUISITION HISTORY: —
MEASUREMENTS: Height: 24 cm. Width: 22 cm. Depth: 13 cm.
MATERIAL: Limestone, white.
PRESERVATION: Only part of the background around the figure is preserved. The central part of the headdresses and the face are weathered. The edge of the veil is chipped. The figure is broken off below the shoulders.
TECHNICAL DESCRIPTION: —
DATE: A.D. 150–200.

REFERENCES: Gawlikowski 1984, 107 cat. 59 pl. 89, 193; Albertson 2014, 32 cat. 29; Krag 2018, 47 n. 214; 51 n. 241; 101 n. 61; 103 n. 74; 312 cat. 550.

OBJECT DESCRIPTION
The fragment depicts a female bust. The edge of the relief has a moulding of beads following by stylized leaves. They are arranged in two rows, and are wide and pointed, with the midribs indicated by oblique grooves forming a triangle at the centre of the leaf.

PORTRAIT
The figure is shown frontally.

She wears three headdresses: a headband, a turban, and a veil. The headband is placed high on the forehead and is divided into rectangular, decorated panels separated by vertical, beaded bands. The central panel is badly weathered, but according to Gawlikowski (1984) it was decorated with a rosette. The outer panels have a geometric crisscross design. The turban is coiled. It is rendered in three twisting layers with horizontal and oblique grooves indicating the coiling of the fabric. The centre is badly weathered, but the direction of the grooves indicates that the two lower layers were twisted into each other, creating a central knot. The veil is heavy. It falls over both shoulders and covers the upper arms. Part of the hair is covered by the headdress: several strands of hair above the ears are brushed back over the headband and the edge of the turban, and disappear under the veil.

Her face is round. The eyebrows are curving (other details unclear). The eyes are close-set, round, with heavy eyelids. Only the earlobes are visible under the hair. She wears earrings with a single round bead (Colledge classification: J). The mouth is small. The neck is short and wide. She wears a necklace composed of a string of round beads and a medallion suspended from the centre.

She wears a tunic. The tunic has a small, round neckline. The folds of the tunic are indicated by wide, curving grooves.

A.D. 170–200

702. FRAGMENT OF A BANQUETING RELIEF

DATABASE NUMBER: PM294.
LOCATION: Palmyra, Palmyra Museum, inv. no. CD 144.
CONTEXT: Secondary context: Found (25.10.1960) at the north-eastern side of the Tetrapylon in the Camp of Diocletian.
ACQUISITION HISTORY: —
MEASUREMENTS: Height: 35 cm. Width: 36 cm. Depth: 20 cm.
MATERIAL: Limestone, grey.
PRESERVATION: The right and the upper sides of the relief are broken off. The lower left corner is chipped. Only part of the torso, arms, and upper legs are preserved. The right arm and the left knee are chipped.

Cat. 701

TECHNICAL DESCRIPTION: —
DATE: A.D. 170–200.
REFERENCES: Michalowski 1962, 159 f. cat. 29 fig. 174.

OBJECT DESCRIPTION
The object depicts a reclining male. The relief has a plain band frame on the left and lower sides, and an inner frame with a leaf-and-dart pattern. The midribs in the leaves are incised. Beneath the figure, there is a mattress. It is decorated with two bands set between two beaded bands: the right band with running scroll and rosettes, and the left with leaves on a stem. Curving grooves indicate the texture of the fabric. The figure rests on a round cushion. The cushion is decorated with a wide band with circular motifs. Curving grooves indicate the texture of the fabric.

PORTRAIT
The figure is shown in three-quarter view. His right arm appears short in relation to the body. The right arm is bent and rests on his right thigh. The left arm is bent, resting against a cushion. His right leg is bent. The left leg is slightly bent, and the knee is visible under the drapery.

He wears a >Parthian-style< tunic and a chlamys. The tunic has a round neckline, and long, tight-fitting sleeves. The cuffs are decorated with a band (details unclear). The tunic has a band with a vegetal motif extending downwards from

Cat. 702

the middle of the neckline. The tunic ends at the middle of the thighs and the hem is decorated with a band of leaves. The folds of the tunic are rendered by curving grooves on the torso and horizontal grooves on the upper legs. He also wears a plain band belt, knotted in the centre with the ends looped under on either side of the waist. Over the tunic, he wears a chlamys that falls over both shoulders and the chest in a curving fold, and covers the left side of the chest. It is fastened at the right shoulder with a circular brooch with an incised circle (Colledge classification: h). A fold of the chlamys falls from the brooch in an s-shape. A fold of the chlamys falls under his left arm onto the cushion and mattress, and forms two large, zigzag-shaped folds. Under the right arm, along the right thigh he has an object with a rectangular body and two lateral angular protrusions: a sheathed dagger.

703. FRAGMENT OF A BANQUETING RELIEF

DATABASE NUMBER: PM790.
LOCATION: Palmyra, Palmyra Museum, inv. no. A 133.
CONTEXT: —
ACQUISITION HISTORY: —
MEASUREMENTS: —
MATERIAL: Limestone.
PRESERVATION: The right and the upper sides of the relief are broken off. Only part of the torso, the right upper arm, and the left arm are preserved. The right lower arm and hand, the left hand, the head, and the legs are missing. The surface is chipped and weathered.
TECHNICAL DESCRIPTION: —
DATE: A.D. 170–200.

Cat. 703

REFERENCES: Ingholt Archives, PS 941.

OBJECT DESCRIPTION

The object depicts a reclining male. The relief has a plain band frame on the left and lower sides, and an inner frame with a leaf-and-dart pattern. The midribs in the leaves are incised. Beneath the figure, there is a mattress visible on the left lower edge. It is decorated with a band with a vegetal motif set between two plain bands. Curving grooves indicate the texture of the fabric. The figure rests on a round cushion. The cushion is decorated with a wide band with a vegetal motif. Curving grooves indicate the texture of the fabric.

PORTRAIT

The figure is shown in three-quarter view. His right arm is stretched and most likely resting on his right knee or thigh. The left arm is bent, resting against a cushion.

He wears a ›Parthian-style‹ tunic and a chlamys. The tunic has a round neckline, and long, tight-fitting sleeves. The tunic has a band with a vegetal motif extending downwards from the middle of the neckline and a decorated band around the right upper arm (details unclear). The folds of the tunic are rendered by oblique and pointed grooves on the torso. He also wears a plain band belt, knotted in the centre with the ends looped under on either side of the waist. Over the tunic, he wears a chlamys that falls over both shoulders and the chest in a curving fold, and covers the left side of the chest. It is fastened at the right shoulder with a brooch (details unclear). A fold of the chlamys falls under his left arm onto the cushion and mattress, and forms two large, s-shaped folds.

In his left hand, he holds a large bowl (visible in outline).

A.D. 180–240

704. FRAGMENT OF A BANQUETING RELIEF

DATABASE NUMBER: BaronPoche004.
LOCATION: Aleppo, Baron Poche private collection (Belgian Consul Adolphe Poche) (last known location).
CONTEXT: —
ACQUISITION HISTORY: —
MEASUREMENTS: —
MATERIAL: Limestone, white/yellow.
PRESERVATION: The relief is broken vertically to the left of the figure and horizontally through the upper legs. The surface of the face is chipped.
TECHNICAL DESCRIPTION: —
DATE: A.D. 180–240.
REFERENCES: Ingholt Archives, PS 531A.

OBJECT DESCRIPTION

The relief is rectangular in shape and depicts a standing male. The frame of the relief is decorated with a leaf-and-dart band with incised midribs. The leaves are oval-shaped followed by a row of pointy leaves.

PORTRAIT

The figure is shown frontally. The right arm is bent and held to the torso.

Cat. 704

His hair is straight, brushed away on either side of the head. His head is round. The ears are large and protruding. The neck is wide and there are two curving grooves.

He wears a tunic with a round neckline decorated with a beaded band, and long sleeves. In the middle, the tunic has a wide band extending downwards and decorated with large, round elements. The folds of the tunic are rendered by curving and oblique grooves.

He may hold an object in his hands (details unclear).

705. FRAGMENT OF A BANQUETING RELIEF

DATABASE NUMBER: PM592.
LOCATION: Palmyra, Palmyra Museum, inv. no. unknown.
CONTEXT: —
ACQUISITION HISTORY: —
MEASUREMENTS: —
MATERIAL: Limestone.
PRESERVATION: The upper, the left side, and the lower side are broken off. The relief background is weathered. Portrait A: The surface of the head, of the torso, and of the left arm are chipped. Portrait B: Only part of the lower leg survives.
TECHNICAL DESCRIPTION: —
DATE: A.D. 180–240.
REFERENCES: Ingholt Archives, PS 1028.

OBJECT DESCRIPTION
The fragment was originally rectangular in shape and depicts a standing male next to a reclining male. The relief has an outer plain frame and an inner frame composed of a stylized leaf-and-dart pattern. The midribs of the leaves are incised.

PORTRAIT A: STANDING MALE
The figure is shown in frontal view. The head appears large. The arms appear small in relation to the body. The right arm is bent and held in front of the torso. The left leg is obscured by the reclining figure to the right.

His hair is arranged in snail-shell curls. The ears are protruding, and the helix, tragus, and earlobe are depicted. The neck is short and wide.

He wears a >Parthian-style< tunic and >Parthian-style< trousers. The tunic has a round neckline decorated with a beaded band, and long, tight-fitting sleeves. The tunic has a beaded band extending downwards from the middle of the neckline. The tunic ends at the knees and the hem is decorated with a beaded band. The folds of the tunic are rendered by vertical and oblique grooves. The tunic is depicted with a horizontal fold at the waist, possibly indicating an overfold. The trouser legs are decorated in the middle with a beaded band extending downwards.

PORTRAIT B: RECLINING MALE
The right lower leg of the figure is shown in profile. It is raised.

Cat. 705

He wears >Parthian-style< trousers. The folds of the trousers are depicted by oblique grooves.

706. FRAGMENT OF A BANQUETING RELIEF

DATABASE NUMBER: PM769.
LOCATION: Palmyra, Palmyra Museum, inv. no. B 1818.
CONTEXT: Secondary context: Found (04.09.1954) north of the Temple of Baalshamin.
ACQUISITION HISTORY: —
MEASUREMENTS: Height: 24 cm. Width: 22 cm. Depth: 6 cm.
MATERIAL: Limestone.
PRESERVATION: The upper side, the left side, and the lower right corner are broken off. The surface of the frame and of the mattress is chipped. Portrait A: The head, the arms, and the torso are broken off. The surface of the legs is chipped.
TECHNICAL DESCRIPTION: —
DATE: A.D. 180–240.
REFERENCES: Dunant – Stucky 2000, 112 cat. 120 pl. 28.

OBJECT DESCRIPTION

The object is rectangular in shape and depicts a standing figure and a reclining figure. A projecting band is carved on the lower side. On the right side is a frame with a dart-and-leaf moulding with the midribs indicated with incised lines. Beneath the figures is a mattress. Curving grooves indicate the texture of the fabric.

PORTRAIT A: STANDING FIGURE

The figure is shown in three-quarter view. He stands with the right foot on the relief ground; the left leg and the foot are obscured by the mattress and the reclining figure to his left.

He wears a tunic. The tunic ends at the knees, and the folds of the tunic are rendered by curving and vertical grooves. He has bare legs under the tunic and is barefooted. The toes are indicated with incised lines.

PORTRAIT B: RECLINING FIGURE

The figure wears a himation that covers the lower legs. The left leg is indicated in the drapery. The folds of the himation are rendered by curving grooves.

707. FRAGMENT OF A BANQUETING RELIEF

DATABASE NUMBER: PM772.
LOCATION: Palmyra, Palmyra Museum, inv. no. B 1922.
CONTEXT: Secondary context: Found (30.09.1956) north-west of the large court of the Temple of Baalshamin.
ACQUISITION HISTORY: —
MEASUREMENTS: Height: 26 cm. Width: 36.5 cm. Depth: 16 cm.
MATERIAL: Limestone.
PRESERVATION: All sides of the object are broken off. The surface of the left side of the mattress is chipped. Portrait A: The upper part of the figure is broken off at the shins. Portrait B: Only part of the lower legs is preserved. The surface of the left knee is chipped.
TECHNICAL DESCRIPTION: —
DATE: A.D. 180–240.
REFERENCES: Dunant – Stucky 2000, 112 cat. 121 pl. 28.

OBJECT DESCRIPTION

The object is rectangular in shape and depicts a standing figure and a reclining figure. At the lower side, there is a plain frame. Beneath the figures is a mattress: it is decorated with a wide band with a crisscross pattern with a central punch hole in each lozenge, set between two beaded bands. Curving grooves indicate the texture of the fabric.

PORTRAIT A: STANDING FIGURE

He stands with the right foot on the lower plain frame; the left foot is obscured by the mattress and the reclining figure to his left.

He wears >Parthian-style< trousers. The folds are indicated by vertical grooves. He wears plain closed-toe ankle boots.

PORTRAIT B: RECLINING FIGURE

The right leg is bent and the right foot rests on the mattress. The left knee is visible under the drapery.

The figure wears a himation and shoes. The himation covers both legs and ends at the ankles. The folds of the himation are rendered by oblique grooves. He wears a shoe or a sandal: incised lines indicate straps and a circular element.

A.D. 200–220

708. FRAGMENT OF A BANQUETING RELIEF

DATABASE NUMBER: Christie's040.
LOCATION: New York, Christie's (last known location).
CONTEXT: —
ACQUISITION HISTORY: Previously in the Sobernheim collection, Berlin. Later in the collection of Neil F. Phillips, sold through Christie's in 1997.
MEASUREMENTS: Height: 26.65 cm.
MATERIAL: Limestone, yellow.
PRESERVATION: The upper left corner and the right and lower sides of the relief are broken off. The nose is broken off.
TECHNICAL DESCRIPTION: —
DATE: A.D. 200–220.
REFERENCES: Ingholt Archives, PS 1077; Ingholt 1938, 99 f. pl. 36.2; Christie's 1997, 18th December, New York, lot 291.

OBJECT DESCRIPTION

The relief is rectangular in shape and depicts a reclining male. The scene is framed by a moulding on the upper and left side. The moulding has a beaded band visible on the upper left side, a plain band, and outermost a band with leaf-and-dart design.

INSCRIPTION

SCRIPT: Palmyrene Aramaic.
LOCATION ON RELIEF: To the right of the figure.
TRANSCRIPTION: —
TRANSLATION: —

CIS no. —; PAT no. —.

PORTRAIT

The reclining figure is shown in three-quarter view, with the head slightly turned to his left. His head is large and the left hand is small in relation to the body. The right arm is bent; the left arm is bent and rests on a cushion. The cushion is decorated with a wide band with leaves on a stem and the texture and fabric of the cushion are indicated by curving grooves.

His hair is arranged in four rows of small snail-shell curls. His face is square. The eyebrows are arched. The eyes are large and almond-shaped. The end of the upper eyelids extends beyond that of the lower ones. The pupils are indicated by incised circles. The ears are small and protruding with the tail of the helix, concha, and earlobe depicted. The nose has

Cat. 708

a wide base. The nostrils are drilled. The mouth is small, with full lips. The cheeks are fleshy. The chin is round and the neck is short and wide.

He wears a ›Parthian-style‹ tunic and a chlamys. The tunic has a round neckline and long, tight-fitting sleeves. The neckline is decorated with a beaded band and from the middle of the neckline, a wide band, decorated with leaves on a stem extends downwards. The folds of the tunic are indicated by curving grooves on the right arm and oblique grooves on the chest. The chlamys falls across the chest in a curving fold. The edge of the chlamys is decorated with a beaded band. The chlamys is fastened at the right shoulder with an oval brooch with an incised border (Colledge classification: i). A zigzag-shaped fold falls under the brooch. The folds of the chlamys are indicated by curving grooves.

With his left hand he holds a small wreath. His index finger is extended.

A.D. 200–240

709. FRAGMENT OF A BANQUETING RELIEF

DATABASE NUMBER: PM517.
LOCATION: Palmyra, Palmyra Museum, inv. no. 2787/8708.
CONTEXT: Secondary context: Found at the northern wall of the city.
ACQUISITION HISTORY: —
MEASUREMENTS: Height: 44 cm. Width: 29 cm.
MATERIAL: Limestone, yellow.
PRESERVATION: The entire right side and part of the lower side are broken off. The surface of the nose, of the mouth, and of the chin are chipped. The figure is broken off at the upper right arm and diagonally across the torso.
TECHNICAL DESCRIPTION: —
DATE: A.D. 200–240 (al-Asʿad et al. 2012: A.D. 200–250).
REFERENCES: al-Asʿad et al. 2012, 172 cat. 29; Cussini 2016a, 141 fig. 2; <https://virtual-museum-syria.org/palmyra/upper-right-corner-of-a-framed-plaque/> (06.05.2022). Inscription: al-Asʿad et al. 2012, 172 cat. 29.

OBJECT DESCRIPTION

The object is rectangular in shape and depicts a reclining male. The relief has an upper plain frame and an inner frame on the upper and left side with a leaf-and-dart pattern, a plain, narrow band, and a beaded band. The male rests against a cushion. Curving grooves indicate the texture of the fabric.

INSCRIPTION

SCRIPT: Palmyrene Aramaic.
LOCATION ON RELIEF: On the plain panel on the upper side.
TRANSCRIPTION: MLKW BR ʿBDNḤS [- - -].
TRANSLATION: Malkû, son of ʿAbdnaḥas - - -.

CIS no. —; PAT no. —.

PORTRAIT: MALKÛ

The figure is shown in frontal view. The head appears large. His left arm is bent and raised to his head and rests against a cushion.

His hair is arranged in four rows of snail-shell curls around the head. Individual strands of hair are indicated with incised lines. His face is oval. The eyebrows are curving. His eyes are closed, and the eyelids are large. The nose is wide at the base. He has a beard that starts at the temples and covers the outer cheeks and the chin. The facial hair is rendered by comma-shaped locks. The neck is wide and has a curving groove.

He wears a tunic and a himation. The tunic has a wide, v-shaped neckline and long, tight-fitting sleeves. The folds of the tunic are rendered by curving grooves on the chest and oblique grooves on the sleeve. The himation falls over his left shoulder and is wrapped in a large fold around his left arm. It continues along the left side of the torso. The folds of the himation are indicated by vertical and curving grooves.

His right hand is lifted to the left cheek and supports his head. The fingers are extended.

A.D. 200–273

710. BANQUETING RELIEF

DATABASE NUMBER: PM653.
LOCATION: Palmyra, Palmyra Museum, inv. no. CD 78/65.
CONTEXT: Secondary context: The exterior of Temple of the Standards (Temple des Enseignes), Camp of Diocletian.
ACQUISITION HISTORY: —
MEASUREMENTS: Height: 46 cm. Width: 51 cm. Depth: 17 cm.
MATERIAL: Limestone, white.
PRESERVATION: The relief is badly weathered. The right side is broken off. The surface of the right side of the mattress is chipped. The entire lower right corner is chipped. Portrait A: Only the possible outline of the hand and attribute are preserved. Portrait B: The surface of the whole figure is chipped and weathered.
TECHNICAL DESCRIPTION: —
DATE: A.D. 200–273.
REFERENCES: Gawlikowski 1984, 107 cat. 58 pl. 88, 192.

OBJECT DESCRIPTION

The object is rectangular in shape and depicts a, possibly standing, figure and a reclining figure. It is framed by a plain panel on the lower side. Beneath the figures is a mattress:

Cat. 709

Cat. 710

curving grooves indicate the texture of the fabric. The male rests against a round cushion (no details visible).

PORTRAIT A: FIGURE
A possible outline of hand and attribute is visible to the right of the knee of the reclining figure.

PORTRAIT B: RECLINING MALE
The figure is shown in three-quarter view, the head in frontal view. The head appears large. The right arm is bent and raised toward the upper edge of the relief. The left arm is bent in front of the chest and rests on a cushion. The right leg is bent and raised. The left leg rests on the mattress.

Two large folds fall from under the left arm onto the cushion and mattress, possibly part of a himation or chlamys.

711. FRAGMENT OF A BANQUETING RELIEF

DATABASE NUMBER: DGAM050.
LOCATION: Palmyra, Directorate of Antiquities.
CONTEXT: —
ACQUISITION HISTORY: Confiscated and surrendered to the Directorate of Antiquities in Palmyra on 12.06.2014.
MEASUREMENTS: —
MATERIAL: Limestone.
PRESERVATION: The upper left edge of the relief is broken off, the lower left edge of the relief is chipped. The relief is broken diagonally from the upper right edge to the lower edge, including the lower left corner.
TECHNICAL DESCRIPTION: Portrait A: There are traces of red pigment on the neckline, the cuffs, and the central band of the tunic, as well as on the shallow bowl. Portrait B: There are traces of red pigment on the neckline, the cuffs, the central band, and the lower border of the tunic, the central band of the trouser leg, as well as on the bowl. There are traces of yellow pigment on the dagger.
DATE: A.D. 200–273.
REFERENCES: Ali 2015, 50 cat. 12.

OBJECT DESCRIPTION
The relief is rectangular in shape and depicts a standing male and a reclining male. The relief is framed on all sides by a plain band and has an inner frame on the right, upper, and left sides composed of a leaf-and-dart band with incised midribs in the leaves, a plain, narrow band, and a beaded band.

PORTRAIT A: STANDING MALE
The figure is shown in frontal view; the head is turned slightly to his right. The head appears large in relation to the body. The right arm falls to the side of his body. The left arm is bent and held upwards at the height of the cheek.

His hair is short. It is arranged in rows of curls around his head (other details unclear). His face is oval. The eyebrows are slightly curving and indicated by ridges. The eyes are almond-shaped, with the upper eyelid depicted. The eyeballs are blank. The ears appear to be covered by the hair. The nose is straight. The mouth is small, with full lips. The chin is pointed. The neck is wide and short.

He wears a >Parthian-style< tunic. The tunic has a decorated, round neckline (other details unclear). The tunic has long, tight-fitting sleeves. The cuffs are decorated with a wide band (other details unclear). The tunic has a decorated band extending downwards from the middle of the neckline (other details unclear). The folds of the tunic are rendered by oblique grooves.

With the palm of the left hand, he holds a shallow bowl with a small object, perhaps a small animal.

PORTRAIT B: RECLINING MALE
The torso and left arm of the reclining figure are shown in three-quarter view, the right arm and leg in profile. His head is turned slightly to the left. The head appears large. The right arm is slightly bent and rests against the leg. The left arm is bent and raised in front of the chest, the elbow resting on a cushion. The right leg is bent and raised, and the left leg is extended.

His hair is arranged in rows of snail-shell curls around the head. His face is oval. The eyebrows are curving. The eyes are almond-shaped. The eyeballs are blank. The ears are protruding and the helix, antihelix, concha, scapha, and lobe are depicted. The nose has a wide base. The mouth is small, with full lips. The chin is pointed. The neck is wide and long.

He wears a >Parthian-style< tunic, a chlamys, and >Parthian-style< trousers. The tunic has a wide, round neckline and long, tight-fitting sleeves. The neckline has a wide, decorated band (other details unclear). The cuffs and the lower border have a wide, decorated band (other details unclear). The tunic has a decorated band extending downwards from the middle of the neckline (other details unclear).

He holds a bowl with the fingertips of the right hand. It has convex walls (other details unclear). The left hand rests on the knee.

712. BANQUETING RELIEF

DATABASE NUMBER: PM652.
LOCATION: Palmyra, Palmyra Museum, inv. no. CD 50/66.
CONTEXT: Secondary context: Found at the steps of the Great Gate in the Camp of Diocletian.
ACQUISITION HISTORY: —
MEASUREMENTS: Height: 19 cm. Width: 23 cm. Depth: 7 cm.
MATERIAL: Limestone, white.
PRESERVATION: All sides of the object are broken off. The surface of the hair, of the face, and of the chest are chipped. Only the head, part of the right arm, and torso are preserved.
TECHNICAL DESCRIPTION: —
DATE: A.D. 200–273.
REFERENCES: Gawlikowski 1984, 107 cat. 57 pl. 88, 191.

OBJECT DESCRIPTION
The object is rectangular in shape and depicts a reclining male. The relief is framed by a leaf-and-dart pattern; the midribs of the leaves are indicated by incised lines.

PORTRAIT
The figure is shown in frontal view. The right arm is extended to the right.

His hair is arranged in three rows of flame-shaped curls around the head. Individual locks of hair are rendered by incised lines. The neck is wide and short.

He wears a tunic and a chlamys. The tunic has a round neckline, and long, tight-fitting sleeves. The folds of the tunic are rendered by oblique and curving grooves. The chlamys falls over both shoulders, and around the left upper arm. It is fastened at the right shoulder with a plain, circular brooch (Colledge classification: i). An s-shaped fold falls underneath the brooch. The edge of the chlamys is scalloped, visible on the diagonal fold across the chest. The folds of the chlamys are rendered by curving grooves.

The outline of a bowl is visible in front of the chest, held by the left hand.

Cat. 712

A.D. 220–240

713. BANQUETING RELIEF

DATABASE NUMBER: PM045.
LOCATION: Palmyra, Palmyra Museum, inv. no. 2216/7882.
CONTEXT: Secondary context: Found under the foundations of a wall in the south-east corner of the forum in the Camp of Diocletian.
ACQUISITION HISTORY: —
MEASUREMENTS: Height: 55 cm. Width: 91 cm. Depth: 18 cm.
MATERIAL: Limestone, yellow.
PRESERVATION: Portrait A: The surface of the right hand is chipped. Portrait B: The surface of the right hand and of the attribute is chipped. The nose is chipped.
TECHNICAL DESCRIPTION: —
DATE: A.D. 220–240.
REFERENCES: Michalowski 1966, 50 f. cat. 4 figs. 58–60; Colledge 1976, 79. 116. 134. 139. 145. 153 pl. 109; Taha 1982, 127 fig. 13; Tanabe 1986, 43 pl. 434; Stoneman 1999, pl. 19; <https://virtual-museum-syria.org/palmyra/palmyrene-man-with-his-servant/> (06.05.2022).

OBJECT DESCRIPTION
The relief is rectangular in shape and depicts a standing male and a reclining male. The relief is framed on all sides by a plain band. On the upper and the lower side is a decorated band with a floral motif, possibly buds with two petals. An inner frame is on the right, upper, and left side. It is composed of a leaf-and-dart band with incised midribs in the leaves, and a beaded band. Beneath the figures is a mattress, decorated with three bands. The central band is decorated with a running scroll with central rosettes. One rosette has hollowed petals. This band is set between two beaded bands. The bands on either side are decorated with leaves with incised midribs, set between two beaded bands. Curving grooves indicate the texture of the fabric. The second male (portrait B) rests against two round cushions. The cushions are decorated with bands. The upper cushion has a band with a running scroll with alternating leaves and rosettes. The petals of the rosettes are hollowed. This band is set between two beaded bands. The lower cushion has a vertical band with a running scroll and rosettes set between two beaded bands. Curving grooves indicate the fabric of the cushions.

PORTRAIT A: STANDING MALE
The figure is shown in frontal view. The head appears large. The right arm is slightly bent and lifted towards the left, across the body. The left arm is bent and held at the left side. He stands on the relief ground with the right foot. The left foot and the lower leg are obscured by the mattress and the reclining figure to the left.

The hair is arranged in two rows of snail-shell curls around the head. The individual strands of hair are indicated by incised lines. His face is oval. The eyebrows are slightly curving and indicated by incised lines, which meet above the nose in a wide angle. The eyes are almond-shaped, with thick eyelids. The irises are indicated by incised circles. The upper eyelids extend beyond the end of the lower ones. The ears are not visible under the hair. The nose is straight and pointed with a wide base. The alae are incised and the nostrils carved. The mouth is small, with full lips. The chin is oval. The neck has a slightly curving groove.

He wears a ›Parthian-style‹ tunic and ›Parthian-style‹ trousers. The tunic has a round neckline decorated with a beaded band. It has long sleeves, and the cuffs are decorated with a beaded band. The tunic covers his body and ends at the middle of the thighs. The lower border is decorated with a band with a running grapevine, with alternating grapes and leaves. The tunic is slit on the right side and the borders of the slit are decorated with a beaded band. The folds of the tunic are indicated by curving grooves down the middle of the torso and vertical grooves on the sides of the body. He also wears a plain band belt, knotted at the centre with the ends looped under on either side of the waist. Along the right thigh he has an object with a rectangular body and a round upper end: a sheathed dagger. The trousers are visible from above the knee to the ankles, and each trouser leg is decorated at the middle by a band with a running scroll with rosettes, set between two beaded bands, extending downwards. The petals of the rosettes are hollowed. He wears a closed-toe pointed ankle boot. The boot is plain, but the shaft is decorated with a beaded band.

His right hand is raised to the left of his body at the height of the shoulder, and the palm is turned towards the reclining figure to his left. The left hand is bent at the height of his waist and he holds a jug by the handle. The jug has a conical foot and a single horizontal incised line across the body.

PORTRAIT B: RECLINING MALE
The reclining figure is shown in three-quarter view, with the head turned slightly to the right. The head appears large. The arms appear short in relation to the body. The right arm is slightly bent and lifted towards the right. The left arm is bent and rests on two cushions. His right leg is bent and raised; the right foot is resting on the mattress. The left leg is bent under the right leg and is obscured by it.

His hair is parted in the centre of the forehead and brushed to the sides in waves. At the sides of the head, the hair is rendered by several snail-shell curls, with the individual strands of hair indicated by incised lines. His face is round. The eyebrows are slightly curving, indicated by incised lines, which meet above the nose in a pointed angle. The eyes are almond-shaped, with thick eyelids. The irises are indicated by incised circles. The nose has a wide base and the alae are incised. The mouth is small, with full lips. The cheeks are fleshy and the chin is pointed. The neck is short and wide and has a curving groove.

He wears a ›Parthian-style‹ tunic, a chlamys, and ›Parthian-style‹ trousers. The tunic has a round neckline decorated with a beaded band with a knot at the left side of the shoulders. A beaded band continues downwards from the knot, visible until the chlamys. The tunic has long, tight-fitting sleeves;

the cuffs are decorated with a beaded band and a band with a running scroll. The tunic has a wide band of leaves on a stem, set between two beaded bands extending downwards from the middle of the neckline. The tunic ends at the middle of the thighs, and the hem is decorated with a band with a running scroll and rosettes, whose petals have a depression, and a beaded band. The tunic is slit at the left side, and the border of the slit is decorated with a beaded band. The folds of the tunic are rendered by oblique grooves. He also wears a plain band belt, knotted at the centre with the ends looped under on either side of the waist. Along the right thigh he has an object with a rectangular main body and three lateral triangular protrusions: a sheathed dagger. Over the tunic, he wears a chlamys that falls over the right shoulder and left upper arm and is folded around the left lower arm. It is fastened at the right shoulder with a circular brooch with an incised circle (Colledge classification: h). The edge of the chlamys is decorated with a beaded band, which is visible on the fold across the chest and the corners. The folds of the chlamys are depicted with oblique grooves on the chest and curving grooves at the left hand. The trousers are visible from the thighs to the ankles. The middle of each trouser leg is decorated with a band of spiralling grapevines, set between two beaded bands extending downwards. The folds of the trousers are indicated by curving grooves. He wears a pointed ankle boot. The sole is indicated by a horizontal, incised line. The boot is decorated by incised rosettes and circles and beaded bands that run from the shaft down the boot and end in curls. Just above the ankle is a plain band with a button. The shaft is decorated with a beaded band.

With the upturned palm of the right hand he holds a bowl (visible in outline). The left hand holds a looped fold of the chlamys. Two large s-shaped folds of the chlamys fall from his hand onto the mattress and a round object is attached in both corners, possibly weights. The left index and the little finger are extended, and the nails are indicated by incised lines.

Cat. 713

714. BANQUETING RELIEF

DATABASE NUMBER: CMA001.
LOCATION: Ohio, Cleveland Museum of Art, inv. no. 1964.359.
CONTEXT: —
ACQUISITION HISTORY: Purchased by Leonard C. Hanna Jr. Fund.
MEASUREMENTS: Height: 55.3 cm. Width: 73.7 cm. Depth: 18.5 cm.
MATERIAL: Limestone, yellow.
PRESERVATION: All corners are chipped. Portrait B: The nose and the mouth are chipped.
TECHNICAL DESCRIPTION: Drilling in outer frame panels.
DATE: A.D. 220–240.
REFERENCES: Ingholt Archives, PS 1489; Vermeule 1981, 386 cat. 335; Equini Schneider 1993, 120 fig. 27; Parlasca 1984, 285 fig. 2; Parlasca 1989b, 546 f. fig. 203; <https://www.clevelandart.org/art/1964.359> (06.05.2022).

OBJECT DESCRIPTION

The relief is rectangular in shape and depicts a standing male and a reclining male. The relief has multiple frames. On the upper and lower side there is a band decorated with bead-and-reel design and a wide band with possible vegetal motif, separated from the relief by a plain band. The inner frame is composed of a leaf-and-dart band with incised midribs of the leaves and a beaded band. Beneath the figures is a mattress, decorated with three bands. The central band with vegetal motif set between two bands, decorated with circles centred in squares, separated by three circles. The bands on either side have lobed leaves where the midribs are rendered with fine, incised lines, set between two beaded bands. Curving grooves indicate the texture of the fabric. The reclining male rests on two round cushions. The cushions are decorated: the upper cushion has a band decorated with a crisscross pattern with circles in the centre of the squares. The lower cushion has a band decorated with a floral motif, set between two beaded bands. Curving grooves indicate the texture of the fabric.

PORTRAIT A: STANDING MALE

The figure is shown in three-quarter view. The head is large. The right arm is extended towards the right in front of his body; the left is bent and held at the height of the waist. He stands with the right foot on the relief ground; the left leg is obscured by the reclining figure to his left.

His hair is parted in the centre of the forehead and brushed to the sides, rendered by wavy, incised lines. On each side of the head the hair is rendered with four rows of snail-shell curls, with each strand of hair indicated with incised lines. His face is oval and the eyebrows are slightly curving. The eyes are almond-shaped, with thick eyelids. The irises and pupils are indicated by concentric, incised circles. Only the earlobes are visible under the hair. At the earlobes two round elements with a deep depression are rendered, possibly earrings. The nose is wide with incised alae. The cheeks are fleshy and the mouth small with full lips. The chin is round with a cleft. The neck has a curving groove.

He wears a >Parthian-style< tunic and >Parthian-style< trousers. The tunic has a round neckline decorated with a beaded band. The beaded band continues downwards on the left side of his chest until it extends behind his arm. The tunic has long, tight-fitting sleeves; the right cuff is decorated with a band of circles centred in squares, separated by three vertical circles. The lower hem of the tunic has a band decorated with circles centred in squares, separated by three vertical circles. The tunic is slit on the right side, and the borders of the slit are decorated with beaded bands. The folds of the tunic are rendered by curving grooves down the middle. He wears a plain band belt, knotted at the centre with the ends looped under on either side of the waist. Attached to the belt along his right thigh is an object with a triangular lower end, a rectangular main body, a lateral angular protrusion, and a round upper end: a sheathed dagger. The trousers are visible from the knee. They are decorated in the middle with a band with a running scroll set between two beaded bands extending downwards. The central bands are narrower towards the ankles. The folds of the garments are indicated by oblique grooves. He wears a closed-toe ankle boot. It is plain with a strap across the ankle.

With the upturned palm of the right hand, he holds a bowl with his fingertips. The body of the bowl is decorated with hollowed-out lozenges, and the rim is indicated by a horizontal, incised line. The left hand holds a bunch of cloth, with the ends falling under his hand in large zigzag-shaped folds. The nails are rendered by fine, incised lines.

PORTRAIT B: RECLINING MALE

The reclining figure is shown in three-quarter view, with the head slightly turned to his left. The head is large. The arms appear short in relation to the body. The right arm is bent and lifted, and rests upon his head. The left is bent and rests against two cushions. His right leg is bent, and the left is extended along the mattress. The right foot is obscured by the left leg.

His hair is arranged in three rows of snail-shell curls around his head, each lock of hair is indicated with incised lines. His face is oval. The eyebrows are slightly curving, rendered by incised lines starting at the root of the nose. The eyes are almond-shaped, with thick eyelids. The upper eyelids extend slightly beyond the end of the lower ones. The pupils and irises are indicated by concentric, incised circles. Only the earlobes are visible under the hair. The nose is wide and short with the alae incised. The mouth is small. The neck is short and wide. The neck musculature is indicated by a v-shaped depression.

He wears a >Parthian-style< tunic, a chlamys, and >Parthian-style< trousers. The tunic has a round neckline decorated with a beaded band. The beaded band continues downwards at the left side, but is obscured by the chlamys. A knot is rendered on the left side of the neckline. The tunic has long sleeves; the cuffs are decorated with a band with a vegetal motif, set between two beaded bands. The tunic has a wide band decorated with five-petal flowers and lobed leaves, extending downwards from the middle of the neckline. The midribs of the leaves are rendered with incised lines. The tunic ends above the knees and has a decorated border with a running scroll with alternating serrated leaves and round objects with circles between. A beaded band runs along the hem. The tunic is slit on the right side: the hem at the slit is decorated with a beaded band. The folds of the tunic are rendered by curving and oblique grooves. Over the tunic, he wears a chlamys that falls over the right shoulder, covers the left side of the chest and left arm, and is wrapped around the left wrist. It is fastened at the right shoulder with a circular brooch with an incised circle (Colledge classification: h). The folds of the chlamys are indicated by wide, oblique grooves. He also wears a belt across the lower torso: a plain band belt, knotted at the centre with the ends looped under on either side of the waist. Along his right thigh he has an object with a round lower end, a rectangular body, two triangular protrusions, and rhomboid upper end: a sheathed dagger. He wears trousers: each trouser leg is decorated in the middle with a wide band extending downwards. The band is decorated with a running scroll and five-petal flowers, set between two bands with circles centred in squares, separated by beaded elements. The folds of the garments are indicated by curving grooves. He wears closed-toe ankle boots. They are plain with a strap and button across the ankle. The shaft of the boot is decorated with a beaded band.

He rests his right hand on the top of his head. With his left hand, he lightly holds the fold of the chlamys. The ends of the chlamys fall under his left hand in zigzag-shaped folds. A drop-shaped object is depicted at the corner of the chlamys, possibly a weight. His left thumb, index, and the little finger are extended. On the little finger of the left hand, he wears a thick hoop ring with a round bezel. At the centre of the bezel there is a round raised element, perhaps indicating a stone.

Cat. 714, Pl. 100

715. BANQUETING RELIEF

DATABASE NUMBER: KMB001.
LOCATION: Budapest, Museum of Fine Arts, inv. no. 2004.1.A.
CONTEXT: —
ACQUISITION HISTORY: Purchased by Professor Rostovtzeff in 1931 for Yale University Art Gallery, inv. no. 1931.139.
MEASUREMENTS: Height: 44 cm. Width: 54 cm. Portrait A: Height: 31 cm. Width: 14 cm. Depth: 8 cm. Head height: 8.5 cm. Head width: 7 cm. Head depth: 5.5 cm. Portrait B: Height: 13 cm. Width: 14.5 cm. Depth: 4.5 cm. Head height: 6 cm. Head width: 6 cm. Head depth: 3.5 cm. Portrait C: Height: 33 cm. Width: 44.5 cm. Depth: 8 cm. Head height: 10 cm. Head width: 9 cm. Head depth: 6.5 cm.
MATERIAL: Limestone, yellow.
PRESERVATION: The upper and lower sides of the frame are chipped. Portrait A: The headdresses, the forehead, the left eye, and the right hand are chipped. Portrait B: The forehead and the nose are chipped. Portrait C: The nose, the mouth, the chin, the left hand, the bowl, and the fold from the garment under the left arm are chipped.
TECHNICAL DESCRIPTION: —
DATE: A.D. 220–240 (Ingholt 1954: A.D. 200–273).
REFERENCES: Ingholt Archives, PS 1341; Ingholt 1935, 70. 74 n. 90; Ingholt 1954, cat. 8; Sotheby Parke Bernet 1977, 21st May lot 220; Sotheby's New York 1983, 10th & 11th June lot 165; Seaby Antiquities Gallery London 2003, seen in MINERVA 2003 SEP/OCT; Royal-Athena Galleries New York & London 2004, lot 37; Albertson 2014, 31 appendix cat. 2; Cussini 2016a, 141 n. 15; 142 n. 19; Krag – Raja 2017, 199 n. 23–25; 201 n. 28; 203 n. 43. 47. 48. 50. 55; 213 cat. 3 fig. 1; Krag 2018, 28 n. 9; 59 n. 324; 60 n. 331; 62 n. 353; 65 n. 377; 87 n. 182. 185; 88 n. 193. 195. 197; 89 n. 206; 106 n. 106; 354 cat. 791; <https://www.mfab.hu/artworks/funerary-stele-of-a-palmyrean-couple/> (06.05.2022). Inscription: Albertson 2014, 31 appendix cat. 2; Krag 2018, 354 cat. 791.

OBJECT DESCRIPTION

The relief is rectangular in shape and depicts a seated female, a standing male, and a reclining male. The relief has an outer plain frame and an inner frame on the right, upper, and left side. The inner frame is decorated by a leaf-and-dart design, with the midribs incised in the leaves, a plain band, and a beaded band. Beneath the figures is a mattress decorated with three bands. The central band has vegetal motifs set between two beaded bands. The bands on either side have a crisscross pattern. Curving grooves indicate the texture of the fabric. The female sits on two cushions. Curving grooves indicate the texture of the fabric. The reclining male rests against a round cushion. The cushion is decorated with a wide band with lanceolate leaves on a stem. Curving grooves indicate the fabric of the cushion.

INSCRIPTIONS
INSCRIPTION 1
SCRIPT: Palmyrene Aramaic.
LOCATION ON RELIEF: Between the seated female and standing male, at the height of their heads.
TRANSCRIPTION: MRTY | ʾTTH.
TRANSLATION: Martî, his wife.

INSCRIPTION 2
SCRIPT: Palmyrene Aramaic.
LOCATION ON RELIEF: Between the standing male and reclining male, at the height of their heads.
TRANSCRIPTION: ʿBDBL | RBʾ.
TRANSLATION: ʿAbdibel, the elder.

CIS no. —; PAT no. 1660.

COMMENT: Inscription 2: L.1: ZBDBL PAT (no text in Ingholt 1954). The first letter has the slanted shape typical of ʿ.

PORTRAIT A: SEATED FEMALE

The figure is shown in frontal view. The head is turned slightly to the right. The arms appear large in relation to the body. The right arm is bent and rests between the knees. The left arm is bent and raised to the neck. She sits with the legs apart with the knees visible under the drapery. The right foot is resting on the mattress; the left is obscured by the reclining figure to her left.

She wears two headdresses: a turban and a veil. The veil is placed high on the head. It falls over her shoulders and in a wide fold around her right arm. The turban is placed high on the head (details unclear). The hair is parted in the centre of the forehead and brushed to either side, and disappears under the veil. The individual strands of hair are indicated by incised lines. His face is round. The eyebrows are curving. The eyes are almond-shaped, with thick upper eyelids. The eyeballs are blank. Only the earlobes are visible under the hair, and she wears earrings composed of three juxtaposed beads: two round ones on either side of a biconical one (Colledge classification: K). The nose is short. The cheeks are fleshy. The mouth is small, with full lips. The chin is small. The neck is wide.

She wears a tunic and a himation. The tunic has a round neckline and short, loose sleeves. The folds of the tunic are depicted with v-shaped grooves on the chest. The himation crosses the chest diagonally from the left shoulder to the right side, and covers the left breast. It is fastened at the left shoulder with a circular brooch decorated with an incised circle (Colledge classification: h). The edge of the himation is scalloped, visible at the diagonal fold across the chest. The himation covers her lower body and legs and ends at the ankles. The folds of the himation are rendered by oblique grooves. She wears a round-toe shoe.

She rests her right hand on her right thigh, and she holds a fold of the veil. The left hand is raised to the neck and she lightly pulls the edge of the veil. The index finger is slightly extended.

PORTRAIT B: STANDING MALE

The figure is shown in frontal view. His arms appear short in relation to the body. The right arm is bent and held in front of the chest. The left arm is bent and held towards the left. The lower body and legs are obscured by the reclining figure to his left.

His hair curls around his head, each lock of hair is indicated with incised lines. His face is oval. The eyebrows are curving. The eyes are large and almond-shaped. The eyeballs are blank. The ears are protruding and helix, tragus, concha, and earlobe are depicted. The nose is short with a wide base. The mouth is small, with full lips. The chin is pointed. The neck is short and wide.

He wears a tunic and a himation. The tunic has a wide, v-shaped neckline. The folds of the tunic are depicted by curving grooves. The himation covers most of the body: it is wrapped around the right shoulder and arm, leaving only part of the upper chest and hands free. One fold of the himation crosses the chest diagonally and falls over the left shoulder (›arm-sling‹ type). The folds of the himation are indicated by diagonal and vertical grooves.

His right hand lightly holds the diagonal fold of the himation, with the index, middle, ring, and the little finger extended. The left hand is placed on the upper right arm of the reclining figure, with all fingers extended.

PORTRAIT C: RECLINING MALE

The body is shown in frontal view; the head is turned slightly to the left. The head appears large. The arms appear short in relation to the body. The right arm is extended and rests on his raised right knee. The left arm is bent in front of the chest, and rests on a cushion. His right leg is bent and the right foot rests on the mattress. The left leg is bent under the right, and the knee is visible under the drapery as pointing forwards. The left foot is obscured by the right leg.

Cat. 715

His hair is arranged in two rows of flame-shaped curls around his head. The individual strands of hair are indicated with incised lines. His face is oval, and the eyebrows are slightly curving. The eyes are almond-shaped, with thick upper eyelids. The eyeballs are blank. The ears are rendered with the tail of the helix and earlobe. The nose is wide and short. He has a beard: it starts at the temples, covers the outer side of the cheeks, and the chin. The facial hair is rendered as individual curls by incised lines. The mouth is small, with a full lower lip. The chin is pointed and the neck is short and wide.

He wears a ›Parthian-style‹ tunic and a himation. The tunic has a round neckline decorated with a beaded band between two narrow bands. The tunic has long sleeves. The cuffs are decorated with a band with a crisscross pattern between two narrow bands. The tunic has a wide band decorated with lanceolate leaves on a stem extending downwards from the middle of the neckline. The folds of the tunic are depicted by vertical grooves on the arm and curving grooves on the body. He wears a plain band belt, knotted at the centre with the ends looped under on either side of the waist. The himation is folded around his left arm, falls along the left side of his body, and is wrapped across the waist. It covers the lower body and legs until the ankles. A folded edge of the himation falls from under the left hand onto the mattress in two large, zigzag-shaped folds. The folds of the himation are rendered by oblique grooves on the lower body, and curving grooves on the arm and at the waist. He wears a plain, closed ankle boot. A lace is tied around the ankle, and is fastened to the boot around the heel.

He rests his right hand on his right knee. With the upturned palm of the left hand, he holds a bowl with the fingertips in front of his chest. The bowl has a plain surface.

716. BANQUETING RELIEF

DATABASE NUMBER: UAG006.
LOCATION: New Haven, Yale University Art Gallery, inv. no. 1931.138.
CONTEXT: —
ACQUISITION HISTORY: Purchased for Yale University by Professor Rostovtzeff in 1931.
MEASUREMENTS: Height: 52 cm. Width: 56 cm. Depth: 8 cm. Depth of figure: 4 cm.
MATERIAL: Limestone, white/yellow.
PRESERVATION: The edges of the relief are chipped. Portrait A: The left cheek is chipped. Portrait B: The headdress, forehead, right eye, nose, mouth, and left hand are chipped.
TECHNICAL DESCRIPTION: There are flat chisel marks on the background. Portrait A: There are flat chisel marks on the face, on the clothing, and on the hat. The lower eyelids are not carved. Portrait B: There are flat chisel marks on the face, on the clothing, and on the hat. The lower eyelids are not carved.
DATE: A.D. 220–240 (Ingholt 1954: A.D. 200–273).

REFERENCES: Ingholt Archives, PS 1347; Ingholt 1954, cat. 11; Vermeule 1964, 107; Yale University Art Gallery 1992, 267; Brody – Hoffman 2011, 376 cat. 75; Raja 2017a, 219. 221. 226 cat. 15 fig. 19.25; Raja 2019e, 97. 99. 111 cat. 24 fig. 19; Raja 2017h, 63–65. 73 cat. 15 fig. 9; <https://artgallery.yale.edu/collections/objects/4729> (06.05.2022).

OBJECT DESCRIPTION
The relief is rectangular in shape and depicts a standing male and a reclining male. It has a plain frame along all sides, and an inner frame at the upper, left, and the right side decorated with a leaf-and-dart moulding, an undecorated narrow band, and a beaded band. A male figure stands on the right side of the relief, next to a male figure that reclines on a mattress divided into four sections by three bands. The left and the right band are decorated with serrated leaves in an opposite arrangement on the stem, set between two narrow beaded bands. The central band is decorated with rosettes inside circles, also set between two beaded bands. The reclining figure rests on a round cushion decorated with a central band decorated with alternating squares with six-petal rosettes and flowers with serrated petals divided by beaded bands. The folds of the cushion are indicated by wide, curving grooves. A pedestal crowned with a Doric capital is located behind the legs of the reclining figure. A tall, cylindrical, flat-top headdress divided into three sections by two vertical grooves is placed on top of the pedestal: a Palmyrene priestly hat. A band divided into three sections by two horizontal, incised lines with an oval with an incised centre is located at the lower part of the headdress. Two swathes of fabric fall down from the headdress across the pedestal in a zigzag-shaped fold and a wide, looped fold.

PORTRAIT A: STANDING MALE
The body of the figure is shown in a three-quarter view, while the head is shown frontally. The hands are bent and crossed in front of the torso. The left leg is obscured by the mattress and the left foot of the reclining figure.

He wears a tall, conical headdress. The headdress is decorated with a beaded band. A series of oblique grooves radiating from the bottom indicate the folds of the headdress. His hair is short, voluminous, and slightly wavy. It is centrally parted and combed backwards with overlapping locks of hair that cover the edges of the headdress. The individual strands of hair are indicated by incised lines. His face is square. The eyebrows are depicted as thin, curving ridges. The eyes are large and almond-shaped, with thick upper eyelids. The lower eyelids are not carved. The eyeballs are blank. The nose is straight and wide. The mouth is small, with a full lower lip. The chin is square. The neck is short and wide.

He wears a ›Parthian-style‹ tunic and ›Parthian-style‹ trousers. The tunic has a small, round neckline and long, tight-fitting sleeves. A central band extends downwards from the middle of the neckline; it is decorated with a branch of serrated leaves. The cuffs of the sleeves are decorated with a wide, undecorated band. The edge of the tunic is decorated with a wide band with alternating four-petal rosettes and flowers with serrated petals. On the right side of the tunic, there is a slit. The folds of the tunic are indicated by wide, oblique grooves. A thin band belt is tied with a double knot at the waist, and the ends of the belt are looped under the sides. Along the right thigh he has an object with a trapezoidal main body, a lateral angular protrusion, and a rhomboid upper end: a sheathed dagger. The trousers are decorated with a central, wide band with a vegetal motif extending downwards. He wears closed, pointed shoes.

His hands are folded over at the height of the waist.

PORTRAIT B: RECLINING MALE

The figure is shown reclining with his right leg in profile, his left leg shown frontally, his torso and head in three-quarter view, his head turned slightly to his left. Both arms are bent to the sides, the right resting on the raised right knee. The right leg is raised and bent, and the left extends along the mattress. The right foot is obscured by the left leg.

He wears a plain, tall, conical headdress. His hair is short, voluminous, and wavy. It is arranged in three rows of snail-shell curls, except over the forehead, where it falls in a single row of curls. His face is oval. The eyebrows are depicted as thin, low, curving ridges. The eyes are almond-shaped, with thick

Cat. 716, Pl. 101

eyelids. The lower eyelids are not carved. The eyeballs are blank. The nose is straight and wide. The mouth is small, with full lips. Two incised lines extend downwards at the corners of the mouth. The chin is pointed. The neck is short and wide with a curving groove.

He wears a ›Parthian-style‹ tunic, a chlamys, and ›Parthian-style‹ trousers. The tunic has a wide, round neckline. A central, wide band extends downwards from the middle of the neckline decorated with four-petal rosettes inside a running scroll motif between two narrow, beaded bands. The tunic has tight-fitting, long sleeves with cuffs decorated with a wide band with a leafy branch motif. The hem of the tunic has a wide band decorated with a running scroll with ivy leaves and a beaded band between two narrow bands. The folds of the tunic are indicated by curving grooves. A wide band belt is tied with a ribbon tied in a double knot at the waist. Along his right thigh he has an object with a rectangular main body, a square lateral protrusion, and a triangular upper end: a sheathed dagger. He wears a chlamys over the tunic. It is folded over the chest and covers the left shoulder and arm. It falls under the left elbow over the cushion and the mattress in two zigzag-shaped folds. It is fastened at the right shoulder with a circular brooch (Colledge classification: i). The folds of the chlamys are indicated by wide, oblique grooves. The trousers are decorated in the middle with a wide band extending downwards. The band has alternating square and circular elements with an incised centre that are divided by beaded bands. He wears a boot decorated with two beaded bands between two narrow bands: one across the top of the boot and one extending downwards. The rest of the boot is decorated with a running dog motif.

His right hand is bent and resting on the knee. He holds a plain, rhomboid object in his hand, possibly fruit. With the upturned palm of his left hand, he holds an undecorated bowl with steep sides with his fingertips in front of the chest.

717. BANQUETING RELIEF

DATABASE NUMBER: MLP032.
LOCATION: Paris, Musée du Louvre, inv. no. AO 4999.
CONTEXT: —
ACQUISITION HISTORY: Acquired in 1886.
MEASUREMENTS: Height: 40 cm. Width: 50 cm. Depth: 18 cm.
MATERIAL: Limestone, yellow.
PRESERVATION: The right and left sides are chipped. Portrait A: The left arm is chipped. Portrait B: The forehead, the nose, the mouth, the left shoulder, and the left leg are chipped.
TECHNICAL DESCRIPTION: The relief was restored in 1997 when the surface was treated and cleaned. There are tooth chisel marks on the sides of the relief.
DATE: A.D. 220–240 (Dentzer-Feydy – Teixidor 1993: A.D. 200–273).
REFERENCES: Ingholt Archives, PS 848; Ingholt 1928, 43; Dentzer-Feydy – Teixidor 1993, 203 cat. 201.

OBJECT DESCRIPTION
The relief is rectangular in shape and depicts a standing male and a reclining male. The scene is framed by a moulding on the upper, right, and left side. The moulding has a beaded band, a plain band, and outermost a band with leaf-and-dart design. A triangular midrib is incised on the frontal leaves. Beneath the two figures is a mattress. It is decorated with three bands. The central band is decorated with a running scroll and six-petal rosettes. The bands on either side are decorated with leaves on a stem. Curving grooves indicate the texture of the fabric. The reclining figure rests on a round cushion. The cushion is decorated with a band with lanceolate leaves arranged on a stem. The midribs on the leaves are indicated with fine, incised lines. Curving grooves indicate the texture of the fabric.

PORTRAIT A: STANDING MALE
The figure is shown in three-quarter view, with the head in frontal view. The arms appear short in relation to the body. The head appears large. His right arm is slightly extended towards the right, in front of his body. The left arm is slightly extended to the right. The lower legs of the figure are obscured by the figure to his left.

His hair is arranged in four rows of crescent-shaped curls around his head, with the individual locks rendered by incised lines. His face is round, and the eyebrows are curving. The eyes are large and almond-shaped; the lower edge of the eye and lower eyelid are not carved. The upper eyelid is indicated by a curving, incised line. The eyeballs are blank. The ears are large and protruding with the tail of the helix, tragus, and lobe depicted. The nose is straight and short, with a wide base and incised alae. The mouth is small, with full lips. The chin is wide and round and the neck is wide and short.

He wears a ›Parthian-style‹ tunic. The tunic has a round neckline decorated with a beaded band and long, tight-fitting sleeves. A band with a vegetal motif extends downwards from the middle of the neckline. The cuff of the left sleeve is decorated with a beaded band. A horizontal groove at the waist possibly indicates an overfold. The folds of the tunic are rendered by vertical and oblique grooves.

With the upturned palm of the right hand, he holds a bowl with the fingertips in front of his body. The bowl is round with an undecorated body. His left hand and lower arm support two bowls. The lower bowl is round with an undecorated body; the upper bowl is placed on the lower. The upper bowl is steeper with an undecorated body.

PORTRAIT B: RECLINING MALE
The reclining figure is shown in three-quarter view with the head slightly turned to his left. The left arm appears short in relation to the body. His head is large. The right arm is bent and rests on his raised right knee; the left arm is bent and rests on a cushion. His right leg is bent; the left appears to be bent under the right leg. The left lower leg is obscured by the right leg and the himation.

His hair is arranged in three rows of flame-shaped locks of hair, each lock indicated by incised lines. His face is oval. The eyebrows are slightly curving. The eyes are large and almond-shaped; the lower edge of the eye and the lower eyelid are not carved. The upper eyelid is indicated by a curving, incised line. The eyeballs are blank. The ears are large and protruding with the tail of the helix, tragus, and earlobe depicted. The nose has a wide base with alae incised. The mouth is small, with full lips. The cheeks are fleshy. The chin is round, and the neck is short and wide.

He wears a ›Parthian-style‹ tunic and a himation. The tunic has a round neckline decorated with a beaded band of square beads. The tunic has long, tight-fitting sleeves and the right cuff is decorated with a band of lanceolate leaves on a stem. The tunic has a wide band, decorated with lanceolate leaves on a stem extending downwards from the middle of the neckline.

The midribs of the leaves are indicated with fine, incised lines. The himation is folded around the left arm, falls along the left side of the body, and is wrapped across his waist. It is fastened at the right shoulder with a circular brooch with an incised border (Colledge classification: h), and an s-shaped fold falls underneath. The edge of the himation is scalloped, visible on the edges that cross the chest. One end of the himation falls under his left hand onto the cushion and mattress in two zigzag-shaped folds. The folds of the himation are indicated by oblique and curving grooves. He wears a round-toe shoe.

He rests his right hand on his right knee, and with it he holds a circular object, possibly a pinecone. All the fingers are extended. With his left hand, he lightly holds the fold of the himation. The thumb and the index finger are extended.

Cat. 717

718. BANQUETING RELIEF

DATABASE NUMBER: AMI074.
LOCATION: Istanbul, İstanbul Arkeoloji Müzesi, inv. no. 3728/180.
CONTEXT: —
ACQUISITION HISTORY: Confiscated in Damascus in 1893.
MEASUREMENTS: Height: 45 cm. Width: 40 cm.
MATERIAL: Limestone, yellow.
PRESERVATION: The right side and lower right corner is chipped. The upper left corner is chipped. Portrait B: The surface of the feet is chipped.
TECHNICAL DESCRIPTION: The finish is smooth.
DATE: A.D. 220–240.
REFERENCES: Ingholt Archives, PS 529; Musée Impérial Ottoman 1895, 72 cat. 180; Ingholt 1928, 43 n. 2; Mackay 1949, 164 pl. 53, 1; Albertson 2014, 32 appendix 23 pl. 3, 3; Krag 2018, 49 n. 229; 53 n. 255. 260; 62 n. 353; 64 n. 361. 362; 65 n. 372. 373; 73 n. 47; 103 n. 73; 375 f. cat. 788.

OBJECT DESCRIPTION

The object is rectangular in shape and depicts a standing female and a reclining female. It has an outer plain frame on all four sides. There is an inner frame on the right, upper, and left side, composed of a leaf-and-dart pattern, a plain band, and a beaded band. On the relief background, between the two figures, is a pedestal with a dual plinth and upon this a round vase, possibly a lebes. The vase is decorated with a crisscross pattern. Beneath the figures is a mattress with three bands: the central one is decorated with a running scroll and six-petal rosettes. The petals of the upper rosette have depressions. The bands on either side are decorated with squares of plain bands, with circles as corners, and central four-petal flowers. The right end of the mattress is indicated by an oval incision. Curving grooves indicate the texture of the fabric. The reclining female rests on two cushions: the upper cushion is decorated with a band of leaves on a stem. The lower cushion is decorated with a band with a running scroll. Curving grooves indicate the texture of the fabric.

PORTRAIT A: STANDING FEMALE

The figure is shown in frontal view, with the head turned slightly to the left. The right arm is bent and held in front of the torso. The lower legs are obscured by the reclining figure to her left.

Her hair is parted at the centre and combed back over the ears. Individual strands of hair are indicated by incised lines. Her face is oval. The eyebrows are curving. The eyes are large and almond-shaped. The eyeballs are blank. The ears are not visible under the hair. The nose is short with a wide base. The alae are incised, and the nostrils carved. The mouth is small, with thin lips. The chin is oval. The neck is short and has a curving groove.

She wears a tunic. The tunic has a small, round neckline and wide sleeves reaching the elbows. A large overfold is depicted across the waist. The folds of the tunic are rendered by curving grooves.

With the right hand, she holds a square box in front of her torso. The sides of the box have incised squares and the front side has a five-petal flower in the centre of the square. The lid of the box is indicated by a horizontal, incised line. It is possibly a jewellery box.

PORTRAIT B: RECLINING FEMALE

The body of the figure is shown in frontal view; the head is turned slightly to the left. The head appears large. The right arm is extended and rests on the right knee. The left arm is bent and raised to the neck, and rests on the cushions. The right leg is bent and raised. The left leg is slightly bent, resting along the mattress, and the knee is rendered under the drapery. The left leg obscures the right foot.

She wears three headdresses: a headband, a turban, and a veil. The headband is decorated with square panels with central incised circles, separated by vertical, narrow bands. The turban is coiled. It is composed of one layer, and oblique grooves indicate the coiling of the fabric. The veil is heavy. It falls behind her shoulders. Part of the hair is covered by the headdress: several strands of hair above the ears are pushed back over the headband and disappear under the veil. The individual strands of hair are indicated by incised lines. Her face is oval. The eyebrows are slightly curving. The eyes are round with thick upper eyelids. The eyeballs are blank. The right earlobe is visible, and she wears earrings composed of two juxtaposed beads; a round, upper bead and a lower, bell-shaped bead (Colledge classification: L). The nose is short and wide, with incised alae and carved nostrils. The cheeks are fleshy. The mouth is small, and the lips are full. The chin is oval. The neck has a horizontal groove. She wears a necklace: a string of round beads worn at the base of her neck.

She wears a tunic and a himation. The tunic has a wide, v-shaped neckline and loose sleeves reaching the elbows. The folds of the tunic are rendered as curving grooves on the chest and oblique grooves on the sleeve. The himation crosses the body horizontally just under the breasts, and is folded around the left arm. A fold of the himation falls underneath the left arm onto the cushions and ends in an s-shaped fold. At the corner of the fold is a triangular-shaped object, possibly a tassel. The himation covers her lower body and legs, and ends at the ankles. The folds are rendered by curving grooves. She wears sandals, with the strap fastened between the big toe and index toe. The toes are indicated by deep, incised lines.

The right hand rests on the right knee, and she holds a round object with a punch hole, possibly fruit. The left hand is supporting the head at the chin and cheek. On each wrist she wears a bracelet composed of twisted, plain wires.

Cat. 718

719. BANQUETING RELIEF

DATABASE NUMBER: NMD044.
LOCATION: Damascus, National Museum of Damascus, inv. no. 2153/4523.
CONTEXT: —
ACQUISITION HISTORY: —
MEASUREMENTS: Height: 47 cm. Width: 55 cm.
MATERIAL: Limestone, yellow.
PRESERVATION: The upper right corner is broken off. The upper side is chipped. The surface of the right half of the mattress is chipped. Portrait A: The surface of the head and of the right side of the body is chipped. Portrait B: The surface of the forehead, nose, mouth, and of the chest is chipped. The right foot is chipped. The lower right arm and the left hand are broken off.
TECHNICAL DESCRIPTION: —
DATE: A.D. 220–240 (Abdul-Hak – Abdul-Hak 1951: A.D. 200–273).
REFERENCES: Ingholt Archives, PS 684; Abdul-Hak – Abdul-Hak 1951, 35 cat. 17 pl. 14, 1; Colledge 1976, 63. 79. 132. 136. 139. 150. 155 f. 215. 240 f. pl. 107; Tanabe 1986, 43 pl. 438; el-Chehadeh 1987, 193 fig. 1; Ploug 1996, fig. on p. 63; Albertson 2014, 32 appendix 22; Krag – Raja 2017, 201 f. fig. 3; Krag 2018, 49 n. 229; 53 n. 255. 260; 62 n. 353; 64 n. 361. 362; 65 n. 372. 373; 73 n. 47. 53; 103 n. 73; 108 n. 125; 376 cat. 790; Krag 2019, 123 fig. 8.8.

OBJECT DESCRIPTION

The object is rectangular in shape and depicts a standing female and a reclining female. There is a plain frame on all four sides of the relief. There is an inner frame on the right, upper, and left side composed of a leaf-and-dart design, a plain band, and a beaded band. The midribs of the leaves are indicated with incised lines. Between the two figures, on the relief background, is a polygonal pedestal with coffers and a dual plinth. On top of this is a round object: the lower half is decorated with a crisscross pattern, and the upper half has very fine, incised lines. The two halves are separated by two horizontal, narrow bands (according to Colledge 1976, this is a ball of wool). Beneath the figures is a mattress. It is decorated with an intersecting lozenge pattern with six-petal flowers in the lozenges. The corners of the lozenges have round elements. The reclining female rests on a cushion: the cushion is decorated with a band with a running scroll and rosettes. The petals of the rosettes have depressions. Curving grooves indicate the texture of the fabric.

PORTRAIT A: STANDING FEMALE

The figure is shown in three-quarter view. The arms appear large in relation to the body. The right arm is bent and held in front of the torso. The left arm is bent and held to the left side. She stands with the right foot on the mattress, the left leg and foot are obscured by the reclining figure to her left.

Her hair is parted at the centre and brushed back. Individual locks of hair are indicated by wavy, incised lines. The chin is oval and prominent. The neck is wide.

She wears a tunic. The tunic has a wide, v-shaped neckline and wide sleeves reaching the elbows. A large round fold of the sleeve at the left arm is rendered on the relief background. A wide, horizontal fold is depicted across the waist. The folds of the tunic are rendered by curving grooves on the chest.

With the upturned palm of the left hand, he holds a square box. The box is decorated with incised squares on the front. The lid is lifted and the box is open towards the reclining figure to the left. Two necklaces hang on the outer side of the box: the lower necklace is composed of a loop-in loop chain with a triangular pendant suspended from the centre. The upper necklace is composed of round beads, with a trapezoidal pendant suspended from the centre.

PORTRAIT B: RECLINING FEMALE

The figure is shown in frontal view. The head appears large. The arms appear small in relation to the body. The right arm is bent across the torso. The left arm is bent and raised to the neck and rests on a cushion. The right leg is bent and the right foot rests on the mattress. The left leg is bent under the right, and the knee is rendered under the drapery. The lower left leg is obscured by the right leg.

She wears three headdresses: a headband, a turban, and a veil. The headband is placed low on the forehead (details unclear). The turban is coiled. It is arranged in a single layer and horizontal grooves indicate the coiling of the fabric. The veil is heavy. It falls behind her shoulders. She also wears a head-chain that is attached under the centre of the turban and runs to the sides disappearing under the veil. It is composed of circular pendants joined by beaded elements. Part of the hair is covered by the headdress: several strands of hair above the ears are pushed back over the headband and disappear under the veil. The individual strands of hair are indicated by incised lines. Her face is oval and the eyebrows slightly curving. The eyes are almond-shaped, with thick upper eyelids. She wears dumbbell-shaped earrings (Colledge classification: H). The chin is oval. The neck has a curving groove.

She wears a tunic and a himation. The tunic has loose sleeves reaching just below the elbows. The folds of the tunic are rendered by curving grooves on the chest and sleeve. The himation crosses the chest diagonally from the left shoulder to the right side and covers the left breast. It is fastened at the shoulder with a circular brooch with an incised border (Colledge classification: h). A fold of the himation falls along the left side of her body onto the mattress in a zigzag-shaped fold. The himation covers her lower body and legs and ends at the ankles. She wears footwear: a sole is indicated by an incised, horizontal line.

The right hand rests on the cushion and the fingers are extended. The left hand lightly pulls the edge of the veil at the height of her neck.

BANQUETING RELIEFS 949

Cat. 719, Pl. 102

720. FRAGMENTS OF A BANQUETING RELIEF

DATABASE NUMBER: PM293.
LOCATION: Palmyra, Palmyra Museum, inv. no. CD 9, CD 42.
CONTEXT: Secondary context: Found (03/04.05.1960) four metres west of the Tetrapylon in the Camp of Diocletian.
ACQUISITION HISTORY: —
MEASUREMENTS: Height: 64 cm. Width: 47 cm. Depth: 16 cm.
MATERIAL: Limestone, yellow.
PRESERVATION: The object is composed of three fragments. The upper and left side is chipped. Portrait A: The lower part is broken off at the chest. Portrait B: The lower right arm and the legs are broken off. The surface of the forehead and of the right hand is chipped.
TECHNICAL DESCRIPTION: The fragments are joined together.
DATE: A.D. 220–240.
REFERENCES: Michalowski 1962, 158 f. cat. 28 fig. 173; Albertson 2014, 32 appendix 24; Krag 2018, 49 n. 229; 53 n. 255. 260; 62 n. 353; 64 n. 361. 362; 65 n. 370; 73 n. 47. 53. 54; 103 n. 73; 376 cat. 789.

OBJECT DESCRIPTION
The object is rectangular in shape and depicts a standing female and a reclining female. On the upper and lower side,

Cat. 720

there is an outer plain frame. On the right, upper, and left side an inner frame is depicted. The inner frame is composed of a leaf-and-dart design, a plain band, and beaded band. Beneath the figures is a mattress. The mattress is decorated with an intersecting lozenges pattern with rosettes and flowers in the lozenges. There are round elements at the corners of the lozenges. The petals of the rosettes have depressions. The reclining female rests on a cushion. Curving grooves indicate the texture of the fabric.

PORTRAIT A: STANDING FEMALE

The figure is shown in three-quarter view. The left hand is bent and held to the left.

Her hair is parted at the centre and brushed to the sides. It is collected in a round knot in the back. The individual locks of hair are indicated by incised lines. Her face is oval. The eyebrows are curving. She has almond-shaped eyes with thick upper eyelids. The eyeballs appear blank. The earlobes are visible under the hair. The nose bridge is narrow. The mouth is small, with full lips. The chin is round. The neck is wide.

She wears a tunic. The tunic has a round neckline and is fastened at both shoulders with circular brooches (details unclear).

With the left hand, she holds an object: the object is round with a round incision, indicating a round frame. Possibly a mirror or tambourine.

PORTRAIT B: RECLINING FEMALE

The figure is shown in frontal view, with the head turned slightly to the left. The head appears large. The right arm is slightly bent. The left arm is bent and raised to the head and rests on the cushion.

She wears a veil. The veil is heavy and falls over the right shoulder and upper arm and behind the left shoulder. The hair is arranged in crescent-shaped curls and is brushed back under the veil. The individual locks of hair are rendered by incised lines. Her face is oval. The eyebrows are curving. The eyes are large and almond-shaped. The eyeballs are blank. The nose is short, with a wide base. The alae are incised. The mouth is small, with full lips. The chin is oval. The neck has a single curving groove.

She wears a tunic and a himation. The tunic has a round neckline and sleeves reaching the elbows. The folds of the tunic are rendered by oblique grooves on the chest. The himation is fastened at the left shoulder with a circular brooch (details unclear). It falls along the left arm and is wrapped around her waist. The himation covers the lower body and legs. The edge of the himation is scalloped, indicated on the edge that falls on the mattress. The folds of the himation are rendered by oblique grooves.

With her left hand she touches her cheek and temple. She wears a plain band bracelet on her left wrist.

721. FRAGMENT OF A BANQUETING RELIEF

DATABASE NUMBER: PM276.
LOCATION: Palmyra, Palmyra Museum, inv. no CD 27.
CONTEXT: Secondary context: Found in the south building in front of the staircase to Temple of the Standards (Temple des Enseignes), Camp of Diocletian.
ACQUISITION HISTORY: —
MEASUREMENTS: Height: 40 cm. Width: 29 cm. Depth: 14 cm.
MATERIAL: Limestone, white.
PRESERVATION: Only the upper right corner, upper right side, and central part survive. Portrait A: The surface is weathered and chipped, especially on the right side of the face and the chin. Portrait B: The knees are chipped.
TECHNICAL DESCRIPTION: Portrait A: The lower eyelids have not been carved.
DATE: A.D. 220–240.
REFERENCES: Ingholt Archives, PS 1495; Michalowski 1966, 49 f. cat. 3 fig. 57; Tanabe 1986, 43 pl. 439; Raja 2017a, 219. 222. 226 cat. 14; Raja 2017h, 63 f. 72 f. cat. 14 fig. 8; Raja 2019e, 97. 112 cat. 26 fig. 20.

OBJECT DESCRIPTION

The relief has a frame along its upper and right side composed of a leaf-and-dart moulding, a narrow, undecorated band, and a beaded band. A male figure stands on the right side of the relief, next to a male figure that reclines on a mattress. The mattress is divided into sections by two wide bands: a band decorated with a continuous vegetal motif framed by a beaded band to the right, and a band with a running scroll with different types of rosettes (four-petal, five-petal) framed by a beaded band. The folds of the mattress are indicated by wide, curving grooves. Behind the thigh of the reclining figure is a narrow pillar pedestal crowned by a three-stepped moulding. The pillar is decorated with a rectangular frame with a curved narrow edge; the frame has an incised border and is decorated with a continuous vegetal motif. A tall, cylindrical, flat-top headdress that is divided into three sections by two vertical grooves is shown on top of a pedestal: a Palmyrene priestly hat. A wreath of leaves pointing towards a central decoration (medallion?) is depicted at the lower part of the headdress.

PORTRAIT A: STANDING MALE

The figure is shown in a three-quarter view, turned towards the left. His head is raised upwards. His left arm is bent and raised to the height of the face; the right hand falls to the side. The left leg is obscured by the right foot of the figure and the mattress.

His hair is arranged in rows of snail-shell curls that reach up to the nape. His face is oval. The eyebrows are depicted by thin, curving grooves. The eyes have not been carved. The nose is short. The neck is short.

He wears a >Parthian-style< tunic. The tunic has long, tight-fitting sleeves. The tunic has a wide, round neckline decorated with a beaded band. A central band composed of squares and circles with incised borders extends downwards

Cat. 721

from the middle of the neckline. The folds of the tunic are indicated by wide, oblique grooves over the body and curving ones over the arms. A band belt is tied around the waist and the ends are looped under on both sides with a central double knot.

In his raised left hand, he holds a curved horn-shaped object decorated with ridges (rhyton). The mouth is circular and indicated by an incised circle.

PORTRAIT B: RECLINING MALE

The figure is shown reclining with his right leg in profile. The right leg is bent, with the foot on the mattress, and the left leg rests on the mattress, extending towards the back under the raised right leg. The left lower leg is obscured by the right leg and the himation.

He wears a himation. The himation is decorated with a pleated band at the hem. The folds are indicated by wide, oblique grooves.

722. FRAGMENT OF A BANQUETING RELIEF

DATABASE NUMBER: DGAM012.
LOCATION: Damascus, Directorate-General of Antiquities and Museums, inv. no. unknown.
CONTEXT: —
ACQUISITION HISTORY: Confiscated by authorities in Mudbnh, March 2014.
MEASUREMENTS: —
MATERIAL: Limestone.
PRESERVATION: Only the upper right side of the relief has been preserved. The surface is lightly weathered. Portrait A: The portrait is preserved from the knees up. The surface is chipped. Portrait B: Only the right leg and arm have been preserved. The surface is lightly chipped.
TECHNICAL DESCRIPTION: —
DATE: A.D. 220–240.
REFERENCES: Ali 2011, 53 cat. 9 fig. 71; Ali 2015, 50 cat. 9 fig. 70; Raja 2017a, 219–220. 222. 226 cat. 17; Raja 2017h, 63–65. 75 cat. 17; Raja 2019e, 97. 112 cat. 27.

OBJECT DESCRIPTION

The relief is square in shape and depicts a male figure standing and a reclining figure. It has a frame along its upper and right side with a plain outer border, a band with a leaf-and-dart motif in the middle, and a beaded band between two undecorated, narrow bands on the inside. A tall, cylindrical, flat-top headdress (details unclear), a Palmyrene priestly hat, is resting on a looped fold of fabric visible on the left side of the relief.

PORTRAIT A: STANDING MALE

The figure is depicted in frontal to three-quarter view. The right arm is held to the side. The left arm is bent and raised to the height of the shoulder.

His hair is centrally parted and long. It is straight at the top and curly at the sides with snail-shell curls arranged in four rows. His face is square. The eyebrows are rendered by wide, curving ridges. The eyes are small. The nose is wide and straight. The mouth is small, with full lips. His chin is wide. The neck is wide.

He wears a ›Parthian-style‹ tunic with a round neckline decorated with a beaded band and long, tight-fitting sleeves. A central, wide band decorated with floral patterns extends downwards from the neckline. The cuffs of the sleeves are decorated with a wide band. He also wears a narrow, band belt tied with a double knot at the waist and with the ends of the belt looped under on either side of the knot.

In the right hand, he holds an elongated object (bag?). The index finger is extended. In his left hand, he holds a round, undecorated bowl filled with irregular objects, possibly food.

PORTRAIT B: RECLINING MALE

His right arm is extended and rests on the raised right knee. The right leg is bent.

He wears a ›Parthian-style‹ tunic and a himation. The sleeves of the tunic are decorated with a broad band at the cuffs. Oblique folds on the knee indicate a himation.

With his right hand, he holds a circular object, possibly fruit.

723. BANQUETING RELIEF

DATABASE NUMBER: Sarrafian006.
LOCATION: Beirut, Sarrafian (antiquities dealer) (last known location).
CONTEXT: —
ACQUISITION HISTORY: —
MEASUREMENTS: —
MATERIAL: Limestone.
PRESERVATION: All four sides of the relief are broken off. A part of the relief ground is preserved next to the figure's head and upper torso. Only the head, torso, and part of the right arm are preserved. The surface of the face is chipped.
TECHNICAL DESCRIPTION: —
DATE: A.D. 220–240.
REFERENCES: Ingholt Archives, PS 577.

OBJECT DESCRIPTION

The fragment depicts a standing male. The relief has a frame along its upper and right side with a plain outer border, a band with a leaf-and-dart motif in the middle, and a beaded band. A male figure stands on the right side of the relief.

PORTRAIT

The figure is depicted in a three-quarter view, with the body turned towards his left and the head towards his right. His right arm is slightly bent and raised to the height of the shoulder; the left arm is bent to the side at the height of the waist.

He has long hair, centrally parted, straight at the top and curly at the sides, arranged in rows of snail-shell curls. His face is square. The eyebrows are rendered by ridges. The eyes are

Cat., 723

large (details unclear). The nose is wide. The mouth is small, with full lips. His chin is square. The neck is short and wide.

He wears a ›Parthian-style‹ tunic. The tunic has a round neckline decorated with a beaded band and long, tight-fitting sleeves. A central, wide band decorated with leaves extends downwards from the middle of the neckline. The cuffs of the sleeves are decorated with a narrow band. A thin band belt is tied with a double knot at the waist, with the ends of the belt secured on either side of the knot.

724. FRAGMENT OF A BANQUETING RELIEF

DATABASE NUMBER: NMD047.
LOCATION: Damascus, National Museum of Damascus, inv. no. 2793/7864.
CONTEXT: —
ACQUISITION HISTORY: —
MEASUREMENTS: Height: 55 cm. Width: 33 cm.
MATERIAL: Limestone, yellow.
PRESERVATION: The right and the upper side are chipped. The left side and the bottom are broken off. The feet are broken off at the ankles. The surface of the head, the nose, the mouth, and of the hands are chipped.
TECHNICAL DESCRIPTION: —
DATE: A.D. 220–240 (Parlasca 1982a: A.D. 175–225).
REFERENCES: Parlasca 1982a, 200 cat. 179; Parlasca 1985, 399 f. cat. 191; Albertson 2000, 162.

OBJECT DESCRIPTION

The object is rectangular in shape and depicts a standing female. The object has a plain frame on the right and the upper side, and an inner frame composed of leaf-and-dart design, a plain band, and a beaded band. The midribs of the leaves are rendered by incised lines.

INSCRIPTION

SCRIPT: Palmyrene Aramaic.
LOCATION ON RELIEF: To the left of the female, at the height of the legs.
TRANSCRIPTION: [- - -]Ḥʾ | [BRT] ʾBNT | [- - -]H BR | [- - -]Y BR | - - -.
TRANSLATION: - - - son of Abanit son of - - - son of - - -.

CIS no. —; PAT no. 1126.

COMMENTS: L.2: ʾBNT is new (only ʾBNYT was previously attested). L.3: [BR ʾL]HBL ›son of Elahbel‹ PAT. L.4: [- - -] ḤBL ›alas‹ PAT.

PORTRAIT

The figure is shown in frontal view; the head is turned slightly to the left. The head appears large. The arms appear short in relation to the body. The right arm is bent and held at the chest. The left arm is slightly bent to the left.

The hair is short and voluminous. The individual strands of hair are indicated by incised lines. Her face is oval. The eyebrows are curving and indicated with incised lines starting from the root of the nose. The eyes are almond-shaped, with thick eyelids. The irises are indicated by punch holes. The ears are small and protruding and the helix, scapha, tragus, and earlobe are depicted. She wears dumbbell-shaped earrings (Colledge classification: H). The nose is short with a wide base. The alae are incised, and the nostrils are carved. The mouth is small, with a full lower lip. The chin is oval. The neck is wide, and she wears a necklace. The necklace is composed of a plain hoop with three pendants: the central pendant is circular and is suspended by a wide sleeve, and on either side is a crescent-shaped pendant suspended by smaller, beaded elements.

She wears a tunic and a mantle. The tunic has a small, round neckline and wide sleeves reaching the elbows. The tunic falls to the ankles. It covers her lower body and legs, and a large fold across the waist is depicted. The folds of the tunic are rendered by curving grooves on the legs. The mantle falls over both her shoulders, and covers most of the upper body. A fold of the mantle is depicted ending at the waist, and a tassel is rendered in the corner. The folds of the mantle are rendered by curving grooves.

With the right hand, she holds an object with a semicircular body and an angular element added to the upper side, possibly a bird. She wears bracelets around both wrists, each rendered as a stem with serrated leaves.

A.D. 240–273

725. BANQUETING RELIEF

DATABASE NUMBER: PA001.
LOCATION: Damascus, Palais d'Azem, inv. no. unknown.
CONTEXT: Secondary context: Fastened above the door of one of the houses located in the Temple of Bel, and later removed.
ACQUISITION HISTORY: —
MEASUREMENTS: —
MATERIAL: Limestone, light brown.
PRESERVATION: The relief is badly weathered. The upper, the left, and most of the right side are broken off. The surface is chipped in multiple areas. Portrait A: The head, the back, and the arms of the figure are broken off. Portrait B: The head, the lower arms, and the hands are broken off. Portrait C: The head, the lower right arm, and the right hand are broken off. The surface of the upper body is chipped. Portrait D: The face and the lower left arm and hand are broken off. The surface of the upper body is chipped.
TECHNICAL DESCRIPTION: —
DATE: A.D. 240–273.
REFERENCES: Ingholt Archives, PS 22A; Ingholt 1928, 42–47 pl. 7, 1. 2.

OBJECT DESCRIPTION

The relief is rectangular in shape and shows four figures on a mattress. The pillow on the left side is depicted as a cylindrical object with wide-spaced grooves. The mattress is depicted as a rectangle with curving grooves. The three reclining males rest against cushions. The texture and the fabric of the cushions are indicated by deep oblique grooves. The cushion next to portrait C is decorated with a wide band with a running scroll. On the upper and right side, the relief is framed by a

Cat. 725

wide cavetto moulding with two rows of pointed leaves and a narrow moulding with beaded elements (>astragal<). On the left and lower side of the relief there is only a raised, plain band functioning as a frame.

PORTRAIT A: SEATED FIGURE

The figure is shown in three-quarter view, turned towards the left. The head and stomach are too large for the body. The left arm is raised to the height of the shoulder. The legs are parted. The right foot rests on the mattress of the kline.

The figure is dressed in an ankle-length tunic. No other details are visible.

PORTRAIT B: RECLINING MALE

The figure is shown frontally with the torso and in three-quarter view below the waist. His arms appear too short for the body. His arms are bent, the left to the side and the right in front of the torso. The legs are obscured by the seated figure to his right.

He has short hair.

He wears a >Parthian-style< tunic and a himation. The tunic has a round neckline with a beaded border and short, tight-fitting sleeves. From the neckline, a band decorated with circular elements extends downwards. The folds of the tunic are indicated by deep, oblique grooves. He wears a band belt low at his waist, knotted at the centre. The himation is folded around the left lower arm, falls along the mattress, and appears to be folded across his waist. A fold of the himation falls below his left arm, onto the cushion and mattress, and ends in a round edge. The folds are indicated by curving grooves.

A chipped area around his chest and right hand suggests he was holding an object (other details unclear). He holds a looped fold of the himation with his left hand.

PORTRAIT C: RECLINING MALE

The figure is shown frontally with the torso and in three-quarter view below the waist. His arms appear too short for the body. His arms are bent, the right raised to the height of his head, the left in front of his chest. The legs are obscured by the reclining figure to his right.

He has short hair.

He wears a >Parthian-style< tunic and a himation. The tunic has a round neckline with a decorated border and short, tight-fitting sleeves. From the neckline, a wide band decorated with leaves on a stem extends downwards. The folds of the tunic are indicated by deep, oblique grooves. He wears a band belt low on his waist. The himation is wrapped around his left lower arm, falls along the body and mattress, and appears to be folded across the waist. A zigzag-shaped fold falls below the left arm onto the cushion and mattress. The folds of the himation are indicated by curving grooves.

His right hand is behind his head. At his left hand, the outline of a bowl is visible.

PORTRAIT D: RECLINING MALE

The figure is shown frontally with the torso and in three-quarter view below the waist. His arms appear too short for the body. His arms are bent in front of the torso. The legs are obscured by the reclining figure to his right.

He has voluminous hair, arranged in rows of thick curls. His face is oval. The eyes are large. The neck is long.

He wears a tunic and a himation. The tunic has a v-shaped neckline and short, wide sleeves. The folds are indicated by deep, oblique grooves. He wears a band belt low at his waist. The himation is wrapped around his left arm and falls along his body on the mattress. The folds of the himation are indicated by curving grooves.

His right hand rests against his stomach. With the upturned palm of the left hand he holds a bowl (details unclear).

726. BANQUETING RELIEF

DATABASE NUMBER: PM443.
LOCATION: Palmyra, Palmyra Museum, inv. no. 2253/8113.
CONTEXT: —
ACQUISITION HISTORY: —
MEASUREMENTS: Height: 49 cm. Width: 52 cm.
MATERIAL: Limestone, yellow.
PRESERVATION: The right side, the upper left corner, and the lower right corner are chipped. Portrait A: The surface of the face is chipped. Part of the attribute is broken off.
TECHNICAL DESCRIPTION: —
DATE: A.D. 240–273 (Charles-Gaffiot et al. 2001: A.D. 200–250).
REFERENCES: Ingholt Archives, PS 1494; Bäärnhielm 1988, 25 f. fig. 14; Charles-Gaffiot et al. 2001, 344 cat. 149; Clauss 2002, 83 fig. 94; Sartre-Fauriat – Sartre 2008, 89; Gawlikowski 2010a, 76; Cussini 2016a, 141 n. 13; Curtis 2017, 62 f. fig. 14; Long 2017, 80 f. fig. 11.

OBJECT DESCRIPTION

The relief is rectangular in shape and depicts a standing male and a reclining male. The relief is framed on all sides by a plain band. There is an inner frame on the right, the upper, and the left side composed of a leaf-and-dart band with incised midribs in the leaves, a plain band, and a beaded band. Beneath the figures is a mattress decorated with three bands. The central band has a vine scroll set between two beaded bands. The bands on either side have running scrolls with rosettes set between two beaded bands. The petals of the rosettes are hollowed out. Curving grooves indicate the texture of the fabric. The male rests on a round cushion. The cushion is decorated with a wide band with a running scroll and flowers. Curving grooves indicate the texture of the fabric.

PORTRAIT A: STANDING MALE

The figure is shown in three-quarter view. The head and hands are large. The right arm is slightly bent and held at the waist. The left arm is bent and held at the chest. He stands with the right foot on the relief ground; the left leg is obscured by the mattress and the reclining figure to his left.

His hair is arranged in snail-shell curls around his head. The individual strands of hair are indicated by incised lines. The neck is long.

He wears a >Parthian-style< tunic and >Parthian-style< trousers. The tunic has a round neckline, decorated with a beaded band. The tunic has long, tight-fitting sleeves; the cuffs are decorated with a band of alternating incised circles and squares separated by three vertical circles. The tunic has a decorated band composed of leaves on a stem, set between two beaded bands extending downwards from the middle of the neckline. The tunic ends above the knees and the lower border is decorated with a running scroll with rosettes and flowers. The petals of the rosettes are hollowed. The tunic is slit on the right side, and the borders of the slit are decorated with plain bands. The folds of the tunic are rendered by vertical grooves along the body and curving grooves on the sleeves. He wears a plain band belt, knotted at the centre with the ends looped under on either side of the waist. He also wears a belt diagonally, under the plain belt. There is a circular element on the band, and a beaded strap continues from this. A long thin object is depicted on the relief ground at his left side, making this and the belt a dagger belt. Along his right thigh he has an object with a lateral triangular protrusion, and a rhomboid upper end: a sheathed dagger. The right trouser leg is decorated with a band in the middle extending downwards, composed of alternating incised circles and squares. He wears a plain closed-toe ankle boot.

Cat. 726

His right arm is held at the right side of his waist, with all fingers extended. With the upturned palm of the left hand, he holds a bowl with his fingertips. The body of the bowl is decorated with hollowed-out lozenges. Incised lines indicate the nails.

PORTRAIT B: RECLINING MALE

The reclining figure is shown in three-quarter view, with the head slightly turned to his left. The head is large. The legs appear small in relation to the body. The right arm is bent and rests on the right knee. The left arm is bent in front of the chest, and rests on a cushion. His right leg is bent, and the left leg is extended along the mattress, obscuring the right foot.

His hair is parted in the centre and brushed to the sides. The individual locks of hair are indicated by wavy incised lines. At the sides of the head, four rows of snail-shell curls are arranged, with each strand of hair depicted by incised lines. His face is oval. The eyebrows are slightly curving, rendered by incised lines starting at the root of the nose. The eyes are almond-shaped, with thick eyelids. The upper eyelids extend slightly beyond the end of the lower ones. The irises are indicated by incised circles, the pupils by punch holes. The nose bridge is narrow. The alae are incised, and the nostrils are carved. He has a beard that starts at the temples, and covers the outer side of the cheeks, the chin, and the upper lip. The facial hair is rendered by comma-shaped locks, indicated by incised lines. The beard ends at the chin with a pointed end. The mouth is large, and the lips are full. The chin is prominent. The neck is long.

He wears a >Parthian-style< tunic, a chlamys, and >Parthian-style< trousers. The tunic has a round neckline decorated with a beaded band. The tunic has long, tight-fitting, sleeves; the cuffs are decorated with a band with leaves, set above a beaded band. The tunic has a wide band decorated with a running scroll and rosettes, set between two beaded bands, extending downwards from the middle of the neckline. The tunic ends above the knees and has a decorated border with leaves on a stem extending downwards from the middle of the neckline. The hem is decorated with a beaded band. The tunic is slit on the right side. The folds of the tunic are rendered by curving and oblique grooves. He also wears a band belt across the lower torso: a plain band belt, knotted at the centre with the ends looped under on either side of the waist. Over the tunic, he wears a chlamys that falls over both shoulders, is wrapped around the left arm and falls onto the cushion and mattress in two large, zigzag-shaped folds. It is fastened at the right shoulder with a circular brooch with an incised border (Colledge classification: h). An s-shaped fold falls under the brooch. The folds of the chlamys are indicated by curving grooves. He wears trousers: each trouser leg is decorated in the middle with a wide band set between beaded bands extending downwards. The band is decorated with alternating circles and squares with central flowers. The folds of the garments are indicated by curving grooves. Along his right thigh he has an object with a round lower end, a rectangular main body, a lateral trapezoidal protrusion, and a rhomboid upper end: a sheathed dagger. He wears closed-toe ankle boots. A strap runs across the ankle with a button attached to it. A beaded band extends down the middle of the boot. The shaft is decorated with a beaded band.

In his right hand, he holds a round object with a punch hole, possibly fruit. The fingers are bent around this object, and incised lines indicate the nails. With the upturned palm of the left hand, he holds a bowl with his fingertips. The body of the bowl is decorated with hollowed-out lozenges and the rim is indicated by an incised horizontal line. Incised lines indicate the nails.

727. BANQUETING RELIEF

DATABASE NUMBER: NMAK002.
LOCATION: Kansas City, Nelson-Atkins Museum of Art, inv. no. 65-2.
CONTEXT: —
ACQUISITION HISTORY: Collection of Marguerite Mallon, Hotel Hassler in Rome. Purchased from Mallon by the Nelson-Atkins Museum of Art in 1965.
MEASUREMENTS: Height: 44.45 cm. Width: 65.1 cm. Depth: 17.78 cm.
MATERIAL: Limestone, white/yellow.
PRESERVATION: The lower right corner is broken off. The sides of the relief are lightly chipped. Portrait A: The surface of the face is lightly chipped. Portrait B: A crack runs across the upper part of the headdress. The right eyebrow, nose, and left cheek are chipped. The lower right arm and hand, and part of the rhyton are broken off.
TECHNICAL DESCRIPTION: —
DATE: A.D. 240–273 (Vermeule 1981: A.D. 200–273).
REFERENCES: Ingholt Archives, PS 1278; Vermeule 1981, 385 cat. 334; Parlasca 1984, 285–287 fig. 3; Raja 2019e, 98. 125 f. cat. 47 fig. 27.

OBJECT DESCRIPTION

The relief is rectangular in shape and depicts a male standing figure and a reclining figure. The relief has a frame along its upper, left, and right side with a plain, outer border, a leaf-and-dart moulding in the middle, and a beaded band. Beneath the figures is a mattress divided into four sections by three bands: two wide bands decorated with a rosettes inside circles or running scroll motif between two narrow, beaded bands at the sides, and a wider band decorated with a vegetal motif, also between two beaded bands. The reclining figure rests on a round cushion decorated with a central band composed of a narrow, beaded band next to a wide band decorated with rosettes inside circles or running scroll motif. The folds of the cushion are indicated by wide, curving grooves.

PORTRAIT A: STANDING MALE

The figure is shown in a three-quarter view, his body turned to his left, the head turned to his right. The left arm is bent to the side, the right arm at the height of the chest. The left leg is obscured by the right leg of the reclining figure and the mattress, the lower right shin is obscured by the mattress.

He wears a tall, almost rectangular headdress with a round top. The headdress is decorated with a beaded band at the bottom and a central band that extends downwards from the top of the headdress. The band seems decorated with a series of squares with a dot in the centre. His hair is centrally parted and falls on either side of the face in a series of rows of snail-shell curls that reach up to the nape. His face is oval. The eyebrows are depicted as thin, curving ridges. The eyes are small and almond-shaped, with thick upper eyelids. The irises are indicated by incised circles and the pupils by punch holes. The nose is wide. The mouth is small, with a full lower lip. The chin is pointed. The neck is short and wide.

He wears a ›Parthian-style‹ tunic and ›Parthian-style‹ trousers. The tunic has a small, round neckline decorated with a beaded band and long, tight-fitting sleeves. A central band extends downwards from the middle of the neckline; it is decorated with rosettes inside circles or a running scroll motif. The cuffs of the sleeves are decorated with narrow rectangles surrounded by beaded borders. The edge of the tunic is decorated with a band with a motif of five-petal rosettes inside circles or a running scroll. On the right side of the tunic there is a slit decorated with a beaded border. The folds of the tunic are indicated by wide oblique grooves. A thin band belt is tied with a double knot at the waist with the ends of the belt looped around it. The trousers are decorated in the middle with a wide band decorated with a vegetal motif extending downwards. He wears closed, pointed shoes.

His right hand is raised to the height of the chest and extended towards his left. The fingers are extended. In his left hand, he holds an oblong object, possibly the hilt of a dagger.

PORTRAIT B: RECLINING PRIEST

The figure is shown with his legs in profile, his torso and head in three-quarter view, head turned slightly to his right. Both arms are bent, the left to the side, the right raised to the height of the neck. The right leg is bent, with the foot on the mattress, and the left is bent under the raised right leg. The left lower leg is obscured by the right leg.

He wears a tall, cylindrical, flat-top headdress that is divided into three sections by two vertical grooves low on his forehead: a Palmyrene priestly hat. A wreath with three

Cat. 727

rows of elliptical (?) leaves pointing towards a central six-petal rosette is depicted at the lower part of the headdress. A horizontal band at the bottom of the headdress suggests a liner. His face is oval and fleshy. The eyebrows are depicted as thin, low, curving ridges. The eyes are almond-shaped, with thick eyelids. The irises are indicated by incised circles and the pupils by punch holes. The nose is straight and wide. The mouth is small, with full lips. The chin is pointed with a cleft. A v-shaped groove on the neck indicates the jugular notch and the sternocleidomastoid muscles.

He wears a ›Parthian-style‹ tunic, a himation, and ›Parthian-style‹ trousers. The tunic has a wide, v-shaped neckline decorated with a beaded border. A central, wide band extends downwards from the middle of the neckline decorated with five-petal rosettes inside circles or a running scroll motif between two narrow beaded bands. The tunic has long sleeves with cuffs decorated with a beaded band border. The folds of the tunic are indicated by curving grooves. A thin band belt is tied with a double knot at the waist, with the ends of the belt secured on either side of the knot. The himation covers the left shoulder and arm. A fold of the himation falls across the left side of the chest, and is wrapped around the lower body. One edge of the himation, visible across the waist is decorated with a pleated band. A fold of the himation is wrapped around the wrist and falls on either side of the arm in two zigzag-shaped folds onto the cushion and the mattress. The folds of the himation are indicated by oblique and curving grooves. The trousers are visible at the right ankle: the folds are indicated by narrow vertical and oblique grooves. He wears a boot with tied laces at the ankle.

His right hand is raised to the height of the head. He holds a horn-shaped cup with a rim decorated with two horizontal grooves underneath a beaded band (rhyton). With his left hand, he holds the fold of the himation that is folded from his left shoulder and down around the lower torso. His thumb, index, and the little finger are extended.

728. BANQUETING RELIEF

DATABASE NUMBER: PM904.
LOCATION: Palmyra, Palmyra Museum, inv. no. unknown.
CONTEXT: —
ACQUISITION HISTORY: —
MEASUREMENTS: —
MATERIAL: Limestone.
PRESERVATION: The surface is weathered. The upper left corner of the relief is broken off. Portrait A: The head and the object in the figure's hand are broken off. Portrait B: The head of the figure and the object in the left hand are broken off. Portrait C: The head of the figure and the object in the left hand are broken off.
TECHNICAL DESCRIPTION: —
DATE: A.D. 240–273.
REFERENCES: Will 1951, 89 fig. 12; Raja 2019e, 98. 126 cat. 48.

OBJECT DESCRIPTION:
The relief is rectangular in shape and depicts a standing figure and two reclining figures. The upper, left, and right sides of the relief have a leaf-and-dart frame and an inner beaded band. Beneath the figures is a mattress decorated with three wide bands: the central decorated with a running scroll with rosettes, the one at either side with a branch with leaves. The fabric and the texture of the mattress are indicated by curving grooves. The reclining figures rest their left arm on round cushions decorated with a wide band at the centre (details unclear). The fabric and texture of the cushions are indicated by curving grooves.

PORTRAIT A: STANDING MALE
The figure is shown in a three-quarter view. His arms are bent and raised to the height of the shoulders.

He seems to wear a conical type of headdress (visible in outline).

He wears a ›Parthian-style‹ tunic and ›Parthian-style‹ trousers. The tunic has long, tight-fitting sleeves and reaches to the knees. The lower hem is decorated with a wide band. The folds of the tunic are indicated by vertical and oblique grooves. The trousers end at the ankles. The folds of the trousers are indicated by oblique and vertical grooves.

He holds a tall, rectangular object with both hands (details unclear).

PORTRAIT B: RECLINING PRIEST
The figure's head, torso, left arm, and leg are shown frontally. The right arm and leg are shown in profile. The right arm is extended to the side and rests on the raised right knee, the left arm is bent and held in front of the chest. The right leg is bent with the foot resting on the mattress, the left leg is bent under the right leg.

He wears a tall, cylindrical, flat-top headdress: a Palmyrene priestly hat (visible in outline).

He wears a ›Parthian-style‹ tunic, a chlamys, and ›Parthian-style‹ trousers. The tunic has a wide, round neckline, long, tight-fitting sleeves, and it ends just above the knees. The tunic has a wide band that extends downwards from the middle of the neckline, decorated with leaves on a stem (details unclear). The lower border of the tunic is decorated with a wide band at the hem. The folds of the tunic are indicated by curving and oblique grooves. A thin band belt is tied with a knot at the waist; the edges of the belt are looped under on each side. Over the tunic he wears a chlamys. It is fastened at the right shoulder with a circular brooch (details unclear). It falls across the chest, over the left shoulder, and covers the left arm. It continues under the left elbow over the cushion and mattress and ends in two zigzag-shaped folds. He wears trousers tucked into boots (visible at the right leg). The folds of the trousers are indicated by oblique grooves.

He rests the right hand on the right knee. He holds a round object (details unclear). With his upturned palm of the left hand, he holds a bowl with his fingers (visible in outline).

PORTRAIT C: RECLINING PRIEST

The figure's head, torso, left arm, and leg are shown frontally. The right arm and leg are shown in profile. The left arm is bent, and held in front of the chest.

He wears a tall, cylindrical, flat-top headdress: a Palmyrene priestly hat (visible in outline).

He wears a tunic and a himation. The tunic has a wide, v-shaped neckline. The folds of the tunic are indicated by ovoid grooves. The himation covers the left arm and falls from under the left elbow down the cushion and the mattress and ends in a zigzag-shaped fold.

He holds a bowl in his left hand (visible in outline).

729. BANQUETING RELIEF

DATABASE NUMBER: PM650.
LOCATION: Palmyra, Palmyra Museum, inv. no. CD 19/66.
CONTEXT: Secondary context: Found in room IIa in the Temple of the Standards (Temple des Enseignes), Camp of Diocletian.
ACQUISITION HISTORY: —
MEASUREMENTS: Height: 36 cm. Width: 28 cm. Depth: 13 cm.
MATERIAL: Limestone, white.
PRESERVATION: The upper and left side are broken off. The surface of the left part of the mattress is chipped. Portrait A: The surface of the torso and of the lower body is chipped. The upper part is broken off at the chest. Portrait B: The left side of the figure is broken off at the waist. The surface of the left leg and of the right hand is chipped.
TECHNICAL DESCRIPTION: —
DATE: A.D. 240–273.
REFERENCES: Gawlikowski 1984, 106 cat. 55 pl. 87, 189.

OBJECT DESCRIPTION

The fragment is rectangular in shape and depicts a standing male and a reclining male. A plain frame is rendered on the right and lower side. Beneath the figures is a mattress: it is decorated with two wide bands set between beaded bands. The right band is composed of circles with central rosettes (the details of the decoration of the band at the left are not clear). Curving grooves indicate the texture of the fabric.

PORTRAIT A: STANDING MALE

The figure is shown in three-quarter view. He stands with his right foot on the relief ground; the left leg and foot are obscured by the mattress and reclining figure to his left.

He wears a >Parthian-style< tunic and >Parthian-style< trousers. The tunic ends at the knees, and the lower border is decorated with a band with alternating incised circles and lozenges. The folds of the tunic are rendered by oblique grooves. The figure also wears a band belt composed of two plain straps. The trousers are undecorated, and the folds are indicated by vertical grooves. The figure wears plain closed-toe boots, and the shaft is decorated with a single horizontal, incised line.

PORTRAIT B: RECLINING MALE

The right leg is shown in profile; the left leg is shown in frontal view. The right arm rests on the right raised knee. The right leg is bent. The left leg extends along the mattress. The right foot is obscured by the left leg.

He wears a >Parthian-style< tunic and >Parthian-style< trousers. The tunic has long, tight-fitting sleeves. The tunic ends above the knees, and the lower border is decorated with a pattern of laurel leaves. The folds of the tunic are rendered by deep, horizontal grooves. The trouser legs are decorated in the middle with a wide band decorated with alternating incised circles and squares extending downwards. The folds of the trousers are rendered by oblique grooves. The figure wears closed-toe ankle boots. The boots are decorated with floral motifs indicated with incised lines, and a beaded band at the shaft.

The outline of an oval object is visible in his right hand.

189

Cat. 729

APPENDIX 1

Lost Dated Reliefs

A.D. 83

FOUNDER BANQUETING RELIEFS

1. FOUNDER BANQUETING RELIEF

DATABASE NUMBER: InSitu119.
LOCATION: Formerly in Palmyra, in situ.
CONTEXT: West necropolis. Valley of the Tombs. Tower tomb no. 51, tower of Yamlikû, ground floor.
ACQUISITION HISTORY: —
MEASUREMENTS: —
MATERIAL: Limestone.
PRESERVATION: The relief is now lost.
TECHNICAL DESCRIPTION: —
DATE: A.D. 83 (dated by inscription).
REFERENCES: Schmidt-Colinet 1996, 361 f. 462 cat. 44 fig. 165. Inscription: Vogüe 1868 40 f. cat. 36; Waddington 1870, 606 cat. 2614; Watzinger 1932, 55; Gawlikowski 1970a, 188 f. cat. 17; Yon 2012, 316–318 cat. 405; Henning 2013b, 193.

OBJECT DESCRIPTION

The object is placed inside an alcove and is a rectangular plaque. The alcove is framed by two unfluted columns with Corinthian capitals and is crowned by a pediment. The relief has three figures: two standing male figures and a male figure reclining on a kline and resting on a round cushion. The kline has a mattress decorated with broad bands with vegetal decoration. The kline has turned legs. The foot is conical. Above is a half-ball, a decorated bell-shaped element, a torus, a thin, rectangular element, a reversed calyx-shaped element, a ball, a neck, a reed, and a flower-like finial.
There are five standing figures between the legs of the kline.

NOTE: The object is now lost, but it had been documented by Louis François Cassas during his trip to Palmyra in 1785. The tower itself was destroyed in 2015 (Cuneo et al. 2015, 6).

INSCRIPTION
INSCRIPTION 1
SCRIPT: Palmyrene Aramaic.
LOCATION ON RELIEF: On a tabula ansata, on the façade of the tomb, below the console supporting the alcove with the relief.
TRANSCRIPTION: BYRḤ NYSN ŠNT 394 | QBRʾ DNH BNʾ YMLKW BR MQYMW ʾQLYŠ BR MLKW | ʾBNYT BR BLʿQB BR MYKʾ BR MTʾ TDMRYʾ LH | WBNWHY WLBNY BNWHY LYQRHN ʿD ʿLMʾ.

App. 1, cat. 1

TRANSLATION: In the month of Nîsan, in the year 394, this tomb was built by Yamlikû son of Moqîmû Aqqalîs son of Malkû Abbanît son of Belʿaqab son of Mîkâ son of Mattâ, the Palmyrene, for him and for his sons and for the sons of his sons, in their honour, until eternity (A.D. 83).

INSCRIPTION 2
SCRIPT: Ancient Greek.
LOCATION ON RELIEF: On a tabula ansata, on the façade of the tomb, below the console supporting the alcove with the relief.
TRANSCRIPTION: Μνημεῖον αἰώνιον γ(έ)ρας ᾠκοδόμ- | ησεν Ιαμλιχος Μοκειμου τοῦ καὶ | Ακκαλεισου τοῦ Μαλιχου εἴς τε | ἑαυτὸν καὶ υἱοὺς καὶ ἐγγόνους, ἔτους δϟτ´ | μηνὶ Ξανδικῷ.

TRANSLATION: This eternal monument of honour was built by Iamlichos son of Mokimos, also called Akkaleisos, for himself, his sons and his descendants, in the year 394, in the month of Xandikos (A.D. 83).

CIS no. 4123bis; PAT no. 0473.

PORTRAIT A: STANDING MALE

The figure is shown frontally. The right arm is bent and held to the torso; the left arm falls along the side. The lower left foot is obscured by the reclining figure.

His hair is short and arranged in curls. His face is square. The eyebrows are straight. The eyes are small. The nose is straight, and the mouth is small. The neck is short and wide.

He wears a tunic. The tunic has a wide, round neckline, tight-fitting sleeves that reach to the middle of the lower arm. The tunic has an overfold at the waist, indicating a belt. The tunic ends at the knees.

His right fist is clenched in front of the torso, and the left arm falls to the side.

PORTRAIT B: STANDING MALE

The figure is shown frontally. The right arm is bent in front of the torso, the left falls along the side. The lower torso and the legs are obscured by the reclining figure. He is reclining with his right leg bent and the right foot resting on the mattress and the left leg bent under the right leg, leaving only the thigh and knee visible. The lower left leg is obscured.

His hair is short and arranged in curls. His face is square. The eyebrows are straight. The eyes are small. The nose is straight, and the mouth is small. The neck is short and wide.

He wears a tunic and a himation. The tunic has a short, round neckline and short, wide sleeves. The himation covers the left shoulder and arm.

PORTRAIT C: RECLINING MALE

The head, torso, upper left arm, and upper left leg of the figure are shown frontally, the right arm and leg are shown in profile, and the left lower arm is shown in a three-quarter view. The right arm is extended along the side, resting on the right leg; the left arm is bent and held in front of the torso. He is reclining with his right leg bent and the right foot resting on the mattress and the left leg bent under the right leg, leaving only the thigh and knee visible. The lower left leg is obscured.

He wears a >Parthian-style< tunic and a himation. The tunic has a wide, round neckline decorated with a band and long, tight-fitting sleeves. Over the tunic, he wears a himation that is wrapped around the waist and covers the legs. One end of the himation is wrapped around the left shoulder and arm, and it falls over the cushion.

PORTRAIT D: STANDING MALE

The figure is shown frontally. The arms fall to the side. The legs are slightly apart.

He has short hair. The face is square. The eyes are small, the nose is straight. He has a beard.

He wears a himation. The himation is wrapped around his whole body.

PORTRAIT E: STANDING MALE

The figure is shown frontally. The left arm falls to the side, the right arm is bent in front of the torso. He stands on the right leg, and the left leg is relaxed.

He has short hair. The face is oval. The eyes are small, the nose is straight, and the mouth is small. The neck is short and wide.

He wears a himation. The himation covers his whole body (possibly >arm-sling< type).

PORTRAIT F: STANDING FIGURE (GENDER UNCLEAR)

The figure is shown frontally. The right arm is bent in front of the chest. The figure stands on the right leg, and the left leg is relaxed.

The figure has short hair. The face is oval. The eyes are small, the nose is straight, and the mouth is small. The neck is short and wide.

The figure wears a garment that covers the body. An over-garment can be distinguished covering the arms, with folds falling down to the sides.

PORTRAIT G: STANDING MALE (?)

The figure is shown frontally. Both arms fall to the side. The figure stands on the right leg, and the left leg is relaxed.

The figure has short hair. The face is oval. The eyes are small, the nose is straight, and the mouth is small. The neck is short and wide.

He wears a tunic and a himation. The tunic has a short, round neckline and short sleeves that reach to the elbows. Over the tunic he wears a himation that falls diagonally from the right shoulder, crosses the chest, and covers the legs.

The arms fall to the sides.

PORTRAIT H: STANDING FIGURE (GENDER UNCLEAR)

The figure is shown frontally. The left arm falls to the side, the right arm is bent in front of the torso. The figure stands on the right leg, and the left leg is relaxed.

The figure has short hair. The face is oval. The eyes are small, the nose is straight, and the mouth is small. The neck is short and wide.

The figure wears a tunic and a himation. The tunic has a short, round neckline and short sleeves that reach to the elbows. Over the tunic, he wears a himation that covers the lower torso and the waist.

The figure holds a fold of the himation with the raised right hand. The end falls in a narrow fold down and over the legs.

APPENDIX 2

Lost Reliefs from Tower Tombs

TOWER TOMB NO. 13, TOWER OF ELAHBEL

SARCOPHAGUS RELIEFS

1. BANQUETING RELIEF

DATABASE NUMBER: InSitu122.
LOCATION: Palmyra, in situ.
CONTEXT: West necropolis. Valley of the Tombs. Tower tomb no. 13, tower of Elahbel.
ACQUISITION HISTORY: —
MEASUREMENTS: —
MATERIAL: —
PRESERVATION: Lost.
TECHNICAL DESCRIPTION: —
DATE: A.D. 103–150.
REFERENCES: Gawlikowski 1970a, 90; Schmidt-Colinet 1996, 365. 471 cat. 57 fig. 186.

OBJECT DESCRIPTION
The object is rectangular in shape and depicts a male figure reclining on a mattress. He rests his arm on a round cushion. The mattress is decorated with broad bands.
The object is now lost, but it had been documented by Louis François Cassas during his trip to Palmyra in 1785.

PORTRAIT
The head is shown frontally. The torso and arms are shown in a three-quarter view. The right leg is shown in profile. The right leg of the figure is raised and bent.
 The head is oval. The figure has short hair and a beard.
 The figure wears a >Parthian-style< tunic and a himation. The tunic has a trapezoidal neckline decorated with a band, and has long, tight-fitting sleeves. Over the tunic, he wears a himation that covers the lower torso and the legs. One fold of the himation is wrapped around the left arm.

App. 2, cat. 1

TOWER TOMB NO. 46

SARCOPHAGI RELIEFS

A.D. 33–170

2. SARCOPHAGI FRAGMENTS

DATABASE NUMBER: —
LOCATION: Palmyra, in situ.
CONTEXT: West necropolis. Tower tomb no. 46.
ACQUISITION HISTORY: —
MEASUREMENTS: —
MATERIAL: Limestone.
PRESERVATION: Lost.
TECHNICAL DESCRIPTION: —
DATE: A.D. 33–170.
REFERENCES: Gawlikowski 1970a, 98; Henning 2013b, 189.

OBJECT DESCRIPTION

The object was rectangular. The contours are visible on the plaster of the wall (Gawlikowski 1970a).

3. SARCOPHAGI FRAGMENTS

DATABASE NUMBER: —
LOCATION: Palmyra, Palmyra Museum, inv. no. B 366.
CONTEXT: West necropolis. Tower tomb no. 46.
ACQUISITION HISTORY: —
MEASUREMENTS: —
MATERIAL: Limestone.
PRESERVATION: Lost.
TECHNICAL DESCRIPTION: —
DATE: A.D. 150–273.
REFERENCES: Henning 2013b, 189.

OBJECT DESCRIPTION

The object was a fragment from a sarcophagus. According to Henning (2013b, 189), it was in the Museum of Palmyra, but it was not possible to locate it.

TOWER TOMB NO. 87

FRAGMENT OF LID OR LID RELIEF

4. SARCOPHAGUS FRAGMENT

DATABASE NUMBER: —
LOCATION: Palmyra, in situ.
CONTEXT: West necropolis. Tower tomb no. 87.
ACQUISITION HISTORY: —
MEASUREMENTS: —
MATERIAL: Limestone.
PRESERVATION: Lost.
TECHNICAL DESCRIPTION: —
DATE: A.D. 150–273.
REFERENCES: Watzinger – Wulzinger 1932, 59; Henning 2013b, 234.

OBJECT DESCRIPTION

The object was a fragment from a sarcophagus. Watzinger and Wulzinger (1932, 59) reported that it had the figure of a reclining male next to an altar and a flying Nike.

PORTRAIT

Reclining male.

TOWER TOMB NO. 101

FRAGMENT OF LID OR LID RELIEF

5. SARCOPHAGI FRAGMENTS

DATABASE NUMBER: —
LOCATION: Palmyra, in situ.
CONTEXT: West necropolis. Tower tomb no. 101.
ACQUISITION HISTORY: —
MEASUREMENTS: —
MATERIAL: Limestone.
PRESERVATION: Lost.
TECHNICAL DESCRIPTION: —
DATE: A.D. 150–273.
REFERENCES: Watzinger – Wulzinger 1932, 61; Henning 2013b, 243.

OBJECT DESCRIPTION

The object was a fragment from a sarcophagus. Watzinger and Wulzinger (1932, 61) reported that it had the figure of a reclining male with a bowl in hand.

PORTRAIT

Reclining male.

APPENDIX 3

Lost Reliefs from Temple Tombs

TEMPLE TOMB NO. 173D

SARCOPHAGI RELIEFS

A.D. 200–273

1. FOUNDER BANQUETING RELIEF

DATABASE NUMBER: InSitu146.
LOCATION: Palmyra, in situ.
CONTEXT: West necropolis. Temple tomb no. 173d.
ACQUISITION HISTORY: —
MEASUREMENTS: —
MATERIAL: Limestone.
PRESERVATION: Lost. Portrait B: The head was broken off by the time of Cassas' visit. Portrait C: The head was broken off by the time of Cassas' visit.
TECHNICAL DESCRIPTION: —
DATE: A.D. 200–273.
REFERENCES: Schmidt-Colinet 1996, 370. 487 cat. 75 fig. 220. Inscription: Yon 2012, 362 f. cat. 475.

OBJECT DESCRIPTION
The object is rectangular in shape and depicts three standing figures and a reclining male. The reclining male rests on a round cushion decorated with a wide band.
The object is now lost, but it had been documented by Louis François Cassas during his trip to Palmyra in 1785.

INSCRIPTIONS
INSCRIPTION 1
SCRIPT: Ancient Greek.
LOCATION ON RELIEF: On the lintel.
TRANSCRIPTION: [- - -] ἀφιέρωσα υἱοῖς καὶ υἱωνοῖς | ἄρσεσι ἐπὶ τῷ κατὰ μηδένα τρόπον κ | οινωνὸν αὐτοῦ προσλαβεῖν καθ᾽ [ἔγραψα].
TRANSLATION: I consecrated for my male (sic!) sons and grandsons, on condition that under no way will they take any associate, according to what I have written …

INSCRIPTION 2
SCRIPT: Palmyrene Aramaic.
LOCATION ON RELIEF: On the lintel.
TRANSCRIPTION: [- - - Q]BRʾ DNH DNBTʾ WʾQDŠT LBNYN WLBNY B | NYN DKRYN WLʾ YHWN [LʾG] WRʾW LMBʿDʾW | LʾḤBWRʾ BH ʾYŠ HYK DY KTBT.
TRANSLATION: This tomb that I have constructed and consecrated for my sons and the sons of my male sons, and that they will not rent or alienate or take anyone in partnership, as I have written.

CIS no. 4214; PAT no. 0570.

PORTRAIT A: STANDING FIGURE
The figure is depicted frontally. The right arm is bent and held in front of the chest, and the left arm falls to the side. The figure stands on the left leg, and the right leg is relaxed. The right knee is rendered under the drapery.
The figure has short hair. The face is oval. The eyes are small. The nose is straight. The mouth is small.
The figure wears a tunic and a himation. The tunic has a wide, round neckline and short, wide sleeves that reach to the elbows. Over the tunic, the figure wears a himation. The himation covers the right shoulder, falls diagonally across the chest, and covers the lower torso and the legs.
With the right hand the figure holds a fold of the himation. The left hand touches the left thigh.

PORTRAIT B: STANDING MALE FIGURE
The figure is depicted frontally. The arms are bent and held next to the torso. The legs are set apart, with the feet firmly on the ground. The left foot is obscured by the foot of the reclining figure.
He wears a tunic and an over-garment. The tunic has a wide, round neckline and reaches to above the knees. Over the tunic, he seems to be wearing an over-garment that covers the upper part of the body and the arms.
With the right hand, he holds a fold of the over-garment. The left hand touches the waist.

PORTRAIT C: RECLINING MALE
The head of the figure was shown frontally. The torso is shown frontally. The right arm, lower left arm, and right leg are shown in profile. The upper left leg is shown frontally. The right arm is extended along the body and rests against the thigh. The left arm rests on a round cushion. The right leg is bent and raised. The left leg is bent and extended under the right leg. The left foot is obscured by the right leg.
He wears a >Parthian-style< tunic. The tunic has a wide, round neckline decorated with a band and long, tight-fitting sleeves. A fold that is wrapped around the left arm, and the way that the legs are covered by a long piece of cloth suggest that he wore a himation over the tunic.

App. 3, cat. 1

PORTRAIT D: STANDING MALE

The figure is shown frontally. The left arm falls to the side, and the right arm is bent and held in front of the chest. His legs are slightly set apart with the feet on the ground.

The figure has short hair. His face is oval. The eyes are small. The nose is straight. The mouth is small. The neck is short and wide.

He wears a tunic and a himation. The tunic has a wide, round neckline. Over the tunic, he wears a himation that covers the left shoulder, falls diagonally down the chest, and covers the lower torso and the legs. One fold of the himation falls under the right arm.

With the right hand he holds a fold of the himation in front of the chest. The left hand is covered by the himation.

APPENDIX 4

Marble Sarcophagi from Attica

A.D. 100–150

1. SARCOPHAGUS BOX

DATABASE NUMBER: PM682.
LOCATION: Palmyra, Palmyra Museum, inv. no. CD 79.
CONTEXT: Secondary context: Found (16.06.1960) at the east corner of the Tetrapylon.
ACQUISITION HISTORY: —
MEASUREMENTS: Height: 68 cm. Width: 46 cm. Depth: 19 cm.
MATERIAL: Marble, white.
PRESERVATION: Broken off on all sides. Portrait A: The head is broken off at the base of the neck. The lower part of the left arm has broken off. The surface is weathered. Portrait B: Only a part of the neck and garment is preserved.
TECHNICAL DESCRIPTION: —
DATE: A.D. 100–150 (Wielgosz 2010: A.D. 225–250; Colledge 1976: A.D. 150–225).
REFERENCES: Michalowski 1962, 141 f. cat. 14 fig. 156; Colledge 1976, 75 fig. 41; Equini Schneider 1993, 118–120 fig. 26; Wielgosz 2010, 84 cat. 35 fig. 31.

OBJECT DESCRIPTION
The object is rectangular in shape and depicts a standing male and an unidentifiable figure.

PORTRAIT A: STANDING MALE
The figure is shown frontally. The right arm is held out from the body. The left arm is held in front of the body. The legs are slightly set apart and he stands in a striding posture. His feet are obscured by the body of a dog.
The figure is naked.
The left arm is wrapped in a chlamys.

PORTRAIT B: FIGURE
Only part of the neck and of the garment survive.

A.D. 150–200

2. FRAGMENT OF A SARCOPHAGUS BOX

DATABASE NUMBER: PM716.
LOCATION: Palmyra, Palmyra Museum, inv. no. CD 17/60.
CONTEXT: Secondary context: Found (14.05.1960) reused as a slab in a wall of a late Byzantine house.
ACQUISITION HISTORY: —

App. 4, cat. 1

MEASUREMENTS: Height: 53.5 cm. Width: 56 cm.
MATERIAL: Marble, white.
PRESERVATION: The object is broken off on all sides. Portrait A: The right side of the figure is broken off horizontally at the right shoulder and the lower part is broken off at the shins. The surface is chipped and weathered. Portrait B: Only the wrist and part of the hand survives.
TECHNICAL DESCRIPTION: —
DATE: A.D. 150–200.
REFERENCES: Michalowski 1962, 142 f. cat. 15 fig. 157; Equini Schneider 1993, 120 fig. 26; Wielgosz 2010, 84 cat. 29 fig. 29.

OBJECT DESCRIPTION
The object depicts an equestrian and a horse. The head, neck, and chest of the horse are preserved. It has a pointed ear and the mane is short and depicted by thin ridges. A neck strap is

App. 4, cat. 2

placed low on the neck of the horse. The upper frame of the sarcophagus box is preserved. It is decorated with acanthus leaves and a floral pattern. To the right of the equestrian is a head of another horse and the hand of a figure.

PORTRAIT A: EQUESTRIAN
The head and right leg of the figure are shown in profile, the torso in three-quarter view. He is turned towards his left.

The figure is wearing headgear, possibly a helmet. He is naked. The chest musculature is indicated by curving grooves.

PORTRAIT B: FIGURE
Only the wrist and part of the hand holding the reins of a horse survives.

A.D. 200–250

3. FRAGMENT OF A SARCOPHAGUS BOX

DATABASE NUMBER: —
LOCATION: Palmyra, Palmyra Museum, inv. no. CD 11/A.
CONTEXT: Secondary context: Found (16.04.1961) at the late wall at the north-west of the Tetrapylon, Camp of Diocletian.
ACQUISITION HISTORY: —
MEASUREMENTS: Height: 56 cm. Width: 46 cm. Depth: 18 cm.
MATERIAL: Marble, white.
PRESERVATION: The object is broken off on all sides. The lower part of the figure is broken off. The surface is chipped and weathered. Comparison with the photograph published by Michalowski reveals that the piece was restored.
TECHNICAL DESCRIPTION: —
DATE: A.D. 200–250.
REFERENCES: Michalowski 1963, 154 cat. 48 fig. 205; Wielgosz 2001, 167–169 fig. 1; Wielgosz 2010, 84 f. cat. 36 fig. 30.

App. 4, cat. 3

OBJECT DESCRIPTION
The object is rectangular and depicts a male figure.

PORTRAIT
The figure is shown in a three-quarter view. The head of the figure falls back. The arms are bent to the sides.

The figure wears a mantle that falls over the left shoulder, crosses the chest diagonally, and covers the lower torso.

The left hand of the figure rests against the middle of the lower torso. The right hand of the figure rests against the torso.

4. FRAGMENT OF A SARCOPHAGUS BOX

DATABASE NUMBER: —
LOCATION: Palmyra, Palmyra Museum, inv. no. CD 187/75.
CONTEXT: Secondary context: Camp of Diocletian.
ACQUISITION HISTORY: —
MEASUREMENTS: —
MATERIAL: Marble, white.
PRESERVATION: The object is broken off on all sides. The head, arms, and lower body of the figure are broken off. The surface is chipped and weathered.
TECHNICAL DESCRIPTION: —
DATE: A.D. 225–250.
REFERENCES: Wielgosz 2001, 170 f. fig. 8; Wielgosz 2010, 85. cat. 37 fig. 32.

OBJECT DESCRIPTION
The object depicts a male figure.

PORTRAIT
The head of the figure is turned towards his left. The torso is shown frontally. The figure is shown standing.

The figure wears a chlamys that is fastened with a brooch (details unclear) over the right shoulder. The musculature of the torso is indicated by curving grooves.

APPENDIX 5

Sarcophagi without Portraits

A.D. 75–150

1. SARCOPHAGUS BOX

DATABASE NUMBER: —
LOCATION: Palmyra, in situ.
CONTEXT: West necropolis. Tower tomb no. 84.
ACQUISITION HISTORY: —
MEASUREMENTS: —
MATERIAL: Limestone.
PRESERVATION: Only the box survives. The upper side of the front is broken off.
TECHNICAL DESCRIPTION: —
DATE: A.D. 75–150.
REFERENCES: Henning 2013b, 231 pl. 67, b.

OBJECT DESCRIPTION

The sarcophagus is rectangular in shape. The interior of the sarcophagus is carved as a rectangle with rounded corners.

A.D. 128–150

2. SARCOPHAGUS BOX

DATABASE NUMBER: —
LOCATION: Palmyra, in situ.
CONTEXT: West necropolis. Tower tomb no. N206.
ACQUISITION HISTORY: —
MEASUREMENTS: —
MATERIAL: Limestone.
PRESERVATION: The box is weathered.
TECHNICAL DESCRIPTION: The box is partly carved.
DATE: A.D. 128–150.
REFERENCES: al-As'ad 2013, 16 fig. 1.

OBJECT DESCRIPTION

The object is rectangular in shape. The outer sides are undecorated and partly carved. A narrow moulding is carved on the inside.
For the sarcophagi in tower tomb no. N206, see image in cat. 4.

3. SARCOPHAGUS BOX

DATABASE NUMBER: —
LOCATION: Palmyra, in situ.
CONTEXT: West necropolis. Tower tomb no. N206.
ACQUISITION HISTORY: —
MEASUREMENTS: —
MATERIAL: Limestone.
PRESERVATION: The box is weathered.
TECHNICAL DESCRIPTION: The box is partly carved.
DATE: A.D. 128–150.
REFERENCES: al-As'ad 2013, 16 fig. 1.

OBJECT DESCRIPTION

The object is rectangular in shape. The outer sides are undecorated and partly carved. A narrow moulding is carved on the inside.

A.D. 150–200

4. SARCOPHAGUS BOX

DATABASE NUMBER: —
LOCATION: Palmyra, in situ.
CONTEXT: North necropolis. Temple tomb no. 146.
ACQUISITION HISTORY: —
MEASUREMENTS: —
MATERIAL: Limestone.
PRESERVATION: The upper part of the sarcophagus box is broken off. The surface is weathered.
TECHNICAL DESCRIPTION: —
DATE: A.D. 150–200.
REFERENCES: al-As'ad 2013, 17 fig. 4.

OBJECT DESCRIPTION

The object is rectangular in shape. Al-As'ad (2013) writes that the surface was decorated originally but the reliefs were completely weathered at the time of the discovery.

5. SARCOPHAGUS BOX

DATABASE NUMBER: —
LOCATION: Palmyra, in situ.
CONTEXT: North necropolis. Temple tomb no. 146.
ACQUISITION HISTORY: —
MEASUREMENTS: —
MATERIAL: Limestone.
PRESERVATION: The upper part of the sarcophagus box is broken off. The surface is chipped and weathered.
TECHNICAL DESCRIPTION: —
DATE: A.D. 150–200.
REFERENCES: al-Asʿad 2013, 17 fig. 4.

OBJECT DESCRIPTION

The object is rectangular in shape. Al-Asʿad (2013) writes that the surface was decorated originally but the reliefs were completely weathered at the time of the discovery.

6. SARCOPHAGUS BOX

DATABASE NUMBER: —
LOCATION: Palmyra, in situ.
CONTEXT: North necropolis. Temple tomb no. 146.
ACQUISITION HISTORY: —
MEASUREMENTS: —
MATERIAL: Limestone.
PRESERVATION: The upper part of the sarcophagus box is broken off. The surface is chipped and weathered.
TECHNICAL DESCRIPTION: —
DATE: A.D. 150–200.
REFERENCES: al-Asʿad 2013, 17 fig. 4.

OBJECT DESCRIPTION

The object is rectangular in shape. Al-Asʿad (2013) writes that the surface was decorated originally but the reliefs were completely weathered at the time of the discovery.

7. SARCOPHAGUS BOX

DATABASE NUMBER: —
LOCATION: Palmyra, in situ.
CONTEXT: North necropolis. Temple tomb no. 174.
ACQUISITION HISTORY: —
MEASUREMENTS: —
MATERIAL: Limestone.
PRESERVATION: The sides of the sarcophagus are broken off. Only part of the reverse and the bottom of the sarcophagus remain.
TECHNICAL DESCRIPTION: —
DATE: A.D. 150–200.
REFERENCES: Ingholt Archives, PS 874; Gawlikowski 1970a, 133; al-Asʿad 2013, 18.

OBJECT DESCRIPTION

The object is rectangular in shape.

App. 5, cat. 7

8. SARCOPHAGUS BOX

DATABASE NUMBER: —
LOCATION: Palmyra, in situ.
CONTEXT: South-west necropolis. Hypogeum AC.
ACQUISITION HISTORY: —
MEASUREMENTS: —
MATERIAL: Limestone.
PRESERVATION: The sarcophagus appears intact in the photograph.
TECHNICAL DESCRIPTION: The decoration is partly carved.
DATE: A.D. 150–200.
REFERENCES: Ingholt Archives, IA_NCG_Miscellaneous2016_062; Raja et al. 2021a, Diary 5, 123.

OBJECT DESCRIPTION
The object is rectangular in shape. It is decorated with a continuous garland suspended on round elements, with two ribbons hanging down.

INSCRIPTION
SCRIPT: Palmyrene Aramaic.
LOCATION ON RELIEF: Across the top, over the garland.
TRANSCRIPTION: whbʾ wšmʿwn bnyʾ mlʾ ʿbd lʾqmʾ bt-tbrn ʾmhn lyqrh.
TRANSLATION: Vahbâ and Šimʿôn sons of Malê have made (this) for ʾAqmê daughter of T, their mother, in her honour.

According to Ingholt, the inscription had red colour in the letters (Raja et al. 2021a, Diary 5, 123).

A.D. 200–273

9. SARCOPHAGUS BOX

DATABASE NUMBER: —
LOCATION: Palmyra, in situ.
CONTEXT: Secondary context: Reused in the Basilica in the area north of the Great Colonnade.

App. 5, cat. 8

ACQUISITION HISTORY: —
MEASUREMENTS: —
MATERIAL: Limestone.
PRESERVATION: The upper left corner is chipped.
TECHNICAL DESCRIPTION: —
DATE: A.D. 200–273.
REFERENCES: Majcherek 2012, 465 fig. 4.

OBJECT DESCRIPTION

The object is rectangular. It is incorporated into the pavement of a later basilica church and it is not possible to determine whether it carried decoration or not.

10. SARCOPHAGUS BOX WITH MYTHOLOGICAL FIGURES

DATABASE NUMBER: —
LOCATION: Palmyra, in situ.
CONTEXT: Secondary context: Used as a water trough at a Byzantine house at the Camp of Diocletian.
ACQUISITION HISTORY: —
MEASUREMENTS: Length: 2.32 cm. Width: 1.20 m.
MATERIAL: Limestone.
PRESERVATION: The upper part of the sarcophagus is broken off on all sides.
TECHNICAL DESCRIPTION: —
DATE: A.D. 200–273.

App. 5, cat. 10

REFERENCES: Michalowski 1963, 53 figs. 57–59.

OBJECT DESCRIPTION
The object is rectangular in shape.
There are five niches on the long sides, and two on the narrow side, all enclosing statues on pedestals. On one of the niches of the narrow side Michalowski (1963) identified a representation of the statue of Artemis of Ephesus.

App. 5, cat. 10

App. 5, cat. 10

A.D. 220–240

11. FRAGMENT OF A SARCOPHAGUS BOX RELIEF

DATABASE NUMBER: —
LOCATION: Doha, Sheikh Saoud bin Mohammed Foundation.
CONTEXT: —
ACQUISITION HISTORY: From a European private collection. Sold by Christie's, New York in 2002.
MEASUREMENTS: Height: 62 cm. Width: 69 cm. Depth: 15 cm.
MATERIAL: Limestone.
PRESERVATION: The left side of the box relief is broken off. The upper and lower edges of the relief are chipped. The palm tree branches, the kline leg, the head, and right foreleg of the camel are chipped.
TECHNICAL DESCRIPTION: —
DATE: A.D. 220–240.
REFERENCES: Kohlmeyer 2018, 70 cat. 22.

OBJECT DESCRIPTION
The object is a sarcophagus box in the shape of a kline on a projecting plinth. The central stretcher of the kline is decorated with alternating square and rectangular panels. The panel at the right corner of the stretcher is square with an incised border, and is decorated with the image of a crouching bull. The next panel is rectangular with a moulding and is followed by a square panel decorated with a cruciform flower with eight petals. The last panel is rectangular and is divided into two registers. The lower register is decorated with a series of tongues, while the upper is decorated with geometric motifs (other details unclear). The kline legs are turned. They are composed of a plinth, above is a concave quarter, a long reversed concave quarter, a concave quarter, a torus, and a reversed concave quarter. The convex finials of the legs are visible over the stretcher. All elements are decorated with a tongue pattern.

The surface of the relief is decorated with a palm tree at the right and a camel. The trunk of the palm tree is decorated with a continuous rhomboid pattern, indicating the scars of the leaves. There are seven branches stemming out of the trunk, one vertical at the centre and three branches projecting downwards on either side of the central branch. The midribs, the rachis, and the leaflets of the leaves are shown. Two bunches of fruit are hanging from either side of the stem; the fruit is depicted by elongated, oval elements.

To the left of the tree a camel is shown moving towards its left. The front left leg is slightly forward, while it takes a step forward with the back left leg. The head of the camel is shown in profile. It wears a harness that is tied along the muzzle over the nostrils, and around the upper part of the neck. One end of the harness is shown between the camel's neck and the saddle, presumably tied at the saddle. Over its back it wears a cloth decorated with hollowed-out rhombi and a beaded band at the edges. Over the cloth it has a riding saddle tied with thick bands to the camel's body. It is covered with the fur of an animal: the head of the animal is shown frontally; it has two small, triangular ears, and elongated eyes and nose. The fur is depicted by small, crescent-shaped curls set between seven vertical grooves. The paws of the animal fall from the edges of the fur. There are several objects attached to the saddle: a soft object with a crease is tied at the back, perhaps a cushion, a cylindrical container decorated with a crisscross pattern and a beaded band, perhaps a closed quiver, and a long, narrow object, perhaps a sheathed sword. A rectangular saddlebag hangs by three straps from the saddle next to the belly of the camel.

12. FRAGMENT OF A SARCOPHAGUS RELIEF

DATABASE NUMBER: —
LOCATION: Istanbul, İstanbul Arkeoloji Müzesi, inv. no. 3804.
CONTEXT: —
ACQUISITION HISTORY: —
MEASUREMENTS: Height: 42 cm. Width: 37.5 cm. Depth: 15 cm.
MATERIAL: Limestone.
PRESERVATION: Only the fulcrum survives. The upper part of the fulcrum is broken off.
TECHNICAL DESCRIPTION: —
DATE: A.D. 220–240.
REFERENCES: Ingholt Archives, PS 729; Parlasca 1992, 260 pl. 42 c.

OBJECT DESCRIPTION

The fulcrum of the sarcophagus kline depicts Dionysiac figures. The fulcrum shows the bust of a bearded and hairy Silenus holding a cup inside the medallion at the lower end. At the body, there is a long-haired male figure dressed in a himation that is wrapped around his lower body shown reclining on a panther. Above him, a second panther with a female figure

App. 5, cat. 12

who sits on the animal's back. The figure wears a sleeveless himation; the himation is fastened with a round button or brooch that has slipped from the shoulder to the upper arm. She has her arms wrapped around the neck of the panther.

13. FRAGMENT OF A SARCOPHAGUS RELIEF

DATABASE NUMBER: —
LOCATION: Istanbul, İstanbul Arkeoloji Müzesi, inv. no. 3819/OM 320.
CONTEXT: —
ACQUISITION HISTORY: Confiscated in Damascus in 1902.
MEASUREMENTS: Height: 62 cm. Width: 69 cm. Depth: 15 cm.
MATERIAL: Limestone.
PRESERVATION: The fragment is well-preserved.
TECHNICAL DESCRIPTION: —
DATE: A.D. 220–240.
REFERENCES: Ingholt Archives, PS 730.

OBJECT DESCRIPTION
The section of the stretcher that survives shows a rectangular frame with a kneeling bull.

14. FRAGMENT OF A SARCOPHAGUS RELIEF

DATABASE NUMBER: —
LOCATION: Possibly Istanbul, İstanbul Arkeoloji Müzesi, inv. no. 3819 / 321.
CONTEXT: —
ACQUISITION HISTORY: —
MEASUREMENTS: —
MATERIAL: Limestone.
PRESERVATION: The fragment is broken off at the upper edge.
TECHNICAL DESCRIPTION: —
DATE: A.D. 220–240.
REFERENCES: Ingholt Archives, PS 1098.

OBJECT DESCRIPTION
The section of the stretcher that survives shows a rectangular frame with a kneeling bull.

15. FRAGMENT OF A SARCOPHAGUS RELIEF

DATABASE NUMBER: —
LOCATION: Istanbul, İstanbul Arkeoloji Müzesi, inv. no. 3819/OM 321.
CONTEXT: —
ACQUISITION HISTORY: Confiscated in Damascus in 1902.
MEASUREMENTS: Height: 62 cm. Width: 69 cm. Depth: 15 cm.
MATERIAL: Limestone.
PRESERVATION: The fragment is well-preserved.
TECHNICAL DESCRIPTION: —
DATE: A.D. 220–240.
REFERENCES: Ingholt Archives, PS 730.

App. 5, cat. 13

APPENDIX 5 – SARCOPHAGI WITHOUT PORTRAITS   979

OBJECT DESCRIPTION
The section of the stretcher that survives shows a rectangular frame with a kneeling calf.

NOTE: there are two archive sheets with the same number (PS 730), but they depict different fragments, possibly from the same sarcophagus, since they were all confiscated in Damascus in 1902 and have the same theme.

App. 5, cat. 14

App. 5, cat. 15

16. FRAGMENT OF A SARCOPHAGUS RELIEF

DATABASE NUMBER: —
LOCATION: Possibly Istanbul, İstanbul Arkeoloji Müzesi, inv. no. 3802.
CONTEXT: —
ACQUISITION HISTORY: —
MEASUREMENTS: —
MATERIAL: Limestone.
PRESERVATION: The fragment is well-preserved.
TECHNICAL DESCRIPTION: —
DATE: A.D. 220–240.
REFERENCES: Ingholt Archives, PS 1097.

OBJECT DESCRIPTION

The object is the fragment of a kline. The kline has a turned leg that stands on a small plinth. The leg is composed of a reversed bell-shaped element, a convex quarter, a biconical element, a thick torus, a biconical element, a reversed bell-shaped element, and a biconical element over the stretcher. All the elements are decorated with a tongue pattern. The stretcher of the kline is decorated with a square frame with a four-petal rosette, a rectangular frame with a running dog pattern, a section divided into two parts by a line, the upper part with oblique lines that run to the left and right from the centre and two straight, thin bands near the ends, and the lower with a wreath pattern. Another rectangular frame with a running dog motif follows. Next to the leg of the kline is a panther's head: the animal holds a ring in its open mouth. The head is framed by a thick garland of leaves, whose midribs are incised, with a six-petal rosette at the lower end. The wreath is held up by two eagles that face each other. The mattress is decorated with a band with a vegetal motif.

NOTE: Ingholt does not record the location of the object. The full inventory number is given as >I.N. 3802<, and usually >I.N.< denotes objects in the Ny Carlsberg Glyptotek, Copenhagen. This piece has not been identified as one belonging to the Ny Carlsberg Glyptotek's collection. In PS 1098, however, there are two photographs of fragments from sarcophagi: the upper can be identified with the piece in the İstanbul Arkeoloji Müzesi, inv. no. 3819/OM 320, while the lower has the inventory number >I.N. 3819 (321)<, indicating that it is also part of the collection of the İstanbul Arkeoloji Müzesi. This makes the relief depicted on PS 1097 likely another part of the İstanbul Arkeoloji Müzesi collection.

17. FRAGMENT OF A SARCOPHAGUS RELIEF

DATABASE NUMBER: —
LOCATION: Palmyra, Palmyra Museum, inv. no. CD 69.
CONTEXT: Secondary context: Camp of Diocletian, found (27.04.1961) in the rubble of the Praetorian Way in front of the Great Gate.
ACQUISITION HISTORY: —
MEASUREMENTS: Height: 38 cm. Width: 27 cm. Depth: 16 cm.
MATERIAL: Limestone, white.
PRESERVATION: Only the lower left side of a sarcophagus relief survives.
TECHNICAL DESCRIPTION: —
DATE: A.D. 220–240.
REFERENCES: Michałowski 1963, 160 cat. 55 fig. 212.

OBJECT DESCRIPTION

The object is the fragment of a kline. The kline has a turned leg that stands on a small plinth. The leg is composed of a biconical element, and another element. All the elements are decorated with a tongue pattern.

18. FRAGMENT OF A SARCOPHAGUS RELIEF

DATABASE NUMBER: —
LOCATION: Palmyra, Palmyra Museum, inv. no. CD 77.
CONTEXT: Secondary context: Camp of Diocletian, found (29.04.1961) in the rubble of the Praetorian Way in front of the Great Gate.
ACQUISITION HISTORY: —
MEASUREMENTS: Height: 17 cm. Width: 13 cm.
MATERIAL: Limestone, white.
PRESERVATION: Only a fragment of a turned leg survives.
TECHNICAL DESCRIPTION: —
DATE: A.D. 220–240.
REFERENCES: Michałowski 1963, 161 cat. 56 fig. 213.

OBJECT DESCRIPTION

The object shows part of a biconical element from the turned leg of a kline. It is decorated with a tongue pattern.

NOTE: Michałowski 1963, 161 suggests that it may be part of the same relief as cat. appendix 5, cat. 16.

App. 5, cat. 16

APPENDIX 6

Objects Known Only through Publications

SARCOPHAGI

A.D. 100–200

1. COMPLETE SARCOPHAGUS

DATABASE NUMBER: InSitu201.
LOCATION: Palmyra, in situ.
CONTEXT: South-west necropolis. Hypogeum of Julius Aurelius Malê.
ACQUISITION HISTORY: —
MEASUREMENTS: —
MATERIAL: Limestone.
PRESERVATION: Ingholt describes the sarcophagus as »badly damaged«.
TECHNICAL DESCRIPTION: —
DATE: A.D. 100–200.
REFERENCES: Ingholt 1935, 81 f.

OBJECT DESCRIPTION

The sarcophagus lid depicts a banquet scene with a seated female, two men reclining on a couch, and behind the men two children. The box has four busts.
The object is not known through photographs.

INSCRIPTIONS
INSCRIPTION 1
SCRIPT: Palmyrene Aramaic.
LOCATION ON RELIEF: Under the male figure to the left.
TRANSCRIPTION: ḤBL ŠʿDY | BR ḤNYNʾ | ḤNYNʾ YRQ.
TRANSLATION: Alas, Šaʿadaî, son of Ḥanînâ Ḥanînâ Yaroq.

INSCRIPTION 2
SCRIPT: Palmyrene Aramaic.
LOCATION ON RELIEF: On the knee of the second male figure.
TRANSCRIPTION: ḤBL ŠʿDY BR ʿBSY | BR ḤNYNʾ YRQ.
TRANSLATION: Alas, Šaʿadaî, son of ʿAbissaî, son of Ḥanînâ Yaroq.

INSCRIPTION 3
SCRIPT: Palmyrene Aramaic.
LOCATION ON RELIEF: On the boot of the second male figure.
TRANSCRIPTION: ṢLM ŠLʾ BRT | ḤNYNʾ ḤNYNʾ YRQ.
TRANSLATION: Image of Šalâ, daughter of Ḥanînâ Ḥanînâ Yaroq.

CIS no. —; PAT no. —.

A.D. 219–250

2. COMPLETE SARCOPHAGUS

DATABASE NUMBER: InSitu199.
LOCATION: Palmyra, in situ.
CONTEXT: South-west necropolis. Hypogeum of Julius Aurelius Malê.
ACQUISITION HISTORY: —
MEASUREMENTS: —
MATERIAL: Limestone.
PRESERVATION: According to Ingholt, the faces are broken off.
TECHNICAL DESCRIPTION: —
DATE: A.D. 219–250.
REFERENCES: Ingholt 1935, 79 f. Inscription: Ingholt 1935, 79.

OBJECT DESCRIPTION

The sarcophagus lid depicts a banquet scene with a seated female, two men reclining on a couch, and behind the men a boy and a girl. The box has four busts.
The object is not known through photographs.

INSCRIPTIONS
INSCRIPTION 1
SCRIPT: Palmyrene Aramaic.
LOCATION ON RELIEF: Under the reclining male figure on the right.
TRANSCRIPTION: ṢLM ʿBSY | BR ḤNYNʾ | ḤNYNʾ YRQ.
TRANSLATION: Image of ʿAbissaî, son of Ḥanînâ Ḥanînâ Yaroq.

INSCRIPTION 2
SCRIPT: Palmyrene Aramaic.
LOCATION ON RELIEF: Under the reclining male figure on the left.
TRANSCRIPTION: ḤBL ḤNYNʾ BR | ḤNYNʾ ʿGʾ | YRQʾBWN.
TRANSLATION: Alas, Ḥanînâ, son of Ḥanînâ ʿOggâ Yaroq, our father.

INSCRIPTION 3
SCRIPT: Palmyrene Aramaic.
LOCATION ON RELIEF: Under the foot of the male figure on the right.
TRANSCRIPTION: ṢLM MRTY | BRT YRḤBWLʾ | ʾTT ʿBSY.
TRANSLATION: Image of Martî, daughter of Yarḥibôlâ, wife of ʿAbissaî.

CIS no. —; PAT no. —.

PORTRAIT A: SEATED FEMALE, MARTÎ

PORTRAIT B: STANDING BOY

PORTRAIT C: STANDING GIRL

PORTRAIT D: RECLINING MALE, ʿABISSAÎ
According to Ingholt the figure wears a »Persian costume« and holds a drinking bowl.

PORTRAIT E: RECLINING MALE, ḤANÎNÂ
According to Ingholt the figure wears a »Persian costume« and holds a drinking bowl.

PORTRAIT F: FEMALE BUST

PORTRAIT G: BUST OF PRIEST

PORTRAIT H: BUST OF PRIEST
According to Ingholt, the figure wears a »modius«, so, a Palmyrene priestly hat.
  He is dressed in a »Persian coat«. The garment has a neckline decorated with a beaded band, and a decorated band between two beaded bands extending downwards from the neckline. A rectangle decorated with a beaded border extends from one side of the neckline downwards, adjacent to the central band.

PORTRAIT I: FEMALE BUST

3. COMPLETE SARCOPHAGUS

DATABASE NUMBER: InSitu200.
LOCATION: Palmyra, in situ.
CONTEXT: South-west necropolis. Hypogeum of Julius Aurelius Malê.
ACQUISITION HISTORY: —
MEASUREMENTS: —
MATERIAL: Limestone.
PRESERVATION: Ingholt does not give any indications of the state of preservation of the sarcophagus. Presumably it was not damaged.
TECHNICAL DESCRIPTION: —
DATE: A.D. 219–250.
REFERENCES: Ingholt 1935, 80 f.

OBJECT
The sarcophagus lid depicts a banquet scene with a seated female, two men reclining on a couch, and behind the men a girl and a boy. The box has four busts.
The object is not known through photographs.

INSCRIPTIONS
INSCRIPTION 1
SCRIPT: Palmyrene Aramaic.
LOCATION ON RELIEF: Across the torso of the reclining male to the right.
TRANSCRIPTION: ḤBL ḤNYNʾ BR | ḤNYNʾ ḤNYNʾ YRQ.
TRANSLATION: Alas, Ḥanînâ, son of Ḥanînâ Ḥanînâ Yaroq.

INSCRIPTION 2
SCRIPT: Palmyrene Aramaic.
LOCATION ON RELIEF: Between the seated female and the girl.
TRANSCRIPTION: ḤBL BTŠMYʾ | BRT ʿBSY.
TRANSLATION: Alas, Batšamayâ, daughter of ʿAbissaî.

INSCRIPTION 3
SCRIPT: Palmyrene Aramaic.
LOCATION ON RELIEF: Under the foot of the male figure on the right.
TRANSCRIPTION: ṢLM ʾQMT | BRT ŠʿDY ʾMWN.
TRANSLATION: Image of Aqamat, daughter of Šaʿadaî, our mother.

CIS no. —; PAT no. —.

PORTRAIT A: SEATED FEMALE, AQAMAT

PORTRAIT B: STANDING GIRL, BATŠAMAYÂ

PORTRAIT C: STANDING BOY

PORTRAIT D: RECLINING MALE, ḤANÎNÂ
According to Ingholt the figure wears a »Persian costume« and holds a drinking bowl.

PORTRAIT E: RECLINING MALE

PORTRAIT F: FEMALE BUST

PORTRAIT G: BUST OF PRIEST
According to Ingholt, the figure wears a »modius«, so, a Palmyrene priestly hat.

PORTRAIT H: MALE BUST
According to Ingholt, the male has hair arranged »in snail curls«.

PORTRAIT I: FEMALE BUST

SARCOPHAGUS LIDS

A.D. 219–250

4. FRAGMENT OF A SARCOPHAGUS LID

DATABASE NUMBER: —
LOCATION: Palmyra, in situ.
CONTEXT: West necropolis. Tower tomb no. 21a.
ACQUISITION HISTORY: —
MEASUREMENTS: —
MATERIAL: Limestone, pink.
PRESERVATION: Only part of the sarcophagus remains.
TECHNICAL DESCRIPTION: —
DATE: A.D. 219–250.
REFERENCES: Watzinger – Wulzinger 1932, 49; Henning 2013b, 165.

OBJECT DESCRIPTION

Only part of the object is preserved. According to Henning (2013b) the object depicted a reclining figure.
　The object is not known through photographs.

SARCOPHAGUS BOXES

A.D. 75–100

5. SARCOPHAGUS BOX

DATABASE NUMBER: —
LOCATION: Palmyra, in situ.
CONTEXT: West necropolis. Tower tomb no. 84, ground floor.
ACQUISITION HISTORY: —
MEASUREMENTS: —
MATERIAL: Limestone, yellow/white.
PRESERVATION: Only the box is preserved.
TECHNICAL DESCRIPTION: The inner narrow sides are rounded.
DATE: A.D. 75–100.
REFERENCES: Henning 2013b, 231.

OBJECT DESCRIPTION

The object is rectangular, in the shape of a kline. The front of the box was undecorated.
　The object is not known through photographs.

A.D. 75–150

6. FRAGMENT OF A SARCOPHAGUS BOX

DATABASE NUMBER: InSitu177.
LOCATION: Palmyra, in situ.
CONTEXT: North necropolis. Tower tomb no. 160.
ACQUISITION HISTORY: —
MEASUREMENTS: Width: 185 cm. Depth: 45 cm.
MATERIAL: Limestone.
PRESERVATION: Possibly lost.
TECHNICAL DESCRIPTION: —
DATE: A.D. 75–150.
REFERENCES: Henning 2013b, 272 f. Inscription: Vogüe 1868, 52 cat. 72; Sachau 1881, 735 f. cat. 2; Müller 1898, 4 cat. 4; Cantineau 1931, 17 f. cat. 8; Milik 1972, 113; Henning 2013b, 273.

OBJECT DESCRIPTION

Only part of the sarcophagus box was preserved when seen. According to CIS, there were two sculpted images on the front, a male at the right, and a female at the left.
　The object is not known through photographs.

INSCRIPTIONS

INSCRIPTION 1
SCRIPT: Palmyrene Aramaic.
LOCATION ON RELIEF: To the right.
TRANSCRIPTION: MLKW BR MLKW | MQYMW ḤBL.
TRANSLATION: Malkû, son of Malkû Moqîmû, alas!

INSCRIPTION 2
SCRIPT: Palmyrene Aramaic.
LOCATION ON RELIEF: To the left.
TRANSCRIPTION: ʾQMʾ BT | BWLMʾ ʾTTH | ḤBl.
TRANSLATION: Aqmê, daughter of Bôlmâ, his wife, alas!

CIS no. 4237; PAT no. 0593.

PORTRAIT A: MALKÛ

PORTRAIT B: AQMÊ

A.D. 100–150

7. SARCOPHAGUS BOX

DATABASE NUMBER: —
LOCATION: Palmyra, in situ.
CONTEXT: West necropolis. Temple tomb no. 171.
ACQUISITION HISTORY: —
MEASUREMENTS: —
MATERIAL: Limestone.
PRESERVATION: Only part of the sarcophagus remains.
TECHNICAL DESCRIPTION: —
DATE: A.D. 100–150.
REFERENCES: Henning 2013b, 281.

OBJECT DESCRIPTION
Only part of a stone sarcophagus is preserved.
The object is not known through photographs.

A.D. 100–200

8. SARCOPHAGUS BOX

DATABASE NUMBER: —
LOCATION: Palmyra, in situ.
CONTEXT: West necropolis. Tower tomb no. 21a.
ACQUISITION HISTORY: —
MEASUREMENTS: —
MATERIAL: Limestone, pink.
PRESERVATION: Only part of the sarcophagus remains.
TECHNICAL DESCRIPTION: —
DATE: A.D. 100–200.
REFERENCES: Watzinger – Wulzinger 1932, 49; Henning 2013b, 165.

OBJECT DESCRIPTION
The object is rectangular. According to Watzinger – Wulzinger (1932) there were remains of a mattress at the top of the box, and of five busts on the box.
The object is not known through photographs.

9. SARCOPHAGUS BOX

DATABASE NUMBER: —
LOCATION: Palmyra, in situ.
CONTEXT: West necropolis. Tower tomb no. 68, in front of the east wall of the ground floor chamber.
ACQUISITION HISTORY: —
MEASUREMENTS: —
MATERIAL: Limestone.
PRESERVATION: Only part of the sarcophagus remains.
TECHNICAL DESCRIPTION: —
DATE: A.D. 100–200.
REFERENCES: Henning 2013b, 210.

OBJECT DESCRIPTION
Only remains of the stone sarcophagus are preserved.
The object is not known through photographs.

10. FRAGMENT OF A SARCOPHAGUS BOX

DATABASE NUMBER: —
LOCATION: Palmyra, in situ.
CONTEXT: North necropolis. Tower tomb no. 123.
ACQUISITION HISTORY: —
MEASUREMENTS: —
MATERIAL: Limestone.
PRESERVATION: Only the upper part of the sarcophagus remains.
TECHNICAL DESCRIPTION: —
DATE: A.D. 100–200.
REFERENCES: Henning 2013b, 252.

OBJECT DESCRIPTION
The object is rectangular, in the shape of a kline. Only the upper part of a stone sarcophagus is preserved.
The object is not known through photographs.

11. FRAGMENT OF A SARCOPHAGUS BOX

DATABASE NUMBER: —
LOCATION: Palmyra, in situ.
CONTEXT: North necropolis. Tower tomb no. 138a, ground floor.
ACQUISITION HISTORY: —
MEASUREMENTS: —
MATERIAL: Limestone.
PRESERVATION: Only part of the sarcophagus box is preserved.
TECHNICAL DESCRIPTION: —
DATE: A.D. 100–200.
REFERENCES: Watzinger – Wulzinger 1932, 64; Henning 2013b, 261.

OBJECT DESCRIPTION
The object is rectangular, in the shape of a kline. According to Watzinger – Wulzinger (1932) it was decorated with busts between the legs of the kline.
The object is not known through photographs.

12. FRAGMENT OF A SARCOPHAGUS BOX

DATABASE NUMBER: —
LOCATION: Palmyra, in situ.
CONTEXT: North necropolis. Tower tomb no. 143, ground floor.
ACQUISITION HISTORY: —
MEASUREMENTS: —
MATERIAL: Limestone.
PRESERVATION: Only part of the sarcophagus box is preserved.
TECHNICAL DESCRIPTION: —
DATE: A.D. 100–200.
REFERENCES: Watzinger – Wulzinger 1932, 64; Henning 2013b, 262.

OBJECT DESCRIPTION
The object is rectangular, in the shape of a kline. According to Watzinger – Wulzinger (1932) it was decorated with busts.
The object is not known through photographs.

13. SARCOPHAGUS BOX

DATABASE NUMBER: —
LOCATION: Palmyra, in situ.
CONTEXT: South-east necropolis. Hypogeum of Taʿaî, west exedra.
ACQUISITION HISTORY: —
MEASUREMENTS: —
MATERIAL: Limestone.
PRESERVATION: According to the description, it appears that the box was well-preserved.
TECHNICAL DESCRIPTION: —
DATE: A.D. 100–200.
REFERENCES: Abdul-Hak 1952, 200.

OBJECT DESCRIPTION
The sarcophagus box was in the shape of a kline. There was no decoration between the legs of the kline. The fulcrum had a seated lion next to the bust of a priest inside a medallion.
The object is not known through photographs.

A.D. 150–200

14. FRAGMENT OF A SARCOPHAGUS BOX

DATABASE NUMBER: —
LOCATION: Palmyra, in situ.
CONTEXT: North necropolis. Temple tomb no. 159, ground floor.
ACQUISITION HISTORY: —
MEASUREMENTS: —
MATERIAL: Limestone.
PRESERVATION: Only part of the sarcophagus box is preserved.
TECHNICAL DESCRIPTION: —
DATE: A.D. 150–200.
REFERENCES: Watzinger – Wulzinger 1932, 65; Henning 2013b, 272.

OBJECT DESCRIPTION
The object is rectangular, in the shape of a kline. According to Watzinger – Wulzinger (1932) it was decorated with four busts between the kline legs.
The object is not known through photographs.

15. FRAGMENT OF A SARCOPHAGUS BOX

DATABASE NUMBER: —
LOCATION: Palmyra, in situ.
CONTEXT: North necropolis. Temple tomb no. 159, ground floor.
ACQUISITION HISTORY: —
MEASUREMENTS: —
MATERIAL: Limestone.
PRESERVATION: Only part of the sarcophagus box is preserved.
TECHNICAL DESCRIPTION: —
DATE: A.D. 150–200.
REFERENCES: Watzinger – Wulzinger 1932, 65; Henning 2013b, 272.

OBJECT DESCRIPTION
The object is rectangular, in the shape of a kline. According to Watzinger – Wulzinger (1932) it was decorated with four busts between the kline legs.
The object is not known through photographs.

16. FRAGMENT OF A SARCOPHAGUS BOX

DATABASE NUMBER: —
LOCATION: Palmyra, in situ.

CONTEXT: North necropolis. Temple tomb no. 159, ground floor.
ACQUISITION HISTORY: —
MEASUREMENTS: —
MATERIAL: Limestone.
PRESERVATION: Only part of the sarcophagus box is preserved.
TECHNICAL DESCRIPTION: —
DATE: A.D. 150–200.
REFERENCES: Watzinger – Wulzinger 1932, 65; Henning 2013b, 272.

OBJECT DESCRIPTION

The object is rectangular, in the shape of a kline. According to Watzinger – Wulzinger (1932) it was decorated with four busts between the kline legs.

The object is not known through photographs.

The three sarcophagi from tomb no. 159 were arranged in a triclinium.

17. SARCOPHAGUS BOX

DATABASE NUMBER: —
LOCATION: Palmyra, in situ.
CONTEXT: North necropolis. Tower tomb no. 161.
ACQUISITION HISTORY: —
MEASUREMENTS: —
MATERIAL: Limestone, yellow/white.
PRESERVATION: Only part of the sarcophagus remains.
TECHNICAL DESCRIPTION: —
DATE: A.D. 150–200.
REFERENCES: Watzinger – Wulzinger 1932, 66; Henning 2013b, 274.

OBJECT DESCRIPTION

The object is in the shape of a kline. There are busts between the kline legs, according to Watzinger – Wulzinger (1932).

The object is not known through photographs.

18. SARCOPHAGUS BOX

DATABASE NUMBER: —
LOCATION: Palmyra, in situ.
CONTEXT: North necropolis. Tower tomb no. 161.
ACQUISITION HISTORY: —
MEASUREMENTS: —
MATERIAL: Limestone, yellow/white.
PRESERVATION: Only part of the sarcophagus remains.
TECHNICAL DESCRIPTION: —
DATE: A.D. 150–200.
REFERENCES: Watzinger – Wulzinger 1932, 66; Henning 2013b, 274.

OBJECT DESCRIPTION

The object is in the shape of a kline. There are four busts between the legs of the kline.

The object is not known through photographs.

According to Watzinger – Wulzinger (1932) one of the sarcophagi had two busts between the legs of the kline, and according to Henning (2013b), both sarcophagi had four busts between the legs of the kline.

The two sarcophagi were arranged in a triclinium.

The object is not known through photographs.

19. SARCOPHAGUS BOX

DATABASE NUMBER: —
LOCATION: Palmyra, in situ.
CONTEXT: North necropolis. Tower tomb no. 171.
ACQUISITION HISTORY: —
MEASUREMENTS: —
MATERIAL: Limestone.
PRESERVATION: Only part of the sarcophagus remains.
TECHNICAL DESCRIPTION: —
DATE: A.D. 150–200.
REFERENCES: Henning 2013b, 281.

OBJECT DESCRIPTION

Only remains of the stone sarcophagus are preserved.

The object is not known through photographs.

20. SARCOPHAGUS BOX

DATABASE NUMBER: —
LOCATION: Palmyra, in situ.
CONTEXT: South-west necropolis. Hypogeum of ʿAqraban.
ACQUISITION HISTORY: —
MEASUREMENTS: —
MATERIAL: Limestone.
PRESERVATION: —
TECHNICAL DESCRIPTION: —
DATE: A.D. 150–200.
REFERENCES: Al-Hariri 2013, 149.

OBJECT DESCRIPTION
Al-Hariri reports that a sarcophagus closed the end of the exedra at the end of the main gallery.
The object is not known through photographs.

21. SARCOPHAGUS BOX

DATABASE NUMBER: —
LOCATION: Palmyra, in situ.
CONTEXT: South-west necropolis. Hypogeum AC.
ACQUISITION HISTORY: —
MEASUREMENTS: —
MATERIAL: Limestone.
PRESERVATION: —
TECHNICAL DESCRIPTION: —
DATE: A.D. 150–200.
REFERENCES: Raja et al. 2021a, Diary 1, 100, Diary 5, 121.

OBJECT DESCRIPTION
According to Ingholt's excavation diaries (Raja et al. 2021a, Diary 1, 100, Diary 5, 121), two animals, dogs or panthers were standing on either side of a bowl. The object is not known through photographs.

A.D. 200–273

22. FRAGMENT OF A MALE HEAD

DATABASE NUMBER: PM902.
LOCATION: Palmyra, Palmyra Museum, inv. no. IV.13.
CONTEXT: West necropolis. Valley of the Tombs. Temple tomb no. 36.
ACQUISITION HISTORY: —
MEASUREMENTS: Height: 17 cm.
MATERIAL: Limestone.
PRESERVATION: Only a part of the right side of the head survives with the ear, temple, and part of the hair.
TECHNICAL DESCRIPTION: —
DATE: A.D. 200–273.
REFERENCES: Schmidt-Colinet 1992, vol. I, 154 cat. K 18.

OBJECT DESCRIPTION
The fragment depicts the head of a male figure.
The object is mentioned but not depicted in Schmidt-Colinet 1992.

PORTRAIT
Part of a male head. He has a beard.

23. FRAGMENT OF A FEMALE HEAD

DATABASE NUMBER: PM875.
LOCATION: Palmyra, Palmyra Museum, inv. no. 83.31.5.
CONTEXT: West necropolis. Valley of the Tombs. Temple tomb no. 36.
ACQUISITION HISTORY: —
MEASUREMENTS: Height: 15 cm.
MATERIAL: Limestone.
PRESERVATION: Only a part of the head with the hair survives.
TECHNICAL DESCRIPTION: —
DATE: A.D. 200–273.
REFERENCES: Schmidt-Colinet 1992, vol. I, 155 cat. K 36.

OBJECT DESCRIPTION
The fragment depicts the head of a female figure.
The object is mentioned but not depicted in Schmidt-Colinet 1992.

PORTRAIT
Left side of head with hair.

SARCOPHAGI RELIEFS

A.D. 200–273

24. SARCOPHAGUS LID RELIEF WITH BANQUETING SCENE

DATABASE NUMBER: InSitu145.
LOCATION: Palmyra, Palmyra Museum, inv. no. unknown.
CONTEXT: West necropolis. Temple tomb no. 173d.
ACQUISITION HISTORY: —
MEASUREMENTS: —
MATERIAL: Limestone.
PRESERVATION: Weathered.
TECHNICAL DESCRIPTION: —
DATE: A.D. 200–273.
REFERENCES: Schmidt-Colinet 1996, 370 cat. 75.

OBJECT DESCRIPTION
The sarcophagus lid is rectangular in shape and depicts at least one reclining male next to an altar-like object.
The object is mentioned but not depicted in Schmidt-Colinet 1996.

PORTRAIT
Reclining male figure.

BANQUETING RELIEFS

A.D. 200–273

25. FRAGMENT OF A BANQUETING RELIEF

DATABASE NUMBER: PM1020.
LOCATION: Palmyra, Palmyra Museum, inv. no. CD 246/65.
CONTEXT: Secondary context: Found in the chapel of the Temple of the Standards, Temple des Enseignes, Camp of Diocletian.
ACQUISITION HISTORY: —
MEASUREMENTS: Height: 44 cm. Width: 16 cm. Depth: 20 cm.
MATERIAL: Limestone, white.
PRESERVATION: The relief is broken off on all sides. Only part of the waist and thigh of the figure survives in two joining pieces.
TECHNICAL DESCRIPTION: Traces of red in the band of the trouser leg.
DATE: A.D. 200–273.
REFERENCES: Gawlikowski 1984, 109 cat. 72.

OBJECT DESCRIPTION
The object depicts a kline decorated with rosettes between the legs against a net pattern.

PORTRAIT
The figure is shown in profile.
He wears >Parthian-style< trousers. The trouser legs are decorated with a band. He also wears a boot.
The object is not known through photographs.

26. FRAGMENT OF A BANQUETING RELIEF

DATABASE NUMBER: PM957.
LOCATION: Palmyra, Palmyra Museum, inv. no. CD 45/73.
CONTEXT: Secondary context: Found in a late wall, at the north side of the east Via Praetoria.
ACQUISITION HISTORY: —
MEASUREMENTS: Height: 25 cm. Width: 23 cm.
MATERIAL: Limestone, white.
PRESERVATION: The relief is broken off on all sides. Only the torso survives. The surface is heavily chipped.
TECHNICAL DESCRIPTION: —
DATE: A.D. 200–273.
REFERENCES: Gawlikowski 1984, 108 cat. 67.

OBJECT DESCRIPTION
The object depicts the torso of a standing male.

PORTRAIT
The figure is shown frontally. The arms fall to the sides and the hands rest on the hips.
He wears a tunic. The tunic has short sleeves and a belt. With his left hand he holds an object, identified as a cup by Gawlikowski (1984).
The object is not known through photographs.

27. FRAGMENT OF A BANQUETING RELIEF

DATABASE NUMBER: PM1018.
LOCATION: Palmyra, Palmyra Museum, inv. no. CD 245/65.
CONTEXT: Secondary context: Found in the chapel of the Temple of the Standards, Temple des Enseignes, Camp of Diocletian.
ACQUISITION HISTORY: —
MEASUREMENTS: Height: 44 cm. Width: 38 cm. Depth: 12 cm.
MATERIAL: Limestone, white.
PRESERVATION: The relief is broken off on all sides. Only part of the thigh survives.
TECHNICAL DESCRIPTION: —
DATE: A.D. 200–273.
REFERENCES: Gawlikowski 1984, 108 f. cat. 70.

OBJECT DESCRIPTION
The object depicts a reclining figure from a banqueting relief. He rests on a mattress decorated with an intersecting lozenges pattern with flowers in the lozenges.

PORTRAIT
The figure is shown frontally.
He wears a >Parthian-style< tunic and >Parthian-style< trousers. The tunic has a broad band between two beaded bands extending downwards. The band is decorated with a running scroll with flowers: the flowers alternate between six-petal, four-petal, and twisted-petal ones.
The object is not known through photographs.

28. MALE FIGURE

DATABASE NUMBER: PM853.
LOCATION: Palmyra, Palmyra Museum, inv. no. CD 3/73.
CONTEXT: Secondary context: Found to the north of the Praetorian Gate.
ACQUISITION HISTORY: —
MEASUREMENTS: Height: 37 cm. Width: 50 cm. Depth: 32 cm.
MATERIAL: Limestone, white.
PRESERVATION: The relief is broken off on all sides.
TECHNICAL DESCRIPTION: —
DATE: A.D. 200–273.
REFERENCES: Gawlikowski 1984, 100 cat. 27.

OBJECT DESCRIPTION
The object depicts an armless male bust.
Gawlikowski (1984) writes that a trace of a strip at the back shows that it was from a sarcophagus box.

PORTRAIT
The figure is shown frontally.
He wears a tunic and a chlamys. The tunic has short sleeves. The chlamys is fastened at the right shoulder with a round brooch with a beaded border (Colledge classification: f).
The object is not known through photographs.

A.D. 240–273

29. FRAGMENTS OF A BANQUETING RELIEF

DATABASE NUMBER: PM878.
LOCATION: Palmyra, Palmyra Museum, inv. no. 307/660.
CONTEXT: West necropolis. Valley of the Tombs. Temple tomb no. 36.
ACQUISITION HISTORY: —
MEASUREMENTS: Height: 83 cm. Length: 50 cm.
MATERIAL: Limestone.
PRESERVATION: Composed of several fragments. Fragment of torso of reclining figure.
TECHNICAL DESCRIPTION: The cushion, himation, mattress, and fulcrum are not finished.
DATE: A.D. 240–273 (Schmidt-Colinet 1992: A.D. 230–260).
REFERENCES: Schmidt-Colinet 1992, vol. I, 108. 135. 151 cat. B 14.

OBJECT DESCRIPTION
Banqueting relief with one reclining figure resting on a cushion and lying on a mattress.

PORTRAIT: RECLINING MALE
The figure wears a tunic and a himation.
The object is not known through photographs.

FRAGMENT OF LID, LID RELIEF, OR BANQUETING RELIEF

30. FRAGMENTS OF RELIEF

DATABASE NUMBER: —
LOCATION: Palmyra, in situ.
CONTEXT: West necropolis. Valley of the Tombs. Tower tomb no. 39d, ground floor.
ACQUISITION HISTORY: —
MEASUREMENTS: —
MATERIAL: Limestone.
PRESERVATION: Fragmentary, very weathered.
TECHNICAL DESCRIPTION: —
DATE: A.D. 150–273.
REFERENCES: Henning 2013b, 181.

OBJECT DESCRIPTION
Fragment of relief with reclining male.

PORTRAIT: RECLINING MALE
The figure's garments are richly ornamented according to Henning (2013b, 181).
The object is not known through photographs.

APPENDIX 7

Reliefs with Frame, without Portraits

1. RELIEF WITH KNEELING BULL

DATABASE NUMBER: —
LOCATION: Paris, Musée du Louvre, inv. no. 3983.
CONTEXT: —
ACQUISITION HISTORY: It was acquired by Bernard and entered the museum's collection in 1902.
MEASUREMENTS: Height: 35 cm. Width: 46 cm.
MATERIAL: Limestone.
PRESERVATION: The relief is chipped along the right and lower edges.
TECHNICAL DESCRIPTION: Traces of flat chisel on the left side of the relief.
DATE: A.D. 240–273.
REFERENCES: Ingholt Archives, PS 532; Dentzer-Feydy – Teixidor 1993, 137 cat. 147.

OBJECT DESCRIPTION
The object depicts a kneeling bull. The relief has a plain band frame on the left and lower sides, and an inner frame with a leaf-and-dart pattern. The midribs in the leaves are incised. The bull faces towards the left.

App. 7, cat. 1

NOTE: The relief is described as »relief cultuel« in Dentzer-Feydy – Teixidor 1993, 137 cat. 147, but it could also come from a funerary monument.

2. RELIEF WITH KNEELING BULL

DATABASE NUMBER: —
LOCATION: Qaryatein.
CONTEXT: —
ACQUISITION HISTORY: —
MEASUREMENTS: Height: 38 cm. Width: 31 cm.
MATERIAL: Limestone.
PRESERVATION: The right edge of the relief is lightly chipped.
TECHNICAL DESCRIPTION: —
DATE: A.D. 240–273.
REFERENCES: Ingholt Archives, PS 533; Savignac 2001, 164.

OBJECT DESCRIPTION
The object depicts a kneeling bull. The relief has a plain band frame, and an inner frame with a leaf-and-dart pattern. The midribs in the leaves are incised. The bull faces towards the right.

App. 7, cat. 2

3. RELIEF WITH LIONS'S HEAD

DATABASE NUMBER: —
LOCATION: Beirut, American University Museum, inv. no. 4808.
CONTEXT: —
ACQUISITION HISTORY: —
MEASUREMENTS: Height: 43 cm. Width: 36 cm.
MATERIAL: Limestone.
PRESERVATION:
TECHNICAL DESCRIPTION: —
DATE: A.D. 240–273.
REFERENCES: Ingholt Archives, PS 1076.

OBJECT DESCRIPTION
The object depicts a lion's head inside a wreath. The relief has a plain band frame, and an inner frame with a leaf-and-dart pattern. The midribs in the leaves are incised. The wreath is composed of leaves and it is tied with a ribbon at the lower part. The upper part has a six-petal rosette.

App. 7, cat. 3

Catalogue Image Credits

Cat. 278 (author not known): © Rubina Raja and Palmyra Portrait Project, Ingholt Archive at Ny Carlsberg Glyptotek, PS 974.

Cat. 279 (author not known): © Rubina Raja and Palmyra Portrait Project, Ingholt Archive at Ny Carlsberg Glyptotek, PS 647.

Cat. 280 (author not known): © Rubina Raja and Palmyra Portrait Project, Ingholt Archive at Ny Carlsberg Glyptotek, PS 534.

Cat. 282 (J.-B. Yon): © Jean-Baptiste Yon, 2001.

Cat. 283 (author not known): © Rubina Raja and Palmyra Portrait Project, Ingholt Archive at Ny Carlsberg Glyptotek, PS 1013.

Cat. 284 (author not known): © Rubina Raja and Palmyra Portrait Project, Ingholt Archive at Ny Carlsberg Glyptotek, PS 1318.

Cat. 285: Gawlikowski 1970b, fig. 15.

Cat. 286 (author not known): © Rubina Raja and Palmyra Portrait Project, Ingholt Archive at Ny Carlsberg Glyptotek, PS 70.

Cat. 287 (author not known): © Rubina Raja and Palmyra Portrait Project, Ingholt Archive at Ny Carlsberg Glyptotek, PS 265.

Cat. 288 (V. Iserhardt – R. Müller): © Römisch-Germanisches Zentralmuseum / Iserhardt, V., Müller, R.

Cat. 290 (M. Gawlikowski): Courtesy of Michał Gawlikowksi.

Cat. 290 (A. Schmidt-Colinet): © Andreas Schmidt-Colinet. Schmidt-Colinet 2009, fig. 3.

Cat. 290 (A. Schmidt-Colinet): © Andreas Schmidt-Colinet. Schmidt-Colinet 2009, fig. 7.

Cat. 290 (A. Schmidt-Colinet): © Andreas Schmidt-Colinet. Schmidt-Colinet 2009, fig. 2.

Cat. 290 (A. Schmidt-Colinet): © Andreas Schmidt-Colinet. al-As'ad – Schmidt-Colinet 2005, fig. 64.

Cat. 290 (A. Schmidt-Colinet): © Andreas Schmidt-Colinet. al-As'ad – Schmidt-Colinet 2005, fig. 65.

Cat. 291 (S. Hoss and A. Paetz gen. Schieck): Courtesy of DAI – Orient-Abteilung.

Cat. 292 (author not known): © Rubina Raja and Palmyra Portrait Project, Ingholt Archive at Ny Carlsberg Glyptotek, PS 61.

Cat. 298 (A. Sune Berg): Copenhagen, Ny Carlsberg Glyptotek, IN 1048. © Ny Carlsberg Glyptotek, Copenhagen / Anders Sune Berg.

Cat. 300 (author not known): © Rubina Raja and Palmyra Portrait Project, Ingholt Archive at Ny Carlsberg Glyptotek, PS 98.

Cat. 303 (author not known): © Rubina Raja and Palmyra Portrait Project, Ingholt Archive at Ny Carlsberg Glyptotek, PS 611.

Cat. 304 (J.-B. Yon): © Jean-Baptiste Yon, 2003.

Cat. 306 (A. Schmidt-Colinet): © Andreas Schmidt-Colinet. Schmidt-Colinet 2009, fig. 10.

Cat. 306 (A. Schmidt-Colinet): © Andreas Schmidt-Colinet. Schmidt-Colinet 2009, fig. 9.

Cat. 306 (A. Schmidt-Colinet): © Andreas Schmidt-Colinet. Schmidt-Colinet 2009, fig. 14.

Cat. 306 (A. Schmidt-Colinet): © Andreas Schmidt-Colinet. Schmidt-Colinet – al-As'ad 2007, pl. 90, 3.

Cat. 307 (S. Hoss and A. Paetz gen. Schieck): Courtesy of DAI – Orient-Abteilung.

Cat. 313 (B. Jacot-Descombes): © Musées d'Art et d'Histoire, Ville de Genève / Bettina Jacot-Descombes.

Cat. 314 (author not known): © Rubina Raja and Palmyra Portrait Project, Ingholt Archive at Ny Carlsberg Glyptotek, Portrait2016_051.

Cat. 316 (author not known): © Rubina Raja and Palmyra Portrait Project, Ingholt Archive at Ny Carlsberg Glyptotek, PS 124.

Cat. 317 (author not known): © Rubina Raja and Palmyra Portrait Project, Ingholt Archive at Ny Carlsberg Glyptotek, Portrait2016_060.

Cat. 318 (author not known): © Rubina Raja and Palmyra Portrait Project, Ingholt Archive at Ny Carlsberg Glyptotek, PS 722.

Cat. 323 (T. Biniewski): Courtesy of the Polish Centre of Mediterranean Archaeology of the University of Warsaw.

CATALOGUE IMAGE CREDITS

Cat. 325 (author not known): © Rubina Raja and Palmyra Portrait Project, Ingholt Archive at Ny Carlsberg Glyptotek, PS 152.

Cat. 326 (S. Hoss and A. Paetz gen. Schieck): Courtesy of DAI – Orient-Abteilung.

Cat. 327 (author not known): © »Funerary bust of a banqueting youth, y1962-92«, Princeton University Art Museums collections online, 12th July 2022, <https://artmuseum.princeton.edu/collections/objects/28889> (15.11.2022).

Cat. 328 (author not known): © Rubina Raja and Palmyra Portrait Project, Ingholt Archive at Ny Carlsberg Glyptotek, PS 646.

Cat. 329 (author not known): © Rubina Raja and Palmyra Portrait Project, Ingholt Archive at Ny Carlsberg Glyptotek, PS 520.

Cat. 330 (Petegorsky – Gipe): © Unknown. Funerary figure of a man reclining at a banquet, 2nd–3rd cent. A.D. Limestone with pigment. Purchase with the Nancy Everett Dwight Fund, Mount Holyoke College Art Museum, South Hadley, Massachusetts. Photograph Petegorsky / Gipe. 1932.2.C.OII.

Cat. 331 (author not known): © Rubina Raja and Palmyra Portrait Project, Ingholt Archive at Ny Carlsberg Glyptotek, PS 121.

Cat. 332 (author not known): © Rubina Raja and Palmyra Portrait Project, Ingholt Archive at Ny Carlsberg Glyptotek, PS 723.

Cat. 333 (A. Sune Berg): Copenhagen, Ny Carlsberg Glyptotek, IN 1149. © Ny Carlsberg Glyptotek, Copenhagen / Anders Sune Berg.

Cat. 335 (author not known): © Rubina Raja and Palmyra Portrait Project, Ingholt Archive at Ny Carlsberg Glyptotek, PS 1152.

Cat. 336 (author not known): © Rubina Raja and Palmyra Portrait Project, Ingholt Archive at Ny Carlsberg Glyptotek, PS 955.

Cat. 337 (A. Dziewanowski): Gawlikowski 1984, pl. 90, 196.

Cat. 338 (T. Biniewski): Courtesy of the Polish Centre of Mediterranean Archaeology of the University of Warsaw.

Cat. 342 (author not known): © Rubina Raja and Palmyra Portrait Project, Ingholt Archive at Ny Carlsberg Glyptotek, PS Portrait_013.

Cat. 345 (author not known): © Rubina Raja and Palmyra Portrait Project, Ingholt Archive at Ny Carlsberg Glyptotek, PS 1146.

Cat. 346 (F. Raux): Paris, Musée du Louvre, inv. no. AO 5001. © 2009 RMN-Grand Palais, Musée du Louvre / Franck Raux: <https://collections.louvre.fr/ark:/53355/cl010127830> (15.11.2022).

Cat. 347 (author not known): Metropolitan Museum of Art, acc. no. 01.25.5. Purchase, 1901. <https://www.metmuseum.org/art/collection/search/322371> (23.05.2022). Licensed under CC0 1.0.

Cat. 348 (author not known): © Rubina Raja and Palmyra Portrait Project, Ingholt Archive at Ny Carlsberg Glyptotek, PS Miscellaneous2016_092.

Cat. 349 (author not known): © Rubina Raja and Palmyra Portrait Project, Ingholt Archive at Ny Carlsberg Glyptotek, PS Miscellaneous2016_092.

Cat. 351 (A. Sune Berg): Copenhagen, Ny Carlsberg Glyptotek, IN 1082. © Ny Carlsberg Glyptotek, Copenhagen / Anders Sune Berg.

Cat. 352 (author not known): © Rubina Raja and Palmyra Portrait Project, Ingholt Archive at Ny Carlsberg Glyptotek, Miscellaneous2016_079.

Cat. 353 (author not known): © Rubina Raja and Palmyra Portrait Project, Ingholt Archive at Ny Carlsberg Glyptotek, PS 1395.

Cat. 354 (author not known): © Rubina Raja and Palmyra Portrait Project, Ingholt Archive at Ny Carlsberg Glyptotek, PS 125.

Cat. 355 (J.-B. Yon): © Jean-Baptiste Yon, 2011.

Cat. 356 (author not known): © Rubina Raja and Palmyra Portrait Project, Ingholt Archive at Ny Carlsberg Glyptotek, PS 934.

Cat. 357 (author not known): © Rubina Raja and Palmyra Portrait Project, Ingholt Archive at Ny Carlsberg Glyptotek, PS 587.

Cat. 358 (A. Sune Berg): Copenhagen, Ny Carlsberg Glyptotek, IN 1125. © Ny Carlsberg Glyptotek, Copenhagen / Anders Sune Berg.

Cat. 360 (A. Sune Berg): Copenhagen, Ny Carlsberg Glyptotek, IN 1150. © Ny Carlsberg Glyptotek, Copenhagen / Anders Sune Berg.

Cat. 361 (T. Biniewski): Courtesy of the Polish Centre of Mediterranean Archaeology of the University of Warsaw.

Cat. 365 (A. Sune Berg): Copenhagen, Ny Carlsberg Glyptotek, IN 1065. © Ny Carlsberg Glyptotek, Copenhagen / Anders Sune Berg.

Cat. 366 (author not known): © Rubina Raja and Palmyra Portrait Project, Ingholt Archive at Ny Carlsberg Glyptotek, IA_NCG_Portrait2016_020.

Cat. 367 (author not known): © Rubina Raja and Palmyra Portrait Project, Ingholt Archive at Ny Carlsberg Glyptotek, IA_NCG_Portrait2016_020.

Cat. 370 (author not known): © Rubina Raja and Palmyra Portrait Project, Ingholt Archive at Ny Carlsberg Glyptotek, IA_NCG_Portrait2016_097.

Cat. 371 (author not known): © Rubina Raja and Palmyra Portrait Project, Ingholt Archive at Ny Carlsberg Glyptotek, PS 1017.

Cat. 372 (author not known): © Rubina Raja and Palmyra Portrait Project, Ingholt Archive at Ny Carlsberg Glyptotek, Portrait2016_032_1.

Cat. 373 (author not known): © Rubina Raja and Palmyra Portrait Project, Ingholt Archive at Ny Carlsberg Glyptotek, Portrait2016_032Pic1_2.

996 CATALOGUE IMAGE CREDITS

Cat. 374 (author not known): © Rubina Raja and Palmyra Portrait Project, Ingholt Archive at Ny Carlsberg Glyptotek, PS 1080.

Cat. 375 (author not known): © Rubina Raja and Palmyra Portrait Project, Ingholt Archive at Ny Carlsberg Glyptotek, Portrait2016_032Pic1_3.

Cat. 376 (author not known): © Rubina Raja and Palmyra Portrait Project, Ingholt Archive at Ny Carlsberg Glyptotek, PS 923.

Cat. 377 (W. Jerke): Gawlikowski 1984, pl. 80, 168.

Cat. 379 (T. Biniewski): Courtesy of the Polish Centre of Mediterranean Archaeology of the University of Warsaw.

Cat. 382 (W. Jerke): Gawlikowski 1984, pl. 92, 204.

Cat. 383 (A. Dziewanowski): Gawlikowski 1984, pl. 92, 203.

Cat. 384 (W. Jerke): Gawlikowski 1984, pl. 92, 202.

Cat. 385 (author not known): KHM-Museumsverband.

Cat. 386 (F. Raux): Paris, Musée du Louvre, inv. no. AO 22249. © 2009 RMN-Grand Palais, Musée du Louvre / Franck Raux: <https://collections.louvre.fr/ark:/53355/cl010198061> (15.11.2022).

Cat. 387 (A. Sune Berg): Copenhagen, Ny Carlsberg Glyptotek, IN 1066. © Ny Carlsberg Glyptotek, Copenhagen / Anders Sune Berg.

Cat. 388 (J.-B. Yon): © Jean-Baptiste Yon, 2009.

Cat. 389 (J. Aliquot): © Jean-Baptiste Yon and Julien Aliquot, 2002.

Cat. 390 (J. Aliquot): © Jean-Baptiste Yon and Julien Aliquot, 2002.

Cat. 391 (J. Aliquot): © Jean-Baptiste Yon and Julien Aliquot, 2002.

Cat. 392 (J. Aliquot): © Jean-Baptiste Yon and Julien Aliquot, 2002.

Cat. 393 (author not known): © Rubina Raja and Palmyra Portrait Project, Ingholt Archive at Ny Carlsberg Glyptotek, PS 969.

Cat. 396 (author not known): © Rubina Raja and Palmyra Portrait Project, Ingholt Archive at Ny Carlsberg Glyptotek, PS 906.

Cat. 397 (author not known): © Rubina Raja and Palmyra Portrait Project, Ingholt Archive at Ny Carlsberg Glyptotek, PS 929.

Cat. 399 (author not known): © Rubina Raja and Palmyra Portrait Project, Ingholt Archive at Ny Carlsberg Glyptotek, Portrait2016_032.

Cat. 400 (author not known): © Rubina Raja and Palmyra Portrait Project, Ingholt Archive at Ny Carlsberg Glyptotek, PS 864.

Cat. 402 (author not known): © The Trustees of the British Museum. All rights reserved.

Cat. 403 (F. Raux): Paris, Musée du Louvre, inv. no. AO 2630. © 2009 RMN-Grand Palais, Musée du Louvre / Franck Raux: <https://collections.louvre.fr/ark:/53355/cl010127817> (15.11.2022).

Cat. 404 (author not known): © The Trustees of the British Museum. All rights reserved.

Cat. 405 (author not known): © Iris & B. Gerald Cantor Center for Visual Arts at Standford University, Standford Family Collections.

Cat. 406 (author not known): © Rubina Raja and Palmyra Portrait Project, Ingholt Archive at Ny Carlsberg Glyptotek, PS 693.

Cat. 407 (author not known): © The Fitzwilliam Museum, Cambridge.

Cat. 408 (author not known): © Rubina Raja and Palmyra Portrait Project, Ingholt Archive at Ny Carlsberg Glyptotek, PS 666.

Cat. 409 (author not known): © Rubina Raja and Palmyra Portrait Project, Ingholt Archive at Ny Carlsberg Glyptotek, PS 669.

Cat. 410 (author not known): © Rubina Raja and Palmyra Portrait Project, Ingholt Archive at Ny Carlsberg Glyptotek, PS 726.

Cat. 411 (author not known): © Rubina Raja and Palmyra Portrait Project, Ingholt Archive at Ny Carlsberg Glyptotek, PS 384.

Cat. 412 (author not known): © Rubina Raja and Palmyra Portrait Project, Ingholt Archive at Ny Carlsberg Glyptotek, PS 672.

Cat. 413 (author not known): © Rubina Raja and Palmyra Portrait Project, Ingholt Archive at Ny Carlsberg Glyptotek, PS 933.

Cat. 414 (author not known): © Rubina Raja and Palmyra Portrait Project, Ingholt Archive at Ny Carlsberg Glyptotek, PS 668.

Cat. 415 (author not known): © Rubina Raja and Palmyra Portrait Project, Ingholt Archive at Ny Carlsberg Glyptotek, PS 567.

Cat. 416: (author not known): © Rubina Raja and Palmyra Portrait Project, Ingholt Archive at Ny Carlsberg Glyptotek, PS 1348.

Cat. 417 (F. Raux): Paris, Musée du Louvre, inv. no. AO 4450. © 2009 RMN-Grand Palais, Musée du Louvre / Franck Raux: <https://collections.louvre.fr/ark:/53355/cl010127825> (15.11.2022).

Cat. 418 (author not known): © Rubina Raja and Palmyra Portrait Project, Ingholt Archive at Ny Carlsberg Glyptotek, PS 1145.

Cat. 419 (author not known): © Rubina Raja and Palmyra Portrait Project, Ingholt Archive at Ny Carlsberg Glyptotek, PS 316.

Cat. 420 (B. Jacot-Descombes): © Musée d'Art et d'Histoire, Ville de Genève / Bettina Jacot-Descombes.

Cat. 421 (author not known): © Rubina Raja and Palmyra Portrait Project, Ingholt Archive at Ny Carlsberg Glyptotek, PS 666.

Cat. 422 (author not known): © Rubina Raja and Palmyra Portrait Project, Ingholt Archive at Ny Carlsberg Glyptotek, PS 547.

Cat. 424 (F. Raux): Paris, Musée du Louvre, inv. no. AO 4084. © 2009 RMN-Grand Palais, Musée du Louvre / Franck Raux: <https://collections.louvre.fr/ark:/53355/cl010127820> (15.11.2022).

Cat. 427 (author not known): © Rubina Raja and Palmyra Portrait Project, Ingholt Archive at Ny Carlsberg Glyptotek, PS 562.

Cat. 428 (author not known): © Rubina Raja and Palmyra Portrait Project, Ingholt Archive at Ny Carlsberg Glyptotek, PS 568.

Cat. 429 (author not known): © Rubina Raja and Palmyra Portrait Project, Ingholt Archive at Ny Carlsberg Glyptotek, PS 495.

Cat. 430 (F. Raux): Paris, Musée du Louvre, inv. no. AO 15556. © 2009 RMN-Grand Palais, Musée du Louvre / Franck Raux: <https://collections.louvre.fr/ark:/53355/cl010127849> (15.11.2022).

Cat. 432 (F. Raux): Paris, Musée du Louvre, inv. no. AO 1010. © 2009 RMN-Grand Palais, Musée du Louvre / Franck Raux: <https://collections.louvre.fr/ark:/53355/cl010127782> (15.11.2022).

Cat. 433 (author not known): © Rubina Raja and Palmyra Portrait Project, Ingholt Archive at Ny Carlsberg Glyptotek, PS 560.

Cat. 434 (author not known): © Rubina Raja and Palmyra Portrait Project, Ingholt Archive at Ny Carlsberg Glyptotek, PS 563.

Cat. 436 (author not known): © Rubina Raja and Palmyra Portrait Project, Ingholt Archive at Ny Carlsberg Glyptotek, PS Miscellaneous2016_058.

Cat. 438 (F. Raux): Paris, Musée du Louvre, inv. no. AO 5000. © 2009 RMN-Grand Palais, Musée du Louvre / Franck Raux: <https://collections.louvre.fr/ark:/53355/cl010127829> (15.11.2022).

Cat. 439 (author not known): © Rubina Raja and Palmyra Portrait Project, Ingholt Archive at Ny Carlsberg Glyptotek, PS 1279.

Cat. 440 (author not known): © Rubina Raja and Palmyra Portrait Project, Ingholt Archive at Ny Carlsberg Glyptotek, PS 569.

Cat. 442 (P. Groß): © Staatliche Museen zu Berlin, Vorderasiatisches Museum, photo: Universität zu Köln, Archäologisches Institut, CoDArchLab, 214771_FA-SPerg-005151-01_Philipp Groß.

Cat. 443 (author not known): © Rubina Raja and Palmyra Portrait Project, Ingholt Archive at Ny Carlsberg Glyptotek, PS 1149.

Cat. 444 (A. Dziewanowski): Gawlikowski 1984, pl. 93, 205.

Cat. 445 (S. Hoss and A. Paetz gen. Schieck): Courtesy of DAI – Orient-Abteilung.

Cat. 445 (S. Hoss and A. Paetz gen. Schieck): Courtesy of DAI – Orient-Abteilung.

Cat. 446 (author not known): © IFPO and Jean-Baptiste Yon.

Cat. 447 (J. Zbinden): © Andreas Schmidt-Colinet. Schmidt-Colinet 1992, pl. 69, d.

Cat. 448 (T. Biniewski): Courtesy of the Polish Centre of Mediterranean Archaeology of the University of Warsaw.

Cat. 452 (H. Romanowski): Courtesy of the Polish Centre of Mediterranean Archaeology of the University of Warsaw.

Cat. 457 (author not known): © Rubina Raja and Palmyra Portrait Project, Ingholt Archive at Ny Carlsberg Glyptotek, PS 858.

Cat. 458 (A. Dziewanowski): Gawlikowski 1984, pl. 91, 199.

Cat. 460 (author not known): © Rubina Raja and Palmyra Portrait Project, Ingholt Archive at Ny Carlsberg Glyptotek, PS. 920.

Cat. 461 (T. Biniewski): Courtesy of the Polish Centre of Mediterranean Archaeology of the University of Warsaw.

Cat. 462 (author not known): © Rubina Raja and Palmyra Portrait Project, Ingholt Archive at Ny Carlsberg Glyptotek, PS 1150.

Cat. 463 (A. Dziewanowski): Gawlikowski 1984, pl. 76, 160.

Cat. 466 (author not known): © Rubina Raja and Palmyra Portrait Project, Ingholt Archive at Ny Carlsberg Glyptotek, PS 942–943.

Cat. 467 (W. Jerke): Gawlikowski 1984, pl. 84, 182.

Cat. 468 (author not known): © Rubina Raja and Palmyra Portrait Project, Ingholt Archive at Ny Carlsberg Glyptotek, PS Portrait2016_088.

Cat. 469 (C. Larrieu): Paris, Musée du Louvre, inv. no. AO 18174. © Musée du Louvre / Christian Larrieu: <https://collections.louvre.fr/ark:/53355/cl010127850> (15.11.2022).

Cat. 470 (A. Dziewanowski): Gawlikowski 1984, pl. 90, 197.

Cat. 473 (author not known): © Rubina Raja and Palmyra Portrait Project, Ingholt Archive at Ny Carlsberg Glyptotek, PS 921.

Cat. 474 (A. Dziewanowski): Gawlikowski 1984, pl. 87, 190.

Cat. 475 (A. Dziewanowski): Gawlikowski 1984, pl. 90, 198.

Cat. 476 (author not known): © Museum of Fine Arts, Boston.

Cat. 477 (S. Hoss and A. Paetz gen. Schieck): Courtesy of DAI – Orient-Abteilung.

Cat. 478 (author not known): © Yale University Art Gallery. Gift of Mr and Mrs Fred Olsen.

Cat. 479 (M. Versteegh): Gawlikowski 1984, pl. 81, 170.

Cat. 480 (author not known): © Rubina Raja and Palmyra Portrait Project, Ingholt Archive at Ny Carlsberg Glyptotek, PS 1035.

Cat. 482 (author not known): © Rubina Raja and Palmyra Portrait Project, Ingholt Archive at Ny Carlsberg Glyptotek, PS 1151.

Cat. 485 (S. Hoss and A. Paetz gen. Schieck): Courtesy of DAI – Orient-Abteilung.

Cat. 487 (A. Dziewanowski): Gawlikowski 1984, pl. 91, 201.

Cat. 488 (author not known): © Staatliche Museen zu Berlin, Vorderasiatisches Museum; Fotograf: unbekannt.

Cat. 491 (W. Jerke): Gawlikowski 1984, pl. 74, 155.

Cat. 492 (T. Biniewski): Courtesy of the Polish Centre of Mediterranean Archaeology of the University of Warsaw.

Cat. 493 (author not known): © Rubina Raja and Palmyra Portrait Project, Ingholt Archive at Ny Carlsberg Glyptotek, PS 949.

Cat. 494 (A. Sune Berg): Copenhagen, Ny Carlsberg Glyptotek, IN 1108. © Ny Carlsberg Glyptotek, Copenhagen / Anders Sune Berg.

Cat. 495 (A. Sune Berg): Copenhagen, Ny Carlsberg Glyptotek, IN 1123. © Ny Carlsberg Glyptotek, Copenhagen / Anders Sune Berg.

Cat. 496 (M. Sjöblom): © Medelhavsmuseet.

Cat. 497 (W. Jerke): Gawlikowski 1984, pl. 75, 156.

Cat. 498 (A. Sune Berg): Copenhagen, Ny Carlsberg Glyptotek, IN 1116. © Ny Carlsberg Glyptotek, Copenhagen / Anders Sune Berg.

Cat. 499 (author not known): Copenhagen, Ny Carlsberg Glyptotek, IN 1024. © Ny Carlsberg Glyptotek, Copenhagen / Palmyra Portrait Project.

Cat. 501 (author not known): © State Hermitage Museum, St Petersburg.

Cat. 503 (author not known): © The Walters Art Museum.

Cat. 504 (A. Sune Berg): Copenhagen, Ny Carlsberg Glyptotek, IN 1162. © Ny Carlsberg Glyptotek, Copenhagen / Anders Sune Berg.

Cat. 505 (A. Sune Berg): Copenhagen, Ny Carlsberg Glyptotek, IN 1101. © Ny Carlsberg Glyptotek, Copenhagen / Anders Sune Berg.

Cat. 506 (W. Jerke): Gawlikowski 1984, pl. 76, 158.

Cat. 507 (author not known): © State Hermitage Museum, St Petersburg.

Cat. 508 (A. Sune Berg): Copenhagen, Ny Carlsberg Glyptotek, IN 1124. © Ny Carlsberg Glyptotek, Copenhagen / Anders Sune Berg.

Cat. 509 (author not known): © Rubina Raja and Palmyra Portrait Project, Ingholt Archive at Ny Carlsberg Glyptotek, PS 950.

Cat. 510 (A. Sune Berg): Copenhagen, Ny Carlsberg Glyptotek, IN 1112. © Ny Carlsberg Glyptotek, Copenhagen / Anders Sune Berg.

Cat. 511 (A. Sune Berg): Copenhagen, Ny Carlsberg Glyptotek, IN 1122. © Ny Carlsberg Glyptotek, Copenhagen / Anders Sune Berg.

Cat. 513 (A. Sune Berg): Copenhagen, Ny Carlsberg Glyptotek, IN 1117. © Ny Carlsberg Glyptotek, Copenhagen / Anders Sune Berg.

Cat. 517 (author not known): © Governorate of the Vatican City State-Directorate of the Vatican Museums.

Cat. 518 (F. Raux): © 2009 RMN-Grand Palais, Musée du Louvre / Franck Raux: <https://collections.louvre.fr/ark:/53355/cl010127832> (15.11.2022).

Cat. 519 (author not known): © Governorate of the Vatican City State-Directorate of the Vatican Museums.

Cat. 520 (A. Sune Berg): © Ny Carlsberg Glyptotek, Copenhagen / Anders Sune Berg.

Cat. 524 (F. Raux): © 2009 RMN-Grand Palais, Musée du Louvre / Franck Raux: <https://collections.louvre.fr/ark:/53355/cl010127799> (15.11.2022).

Cat. 525 (author not known): © Rubina Raja and Palmyra Portrait Project, Ingholt Archive at Ny Carlsberg Glyptotek, PS 938.

Cat. 526 (author not known): © Great North Museum, Newcastle upon Tyne, Shefton Collection.

Cat. 527 (author not known): © Rubina Raja and Palmyra Portrait Project, Ingholt Archive at Ny Carlsberg Glyptotek, PS 328.

Cat. 528 (author not known): © Rubina Raja and Palmyra Portrait Project, Ingholt Archive at Ny Carlsberg Glyptotek, PS 319.

Cat. 529 (author not known): © Rubina Raja and Palmyra Portrait Project, Ingholt Archive at Ny Carlsberg Glyptotek, PS 313.

Cat. 530 (author not known): © Rubina Raja and Palmyra Portrait Project, Ingholt Archive at Ny Carlsberg Glyptotek, PS 327.

Cat. 533 (author not known): © »Head of a man, y1930–447«, Princeton University Art Museums collections online, 12th July 2022, <https://artmuseum.princeton.edu/collections/objects/19704> (15.11.2022).

Cat. 534 (author not known): © Rubina Raja and Palmyra Portrait Project, Ingholt Archive at Ny Carlsberg Glyptotek, PS 634.

Cat. 535 (author not known): © Rubina Raja and Palmyra Portrait Project, Ingholt Archive at Ny Carlsberg Glyptotek, PS 614.

Cat. 537 (author not known): © Rubina Raja and Palmyra Portrait Project, Ingholt Archive at Ny Carlsberg Glyptotek, PS 823.

Cat. 538 (author not known): © »Head of a banquet attendant, y1930–441«, Princeton University Art Museums collections online, 12th July 2022, <https://artmuseum.princeton.edu/collections/objects/19694> (15.11.2022).

Cat. 539 (author not known): © Museum of Cultural History, Oslo. Licensed under CC BY-SA 4.0. <https://www.unimus.no/portal/#/things/57d2600b-4b86-425f-8ee8-5ae4387a8e50> (12.07.2022).

Cat. 540 (T. Biniewski): Courtesy of the Polish Centre of Mediterranean Archaeology of the University of Warsaw.

Cat. 543 (W. Jerke): Gawlikowski 1984, pl. 75, 157.

Cat. 544 (author not known): © Rubina Raja and Palmyra Portrait Project, Ingholt Archive at Ny Carlsberg Glyptotek, PS 642.

Cat. 545 (A. Dziewanowski): Gawlikowski 1984, pl. 72, 145.

Cat. 547 (author not known): © Rubina Raja and Palmyra Portrait Project, Ingholt Archive at Ny Carlsberg Glyptotek, PS 718.

Cat. 548 (author not known): © Museum of Cultural History, Oslo. Licensed under CC BY-SA 4.0. <https://www.unimus.no/portal/#/things/c4d3a0ef-4653-44fd-bf3f-6f41c06a992d> (12.07.2022).

Cat. 549 (A. Dziewanowski): Gawlikowski 1984, pl. 70, 139.

Cat. 550 (A. Sune Berg): Copenhagen, Ny Carlsberg Glyptotek, IN 1128. © Ny Carlsberg Glyptotek, Copenhagen / Anders Sune Berg.

Cat. 552 (A. Sune Berg): Copenhagen, Ny Carlsberg Glyptotek, IN 1131. © Ny Carlsberg Glyptotek, Copenhagen / Anders Sune Berg.

Cat. 553 (author not known): © The Trustees of the British Museum. All rights reserved.

Cat. 554 (author not known): © Musée du Louvre / Anqituités orientales: <https://collections.louvre.fr/ark:/53355/cl010361176> (15.11.2022). Paris, Musée du Louvre, inv. no. AO 6213.

Cat. 555 (author not known): © Martin von Wagner Museum.

Cat. 556 (A. Dziewanowski): Gawlikowski 1984, pl. 71, 142.

Cat. 557 (author not known): © The Trustees of the British Museum. All rights reserved.

Cat. 558 (author not known): © The Trustees of the British Museum. All rights reserved.

Cat. 559 (author not known): © Rubina Raja and Palmyra Portrait Project, Ingholt Archive at Ny Carlsberg Glyptotek, PS 613.

Cat. 560 (A. Sune Berg): Copenhagen, Ny Carlsberg Glyptotek, IN 1163. © Ny Carlsberg Glyptotek, Copenhagen / Anders Sune Berg.

Cat. 561 (A. Sune Berg): Copenhagen, Ny Carlsberg Glyptotek, IN 1130. © Ny Carlsberg Glyptotek, Copenhagen / Anders Sune Berg.

Cat. 565 (A. Sune Berg): Copenhagen, Ny Carlsberg Glyptotek, IN 1126. © Ny Carlsberg Glyptotek, Copenhagen / Anders Sune Berg.

Cat. 566 (author not known): © Rubina Raja and Palmyra Portrait Project, Ingholt Archive at Ny Carlsberg Glyptotek, PS 622.

Cat. 567 (author not known): © Rubina Raja and Palmyra Portrait Project, Ingholt Archive at Ny Carlsberg Glyptotek, PS 578.

Cat. 568 (W. Jerke): Gawlikowski 1984, pl. 74, 153.

Cat. 569 (author not known): © Rubina Raja and Palmyra Portrait Project, Ingholt Archive at Ny Carlsberg Glyptotek, PS 581.

Cat. 570 (author not known): © Rubina Raja and Palmyra Portrait Project, Ingholt Archive at Ny Carlsberg Glyptotek, PS 945.

Cat. 571 (author not known): © Rubina Raja and Palmyra Portrait Project, Ingholt Archive at Ny Carlsberg Glyptotek, PS 233.

Cat. 572 (A. Dziewanowski): Gawlikowski 1984, pl. 71, 143.

Cat. 573 (author not known): © Rubina Raja and Palmyra Portrait Project, Ingholt Archive at Ny Carlsberg Glyptotek, PS 615.

Cat. 574 (author not known): © Rubina Raja and Palmyra Portrait Project, Ingholt Archive at Ny Carlsberg Glyptotek, PS 573.

Cat. 575 (author not known): © Rubina Raja and Palmyra Portrait Project, Ingholt Archive at Ny Carlsberg Glyptotek, PS 576.

Cat. 576 (F. Raux): © 2009 RMN-Grand Palais, Musée du Louvre / Franck Raux: <https://collections.louvre.fr/ark:/53355/cl010127868> (15.11.2022).

Cat. 577 (A. Sune Berg): © Ny Carlsberg Glyptotek, Copenhagen / Anders Sune Berg.

Cat. 578 (T. Biniewski): Courtesy of the Polish Centre of Mediterranean Archaeology of the University of Warsaw.

Cat. 579 (author not known): © Rubina Raja and Palmyra Portrait Project, Ingholt Archive at Ny Carlsberg Glyptotek, PS 1060.

Cat. 581 (author not known): © Szépművészeti Múzeum / Museum of Fine Arts, Budapest, 2021.

Cat. 583 (author not known): © KHM-Museumsverband.

Cat. 584 (A. Sune Berg): Copenhagen, Ny Carlsberg Glyptotek, IN 1097. © Ny Carlsberg Glyptotek, Copenhagen / Anders Sune Berg.

Cat. 585 (T. Biniewski): Courtesy of the Polish Centre of Mediterranean Archaeology of the University of Warsaw.

Cat. 586 (author not known): © Rubina Raja and Palmyra Portrait Project, Ingholt Archive at Ny Carlsberg Glyptotek, PS 133.

Cat. 590 (S. Hoss and A. Paetz gen. Schieck): Courtesy of DAI – Orient-Abteilung.

Cat. 591 (T. Biniewski): Courtesy of the Polish Centre of Mediterranean Archaeology of the University of Warsaw.

Cat. 592 (A. Sune Berg): Copenhagen, Ny Carlsberg Glyptotek, IN 1145. © Ny Carlsberg Glyptotek, Copenhagen / Anders Sune Berg.

Cat. 593 (A. Sune Berg): Copenhagen, Ny Carlsberg Glyptotek, IN 1121. © Ny Carlsberg Glyptotek, Copenhagen / Anders Sune Berg.

Cat. 594 (author not known): © Rubina Raja and Palmyra Portrait Project, Ingholt Archive at Ny Carlsberg Glyptotek, PS 1087.

Cat. 595 (author not known): © Rubina Raja and Palmyra Portrait Project, Ingholt Archive at Ny Carlsberg Glyptotek, PS 1159.

Cat. 596 (author not known): © Rubina Raja and Palmyra Portrait Project, Ingholt Archive at Ny Carlsberg Glyptotek, PS 1158.

Cat. 598 (A. Dziewanowski): Gawlikowski 1984, pl. 73, 149.

Cat. 599 (author not known): © Rubina Raja and Palmyra Portrait Project, Ingholt Archive at Ny Carlsberg Glyptotek, PS 240.

Cat. 600 (author not known): © Rubina Raja and Palmyra Portrait Project, Ingholt Archive at Ny Carlsberg Glyptotek, PS Portrait_058.

Cat. 602 (author not known): © Rubina Raja and Palmyra Portrait Project, Ingholt Archive at Ny Carlsberg Glyptotek, Portrait2016_058.

Cat. 603 (author not known): © Rubina Raja and Palmyra Portrait Project, Ingholt Archive at Ny Carlsberg Glyptotek, PS 635.

Cat. 604 (author not known): © Rubina Raja and Palmyra Portrait Project, Ingholt Archive at Ny Carlsberg Glyptotek, Portrait2016_037.

Cat. 605 (A. Dziewanowski): Gawlikowski 1984, pl. 70, 140.

Cat. 606 (author not known): © Rubina Raja and Palmyra Portrait Project, Ingholt Archive at Ny Carlsberg Glyptotek, PS 585.

Cat. 607 (A. Dziewanowski): Gawlikowski 1984, pl. 81, 172.

Cat. 608 (author not known): © Rubina Raja and Palmyra Portrait Project, Ingholt Archive at Ny Carlsberg Glyptotek, PS 659.

Cat. 609 (B. Jacot-Descombes): © Musée d'Art et d'Histoire, Ville de Genève, photographe: Bettina Jacot-Descombes.

Cat. 510 (author not known): © Rubina Raja and Palmyra Portrait Project, Ingholt Archive at Ny Carlsberg Glyptotek, PS 658.

Cat. 611 (author not known): J. P. Getty Museum, inv. no. 81. AA.170. Image in the public domain: <https://www.getty.edu/art/collection/object/105YZG?altImage=af00565e-ffce-4976-9128-bfb791ee7022> (12.07.2022).

Cat. 614 (A. Sune Berg): Copenhagen, Ny Carlsberg Glyptotek, IN 1109. © Ny Carlsberg Glyptotek, Copenhagen / Anders Sune Berg.

Cat. 616 (A. Sune Berg): Copenhagen, Ny Carlsberg Glyptotek, IN 1110. © Ny Carlsberg Glyptotek, Copenhagen / Anders Sune Berg.

Cat. 617 (author not known): © KHM-Museumsverband.

Cat. 621 (author not known): © Bryn Mawr College.

Cat. 622 (A. Sune Berg): Copenhagen, Ny Carlsberg Glyptotek, IN 1090. © Ny Carlsberg Glyptotek, Copenhagen / Anders Sune Berg.

Cat. 624 (author not known): © Rubina Raja and Palmyra Portrait Project, Ingholt Archive at Ny Carlsberg Glyptotek, PS 502.

Cat. 625 (author not known): © Rubina Raja and Palmyra Portrait Project, Ingholt Archive at Ny Carlsberg Glyptotek, PS 503.

Cat. 626 (Y. Siza): © Musée d'Art et d'Histoire. Photograph by Yves Siza.

Cat. 627 (T. Biniewski): Courtesy of the Polish Centre of Mediterranean Archaeology of the University of Warsaw.

Cat. 630 (author not known): © Rubina Raja and Palmyra Portrait Project, Ingholt Archive at Ny Carlsberg Glyptotek, PS 691.

Cat. 631 (H. Romanowski): Courtesy of the Polish Centre of Mediterranean Archaeology of the University of Warsaw.

Cat. 632 (author not known): © Herbert F. Johnson Museum of Art, Cornell University.

Cat. 634 (L. Kheifets): © State Hermitage Museum, St Petersburg.

Cat. 635 (author not known): © Rubina Raja and Palmyra Portrait Project, Ingholt Archive at Ny Carlsberg Glyptotek, PS 688.

Cat. 636 (A. Dziewanowski): Gawlikowski 1984, pl. 81, 171.

Cat. 637 (A. Sune Berg): Copenhagen, Ny Carlsberg Glyptotek, IN 1132. © Ny Carlsberg Glyptotek, Copenhagen / Anders Sune Berg.

Cat. 638 (F. Raux): © 2006 RMN-Grand Palais, Musée du Louvre / Franck Raux: <https://collections.louvre.fr/ark:/53355/cl010127841> (15.11.2022).

Cat. 644 (A. Sune Berg): © Ny Carlsberg Glyptotek, Copenhagen / Anders Sune Berg.

Cat. 645 (H. Romanowski): Courtesy of the Polish Centre of Mediterranean Archaeology of the University of Warsaw.

CATALOGUE IMAGE CREDITS 1001

Cat. 651 (author not known): © Rubina Raja and Palmyra Portrait Project, Ingholt Archive at Ny Carlsberg Glyptotek, PS 706.

Cat. 653 (author not known): © Rubina Raja and Palmyra Portrait Project, Ingholt Archive at Ny Carlsberg Glyptotek, PS 504.

Cat. 655 (A. Sune Berg): Copenhagen, Ny Carlsberg Glyptotek, IN 1104. © Ny Carlsberg Glyptotek, Copenhagen / Anders Sune Berg.

Cat. 656 (author not known): © Rubina Raja and Palmyra Portrait Project, Ingholt Archive at Ny Carlsberg Glyptotek, PS 698.

Cat. 657 (H. Romanowski): Courtesy of the Polish Centre of Mediterranean Archaeology of the University of Warsaw.

Cat. 660 (P. Fuzeau): © 2017 Musée du Louvre / Philippe Fuzeau: <https://collections.louvre.fr/ark:/53355/cl010127781> (15.11.2022).

Cat. 661 (M. Versteegh): Gawlikowski 1984, pl. 83, 177.

Cat. 663 (author not known): © Yale University Art Gallery. Image in the public domain: <https://artgallery.yale.edu/collections/objects/4726> (12.07.2022).

Cat. 664 (M. Versteegh): Gawlikowski 1984, pl. 82, 176.

Cat. 666 (A. Sune Berg): Copenhagen, Ny Carlsberg Glyptotek, IN 1091. © Ny Carlsberg Glyptotek, Copenhagen / Anders Sune Berg.

Cat. 667 (Y. Siza): © Musées d'Art et d'Histoire, Ville de Genève.

Cat. 669 (author not known): © Rubina Raja and Palmyra Portrait Project, Ingholt Archive at Ny Carlsberg Glyptotek, PS 704.

Cat. 670 (author not known): © Rubina Raja and Palmyra Portrait Project, Ingholt Archive at Ny Carlsberg Glyptotek, PS 696.

Cat. 671 (author not known): © Rubina Raja and Palmyra Portrait Project, Ingholt Archive at Ny Carlsberg Glyptotek, PS 1085.

Cat. 672 (author not known): © Rubina Raja and Palmyra Portrait Project, Ingholt Archive at Ny Carlsberg Glyptotek, Portrait2016_058_f_3.

Cat. 673 (author not known): © Rubina Raja and Palmyra Portrait Project, Ingholt Archive at Ny Carlsberg Glyptotek, PS 728.

Cat. 674 (author not known): © Rubina Raja and Palmyra Portrait Project, Ingholt Archive at Ny Carlsberg Glyptotek, Portrait2016_037.

Cat. 675 (author not known): © Rubina Raja and Palmyra Portrait Project, Ingholt Archive at Ny Carlsberg Glyptotek, PS 500.

Cat. 676 (author not known): © Rubina Raja and Palmyra Portrait Project, Ingholt Archive at Ny Carlsberg Glyptotek, PS 699.

Cat. 677 (author not known): © Rubina Raja and Palmyra Portrait Project, Ingholt Archive at Ny Carlsberg Glyptotek, PS 1336.

Cat. 678 (author not known): © Rubina Raja and Palmyra Portrait Project, Ingholt Archive at Ny Carlsberg Glyptotek, PS 727.

Cat. 679 (author not known): © Rubina Raja and Palmyra Portrait Project, Ingholt Archive at Ny Carlsberg Glyptotek, PS 702.

Cat. 680 (author not known): © Rubina Raja and Palmyra Portrait Project, Ingholt Archive at Ny Carlsberg Glyptotek, PS 701.

Cat. 681 (author not known): Metropolitan Museum of Art, acc. no. 65. 77. Gift of Harry Jones, 1965. <https://www.metmuseum.org/art/collection/search/255206> (23.05.2022). Licensed under CC0 1.0.

Cat. 682 (author not known): © Rubina Raja and Palmyra Portrait Project, Ingholt Archive at Ny Carlsberg Glyptotek, PS 707.

Cat. 683 (author not known): © Rubina Raja and Palmyra Portrait Project, Ingholt Archive at Ny Carlsberg Glyptotek, PS 694.

Cat. 684 (author not known): © Rubina Raja and Palmyra Portrait Project, Ingholt Archive at Ny Carlsberg Glyptotek, PS 1032.

Cat. 686 (author not known): © Rubina Raja and Palmyra Portrait Project, Ingholt Archive at Ny Carlsberg Glyptotek, PS Portrait2016_032.

Cat. 687 (author not known): © Rubina Raja and Palmyra Portrait Project, Ingholt Archive at Ny Carlsberg Glyptotek, PS 720.

Cat. 688 (author not known): © Rubina Raja and Palmyra Portrait Project, Ingholt Archive at Ny Carlsberg Glyptotek, PS 719.

Cat. 689 (author not known): © The Fitzwilliam Museum, Cambridge.

Cat. 690 (author not known): © Rubina Raja and Palmyra Portrait Project, Ingholt Archive at Ny Carlsberg Glyptotek, PS 72.

Cat. 691 (author not known): © Rubina Raja and Palmyra Portrait Project, Ingholt Archive at Ny Carlsberg Glyptotek, PS 262.

Cat. 692 (M.-P. Chuzeville): © 1988 RMN-Grand Palais, Musée du Louvre / Maurice et Pierre Chuzeville: <https://collections.louvre.fr/ark:/53355/cl010127798> (15.11.2022). Paris, Musée du Louvre, inv. no. AO 2000.

Cat. 693 (F. Raux): © 2009 RMN-Grand Palais, Musée du Louvre / Franck Raux: <https://collections.louvre.fr/ark:/53355/cl010127804> (15.11.2022). Paris, Musée du Louvre, inv. no. AO 2093.

Cat. 694 (author not known): © The Trustees of the British Museum. All rights reserved.

Cat. 695 (A. Sune Berg): Copenhagen, Ny Carlsberg Glyptotek, IN 1157. © Ny Carlsberg Glyptotek, Copenhagen / Anders Sune Berg.

Cat. 696 (A. Dziewanowski): Gawlikowski 1984, pl. 73, 148.

Cat. 697 (A. Dziewanowski): Gawlikowski 1984, pl. 90, 195.

Cat. 698 (A. Dziewanowski): Gawlikowski 1984, pl. 91, 200.

Cat. 700 (Hervé Deschamps-Dargassies): © Musée Saint-Raymond, Toulouse. Licensed under CC BY-SA 4.0: <https://commons.wikimedia.org/wiki/File:2003-2-1-HDD.jpg> (13.07.2022).

Cat. 701 (W. Jerke): Gawlikowski 1984, pl. 89, 193.

Cat. 702 (H. Romanowski): Courtesy of the Polish Centre of Mediterranean Archaeology of the University of Warsaw.

Cat. 703 (author not known): © Rubina Raja and Palmyra Portrait Project, Ingholt Archive at Ny Carlsberg Glyptotek, PS 941.

Cat. 704 (author not known): © Rubina Raja and Palmyra Portrait Project, Ingholt Archive at Ny Carlsberg Glyptotek, PS 531A.

Cat. 705 (author not known): © Rubina Raja and Palmyra Portrait Project, Ingholt Archive at Ny Carlsberg Glyptotek, PS 1028.

Cat. 708 (author not known): © Rubina Raja and Palmyra Portrait Project, Ingholt Archive at Ny Carlsberg Glyptotek, PS 1077.

Cat. 709 (J.-B. Yon): © Jean-Baptiste Yon, 2011.

Cat. 710 (A. Dziewanowski): Gawlikowski 1984, pl. 88, 192.

Cat. 712 (A. Dziewanowski): Gawlikowski 1984, pl. 88, 191.

Cat. 713 (author not known): © Rubina Raja and Palmyra Portrait Project, Ingholt Archive at Ny Carlsberg Glyptotek.

Cat. 714 (author not known): © The Cleveland Museum of Art.

Cat. 715 (author not known): © Szépművészeti Múzeum / Museum of Fine Arts, Budapest, 2021.

Cat. 716 (author not known): © Yale University Art Gallery. Image in the public domain: <https://artgallery.yale.edu/collections/objects/4729> (12.07.2022).

Cat. 717 (F. Raux): © 2009 RMN-Grand Palais, Musée du Louvre / Franck Raux: <https://collections.louvre.fr/ark:/53355/cl010127828> (15.11.2022). Paris, Musée du Louvre, inv. no. AO 4999.

Cat. 718 (author not known): © Rubina Raja and Palmyra Portrait Project, Ingholt Archive at Ny Carlsberg Glyptotek, PS 529.

Cat. 719 (S. Hoss and A. Paetz gen. Schieck): Courtesy of DAI – Orient-Abteilung.

Cat. 720 (H. Romanowski): Courtesy of the Polish Centre of Mediterranean Archaeology of the University of Warsaw.

Cat. 721 (M. Niepokólczycki): Courtesy of the Polish Centre of Mediterranean Archaeology of the University of Warsaw.

Cat. 723 (author not known): © Rubina Raja and Palmyra Portrait Project, Ingholt Archive at Ny Carlsberg Glyptotek, PS 577.

Cat. 725 (author not known): © Rubina Raja and Palmyra Portrait Project, Ingholt Archive at Ny Carlsberg Glyptotek, PS 22A.

Cat. 726 (author not known): © Rubina Raja and Palmyra Portrait Project, Ingholt Archive at Ny Carlsberg Glyptotek, PS 1494.

Cat. 727 (author not known): © Rubina Raja and Palmyra Portrait Project, Ingholt Archive at Ny Carlsberg Glyptotek, PS 1278.

Cat. 729: Gawlikowski 1984, pl. 87, 189.

Appendix 1

C651_App. 1_cat. 1 (drawing by L.-F. Cassas; photographer not known): © Andreas Schmidt-Colinet. Schmidt-Colinet 1996, fig. 165.

Appendix 2

C652_App. 2_cat. 1 (drawing by L.-F. Cassas; photographer not known): © Andreas Schmidt-Colinet. Schmidt-Colinet 1996, fig. 186.

Appendix 3

C653_App. 3_cat. 1 (drawing by L.-F. Cassas; photographer not known): © Andreas Schmidt-Colinet. Schmidt-Colinet 1996, fig. 220.

Appendix 4

C654_App. 4_cat. 1 (H. Romanowski): Courtesy of the Polish Centre of Mediterranean Archaeology of the University of Warsaw.

C655_App. 4_cat. 2 (H. Romanowski): Courtesy of the Polish Centre of Mediterranean Archaeology of the University of Warsaw.

C656_App. 4_cat. 3 (T. Biniewski): Courtesy of the Polish Centre of Mediterranean Archaeology of the University of Warsaw.

Appendix 5

C657_C658_App. 5_cat. 7 (author not known): © Rubina Raja and Palmyra Portrait Project, Ingholt Archive at Ny Carlsberg Glyptotek, PS 874.

C658_App. 5_cat. 8 (author not known): © Rubina Raja and Palmyra Portrait Project, Ingholt Archive at Ny Carlsberg Glyptotek, Miscellaneous2016_062.

C659_ App.5_cat. 10 (T. Biniewski): Courtesy of the Polish Centre of Mediterranean Archaeology of the University of Warsaw.

C660_App.5_cat. 10 (T. Biniewski): Courtesy of the Polish Centre of Mediterranean Archaeology of the University of Warsaw.

C661_App.5_cat. 10 (T. Biniewski): Courtesy of the Polish Centre of Mediterranean Archaeology of the University of Warsaw.

C662_App. 5_cat. 12 (author not known): © Rubina Raja and Palmyra Portrait Project, Ingholt Archive at Ny Carlsberg Glyptotek, PS 729.

C663_ App. 5_cat. 13 (author not known): © Rubina Raja and Palmyra Portrait Project, Ingholt Archive at Ny Carlsberg Glyptotek, PS 730.

C664_ App. 5_cat. 14 (author not known): © Rubina Raja and Palmyra Portrait Project, Ingholt Archive at Ny Carlsberg Glyptotek, PS 1098.

C665_ App. 5_cat. 15 (author not known): © Rubina Raja and Palmyra Portrait Project, Ingholt Archive at Ny Carlsberg Glyptotek, 730.

C666_ App. 5_cat. 16 (author not known): © Rubina Raja and Palmyra Portrait Project, Ingholt Archive at Ny Carlsberg Glyptotek, PS 1097.

Appendix 7

C667_ App. 7_cat. 1 (author not known): © Rubina Raja and Palmyra Portrait Project, Ingholt Archive at Ny Carlsberg Glyptotek, PS 532.

C668_ App. 7_cat. 2 (author not known): © Rubina Raja and Palmyra Portrait Project, Ingholt Archive at Ny Carlsberg Glyptotek, PS 533.

C669_ App. 7_cat. 3 (author not known): © Rubina Raja and Palmyra Portrait Project, Ingholt Archive at Ny Carlsberg Glyptotek, PS 1076.

STUDIES IN PALMYRENE ARCHAEOLOGY AND HISTORY

All volumes in this series are evaluated by an Editorial Board, strictly on academic grounds, based on reports prepared by referees who have been commissioned by virtue of their specialism in the appropriate field. The Board ensures that the screening is done independently and without conflicts of interest. The definitive texts supplied by authors are also subject to review by the Board before being approved for publication. Further, the volumes are copyedited to conform to the publisher's stylebook and to the best international academic standards in the field.

Titles in Series

Studies on Palmyrene Sculpture: A Translation of Harald Ingholt's Studier over Palmyrensk Skulptur, *Edited and with Commentary*, ed. by Olympia Bobou, Jesper Vestergaard Jensen, Nathalia Breintoft Kristensen, Rubina Raja, and Rikke Randeris Thomsen (2021)

Production Economy in Greater Roman Syria: Trade Networks and Production Processes, ed. by Rubina Raja and Julia Steding (2021)

Individualizing the Dead: Attributes in Palmyrene Funerary Sculpture, ed. by Maura Heyn and Rubina Raja (2021)

Rubina Raja, Julia Steding, and Jean-Baptiste Yon, *Excavating Palmyra. Harald Ingholt's Excavation Diaries: A Transcript, Translation, and Commentary* (2 vols) (2021)

The Small Stuff of the Palmyrenes: Coins and Tesserae from Palmyra, ed. by Rubina Raja (2022)

Palmyra and the East, ed. by Kenneth Lapatin and Rubina Raja (2022)

Julia Steding, *Carvers and Customers in Roman Palmyra: The Production Economy of Limestone Loculus Reliefs* (2022)

Odds and Ends, ed. by Maura K. Heyn and Rubina Raja (2023)

In Preparation

Palmyra in Perspective, ed. by Rubina Raja